LABYRINTH
of
RUINS

Francis Bacon's Encrypted Sonnet Sequence

Volume I

Richard B. Shapiro

LABYRINTH
of
RUINS

Francis Bacon's Encrypted Sonnet Sequence

Volume I

Leonidas Press

Published in the United States of America
Leonidas Press
6 Liberty Square #2128
Boston, MA 02109

www.Hekatompathia.com

Editor: Kelly Clody
Proofreader: Penelope Wayne-Shapiro
Cover Design: David Moratto

Second and Complete Edition

First printed June, 2023

9 8 7 6 5 4 3 2 1

ISBN: 978-1-7353651-2-1 (Hardcover)

ISBN: 978-1-7353651-3-8 (Softcover)

Sed nos quos crassa Minerva dedecet,
non patiamur abstrusa esse adyta sacri poematis,
sed arcanorum sensuum investigato aditu,
doctorum cultu celebranda praebeamus reclusa penetralia.

—Macrobius, *Saturnalia* (1.24.13)

(But we who disdain a shallow understanding, will not allow
the innermost recesses of the sacred poem to remain concealed,
but instead will expose them by finding the pathway to their
secret significance, and reveal their deepest meaning, so that by
the veneration of scholars, they may be duly honored.)

Acknowledgments

The inspiration to embark on this study arose from the lectures of my teacher at Brandeis, poet and scholar Allen Grossman (1932–2014), who left an indelible mark upon me and my fellow students. I was truly fortunate to receive excellent counsel from many scholars at various stages of this project. The ideas, corrections, and support that I received from the following modern language professors were essential to my undertaking. I am most grateful for the help that I received from Adam Rzepka, who provided sound advice and many detailed comments that shaped both the style and content of this study. Gerhard F. Strasser, a scholar with expertise in the cryptography of the early modern period, provided detailed feedback that resulted in many important improvements to my study. My friend of fifty years, Richard B. Freadman, dispensed valuable advice and answered many of the literary questions that I posed over the past decade. Steven Monte read an early draft of this study: his comments led to changes in its presentation. William Junker provided me with a critique that both refined arguments and initiated new explorations. Finally, James Kee read an earlier study on a related topic, providing essential feedback and encouragement.

The cryptographic aspects of this study led me to consult with a different group of scholars: mathematicians. I owe a great debt to Jacques Cohen, who founded the Computer Science Department at Brandeis. On many occasions, usually over lunch, he provided essential advice on how to move my project forward. Another emeritus professor from Brandeis, Martin Cohn, advised me on certain cryptographic details and mathematical arguments. Chris Thorpe, a mathematician and computer industry entrepreneur, offered many helpful suggestions at an early stage of this project. Finally, the late Steven J. Schwartz, a colleague in the computer industry, taught me to use models to tackle difficult problems.

I also owe a dept to classicists, especially Neo-Latinist Dana Sutton, whose textual work and insights into the *Hekatompathia* proved extraordinarily valuable. I am indebted to Patricia A. Johnston, a Latinist, who kindly allowed me to attend her classes as an elder student. Latinist Chris Cochran provided essential feedback on my translations of the *Hekatompathia*'s Neo-Latin texts. Hellenist Emrys Schlatter helped me in my early work in translating Trithemius. My thanks also to historian Benedek Láng, librarian Andrew Moore, Sarah A. Lang, and my son Benjamin for his clerical help.

My thanks to Philosopher Palle Yourgrau, my instructor in ancient philosophy, who aided me in my study of Plato and Aristotle. In my undergraduate days, the intellectual history department at Brandeis helped to develop my critical thinking skills: philosopher Alasdair MacIntyre was an inspiring teacher; Gerald Izenberg excited my interest in intellectual history. At an even earlier point in my education, my biology teacher, Harvey Lawrence, sparked my desire to learn.

I deeply appreciate the diligence and thoughtful advice of my editor, Kelly Clody. Her push toward greater clarity and attention to detail were essential to making this complex study accessible. My wife, Penelope, was the editor of the early drafts of this study and provided valuable advice on many critical editorial decisions. Most importantly, she was extremely supportive overall of my pursuit of this project, which consumed considerable time and resources.

Contents (Vol. I)

Contents (Vol. II)

Reader's Guide:
Objectives, organization,
conventions, and abbreviations

Literary critics do not write two-volume monographs on rarely read works—an explanation is in order. The *Hekatompathia*, the first English sonnet sequence, presents an extensive and complex puzzle that defines a new order for most of the work's sonnets, revealing a radically changed sonnet sequence. The "Puzzle" (the term used throughout this study) also references a set of tables in an influential cryptography manual and asserts that the reader may "decypher" something "cunningly conveighed" by the "secret transposition of letters." The present study solves this literary-cryptographic Puzzle by leading the reader on a step-by-step labyrinthine journey that shows exactly how and why the work's text is rearranged.

The concept of a reader-transformed text has its origins in the medieval and Renaissance practice of "ruined" poetry, which the *Hekatompathia* takes to its ultimate limit. The Puzzle yields a finely detailed blueprint from which the reader produces a new sequence organized around a heterodox cosmology. The Puzzle's directives include prefaces, sonnet headnotes, intratextual links, contradictions in the poetic text that require resolution, and cryptographic messages. As explained in the first chapter, the Puzzle's cryptography stabilizes the interpretation of the Puzzle's literary components.

Solving the Puzzle requires that literary hermeneutics and cryptographic skills be applied in tandem, a task unlike any found in other literary works. In the *Hekatompathia*, cryptography may be thought of as another form of literary communication, like symbolism or allegory. But from our contemporary viewpoint, the work is a chimera, marrying two disparate disciplines, one an art and the other a science. As a result, this study often appears to be eccentric, suddenly (but unavoidably) shifting gears from literary interpretation to codebreaking and back again. Whenever possible, I have separated these disciplines (for example, Chapter 2 is primarily cryptographic; Chapters 3 and 4 are primarily literary). However, this study's order is necessarily determined by the step-by-step process required to solve the Puzzle, an order established by the Puzzle's creator.

This study's essential task is to win acceptance for the restored text, and toward that end, every detail of the Puzzle's solution must be documented, which requires two volumes. While a relatively complete view of the *Hekatompathia* is presented in this study's first volume, many of the cryptographic details and much of the commentary on individual sonnets are reserved for the second volume. This allows the reader to read only the first volume and refer to the second volume only if greater detail is desired. As the second volume is primarily intended as a reference work, it has been made publicly available on this study's website (Hekatompathia.com).

The first volume solves the Puzzle, step by step, through its seven distinct stages, each of which produces a cryptographic message. The first volume contains all details of the solutions to the first and seventh stages, but for the second through sixth stages, the details appear in Addenda 1–11 of the second volume. The second volume also includes appendices, excursus, and the complete restored text of the *Hekatompathia*. The first volume references the second volume by referring to "Appendix A," "Addendum 1," "Excursus 1," and so forth. (See the table of contents for the second volume, which also appears in this volume.)

Literary criticism has one set of editorial standards; the presentation of technical materials (e.g., mathematics and cryptography) follow different editorial standards. As part of its deciphering process, *Labyrinth of Ruins* uses symbols, numbers, and abbreviations that are not easily handled by the usual editorial standards in the humanities. For example, numbers appear in Arabic numerals, rather than being written out (the standard in the humanities). I have adopted standards, as described below, that are most practical for this study, borrowing from the editorial practices of both fields.

Objectives

The first objective of this study is to win acceptance for the restored text of the *Hekatompathia*. Achieving this goal will grant scholars access to a precisely structured sonnet sequence, with extensive authorial annotations that reveal how this Renaissance poet constructed his sonnet sequence. Indeed, the purpose of the sequence and its Puzzle is to teach its readers how poetry is written and how it is to be read—the hermeneutics of Renaissance poetry (see Chapter 1). Its organization around an Epicurean cosmology will provide new insights into the intellectual history of the early modern period (see Chapter 14). Its practice of early modern rhetorical strategies will aid us in reading other early modern poetry (see Chapter 1).

Nevertheless, I am concerned that my claim of Bacon's authorship—unexpected, sensational, and thus likely to be met with skepticism—will overshadow the restoration of the sequence. This restoration occurs in the Puzzle's first four stages, and thus may be considered independently from Bacon's authorship, which is only revealed in the seventh stage. Taken together, the Puzzle's stages present such a novel—indeed freakish—contraption to which one's first reaction may be rejection of the Puzzle as a mirage. However, if this study's readers evaluate the Puzzle in a dispassionate and scrupulous manner, considering the detailed evidence presented here for each of its incremental stages, the Puzzle—a marvel and wonder—will gain acceptance.

Online resources at Hekatompathia.com

This study's website, Hekatompathia.com, provides these resources:

- This study's edition of the original and restored versions of the *Hekatompathia*.

- This study's second volume, a reference volume, is made freely available.

- This study's endnotes (to allow for quick access while reading a hardcopy).

- Links to *Hekatompathia* editions at Hathitrust, including the 1582 edition and the Spenser Society 1869 edition (an accurate reproduction).

- Links to Dana Sutton's *The Complete Works of Thomas Watson (1556–1592)*, available in modified form at the University of Birmingham's Philological Museum.

- Links to various editions of Trithemius's *Polygraphiae VI* at the Library of Congress, the Herzog August Bibliothek Wolfenbüttel, and the Bayerische Staatsbibliothek.

Conventions in citing the *Hekatompathia*

I place the *Hekatompathia*'s text in italics rather than quotation marks, following the practice that Helen Vendler adopted in her edition of Shakespeare's *Sonnets*. Because the sonnet text is referenced so frequently, using italics avoids what she calls pages "littered with quotation marks" (xvi). These italicized quotations are followed by the sonnet and line number in parentheses, or only the line number if the sonnet being referenced is clear.

The Puzzle's reordering of the *Hekatompathia*'s sonnets required the construction of a special numbering system that reflects the structure and divisions of the new sonnet order, as described in Chapter 5. Sometimes references use the original sonnet number (in Arabic rather than Roman numerals), and at other times the new numbering convention is used—whichever is more likely to be convenient for the reader. "Sonnet Number Converters" allow for quick translation from one numbering system to the other (located at the end of this volume and in Appendix A of Vol. II). The converters also provide a page number reference for the sonnet's text in the addenda of Vol. II. The abbreviations used in the sonnet references are as follows:

H	Head sonnet of a Series (a subgroup of sonnets, as explained in Chapter 5).
HN	Headnote: a headnote appears above every sonnet.
Sz	Stanza: The *Hekatompathia*'s 18-line sonnets have 3 stanzas: Sz1, Sz2, and Sz3.

The editions of the *Hekatompathia*

All published and dissertation editions of the *Hekatompathia* are listed in the "List of Primary Sources" and are identified by the author's or editor's name: Sutton Edition, Heninger Edition, Murphy Dissertation, Phillips Dissertation, and so forth.

The *Hekatompathia*'s three typefaces

The *Hekatompathia*, printed in a single edition in 1582, uses three different typefaces in its text: Old English, a standard serif font, and italics. The use of these three fonts is deliberate, as explained in Chapter 3 and Appendix D, "Notes on the text." All non-facsimile editions, except the 1869 edition, have consolidated the text into two fonts. This loss of fidelity to the original text is not acceptable, and thus this study utilizes three different fonts in its reproduction of the text. To make reading less laborious, the Old English font is rendered in a semibold serif font, the serif font is rendered in a light serif font, and the italics remain unchanged. However, when the *Hekatompathia*'s text is reproduced in short excerpts, only italics are used and all distinction is lost.

Appendices A, B, C, and D (Vol. II)

Appendix A presents the structure of the *Restored Hekatompathia*. Fig. A.1 is a diagram of the work's 3 Subsequences and 10 Series—a useful overview. Appendix B reproduces the cryptographic tables that are discovered and used throughout the solution to the Puzzle. Appendix C lists the deciphering details for all encrypted messages—a summary of the decryptions made throughout the study. Appendix D includes a description of the text's use of its three typefaces, a list of emendations to the text, and a summary of the press variants among the 11 extant copies.

Addenda 1–11 (Vol. II)

These addenda present the sonnet text, including its headnotes, sidenotes, and designs, on a verso page, with both the literary and cryptographic analyses of the sonnet presented on the opposite, recto page. This allows the sonnets to be viewed at the same time as the commentary—like a facing translation.

Excursus 1–12 (Vol. II)

In some instances, background or ancillary materials have been placed in an excursus.

The *Restored Hekatompathia* (Vol. II)

The restored sequence appears at the end of the second volume. Although the sonnets also appear in Addenda 1–11, they are interspersed with my commentary and organized in accordance with the process of their discovery. The text of the restored sequence appears uninterrupted and complete with all prefaces.

Cryptography

Many readers will have no prior experience with cryptography, and therefore, I have included certain basic information about cryptography, which appears in Chapters 1 and 2. An introduction to the process of codebreaking and the method by which cryptograms are validated is presented in Excursus 3, "Cryptanalysis and the validation of deciphered texts." As this study's central claims are cryptographic, this excursus is worth examining.

For those interested in learning more about the role and practice of cryptography in this period, I recommend Gerhard F. Strasser's *The Rise of Cryptology in the European Renaissance* and two of his other contributions to the field (see the List of Secondary Sources). A fascinating compendium of early modern cryptographic practices can be found in *Cryptomenytices* (1623) by Gustavus Selenus (Duke August of Wolfenbüttel). Another valuable resource is *A Material History of Medieval and Early Modern Ciphers*, edited by Katherine Ellison and Susan Kim.

Translations

The Latin translations are mine unless otherwise noted. My translations are deliberately literal, and for poetry, usually maintain line boundaries. Translations of other languages are from the texts found in the List of Primary Sources, unless otherwise noted.

Abbreviations

OED for Oxford English Dictionary, 2nd edition; OLD for Oxford Latin Dictionary; LS for the Lewis and Short Latin Dictionary; STC for Short Title Catalog; *Works*, for the works of Francis Bacon (see the List of Primary Sources).

The appearance of numbers

As mentioned above, I have broken with the standard convention for formatting numbers in this study. I made this decision because the representation of numbers by words rather than Arabic numerals is problematic since this study continuously engages in arithmetic operations. Thus, all numbers greater than 9 appear in Arabic numerals; single digit numbers may or may not appear in Arabic numerals, depending upon their context.

Labyrinth of Ruins editions

Prior to this publication, I privately circulated a small number of copies of an earlier edition, titled *Labyrinth of Ruins: Thomas Watson's Self-Restoring Masterpiece.* That work was written at a time when I had solved only three of the puzzle's seven stages. I refer to the present, two-volume edition as the "Second and Complete Edition."

1

Introduction:

A Systematically Concealed Text

Everything that is deep loves the mask.

–Nietzsche

The *Hekatompathia* (1582), the first English sonnet sequence, surprises its readers with a cryptographic puzzle at a critical juncture in the text. The puzzle's instructions, enumerated in five points, promise that a message can be deciphered using a specific set of published cryptographic tables. This odd, indeed unique, interruption of a poetic text has long baffled critics. Some have dismissed the puzzle as esoterica; one critic argued that the puzzle is unsolvable because its construction is flawed; what no one has previously done is to solve the puzzle. And so, until now, the mystery has remained. However, by applying both cryptographic and literary skills, this study has uncovered the solution to this extraordinarily elaborate seven-stage puzzle, in which each stage produces a cryptographic message. Even more surprising, the seventh stage's cryptographic message reveals that the work's author is not actually he whose name appears on the title page, Thomas Watson, but rather the philosopher, statesman, and harbinger of scientific progress, Francis Bacon.

Unfortunately, specious claims of cryptographic messages embedded in Elizabethan texts constitute almost a cottage industry. Shakespearean texts seem to particularly attract such illusory notions. However, none of these pseudo-cryptographic claims are based on an actual cryptographic system; instead, they rely on a fanciful and unsystematic extraction of letters to produce the message that the "decipherer" anticipated at the start. In fact, in most of these pseudo-cryptographic claims, there is usually no reason to suspect that the examined text contains a hidden message in the first place. In contrast, the *Hekatompathia* openly asserts that a hidden message is present and provides the instructions and cryptographic tables required to decipher it. This study follows those instructions to solve the "Puzzle" (the term used throughout this study), which leads to the deciphering of seven messages. Modern-day mathematical techniques are then used to validate the messages.

Given the history of ludicrous assertions that hidden messages are embedded in Elizabethan texts, this study's reader will naturally be skeptical; however, my hope is that he or she will recognize the categorical differences between its argument and those made under the guise of cryptography. As such, I ask that readers take the proper approach to this study's cryptographic arguments, which is to evaluate them based on the tenets of cryptographic science. These arguments are quantifiable, unlike any matters of literary interpretation or authorship attribution based on the historical record. Indeed, false claims based on a true cryptographic system are difficult to concoct because such systems impose significant constraints. In this sense, the evidence presented here to validate the *Hekatompathia*'s deciphered messages bears some resemblance to the evidence available in certain types of DNA testing in which the discovered correlations could not have arisen by chance (assuming uncorrupted samples and full sequencing). Both DNA and cryptographic tests rely on a coincidence of quantifiable information: the sequences of base pairs (A, T, G, C) in the former and the sequence of letters that form words in the latter.

Past scholarship quite naturally accepted the authority of the *Hekatompathia*'s title page and its authorial attribution to Thomas Watson. However, as discussed below, scholars recognize that a culture of literary anonymity was developed in Elizabethan England, especially among lyric poets. One form of anonymity is to write under a pseudonym, either a fictional name or the borrowed name of an actual person. Thus, even though Watson's authorship appears to be supported by contemporary documents, the purpose of writing under a pseudonym is often to mislead one's contemporaries, which the *Hekatompathia* seems to have successfully done.

As my audience will include literary critics who are not familiar with cryptographic science, this introductory chapter begins with a description of the *Hekatompathia*'s cryptography (no prior knowledge of cryptography is assumed). The fundamental difference between the *Hekatompathia*'s cryptography and the pseudo-cryptographic applied to various Shakespearean texts is considered. Turning to literary matters, the *Hekatompathia* and its reception are briefly described, and an overview of this study's course and its primary concerns are then presented.

Cryptography contrasted with pseudo-cryptography

Unfortunately, the term "cryptography" has been badly abused: various pseudo-scholarly claims have been advanced in which ciphers are "found" when in fact none exist. There are many notorious examples of amateur scholars finding "cryptograms" hidden in Shakespeare's works, and these are purported to reveal that his works were written by someone other than the William Shakespeare born in Stratford. Typically, an enthusiastic proponent of an alternative authorship claim believes that a secret message is embedded in an ordinary text. As Katherine Ellison notes, "The imagination can begin to form connections where they are in fact not present."[1] This is an example of pareidolia, the psychological tendency to find patterns where none exist.

Many such claims were examined in 1958 by two distinguished cryptographers, William F. Friedman and Elizebeth S. Friedman, and they debunked all of the claims they reviewed.[2] Often, they found that these imagined cryptograms stemmed from a reliance on an unsystematic selection or rearrangement of the letters of an ordinary text, as opposed to a valid message deciphered using a clearly defined cryptographic system. Mathematical validations rarely accompany such claims because without a cryptographic system, the process of validation is often impossible to define. In the few cases in which validations are provided, serious flaws are evident. In contrast to such pseudo-cryptography, a cryptographic system operates under clearly defined rules, and the system's properties can be quantitatively analyzed.

One might ask how many claims have been asserted in which a Shakespearean text has been deciphered using a cryptographic system. The answer is none: no true cryptographic claims (i.e., ones based on a cryptographic system) have been proffered at all—not even any false ones.[3] That is because it is difficult to make false cryptographic claims: unless a message is really enciphered in a text, any plausible cryptographic system will deliver nothing other than gibberish. To appreciate the ironclad strength of this study's claim, it is essential to understand the difference between these pseudo-cryptographic claims and a true cryptographic system, such as the one employed in the *Hekatompathia*. We therefore will examine one of the pseudo-cryptographic claims as a foil.

One such claim concerns the enigmatic dedication to Shakespeare's *Sonnets*, which appears in the form of a Roman tombstone (all letters capitalized; interpuncts between words). This unusual format has invited speculation that it hides a secret message. One investigator, John Rollett, arranged the dedication's 144 letters into a rectangle of 8 by 18, as shown in Fig. 1.1. He then concatenated certain letters (highlighted in Fig. 1.1), and by reading either downward or upward, he formed the name WRIO-THESLEY. Many scholars believe that Henry Wriothesley, 3rd Earl of Southampton, is the dedicatee of the *Sonnets*. Rollett claims that the probability of finding this name is one in 20,000 (a calculation that he fails to provide) and that this validates his discovery.[4]

T	O	T	H	E	O	N	L	I	E	B	E	G	E	T	T	E	R
O	F	T	H	E	S	E	I	N	S	V	I	N	G	S	O	N	N
E	T	S	M	r	W	H	A	L	L	H	A	P	P	I	N	E	S
S	E	A	N	D	T	H	A	T	E	T	E	R	N	I	T	I	E
P	R	O	M	I	S	E	D	B	Y	O	V	R	E	V	E	R	L
I	V	I	N	G	P	O	E	T	W	I	S	H	E	T	H	T	H
E	W	E	L	L	W	I	S	H	I	N	G	A	D	V	E	N	T
V	R	E	R	I	N	S	E	T	T	I	N	G	F	O	R	T	H

Fig. 1.1 **A rectangular view of the Dedication in Shakespeare's** *Sonnets*

Rollett's discovery is not based on a cryptographic system, and indeed, the degree of freedom or latitude in his selection of letters is wide and arbitrary. To begin with, the 11-letter name WRIOTHESLEY could have appeared in 11 contiguous letters, or been split into two or four groups rather than the three that he conveniently settles upon to obtain his desired result. Reading upward or downward is an arbitrary choice. The placement of the segments within the rectangle is also arbitrary. The letters might have appeared diagonally instead of vertically, or even horizontally (for a small number of characters, as the open text appears horizontally). The 144 letters could have instead been used to form a rectangle of different dimensions, including 6 by 24, 9 by 16, 12 by 12, 16 by 9, 18 by 8, and so forth. Finally, there are at least a dozen other dedicatee candidates in addition to Henry Wriothesley, and thus any search should not be restricted to only Wriothesley. When we factor the foregoing variations into the calculation, we find that the true probability is closer to one out of two—which is no validation at all—and far from the one in 20,000 that Rollett claims.[5] Moreover, if the dedication's author really wished to embed someone's name by this method, the dedication's text (Fig. 1.1 read horizontally) could have been easily edited to produce WRIOTHESLEY in a contiguous 11-letter span rather than divided into three segments. Indeed, the arbitrary concatenation of three segments to form WRIOTHESLEY should arouse our skepticism. Such free ranging and non-systemic assumptions permit the arbitrary production of a vast range of texts—the fundamental flaw at the center of pseudo-cryptography. Unlike these so called "Shakespearean ciphers," the cryptography presented in this study of the *Hekatompathia* is based on a proper cryptographic system and the work's explicit reference to a set of tables in a widely available cryptographic textbook.

The validation of deciphered texts

Given that the unprecedented claim of Bacon's authorship rests upon the validation of a deciphered message, an explanation of how cryptograms are validated is now provided. An essential cryptographic term is "cryptanalysis": the deciphering of a cryptogram by someone who does not have access to the key. For example, if an enemy courier with an encrypted message is intercepted, an attempt may be made to decipher the message without access to the cryptographic key—often referred to as "cracking" the cipher. In such cases, how do we know that the deciphered message is valid?

When a proper cryptographic system is employed, a deciphered message may be validated using a standard mathematical method. To appreciate how these validations are made, and the level of certainty that they yield, I present a simple example. We examine a 12-letter enciphered message, ZOUMQLDOXMEU, which we suspect was enciphered using the simplest of cryptographic methods, known as a "Caesar shift." In this method, each letter is shifted alphabetically by a fixed number of places. For example, if the shift or key is equal to 3, then the letter that typically occupies position 4 in the alphabet, the letter "D," is encrypted by "shifting" back three letters, and thus the letter "D" is substituted by the letter "A." Similarly, "E" is substituted by "B," "F" by "C," and so on. To decipher the message, one simply reverses the process, substituting D for A, E for B, and so on. In this example, as in all the cryptography of this study, the 24-letter Elizabethan alphabet was used. If our intercepted 12-letter cryptogram is a simple Caesar shift, then the unknown key must be a number between 1 and 23 (24 would be no shift at all). Without knowledge of the key, we may nevertheless decipher our cryptogram (ZOUMQLDOXMEU), commonly called a "ciphertext," by simply iterating through all possible keys, as shown in Fig. 1.2.

Ciphertext:	Z	O	U	M	Q	L	D	O	X	M	E	U
Key = 1	A	P	W	N	R	M	E	P	Y	N	F	W
Key = 2	B	Q	X	O	S	N	F	Q	Z	O	G	X
Key = 3	**C**	**R**	**Y**	**P**	**T**	**O**	**G**	**R**	**A**	**P**	**H**	**Y**
Key = 4	D	S	Z	Q	U	P	H	S	B	Q	I	Z

(Keys 5 through 23 are omitted)

Fig. 1.2 Cryptanalysis of Caesar shift cipher

A key value of 3, shown in bold in Fig. 1.2, produces the deciphered text CRYPTOGRAPHY; all other keys produce gibberish. Even though we do not have direct knowledge that the encipherer used a key value of 3, our sense is that our deciphered message must be correct because the disorder created by all the other alphabetic shifts is so high that an English word or phrase is extremely unlikely to be produced purely by chance. Alphabetic shifts are essentially a randomizing process and are foreign to any natural communicative use of the English language.

We now quantify the probability of the unlikely event that a valid message is produced serendipitously, that is, purely by chance. Is it possible, for example, that a different key value would yield another 12-letter word, say, WICKETKEEPER? What is the probability that when cracking a 12-letter cryptogram enciphered by a Caesar shift, we obtain a valid English message that was not intentionally enciphered? To calculate this probability, we first determine the number of all possible ciphertext messages. The ciphertext could have any of 24 letters as its first character, any of 24 letters as its second character, etc. Cryptographers refer to this as the "absolute rate of language," and it is equal to the number of characters in the alphabet, 24, raised to the power of the number of characters in the message. In our example, the number of all possible 12-letter texts (the absolute rate of language) is 24^{12}, equal to approximately 36,520 trillion. We now must calculate the number of valid messages. For the purpose of illustration, we will make the simplifying (but inexact) assumption that the message can only be a 12-letter word rather than a phrase. (In this study's validations, a more sophisticated calculation is made that allows for multiple words in the deciphered messages.) The number of 12-letter English words is approximately 20,000. What is the probability that one of the 36,520 trillion possible ciphertexts will produce one of these 20,000 12-letter English words?

This probability calculation may be analogized as the purchase of lottery tickets. Suppose that there is a one in one billion chance that any single lottery ticket is a winner. Suppose further that we purchase one thousand lottery tickets. What then is the probability that one of our one thousand tickets wins the lottery? It is approximately one thousand divided by one billion, which is equal to one in one million.[6] Applying this simple division to our 12-letter cryptogram, the probability that any Caesar shift will produce one of the 20,000 12-letter words is 20,000 divided by the number of possible ciphertexts (the absolute rate of language or 36,520 trillion), which is equal to approximately one in 1.8 trillion. Thus, the probability of serendipitously deciphering an unintended message with a given key is very remote. However, we must also account for our examination of all 23 possible keys in the deciphering process (known as "key equivocation"). This has the effect of increasing the probability by a factor of 23. The probability that any of our 23 keys might serendipitously generate a valid message is thus one in 79 billion (23 divided by 1.8 trillion). For all practical purposes, a probability of one in 79 billion describes an event that will never happen.

In this example, three factors enter the calculation: the absolute rate of language (the full range of the ciphertext), the number of valid messages (all valid 12-letter words), and the range of the key (23). This calculation applies the standard methods developed by the founder of Information Theory, Claude Shannon (1916–2001). The basic principle behind the validation of cryptograms is that there are only two circumstances that can produce a valid message: either someone actually encrypted the message using the key, or by some freakish chance, a valid message serendipitously emerged. If one can show that the probability of the second circumstance is sufficiently remote, then the deciphered message must be the encipherer's authentic and intended message. Put another way, a cryptogram is validated by showing that the chance of its accidental generation is essentially nil.

We now consider the difference between the above Caesar shift example and the pseudo-cryptography applied by Rollett to the dedication in the *Sonnets*. In the former, a standard method was applied, and the key had a very narrow range (1 to 23). In the latter, an ad hoc method was applied, and the key effectively had a very wide range. In Rollett's deciphering, the key range is essentially a product of his varied and not-well-defined methods, resulting in an astronomical key range: he arbitrarily selected the rectangle size, the number of segments, the place of each segment, the direction of reading, and so forth. If we multiply the range of each of these arbitrary choices together (as probability theory dictates), the result is billions of keys. In his process of deciphering, Rollett worked backward, looking for the name WRIOTHESLEY (one of two prominently suspected dedicatees of the *Sonnets*) and making key or method choices that result in that name. This is the operative principle behind Shakespearean pseudo-cryptography: the cumulative and wide-ranging arbitrary choices made in the process of deciphering allow for almost anything to be discovered.

In contrast, a true cryptographic system applies a key with a clearly defined range. This clearly defined key range allows for an authoritative calculation of the probability that a deciphered message is valid. Unlike pseudo-cryptography, the messages deciphered in this study are based on a cryptographic system, and the components of that system can be found in various sixteenth-century cryptographic manuals. These deciphered messages are examined mathematically, using the standard methods of Shannon and probability theory.

Unlike pseudo-cryptographic claims, this study discovers Bacon's name only subsequent to the discovery of other deciphered messages. These Latin messages explain the author's poetic purpose, and Bacon's name is revealed only at the end—and with extraordinary flair. The Puzzle's 7-Stage labyrinth design makes it impossible to work in reverse: one cannot start with an assumed name and then choose keys or methods that produce that name. Moreover, the deciphered messages in two of the Stages appear elsewhere in the text, which verify the cryptographic system. In short, the *Hekatompathia*'s cryptography has nothing at all in common with the pseudo-cryptography used in spurious claims of hidden messages in Elizabethan literature.

The *Hekatompathia* and its reception

The *Hekatompathia* ("one hundred love passions") is an unusual work in many respects, beginning with its name, which, as it appears on the title page, includes a word in Greek: Ἑκατομπαθία or *Passionate Centurie of Loue*. The *Hekatompathia* (as it is known) consists of 100 poems, which the author refers to as either "passions" or "sonnets."[7] Most are 18 lines long and consist of three sestets with a rhyme pattern of ababcc; 6 are Neo-Latin poems. I have chosen to refer to all of its poems as sonnets, followed by the number designated in the text. Although this terminology improperly characterizes the Neo-Latin poems as sonnets, it allows for a simple and consistent reference system.[8] For convenience, I use Arabic numerals rather than the original's Roman numerals.

The sonnets draw heavily from both classical and Renaissance sources. Occasionally, they offer a direct translation of an earlier poem, but more often, the poem is a synthesis of tropes or ideas from the source material. The poet displays an extraordinary level of erudition in drawing upon over two hundred sources,[9] exhibiting a profound "knowledge of Greek, Roman, Italian, French, and Continental Latin literature."[10] The *Hekatompathia* provides details on these sources in the headnotes, which precede every sonnet, and sometimes in sidenotes. The headnotes often include lines from the source or sources in their native language and frequently point out differences between the poem and its source. According to A. E. B. Coldiron, the poet's "highly visible commentary elevates lyric to an object of careful study."[11] Some scholars find these headnotes similar to the glosses of E. K. in Spenser's *Shepheardes Calender* (1579).[12] In both E. K.'s glosses and those found in the *Hekatompathia*, one sometimes encounters a peculiar viewpoint or inconsistency, and this presses the reader to a closer reading of the text and to consider various rhetorical and hermeneutic practices, which are taken up in Chapter 4.

A significant bibliographic feature of the *Hekatompathia* is the placement of woodcut figures or designs below most of the sonnets. Throughout this study, they will be referred to as "Designs." There are 18 different Designs, some appearing as often as a dozen times, but others appearing only once. Some Designs seem to consist of flowers or other parts of a plant while others are elaborate drawings.

The *Hekatompathia* comes to us from a single edition published in 1582, of which 11 copies survive.[13] The work has been republished five times (see this study's List of Primary Sources). Dana Sutton's *Complete Works* (1996) is the most recent edition: it is set in modern type and includes valuable notes and commentary. Sutton details the differences between the printed edition and a surviving manuscript. This manuscript is an earlier version of the work, titled "A Looking glasse for Loovers," but only 80 of the *Hekatompathia*'s 100 poems appear in it.[14] There are two unpublished critical editions that contain much helpful material: dissertations by William M. Murphy (1947) and Wendy Phillips (1989).

Unfortunately, there are few, if any, studies focused on interpreting the work itself, as opposed to understanding its place within literary history or how it exemplifies some feature of Elizabethan poetry. Critics have usually lauded its poetic technique: the poet is said to display excellent diction, his rhymes are rarely forced, and his metrical practice "is notable for the unwavering regularity of its meter; even a simple trochaic substitution is extremely rare."[15] On the other hand, with respect to artistic merit, critical judgment varies considerably. Edward Arber counts him a vastly underrated poet, arguing that "in power of gifts, genius, and learning, we would put Spenser first; Watson, second; and Sidney, third."[16] In contrast, more recent scholarship has often been reserved, sometimes taking a dim view of its borrowings from earlier poets. These critics see such direct adaptations of earlier works as lacking originality. No critic has been stronger in his censure than Murphy:

> For the *Hecatompathia* is nothing but a mosaic of Petrarchan conventions, affirmed and reaffirmed through hundreds of lines of precise but unilluminated verse. Watson was not a creative thinker, but rather the inheritor and warden of a sterile culture, who tried to keep alive a tradition whose possibilities had already been fully exploited. ... To study Watson is to study "pure" literature—literature divorced from emotion, philosophy, and human nature, wedded to scholarship and the outworn ideas of the past.[17]

Here Murphy greatly misjudges the work by wrongly applying present-day aesthetic standards to a very different era. The work's borrowings of poetic lines and ideas from other poets, with credit given in his extensive head-notes, follows the Renaissance practice of *translatio*, which is by no means unoriginal replication.[18] Cesare Cecioni sees this practice of borrowing from other works as part of the Petrarchan tradition:

> But the Petrarchan is not a plagiarist in the modern sense of the word: he is a Renaissance poet, i.e. a rational imitator of what he considers the best in the works he takes as models.[19]

Unlike Murphy, other scholars have recognized the work's creativity. After all, intertextual appropriations, ubiquitous in poetry, do not exclude originality. Phillips believes that "his treatment of sources is far from slavish imitation."[20] A. E. B. Coldiron deftly critiques the work's use of sources:

> Watson seems much more willing to force the sources to accommodate to his structures than the other way around, since he so variously rejects replicativity and so often subordinates sources, chopping them up and altering their essential features, even while putting them on display. ... Watson fragments, decontextualizes, and radically recontextualizes the bits and pieces he translates.[21]

Stephen Clucas writes, "Watson emphasizes, then, the plasticity of his sources, and... he is perfectly happy to vary his sources for 'more allowable' considerations of invention or expressivity." He notes that it was popular in sixteenth-century Italy to fabricate poems from fragments of other poems, like mosaics, and is critical of Murphy's dismissive comments about the *Hekatompathia*, believing the work to be undervalued.[22] Edgar Wind insists that "one must abandon the common prejudice that imitation is always a cold and uninspired performance, and hence incompatible with a creative spirit."[23]

Another reason that the *Hekatompathia* has been undervalued is its putative impersonal quality— "divorced from emotion," as Murphy asserts. It disclaims autobiographical truth and lacks the narrative details that can make fictions seem real. This is unfavorably compared with the emotional immediacy found in the sequences of Sidney and Shakespeare. In a sense, the *Hekatompathia* seems akin to mannerist art in its artificiality, self-consciousness, and dependence upon an elaborate and complex set of conventions. Yet these are features, not faults, of certain sixteenth-century poetry, and an issue to which we will return.

But regardless of how we judge the work's artistic merits, a closer analysis of the *Hekatompathia* is warranted because of its extensive influence. It was a progenitor of the many sonnet cycles of the 1590s and of

Shakespeare's *Sonnets* in the following decade.[24] Phillips documents a number of strong connections, mostly borrowed tropes and words, that connect the *Hekatompathia* to Shakespeare's *Sonnets*.[25] C. S. Lewis writes, "Watson is perhaps closer to Shakespeare than to any other sonneteer in his conception of the sonnet."[26] Lisle John believes that the *Hekatompathia* is "one of the most important but least-read books of the century."[27]

The authorship of the *Hekatompathia*

The *Hekatompathia*, according to its title page, was "composed by Thomas Watson, Gentleman," which has long gone unquestioned by scholars. The *Hekatompathia*'s poet is recognized as having been both a polymath and polyglot.[28] Much of his work was written in Latin and directed toward an elite, well-educated audience.[29] Michael Hirrel reports that "Watson's learning and writing, especially *Amyntas* and [his translation of] *Antigone*, were highly esteemed by his contemporaries, both during his life and long after. A great many encomia survive."[30] Moreover, he "not only helped shape modern drama in general, but directly touched the plays of Kyd, Marlowe and Shakespeare."[31] Watson appears to have been a member of the Philip Sidney literary circle, in which he apparently developed a close relationship with Sidney and possibly Edmund Spenser.[32] Dana Sutton argues that "his literary output serves to present a cumulative portrait of Watson as first and foremost a philosophical moralist and apostle of Continental culture."[33]

Judgments about Watson's personal life, however, are not complimentary: "He was in his personal life, truly, a rogue."[34] In 1579 he accepted a fee from a mentally unstable woman for soothsaying, which fed her delusion and ultimately caused her to suffer.[35] He was a friend of Christopher Marlowe, and in 1589 interceded in a duel between Marlowe and another man, Bradley. After being seriously wounded by Bradley, Watson killed him, saving both his own life and Marlowe's, though doing so landed him in jail for several months. In another unsavory affair, he participated in a scheme to defraud his employer.[36] Perhaps this should alert us that something is afoot: it seems odd that a man with such deep intellectual pursuits and "a philosophical moralist" should have engaged in these illicit activities.

The *Hekatompathia*'s four separate authorial prefaces (an extraordinary number for any time period) assert that the work may be read in two possible ways: either as a "toy," or in some other, more serious manner. In the last of these prefaces, just prior to the first sonnet, the poet addresses his book as if it were a person and then makes this enigmatic statement:

> **But still observe this rule where ere thou staye,**
> **In all thou mai'st tender thy father's fame,**
> „ Bad is the Bird, that fileth his own nest.   (*Quatorzain*, 8–10)

Many books were published anonymously in this period, either without any author's name, with initials only, or under a pseudonym. The above lines suggest that the author is concerned about his reputation, and that the book adheres to some unspecified *rule*, presumably to protect the author's reputation, for *Bad is the Bird, that fileth his own nest*. However, *in all*, the book shall *tender* the poet's *fame*. Solving the Puzzle's seventh and final Stage elucidates the meaning of these words, for that Stage's cryptographic message reveals that Francis Bacon is, in fact, the *Hekatompathia*'s author, not Watson.

Bacon wrote under a pseudonym on a few occasions, and here wrote under the name Thomas Watson, a real person.[37] The lives of Bacon and Watson coincide in several respects: both were believed to be playwrights (Bacon wrote a masque); both were close to Francis Walsingham, England's spymaster, and likely part of Walsingham's intelligence network in France in the late 1570s; both were lawyers; both were members of the Sidney-Leicester literary circle.

There are a few scattered indications that Bacon wrote poetry. In one letter, he refers to himself as a concealed poet.[38] A poem written after his death, found among the papers of Bacon's chaplain (Rawley), identifies him as a poet.[39] He was a master of rhetoric, and sonnet sequences are a form of rhetoric (epideictic). His *Wisdom of the Ancients*, an interpretation of ancient myth, displays considerable literary knowledge. He was a close associate of members of the Sidney-Leicester literary circle and is believed to have written masques at Gray's Inn.[40] None of this provides even circumstantial evidence that Bacon wrote the *Hekatompathia*, and certainly not, as some might claim, the works of Shakespeare. My purpose in listing these references is to show that his contemporaries would not have been surprised to learn that he wrote poetry. However, as discussed above, my argument that he wrote the *Hekatompathia* is not based on historical evidence, but on the mathematically validated deciphered message that identifies him as the author.

However, if Bacon wrote the *Hekatompathia*, why does Thomas Watson's name appear on its title page? The appearance of a false name is a form of anonymity, which was widely practiced in this period, according to Marcy North:

> The modern neglect of anonymity as a subject of study is somewhat
> surprising given how popular and interpretable anonymity was in

early modern England. ... Whether for reasons of personal safety, social decorum, or political and rhetorical effectiveness, early modern authors and book producers manipulated anonymity in remarkably diverse ways, sometimes looking back to medieval conventions of anonymity, sometimes responding directly to the demands of print culture and Tudor-Stuart politics, and often employing age-old conventions of anonymity in unique and surprising ways.[41]

North reports that literary anonymity was "cultivated" and "became very popular among the lyric poets." She gives several examples of the use of false names, including that of dramatist John Bale.[42] Often when the author's name is suppressed, no attribution is possible due to the lack of historical evidence. The use of a false name is especially problematic because there may be no indication of the deception.

An intriguing case of authorship suppression is found in *The Arte of English Poesie* (1589), published anonymously, but later attributed to George Puttenham. Paradoxically, *The Arte*'s author advises authors to shun anonymity, which directly conflicts with his own decision to publish anonymously. Yet this ambiguous depiction of anonymity is consistent with the conflicting social aims of discretion and the desire for recognition for the purpose of advancement.[43] North argues that Puttenham's suppression of his own name, his advice against doing so, and his story of how the manuscript arrived with no author's name at a printer is indicative of a literary game of concealment and revelation:[44]

> Although anagrams, name games, and even anonymity occupy a space that is more internal than that of a modern signature, Puttenham consistently expects the disguised names and the anonymity that propels them to identify subjects and authors in a complex bi-directional process. ... When addressing elite audiences, authors were especially dependent on the audience's willingness to respect the guise of anonymity and see through it simultaneously.[45]

Bacon had many reasons for not publishing the *Hekatompathia* under his own name. He was beset by various difficulties stemming from his father's recent death, and he was attempting to begin a political career, which required discretion. One might ask why he used another person's name rather than publishing under "Anon" or "Ignoto." One advantage of using Watson's name is that it might act to deflect speculation about authorship that publication under "Anonymous" might encourage. The *Hekatompathia* displays an extraordinary learning that borrows from hundreds of sources, and if the question of the work's authorship had been left completely open, then the coincidence of certain biographical details (Bacon's role in an embassy to France and his close connection to Walsingham) may easily have led to speculation that Bacon was the author.

A potentially graver concern was that his text might easily be read as blasphemous: its cosmogony contradicts Christian doctrine, and thus Bacon had good reason to obscure his authorship. In such circumstances, an author may wish to communicate two different messages within the same text: one to the general public and another to an elite group sympathetic to his dangerous ideas. An obvious technique for accomplishing this is the use of cryptography—something at which Bacon excelled. Richard Serjeanston, in his analysis of Bacon's use of a pseudonym to conceal his authorship of *Valerius Terminus*, explains that pseudonymity was commonly practiced by Bacon's associates:

> Pseudonymity served a similarly protective function in the indistinct world of Elizabethan epistolary espionage that was inhabited by Bacon's early friend Thomas Phelippes and by his brother Anthony Bacon. A more contrived form of pseudonymity was also prominent among writers of verse in the Elizabethan court, where perhaps its most notable exponent was Sir Philip Sidney, whose sonnet sequence is addressed by the figure of "Astrophel" (star-lover) to a lady called, just like Bacon's annotator, "Stella." Bacon was no stranger to these worlds, having moved in all of them since his youth.[46]

Both North and Serjeanston see the practice of pseudonymity as a natural response to the political and social dangers of this period.

Francis Bacon

Bacon was a philosopher, theorist of experimental science, statesman, and lawyer. In an often-quoted letter to his uncle, William Cecil, he brashly states, "I have taken all knowledge to be my province."[47] He proposed fundamental changes in application of common law that allowed more recent case law to supersede older and less relevant law—a fundamental reform that remains with us to this day. He initiated the idea of the modern research university. He believed in a future in which man would learn to harness the forces of nature, which would result in technological innovations greatly benefiting mankind. Most relevant to this study, he developed the experimental methods that are the foundation of modern science. Andrew Hiscock asserts that Bacon has been characterized, both by scholars and himself, as "the High Priest presiding at the dawn of a new age of intellectual discovery."[48]

As this study unfolds the *Hekatompathia*'s complex, multistage Puzzle, the genius that went into its creation will become apparent. Surprisingly, some of the Puzzle's components utilize techniques found in modern-day software systems. Only the rarest of geniuses could have created such a Puzzle. Bacon made extraordinary contributions to several fields and saw far beyond his own time—a comparison might rightly be made to Leonardo da Vinci, who foresaw inventions that only became practical centuries later. The rare incidence of such talent severely limits the number of potential authors of the *Hekatompathia*, should we suspect that Watson is not the true author, because only a truly exceptional mind could have created its unprecedented Puzzle. To demonstrate the unusual fecundity of Bacon's mind in his practice of cryptography, we can examine an invention that he developed in his youth, the "biliteral cipher" (the biliteral cipher plays no role in the *Hekatompathia*).[49]

Bacon's "biliteral cipher" uses a subtle difference in the appearance of text to encode a message. In this technique, two different styles are used in the composition of a letter. An example of a biliteral cipher is shown in Fig. 1.3, which employs two different styles of type, one bold and the other light. The difference in style has been made obvious in the figure for the sake of clarity; in practice, the difference must be subtle enough to go unnoticed by all but those who know to look for it.

EVERYTHING IS **PEACEFUL**

EVERY	THING	IS **PEA**	CEFUL
00110	10100	00111	00101
6	20	7	5
F	U	G	E

Fig. 1.3 An example of a biliteral cipher

The open message, "everything is peaceful," hides a secret message: each group of 5 letters encodes one letter of a secret message. The differences in type style produce a binary number, shown in the second tabular row of Fig. 1.3. The third row converts this to a decimal number, and the fourth row translates this to a letter in the Elizabethan alphabet (e.g., 6 designates "F," the sixth letter of the alphabet). The secret message, FUGE (Latin: flee), warns the decipherer that everything is *not* peaceful and that he or she had better flee.

Bacon recognized that 5 bits of information can encode an alphabet of up to 32 letters ($2^5 = 32$). The use of binary numbers to designate letters is a fundamental computer technology (ASCII) developed in the twentieth century, and to find it used in the sixteenth century is surprising. Adding to our surprise, Bacon points out that the information content of the open text is 5 times the size of the secret text: "The infolding writing shall contain at least five times as many letters as the writing infolded."[50] In other words, the ratio of the information in the open text to that in the secret text is 5:1. Bacon has quantified the amount of information a message holds logarithmically, a concept that only reemerged four centuries later when Claude Shannon developed his Information Theory, a staple of modern computer and communications technology.[51]

Bacon saw himself as presiding over an intellectual revolution. He rejected the deference given to the authorities of antiquity, "how men are ever saying and doing what has been said and done before."[52] In *The Refutation of Philosophies*, Bacon's speaker derides Plato and Aristotle, placing them "among the Sophists."[53] Bacon's natural philosophy rejects Platonist and Aristotelean conceptions of the natural world, instead reaching back to the views of certain pre-Socratic philosophers.

Overview of the Puzzle

The Puzzle abruptly appears at a critical juncture in the *Hekatompathia*, at the beginning of its second subsequence. The reader is explicitly challenged to decipher an encrypted message using a specific set of tables. The Puzzle provides a set of instructions on a page numbered as if it were the 80th sonnet, followed by an acrostic sonnet presented in two different formats on subsequent pages. This interruption of a poetic collection to present a cryptographic puzzle is bizarre and unprecedented. Commentators, lacking any literary context in which this might fit, have either ignored it or attempted to explain it as some mystical or esoteric digression. To my knowledge, no one has previously attempted to solve it.

The Puzzle's instructions are only the beginning of a journey through a complex, hierarchically structured labyrinth that, in certain respects, bears a surprising resemblance to a modern computer adventure game. The Puzzle tests the would-be-solver's poetic knowledge, inductive reasoning skills, and cryptographic expertise. Each step in its solution advances the puzzle-solver along a labyrinthine course through the Puzzle's seven levels or "Stages." Knowledge acquired in each Stage of this hierarchy aids the puzzle-solver in subsequent Stages. Remarkably, some of the Puzzle's mechanisms resemble features found in present-day computer software: a network of interdependent tables, redundant indices, linked lists, inheritance, and recursion. Although the appearance of this technology in the sixteenth century might seem highly improbable, these technological mechanisms are improvements upon, or intensifications of, existing late

Renaissance practices: elaborate indexing methods, the place-logic of influential Dutch humanist Rodolphus Agricola, and the *Ars Memoriae* (mnemonic techniques). These methods, widely practiced during the Renaissance, are combined with sixteenth-century cryptographic methods to form an unusual hermeneutic system—the Puzzle. It pushes the reader to closely evaluate the poetic text, which leads to its radical rearrangement: 83 of the sequence's 100 sonnets are reordered. This reordering completely transforms the significance of the text: effectively, a new sixteenth-century sonnet sequence is revealed. Thus the occlusion of Bacon's authorship is part of a larger obfuscation: that of the correct order of the text itself.

The Puzzle resembles a jigsaw puzzle: each piece—or sonnet—must be placed in its proper, predetermined location. This location is established by the sequence's well-defined structure and by multiple systems of intratextual links, including links between adjacent sonnets. The *Hekatompathia* also resembles a labyrinth: solving the Puzzle requires the navigation of the sequence's tightly defined structure toward a predetermined endpoint. After the sequence is reordered, each sonnet's context—the newly adjacent poems and its overall position within the sequence—often radically alters our reading of it. Thus, the new order and its finely articulated architecture re-signifies its component parts, its sonnets. As such, the sequence is utterly transformed, and its new order exhibits a thematic development that ends quite differently from the work in its published order.

The scrambling of the sonnet order and the provision of the Puzzle that allows the reestablishment of the true order serve two purposes: the work's heretical cosmology is hidden and the puzzle-solver is forced into an intimate engagement with the details of the text. This close reading of the text is concomitant with the work's didactic intent: the reader is fully immersed in the sequence's architecture and the significance of its poetry.

How is it possible to rigorously specify the order of the 83 sonnets that have been scrambled? The number of permutations in which 83 sonnets may be ordered is an astronomical number ($83! \approx 4 \times 10^{124}$). If the new order is to be rigorously defined, then some special apparatus is required. This apparatus, the Puzzle, consists of two systems, which I call the Heuristic System and the Precision System, as shown in Fig. 1.4. The Heuristic System provides various mechanisms that allow the puzzle-solver to restore the sonnets to their proper order. These mechanisms include indices, intratextual links, thematic subdivisions, the poet's glosses, semiotic designs, ring patterns, and thematic progression. All of the foregoing mechanisms were in use in the sixteenth century and some much earlier. I have characterized this system as heuristic because it depends on language and interpretation, which are inexact. For example, the index mechanism requires that the puzzle-solver match phrases from a list to sonnet lines, in a manner similar to how a crossword puzzle's clues link to its words—an interpretive judgment must be made.

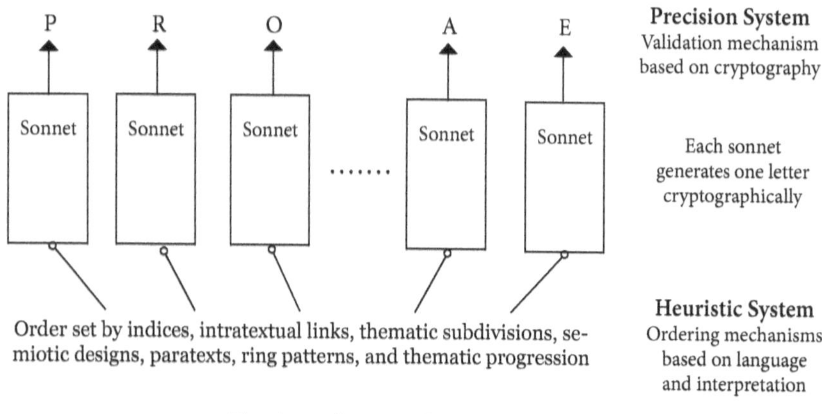

Fig. 1.4 The Puzzle's architecture

However, the question may arise: will different interpretations result in different restorations of the sonnet order? The Heuristic System protects against this by using multiple mechanisms to specify a sonnet's location. These overlapping mechanisms increase the puzzle-solver's confidence in their decision to place a sonnet in its new position. Indeed, often an initial interpretation will be made, only to later find that it conflicts with what is indicated by another one of the Heuristic System's mechanisms. An interpretation must then be found that satisfies both mechanisms. In this way, the Heuristic System requires interpretation but guards against misinterpretation, which follows Bacon's pedagogical model (see "Poetry and pedagogy" section below). The ultimate purpose of the Heuristic System is to instruct readers in hermeneutics—the art of reading poetry.

The Heuristic System's overdetermination is augmented by the Precision System, which further ensures the correctness of the reordering process. It utilizes various cryptographic techniques practiced in the sixteenth century, as will be discussed in Chapter 6. It validates the sonnet order by having each sonnet generate a single letter in a cryptographic message. If the message is coherent, then the sonnets must be in their correct order; if they are not correctly ordered, then the message is garbled. Fig. 1.4 depicts the beginning and ending letters of the message enciphered in the Puzzle's second Stage: the first three letters are PRO and the final two are AE. The complete message is PRODIGA LIBERTAS ANIMAE (an overly free state of mind), which appears in one of the work's Neo-Latin poems, as will be discussed in Chapter 7. The message enciphered in Stage 3 is also a known text; the messages in Stages 4 through 6 are unknown texts that help the puzzle-solver's advance through the Puzzle; the message in Stage 7 contains Bacon's name.

The genius of the Puzzle's design is its incorporation of two systems that work in tandem, one heuristic and one reasonably precise. The Heuristic System tests and develops the puzzle-solver's understanding of poetry: poems must be reordered to make the sequence coherent. Hints about order are provided in many forms, including phrase lists that serve as indices, links between adjacent sonnets, hints in sonnet headnotes, and repetitive structures. Nevertheless, the great number of permutations and the uncertainties of language make the reordering process challenging and somewhat uncertain. The Precision System is an adjunct that stabilizes interpretation, akin to an answer key: if the reordering is incorrect, the deciphered message is incoherent. The deciphered message acts like the combination lock on a safe: the exact numbers must be entered if the safe is to be opened. If the puzzle-solver has not correctly ordered the sonnets, he or she must return to the Heuristic System to find and correct his or her mistakes in ordering the sonnets. A clever mechanism, later explained, makes it difficult to use the Precision System in reverse, that is, to derive the sonnet order from the deciphered message. The Puzzle is designed to force the reader into a close engagement with the text, interpreting it under the guidance of the Heuristic System. The Precision System acts like a good instructor: it refuses to give the student the answer directly, and instead indicates where the student's work is correct and where deficiencies require further effort. In effect, the Precision System acts as a proxy for the absent poet.

The Precision System is not entirely free of language judgments, that is, it has some overlap with the Heuristic System. As will be later explained in Chapter 4, it uses linguistic links to designate certain lines that are then employed as ciphertext. Nevertheless, the Precision System's mechanisms are robust enough to allow a mathematical validation of its cryptographic results. The Puzzle is crafted so that the discovery of the work's hidden significance is very challenging, yet once discovered, that significance can be verified mathematically and recognized as the author's true intent.

The primary mode of solving the Puzzle is unlike cryptanalysis (code-breaking). The cryptanalyst usually has the ciphertext in hand but must discover the tables by which it was encrypted. In the Puzzle, as shown in Fig. 1.4, the ciphertext is generated from scrambled sonnets, and until those sonnets have been properly reordered using the Heuristic System, no ciphertext is available. On the other hand, the initial encryption tables are given to the puzzle-solver, as described in Chapter 2.

The obscured text

Often an author wished to communicate two messages within a single text, each to a different audience: a public message that anyone could read, and a hidden message, often contradictory to the apparent message, that was directed toward a select audience. The belief that art could be used to speak both falsity and truth was also prevalent in antiquity. The muses tell Hesiod that "we know how to speak many false things as though they were true; but we know, when we wish, to proclaim true things."[54] A poet must follow this example of the muses, and rather than simply revealing the truth, the truth must be rhetorically hidden under a cover of lies. Philosophy may also make good use of lies, something not lost on Plato, according to Stanley Rosen:

> Throughout Plato's dialogues, one finds a continuous interest in false-hood, suspicion, deception, and concealment, an interest that is curiously unnoticed in the secondary literature. For an appreciation of this side of Plato, one must turn to Nietzsche, who is the first major thinker of my acquaintance to appreciate explicitly the connection between spiritual nobility and the mask. [In the *Republic*], Socrates makes the interesting assertion that falsehood is not useful for the gods, whereas it is useful for mortals in the form of a medicine [*pharmakon*].[55]

Pharmakon can mean a magic potion or a poison, and we are reminded of Plato's "noble [or medicinal] lies," necessary falsehoods that his ideal republic requires in order to function. We will find that the outer form of the *Hekatompathia*, its necessary lies, serve an educational purpose: the reader must identify and eradicate these lies by solving the Puzzle, which reveals the hidden truths within.

Leo Strauss recognized that radical ideas can only be safely expounded by means of an obfuscated text. In his *Persecution and the Art of Writing*, he describes how Maimonides, Judah Halevi, and Spinoza hid the expression of ideas that would have endangered their lives. "Ordinary language is utterly insufficient" for this purpose, and the writer must resort to "parabolic and enigmatic speech." Yet understanding these writers centuries later is extraordinarily difficult: "However greatly we may think of the qualities of the modern historian, he certainly is neither per se able to understand esoteric texts nor is he an esoteric writer."[56] According to Strauss, Maimonides recognized certain formal deficiencies in the Torah (e.g., abrupt changes, unnecessary repetitions, contradictions), and his method of embedding hidden meaning is based upon intentional formal deficiencies in his own text. The reader of Maimonides's *Guide for the*

Perplexed must therefore recognize textual deficiencies and figure out why they appear.[57] Indeed, according to Strauss, Maimonides implies that the Bible itself is an example of parabolic literature.[58]

The obfuscation of literary texts was common in the sixteenth century, an era of religious strife. Erasmus, "the West's chief humanist at the dawn of humanism," thought that certain beliefs should be treated as "mysteries reserved for the initiated."[59] Those who were erudite could be trusted with such secrets, but a mass audience could not.[60] The *Hekatompathia* not only hides meaning using cryptography but also follows a long tradition of hiding its secrets by means of rhetorical practices.[61]

In Bacon's *De Augmentis*, immediately after detailing his biliteral cipher, he describes methods of communication that differentiate between "vulgar" and "select" auditors. The former is addressed using an "Exoteric" method and the latter by an "Acroamatic," or esoteric, method. He explains that the ancients usually prepared different texts for each group, but that, in "later times," the obscurity of the delivered message is used "to exclude the vulgar (that is the profane vulgar) from the secrets of knowledges, and to admit those only who have either received the interpretation of the enigmas through the hands of the teachers, or have wits of such sharpness and discernment as can pierce the veil."[62] Bacon depicts these two opposed methods of communication on many occasions. In "Cassandra," the first myth in his *Wisdom of the Ancients*, he makes clear that presenting certain topics indiscreetly risks damaging one's reputation.[63] Bacon's *New Atlantis* "can easily be seen as an allegory for this relationship between secrecy and publicity," according to David Colclough.[64] In *The Refutation of Philosophies*, he describes a speech delivered in a secluded location to a select group of learned men, in which the speaker launches a radical attack against the Western philosophical tradition.

The *Hekatompathia*'s authorial prefaces suggest that the work may be read in two different modes, one exoteric and the other esoteric: in one mode, the work is frivolous (*A toye*), and in the other, it is taken seriously, but the manner of reading is left unspecified.[65] The second of these modes is only accessible through the Puzzle, which allows the reader to pierce its "veils" and restore the text to its proper order. In the first mode, reading the *Hekatompathia* in its published order, love is a powerful and debilitating force that the speaker rejects. In the second mode, reading the sequence in its restored order, love is a primordial and insurmountable natural force that appears to rival or even supplant the Christian belief in God.

The Puzzle is extremely complex and places inordinate demands upon the exegete. Why make things so difficult? One reason, according to a belief that dates back to antiquity, is that the difficulty of interpreting a text made the discoveries all the more memorable.[66] One fifteenth-century

Italian humanist tells us that "what is described by the poets with the highest artifice is at length sought out with great industry and labor, and once discovered is more valued."[67] Aquinas argues that "the darkness of figures serves to exercise those eager to learn."[68] Macrobius, in the quotation that prefaces this study, sees the unveiling of hidden truths in a text as the true office of a scholar. According to Augustine, "what is attended with difficulty in the seeking gives greater pleasure in the finding," a sentiment also found in Arthur Golding, who believed that overcoming difficulty "makes the mynde more glad."[69] Anthony Bacon concurs when he writes *Difficilia quae pulchra* (difficulties make for beauty/nobility).[70]

According to Kenneth Borris, Platonizing allegory was common in the early modern period, and included "the soul's nature and its path to knowledge, true self-recognition, and the fruition of its highest capacities; its quest for reality and truth amidst the bewildering welter of appearances, and its means of returning to heaven; ... ideal imitation and icastic truth, as opposed to their misleading counterparts; and the universal correspondences supposed to structure reality."[71] Such esoteric wisdom, it was believed, did not come easily, and thus, it was appropriate to dispense it only in a veiled manner. Such veils are made difficult to remove—for to do otherwise would devalue the esoteric knowledge that is hidden, as Boccaccio instructs us:

> Surely no one can believe that poets invidiously veil the truth with fiction, either to deprive the reader of the hidden sense, or to appear the more clever; but rather to make truths which would otherwise cheapen by exposure the object of strong intellectual effort and various interpretation, that in ultimate discovery they shall be more precious. ... As saith Francis Petrarch ... "what we acquire with difficulty and keep with care is always the dearer to us." ... But I repeat my advice to those who would appreciate poetry, and unwind its difficult involutions. You must read, you must persevere, you must sit up nights, you must inquire and exert the utmost power of your mind. If one way does not lead to the desired meaning, take another; if obstacles arise, then still another, until, if your strength holds out, you will find that clear which at first looked dark.[72]

The last two sentences describe the challenges faced in solving the Puzzle: the unwinding of "difficult involutions," the false paths that lead only to frustration, and, above all, the need to persevere. Although on first encountering the Puzzle one might judge its complexity and scope to be idiosyncratic, its intricacy and entanglements with multiple modes of signification were not uncommon in this era. As C. S. Lewis points out, the intellects of this period delighted in building large, ordered models, especially in cosmology and philosophy.[73] Such works as the *Roman de la Rose* and *The Faerie Queene* attest to the complexity of the literary canon of the medieval and early modern periods.

Erasmus's Silenic literary model

The concept of two reading modes, one public and the other secret, is found in Erasmus, who posited a literary model in which a shell of outer meaning obfuscates a text's inner meaning. Erasmus's "The Sileni of Alcibiades," published in a 1515 edition of *Adages*, was widely available and had a considerable influence in England.[74] The title refers to Alcibiades's speech in the *Symposium* in which he compares Socrates to "those little Sileni that you see on the statuaries' stalls... they're modeled with pipes or flutes in their hands, and when you open them down the middle there are little figures of the gods inside" (215b). Silenus, a satyr (a ludicrous figure), was the tutor of Dionysius, and the statue of Silene appears "worthless or ridiculous," according to Erasmus, but "on closer and inward consideration, [it] proves admirable."[75] Erasmus explains that Socrates "had the face of a country bumpkin, a bit like that of an ox, and a snub nose always running with snot." Nevertheless, he writes, "if you open up this Silenus, who is outwardly so ridiculous, you find within someone who is closer to being a god than a man, a great and lofty spirit, the epitome of a true philosopher."[76] In this "statue of Silenus" model, an ugly outward appearance hides inner beauty, a concept that here is applied to a person but could easily also pertain to a literary work.

This "Silenic" rhetorical model is especially applicable to the *Hekatompathia*. Other sixteenth-century works also employ this model, including Erasmus's *Moriae Encomium* (*In Praise of Folly*), which, like the *Hekatompathia*, confronts the reader with ambiguity and contradiction that the reader must resolve to make sense of the work. Erasmus's personified Folly describes pairs of contradictory images that must be "undone" in order to disclose "a new semblance."

> For fyrst it is not vnknowen, how all humaine thyngs lyke the Silenes or duble images of Alcibiades, haue two faces muche vnlyke and dissemblable, that what outwardly seemed death, yet lokyng within ye shulde fynde it lyfe: and on the other side what semed life, to be death: what fayre, to be foule: what riche, beggerly: what cunnyng, rude: what strong, feable: what noble, vile. ... Briefely the Silene ones beyng vndone and disclosed, ye shall fynde all thyngs tourned into a new semblance.[77]

Arthur Kinney argues that Erasmus converts a rhetorical sophistry into a poetics, pushing "his reader to work at the task of reconciliation" of the opposites that Folly presents.[78] David Wootton, in his introduction to "The Sileni of Alcibiades," asserts that the Silenus statue trope "implies that every text participates in a debate about how to interpret the world, and that the language in which texts are written is slippery, with the meanings of words... constantly liable to turn into their opposites."[79] This Silenic rhetorical model was also taken up by Rabelais, who in his prologue to *Gargantua* pays homage to Erasmus's "The Sileni of Alcibiades." He recommends that the reader have "a sagacious flair for sniffing and smelling out and appreciating such fair and fatted books, to be swift in pursuit and bold in the attack, and then, by careful reading and frequent meditation, to crack open the bone and seek out the substantifical marrow."[80] Thus, he defines his text as a quest, challenging the reader to ferret out the work's "marrow" or substance, which, he promises, will be no easy task.

The *Hekatompathia*'s hidden "marrow" only becomes visible after the reader restores the sonnet sequence to its proper order. Its poet has scrambled the order of its sonnets, building upon a prevalent literary mode, the "ruined text," that emerged in the sixteenth century. Just as Rabelais in the prologue to *Gargantua* alerts the reader to hidden meaning, the *Hekatompathia*'s prefaces point to hidden significance that the reader must uncover to arrive at a deeper understanding of the work. Like *In Praise of Folly* and *Gargantua*, the *Hekatompathia* is a tissue of violations of grammar, logic, and decorum, and the reader's task is to puzzle through these anomalies in order to reach the "marrow" that is secreted within the text. However, unlike those works, or any other known work, the *Hekatompathia* contains a precise device, the Puzzle, that allow the reader to cut through to the "marrow," and this leads to a comprehensive and authenticated restoration of the ruined work. Only the later Stages of the Puzzle are devoted to hiding the poet's name; the purpose of the earlier Stages is to restore the order of the *Hekatompathia*'s scrambled sonnets, revealing a very different sonnet sequence. The poetics of the ruined text will be taken up in Chapter 4.

How could Francis Bacon, who railed against the excesses of poetic fictions, be himself a lyric poet? On closer examination, however, Bacon expressed sharply divergent attitudes towards poetry, and this self-contradiction (which occurs in Bacon's preface to *Wisdom of the Ancients*) was noticed long ago by a contemporary, Henry Reynolds:

What shall we make of such willing contradictions, when a man to vent a few fancies of his owne shall tell vs first, they are the wisdome of the Auncients, and next, that those Auncient fables were

but meere fables, and without wisdom or meaning til their exposi-
tours gaue them a meaning; & then scornefully and contemptu-
ously (as if all Poetry were but Play-vanity) shut vp that discourse of
his of Poetry with *It is not good to stay too long in the Theater.*[81]

This contradiction has frustrated many contemporary critics in addition
to Reynolds. What many critics seem to have missed is that Bacon practices esotericism in his discussion of esotericism. Indeed, contradiction is
central to esoterism because although it obscures the truth, it also reveals
the means by which the truth may be discovered: the resolution of the
contradiction. Bacon is a "master practitioner of the esoteric," an art that
he likely learned from multiple sources, including Plato and Montaigne.[82]
His aphoristic writing is a "knowledge broken" that can only be understood if the reader mends the work (as this study has done for the *Hekatompathia*). Thus, fragmentation serves Bacon's didactic purposes.[83]
Ronald Levao describes a critical tradition that has had difficulty grappling with Bacon's apparent self-contradiction:

> Bacon's wavering reveals a split found throughout his work that has
> produced a critical tradition of two fundamentally opposed portraits:
> Bacon as the enthusiast of both "powers of imagination and under-
> standing" and Bacon as harbinger of narrow objectivism, the "dissoci-
> ation of sensibility," and worse.[84]

For Bacon, poetry, and imagination are both necessary and dangerous.[85]
Poetry, a form of rhetoric, appeals to the reader's imagination, and it car-
ries the force of persuasion, which is necessary for its effectiveness. However, it has no claim upon the truth (also Plato's concern in his *Republic*).
Bacon's ambiguous attitude to poetry may be better understood by considering his treatment of an analogous problem that presents itself in scientific advancement:

> The understanding must not however be allowed to jump and fly from
> particulars to remote axioms and of almost the highest generality (such
> as the first principles, as they are called, of art and things), and taking
> stand upon them as truths that cannot be shaken, proceed to prove and
> frame the middle axioms by reference to them; which has been the
> practice hitherto; the understanding being not only carried that way
> by a natural impulse, but also by the use of syllogistic demonstration
> trained and inured to it. But then, and then only, may we hope well of
> the sciences, when in a just scale of ascent, and by successive steps not
> interrupted or broken, we rise from particulars to lesser axioms; and

then to middle axioms, one above the other; and last of all to the most general. ... The understanding must not therefore be supplied with wings, but rather hung with weights, to keep it from leaping and flying. Now this has never yet been done; when it is done, we may entertain better hopes of the sciences.[86]

In both poetry and experimental science, the imagination is necessary, but needs to be fettered. The Puzzle is a "weight" that controls and stabilizes the interpretation of the text. Solving the Puzzle requires a process similar to that used in scientific investigation: one must proceed step by step, Stage by Stage, through the Puzzle in a slow ascent. Bacon intentionally created locks between the Puzzle's Stages to enforce this slow ascent, and indeed, whenever I attempted to "jump and fly," bypassing a step or Stage, I was blocked. The Puzzle's Heuristic System often requires the puzzle-solver's imagination to progress; the Precision System is the weight that stabilizes and validates meaning. Solving the Puzzle requires shuttling back and forth between these systems, which was fundamental to Bacon's new approach to learning, according to Levao:

> What keeps this mental shuttling between affirmation and hypothesis in motion is the stimulus of unresolved contradiction, the sustaining of opposed intellectual motions. Intellectual heat, no less than physical heat, requires a prolonged contest—"perpetually quivering, striving and struggling, and irritated by repercussion." ... The new organon he offers seeks out its adversary, whether it is the world of brute, unexplained "nature" or the "mimic and fabulous worlds" of theologians and poet-philosophers. If the lines of opposition are initially set by the renovating force, that force is itself contingent on and revised by successive acts of opposition.[87]

The Heuristic System, poetic and hypothetical, and the Precision System, scientific and affirmative, fulfill complementary roles. The "obsessive modern opposition between scientific and poetic knowledge" makes this difficult for us to grasp today, but the *Hekatompathia*'s Puzzle achieves a harmony between these two opposed forms of knowledge.[88]

Andrew M. Cooper claims that for Bacon, a fable (a fiction like myth and poetry) might serve as "a collective repository of common sense [and] supply a model for the new organon based on induction and shared enterprise."[89] He concludes that the "fable is a prototype of inductive empiricism."[90] Christopher Crosbie argues that Bacon's "approach to the fable [was] compatible with his project of reforming natural philosophy [and] remains in this regard rather consistent throughout his writing life."[91]

The Puzzle is a rigorous test of one's skill in inductive reasoning: it requires the puzzle-solver to make inferences—sometimes imaginative ones.

William Eamon recognizes the importance of a creative imagination in Bacon's method, which included analogy, conjecture, and a search for clues, which Bacon called "prerogative instances." Sometimes the investigator "must make intuitive leaps from the seen to the unseen."[92] However, such leaps must always be tested. In the case of the Puzzle, testing is performed using the Precision System and progress only occurs when hypotheses are validated. Only then can we accept as valid an axiom about the Puzzle's operation or make an entry into one of its numerous tables. The Puzzle, like the physical world in which scientific hypotheses are tested, governs the interpretation of the text. According to Eamon, Baconian induction was an attempt to translate *metis*—"the artisan's cunning or the natural magician's intuition—into a method." Bacon attempted "to define a rigorous methodology for conjecturing from the seen to the unseen aspects of nature, and from effects to causes."[93]

Reading rhetorically

How does one read esoteric works? The most important lesson I learned in solving the Puzzle was that one must assiduously pursue the quest for coherence despite the appearance of disorder, or rather, because of the appearance of disorder. The section in Chapter 4 titled "Alerting the reader: breaches of decorum" provides examples of how contradictions, irrelevant digressions, and other breaches of decorum are flagrant signals that should not be ignored. Such breaches must be pursued because they point to a solution, and if tenacious enough, the reader will prevail and discover underneath an exterior cloak of chaos, a unified work.

This argument suggests that Bacon's work is closed rather than open, which runs against the trend in contemporary criticism. David Parry believes that this has led to misreading Bacon:

> Given Bacon's recognition of the contingency of human knowledge and his anxieties about the capacities of language to mislead, it is tempting for literary scholars after Derrida to read Bacon as an anti-teleological advocate of the perpetual free play of signifiers with no final resolution, but this would be to misread Bacon, since Bacon holds that "that vse of wit and knowledge is to be allowed which laboureth to make doubtfull thinges certaine, and not those which labour to make certaine things doubtfull" (*Advancement* 91).[94]

The Puzzle is a device that allows us to make "doubtfull thinges," the heuristic reordering of the text, "certaine." It closes an open text and enables the work's teleological purpose to be realized.

Our understanding of esotericism has been greatly enhanced by Nietzsche, whose long practice of philology greatly influenced not only his own work, but that of later scholars. He advises readers:

> Philology is that venerable art which demands of its votaries one thing above all: to go aside, to take time, to become still, to become slow. ... It teaches to read well, that is to say, to read slowly, deeply, looking cautiously fore and aft, with reservations, with doors left open, with delicate eyes and fingers.[95]

The practice of "close reading," promoted by I. A. Richards and William Empson in the first half of the twentieth century, deserves our consideration today. The process of solving the Puzzle required that I practice close reading. Every sonnet had to be read carefully to discover its structure, links to other sonnets, relationship to source material cited in the headnote, and its place within the sequence's finely specified architecture. This resulted in the present study, which in filling two volumes, seems out of proportion for a sonnet sequence that is not often read. Nevertheless, this was required to solve the Puzzle.

In addition to close reading and careful attention to contradictions, the exegesis of esoteric works often benefits from an examination of the work's structure. The Puzzle, of course, is welded to the structure of the work, which was fundamental to Bacon's plan. In the *Novum Organon*, he contrasts his own writing with that of the ancients, whom he is criticizing:

> [The ancients] thought it superfluous and inconvenient to publish their notes and minutes and digests of particulars; and therefore did as builders do,—after the house was built they removed the scaffolding and ladders out of sight. (*Works*, 4.111)

In contrast, Bacon leaves his scaffolding in place, or at least partially visible, and the skilled reader uses it to extract the work's esoteric significance. Bacon is a master builder, and the method by which he constructed a text cannot be separated from the text itself. The Puzzle is valuable because it reveals the methods by which other texts (even though they lack puzzles) may be mined for their esoteric content. The Puzzle hides not only the author's name, but a radical materialist philosophy. It lays bare the scaffolding used to construct a complex poetic collection and reveals its secret significance.

Cryptography as a poetic device

The use of a cryptographic system as the stabilizing backbone of a poetic collection is unprecedented. Sometimes cryptography is confused with numerology (a form of symbolism), esotericism, or the occult; however, it is really a practical science. Although it was sometimes associated with the occult during the Renaissance, it is first and foremost a technology that allows for secure communication. It was used extensively in military and diplomatic operations, as well as in private correspondence.

The literary uses of cryptography have typically been limited to the hiding of an author's name (e.g., in acrostics), which dates as far back as Anglo-Saxon literature (see "The uses of cryptography in literature," Excursus 1). The *Hypnerotomachia Poliphili* (1499) hides a message (which may or may not include the author's name) using steganography, a form of cryptography.[96] Steganography refers to the hiding of one text within another, a technique used by the Puzzle, as described in the next chapter and in "Steganography: Exterior and interior writing methods," Excursus 2. The *Hekatompathia*'s expansive use of cryptography has, to my knowledge, no known predecessor.

The Puzzle's design allows for the puzzle-solver to discover the true order of the work's sonnets. Each sonnet may be thought of as a *topos* (topic or place), a discrete packet of knowledge. Terence Cave sees *topoi* as a major concern of sixteenth-century French literature:

> The redeployment or re-grounding of topoi is, of course, a major pre-occupation of French Renaissance writing in general. Rabelais, Ronsard, and Montaigne are all caught, in their different ways, in the same problem: the resistance of alien fragments within a new formal context tends to disrupt the movement of the text towards a stable meaning, and thus draws attention to the mode of operation rather than to the product of the writing system. As a corollary, this same phenomenon blocks the possibility of full thematic closure.[97]

A cornucopia of diverse materials extracted from earlier writers proves difficult for a writer to integrate in a manner that leads to stable meanings and thematic closure. Cave believes this results in an open text—a plurality of possible meanings—a position consistent with modern literary theory. He argues that "the absence of any extra-linguistic criterion ruins the possibility of a reassuring dialectic and imprisons the speaker or writer in the labyrinthine detours of language, in its surface or *species*."[98]

In contrast to this characterization of French Renaissance literature, Bacon hopes that his reader will escape the labyrinth and arrive at "full thematic closure." Although this may have been unattainable for those French writers discussed by Cave because they lacked "any extra-linguistic criterion," the *Hekatompathia*'s cryptography, its Precision System, is an extra-linguistic device that allows for definitive thematic closure. Bacon has presented his readers with scattered poetic fragments—ruins—and expects them to build a "sonnet palace" based on the blueprints he provides. Those blueprints include the Heuristic System, in which order and interpretation emerge, and the Precision System that regulates and validates the order derived from the Heuristic System.

Poetry and pedagogy

Poetry was considered a form of rhetoric, and sonnet sequences fall under the category of epideictic poetry: the good is praised and practical knowledge is instilled in the reader. The title of an incomplete manuscript version of the *Hekatompathia*, "A Looking glasse for Loovers," indicates that the work follows the literary tradition of *specula principum* (mirrors for princes). This genre reflects back to the reader (or prince) his faults and also presents an ideal image to which the reader should aspire. Solving the *Hekatompathia*'s Puzzle is foremost an educational exercise that is meant to instruct the reader about the nature of love, and at the same time, test and develop the reader's reasoning and inductive skills.

Bacon distinguishes between two pedagogical methods or modes of communication: magistral and probative. In the former, an eminent authority disburses knowledge to the student, who readily accepts it. Bacon describes the giver and receiver of knowledge in this magistral mode of communication:

> For he who delivers knowledge desires to deliver it in such form as may be best believed, and not as may be most conveniently examined; and he who receives knowledge desires present satisfaction, without waiting for due inquiry... sloth making the receiver unwilling to try his strength.[99]

Bacon rails against this approach: "The sciences are presented in such a way as to enslave belief instead of provoking criticism; the intervention of a blighting authority precludes fruitful research."[100] In contrast, in the probative method of transmission, according to David Colclough's description of it, "the reader's understanding is facilitated by a reproduction of the writer's arrival at his conclusions."[101] In the probative mode, the communication from giver to receiver is subtle and insinuative. Bacon describes it thus:

> But knowledge that is delivered to others as a thread to be spun on ought to be insinuated (if it were possible) in the same method wherein it was originally invented. And this indeed is possible in knowledge gained by induction; but in this same anticipated and premature knowledge (which is in use) a man cannot easily say how he came to the knowledge which he has obtained. Yet certainly it is possible for man in a greater or less degree to revisit his own knowledge, and trace over again the footsteps both of his cognition and consent; and by that means to transplant it into another mind just as it grew in his own.[102]

For Bacon, a reader must understand a writer's thinking, and follow it step by step in a manner that imitates the writer's invention of his material. This is the very method of the Puzzle: it forces the reader to rethink the creation of the *Hekatompathia*, mimicking the process by which the poet ordered and arranged his sonnet sequence. According to Rhodri Lewis, for Bacon, "any text that purports to impart true learning must do so heuristically, thereby initiating the student into the true significance of what was being taught." Lewis suggests that Bacon, in his *Thoughts and Conclusions*, "heaped praise on the pre-Socratic philosophers for the aphoristic form of their fragments, and it is no coincidence that, in [his *Advancement of Learning*], King Solomon is depicted as teaching through 'excellent Parables and Aphorismes.'"[103] The fragmentary nature of aphoristic writing forces the reader to make connections, just as allegory or parables demand interpretation. In both cases, the reader must heuristically create a fully formed work in his or her own mind that is organic and coherent, to whatever extent possible.

Bacon's promotion of probative over magistral instruction is derivative of Plato's educational method. Plato's intellectual opponents, the Sophists, taught oratorical skills and rhetoric for the purpose of persuasion. In contrast, Plato believed that students should be taught how to think for themselves: when thoughts or knowledge is handed down, there must be a renewal of that knowledge (see *Symposium* 207e). Unlike a Sophist instructor, a good writer...

> will sow his seed in literary gardens... collecting a store of refreshment both for his own memory, against the day 'when age oblivion comes,' and for all such as tread in his footsteps. ... The dialectician selects a soul of the right type, and in it he plants and sows his words founded on knowledge, words which can defend both themselves and him who planted them, words which instead of remaining barren contain a seed whence new words grow up in new characters, whereby the seed is vouchered immortality, and its possessor the fullest measure of blessedness that man can attain unto. (*Phaedrus* 276d–277a)

Bacon is a rhetorical Platonist: dialectic argument, unresolved paradox, and rhetorical complexities all provoke the engagement of the reader, who, through the interpretive process, breathes new life into the work. The *Hekatompathia* delivers "seeds," scrambled sonnets, relatively barren of meaning in their disordered state, which the puzzle-solver must bring to an ordered state. In the *Theaetetus*, Socrates compares his method to that of a midwife, who does not create the child but assists in the process of bringing it forth into the world (150bcd). M. F. Burnyeat, in his reading of the *Theaetetus*, explains the difference between the educational method of the Sophists and that advocated by Socrates:

> The Sophist treats his pupil as an empty receptacle to be filled from the outside with the teacher's ideas. Socrates respects the pupil's own creativity, holding that, with the right kind of assistance, the young man will produce ideas from his own mind and will be enabled to work out for himself whether they are true or false.[104]

The *Hekatompathia*'s exegete, like Socrates's "young man," must "work out for himself [what is] true or false." The puzzle-solver engages in no ordinary reading experience, but becomes the poet's apprentice and, under the guidance of the poet's hidden blueprint, must reconstruct the poetic text. The great advantage of this scheme is that it immerses the puzzle-solver in the details of a poetic collection's creation: deciphering the poet's rhetorical glosses, discovering intertextual sources, recognizing the links in its concordantial text, interpreting symbols and figures, perceiving metric anomalies, and unraveling the overarching structure that governs the work. The puzzle-solver is forced to engage with the work at both the architectural level and down to the smallest of details, providing comprehensive lessons in the art of poetic creation. Thus, the *Hekatompathia* practices the Platonic ideal of active participation of the student, and, it must be acknowledged, on an extraordinarily expansive scale.

Bacon derived his pedagogical methods not only from Plato but also from sixteenth-century humanists, including Erasmus (the Silenic literary model, discussed above). Philip Sidney begins his *Defence of Poesie* with a discussion of horsemanship: the relationship between rider and horse is a metaphor for the relationship between poet and reader. Rather than provide direct instruction, the poet ought to instruct the reader (i.e., the horse) in such a manner that he or she still feels as if they are in control. Yet, at the same time, the poet (i.e., the rider) exercises significant control over which direction the reader takes.[105] In Rabelais, Gérard Defaux finds "a special kind of dialogue, in which the author dictates both the questions and the answers and keeps the reader, so to speak, on a leash."[106]

Bacon not only promoted this probative mode of writing but practiced it himself. According to Julianne Werlin, Bacon "reserves his highest praise for 'Parabolical' poetry, because it demands intensive and skilled interpretation: it conceals and 'infold[s]' its teaching, allowing authors to write about subjects whose 'dignity… requires that they should be seen as it were through a veil.'" Yet he was concerned that readers might stray too far in their interpretations, and thus, he "hedged his writing with additional layers of authorial direction."[107] In his *Wisdom of the Ancients*, he pushes the reader to reconsider the traditional readings of ancient mythology, offering new allegorical interpretations for the reader's consideration. Lewis argues:

> [In Bacon's critical vision, the] student of mythopoeic allegory is a heuristic and creative agent, completing the poem's field of reference for himself through an act of rational reconstruction. In its turn, this reflects Bacon's preferred mode of initiative or probative rhetoric, but it also implies that no single mythographic interpretation could be definitive. … The mythographer's true task is to identify and assess the wisdom that lies behind the allegories of the textual record, not within them.[108]

Mythographic and allegorical interpretation are obviously subject to multiple interpretations and misinterpretation, which may conflict with a poet's desire to clearly convey a single or unified meaning. The challenge the poet faces is to harness the great energy inherent in allegory and myth, and at the same time, subtly inform the reader which meaning among several potential meanings is the intended one. The poet has various methods at his disposal, including prefaces (and other paratexts) that offer direct guidance, rhetorical signals within a text, and the work's organizational structure. The need for coherence across a text restricts the range in which the reader may rationally reconstruct meaning and may be sufficiently restrictive to recover hidden meaning with a high degree of confidence.

Colclough believes that "the proleptic gesture is present almost everywhere in [Bacon's] writings."[109] *The Refutation of Philosophies* practices this probative mode through a "rhetorical refiguring," in which a received text "is accorded authority, then framed by a commentary and a contextualizing preface only in order for it ultimately to be superseded."[110] This strategy is similar to that used in the *Hekatompathia*, where four authorial prefaces and the headnotes that precede each sonnet provide context for reading the text. Further, the *Hekatompathia* explicitly builds upon others' poetry, often Petrarchan sonnets, but modifies and reorganizes these materials for its own ends. Building upon a root stock—Petrarchan poetry—that is deeply established, Bacon gains at the outset a receptive audience. Yet, the ordering and glossing of these materials allow him to subvert his source texts, and as I later argue, expound a counter-Petrarchan philosophy.

Bacon's poetic practice may be understood in the context of Gadamer's phenomenological thesis concerning works of art, which was derived both from his reading of Plato's dialogues and Heidegger. According to Gerald Bruns, Gadamer sees a work of art as "an event as well as an object."[111] Gadamer argues that like music, "it is in performance and only in it... that we encounter the work itself."[112] Bruns describes Gadamer's thought:

> On this theory it is a mistake to think of the work as a self-contained formal object that merely persists in time and retains its identity as a relic that fills up museums and standard editions. The work of art is not (or not just) an aesthetic object. ... Hermeneutic identity is not something to be construed like a meaning, but something to be constructed as the form that occasions the event of the work. In *Truth and Method* Gadamer calls this event "transformation into structure," a taking shape in which the work materializes as the thing it is in our experience of it—something that happens again and again each time we experience the work.[113]

The Puzzle induces the reader to effect a "transformation into structure." The *Hekatompathia* has been read as an aesthetic object, without much consideration given to its structure, and obviously its ruined state deserves much blame. Nonetheless, even in its ruined state, the first 17 properly ordered sonnets should have been analyzed for their structure, as this study does (see Chapter 3). Also, little attention has been paid to the structure of individual sonnets. Nor do critics read the work as a performance; instead, it has been treated as a cultural artifact or museum piece. Although thoroughly cataloged by curators, attempts at exegesis have been rare, even though there is much to consider even without solving the Puzzle.

Nietzsche argued that art is "not knowing but schematizing, superimposing as much regularity and as many forms onto chaos as suffices our practical needs."[114] For Nietzsche, like Bacon, the schematizing function is a product of the imagination.[115] Human beings must live in illusion (*das Leben im Schein*), which may be realized by the creation of their own little worlds.[116] Art is making for Nietzsche, as it is for Sidney in his *Defence* and in the *Hekatompathia* as well: the Puzzle's fundamental purpose is to teach the art of making. Stanley Rosen argues that "From Descartes to Kant, Fichte, and Hegel... if in different ways... the identification of knowledge as construction or projection is regulated by the mathematical conception of identity and order but therefore implicitly by the Platonist doctrine of formal unity."[117] The Puzzle, most remarkably, develops the reader's imagination and ability to schematize, while at the same time, compelling the restoration of the work to its predetermined end state, in which formal unity is realized.

The *Hekatompathia* practices the probative mode of communication at its extreme limit: it destroys the order of 83 sonnets but provides the reader the tools by which he or she may effect a perfect restoration. The Precision System is the essential technological apparatus that makes this radical practice possible. Only by means of a quantitative technology such as cryptography can such a massive reconstruction of sonnet order be reliably specified. The Puzzle, with its paired Heuristic and Precision Systems, allows the poet to both insinuate meaning in its initiative or probative rhetoric, and at the same time, guarantee perfect fidelity in the transmission of meaning. Werlin argues that Bacon's goal is to avoid misinterpretation: "*New Atlantis* reveals that Bacon is a theorist of a complexly disseminated system of written knowledge, which notwithstanding its power could introduce, as well as eliminate, misinterpretations."[118] The *Hekatompathia*'s Precision System guarantees correct interpretation, that is, the proper reconstitution of sonnet order, which profoundly changes our reading of the *Hekatompathia*'s individual sonnets as well as the sequence as a whole. In the restored order, the work's conclusion is completely inverted: love is a blessing rather than a curse.

The Puzzle and Baconian experimental science

The Puzzle and the method of its solution are best understood in the context of Bacon's views on scientific discovery, even though they were published decades after the *Hekatompathia*. In antiquity, nature was viewed as hiding behind a veil: one medical treatise declares that one must do violence to Nature to force her to reveal her secrets.[119] This metaphor of a veiled nature that must be forcefully interrogated continues through to the early modern period. Bacon, in his recounting of the myth of Pan, describes the "hunt of Pan" (*venatio Panis*):

> The discovery of things useful to life... is not to be looked for from the abstract philosophies... but only from Pan; that is from sagacious experience and the universal knowledge of nature, which will often by a kind of accident, and as it were while engaged in hunting, stumble upon such discoveries.[120]

Bacon describes one method of inquiry that he calls *experientia literata* (literate experience), which proceeds by "extending or transferring or putting together former inventions."[121] Sophie Weeks describes Bacon's *experientia literata*:

> There must be a first digestion of materials to reduce the mind's confusion when confronted with the disorganised and seemingly infinite range of materials that constitute the primary history. ... In Bacon's scheme, *experientia literata* is both a phase of inquiry in itself and an incipient part of a higher phase of inquiry (interpretation of nature) that culminates in the discovery of forms. In its broadest sense, *experientia literata* refers to the primary history drawn into 'titles and tables.' The tables bring 'all the experiments of all the arts... collected and arranged [*digesta*]... within one man's knowledge and judgment.[122]

This closely resembles the process by which the Puzzle is solved. The reader is confronted with anomalies and disorganized materials such as scrambled sonnets, and at first, these difficulties seem intractable. But then one notices certain structures or forms that may offer a path forward. These structures are often in the form of a table whose entries are incomplete. The challenge is to properly interpret and organize the poetic text, a process managed largely by the completion of table entries, which tests one's knowledge and judgment. This process of discovery, analogous to the search for Pan, occurs within the Puzzle's Heuristic System.

As one progresses through the Puzzle, and more table entries are discovered, the Puzzle's overall architecture begins to emerge. The Puzzle's regulatory apparatus, its cryptography-based Precision System, comes into view. The Precision System plays a role analogous to that of axioms in Bacon's theory of scientific discovery, the Heuristic System is akin to experimental testing performed in his theory. Solving the Puzzle requires both Systems, just as there are two independent processes in Bacon's model of scientific inquiry. Weeks describes these two processes or methods:

> First, the range of information assembled forms the input and its structuring in tables (*experientia literata*) provides the equivalent of a directing mechanism, in the sense of homing in on a target. Second, the experimental attempt to confirm the axiom provides the feedback. The positive feedback (production of *nova*) from the experimental testing is the guarantee that the investigation is still pursuing its target in nature (*res*).[123]

The Puzzle's Precision System will either produce a coherent message or gibberish. If a coherent message is obtained, the construction of the tables (the *experientia literata*) using the Heuristic System is validated and one progresses; if gibberish is obtained, the puzzle-solver must descend back to the Heuristic System and correct their errors. I experienced this shuttling up and down many times in the course of solving the Puzzle. Weeks calls this a "cybernetic epistemology:"

> Bacon states time and again that his 'route is not laid on the flat but goes up and down—ascending first to axioms, and then descending to works.' According to Bacon, 'all true and fruitful Natural Philosophy has a double scale or ladder going in different directions, ascendent and descendent.' ... Interpretation of nature is a continual play of error correction that produces a cybernetic epistemology, guaranteed to find the target. ... Bacon's procedures are cybernetic by virtue of his asymmetrical criterion of truth which incorporates negativity in an error-correcting procedure. ... The negative instance excludes useless pursuits and redirects the inquiry back onto a fruitful course. The experiments of philosophical mechanics feed back into the inquiry in a continual play of error correction: this is the basis on which I chose the term 'cybernetic epistemology' to characterise Bacon's blending of error correction and truth production.[124]

The Greek root of "cybernetic" means "governance:" the Precision System governs interpretations derived in the Heuristic System, rejecting any incorrect interpretation. The *Hekatompathia* begins in chaos, as does ancient Greek cosmogony: its sonnets are scrambled and it ends with the death of Cupid—a rather ridiculous end for a collection of Petrarchan love poems. Not only does Nature hide but art does too in this Silenic text. The Heuristic System must be used to repair the text, step by step. The Precision System monitors the reader and excludes false repair. The Puzzle—through the use of these two tandem Systems—are the reader's toolkit for repairing the text.

The course of this study

In the next chapter, we begin our solution of the *Hekatompathia*'s Puzzle, a long labyrinth that requires 12 chapters and 11 addenda to navigate and document each step in our journey. Most of this study's readers have expertise either in literature or cryptography but not both, and therefore it would have pleased most readers if I had fully separated out the literary arguments from the cryptographic work. However, I had no choice but to present the Puzzle linearly, navigating this strange labyrinth along the narrow path that its poet defined long ago. Although I have separated literary and cryptographic arguments wherever possible, the path through the labyrinth (as laid out by the poet) alternates between the two disciplines. Thus I have no choice but to treat literary and cryptographic discoveries as they arise in the step-by-step solution to the Puzzle.

True, this requires that the reader follow the threads of two disciplines, but in many ways, this is the point of the Puzzle. The *Hekatompathia* is scientific poetry, that is, poetry built upon a highly ordered cosmological model in the tradition of Lucretius's *The Nature of Things*. The process of solving the puzzle instructs the puzzle-solver in how to find order within disordered material. It also teaches an intensive reading process by which significance is distilled from a poetic text that is often obscure. Thus the comingling of a literary journey, the restoration of sonnet order, and the deciphering of cryptographic messages serves the poet's pedagogical purposes, as discussed above and in this study's final chapter.

This does not necessarily prevent the deciphering and validation of cryptograms from being evaluated independently, especially in the later Stages. However, it would have been extremely awkward to present decryptions outside of their context—that is, the point in the Puzzle at which they occur. Furthermore, this study cannot skip ahead to later Stages because they are entirely dependent upon the discoveries of earlier Stages. The Puzzle's solution path is locked into a singular set of successive steps; as in a labyrinth, only one path leads toward the exit.

In the next chapter, we solve the Puzzle's first Stage and decipher its encrypted message. The third chapter then takes up the ramifications of this message. It also discusses the *Hekatompathia*'s rhetorical practices, examines its first 17 unscrambled sonnets, and describes the sequence's structure and underlying cosmological model. The fourth chapter considers the traditions and methodologies found in the poetics of ruin and restoration. We then return to the Puzzle, and in Chapters 5 through 13, we solve the Puzzle's second through seventh Stages. Chapter 13 solves the seventh Stage, which reveals Bacon's authorship of the sequence. Chapter 14 then examines the philosophical story that the sequence unfolds. The final chapter considers the *Hekatompathia* in the context of the poetics and intellectual history of the early modern period.

This study's front matter includes a Reader's Guide that provides a description of this study's organization, reference conventions, and other practices. This is essential reading due to the uniqueness of this study's subject: the *Hekatompathia* and its Puzzle.

2

Stage 1: The Puzzle Sonnet

The *Hekatompathia*'s title page declares that the work is *divided into two parts*, which this study refers to as "Subsequences." The title page describes the second Subsequence as a *long farewell to Loue and all his tyrannie*. The headnote of the last sonnet of the first Subsequence, Sonnet 79, states that the sonnets that follow *are all made vpon this Posie, My Loue is past*. This poesy appears in bold capital letters (MY LOVE IS PAST), blazoned at the top of every sonnet in the second Subsequence and also the Epilogue. The term "MLIP Subsequence" is used to refer to this blazoned second Subsequence, which includes the Epilogue. The first Stage of the Puzzle appears on the first three pages of the MLIP Subsequence: the poet's decision to place it at this, the work's critical dividing point, elevates the importance we attach to it. Solving the Puzzle's first Stage reveals the foundation of the cryptographic system that is utilized in all 7 Stages and produces an 18-letter message that is essential to further progress in the Puzzle.

The first three pages of the MLIP Subsequence consist of Sonnets 80 through 82, one on each page. However, Sonnet 80 (Fig. 2.1), though labeled as if it were the 80th sonnet, is not actually a sonnet but the Puzzle's prose instructions. Read literally, the work's title, *Hekatompathia*, promises 100 (*hekatón*) passions (*pátheia*) but actually delivers 99, as Sonnet 80 is not a poem. Two headnotes appear to bolster this contradiction.[1] This violation of decorum also alerts us to the significance of these instructions. A further suggestion of its significance is found in the illumination of its first letter; only two other illuminated letters appear in the work: the dedication to de Vere and the *To the frendly Reader* preface. For convenience, Fig. 2.2 shows Sonnet 80 reset in modern type and reformatted so that its five enumerated "Points" are distinctly set off (the numbers 1 through 5 appear at the left margin in the original).

LXXX.

MY LOVE IS PAST.

ALL such as are but of indifferent capacitie, and haue some skill in Arithmetike, by viewing this Sonnet following compiled by rule and number, into the forme of a piller, may soone iudge, howe much art & study the Authoz hath bestowed in the same. Where in as there are placed many pzeaty obseruations, so these which I will set downe, may be marked foz the pzincipall, if any man haue such idle leasure to looke it ouer, as the Authour had, when he framed it. First therfoze it is to be noted, that the whole piller (except the basis oz foote thereof) is by relation of either halfe to the other Antitheticall oz Antisillabicall. Secondly, how this posie (Amare est insanire) runneth twyse thzough out yᵉ Columne, if ye gather but the first letter of euery whole verse ozdezly (excepting the two last) and then in like manner take but the last letter of euery one of the said verses, as they stand. Thirdly is to bee obserued, that euery verse, but the two last, doth end with the same letter it beginneth, and yet thzough out the whole a true rime is perfectly obserued, although not after our accustomed manner. Fourthly, that the foote of the piller is Orchematicall, yᵗ is to say, founded by transilition oz ouer skipping of number by rule and ozder, as from 1 to 3, 5, 7, & 9: the secret vertue whereof may be learned in * Trithemius, as namely by tables of transilition to decypher any thing that is wzitten by secret transposition of letters, bee it neuer so cunningly conueighed. And lastly, this obseruation is not to be neglected, that when all the fozesaide particulars are perfozmed, the whole piller is but iust 18 verses, as will appeare in the page following it, Per modum expansionis.

* Polygra-
phiæ suæ lib. 5

Fig. 2.1 Sonnet 80: The Puzzle Sonnet instructions
(Reproduced from the 1869 edition)

ALL such as are but of indifferent capacitie, and haue some skill in Arithmetike, by viewing this Sonnet following compiled by rule and number, into the forme of a piller, may soone iudge, howe much art & study the Author hath bestowed in the same. Where in as there are placed many preaty obseruations, so these which I will set downe, may be marked for the principall, if any man haue such idle leasure to looke it ouer, as the Authour had, when he framed it.

1. First therfore it is to be noted, that the whole piller (except the basis or foote thereof) is by relation of either halfe to the other Antitheticall or Antisillabicall.

2. Secondly, how this posie (Amare est insanire) runneth twyse through out ye Columne, if ye gather but the first letter of euery whole verse orderly (excepting the two last) and then in like manner take but the last letter of euery one of the said verses, as they stand.

3. Thirdly is to bee obserued, that euery verse, but the two last, doth end with the same letter it beginneth, and yet through out the whole a true rime is perfectly obserued, although not after our accustomed manner.

4. Fourthly, that the foote of the piller is Orchematicall, that is to say, founded by transilition or ouer skipping of number by rule and order, as from 1 to 3, 5, 7, & 9: the secret vertue whereof may be learned in *Trithemius, as namely by tables of transilition to decypher any thing that is written by secret transposition of letters, bee it neuer so cunningly conueighed.

*Polygraphiae suae lib. 5

5. And lastly, this obseruation is not to be neglected, that when all the foresaide particulars are performed, the whole piller is but iust 18 verses, as will appeare in the page following it, Per modum expansionis.

Fig. 2.2 Sonnet 80: Puzzle Sonnet instructions reformatted for clarity

LXXXI.

MY LOVE IS PAST.

A Pasquine Piller erected in the despite of Loue.

```
          A   1  At
              2  laſt, though
              3  late, farewell
              4  olde well a da: A
         m    5  Mirth or miſchance ſtrike
        a   6  vp  a  newe  alarM,  And   m
           7  Cypria        la        nemica
      r  8  miA  Retire  to  Cyprus  Jle,  a
    e  9  & ceaſe thy waRR, Els muſt thou proue how   r
  E  10  Reaſon can by charmS Enforce to flight thy   e
 s  11  blindfolde bratte & thee. So frames it with mee now,   E
t  12  that I confeſS, The life I ledde in Loue deuoyde   :
I  12  of reſT, It was a Hell, where none felte more then I,   t
 n  11  Nor anye with lyke miſeries forlorN. Since   n
  s  10  therefore now my woes are wered leſS, And   s
    a  9  Reaſon bidds mee leaue olde welladA,  a
      n  8  No longer ſhall the worlde laughe mee
        i  7  to ſcorN; J'le chooſe a path that   n
          r  6  ſhall not leade awrie.  Reſt   i
              5  then with mee from your
              4  blinde Cupids carK   r
          e. 3  Each   one   of
              2  you, that
                 1  ſerue,
              3  and would be
              5  freE. H'is dooble thrall   e.
           7  that liu's as Loue thinks beſt, whoſe
          9  hande ſtill Tyrant like to hurte is preſte.
```

Huius Colum-
næ Baſis, pro
ſillabarum nu-
mero & linea-
rum proporti-
one eſt Orche-
matica.

Fig. 2.3 Sonnet 81: Puzzle Sonnet in "pillar" format
(Reproduced from the 1869 edition)

LXXXII.

MY LOVE IS PAST.

Expanſio Columnæ præcedentis.

A	At laſt, though late, farewell olde wellada;
m	Mirth foꝛ miſchaunce ſtrike vp a newe alarm;
a	And Ciprya la nemica mia
r	Retyꝛe to Cyprus Ile and ceaſe thy warr,
e	Els muſt thou pꝛoue how Reaſon can by charme
E	Enfoꝛce to flight thy blyndfold bꝛatte and thee.
s	So frames it with me now, that I confeſſ
t	The life I ledde in Loue deuoyd of reſt
I	It was a Hell, where none felt moꝛe then I,
n	Noꝛ any with like miſeries foꝛloꝛn.
s	Since therefoꝛe now my woes are wered leſſ,
a	And Reaſon bids me leaue olde wellada,
n	No longer ſhall the woꝛld laugh me to ſcoꝛn:
i	I'le chooſe a path that ſhall not leade awꝛi.
r	Reſt then with me from your blinde Cupids carr
e.	Each one of you, that ſerue and would be free.
"	* His double thꝛall that liu's as Loue thinks beſt
"	Whoſe hand ſtill Tyꝛant like to hurt is pꝛeſt.

τόν τόι τύρα=
νον ἐυσεβἑιν
ὀυ ῥάδιον.
Sophoc. in
Aia. flagell.

Fig. 2.4 Sonnet 82: Puzzle Sonnet in customary format
(Reproduced from the 1869 edition)

Sonnet 81 (Fig. 2.3) is a sonnet whose shape has been strangely distorted. It is labeled *A Pasquine Piller erected in the despite of Loue*, a reference to a statue in Rome that was used to post anonymous messages, as later discussed. Sonnet 82 (Fig. 2.4) shows the same text as Sonnet 81, though reformatted into the sonnet's customary form. In Point 2 (Fig. 2.2), the instructions state that *if ye gather but the first letter* of each line of the sonnet (referring to it in its customary form) except the last two, reading vertically downward yields this poesy: *amare est insanire* (to love is madness). The same is true for the last letters of each line, making this sonnet a double acrostic poem.

The purpose of these three pages (Figs. 2.1, 2.3, and 2.4) is not specified, but they include several strong suggestions that a message is somewhere encrypted. Point 4 of the Puzzle's instructions (reformatted for clarity in Fig. 2.2) makes several references to secret writing: the phrase *tables of transilition*—a likely reference to cryptographic tables; the declaration that there is something to *decypher* by *secret transposition of letters*; the allusion to something *cunningly conueighed*; the sidenote that references Trithemius's *Polygraphia 5*—a well-known cryptography manual. Indeed, this fourth point introduces two key words that Trithemius uses repeatedly to describe his enciphering process: *transposition (transpositionem)* and *Orchematicall (orchemate)*.[2] The title of *Pasquine Piller* (Fig. 2.3) refers to a monument used for the secret transmission of messages. Wendy Phillips addresses the possibility of a hidden message:

> It seems extraordinary that Watson should have referred the reader to Trithemius merely to draw attention to the syllabic count of each line increasing by odd instead of consecutive numbers [in the base], and it is tempting to look for a message encoded along the lines of Trithemius's principles. But, given the existing complexity of the poem, it would be even more extraordinary had Watson managed to include yet another arcane device.[3]

Phillips is skeptical that the poet could add a secret message ("yet another arcane device") to a sonnet that is already severely constrained by its double acrostic. For example, it is hard to imagine that the direct application of Trithemius's tables to the acrostic *amare est insanire* would yield another short text.[4] Nevertheless, as we will discover, Bacon, by means of a clever trick, succeeded at this exactly. Indeed, he boasts in the first sentence of the instructions of *howe much art & study the Author hath bestowed* upon this Puzzle Sonnet.

Roland Greene argues that the Puzzle is an appropriation of a "ritual event for fictional purposes." However, he does not specify what ritual is being appropriated, making it difficult to test his assertion.[5] Nor is there much reason to expect a "ritual event," given that rituals are not found elsewhere in the *Hekatompathia*. On the other hand, there is every reason to read the prose instructions literally. Its five Points are delivered in simple declarative sentences that do not suggest any mystical or other nonliteral interpretation. The references to *Orchematicall* tables (Point 4 and Sonnet 81's sidenote), deciphering (Point 4), and Trithemius's *Polygraphia* 5 (Sonnet 80's sidenote) are details that are unlikely to have any purpose other than cryptographic. The specificity of the instructions and their prominent position invite the diligent reader to undertake the challenge they present.

Puzzle-solving: an inductive process

Puzzle-solving requires an inductive reasoning process that begins with inferences and ends with a hypothesized solution that is quickly recognized as being the correct solution (assuming the puzzle is well-designed). This recognition of a puzzle's validity is based on the solution providing a sense of coherence—puzzles begin in contradiction or disorder, but end in order. The following riddle, perhaps the most prolific folk riddle in the twentieth century, illustrates this point:

What is black and white and rɛd all over?

This riddle is meant to be delivered orally: the word pronounced "rɛd" may be either the color red or its homophone, a participle of the verb "to read." To answer the riddle, one must recognize rɛd as "read." The riddle's solution is a newspaper, whose print is black on white paper and "read" all over. The earlier mention of two colors causes the homophone red/read to be discerned as "red" rather than "read." This is known as a riddle's "block" or "distraction" because it impedes the recipient of a riddle from finding the solution. Once the block is recognized, the incoherence of how something can be black and white and "rɛd" dissolves and we feel confident that we have arrived at the correct solution to the riddle.

At the outset of tackling a puzzle, the puzzle-solver must adopt this fundamental assumption: the puzzle was designed in such a way as to allow the puzzle-solver to find its unique solution. This is true for virtually all puzzles because if a puzzle is not solvable, then it provides nothing more than frustration, and if the solution is not unique, then the puzzle is inelegant, with its multiple answers providing no sense of completion. This fundamental assumption is essentially a hypothesis that coherence can be found, and it is often the starting point in an inductive reasoning process.

Scientists begin with a similar assumption: they presume that their observations of nature will cohere to some model.

Typically, a puzzle's rules are sparsely elaborated (if at all), and this leaves the puzzle-solver with many—indeed, too many—degrees of freedom. Therefore, the puzzle-solver seeks reasonably simple solutions, that is, he or she follows a heuristic process based on a straightforward model. In this case of a cryptographic puzzle, the correctness of the solution is guaranteed by the coherence of the deciphered message.

We now begin our solution to the Puzzle's first Stage. Our attention is likely to be drawn to Point 4 of the Puzzle instructions, which promises that something may be deciphered using Trithemius's tables. Indeed, ultimately it will be possible to decipher a short message. However, the usual starting place for a puzzle is its block, and we should therefore defer the process of deciphering until we have found the block. This will likely be found among the five points of the Puzzle instructions. We must recognize this block or contradiction and then resolve it.

The misordered Puzzle Sonnet

If one examines the Puzzle's instructions, the Points listed in Fig. 2.2, a contradiction is immediately evident in Point 3, which states that *through out the whole a true rime is perfectly obserued, although not after our accustomed manner.* "Accustomed manner" must refer to the work's standard ababcc/dedeff/ghghii rhyme scheme. This rhyme scheme is followed in all of the work's 94 English-language sonnets, excluding only the Puzzle Sonnet.[6] The Puzzle Sonnet does not adhere to any sort of rhyme scheme. However, as Wendy Phillips has observed, it does include potential rhymed endings for every line:

> The meter is impeccably maintained but the rhyme conforms neither to his "accustomed manner" nor to any recognizable scheme. ... Yet if one admits the pronunciation of *mia* with a long "a" no end-word remains without its rhyming counterpart, although that may be considerably separated from it: a,b,[a],c,b,d,e,f,g,h,e,a,h,g,c,d,f,f.[7]

In the worst case, the distance between the "c" rhyme of *warr* and *carr* stretches from line 4 to line 15, an absurdly long gap between rhymed lines. I have calculated the average gap between rhymed lines in this sonnet to be 4.7 lines.[8] This is surely unsuitable for any rhyme scheme, per se, because the human ear generally will not pick up a rhyme after three or four unrhymed lines are heard. Indeed, if one calculates what the gap would be if the poem's lines were ordered by a random process, the average gap would be 4.2 lines.[9] Thus the actual average gap of 4.7 lines is slightly worse than random. In the rhyme pattern given in the above Phillips quotation, there are 6 pairs of rhymed endings (b, c, d, e, g, h) and 2 triplets (a, f), accounting for all 18 lines. The triplets make it impossible for this sonnet to follow the *Hekatompathia*'s customary rhyme scheme, which requires 9 pairs of rhymed endings and permits no triplets. This is acknowledged in Point 3 (*although not after our accustomed manner*). Thus, the Puzzle Sonnet is unique among the sequence's English sonnets, failing to adhere to the rhyme scheme of the other 93 English sonnets. Yet, curiously, the instructions insist that throughout the Puzzle Sonnet, *a true rime is perfectly obserued* (Point 3). This is clearly contradicted by the worse-than-random gap between rhymed lines. Such a large gap between rhymes is well outside of any known practice, and further, it could not possibly fulfill the purpose of the rhyme, an enhanced sense of flow and rhythm.

There are other indications that the lines are misordered. The sonnet lacks any recognizable structure, and sonnets are invariably a highly structured form.[10] Another difficulty is that its order of events appears to be inverted: it begins with a dismissal of love (*farewell olde wellada*; 1) and ends with love's hand pressed upon and hurting the speaker (18). Given that the Subsequence describes a *fall from Love and all his lawes* (79.HN), the sonnet ought instead to start with the speaker being pressed by love's power and end with love's dismissal. The sonnet's final couplet, in which love presses upon the speaker, is at odds with the other ending couplets of the MLIP sonnets, virtually all of which affirm the speaker's freedom from love. It is surprising that the concluding couplet of this first sonnet of the Subsequence contradicts the Subsequence's overall theme.

The apparently counterfactual statement that the Puzzle Sonnet exhibits *true ryme ... perfectly observed* is an obvious block. Riddles, popular in this period, are usually built upon a series of contradictions. Archer Taylor writes:

> The literary riddle ordinarily contains a long series of assertions and contradictions. ... The first assertion and its denial are almost certain to conflict with the next pair. Yet the author goes on and on, while his conception becomes more and more incoherent.[11]

Riddles are solved by resolving their stated contradictions. In word riddles, this is often accomplished by changing the context in which the riddle's words are understood, as in the above folk riddle. In the case of the Puzzle Sonnet, the putative rhyme scheme will only appear if we reorder the sonnet lines. True, the instructions do not explicitly tell the reader to reorder the sonnet lines. However, it would have been inelegant and contrary to the style of puzzles for this to be stated directly. And yet, the instructions hint at this demand in Point 5:

> That **when all the foresaide particulars are performed**, the whole piller is but iust 18 verses, as will appeare in the page following it, *Per modum expansionis.*   [bold added]

These *foresaide particulars* refer to the prior 4 Points, which include descriptions of work done by the poet in framing the Puzzle: the two matching acrostics; the inverse relationship between the top half and bottom half of the pillar (excluding the base); and the syllable count of the base (1, 3, 5, 7, 9). Yet, these *foresaide particulars* also leave work for the reader: *the secret vertue* that may be learned from Trithemius that allows for deciphering (Point 4) is not disclosed. But first we must see that *all the foresaide particulars are performed*, which includes Point 3: *through out the whole a true rime is perfectly observed*. Thus, we begin the first step of the Puzzle's first Stage, the reordering of the Puzzle Sonnet.

Reordering the Puzzle Sonnet

The reordering of the Puzzle Sonnet requires that we find an order that has a reasonable flow from line to line, adheres to a reasonable but unknown rhyme scheme, and is generally consistent with the style and themes of the overall sequence. The task of reordering a poem's scrambled lines is not only difficult, but in some circumstances would be impossible; for if the flow from line to line resembles free association, then multiple orders might be equally valid. At first, the task appears daunting because 18 lines may be reordered in 6,402,373,705,728,000 (18 factorial) permutations. However, sonnets are a structured form, and this significantly eases the task of reordering its lines. If, for example, the sonnet is clearly structured as two 9-line halves, then each half would have a more manageable number of permutations: 362,880 (9 factorial). A principle of computer science can be applied here. Reordering is essentially sorting, and one well-known method of sorting is the so-called "bucket sort." In this procedure, a rough sort into buckets (subsets) is first performed, followed by independent sorts within each bucket. This procedure will be applied in our reordering of the Puzzle Sonnet.

Before attempting to discover the Puzzle Sonnet's true order, we should enumerate the conditions that we expect to be met by the sonnet in its reordered state. These conditions or "Rules" are:

1. It must adhere to a plausible rhyme scheme.

2. The flow from one line to the next must be logical and grammatical, as is the case in the work's other sonnets.

3. For each line, the division of syllables must respect the boundaries of the Pillar Sonnet. That is, multisyllable words cannot overgo the end of any of the Pillar Sonnet's 28 lines.

4. Sonnets are a structured form, and the instructions state that one half of the Puzzle Sonnet is antithetical to the other (Point 1). Thus, our reordered sonnet should exhibit structure, a requirement of the sonnet genre.

5. The reordered sonnet, which is the lead sonnet of the MLIP Subsequence, must be thematically consistent with that Subsequence it introduces.

Of course, there is no simple algorithmic process for applying these Rules. It is a problem akin to cracking the combination of a safe, where one must guess at a series of numbers, and only after dialing in every number of the series can one check to see if the safe will open. It would be relatively easy to crack a safe if after dialing in each number individually, one could determine whether that single number is correct (e.g., by hearing a tumbler fall). Similarly, the challenge in reordering the sonnet lines is difficult because one cannot determine whether the position of any one line is correct independently from the others. Only with a complete reordering of all lines is it possible to fully test the validity of the reordering.

In my attempt to reorder the Puzzle Sonnet's lines, I spent endless hours unmethodically trying countless possibilities until finally one strategy for reordering the sonnet emerged. Point 1 states that *the whole pillar (except the basis or foote thereof) is by relation of either halfe to the other Antitheticall or Antisillabicall*. The opposed relationship of the first 12 lines of the Pillar Sonnet (81) to the next 12 lines is clearly visible in its syllable counts, which increase from 1 to 12 and then decrease from 12 to 1. The relationship between these two halves is thus obviously *antisillabicall*, but the instructions also apply the adjective *antitheticall*. The OED lists the *Hekatompathia* as the first to use "antithetical" and defines it as the use of "antithesis," that is, the "opposition or contrast of ideas" (OED 1). Although the use of *antitheticall* may be merely redundant of *antisillabicall*, it is also possible that it is intended as a hint that the sonnet is structured as two thematically opposite halves. This would hardly be surprising because Petrarchan sonnets are structured around two opposing views, one presented in the octave and the other in the sestet. Adopting this hypothesis seemed warranted given the instructions' probable hint and the dialogic nature of the sonnet form. In any event, following the inductive process that puzzles require means, at some point, one must undertake assumptions, and this one seemed to be a reasonable one with which to start.

The instructions exclude the base of the sonnet from the two halves: *except the basis or foote thereof.* The base consists of 24 syllables (3 + 5 + 7 + 9), a little more than two lines of 10 syllables each. We can only reorder whole lines and therefore must assume the base to be either 2 or 3 lines. We make the more likely assumption of a base of 2 lines because this fits best with the sonnet form, which often ends in a rhyming couplet. This base of only 2 lines is too small to introduce a third theme, or even deliberate between the opposing themes of the 2 halves. Indeed, a structure, consisting of two large halves of 8 lines each, followed by a couplet that injects a new idea or attempts mediation, would be an unbalanced structure.[12] More likely, and consistent with the sonnet form, the couplet ought to provide a strong conclusion, but not introduce any new ideas.

We begin by considering what thesis might divide the sonnet into two antithetical halves. This sonnet is located at the boundary of the two Subsequences, the first of which describes the speaker's suffering under love's power, and the second describes the speaker's escape from love. From this, we might hypothesize that the sonnet's two antithetical themes are (1) the speaker still living under love's tyranny and (2) the speaker being free of love's tyranny. This is consistent with a cursory review of the sonnet's lines: some depict the speaker suffering under love while others show him free from love. We might further hypothesize that the order of these two halves is consistent with the order of the two Subsequences: the speaker first suffers under love and then escapes it. We now adopt this as our working assumption.

We next consider the base, the sonnet's ending couplet. The final couplet in the published order is as follows:

> **H'is double thrall that liu's as** Loue **thinks best**
> **Whose hand still Tyrant like to hurt is prest.**   (17–18)

This depicts the speaker as still living under love's thrall and therefore, under our working assumption, belongs in the first half of the sonnet and not at its end. Moreover, this couplet, as it stands, is inconsistent with the other concluding couplets in the MLIP Subsequence, virtually all of which indicate that love has been dismissed. Finally, these two lines are part of a triplet rhyme (with line 8), an uncommon way of ending a sonnet. The

Puzzle Sonnet contains 6 rhyme pairs and 2 rhyme triplets, as previously discussed. These rhyme groups are assigned numbers in Fig 2.5. The assigned Pair numbers and Triplet numbers are arbitrary; the order in which the lines are presented is also arbitrary.

It was a Hell, where none felt more then I,	Pair 1
I'le choose a path that shall not leade awri.	(9, 14)
So frames it with me now, that I confess	Pair 2
Since therefore now my woes are wexed less,	(7, 11)
Rest then with me from your blinde Cupids **carr**	Pair 3
Retyre to Cyprus **Ile and cease thy warr,**	(15, 4)
Each one of you, that serue and would be free.	Pair 4
Enforce to flight thy blyndfold bratte and thee.	(16, 6)
Els must thou proue how Reason **can by charme**	Pair 5
Mirth for mischaunce strike vp a newe alarm;	(5, 2)
No longer shall the world laugh me to scorn:	Pair 6
Nor any with like miseries forlorn.	(13, 10)
The life I ledde in Loue deuoyd of rest	Triplet 1
H'is double thrall that liu's as Loue **thinks best**	
Whose hand still Tyrant like to hurt is prest.	(8, 17, 18)
At last, though late, farewell olde wellada; *	Triplet 2
And Ciprya la nemica mia †	
And Reason **bids me leaue olde wellada,**	(1, 3, 12)

*wellada: a lamentation (OED A)   †translation: "Venus my enemy"

Fig. 2.5 Puzzle Sonnet rhyme groups

Next, we try to find a good candidate for the concluding couplet among the 6 rhyme pairs in Fig. 2.5. In Pair 1, the speaker has yet to leave love; in Pair 2, he is about to make a confession—no way to conclude a sonnet; Pairs 3 and 4 call out to others—neither sounds conclusive; Pair 5 is deliberative; in Pair 6, however, the speaker makes a bold declaration that applies both to himself and others, striking a note of finality. We now adopt the working assumption that Pair 6 is the concluding couplet in the restored order.

We will now divide the sonnet into two halves, as best we can, in accordance with our hypothesized thematic division. In performing this division, we reorder pair and triplet rhymes as a unit because presumably these lines are proximate to each other. However, this assumption is only adopted on a preliminary basis: it may not hold because a rhyme group could transcend the two halves of the sonnet. In the first half of the sonnet, we might expect to find lines that look back at the speaker's sufferance under love, his condition in the first Subsequence. One rhymed pair and one triplet show the speaker reflecting upon his past condition and therefore ought to fall in the first half of the sonnet:

It was a Hell, where none felt more then I,	Pair 1
I'le choose a path that shall not leade awri.	(9, 14)
The life I ledde in Loue deuoyd of rest	Triplet 1
H'is double thrall that liu's as Loue **thinks best**	
Whose hand still Tyrant like to hurt is prest.	(8, 17, 18)

Fig. 2.6 Lines assigned to first half of the Puzzle Sonnet

In Pair 1, the first line describes the speaker's most intense pain (*Hell*) in the past tense, and its other line (*I'le choose a path*) indicates that he has not yet made the decision to leave love—both reasons to assign Pair 1 to the sonnet's first half. Similarly, Triplet 1 describes intense pain (*devoyd of rest*) in the past tense; continued pain in the present (*to hurt is prest*) seems to indicate that the speaker is not yet free of love. For these reasons, we assign this triplet to the first half. All 5 lines in Fig. 2.6 appear to come before the speaker's complete abandonment of love and therefore ought to fall in the first half. This leaves us 3 lines short of the 8 lines needed for the first half. Later we will discover that these lines are part of a transition between the two halves.

The 5 lines in Fig. 2.6 look back to the prior Subsequence and therefore they seem to be good candidates to occupy the first 5 line positions of the reordered sonnet. After giving consideration to logical sense, likely rhyme schemes, and the restrictions on syllable boundaries, we find only one possible order:

The life I ledde in Loue deuoyd of rest	(8; Position 1)
It was a Hell, where none felt more then I,	(9; Position 2)
H'is double thrall that liu's as Loue **thinks best**	(17; Position 3)
Whose hand still Tyrant like to hurt is prest.	(18; Position 4)
I'le choose a path that shall not leade awri.	(14; Position 5)

We now consider which lines are likely to fall in the second half of the sonnet, in accordance with our working assumption that the second half of the sonnet depicts the speaker as free from love's tyranny. There are 3 rhymed pairs that fit this criterion:

Rest then with me from your blinde Cupids **carr**   Pair 3
Retyre to Cyprus **Ile and cease thy warr,**   (15, 4)

Each one of you, that serue and would be free.   Pair4
Enforce to flight thy blyndfold bratte and thee.   (16, 6)

Els must thou proue how Reason **can by charme**   Pair 5
Mirth for mischaunce strike vp a newe alarm;   (5, 2)

Fig. 2.7 Lines assigned to second half of the Puzzle Sonnet

In Pairs 3 and 4, the speaker also calls on others to abandon love: *Rest then with me from your blinde Cupids carr* (15); *Enforce to flight thy blyndfold bratte and thee* (6). Presumably, these calls to others to join the speaker in a love-free state ought to occur only subsequent to the speaker's departure from love and thus fall in the second half. Pair 5 asserts that the speaker is bound to Reason and therefore has some immunity from the temptation (*newe alarm*) to return to love. Of course, this must refer to a time subsequent to the speaker winning his freedom from love. All 3 pairs are consistent with Pair 6, our assumed final couplet, in which the speaker vows that he will never again suffer under love, and neither will others if they heed his call to abandon love.

We have now assigned 5 lines to the first half, leaving 3 unassigned places; and 6 lines to the second half leaving 2 unassigned places. These 5 unassigned places must be filled with our 5 unassigned lines, the one remaining triplet and the one remaining pair:

At last, though late, farewell olde wellada;   Triplet 2
And Ciprya la nemica mia
And Reason **bids me leaue olde wellada,**   (1, 3, 12)

So frames it with me now, that I confess   Pair 2
Since therefore now my woes are wexed less,   (7, 11)

Fig. 2.8 Lines that remain unassigned

Assuming our work to this point is correct, these 5 lines must span the two halves, with 3 lines falling in the first half and 2 in the second half, as shown in Fig. 2.9.

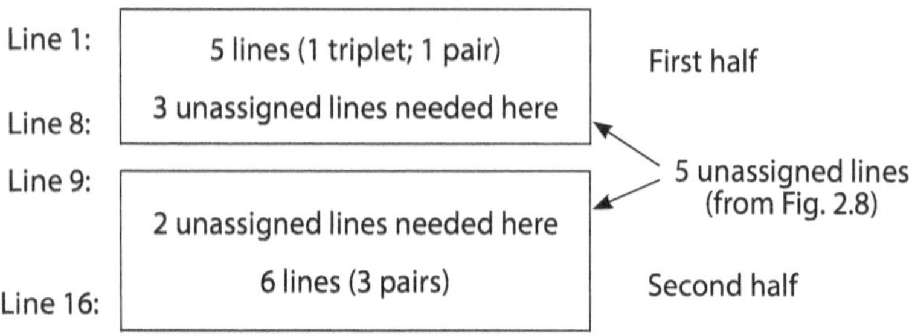

Fig. 2.9 Division of Puzzle Sonnet into halves

Returning to Fig. 2.8, in line 1 of Triplet 2 the speaker bids farewell to love (*wellada*). This avowal in the present tense belongs in the second half of the sonnet because the speaker's mind is finally resolved. Line 12 belongs in the first half because the speaker is still contemplating leaving love in the future. Line 3's position cannot be distinguished based on its content. We now consider Pair 2 in Fig. 2.8. One of its lines, *Since therefore now my woes are wexed less* (11), depicts the speaker still deliberating about leaving love, and therefore it belongs in the first half. Pair 2's other line, *So frames it with me now, that I confess* (7), includes the significant word, *confess. Confess* in the present tense implies that the moment of avowal or conversion is at hand. The use of *now* adds to the sense of immediacy of this confession. The speaker is here announcing his farewell to love, making this line a good candidate to be positioned as the first line of the second half. This position is known as the *volta* in a Petrarchan sonnet. The first line of a Petrarchan sonnet's sestet (the second stanza) is thought of as a *volta* (jump) from the octave (the first stanza).

Where does this leave us? We have assigned line 12 (Triplet 2) and line 11 (Pair 2) to the first half, filling 2 of the 3 open positions. We have assigned line 1 (Triplet 2) and line 7 (Pair 2) to the second half, filling both of the 2 open positions. The one line whose position could not be distinguished, line 3 (Triplet 2), can now be assigned to the only open position, which is in the first half. This summarizes our sorting of these 5 lines into the two halves (the position of lines within each half is arbitrary):

First half:
Since therefore now my woes are wexed less   (11)
And Ciprya la nemica mia   (3)
And Reason **bids me leaue olde wellada,**   (12)

Second half:
At last, though late, farewell olde wellada;   (1)
So frames it with me now, that I confess   (7)

The number of permutations is now vastly reduced. For the two second half lines, there are only two possible orders. *Confess* (7), meaning "avow," indicates that this line ought to precede the speaker's dismissal of love: *At last, though late, farewell olde wellada* (1). This is consistent with the prior discussion in which line 7 was determined to be the *volta*, the first line of the second half. Then, the order that begins the second half is:

So frames it with me now, that I confess   (7)
At last, though late, farewell olde wellada;   (1)

We now consider the 3 lines above that end the first half. There are 6 possible orders for these three lines. We begin by considering which line might precede line 7, the first line of the second half. *So frames* (7) limits the choice of the preceding line. "Frames" (*OED*, 5c, "to shape the action, faculties, or inclinations of a person") refers to the forces acting upon the speaker's mind prior to the speaker's avowal. Neither line 11 nor 12 fits prior to line 7, but line 3 fits perfectly: placing it before line 7 specifies Venus, or love's painful effects, as the force that *frames* the speaker's mind to depart from love. Now only the order of lines 11 and 12 must be determined. If line 11 is placed first, then the rhyme scheme is an awkward abbba—a triple repetition of a rhyme; if line 12 is placed first, then the rhyme scheme is a reasonable ababa. We now have reordered lines 6 through 10 of the sonnet:

And Reason bids me leaue olde wellada,   (12; Position 6)
Since therefore now my woes are wexed less,   (11; Position 7)
And Ciprya la nemica mia   (3; Position 8)
So frames it with me now, that I confess   (7; Position 9, the *volta*)
At last, though late, farewell olde wellada;   (1; Position 10)

We now turn our attention to line positions 11 through 16, the remainder of the second half of the sonnet. From Fig. 2.7, Pairs 3, 4, and 5 provide the 6 lines that we must now order. A careful examination of Pair 5 will show that it is a continuation of the speaker's avowal, *At last, though late, fare-well olde wellada*. Pair 5 is presented as contiguous and in its likely order:

> **Els* must thou proue how** Reason **can by charme**   (Position 11)
> ****Mirth for**[13] **mischaunce strike vp a newe alarm;** (Position 12)
>
> [*for it to be otherwise; **only then might...]

The speaker declares that his vow will hold unless you can *proue* to him that *Reason* can once again be overtaken by (a lover's) *charme*. Only then might pleasure (*Mirth*) or ill-luck (*mischaunce*) initiate a new war (*alarm* means a call to arms). The implication is that the speaker has embraced Reason, and he is safe as long as Reason is immune from a beloved's charm.

Only Pairs 3 and 4 remain unassigned, and only positions 13 through 16 are open. Pairs 3 and 4 have this in common: they call upon others to join the speaker in his avowal to forswear love: *Each one of you, that serve* love should remove yourself from *Cupid's carr*, and *enforce to flight thy blynd-fold bratte* [Cupid]. Restrictions of rhyme order, logical flow, and syllable boundaries allow for only one ordering of these 4 lines from Pairs 3 and 4:

> **Retyre to** Cyprus **Ile and cease thy warr,**   (Position 13)
> **Enforce to flight thy blyndfold bratte and thee.**   (Position 14)
> **Rest then with me from your blinde** Cupids **carr**   (Position 15)
> **Each one of you, that serue and would be free.**   (Position 16)

The reordering of Sonnet 82, now complete, is presented in Fig. 2.10. It follows a reasonable rhyme scheme, abaab cdcdc eefgfg hh.[14] The speaker progresses from a life led subject to love to one led free from love. This progressive development allows for some confidence in our reordering. (Full confidence will come after deciphering the message that results from this reordering, later in this chapter.) The first 4 lines describe the torments of living under love's influence, which include restlessness (1), being subject to a double thrall (3), and painful oppression (4). In the next 4 lines, the speaker declares that he will leave love (5) and then gives reasons for leaving: Reason has led him to this decision (6); he is now in less pain (7); Venus has in some way affected his thinking (8). The second half begins with the *volta*, a declaration that he is now making a confession (9) and his declaration that he has at last left love (10). In the next two lines (11–12), anticipating an (unstated) objection that he might yet return to love someday, he explains that his adherence to *Reason* will likely prevent any such possibility. In the next 4 lines, he calls for others to follow his lead in abandoning love. In the sonnet's final 2 lines (the base section), he concludes that love will no longer control his life or that of others.

The life I ledde in Loue deuoyd of rest
It was a Hell, where none felt more then I,
H'is double thrall that liu's as Loue thinks best
Whose hand still Tyrant like to hurt is prest.
I'le choose a path that shall not leade awri.   5
And Reason bids me leaue olde wellada,
Since therefore now my woes are wexed less,
And Ciprya la nemica mia
So frames it with me now, that I confess
At last, though late, farewell olde wellada;   10
Els must thou proue how Reason can by charme
Mirth for mischaunce strike vp a newe alarm;
Retyre to Cyprus Ile and cease thy warr,
Enforce to flight thy blyndfold bratte and thee.
Rest then with me from your blinde Cupids carr   15
Each one of you, that serue and would be free.
No longer shall the world laugh me to scorn:
Nor any with like miseries forlorn.

Fig. 2.10 Reordered Sonnet 82

The sonnet exhibits both a logical and chronological flow. The speaker begins by telling us of his past pain in love, an obvious starting point. Moving forward in time, using the present tense, he declares his departure from love. Finally, looking to the future, he calls on others to follow his course. Any change to the order of these sections would break the logical flow of the poem. The progressive development of the reordered Sonnet 82 fits perfectly with its role as the lead sonnet of the MLIP Subsequence. As we will discover in Chapter 5, the MLIP Subsequence follows roughly the same course set by Sonnet 82: beginning with sonnets that describe the woes of love, followed by sonnets that scoff at love, and lastly sonnets that call for others to abandon love. Thus the course of topics in Sonnet 82, the lead sonnet of the Subsequence, foreshadows the course of topics presented in the Subsequence.

Although we reordered the sonnet using a procedure whose starting point was a division into halves plus a closing couplet (the base), other procedures may have produced the same result. For example, a recognition of the sonnet's chronological and logical flow without first dividing it may have achieved the same result. The task of reordering turns the puzzle-solver into a quasi-poet—a "maker" in Sidneian terms. The puzzle-solver becomes engaged with the text at a detailed level in order to understand its structure and even its line-to-line ordering. The reader is made to wander through this labyrinthine Puzzle, and perhaps this makes for some affinity with the sonnet speaker, who is also a wanderer.

How can we be sure that our reordering is exactly the reordering intended by the poet? Ordinarily we would have no way of knowing whether our reordering is the uniquely correct solution; however, because the sonnet hides a cryptogram, and that cryptogram depends upon the sonnet being correctly reordered, the reordering can be verified. Next, we will decipher the cryptogram, and if it produces an intelligible message rather than gibberish, then our reordering is correct (although it will still be subjected to a mathematical test, as later described). Bacon has set before the reader a literary problem—the sonnet reordering—along with a cryptographic system that allows for the definitive verification of whether the reader has correctly performed the reordering task.

The cryptography of the *Polygraphia*

Prior to resuming our efforts to solve the Puzzle's first Stage, a brief description of the *Polygraphia* 5's cryptography is required. This section does not assume that the reader has any prior knowledge of cryptography. The term "ciphertext," introduced in the first chapter, refers to an enciphered text that usually appears to be gibberish. Ciphertexts often lack word boundaries and are therefore conventionally presented in groups of 5 letters as shown:

XJCDA BAEZW KLURD

"Plaintext" refers to the original message, a plainly readable text. A plaintext is enciphered to produce a ciphertext; a ciphertext is deciphered to produce a readable plaintext, as shown in Fig. 2.11.

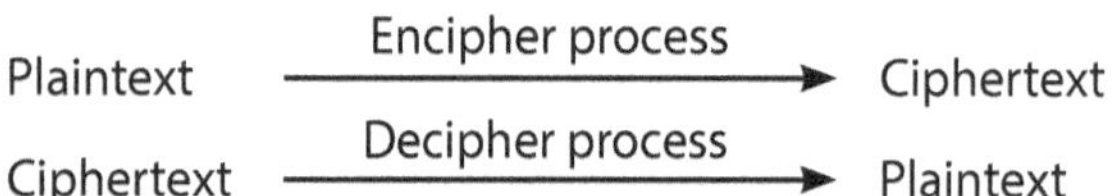

Fig. 2.11 Encipher and decipher processes

The deciphering of a ciphertext may either be authorized—as when an official legitimately has access to the tables needed to decipher a message—or unauthorized—as when someone uses cryptographic techniques to crack a cipher. An unauthorized person who discovers cipher tables by technical tricks (e.g., cracking a cipher by frequency counting or other means) is known as a cryptanalyst.

Ciphering and deciphering in the Renaissance were typically performed using tables that substitute one character for another. For example, whenever an "A" appears, it is substituted with a "K"; whenever a "B" appears, it is substituted with a "T," and so on. Trithemius refers to such a substitution scheme as a "table" (*tabula*) or "Alphabet" (*alphabetum*), and the process of enciphering or deciphering as "transposition" (*transpositio*). The Puzzle's instructions (Point 4) also use the term "transposition," and in the same manner as Trithemius does. However, in modern terminology, "transposition" refers to an altogether different form of encryption, the rearranging of the order of the letters of a text. So, to avoid confusion with this modern usage, I use "Transform" rather than "transposition" to describe the enciphering and deciphering processes employed in the *Polygraphia* and the *Hekatompathia.*

During the Renaissance, most cryptography used only a single Alphabet (monoalphabetic substitution) to Transform all the letters of a text. However, single Alphabetic substitution was vulnerable to cryptanalytic techniques, and this led to the invention of more sophisticated cryptographic techniques. In the fifteenth century, Leon Battista Alberti invented a system that used multiple tables (or Alphabets) in a method known as "polyalphabetic substitution." Trithemius uses this method in his *Polygraphia* 5: the advantage of using multiple tables (or, in our terminology, Transforms) is that it makes for a stronger cryptographic system (meaning that it is hard to crack). The virtue of polyalphabetic cryptography is that one letter is not always Transformed into the same letter, which would otherwise be a vulnerability.

Polygraphia 5 provides three types of tables for implementing polyalphabetic Transforms: Recta, Aversa, and Orchema. The Recta Transforms are the simplest of cryptographic tables and are known as a "Caesar shift." In a Caesar shift, one letter is enciphered into another by shifting a fixed number of letters within an ordered alphabet. Fig. 2.12 shows the *Polygraphia*'s master Recta Transposition Table,[15] which is a collection of 23 Recta tables: each column represents one Recta table. I have inserted column numbers 1 to 23 into Trithemius's master table so that each of the 23 Recta tables may be easily referenced (nothing in the original is obscured). The *Polygraphia*, on subsequent pages, disperses this master table into the 23 Recta tables that appear as 23 pairs of columns: the left-hand columns of each pair repeat the leftmost column of the master table; the right-hand columns of each pair duplicate the 23 columns of the master table in sequential order. The first table implements a Caesar shift of 1, the second a Caesar shift of 2, and so on. In total, Trithemius presents 23 Recta tables, each table shifting between 1 and 23 places in a 24-letter alphabet (a shift of 24, equivalent to no shift at all, is omitted).[16]

Recta transpositionis tabula.

	1	2	3	4	5	6	7	8	9	10	11	12	13	14	15	16	17	18	19	20	21	22	23	
a	b	c	d	e	f	g	h	i	k	l	m	n	o	p	q	r	s	t	u	x	y	z	w	
b	c	d	e	f	g	h	i	k	l	m	n	o	p	q	r	s	t	u	x	y	z	w	a	a
c	d	e	f	g	h	i	k	l	m	n	o	p	q	r	s	t	u	x	y	z	w	a	b	b
d	e	f	g	h	i	k	l	m	n	o	p	q	r	s	t	u	x	y	z	w	a	b	c	c
e	f	g	h	i	k	l	m	n	o	p	q	r	s	t	u	x	y	z	w	a	b	c	d	d
f	g	h	i	k	l	m	n	o	p	q	r	s	t	u	x	y	z	w	a	b	c	d	e	e
g	h	i	k	l	m	n	o	p	q	r	s	t	u	x	y	z	w	a	b	c	d	e	f	f
h	i	k	l	m	n	o	p	q	r	s	t	u	x	y	z	w	a	b	c	d	e	f	g	g
i	k	l	m	n	o	p	q	r	s	t	u	x	y	z	w	a	b	c	d	e	f	g	h	h
k	l	m	n	o	p	q	r	s	t	u	x	y	z	w	a	b	c	d	e	f	g	h	i	i
l	m	n	o	p	q	r	s	t	u	x	y	z	w	a	b	c	d	e	f	g	h	i	k	k
m	n	o	p	q	r	s	t	u	x	y	z	w	a	b	c	d	e	f	g	h	i	k	l	l
n	o	p	q	r	s	t	u	x	y	z	w	a	b	c	d	e	f	g	h	i	k	l	m	m
o	p	q	r	s	t	u	x	y	z	w	a	b	c	d	e	f	g	h	i	k	l	m	n	n
p	q	r	s	t	u	x	y	z	w	a	b	c	d	e	f	g	h	i	k	l	m	n	o	o
q	r	s	t	u	x	y	z	w	a	b	c	d	e	f	g	h	i	k	l	m	n	o	p	p
r	s	t	u	x	y	z	w	a	b	c	d	e	f	g	h	i	k	l	m	n	o	p	q	q
s	t	u	x	y	z	w	a	b	c	d	e	f	g	h	i	k	l	m	n	o	p	q	r	r
t	u	x	y	z	w	a	b	c	d	e	f	g	h	i	k	l	m	n	o	p	q	r	s	s
u	x	y	z	w	a	b	c	d	e	f	g	h	i	k	l	m	n	o	p	q	r	s	t	t
x	y	z	w	a	b	c	d	e	f	g	h	i	k	l	m	n	o	p	q	r	s	t	u	u
y	z	w	a	b	c	d	e	f	g	h	i	k	l	m	n	o	p	q	r	s	t	u	x	x
z	w	a	b	c	d	e	f	g	h	i	k	l	m	n	o	p	q	r	s	t	u	x	y	y
w	a	b	c	d	e	f	g	h	i	k	l	m	n	o	p	q	r	s	t	u	x	y	z	z

Fig. 2.12 "Recta transposition table" from Trithemius's *Polygraphia 5*
(Numbered row added.)   Courtesy of Library of Congress.

A polyalphabetic cipher may be implemented through the use of multiple Recta tables. Trithemius suggests the following simple procedure to produce a polyalphabetic cipher: use the first column (labeled "1") to encipher the first letter of a message (a shift of one letter), then use the second column (labeled "2") to encipher the second letter of the message (a shift of two letters), and so on. This pattern is continued until all 23 columns of Fig. 2.12 are exhausted, at which point one cycles back to the first column.

Trithemius's Recta tables (Fig. 2.12) could, in practice, be treated as either enciphering tables or deciphering tables. The Puzzle treats these tables as deciphering tables: the ciphertext letter is the far-left column, and the plaintext letter is one of the 23 numbered columns to the right. In

	1	2	3	4	5	6	7	8	9	10	11	12
A	B	C	D	E	F	G	H	I	K	L	M	N
B	C	D	E	F	G	H	I	K	L	M	N	O
C	D	E	F	G	H	I	K	L	M	N	O	P
D	E	F	G	H	I	K	L	M	N	O	P	Q
E	F	G	H	I	K	L	M	N	O	P	Q	R
F	G	H	I	K	L	M	N	O	P	Q	R	S
G	H	I	K	L	M	N	O	P	Q	R	S	T
H	I	K	L	M	N	O	P	Q	R	S	T	U
I	K	L	M	N	O	P	Q	R	S	T	U	W
K	L	M	N	O	P	Q	R	S	T	U	W	X
L	M	N	O	P	Q	R	S	T	U	W	X	Y
M	N	O	P	Q	R	S	T	U	W	X	Y	Z
N	O	P	Q	R	S	T	U	W	X	Y	Z	A
O	P	Q	R	S	T	U	W	X	Y	Z	A	B
P	Q	R	S	T	U	W	X	Y	Z	A	B	C
Q	R	S	T	U	W	X	Y	Z	A	B	C	D
R	S	T	U	W	X	Y	Z	A	B	C	D	E
S	T	U	W	X	Y	Z	A	B	C	D	E	F
T	U	W	X	Y	Z	A	B	C	D	E	F	G
U	W	X	Y	Z	A	B	C	D	E	F	G	H
W	X	Y	Z	A	B	C	D	E	F	G	H	I
X	Y	Z	A	B	C	D	E	F	G	H	I	K
Y	Z	A	B	C	D	E	F	G	H	I	K	L
Z	A	B	C	D	E	F	G	H	I	K	L	M

Fig. 2.13 Recta tables

contrast, Trithemius's explanation and examples use the Recta tables as enciphering tables. This minor variation between the Puzzle's and *Polygraphia*'s treatment of the Recta tables is not surprising. Indeed, Trithemius advises his readers that his tables can be used flexibly and that many variations are possible.[17] Fig. 2.13 reproduces the first 12 Recta tables from Fig. 2.12 (called transpositions or Alphabets by Trithemius) in a more easily readable format. Only 12 of the 23 Recta tables or Transforms are reproduced because the Puzzle only uses the first 12, as later discussed. Also, a minor change has been made to the alphabetic order in Fig. 2.13: the position of the letter "W" is made consistent with the English ordering of the alphabet, as opposed to Trithemius's German ordering, in which

"W" is the last letter.[18] The Recta table in Fig. 2.13, which is used through-out this study, is replicated for convenience in Appendix B, Fig. B.1.

To illustrate the use of the Recta tables, we encipher the arbitrary word LOGOS (the plaintext). The Recta tables, following the Puzzle's method, are deciphering tables, so we need to perform a reverse lookup when enciphering. We encipher the first plaintext letter, "L," by looking for that letter in column 1. The letter that appears to its left in the row header is the letter "K." This is the ciphertext letter used to encipher the plaintext letter "L." Column 2 is used to encipher the next plaintext letter, "O," and so on. This process generates the ciphertext KMDKN, as shown below. Note that unlike a monoalphabetic cipher, the letter "O," which appears twice in the plaintext, is transformed into two different ciphertext letters, M and K, which defends against the usual frequency counting technique used to break ciphers. The use of different Transforms for different letters is the defining characteristic of polyalphabetic cryptography.

Plaintext:	L	O	G	O	S
Transform column:	1	2	3	4	5
Ciphertext:	K	M	D	K	N

Deciphering is accomplished by the same process in reverse. We simply find the ciphertext letter among the row headers and its deciphered value in the appropriate column. Alternatively, enciphering and deciphering operations can be performed without tables, using simple arithmetic (the instructions mention arithmetic). The standard practice was to assign a numerical value to each letter in a standard 24-letter alphabet based on their normal order, as shown:

Numeric values of the letters of the Elizabethan alphabet

A	B	C	D	E	F	G	H	I	K	L	M	N	O	P	Q	R	S	T	U	W	X	Y	Z
1	2	3	4	5	6	7	8	9	10	11	12	13	14	15	16	17	18	19	20	21	22	23	24

To encipher, one simply subtracts the Transform number from the plain-text letter's numeric value. To decipher, one adds the Transform number to the ciphertext letter's numeric value. The deciphering operation, used frequently in solving the Puzzle, is performed using the Recta Decipher-ing Formula that appears below. "Mod" refers to modular or clock arith-metic: if the sum obtained by adding the Ciphertext to the Transform number ever exceeds 24, then following the rules of modular arithmetic, one must subtract 24 and use the remainder. For example, if a ciphertext letter T (19) is to be deciphered using a Transform value of 10, then a sum of 29 is obtained. Then applying modular arithmetic, one must subtract 24, which yields 5, which is E. The arithmetic formula for Recta deciphering is given below:

Plaintext = (Ciphertext + Transform number) (mod 24)   Recta Deciphering Formula

	1	2	3	4	5	6	7	8	9	10	11	12
A	Z	Y	X	W	U	T	S	R	Q	P	O	N
B	Y	X	W	U	T	S	R	Q	P	O	N	M
C	X	W	U	T	S	R	Q	P	O	N	M	L
D	W	U	T	S	R	Q	P	O	N	M	L	K
E	U	T	S	R	Q	P	O	N	M	L	K	I
F	T	S	R	Q	P	O	N	M	L	K	I	H
G	S	R	Q	P	O	N	M	L	K	I	H	G
H	R	Q	P	O	N	M	L	K	I	H	G	F
I	Q	P	O	N	M	L	K	I	H	G	F	E
K	P	O	N	M	L	K	I	H	G	F	E	D
L	O	N	M	L	K	I	H	G	F	E	D	C
M	N	M	L	K	I	H	G	F	E	D	C	B
N	M	L	K	I	H	G	F	E	D	C	B	A
O	L	K	I	H	G	F	E	D	C	B	A	Z
P	K	I	H	G	F	E	D	C	B	A	Z	Y
Q	I	H	G	F	E	D	C	B	A	Z	Y	X
R	H	G	F	E	D	C	B	A	Z	Y	X	W
S	G	F	E	D	C	B	A	Z	Y	X	W	U
T	F	E	D	C	B	A	Z	Y	X	W	U	T
U	E	D	C	B	A	Z	Y	X	W	U	T	S
W	D	C	B	A	Z	Y	X	W	U	T	S	R
X	C	B	A	Z	Y	X	W	U	T	S	R	Q
Y	B	A	Z	Y	X	W	U	T	S	R	Q	P
Z	A	Z	Y	X	W	U	T	S	R	Q	P	O

Fig. 2.14 Aversa tables

We use the Recta Deciphering Formula and the numeric values of the Elizabethan alphabet (given above) to decipher the ciphertext, KMDKN of our previous example, as shown below:

Ciphertext:	K	M	D	K	N
Numerical value of letter:	10	12	4	10	13
Transform number to add:	1	2	3	4	5
Sum:	11	14	7	14	18
Plaintext:	L	O	G	O	S

Trithemius also provides tables that he calls *Tabulae Aversae*; a master Aversa table, as implemented in the Puzzle, appears in Fig. 2.14.[19] The Aversa table, which is used throughout the study, is replicated for convenience in Appendix B, Fig. B.2. Trithemius called these tables *"aversa"* because of the descending alphabetic order in each column, rather than the ascending order found in the Recta tables. The arithmetic formula for Aversa deciphering, which may be used instead of looking up values in the Aversa table, is given below:

Plaintext= (50—Ciphertext—Transform number) (mod 24)   Aversa Deciphering Formula

The Pillar Sonnet: a map of cryptographic tables

If the Puzzle is to decipher something, as the instructions state in Point 4 (Fig. 2.2), then it must perform a deciphering operation on a ciphertext. But where is the ciphertext located? The obvious answer is in the Puzzle Sonnet's pair of acrostics—in part because there is no other demarcated text elsewhere in the Puzzle Sonnet. These acrostics, composed of the first and last letters of each line of Sonnet 82, also appear as added letters in the left and right margins of Sonnet 81, placing further emphasis upon them. They are further distinguished by their odd (though not consistent) capitalization in Sonnet 81, as discussed below. Moreover, these acrostics display a Latin sententia (*amare est insanire*), distinguishing this text from the other text in the Puzzle Sonnet, which is in English. Given these accentuations of the acrostics, it is natural to hypothesize that they are the intended ciphertext (indeed, no other possibilities are apparent). Moreover, there is a tradition of placing secret texts in acrostics: an acrostic in a 14-line prefatory poem spells out THOMAS SEBILLET, the only evidence for the work's attribution.[20]

We now turn to the pointed reference to Trithemius's tables (Instructions, Point 4). Which table should be applied to each letter of the acrostics? As discussed above, Trithemius's assignment of tables to cipher-text letters is simple: he assigns the first Recta table (offset of 1) to the first letter of the message, the second Recta table (offset of 2) to the second letter, and so on. The Puzzle Sonnet assigns the Transforms or tables in a different manner, which is specified by the Pillar Sonnet. We carefully examine this oddly shaped sonnet (Fig. 2.3). Its first line contains a single syllable, and each line that follows has one more syllable than the prior line, reaching a maximum count of 12. This process is then reversed as the pillar tapers downward, the syllable count declining from 12 to 1. This is consistent with Point 1, in which the instructions state that *either halfe to the other* [is] *antisillabicall*, excluding the base. The base has syllable counts of 3, 5, 7, and 9. Why does this double acrostic sonnet appear twice, first in this strangely shaped pillar and then in the normal sonnet format on the following page? Has the poet included the Pillar Sonnet merely for its ornamental value? Although Sonnet 81 is nominally a pattern poem, there is no obvious relationship between its visual properties and the poetic text, as one would expect in a pattern poem. Furthermore, its shape barely resembles that of the pillar specified in its title. What column has such girth in its middle and a pointed top? Rather, the poem's shape follows a numerical pattern based on the syllable count: 1 to 12, 12 to 1, 3, 5, 7, 9. What is the significance of this sequence of 28 numbers?

Curiously, the title above this sonnet refers to it as a *Pasquine Piller*. From Elyot's *Dictionary* we learn that Pasquino is "a statue in Rome on whom all libels, railings, detractions, and satirical invectives are fathered."[21] In 1501, a truncated Greek statue was discovered, and after being placed near the Orsini Palace, it was used, under the cover of darkness, to post anonymous messages. From this, the tradition of *sonetti caudati* (tailed sonnets), sonnets that sport an extra half line that delivers a satirical sting, developed. Printed anthologies of these works were called *pasquinate*. Authors of such poems include Serafino, a favorite of Bacon's.[22] The implication of calling this sonnet a *Pasquine Piller* is that some "tail" or message is posted on it. Sonnet 81 might perhaps be thought of as having two tails, the two acrostics that read *amare est insanire*. However, the tailed sonnet tradition suggests something clandestine appearing only after the cover of darkness. Is there a hidden tail, as well?

We begin by examining the numerical sequence that defines the Pillar Sonnet's 28-line pattern: 1 to 12, 12 to 1, 3, 5, 7, 9. These syllable counts are emphasized by their appearrance at the left of each line of the Pillar Sonnet. Although the instructions say nothing about the first 24 syllable counts (1 to 12, 12 to 1), they do tell us that the *foote* or base of the pillar is *Orchematicall*. The instructions define *Orchematicall* as the *ouer skipping of number by rule and order, as from 1 to 3, 5, 7, and 9* (Point 4).

This is further emphasized by a sidenote to the right of the Pillar Sonnet: *Huius Columnae Basis... est orchematica* (The base of this pillar... is orchematical). Point 4 reads:

> Ouer skipping of number by rule and order, as from 1 to 3, 5, 7, and 9: the secret vertue whereof may be learned in *Trithemius, as namely by tables of transilition to decypher any thing that is written by secret transposition of letters, bee it neuer so cunningly conueighed.

[The asterisk links to the sidenote: *Polygraphiae suae lib. 5*]

Bacon thus reveals the significance of the last four numbers of his syllable counts (3, 5, 7, and 9): they somehow relate to the Orchema tables in *Polygraphia* 5. If these last 4 syllable counts point to cryptographic tables, it is a modest extrapolation to infer that the first 24 numbers (on which the instructions are silent) are also associated with the *Polygraphia*'s cryptographic tables. *Polygraphia* 5 contains three sets of cryptographic tables, the previously mentioned Recta and Aversa tables, and the Orchema tables, which are presented in that order. When the instructions state that the Orchema tables are related to the base of the pillar (the last 4 syllabic counts), the puzzle-solver will naturally speculate which tables might be applied to the first 24 syllable counts (1 to 12 and 12 to 1).

A straightforward extrapolation is presented in Fig. 2.15, which is a reproduction of the Pillar Sonnet (Fig. 2.3). It shows the Pillar Sonnet consisting of three regions, an upper half of the pillar (excluding the base) in which the syllable count increases, a lower half of the pillar (excluding the base) in which the syllable count decreases, and the base of the pillar. The solid chevron is drawn to show the assignment of the base to the Orchema tables. Then what tables are to be used above the base? The natural answer is to assign the three depicted Pillar Sonnet regions to the *Polygraphia* 5's three table types in the order in which they appear (Recta, Aversa, Orchema). This is also the natural assignment of the tables, given their names: the Recta (proper) tables are assigned to the increasing numerical sequence (1 to 12, a normal upward count), and the Aversa (turning back) tables to the decreasing sequence (12 to 1). The checkered chevrons in Fig. 2.15 show this inferred assignment of the first two regions to the Recta and Aversa tables.

Fig. 2.16 is another reproduction of the Pillar Sonnet. As in Fig. 2.15, the acrostic letters (the first and last letters of each line in normal sonnet form) are emphasized using large, bold capital letters. This follows the Puzzle's practice of using capital letters in the Pillar Sonnet to emphasize the acrostic letters. For example, as shown in both Fig. 2.3 and 2.16, "alarM," which appears in the sixth line, has its final letter capitalized. The

Puzzle further emphasizes these acrostic letters by replicating them to the left or the right of the Pillar Sonnet. We notice that each of the acrostic letters fall on one of the Pillar Sonnet's 28 lines. In some cases, such as the second and third lines of the Pillar Sonnet, no acrostic appears; on other lines, 1, 2, or 3 acrostic letters appear. Figure 2.16 is annotated to the right of the sonnet with a list of the acrostic letters that appear on each of the Pillar Sonnet's 28 lines. These are the first and last acrostic letters for each of the Puzzle Sonnet's 18 lines (in customary sonnet format, Fig. 2.4). The suffix "F" is used to designate the "First" letter; the suffix "L" is used to designate the "Last" letter. Thus, 7F refers to the first letter of line 7 of the sonnet in its customary form.

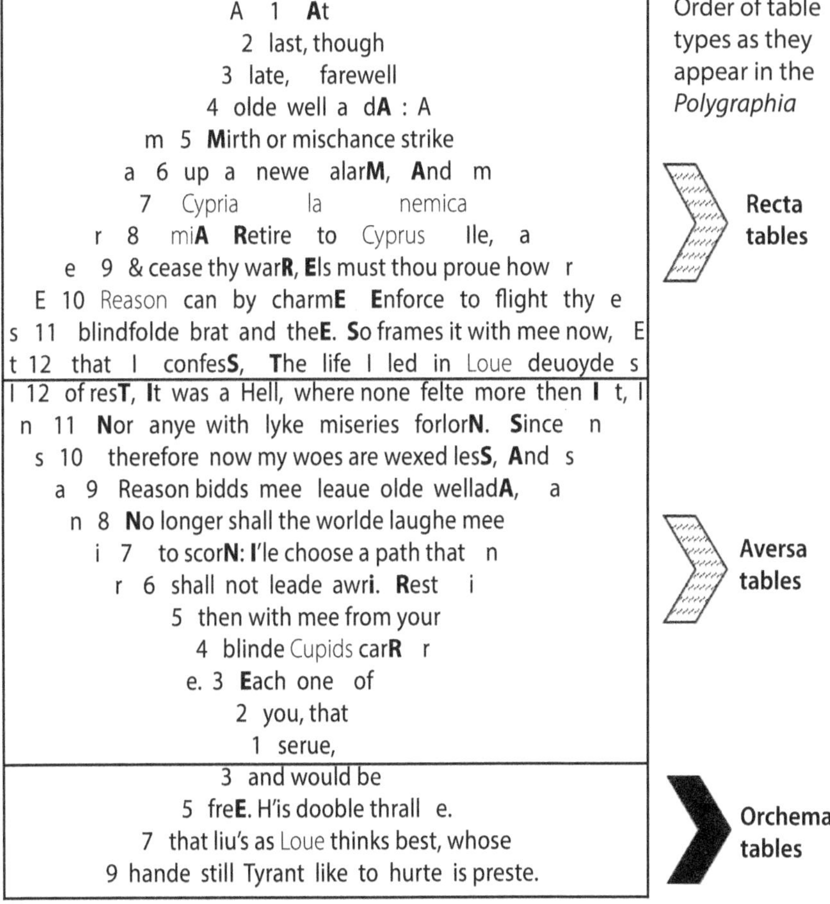

Fig. 2.15 Pillar Sonnet: Table type alignment

```
          A  1  At                                                  1F
             2  last, though                                        --
             3  late,   farewell                                    --
             4  olde well a  dA : A                                 1L
       m  5  Mirth or mischance strike                              2F
     a  6  up  a  newe  alarM,  And  m                              2L, 3F
          7  Cypria        la        nemica                         --
     r  8   miA  Retire  to  Cyprus     Ile,  a                     3L, 4F
    e  9  & cease thy warR, Els must thou proue how  r              4L, 5F
  E 10  Reason  can  by  charmE  Enforce  to  flight  thy  e        5L, 6F
 s 11   blindfolde brat and theE. So frames it with mee now,  E     6L, 7F
 t 12   that  I  confesS,  The  life  I  led  in  Loue  deuoyde  s  7L, 8F
 I 12  of resT, It was a Hell, where none felte more then I  t, I   8L, 9F, 9L
 n 11  Nor  anye  with  lyke  miseries  forlorN.  Since   n         10F, 10L, 11F
  s 10   therefore now my woes are wexed lesS, And  s               11L, 12F
    a  9  Reason bidds mee  leaue olde welladA,   a                 12L
     n  8  No longer shall the worlde laughe mee                    13F
      i  7   to scorN: I'le choose a path that   n                  13L, 14F
       r  6  shall not leade awri. Rest   i                         14L, 15F
             5  then with mee from your                             --
             4  blinde Cupids carR   r                              15L
          e. 3  Each one  of                                        16F
             2  you, that                                           --
             1  serue,                                              --
             3  and would be                                        --
             5  freE. H'is dooble thrall  e.                        16L, 17F
          7  that liu's as Loue thinks best, whose                  17L, 18F
       9  hande still Tyrant like to hurte is preste.               18L
```

Fig. 2.16 Pillar Sonnet: Table to acrostic letter mapping

The Pillar Sonnet acts essentially as a map or table: it assigns acrostic letters to cryptographic tables (i.e., Transforms). Each acrostic letter falls on one of the Pillar Sonnet's 28 lines, which effectively assigns each acrostic letter to one particular number in our 28-number sequence of left margin numbers (1 to 12; 12 to 1; 3, 5, 7, 9). In Fig. 2.15, we assigned each region of the Pillar Sonnet to a table type. We further assume that the left margin numbers provide additional information concerning the assignment of cryptographic tables (which might be inferred from Point 4). The simplest assumption would be that the numbers that were placed at the left margin designate the particular Recta, Aversa, or Orchema table to use. Thus, for the Recta table region of Fig. 2.15, these left margin numbers specify the column number of the master Recta table shown in Fig. 2.13, which is equivalent to the shift value. In other words, a left margin number of 1 specifies the first Recta table (the first column), which shifts by 1. A left margin number of 2 specifies the second Recta table (the second column), which shifts by 2, and so on. Similarly, for the Aversa table, a left margin number of 12 (the 13th line of the Pillar Sonnet) would indicate column 12 (a shift of 12), a left margin number of 11 would indicate column 11 (a shift of 11), etc. The numbers 3, 5, 7, and 9 would make assignments to various Orchema tables. The foregoing assumptions are not only natural, but it is difficult to come up with many reasonable alternatives.[23]

Pillar Line Number	Margin Number	Table Type	Table Name	Acrostic Letter
1	1	Recta	R1	1F
2	2	Recta	R2	--
3	3	Recta	R3	--
4	4	Recta	R4	1L
5	5	Recta	R5	2F
6	6	Recta	R6	2L, 3F
7	7	Recta	R7	--
8	8	Recta	R8	3L, 4F
9	9	Recta	R9	4L, 5F
10	10	Recta	R10	5L, 6F
11	11	Recta	R11	6L, 7F
12	12	Recta	R12	7L, 8F
13	12	Aversa	A12	8L, 9F, 9L
14	11	Aversa	A11	10F, 10L, 11F
15	10	Aversa	A10	11L, 12F
16	9	Aversa	A9	12L
17	8	Aversa	A8	13F
18	7	Aversa	A7	13L, 14F
19	6	Aversa	A6	14L, 15F
20	5	Aversa	A5	--
21	4	Aversa	A4	15L
22	3	Aversa	A3	16F
23	2	Aversa	A2	--
24	1	Aversa	A1	--
25	3	Orchema	O3	--
26	5	Orchema	O5	16L, 17F
27	7	Orchema	O7	17L, 18F
28	9	Orchema	O9	18L

Fig. 2.17 Pillar Sonnet map in tabular form

Fig 2.17 presents the salient information from Fig. 2.16 in tabular form: the first column gives the Pillar Line number (1 to 28); the second column reproduces the number that appears to the left of each sonnet line (the number of syllables); the last column reproduces the annotations from the right side of Fig. 2.16. The assignment of table type, made in Fig. 2.15, is shown in the third column. The fourth column contains an abbreviated table name using R to indicate Recta, A to indicate Aversa, and O to indicate Orchema. Those letters are concatenated with the margin number (the column number, equivalent to the shift value) to produce a concise designator for the table. This fourth column, in conjunction with the last column, shows the mapping of tables to acrostic letters. It is not a one-to-one mapping: some rows in the final column have no values while others have up to 3 values (there is no reason to expect it to be a one-to-one mapping). What is important is that it provides us with a Transform, a cryptographic table, for use with each acrostic letter.

For the purposes of deciphering, it is more convenient to have the information of Fig. 2.17 indexed by acrostic letter rather than by Pillar line number. Fig. 2.18 is a re-indexed version of Fig 2.17; there is no difference in its content. For example, the first letter of line 1, designated as "1F" in Fig. 2.17, has a Transform value of R1 (fourth column of Fig. 2.17). In Fig. 2.18, Acrostic Line Number 1, the first row, shows a Table Name value of R1 for the first letter. Changing the index of a data table or directory is a common practice: for example, reverse-lookup phone directories.

Assigning a different Transform for different letter positions in a text (or as here, for an acrostic letter) is the defining feature of polyalphabetic cryptography. Trithemius's implementation, which uses the overly simple method of assigning consecutive letters to consecutive tables, is not cryptographically robust (it can easily be attacked by a cryptanalyst). Indeed, more sophisticated schemes predate the *Polygraphia*. For example, Alberti's cipher-wheel (ca. 1466) employs a far more complex mechanism to assign tables to ciphertext letters.[24] In the case of the Puzzle, the Pillar Sonnet assigns each letter position of its two acrostics to a Transform or table, in accordance with Fig. 2.18 (which is equivalent to Fig. 2.17).

Naturally, all puzzles require that some inferences be made. I've made some inferences in building the Transform Assignments of Fig. 2.18, but they are minimal. Nevertheless, inferences made in attempting to detect a cryptographic system should be explicitly enumerated.[25] We assumed that the ascending numbers of the Pillar Sonnet (1 to 12) specify Recta tables and that the descending numbers (12 to 1) specify Aversa tables. This assumption was a natural extrapolation of the Puzzle's instructions, which state that the base specifies Orchema tables. We then assumed that the Pillar Sonnet numbers of 1 to 12, which appear at the head of each Pillar Sonnet line (Fig. 2.3 and Fig. 2.16), correspond to the first through twelfth Recta tables, respectively. We made a corresponding assumption for the Aversa tables: the numbers from 12 to 1 at the left margin specify the twelfth through first Aversa tables, respectively. Having given us the cryptographic tables, the Puzzle makes us—after a few minor inferences—essentially authorized decipherers rather than codebreakers (i.e., cryptanalysts).

Acrostic Line No.	Table Name First Letter	Table Name Last Letter
1	R1	R4
2	R5	R6
3	R6	R8
4	R8	R9
5	R9	R10
6	R10	R11
7	R11	R12
8	R12	A12
9	A12	A12
10	A11	A11
11	A11	A10
12	A10	A9
13	A8	A7
14	A7	A6
15	A6	A4
16	A3	O5
17	O5	O7
18	O7	O9

Fig. 2.18 Pillar Sonnet map indexed by acrostic position

Deciphering the reordered sonnet and polyphonic ciphers

We will now attempt to decipher the reordered Puzzle Sonnet based on the assignment of cryptographic tables implied by the Pillar Sonnet. The left and right acrostics of the reordered Puzzle Sonnet (Fig. 2.10) provide our ciphertext. This ciphertext has been copied into Fig. 2.19's two ciphertext columns (under Left Acrostic and Right Acrostic). The Transform tables for each acrostic line number (from Fig. 2.18) have also been copied into Fig. 2.19, in the two Transform table columns. We now apply these Transform tables to the ciphertext, for both the left and right acrostics. The deciphered results appear in the two plaintext columns of Fig. 2.19. Reading these results downward, we are disappointed to find that there is no discernable message. Clearly, there is at least one more step to finding the solution to the Puzzle's first Stage.

Sonnet Line Number	Left Acrostic			Right Acrostic		
	Transform table	Cipher-text	Plain-text	Transform table	Cipher-text	Plain-text
1	R1	T	U	R4	T	Y
2	R5	I	O	R6	I	P
3	R6	H	O	R8	T	C
4	R8	W	E	R9	T	D
5	R9	I	S	R10	I	T
6	R10	A	L	R11	A	M
7	R11	S	E	R12	S	F
8	R12	A	N	A12	A	N
9	A12	S	U	A12	S	U
10	A11	A	O	A11	A	O
11	A11	E	K	A10	E	L
12	A10	M	D	A9	M	E
13	A8	R	A	A7	R	B
14	A7	E	O	A6	E	P
15	A6	R	C	A4	R	E
16	A3	E	S	O5	E	?
17	O5	N	?	O7	N	?
18	O7	N	?	O9	N	?

Fig. 2.19 Puzzle Sonnet deciphered

Cryptographic systems in this period attempted to guard against unauthorized deciphering (cryptanalysis) using a variety of techniques. One method is to assign two ciphertext characters to represent a single high frequency plaintext letter, such as the letter "E," in order to thwart frequency counting. Another less common practice is to assign two plaintext letters to a single ciphertext letter. Such ciphers, known as "polyphonic ciphers," force even an authorized decipherer to select the true plaintext letter out of two or three possibilities for each character. Although on rare occasions this allows for ambiguity in the deciphered message, it usually does not because the constraints of language are too strong, as will be discussed later. The advantage of polyphonic ciphers is that they are very difficult to crack.

A modern-day example of such enciphering is found on telephone keypads, where each number is assigned to multiple letters. This allows telephone numbers to be specified as words as well as numbers. For example, a plumber might acquire the phone number 800-758-6237 and then advertise it as 800-PLUMBER. However, enciphering in this manner can lead to ambiguity, as shown in the example below. The telephone number 794-6437 can be deciphered as two valid words, PYGMIES and SWINGER. However, there are very few phone numbers that would generate multiple seven-letter words; surely much effort was required to discover this example.[26]

Dialpad Numeric:	7	9	4	6	4	3	7
Dialpad Encoding 1:	P	W	G	M	G	D	P
Dialpad Encoding 2:	Q	X	H	N	H	E	Q
Dialpad Encoding 3:	R	Y	I	O	I	F	R
Dialpad Encoding 4:	S	Z					S
Possibility 1:	P	Y	G	M	I	E	S
Possibility 2:	S	W	I	N	G	E	R

Aloys Meister documents various polyphonic ciphers used in the sixteenth century. The polyphonic cipher that appears below was used in 1583 by Cardinal Jacobus Sabellus (1540–87).[27] I have slightly modified it to facilitate my example (e.g., a "W" was added—Sabellus's Italian alphabet lacks that letter). In the table below, every number from 0 to 9 is assigned to two alphabetical characters. This table is used to both encipher and decipher messages.

0	1	2	3	4	5	6	7	8	9	Ciphertext
N	S	R	M	H	U	E	F	A	I	Plaintext1
G	Z	T	P	W	L	C	O	B	D	Plaintext2

We now encipher the name Thomas Watson (the plaintext) using the above polyphonic cipher:

T	H	O	M	A	S	W	A	T	S	O	N	Plaintext
2	4	7	3	8	1	4	8	2	1	7	0	Ciphertext

Next we decipher the above ciphertext, 247381482170. We must examine the two possible plaintext letters for each character of the message as shown below.

2	4	7	3	8	1	4	8	2	1	7	0	Ciphertext
R	**H**	F	**M**	**A**	**S**	H	**A**	R	**S**	F	**N**	Plaintext1
T	W	**O**	P	B	Z	**W**	B	**T**	Z	**O**	G	Plaintext2

Looking at either the Plaintext 1 or Plaintext 2 row alone, the text is gibberish. The cipher can only be read if, for each character, we select one plaintext letter from either one row or the other, depending upon whichever one will produce a coherent message. The letters that allow for a valid message appear in bold, yielding the original plaintext: THOMAS WATSON. Unlike nonpolyphonic ciphers, which produce a definitive plaintext, even the authorized decipherer must select among plaintext alternatives solely based on the coherence of the resulting message.

This might seem to allow for a great deal of indeterminacy in the true plaintext message, but it does not. To understand why, it is helpful to consider such games as "hangman" or the TV show *Wheel of Fortune,* in which a contestant must guess an incomplete short text, often a familiar phrase or aphorism, prior to all letters of the text appearing. The contestants are often able to guess the text with half or even fewer of the letters present. If half the letters are missing, 50% of the text is presented, and 50% is indeterminate. In the case of our polyphonic cipher, the decipherer must make a binary choice between two letters. A simple calculation shows that this is equivalent to 78% of the message being present and 22% being indeterminate.[28] With 78% of the message present, ambiguities are rare. The remaining indeterminacy of 22% will prove to be a modest factor in our validation of the solution to the Puzzle Sonnet's cipher, as discussed later in this chapter.

This inherent indeterminacy, the defining feature of polyphonic ciphers, presents a great hindrance to anyone trying to crack the cipher. When an unauthorized decipherer is examining possible keys, they look for unlikely or wrong letters: the letter K in Latin, rare letters such as Z, or an unlikely trigram of consonants, for example. This allows many hypothetical keys to be eliminated, an essential step in cracking cryptograms. However, if there are *two* possible plaintext letters for each character, rarely will it be possible to eliminate a particular hypothetical key, because usually one of the two plaintext letters will be common rather than rare. Thus, polyphonic ciphers are far stronger. However, this comes at the expense of introducing an additional step for the authorized decipherer.

The double acrostic sonnet subtly hints that a polyphonic cipher is present. The two unconcealed acrostic messages (*amare est insanire*) suggest that both acrostics come into play in the enciphered message. Yet for each acrostic to produce one transparent message in the original order, and also produce an enciphered message in the reordered sonnet, is far too great a constraint to ever be realized. Even for one of the two acrostics to do so would probably be impossible (it would also beg the question of why the unconcealed message appears twice). Indeed, only by means of a polyphonic cipher, with one acrostic or the other coming into play on a per character basis, are the constraints loose enough to allow a third message to be present in the reordered acrostics.

As we will discover, the Puzzle Sonnet's cryptogram is indeed polyphonic (in addition to being polyalphabetic). Polyphony was well suited to Bacon's purposes because without it, the Puzzle would have been fairly easy to solve. If Bacon had enciphered his message in a nonpolyphonic single acrostic, then the puzzle-solver might easily test each sonnet line in different positions, frequently determining that a particular position was unlikely because a rare character was generated, or conversely, fairly likely because a common letter, such as a vowel, was generated. This would have eliminated countless permutations. When combined with other restrictions such as rhyme pattern and logical flow, the Puzzle would be solved quickly by the practiced cryptanalyst. Bacon's use of a polyphonic cipher makes any cryptanalytic attack almost impossible. His clever defense forces the puzzle-solver to instead attack the Puzzle by the only remaining option, a reordering based on poetic sense. As we shall see, polyphonic ciphers are also employed in the other Stages of the Puzzle. The strength of polyphonic ciphers blocks most, if not all, cryptanalytic paths to solving those Stages, and instead the puzzle-solver must follow the path toward a solution that the Puzzle's design allows: the Heuristic System. The Puzzle's cryptography, the Precision System, is a tool used to enforce a unique (i.e., deterministic) solution to the poetic problems that the *Hekatompathia* presents to its readers. At the same time, the Puzzle's design—Bacon's clever use of polyphonic cryptography—prevents the puzzle-solver from operating the Precision System in reverse, that is, using cryptanalytic techniques instead of poetic sense to solve the Puzzle. This essential element of the Precision System forces the puzzle-solver to think creatively like a poet in their effort to reconstruct the work's text.

The Puzzle thus practices the probative mode of communication, as discussed in the "Poetry and pedagogy" section of the first chapter. Yet it addresses the danger inherent in any obscured text: that the exegete will err in his or her construction or interpretation of the text. The Precision System directly addresses this danger, and at the same time, prevents any "cheating"—operating the Precision System in reverse—that would undermine the probative mode of communication. Thus, it alerts the reader to any errors in reconstructing the text but cannot be used as an alternative to the Heuristic System. This forces adherence to the probative mode: the puzzle-solver must engage in a full exploration of the poetic text. Thus, the puzzle-solver is informed of wrong answers, but has no access to the right answers, and must then reconsider wrong answers, find an alternative, and then retest it.

The use of polyphony was also a practical necessity. Phillips, in the passage quoted earlier, questions how the poet could possibly add "yet another arcane device" into this already complex double acrostic sonnet. She is right. To overlay another determinate single acrostic (containing a secret plaintext) onto the original double acrostic (*amare est insanire*) creates so many constraints as to make the inclusion of an enciphered message impossible. Alternatively, allowing either the first or last letter of each line to produce a secret plaintext message produces a less constraining set of conditions.

Deciphering the Puzzle Sonnet's secret message

We now reexamine the two columns of deciphered letters, both labeled "Plaintext," in Fig. 2.19, which for convenience are replicated side by side in Fig. 2.20. Treating the plaintext columns as a polyphonic cipher, we choose one letter from either column for each row. We might first consider whether the cryptogram is more likely to be in English or Latin (the two languages in which the *Hekatompathia*'s poems are written). Latin seems more likely of the two in that the original acrostics are in Latin, and the greater compactness of Latin would make it a more attractive choice for a short message.

In Fig. 2.20, the selection between the two plaintext alternatives in each column is designated by boldface type. This selection is based on finding a coherent Latin expression. We are restricted to 15 of the 18 characters because we have not yet determined the Transform values for the Orchema tables. The first 13 characters produce these words:

VOCES ME. NUO LEA...
(May you invoke me. I waver under the influence of the lioness.)

Our deciphered text begins appropriately enough by addressing the reader, VOCES ME. The poet is exhorting the reader to call upon or invoke the poet himself. An invocation frequently occurs at the beginning of an authoritative text, such as in the *Iliad*'s first line, which includes "Sing goddess."

Homer invokes a muse to allow him to tell a story from centuries prior. The conceit is that he is merely lending his voice to the muse. In this case, the puzzle-solver, as in Homer's conceit, is delivering not his own words, but those of the *Hekatompathia*'s poet, the author of the secret text. The poet is exhorting the decipherer to invoke himself and deliver his message—an encouragement to continue the process of solving the Puzzle.

Sonnet Line Number	Left Acrostic Plaintext	Right Acrostic Plaintext
1	**U**	Y
2	**O**	P
3	O	**C**
4	**E**	D
5	**S**	T
6	L	**M**
7	**E**	F
8	**N**	**N**
9	**U**	**U**
10	**O**	**O**
11	K	**L**
12	D	**E**
13	**A**	B
14	O	P
15	C	E
16	S	?
17	?	?
18	?	?

Fig. 2.20 **Puzzle Sonnet deciphered: A polyphonic cipher**

Indeed, an invocation is a particularly fitting way to begin any ciphered text. Katherine Ellison discusses a notorious "incantation" in Trithemius's *Steganographia*, which involves "the summoning of angels to deliver encrypted messages." While some of Trithemius's contemporaries read this incantation as evidence of black magic, later commentators in the seventeenth century may have understood that his incantation was "itself a secret message for expert readers."[29] This use of incantation or invocation as a prelude to cryptography suggests that *Voces me* follows this convention, signaling the beginning of an enciphered message.

Of course, invocation occurs frequently in sacred texts and liturgy. When Christ is invoked in the sacrament of the Eucharist, it is to make God and His Word present. Invocation is found in 1 Corinthians 1.2, which is here translated from the Vulgate:

> To the church of God that is at Corinth, to those sanctified in Christ Jesus, called (*vocatis*) to be saints, with all that invoke (*invocant*) the name of our Lord Jesus Christ in every place of theirs and ours.

Here the verb *vocare*, in two different forms, is used bidirectionally: to show God or the Church calling upon man, and man invoking the name of God. *Voces me* is also bidirectional. With remarkable concision, the poet calls upon the reader to call upon the poet (*voces* is the second person hortatory subjunctive). Bacon appears to be calling upon the solver-decipherer to continue his work. This cooperative interaction between poet and reader may be an example of what Mary Carruthers calls "hermeneutic dialogue," in which an active reader must complete the work of an absent author.[30]

The next word of the secret text, the verb *nuo* (also written *nuto*) can mean "I nod or command by a signal or other non-verbal means" (*OLD* 1). *Nuo* may also mean "I sway/totter, or I waver in my opinion" (*LS* II). The next word, *lea*, means lioness (ablative case). Therefore, *nuo lea* might be translated in either of the following ways:

> I waver/sway under the influence of the lioness.
> I indicate by means of the lioness.

Just below the Puzzle Sonnet, we find a Design that looks very much like a lion or lioness (see Fig. 2.4), which does much to confirm the validity of our deciphered message. Moreover, there is a link to the closing couplet of Sonnet 82. To the left of that couplet, next to an asterisk, is a curious side-note in which Bacon quotes Sophocles: τόν τοι τύρανον εὐσεβεῖν οὐ ῥᾴδιον (it is difficult for an absolute monarch to show piety). This line occurs very near the end of his play, *Ajax*: Odysseus is making the case to Agamemnon that Ajax should be given a proper burial, despite Agamemnon's continued anger. Of what possible relevance could this be to Sonnet 82, or anything else in the *Hekatompathia*? The only connection is τύρανος, cognate to the English word tyrant, which appears in the final couplet:

> *H'is double thrall that liu's as Loue thinks best
> Whose hand still Tyrant like to hurt is prest.   (82.17–18)

Τύρανος can mean either a "tyrant," or "autocrat" or "absolute monarch" without the pejorative sense of "tyrant." It seems that Bacon is providing the reader with a gloss. Of course, this *tyrant* (*whose hand* is pressing upon the speaker *to hurt*) who is also a monarch can only refer to one thing in the context of the *Hekatompathia*—love. Throughout the work, love is portrayed as the highest power, a supreme god, and a cruel tyrant. Thus, this Design that looks like a lion or lioness—which we shall call a "Lioness Design"—conveys the symbolism of kingship and the image of fierce tyranny. (The identification of lions and monarchy is a symbolism that dates from antiquity.) This connection between the English word "tyrant," glossed as "absolute monarch" by the sidenote, and the proximate Lioness Design, indicates that the placement of this Design was almost certainly an authorial choice and not the arbitrary decision of a printer. The deciphered message, which has the speaker "swaying" (NUO) under pressure from a "lioness" (LEA), is perfectly cognate with what is plainly visible in the text: the Lioness Design, sidenote, and the Puzzle Sonnet's final two lines. This provides strong confirmation of the authenticity of the deciphered message. Moreover, the image of the speaker suffering under love's tyranny is not one of many possible images, but the central image employed by the *Hekatompathia*.

The androgynous lion

The deciphered message identifies the significance of the Lioness Design: it is a symbol of personified, tyrannical Love. Spenser also chose a lion to represent love as a great power in his *Shepheardes Calender* (published three years prior to the *Hekatompathia*), in which Colin says:

> And Sommer season sped him to display
> (For loue then in the Lyons house did dwell)
> The raging fyre, that kindled at his ray.
> A comett stird vp that vnkindly heate,
> That reigned (as men sayd) in *Venus* seate.   (December, lines 56–60)

"Lyons house" refers to the astrological sign Leo (July 23–August 22). The embedded commentary of E. K. in Spenser's *Shepheardes Calender* glosses "Lyons house" with "He imagineth simply that Cupid, which is loue, had his abode in the whote [hot] signe Leo, which is in middest of somer; a pretie allegory, whereof the meaning is, that loue in him wrought an extaordinarie heate of lust." Given that both Spenser and Bacon were members of the Leicester literary circle, Bacon would have likely read the *Shepheardes Calender* and thus be aware of the metaphoric link between Spenser's astrological lion and love, and perhaps of the same metaphor in other sources as well. As I will argue in the next chapter, the Lioness Design, whose semiotic value is love, is the most important of the 18 Design types that appear in the *Hekatompathia*. Sonnets with a Lioness Design play a critical role in the reordering of the *Hekatompathia*'s sonnets, as described in the next chapter, and in the seventh Stage, where they are used to reveal Bacon's name.

Examining the Puzzle Sonnet's final couplet and the deciphered message, we notice a contradiction in the specification of the lion's gender: *H'is* (82.17) versus LEA (feminine). At first glance, the lion or lioness in the Lioness Design seems to have something of a mane (Fig. 2.4), and if this indicates the male of the species, it would conflict with our deciphered *lea* (lioness). However, love in the *Hekatompathia* is sometimes masculine, as when personified by Cupid, at other times feminine, as when personified by Venus. The work's closing apothegm characterizes love as feminine: *The Labour is light, where Loue is the Paimistres* [pay-mistress]. The Puzzle Sonnet's final couplet (situated near the Lioness Design and linked to the sidenote) begins with the contraction *H'is*, an apparent reference to love as masculine. The uncommon contraction, *H'is*, is unlikely to be a misprint of "His" because it appears four times, in both formats of the Puzzle Sonnet (Sonnets 81 and 82), and again twice in the manuscript. This contraction might mean "He is," in which case line 17 reads:

[He is] **double thrall that liu's as** Loue **thinks best**

"He is double thrall" makes little sense because it equates Cupid with his powers, which seems odd and is not consistent with the treatment of Cupid elsewhere in the sequence.[31] Our attention is next drawn to another odd contraction, *liu's*, which given the context of *double thrall*, cannot mean "lives," as thrall does not "live." It almost certainly means "livers": Cupid livers (i.e., delivers) his arrows—his thrall—capriciously, a prolific trope found in the *Hekatompathia* and elsewhere. Indeed, in Sonnet 63, Cupid delivers *double thrall* by means of two kinds of arrows, one gold and one lead: each type corresponds to one of love's two powers, as discussed in Chapter 8. Line 17 might then be read as "Cupid (He) is double thrall that livers as Love thinks best." In this reading, Cupid personifies love's delivery mechanism, as opposed to love itself. This would be analogous to the Renaissance conception of personified Nature (feminine) as a demiurge, carrying out God's orders. Line 17's (somewhat awkward) construction allows for independence between *H'is* and *Loue*, and this permits *Loue* to be read as either androgynous or feminine, despite the masculine *H'is*.

An alternative reading of the contraction *H'is* is suggested by the value of the omitted letters in the line's other contraction, *liu's*, which is "er." If we take the value of the apostrophe in *H'is* to also be "er," the result is "Heris." This might be taken as an androgynous pronoun, hiding a "Her[is]" within the orthographically masculine *H'is*, or it might be "heris," an archaic pronoun that means "hers" or "theirs" (OED, "hers," poss. pron. 1 and 2). *H'is* would then be an orthographic "his" that hides a "hers." If this is true, then Bacon created a gender-ambiguous pronoun meaning "his/her," presumably because neither "his" nor "her" is appropriate to love itself, which is androgynous. If this was Bacon's intention, then it would be the second time that he created an androgynous pronoun in the *Hekatompathia*: in Sonnet 25, he fabricated a gender-ambiguous pronoun because the sonnet required it.[32] Thus, the deciphered LEA (feminine) is not contradicted by *H'is* (82.17), which might at first be taken to be masculine.

Regardless of which of the foregoing readings is accepted, *Loue* is independent of the contraction *H'is*, and this allows *Loue* to be taken as masculine, feminine, or both. Moreover, the Puzzle Sonnet itself includes both masculine and feminine representations of love based on Cupid and Venus.[33] Thus, *Loue*, the ultimate source of the *double thrall* (17), is treated as neither purely masculine nor feminine (a Platonist attitude), and so the appearance of the feminine *lea* in the deciphered message does not contradict the sonnet's text. Indeed, any reference made to the leonine Design that appears below the Puzzle Sonnet (82) must be either masculine or feminine: there is no such word as "*leum*" (a neuter lion) in Latin. Bacon, faced with an arbitrary choice of whether to refer to the lion as masculine or feminine, probably chose *lea* (feminine, ablative) because of its decided advantage: it is significantly more compact than *leone* (masculine, ablative).

This conception of love as androgynous or hermaphroditic is prevalent in Platonism and found elsewhere in Elizabethan literature. For example, an important Platonist doctrine states that *contradictoria concidunt in natura unialis* (contradictions are reconciled in the nature of the one). Derived from the ancient idea that strife between opposites results in a harmony, in Platonist thought, opposites are resolved in the Plotinian "the One." This coincidence of opposites (*coincidentia oppositorum*) can be found in Spenser's *Faerie Queene*, where Venus is described as hermaphroditic:

> But for, they say, she hath both kinds in one,
> Both male and female, both under one name:
> She syre and mother is her selfe alone,
> Begets and eke conceives, ne needeth other none.   (IV.x.41)

For some Platonists, not only might Venus represent both sexes, but God, too, may contain the principles of male and female within his self in a higher unity. That is, because God is the Cause of All, he must himself be comprised of both sexes.[34] C. S. Lewis writes:

> I think that Spenser's Nature is really an image of god himself. … As Nicholas of Cusa reminds us, the ancients call God Nature. … So Spenser's Nature is veiled, some say, to conceal her terror, 'for that her face did like a Lion shew.' (VII.vii.6)[35]

Alastair Fowler, citing the above passage, says that "in the *Mutability Cantos*, Natura herself, the creative Logos, reconciles order and mutability in a veiled mystery uniting solar splendor [the masculine Apollo] and leonine terror."[36] Bacon's hermaphroditic, terrifying Lioness Design is the perfect emblem for love in the *Hekatompathia*. Moreover, elsewhere in the sonnet sequence, love is portrayed as an all-powerful god whose presence is known by the coincidence of opposites, as later discussed.

The final letters of the deciphered message

Returning to our deciphering task, we consider the final letters of the plaintext message, which are enciphered by Orchema Transforms. However, we as yet have insufficient information to decipher these letters because the Orchema Transforms, unlike the Recta and Aversa Transforms, are broadly defined in the *Polygraphia*.[37] The 5 pairs of plaintext characters that follow LEA, found in lines 14–18 of the Puzzle Sonnet, are shown in Fig. 2.21 (these values are taken from Fig. 2.20). The first 5 plaintext values are deciphered from Aversa Transforms; the next 5 values are unknown because they derive from Orchema Transforms and are therefore marked with a question mark.

From Fig. 2.21, we can see that the final word of the plaintext message is 5 letters in length. Examining the first two pairs of polyphonic plaintext letters, the final word in the message may begin with either OC, OE, PC, or PE. The second and third possibilities are unlikely beginnings for Latin words. Although the letters OC might begin a Latin word, no 5-letter word beginning with those letters comes to mind. When we consider the letters PE, or PES (a 50/50 chance), the possibilities narrow. If we assume the word begins with PES, then only two unknown letters remain. In this case, the final word is almost certainly PESUS, a late Latin spelling of the classical Latin *pensus*.[38] It is the masculine singular perfect passive participle of *pendere* (to weigh). *Pesus* means "to be weighed upon," and the now complete second sentence of the deciphered message, NUO LEA PESUS, may be translated:

Weighed upon by the lioness, I waver.

NUO LEA PESUS fits with the conceit that the speaker suffers under tyrannical love, which is found throughout the *Hekatompathia*, as well as in the Puzzle Sonnet's final line: *Whose hand still Tyrant like to hurt is prest.* The notion that the speaker is being pressed (*prest*) upon fits well with *pesus* (weighed upon). However, this guess at the plaintext's final word is uncertain without knowing the value of the Orchema Transforms.

Sonnet Line Number	Left Acrostic Plaintext	Right Acrostic Plaintext
14	O	P
15	C	E
16	S	?
17	?	?
18	?	?

Fig. 2.21 Puzzle Sonnet deciphered: The final five letters

Validating our deciphered message

How can we be sure that our reordered sonnet is in the order intended by the poet? Given the millions of possible line orders, perhaps there are other possibilities that satisfy the five Rules, generate a coherent Latin message, and render a sonnet that has a fine-grain internal structure appropriate to its role as the MLIP Subsequence's lead sonnet. Perhaps—but the foregoing constraints, coupled with several of those imposed by the Rules, are so restrictive that it seems very unlikely, especially given the additional restrictions that the sonnet progress both chronologically and logically. A further constraint, the most critical of all, is that the deciphered plaintext message must be sensible and relevant—all but one among billions of permutations will generate gibberish, as discussed in the mathematical validation section below.

The deciphered message is remarkable in its concision and astonishingly pertinent. It perfectly articulates the relationship between poet and decipherer in its first sentence, VOCES ME. Its second sentence, NUO LEA PESUS, is extraordinary in several respects. LEA matches up with the Lioness Design that appears beneath Sonnet 82, and there is further corroboration by the Greek sidenote about absolute monarchs, lions being a symbol of kingship. This second sentence must have been very carefully chosen by Bacon because it is descriptive of virtually every one of the *Hekatompathia*'s sonnets: the speaker is always affected by love, wavering under the weight of its awesome power. Indeed, these three words might be taken as a hypogram[39] for the entire work.

The validity of NUO LEA PESUS becomes apparent when comparing each of its words to the Puzzle Sonnet's final line in the original order, as shown below:

Deciphered words	*Whose hand still Tyrant like to hurt is prest* (18)
nuo (I waver/totter)	*hurt* (OED 1: to knock or collide violently)
lea (symbol of kingship)	*Tyrant* (monarch gloss in sidenote)
pesus (to be weighed upon)	*prest*

Both NUO LEA PESUS and the sonnet's final line express the conceit that *Love* (17) is a king who physically pressures the speaker. Thus we have near-perfect alignment between the deciphered message and the Puzzle Sonnet's final line, which provides overwhelming evidence of its validity.

To supplement this qualitative evaluation, a quantitative analysis is now performed. Excursus 3, "Cryptanalysis and the validation of deciphered texts," provides an introduction to the quantitative validation of cryptographic solutions. Two other such validations appear in this study, and this excursus is intended for those readers without prior knowledge of the validation process. It includes a brief description of Shannon's Information Theory (see Fig. E3.3).

The process that produced the deciphered message is depicted schematically in Fig. 2.22. After reordering the Puzzle Sonnet, the acrostics were stripped away, treated as numeric values, and shifted by an arithmetic formula (the Transforms indicated by the Pillar Sonnet). The resulting polyphonic plaintext was then resolved to produce a single plaintext.

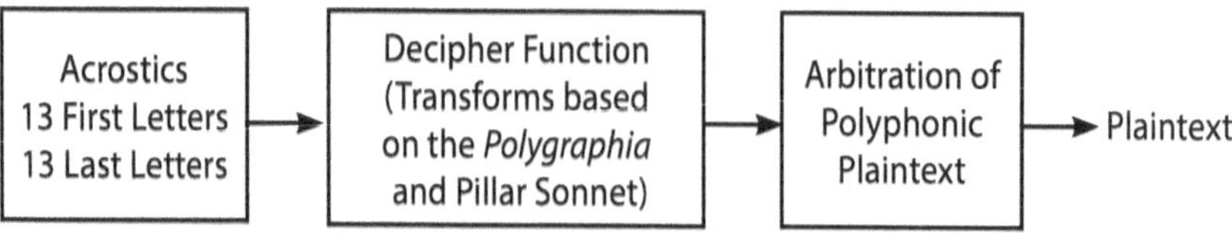

Fig. 2.22 Summary of Puzzle Sonnet deciphering process

As discussed in Chapter 1, three factors must be considered in validating a cryptogram: the absolute rate of language (the full range of the ciphertext), the number of valid messages, and the range of the key. To validate our 13-letter plaintext solution (VOCES ME. NUO LEA...[40]) to the Puzzle Sonnet, we must first calculate the probability that a coherent and relevant plaintext message is produced by what is effectively a random process (apart from the context of the Puzzle). We estimate the number of valid 13-letter plaintext messages, using a Shannon information value of 25% pure information and 75% redundancy.[41] The number of possible valid texts is equal to $24^{(25\% \text{ of } 13)} = 24^{3.25} \approx 30{,}600$. We now divide the number of valid texts by the absolute rate of language, which for our 13-letter ciphertext is 24^{13}, or approximately 8.8×10^{17}:

Ratio of valid texts to all possible texts $\approx 30{,}600 \, / \, 8.8 \times 10^{17} \approx 1$ in 29 trillion

The probability that a valid text has been serendipitously generated is extremely remote; however, we have yet to account for the indeterminacy in polyphonic ciphers, which requires a choice between one of two plaintext letters. For each of 13 lines, a binary decision is required, which makes for 2^{13} or 8,192 permutations. Multiplying 8,192 by the probability calculated above (1 in 29 trillion), we obtain a probability of approximately 1 in 3.5 billion—still extremely remote.[42] This is the probability that any given ciphertext—the reordered acrostics—would generate a coherent plaintext message after polyphonic resolution.

We must now consider the reordering of the Puzzle Sonnet: are there many valid reorderings, and if so, might one of these produce a different plaintext message? In the course of solving the Puzzle, I came up with only one valid reordering to test, and from this perspective, it does not matter if there are many other valid reorderings because, in practice, I only tested one reordering. The probability that the single reordering that I found would produce a coherent plaintext message is the calculated probability that any given ciphertext produces a coherent plaintext: one in 3.5 billion. True, there may be other valid reorderings, but as I discovered and tested only one reordering, the probability that the one I discovered is valid can be considered independently of any other valid reorderings that may exist. Given the improbability of a one in 3.5 billion chance, the coherent plaintext that I found must be the result of my reordering the sonnet as intended by the poet and applying the correct deciphering procedure to its acrostics (the ciphertext).

True, this is dependent upon my testimony that I did not discover and test other valid reorderings. Of course, it would be preferable that the validation be independent of my testimony. This requires that the number of poetically valid reorderings be estimated, which is difficult to do because of the complexity of the constraints in reordering the sonnet: logical flow from line to line, appropriateness to the sonnet's poetic meaning, and adherence to a reasonable rhyme scheme. My estimate of the number of valid Puzzle Sonnet reorderings, really an upper limit, is 16,000.[43] From the many hours I spent attempting to find a valid reordering, I believe that this significantly overestimates the number of valid reorderings. The requirement for a sensible and grammatic flow from line to line, which is extraordinarily restrictive, is difficult to estimate but I believe that the likely number of valid reorderings is orders of magnitude less than this estimate. We now factor this estimate of the number of valid reorderings into our probability calculation. The probability that one of these 16,000 reorderings might produce a coherent 13-letter plaintext is $16,000 (1/3.5 \times 10^9) \approx 1$ in 200,000. This is the probability, at the estimated upper limit of possible reorderings, that our 13-letter plaintext message was produced serendipitously.

One other aspect of this validation requires discussion. Was my restoration of the sonnet's order aided by cryptanalytic techniques, that is, did I eliminate reorderings that would not have generated coherent plaintexts by employing cryptanalytic techniques? This would alter the probability calculation of one in 3.5 billion because applying cryptanalytic techniques is equivalent to testing additional reorderings. Said another way, my claim to have tested only one reordering of the Puzzle Sonnet would be inaccurate because that reordering would have been biased by having restricted my examination of reorderings to only those more likely to produce a coherent plaintext message. However, Bacon's design makes such cryptanalytic techniques difficult to apply due to the Puzzle's polyphony, as previously discussed. The polyphony prevents the puzzle-solver from working backward, that is, in the opposite direction of the arrows shown in Fig. 2.22. If a nonpolyphonic cipher had been used, one could test the plausibility that particular lines would work at particular positions in the Puzzle Sonnet by rejecting alternatives that produced a rare letter and favoring alternatives that produced a common letter.

Indeed, having some technical skills, I attempted a cryptanalytic attack, which I applied to smaller sections of the Puzzle Sonnet of about 4–6 lines each. I tested these smaller sections cryptographically, with the hope that I might eliminate some positions for some sonnet lines, and thus obtain some help in the reordering process. However, I was frustrated by the polyphonic cryptography, which never produced a pair of rare letters (which would allow elimination), and always produced a plausible letter sequence for the groups of 4-6 letters that I tested. I was forced to abandon my attempt and the reordering of the sonnet was accomplished without the use of any cryptanalytic technique.

Thus we have now validated the message deciphered in the Puzzle's first Stage: VOCES ME. NUO LEA PESUS (May you invoke me. Weighed upon by the lioness, I waver.). The probability of serendipitously obtaining a valid and contextually relevant message for my single reordering of the Puzzle Sonnet was calculated to be only one in 3.5 billion. Further, it was demonstrated that even if one somehow uncovered 16,000 poetically valid reorderings of the Puzzle Sonnet, the probability that one of those reorderings would result in a valid message is still extremely remote. Non-mathematicians may prefer the qualitative analysis discussed above. The message's second sentence, NUO LEA PESUS, thematically matches the Puzzle Sonnet's closing couplet and the appearance of love's emblem, the Lioness Design, directly below the couplet. Moreover, "I waver under the weight of the lioness (love)" might aptly serve as a hypogram for the sequence: nearly every sonnet describes the speaker struggling under love's influence.

There is one further piece of evidence: given the amount of work required to solve the Puzzle's first Stage, one would expect some significant revelation. The Puzzle's first Stage must either reveal some great secret (such as the identity of the beloved, if she were a historical person), which it does not, or suggest how next to proceed. Indeed, we have been given the key to the Puzzle's next Stage. NUO, besides meaning "I sway," can also mean "I nod" (or gesture or indicate). This second meaning renders the following: "I indicate by means of the lioness." This is an essential clue, for as we will discover in the next chapter, it provides critical information needed to reorder the sequence. The phrase NUO LEA PESUS exhibits extraordinary concision and polyvalence: it both mirrors the Puzzle Sonnet's final couplet and provides the essential clue for us to advance through the Puzzle. Open questions about the purpose of the Designs below each sonnet and the Orchema tables propel us toward the Puzzle's next Stage.

We have now fulfilled the challenge set by the Puzzle's instructions to decipher something using Trithemius's tables. Although it might seem that there are multiple valid rearrangements of the Puzzle Sonnet, the poetic constraints are highly restrictive. Further, the restrictions imposed by the cryptographic generation of a valid deciphered message guarantee the uniqueness of our rearrangement because the probability that another rearrangement would produce a valid plaintext message is infinitesimal (1 in 3.5 billion). We can now be certain that the *Hekatompathia*'s literary-cryptographic Puzzle is genuine and move forward to its next Stage.

The Puzzle tests our literary skills: this Stage required us to reconstruct a poem from its scrambled lines. This first Stage follows a model similar to the one presented in Fig. 1.4 (which applies to Stages 2 through 7), except that each line of the Puzzle Sonnet generates one letter in the deciphered message. In this Stage, the heuristic challenge was to reorder the Puzzle Sonnet's lines; in Stages 2 through 4, the challenge will be to reorder the sonnets themselves.

3

The *Hekatompathia*'s Foundation: Sonnets 1–17

The *Hekatompathia*'s first 17 sonnets define the work's fundamental concern, which is to discover the nature of love. Love is depicted as a two-pronged cosmological force that operates in two independent realms, one earthly and the other heavenly: a physical world associated with the body and a nonmaterial world associated with the mind or soul. These two realms correspond to two epistemic modes, one sensory or aesthetic, and the other noetic. Love is the center point of a cosmological/epistemological model that is applied throughout the sequence.

The nature of love is explored both scientifically as a physical phenomenon and as the emotional plight that afflicts the speaker. Love is represented poetically as the two forces that imprison the speaker, as for example, in the Puzzle Sonnet's *double thrall* (82.17). The speaker's capture by love is initiated by aesthesis, the sight of the beloved, and then love embeds itself in his heart through noesis. This division between aesthetic and noetic apprehension is a grammar and fundamental structuring mechanism. This is evident in the first 17 sonnets, which divide as follows: the first 6 define the work's subject matter following the precepts of rhetorical invention; the next 4 treat love's first power, the aesthetic or visual episteme; the next 7 treat love's second power, the noetic episteme. This grammar is an essential tool used by the puzzle-solver to reorder the work's sonnets, which are scrambled subsequent to the first 17 sonnets.

The Christian God is difficult to spot in the *Hekatompathia*, and instead, love is the speaker's god. Love resembles the cosmic flux described by pre-Socratic philosophers (e.g., Heraclitus) and Eryximachus in Plato's *Symposium*. This flux is a pathway that connects the physical and noumenal realms, an essential point made by Diotima in her speech in the *Symposium*, as related by Socrates. This fits perfectly with the sonnet genre, especially its core conceit that the beloved is an intermediary to the noumenal world. That is, the beloved is a means of apprehending the divine—a kind of theophany at the center of Petrarchan sonnet sequences. The *Hekatompathia* is a rigorously constructed artifice built upon several bases: a pre-Socratic cosmology, a Petrarchan beloved, medieval textual procedures, and all these tied together by a cryptographic system.

Before tackling the Puzzle's next Stage, we must carefully examine the sequence's foundation, its first 17 sonnets. Further, we must consider the *Hekatompathia*'s rhetorical and poetic practices, for these are often entangled with the Puzzle's cryptographic challenges. The sequence's rhetoric and poetics are deeply indebted to medieval textual practices, which is evident from even a visual examination of the text. The sonnets appear in an Old English font, which is not typical in the 1580s, and this casts the text in an antiquarian light.[1] The work's extensive citations in its headnotes and sidenotes are unusual for an early modern poetic collection but remind us of the commentary placed in the margins of medieval manuscripts.[2] The inclusion of Neo-Latin poems is also characteristic of an earlier time. These features suggest that medieval rhetorical and hermeneutic practices should be considered in both reading the work and solving the Puzzle.

The *Hekatompathia* employs a range of medieval textual practices that include *translatio*, the rhetorical procedures of *circumstantiae*, division, and arrangement, as well as a rhetorical hermeneutics that guides the reader by its alternating adherence to, and breaching of, decorum. This study's close reading of the *Hekatompathia* requires knowledge of these medieval practices; in contrast, most early modern poetry is not so deeply entrenched in medieval rhetorical practices. We will briefly review these practices for they dictate the hermeneutic procedures applied throughout this study's reading of the *Hekatompathia*.

Translation (*translatio*)

As discussed in the introductory chapter, the *Hekatompathia* draws from over 200 sources: sometimes the poet directly translates lines from a French, Italian, or Latin poem, but more often the poem's thematic material is recontextualized for another purpose. Medieval and Renaissance vernacular writers typically borrowed material from earlier texts, written either in another vernacular language or Latin, in a practice known as *translatio*. Renaissance poets appropriated material from earlier poets and reused it in ways that would either newly project its meaning, controvert its original meaning, or, in part, both. In many instances, poets were concerned with the transmission of culture and learning (*translatio studii*) and dynastic succession (*translatio imperii*), desiring to establish their own national poetic heritage. The appropriation of foreign resources has often proven essential to the process of beginning a new literary culture. The most remarkable example is the Roman adoption of Greek literary traditions; an early modern example can be found in the borrowing by French poets from Italian and Latin poets to create their own poetic tradition under the patronage of Francis I (reigned 1515–1547). Bacon, in writing the first English sonnet sequence, has likewise engaged in literary appropriation, building upon earlier literary dynasties (Greek, Latin, Italian, and French). Literary ambitions in England ran high at this time; for example, Edmund Spenser's nearly contemporaneous *Shepheardes Calender* was regarded as a proclamation of high literary ambitions.[3] Two of the *Hekatompathia*'s prefaces, undersigned "C. Downhalus," call for a transfer of poetic skill (*translatio studii*) to England: the first bids Helicon's muses to depart for *Britan soyle* (5); the second recounts the transfer of learning from Greece to Rome to France (Ronsard's poetry), and then foresees a transfer to England, initiated by the *Hekatompathia*.

The term *translatio*, literally "carrying across," has a broad range of meanings: it includes faithful translations (*fides interpres*), texts (or translations of texts) with interwoven commentary, commentaries that include only a small portion of the text, and the refashioning of texts into an original work in which the relationship with the earlier text is tenuous or even contradictory. Medieval commentaries often provide extensive and systematic expositions of the text under study. A key goal of commentators was to organize or divide a text: they would often add guidance in various forms, including headings, marginal notes, running titles, and indices. The *Hekatompathia* incorporates all of the foregoing textual devices, and these practices—hardly the norm for sonnet sequences—merit our attention. Few sonnet sequences include headnotes that comment upon each sonnet, sidenotes, quotations from a sonnet's intertextual source, and semiotic designs, as does the *Hekatompathia*.[4] In the course of this study, we will find that these paratextual and bibliographic features provide essential assistance in the interpretation of the sequence. A consideration of the methods and purposes of medieval *translatio* will orient us in our exegesis of the *Hekatompathia*'s text and embedded commentary, as well as help us to understand Bacon's unusual Puzzle. For a further discussion of the practice of *translatio*, see "Translation and compilation," Excursus 4.

The circumstances (*circumstantiae*)

"Circumstances" denotes a rhetorical scheme used in the exposition of texts (e.g., an *accessus ad auctores*) that begins by asking a set of seven questions: *quis, quid, cur, quomodo, ubi, quando,* and *unde* or *quibus facultatibus* (who, what, why, in what way, where, when, and whence or by what means).[5] The purposes of these questions, which originate with Hermagoras of Temnos (second century BCE), was to delineate a hypothesis, but over time, they became a methodology to determine the status or scope of a work, including the author's intention, the utility of the work, and the work's philosophical underpinnings. According to Rita Copeland, in Cicero's *De inventione*, he "reworks the circumstances into an elaborate system of topics," that is, they become "a procedural function, ... an apparatus for topical invention under proof."[6] Cicero was of paramount importance to Petrarch: he even imagined meeting Cicero, writing to a friend that "Cicero and I spent ten tranquil, leisurely days together, and I think he enjoyed his stay and liked my company." Arthur Kinney believes, "For Petrarch, Cicero held the key to all aspects of civilization."[7] Petrarch's recognition of the value of Ciceronian rhetoric was an important factor in the Renaissance's growing adoption of Ciceronian rhetorical practices and influenced later exegetical theories, including those of Agricola, Erasmus, Melanchthon, and Philip Sidney.[8] Copeland argues that the *circumstantiae* have important consequences for hermeneutics:

> First, as Gadamer suggests, interpretation is an act delimited by particular circumstances, by the historically particular situation of the interpreter and his community. ... This first principle leads to a second: the hermeneutical performance assumes a kind of inventional or heuristic force, and becomes an "independent productive act." These two principles of hermeneutics correspond with the principles of the rhetorical theory of the *circumstantiae*: first, that the circumstances define rhetoric by delimiting the hypothesis; and second, that they define rhetoric by constituting its basic procedure, topical invention.[9]

In the *Hekatompathia*, the seven questions, several of which appear in Sonnets 5 and 6, delimit the scope of the work (as discussed below); topical invention, as this study will show, is a key procedure required to solve the Puzzle. The *circumstantiae*, concomitant with the work's *causa* (case, purpose, or reason) and *intentio auctoris* (author's intent), reveal the work's significance. Copeland writes:

> The discovery of significance in authorial *intentio* invites revaluation of the work's structure according to the meaning that the interpreter has posited. In effect this represents a progression through rhetorical categories: from *inventio*, or the determination of the text's issues and their significance, to *dispositio*, the determination of how meaning provides the work with its structural coherence.[10]

This describes one of the fundamental procedures used in solving the Puzzle: rhetorical categories, including *intentio auctoris* and *inventio* (topical invention), allow for the discovery of the work's structure and, ultimately, facilitate the reordering of the sequence. In rhetorical practice, the author's intention may allow an exegete to discover a work's structure (*dispositio*) and significance, as, for example, in a twelfth-century *accessus* to Ovid's *Heroides*, in which the author's stated intentions allow the unification of an otherwise heterogeneous anthology.[11] Melanchthon, a strong influence on Sidney, believed that the reader must begin by determining a work's *status* or *causa*:

> No part of the art [of rhetoric] is more necessary than the precepts dealing with the status of the case, in respect of which, this is first and foremost: in relation to every problem or controversial question we consider what the status is, that is, what is the chief subject of inquiry, the proposition that contains the gist of the matter toward which all arguments are aimed, in other words, the main conclusion. No matter of debate can be comprehended, nothing can be explained, stated or grasped in an orderly fashion, except some position be formulated which includes the sum total of the case [*summam causae*].[12]

This hermeneutic process will be applied in solving the second and subsequent Stages of the Puzzle. We will find that in the *Hekatompathia*, the "gist of the matter toward which all arguments are aimed" is the nature of love. This is the work's *status* or *causa* and understanding it is essential to the process of discovering the work's structural coherence. The *Hekatompathia* is built upon a logically ordered series of topics that the speaker traverses in his exploration of the nature of love. This mode of exegesis is not unique to solving the Puzzle, but rather a common practice: the grounding of a text in its *circumstantiae* or *status* "is the point at which [the exegete] assumes a productive role in the formation of the text," according to Copeland.[13] Although the Puzzle is unusual in that the exegete reorders scrambled sonnets, a similar productive role is assumed by medieval commentators, by the authors of compilations, and indeed, by readers in general who wish to understand any poetic work beyond its literal meaning.

Division, arrangement, and decorum

Solving the Puzzle results in a massive reordering of the sequence to reveal a highly structured work. This new work has clear divisions, or groups of sonnets, and a precise arrangement of sonnets within each group, a reconstruction that follows medieval practices. In medieval texts, the commentator's perceived divisions of a text were often marked in the margins: red ink is used to indicate sources, headings (rubrics), and subheadings, including *prima* (*secunda*, *tercia*, etc.) *causa*, *obiectio*, and *responsio*. Sometimes a text was prefaced by a *materia operis*, a list of the text's topics.[14] This systematic organization of a text, its *ordinatio* or arrangement, was considered essential to the text's proper exegesis. According to M. B. Parkes, the practice of *compilatio* promoted the development of a new class of apparatus: the *tabula* or alphabetic index. "Because the *compilatio* is essentially a rearrangement, the new *ordinatio* employed by the compiler must be clearly defined and the new division of the material made obvious to the reader." These practices led to a new vernacular literature based on the principles of *compilatio*: the process of *ordinatio* "may be detected in the general schemes of the *Decamerone*, the *Confessio amantis*, *Les Cent Balades* and the incomplete *Canterbury Tales*."[15]

The *Hekatompathia*, given its frequent glossing of its many poetic sources, must be considered within this tradition of *compilatio*. Indeed, its use of different typefaces highlights its appropriations: the headnotes are set in a normal font for this period, the quoted text of the sources appears in italics, and the poetic text appears in old English typeface. Bacon thus casts his poetry in an antiquarian light, which supports consideration of its use of medieval practices such as *compilatio*. Spenser, of course, also engages in antiquarianism in both the *Shepheardes Calender* and the *Faerie Queene*, and both works, it has been argued, employ a medieval structure. Andrew King argues that the *Faerie Queene*, "as it is presented in the Letter to Ralegh, [is] a fundamentally schematic work whose structure may be explained as 'one Book per knight.' [It] presents a structure of discrete parts within a whole, and that its unity of structure can be comprehended not in terms of a beginning, middle, and end but rather in terms of an overall pattern."[16] One might expect that the *Hekatompathia*, given its practice of medieval *compilatio*, would also, in line with medieval practices, exhibit a clear structure appropriate to the work as a whole—that is, aligned with its overall meaning or *causa*.

The relationship of the overall theme or unity of a work to its divisions (i.e., the whole to its parts) is a chief concern of the rhetorical tradition. The whole, which depends upon the intent or *voluntas* (will) of the writer, provides a context for reading the parts. Conversely, the division into parts leads to a better understanding of the whole. The importance of aligning the whole and the parts of a literary work or oration is a practice that dates from antiquity. In the *Phaedrus*, Socrates, having described love as a kind of madness, asserts that there are a pair of procedures to apply to discourses on love:

> The first is that in which we bring a dispersed plurality under a single form, seeing it all together—the purpose being to define so-and-so, and thus to make plain whatever may be chosen as the topic for exposition. [The second procedure is] the reverse of the other, whereby we are enabled to divide into forms, following the objective articulation. ... Believe me, Phaedrus, I am myself a lover of these divisions and collections, that I may gain the power to speak and to think, and whenever I deem another man able to discern an objective unity and plurality, I follow 'in his footsteps where he leadeth as a god.'[17] [265b–266c]

By considering the *causa* and *circumstantiae*, one discovers the unity that holds a work together; the next step in interpreting a work is to understand its divisions. Augustine's *De Doctrina* advocates this view, according to Kathy Eden:

> Augustine, then, outspokenly advocates a hermeneutics in which the meaning of the whole simultaneously depends on and informs the meaning of the parts. ... This circularity looks not only back to the rhetorical arguments and counterarguments for *scriptum* versus *voluntas* but ahead to the circle of understanding at the center of modern hermeneutics.[18]

The process of reordering the *Hekatompathia*'s sonnets, which takes place in the second and subsequent Stages of the Puzzle, requires the discovery of the work's divisions, the arrangement of these divisions within the work, and the ordering of individual sonnets within each division. Bacon provides several devices that allow for the correct (his intended) rearrangement of sonnets; these include an ordered index and links between adjacent sonnets, either verbal or conceptual. Yet in addition to these devices, the requirement that the work exhibit organic coherence drives the puzzle-solver in his or her quest to correctly order the work. The discovery of the work's *causa*, the work's fundamental argument, is indispensable to finding the work's divisions and reordering its sonnets—the whole and its parts must be congruent, and the parts should logically advance the work's argument.

Such congruence is concomitant with "decorum," the last of the Seven Ideas of style of Hermogenes. Annabel Patterson, citing Puttenham and his "philosophical concept" of decorum, argues that decorum can refer to either a matter of style, organic unity, or the imitation of patterns found in the natural world.[19] Puttenham says of decorum:

> This lovely conformity, or proportion, or convenience between the sense and the sensible hath nature herself first most carefully observed in all her own works, then also by kind grafted it in the appetites of every creature... and of man chiefly before any other creature, as well in his speeches as in every other part of his behavior.[20]

Kathy Eden calls decorum "the single most important principle of composition; [it] is the productive counterpart to the receptive or interpretive principle of historical context."[21] The hermeneutic implications of decorum are far reaching—the whole is given priority over the part, as Quintilian advises:

> And it is not enough merely to arrange the various parts: each several part has its own internal economy [the rhetorical concept of *oikonomia*], according to which one thought will come first, another second, another third, while we must struggle not merely to place these thoughts in their proper order, but to link them together and give them such cohesion that there will be no trace of any suture: they must form a body, not a congerie of limbs (*corpus sit, non membra*).[22]

The puzzle-solver's reordering of the *Hekatompathia*'s sonnets is driven by a process of ordering that never loses sight of the work's *causa* and *circumstantiae*. According to Eden, the exegete must "consider both the *whole* text and the *whole* set of circumstances." She quotes Cicero:

> For it is easy to estimate what it is likely that the writer intended from the complete context (*ex omni scriptura*) and from the character of the writer *(ex persona scriptoris)*, and from the qualities which are associated with certain characters.[23]

Of central concern to this study, decorum mandates adherence to a progressive, ordered discourse on a subject defined by its historical context and supplemented by whatever authorial guidance may be provided, either in the text or paratext. In the *To the frendly Reader* preface, Bacon references decorum and describes how his poetry may be affected either by *the nature of the passion* he felt, *or by rule of art*. Patterson quotes the *Hekatompathia*'s *To the frendly Reader* preface at length and reaches this conclusion:

> The whole passage shows how widely, in the late sixteenth century, decorum of style has been recognized as more than just a vague aim, and more than just a way of relating speech to character in the drama. It is seen instead as a complex art affecting all the poetic genres and requiring detailed study... while at the same time the large philosophical center of the concept remains intact.[24]

E. K., in his letter to Harvey that prefaces the *Shepheardes Calender*, says that unlike the loose work of most English writers, this author's work "is well grounded, finely framed, and strongly trussed up together."[25] This desire for order is fundamental to the poetic practice of certain poets and, as we will discover, it is the force that propels the exegete to solve the *Hekatompathia*'s Puzzle. (For a further discussion of hermeneutic practices, see "Hermeneutics: Traditional allegory vs. teleologically guided accommodation," Excursus 5.)

The structure of the sequence

It is essential to determine the *Hekatompathia*'s structure because it guides the puzzle-solver in reordering the sequence. We might ask: how do we know that the sequence requires reordering? Examining the first 17 sonnets will reveal that they adhere to a well-defined structure, and further, that the correctness of their order is guaranteed by clear linkages between one sonnet and the next. Subsequent to Sonnet 17, the sequence's sonnets are scrambled: those sonnets exhibit inexplicable disorder and no linkages between one sonnet and the next can be found.

The solution to the Puzzle's first Stage provides an essential hint that helps us to discover the structure of the first 17 sonnets. The first Stage revealed that the Lioness Design, which is situated below the Puzzle Sonnet and nine other sonnets, is an emblem of love. Furthermore, we might suspect that the second sentence of our deciphered message, NUO LEA PESUS, is intended to aid us in solving the Puzzle's next Stage. In fact, we will discover that the Lioness Design acts as a rubric or header, marking the first sonnet in a group we will regularly refer to as a "Series." This division into Series structures the work: each Series is focused on a topic and represents a progressive step in the work's overall exposition of the nature of love and the speaker's personal struggle with love.

This precisely defined structure follows the medieval and Renaissance rhetorical practices discussed above: the division into topics and adherence to an ordered plan of exposition. The first 17 sonnets consist of an introductory first sonnet followed by two Series, each of which treats one of love's two powers—one, an aesthetic or visual apprehension, and the other, a noetic apprehension. As discussed below, this follows a medieval tradition with ancient roots. The scrambled sonnets that appear after Sonnet 17 follow a practice antithetical to the usual medieval taste for order, the "poetics of ruin," which is discussed in the next chapter. After the *Hekatompathia* is restored to its proper order, its precisely defined divisions—its Series—are evident throughout the work. Moreover, it adheres to a single purpose or *causa*.

The division of the sequence's opening sonnets into two Series is apparent from both the thematic content of the sonnets and a bibliographic signal, the Lioness Design. As discussed in the previous chapter, the Puzzle Sonnet's final line, the Lioness Design beneath it, and the deciphered message establish the Lioness Design as an emblem of tyrannical love. Given the considerable effort required to solve the Puzzle's first Stage, we might expect that the Lioness Design and the deciphered message, NUO LEA PESUS, will lead to further discoveries. The message is suggestive: the speaker is said to waver or bend (NUO) under the weight (PESUS) of personified Love—the lioness (LEA). Does this suggest that the speaker bends or changes his attitude in those sonnets with Lioness Designs? NUO, in addition to meaning "waver/bend," can refer to various forms of nonverbal signaling such as nodding and gesturing. Although I have translated NUO LEA PESUS as "weighed upon by the lioness [love], I waver," it might also be translated as "weighed upon, I signal by means of the lioness,"[26] suggesting that the Lioness Design is a signaling mechanism.[27] Both translations suggest that the "Lioness Sonnets" (sonnets accompanied by a Lioness Design) may demarcate points of change in the text, i.e., a new topic: the speaker's mind "wavers" under love's pressure; alternatively, the poet intentionally "signals" using the Lioness Design. For example, the Puzzle Sonnet (82), a Lioness Sonnet, is the first sonnet (except for the textually identical Pillar Sonnet) of the MLIP Subsequence—a point of change in the speaker's attitude. We will discover that the Lioness Design is a master rubric, demarcating the start of a Series of sonnets. Each Series, which may consist of as few as 7 or as many as 19 sonnets, begins with a Lioness Sonnet and ends immediately prior to the next Lioness Sonnet.

Bacon provides links between consecutive sonnets that gives some assurance that they are ordered correctly. This is accomplished by means of a common word, idea, or theme. He seems to be hinting at this possibility when he discusses links between lines within a sonnet. His headnote to Sonnet 41 discusses this concept of *continuation*:

> This Passion is framed vpon a somewhat tedious or too much affected continuation of that figure in Rhethorique, whiche of the Grekes is called παλιλογία [deliberate repetition] or ἀναδίπλωσις [doubling up], of the Latines *Reduplicatio*: whereof *Susenbrotus* (if I well remember me) alleadgeth this example out of *Virgill*,
> *Sequitur pulcherrimus Austur,*   Aeneid. 10.
> *Austur equo fidens.*

In most of Sonnet 41's lines, a word near the end of one line is repeated near the beginning of the next line. The first stanza, reproduced below, serves as an example (the repeated words are bolded for convenience):

> O Happy men that find no **lacke** in **Loue**
> I **Loue**, and **lacke** what most I do **desire**;
> My deepe **desire** no **reason** can remoue;
> All **reason** shunnes my brest, that's set on **fire**;
>   And so the **fire** mainetaines both **force** and flame,
>   That **force** auayleth not against the same;   (41.1–6)

Curiously, in the headnote, Bacon refers to this rhetorical figure of continuation as *somewhat tedious or too much affected*. Why has he bothered to write a poem in this style if he believes it to be tedious? Moreover, he gives us another poem in this style, Sonnet 64, whose headnote specifically references Sonnet 41 by number. Why *two* such tedious sonnets—has the poet breached decorum? I believe his purpose is to alert the puzzle-solver to the importance of the principle of *continuation* (41.HN). Although this principle is applied from one *sonnet line* to the next in Sonnets 41 and 64, it can also be applied from one *sonnet* to the next. Indeed, Bacon does just that to create links between adjacent sonnets, which will regularly be referred to as "Sequential Ties." In the next two sections of this chapter, these Sequential Ties will provide one set of evidence that confirms that the first 17 sonnets are correctly ordered. In solving subsequent Stages of the Puzzle, Sequential Ties will provide one means of restoring the order of scrambled sonnets.

The first 17 sonnets consist of an introductory sonnet followed by two Series. Sonnet 1 is not part of any Series and serves as an introduction or exordium to the work. The sonnet's headnote, which calls the sonnet an *occasion to open his estate in loue*, confirms its role as an exordium.[28] It is linked to Sonnet 2 by a Sequential Tie: the pitiful state of the speaker.[29] The two Series that follow set forth the *Hekatompathia*'s fundamental cosmological argument: love has two powers, one associated with the sensual realm, and the other with the noetic realm.

First Series: the sequence's rhetorical foundation

The first Series begins with Sonnet 2 (a Lioness Sonnet) and ends with Sonnet 10. Sonnets 2–6 deliver the rhetorical invention of the sequence. Sonnet 2's headnote, reproduced below, uses the phrase *conveyance of his invention* in a suggestive manner. Read in context, *invention* refers to the poet's treatment of the sonnet's subject matter, but the poet appears to be hinting that this sonnet *conveys* the *invention* of the sequence itself. In any case, the headnote sets forth the fundamental conceit that frames the work: the separation of the speaker's heart from his body, an affliction that is not resolved until the sequence's final Series in the restored order.

> In this passion the Author describeth in how pitious a case the hart of
> a louer is, being (as he fayneth heere) seperated from his owne body, &
> remoued into a darksome and solitarie wildernes of woes. The conuey-
> ance of his inuention is plaine & pleasant enough of it selfe, and there-
> fore needeth the lesse annotation before it. (2.HN)

This theme of a divided self is found throughout the work: the speaker's
hart is imprisoned, either by the beloved or personified Love. The speaker
is situated at the edge of death (*on side of Stigian lake*; 8) and appears to
suffer from melancholy (*blacke despaire*; 9). This topos of self-alienation
can also be found in love treatises such as Ebreo's *Dialogues of Love,* in
which the interlocuter Philo asserts:

> Love confuses the mind, where judgment lies; it erases the memory of
> all other things in order to fill the mind only with itself, and utterly
> alienates a man from himself, and makes him a slave of the beloved. ...
> The desire might be so keen and the contemplation so intimate that the
> soul would cast off all fetters and be withdrawn from the body, and by
> reason of the closeness of their union the sprits would be dissolved, so
> that the soul, cleaving in love to the object of its desire and contempla-
> tion, could quickly leave the body without any life at all.[30]

One of the work's most prolific themes is the speaker's feeling that he lives
at the cusp between life and death: waiting for *Charons boate* (2.7); *That
he as yet shall nether live nor die* (2.12). The soul is cut off from the sun
(the heavenly source of life and enlightenment) and is instead a captive of
the beloved: *No sunne comes there, nor any heau'nly sainte / But onely
shee, which in him selfe remaines* (2.16–17). This feeling of isolation and
exile-from-oneself can be found in Ficino's *Commentary on Plato's Symposium*: "The soul of a lover does not exist within the man himself. ... In
this case the lover is completely dead, for he neither lives in himself... nor
does he live in his loved one."[31] In the *Dialogues of Love,* Philo elaborates
on this condition:

> [Love] makes him... full of passions, surrounded by sufferings, tor-
> mented by depression, martyred by desire, nourished by hope, stimu-
> lated by despair, oppressed by thought, anxious from cruelty, afflicted
> by suspicion, pierced through by jealousy, constantly distressed, over-
> tired by restlessness, always in pain and full of sighs, never unbowed
> by grief or wrongs. ... What else can I tell you, save that the lover's part
> is a continual death in life and life in death? ... His mind neither hopes
> nor desires or designs to escape it. Do you think... that a man in such

a labyrinth can recognize the laws of reason or rules of prudence? ...
How then can someone who is not free be governed by reason?[32]

Each of the abovementioned conditions or images—enslavement to the
beloved, suffering, restlessness, insomnia, hopes and fears, life-in-death,
being lost in a labyrinth, loss of reason's law, and incarceration—appear
multiple times in the *Hekatompathia*. This sonnet, at the work's outset,
defines the work's subject as the passion (*passio*) found in humanist literature (the "*pathia*" of the work's title is the Greek root of *passio*). In
Castiglione's *The Book of the Courtier*, such passion is attributed to "sense"
and "youthfull" appetite.

> There is never other thinge felt, but afflictions, tourmentes, greeffes,
> pining, travaile, so that to be wann, vexed with continuall teares, and
> sighes, to lyve with a discontented minde, to be alwaies dumbe, or to
> lament, to covet death, in conclusion to be most unlucky are the pro-
> preties which (they saye) beelonge to lovers. The cause therfore of this
> wretchednesse in mens mindes, is principally sense, whiche in youth-
> full age bereth moste swey.[33]

Sonnet 3 continues to set forth the work's central conceit, introduced in
Sonnet 2, the separation of the speaker from his heart: the speaker's *heart,
beeing nowe through the commandement and force of loue separated from
his bodie miraculouslie* (3.HN). The similar language found in the headnotes of Sonnets 2 and 3 creates a Sequential Tie. Another Sequential Tie
is found in the description of the speaker's heart in Sonnet 2, which links
to the first line of Sonnet 3. The speaker's heart is described as having been
removed into a darksome and solitarie wilderness of woes (2.HN), and
further, that *no flowr but Hiacynth* grows in this *place* (2.15), nor does any
sunne (2.16) shine. This describes the location (*place*) of the speaker's heart
but does not specify it. The first line of Sonnet 3 seeks to discover this
place: Speake gentle heart, where is thy dwelling place? (3.1), and the next
line provides an answer. This is an example of a Sequential Tie in which a
significant word (*place*) is repeated between adjacent sonnets.

Sonnet 3, like its predecessor, practices rhetorical invention, an exposition of the condition of the speaker's heart that will be amplified
throughout the sequence. Its initial question, *where is thy* [the heart's]
dwelling place, is followed by seven other questions, consistent with the
rhetorical practice of setting forth the *circumstantiae*. The sonnet tells us
that the speaker believes that his heart lies with the beloved, and furthermore, that he hopes his heart will return to him, along with the heart of
the beloved. For this to happen, the speaker must convince the beloved to

accept him: *Ile move her heart to purchase thy* [addressing his own heart] *reliefe* (10). This petitioning of the beloved in order to win her heart and regain his own appears throughout the *Hekatompathia* and is a staple of sonnet sequences. Consistent with rhetorical practice, this sonnet announces one of the sequence's principal concerns, acceptance by the beloved, by posing a series of questions.

Sonnet 4's headnote uses the technical language of rhetoric: *the chiefe grounde and matter of this Sonnet standeth vppon the rehearsall of such thinges as by reporte of the Poets, are dedicated vnto Venus.* (*Standeth* suggests *status*, a participle of its Latin root.) This sonnet is an encomium to Venus, rehearsing her traditional emblems (myrtle, the evening star, Cyprus Isle, etc.) and pledging an enduring allegiance to her. It begins by asking Venus's assistance in winning the beloved:

> **Sweete** Venus **as if nowe thou stand my friende,**
> **As once thou didst unto Kinge *** Priams **sonne,**   *Paris.
> **My ioyfull muse shall neuer make an end**
> **Of praising thee, and all that thou hast done:**   (4.1–4)

This conceit of asking for personified Love's help, either Venus's or Cupid's, recurs frequently in the sequence, often employing the same phrase: *stand my friende.* Sonnets 3 and 4 set out the two strategies that the speaker employs throughout the sequence to win the beloved and thus regain his heart: the petitioning of the beloved and the requesting of personified Love's assistance, respectively. Thus, these sonnets form a pair: they represent the two potential remedies for the work's central problem, the alienation of the speaker's heart from his body. Sonnet 4 refers to the aid that Venus gives to Paris in the *Iliad* (2) and to Aeneas (*Anchises sonne*; 9) in the *Aeneid*; the speaker hopes that, similarly, personified Love will aid him. This hope for Venus's aid parallels the *hope* expressed in the final line of Sonnet 3 that the beloved can be moved. Sonnet 4's final line, in which the speaker pledges to praise *No Gods but Love*, expresses the speaker's unalloyed commitment to love, which is not only the *chiefe grounde and matter of this Sonnet* (HN), but the *status* or *causa* of the entire sequence—an investigation into the nature of love.

In their commitment to love, the speaker and the poet are indistinguishable (*wherein the Author talketh with his owne heart*; 3.HN). Sonnet 4 is in a critical position: it follows the description of the sequence's fundamental conceit in Sonnets 2 and 3, and sits immediately prior to Sonnet 5, which enumerates the work's *circumstantiae*. Sonnet 4's opening invocation to Venus ought to be considered carefully, as the opening invocation of any work deserves the reader's special attention. In the second stanza, the speaker eschews Apollo's laurel for Venus's myrtle:

> **My temples hedged in with** Myrtle **bowes**
> **Shall set aside** Apolloes Lawrell **tree,**   * Materna redimitus
> **As did*** Anchises **sonne, when both his browes**   tempora Mirto. Virg.
> **With** Myrtle **hee beset, to honour thee:**   (4.7-10)

The sidenote at line 9 (*Materna redimitus tempora Mirto*), an imprecise quotation that could be from either Virgil's *Aeneid* or *Georgics*, draws further attention to this rejection of Apollo's laurel for Venus's myrtle.[34] Bacon has dispensed with the usual poetic conceit so central to Petrarch's sequence: the Laura-laurel emblem of poetic fame. Why has the poet forsaken Apollo for Venus? The sequence often treats love as a natural phenomenon, a harmony or coincidence of opposites, an idea found among pre-Socratic philosophers, in the *Symposium* in the speech by the physician Eryximachus, and in Cusanus.[35] Thus, the *Hekatompathia* investigates love from a scientific perspective (i.e., as a natural phenomenon), a rational approach that might be associated with Apollo. Yet the sequence's frequent praise of love and beauty is not driven by reason, but by emotion. Curiously, the sidenote that ambiguously quotes Virgil fails to mention the work cited, unlike almost all other sidenotes. This leaves us uncertain as to whether Bacon is quoting the *Aeneid* (5.72) or the *Georgics* (1.28), which may be intentional, allowing the reader to consider both instances.[36] The *Georgics* is concerned with the sometimes rational forces of nature; in contrast, the *Aeneid* frequently depicts Aeneas as suffering under the irrational forces of the gods. In Sonnet 4's second stanza, the poet appears to be placing love (the irrational) above reason. In the *Canzoniere*, the speaker is concerned with poetic fame (the laurel of Apollo) and ultimately places himself in the hands of the Christian God; in contrast, the *Hekatompathia*'s speaker pledges his allegiance to Venus at the outset, and in the reordered sequence's end, it rests not with the Christian God but with numinous love. Although the *Hekatompathia* is heavily indebted to Petrarch, the sequence is radically counter-Petrarchan.

The two previous sonnets imagine the conflict between love and reason as the separation of the speaker from his heart. This pivotal sonnet then adumbrates the resolution of that conflict in the embrace of love at the restored sequence's end. The sonnet's (imprecise) reference to *Aeneid* 5.72 points to a critical juncture in the *Aeneid*, the moment at which Aeneas dons a myrtle wreath at the outset of his trip from Sicily to Italy. He thus embarks on the path that fulfills his destiny, the establishment of a new home for the Trojan race. Similarly, in this sonnet, the speaker begins his sequence with an encomium to Venus, a journey that ends with the complete acceptance of love, fulfilling his pledge to the goddess.

Sonnets 5 and 6 are translations of a famous *Canzoniere* sonnet (132) into English and Latin, respectively. The adjacent repetition of a poem in a poetic collection (even if that repetition is a translation to another language) is rare and alerts us to the poem's importance. This sonnet pair asks multiple questions concerning the nature of love. Sonnet 5 is reproduced below:

IF't bee not loue I feele, what is it then?
If loue it bee, what kind a thing is loue?
  If good, how chance he hurtes so many men?
  If badd, how happ's that none his hurtes disproue?
    If willingly I burne, how chance I waile?   5
    If gainst my will, what sorrow will auaile?
O liuesome death, O sweete and pleasant ill,
Against my minde how can thy might preuaile?
If I bend backe, and but refraine my will,
If I consent, I doe not well to waile;
{ And touching him, whome will hath made a slaue,   { Tuscano
{ The Prouerbe saith of olde, *Selfe doe, selfe haue.*   { hii duo
  Thus beeing tost with windes of sundry sorte   versus.
Through daung'rous Seas but in a slender Boat,
With errour stuft, and driu'n beside the porte,   15
Where voide of wisdomes fraight it lies afloate,
    I waue in doubt what helpe I shall require,
    In Sommer freeze, in winter burne like fire.

(with the marginal note: *Adduntur Tuscano hii duo versus.*)

Surely these multiple questions are the *circumstantiae*, and indeed, this was recognized by Bacon's contemporary, John Lilliat, a choral musician. His heavily annotated copy of the *Hekatompathia* (discussed in the next chapter) includes two lines in his hand, near Sonnet 5, a versification of the *circumstantiae*:

Who, what, and Where; by what help and by whose:
Why, how and when; doe many things disclose.[37]

Sonnet 5 begins the work's inquiry into the nature of love—an exploration carried out both by a quasi-philosophical investigation of love as a coincidence of opposites and by the affective journey of the speaker in his personal quest to come to grips with love's great power. This is the work's *causa* or *status*, and the foundation upon which the work is structured. An initial observation about the nature of love is that it has paradoxical properties: *O liuesome death, O sweete and pleasant ill* (5.7). The paradoxical nature of love—its mysterious ability to combine opposites—is found throughout the sequence. The coincidence of opposites, often represented poetically as oxymorons, is prolific in the *Canzoniere* as well as other sonnet sequences. A good example is the final line of this sonnet, *In Summer freeze, in winter burne like fire* (5.18), and its equivalent in the paired Neo-Latin poem, *Frigeo, dum media est aestas; dum bruma, calesco* (6.14), both of which translate line 132.14 of the *Canzoniere*.

Sonnet 5's headnote advises that it is *wholly translated out of Petrarch* except for *two verses*, drawing attention to Bacon's addition of these two verses. This addition is further emphasized by a bracket placed to the left of the two verses (11–12) and another bracket with a sidenote to the right of the verses, which reads *Adduntur Tuscano hii duo versus* (these two verses are added to those of the Tuscan). The *proverbe* (12), the final four words of line 12, are italicized—the use of italics in the sonnet text, uncommon in the *Hekatompathia*, is used to highlight critical text.[38] These words are further emphasized by their spondaic meter, which breaks metrical decorum. The proverb's bold statement is foreign to the rest of the sonnet, which depicts the speaker's confusion and helplessness. Moreover, it stands in opposition to the characterization found throughout the sonnet of the speaker's will or mind as being overmatched by love: *willingly I burne* (5); *gainst my will* (6); *against my minde* (8); *whome will hath made a slave* (11); *with errour stuft* (15); *voide of wisdomes fraight* (16); *I wave in doubt* (17). This opposition between the speaker's will and love is consonant with the opposition of love and reason, the central conflict of the *Hekatompathia*. The proverb *Selfe doe, selfe haue* projects the opposite of an oppressed will.[39] Indeed, it is foreign to Petrarchan discourse, as well as the unrestored *Hekatompathia*. Bacon has inexplicably dropped this radically dissonant proverb into one of Petrarch's most famous sonnets. And just in case the reader has (somehow) failed to notice these two decorum-breaking lines, he has emphasized his obtrusive, counter-Petrarchan addition using several means to draw the reader's attention: the headnote, brackets, sidenote, and metric deviation. The use of brackets is a medieval exegetical practice known as *distinctio*: brackets or other typographical markings distinguish or accentuate a word or portion of the text.[40] Here, at the outset of the sequence, the poet has markedly broken decorum and thereby suggests that his sequence will radically diverge from the Petrarchan tradition.

By the addition of this proverb, antithetical to Petrarchan discourse, Bacon foreshadows how the central conflict of his sequence will play out. In the published order, the *Hekatompathia* ends with reason prevailing and Cupid's death, but in the restored work's conclusion (revealed in Chapter 9), the speaker's will and love achieve an amiable coexistence. Further discussion must be postponed, but of concern to us at this moment is the poetic technique that authorizes this insertion of an anomalous proverb into an otherwise perfectly ordered translation of a famous poem by a master poet. Anomalies, faults, and incongruities are what Michael Riffaterre calls "ungrammaticality," and they are an invitation to engage in hermeneutic work:

> As always this ungrammaticality is at one and the same time the locus of obscurity and the index to the solution. It signals that the words cannot be taken at face value, that they are forced to conform to a structure other than that of their referents.[41]

> The great error of philological commentary, as it continues to be practiced by many scholars of the sixteenth-century [*sic*], has been to believe that erudite poetry sets out to hide its idea. *It veils it, but it always points to where it is hidden and how it can be revealed.* This is, moreover, a general law of all literary discourse, for literary discourse is a locus of semantic indirection.[42] [my italics]

The poet's anomalous proverb discloses his intent, but in a cursory reading of the sonnet, it is hidden. Even if the reader notices that the proverb is odd, he or she may well skip past it, attributing it to a lapse in poetic judgment. Yet Bacon forewarns the reader in his *To the frendly Reader* preface, that with respect to *the faultes herein escaped*, the reader may either *winke at them, as ouersightes of a blinde Lover*, or *excuse them, as idle toyes proceedinge from a youngling frenzie*, or *lastlie, to defend them, by saying, it is nothing praeter decorum... for a Poete to falter in his Poeme, when his matter requireth it*. Thus, a breach in decorum, rather than an errant lapse, likely points to something hidden. The above pair of Riffaterre quotations succinctly describe the orientation that is essential to any critical reading of the *Hekatompathia*. Breaches are pointers to hidden things, and such intentional ungrammaticality is found throughout the *Hekatompathia*. Sonnet 5's addition of two anti-Petrarchan lines to a Petrarchan sonnet is the best example of such a breach because the poet gives us so many pointers to it—he does everything but mark the lines with a yellow highlighter. Breaches, "semantic indirection," and strange glosses all provide the clues that allow us to navigate Bacon's labyrinthine Puzzle.

Sonnet 5 contains another breach, a long-winded and pedantic gloss in its headnote:

> And it may be noted, that the Author in his first halfe verse of this translation varieth from the sense, which Chawcer useth in translating the selfe same: which he doth upon no other warrant then his owne simple private opinion, which yet he will not greatly stand upon.

The first verse of Sonnet 5, Chaucer's translation of it, and the original, Petrarch's Italian, are reproduced below:

> If't bee not loue I feele, what is it then?   *Hekatompathia, 5.1*
> `If no love is, O god, what fele I so?   *Troilus and Criseyde, 1.400*
> S'amor non è, che dunque è quel ch' io sento?   *Canzoniere, 132.1*

Comparing the first half verse of his translation, as the headnote suggests, to that of Chaucer's, the only substantive difference appears to be Chaucer's insertion of "O god," which has no warrant in Petrarch's text. The headnote's lengthy statement about a minor difference between his translation and that of Chaucer's seems entirely irrelevant. Why does the poet bother with this? A difference with Petrarch might have some relevance, but a minor difference with another translator ought to be inconsequential. I would argue that Bacon digressed at such length because he wished to create a Sequential Tie to the prior sonnet, Sonnet 4. Assuming that "god" in Chaucer's line refers to a sole deity, or any deity other than Venus, then the speaker, by omitting Chaucer's "O god," adheres to his pledge made at the conclusion of the prior sonnet, that he would praise no god but Venus. Am I reading too much into this trivial distinction? The triviality, an indecorous digression, is an invitation to exegesis. It also hints at something far from trivial: Bacon's pointed omission of this call to God is an affirmation of his text's loyalty to a single god, Venus. We will discover that the Christian God is almost completely absent from the *Hekatompathia*, and this is no small matter.

We have now observed that the first 5 sonnets of this Series, Sonnets 2–6, define the sequence at its outset. Sonnet 2 describes the speaker's self-alienation as separation from his own heart, which is the sequence's foundational conceit and the challenge that the speaker must overcome. Sonnets 3 and 4 each express hope that the speaker's heart might be restored by gaining the beloved's acceptance in one of two possible ways: either by directly petitioning the beloved (Sonnet 3), or by requesting that personified Love (Venus) influence the beloved (Sonnet 4). These three sonnets describe the action or quasi-plot of the sequence—its central problem and two paths by which the speaker will attempt a solution. Sonnets 5 and 6 then introduce the philosophical or cosmological mystery that is explored throughout the sequence: the representation of love as paradox, a strange coincidence of opposites. Thus, these 5 sonnets establish the sequence's course with respect to both action and philosophical inquiry.

A shift then occurs in the final 4 sonnets of the Series, Sonnets 7–10, which describe the speaker's captivation through the visual perception of the beloved's physical beauty. The sight of the beloved, frequently analogized here as the sun's blinding light, is overpowering, possibly to the point of decay or death. Thus, the first Series divides into two "Subseries:" in the first Subseries (Sonnets 2–6), questions about the nature of love are posed; in the second Subseries, a preliminary answer is given. This second Subseries describes love as a blinding light that overpowers both men and women, mythical figures, and, indeed, the speaker. A link from the last sonnet of the first Subseries to the second Subseries is provided in Sonnet 6's headnote, which suggests that the reader *survey it here as a probable signe of his dayly sufferance in love*; the sonnets of the next Subseries describe how the speaker suffers by viewing the beloved. The headnote's use of *survey* provides a Sequential Tie to Sonnet 7, a classic blazon of the beloved's features that enumerates (*surveys*) *the person and beautifull ornamentes* (7.HN) of the beloved.

Sonnets 7 and 10 are encomiums to the beloved, beheld in all her beauty and virtue. These sonnets bookend the two middle sonnets of the Subseries, 8 and 9, which portray the (mythical or metaphoric) blindness that results from viewing the beloved. The concern of this Subseries is love experienced visually. Sonnet 10, the final sonnet of the first Series, begins *Myne eyes dye first*, and in the next Series, we discover that the speaker's heart dies second. The final line of this sonnet, which mentions *songes of love* (10.18), provides the perfect segue to the next Series, whose subject is music. Sonnets 7 through 10 clearly form an ordered unit, which is verified by a clever bibliographic mechanism: Sonnet 7's three sidenotes provide an ordered set of intratextual links to Sonnets 8 through 10. (This mechanism is described in "Sonnets 7–10: Sidenote ordering mechanism," Excursus 6.)

Second Series: Love's second power

The headnote of every sonnet of this second Series (11–17) recognizes music as a great power, clearly delineating it as a Series. Sonnet 17's headnote indicates that it is the last sonnet of the Series: *the Authour not yet hauing forgotten the song of his mistrss* (17.HN). Sonnet 18, a Lioness Sonnet, marks the beginning of a new Series. The order of the sonnets of this Series is confirmed by the Sequential Ties that bind each sonnet to the next, as detailed in Addendum 7.

As discussed above, the second Subseries of the first Series, Sonnets 7–10, describes the speaker's subjugation by sight; this second Series describes the speaker's subjugation (and sometimes delight) by music, a nonmaterial force. Music is portrayed as wonderous, heavenly, and as having a mysterious effect on the mind. Every sonnet in the Series is an amplification of, or variation on, this theme of the other worldly nature of music, especially the beloved's singing. The enumeration below describes how each sonnet touches upon music's heavenly nature.

> **Sonnet 11** calls the beloved the *Phenix of our age* (1), and asserts that her voice is *more than earthly voice* (2) and wields a *wondrous* force (3).
>
> **Sonnet 12** describes the beloved's voice as *an Angells voice* (5).
>
> **Sonnet 13** gives examples of the miraculous effect of music and again describes his beloved's voice as heavenly: *For since I heard a secret heav'nly song* (13).
>
> **Sonnet 14** asserts *that musick hauing birth from heau'ns above* (8) can alter the mind and is imagined to have entered into the speaker's ears and possessed his will (16–18).
>
> **Sonnet 15** claims that the beloved's melody outdoes music itself (HN; 1–2) and places her music above that of the gods.
>
> **Sonnet 16** asserts that the beloved's *voice excels those harmonies that fill / Elisian fieldes* (15–16).
>
> **Sonnet 17** calls the beloved a *Sacred Nymph* (5), a *Phoenix* (10), and Apollo's *chiefe delight* (12).

Throughout this Series, the beloved's song dispenses a powerful force— love's second power. Love first captures the speaker through sight (*Myne eyes dye first*; 10.1) and then becomes lodged within the speaker's breast by means of its second power, which enforces the speaker's confinement —a conceit found throughout the sequence. In every sonnet of the Series except the last, the speaker reminds the reader that the beloved's song binds the will of the speaker, as the excerpts below demonstrate:

Of such a songe, as had increast my wound	(11.12)
Through musicks helpe loue hath increast his might	(12.16)
that musick in my minde / Enforceth cause of hurt	(13.11–12)
Transform'd to ayre Loue entred with my will /	
And nowe perforce doth keepe possession still	(14.17–18)
When she shall make replie which rules my heart	(15.16)
And who so mad, as woulde not with his will /	
Leese libertie and life to heare her sing	(16.13–14)

Throughout the *Hekatompathia*, love is portrayed as having two powers that act upon the speaker, a *passio corporis* and a *passio animae*. This model of love is based on a medieval scheme that defines love as the result of two successive passions. Don Monson explains these two passions:

> According to [Andreas Capellanus's] definition, love is the result of two successive *passiones*, an external *passio corporis* followed by an internal *passio animae*. That is the basis of Andreas's distinction between the remote and proximate efficient causes: *ex visione et... cogitatione.* A very similar psychological process is described by Andreas's contemporary, John of Salisbury, in [a passage from] the *Metalogicon.* ... This passage shares with Andreas's definition the view that love is derived from a complex "affect" (*passio*), including an external sense perception and a further psychic manipulation of that perception. Because he is discussing human psychology in general, John speaks of *sensus* rather than *visio*, but, thanks to a long tradition, there can be no doubt that vision is the particular type of sensation to be associated with his example, *amor.*[43]

The second Subseries of the *Hekatompathia*'s first Series presents love as a *passio corporis*: the beauty of the beloved, an image, is apprehended through the eye and thus enters into the speaker's body. This second Series presents love as a *passio animae*, which it represents as the effect of music. In the above notes on each sonnet of the second Series, love as sound is described as heavenly and mysterious, a nonphysical, mental phenomenon that overtakes the speaker's will. The second Subseries of the first Series is governed by sight—a sensual/material apprehension; the second Series is governed by hearing—a cognitive/nonmaterial apprehension. Although music travels through air, which is material, it is a metonym for spiritual transmission.[44] In Leone Ebreo's *Dialogues of Love*, the interlocuter Philo says:

> You know that the world is divided into the corporeal and the spiritual... and that the corporeal world is apprehended by sense and the spiritual world by the intellect. ... Sight alone is the one that knows all bodies; hearing aids the cognition of things.[45]

Let us examine Andreas's definition of love, to which Monson refers in the above quotation. Andreas's definition is found in his *De Amore* (*The Art of Courtly Love*, ca. 1185); it appears at the beginning of the work, under the heading *Quid sit amor* (what might love be):

> Amor est passio quaedam innata procedens ex visione et immoderata cogitatione formae alterius sexus...

> (Love is a certain inborn suffering [*passio*] derived from the sight [*visio*] of, and excessive meditation [*cogitatio*] upon, the beauty of the opposite sex...)[46]

"There is a progression indicated by the terms *visio, cogitatio, passio*," writes D. W. Robertson.[47] Love begins with vision (*visio*), which leads to excessive thought (*immoderata cogitatio*), and ends in *passio*, which might be translated as either passion or suffering. In Andreas's definition of love, for the passion of love to be truly present, the love must proceed from both vision and a subsequent meditation upon the beloved's image. This definition of love was extremely well known: it appears in medieval florilegia and was translated into Old French in the *Roman de la Rose*.[48] The popularity of *De Amore*'s theory of love is revealed by the work's "frequent translations, adaptations, and citations in later works," according to Douglas Kelly. It "provides a norm with which to compare other works and to arrive at an understanding of how courtly love was conceived, at least as an ideal, and what variations in interpretation and application are characteristic of it."[49]

In the second Subseries of the first Series, *passio* proceeds from sight (*ex visione*); in the second Series, it proceeds from hearing music, a cognitive process (*ex cogitatione*). The *Hekatompathia* presents these two processes as two powers of love, and as two epistemic modes: aesthesis and noesis. This study will regularly refer to these two modes or powers of love as "*ex visione* love," or "love's sensual power," and "*ex cogitatione* love," or "love's intellectual power." These two modes of love operate in tandem throughout most of the sequence: the speaker is first entrapped by love's visual power when he catches sight of the beloved, and subsequently, he cogitates upon the remembered image of the beloved, which enforces his imprisonment by love. Just as in Andreas's definition of love, love's modes operate sequentially and then in concert. However, Bacon's treatment of these modes of love differs from Andreas's in one important respect: his *ex cogitatione* is not a courtly love or a rational love that may effectively regulate sensual love.[50] In the *Hekatompathia*, a personified Reason and the speaker's "willfulness" instead play that role.

In the second Series, *ex cogitatione* love is presented independently from *ex visione* love. Elsewhere in the sequence, an individual sonnet may be devoted to one mode of love or another, but often, both modes appear. The motivation for devoting one group of sonnets (the second Subseries of the first Series) to *ex visione* love and another group (the second Series) to *ex cogitatione* love, is, I believe, to clearly define and distinguish these two modes of love at the work's outset. In these two groups, the poet describes each mode of love as belonging to a different cosmic sphere, *ex visione* love to the material world and *ex cogitatione* love to the nonmaterial world. The second Series describes love as incorporeal, *having its birth from heau'ns aboue* (14.8). The headnote to Sonnet 14 offers this *jeu d'esprit*:

> Loue espiyng a time of aduantage, transformed him selfe into the sub-
> stance of aier, and so deceitfullie entered into him with his owne great
> goodwill and desire, and nowe by mayne force still holdeth his possession.

The effect of music is initially depicted as *sweet* and causing *delight*.[51] This
delectatio cogitationis (delight-in-thought) comes from a heavenly power,
and images of heaven abound in this Series: *an Angells voice* (12.5), *secret
heau'nly song* (13.13), *musick hauing birth from heau'ns aboue* (14.8),
harmonies that fill Elisian fieldes (16.15–16). The power of music is characterized as supernatural: a *wondrous force* (11.3); the unworldly power of
Arion's harp by which this sailor controlled a dolphin (12.2–3); the *miracu-
lous good effectes accomplished by* five different musicians enumerated in
Sonnet 13 (HN, 1–10); music's powerful effect on the mood of Alexander
driving him to war or peace (14.1–6). This belief in music's heavenly origin
would come as no surprise to an early modern reader, knowing that Saint
Paul asserts that "faith cometh by hearing" (Romans 10:17).

Music, though often a source of delight, may also cause suffering, just
as visually induced love does (11.17–18). This suffering may result from
immoderata cogitatione (excessive meditation) upon the beloved. Many
of the suffering tropes that characterize love in the first Series are repeated
in the second. The feeling of being on the cusp between life and death
appears again with a reference to *Charon's boate* (11.9). The paradoxical
nature of love is again emphasized: *O bitter sweete, or hunny mixt with
gall* (12.13). The danger of love is made apparent by the speaker's comparison of his mistress's singing to a Siren's song, driving him to madness
(12.17–18). The blindness of the first Series becomes deafness in the second (12.15; 13.17). Love may overpower the lover's will (14.17–18), just as
in the first Series.

The final sonnets of the Series, 16 and 17, draw a distinction between
sight and sound: music, seen as heavenly and virtuous, fills the mind; the
sight of the beloved's face fills the eye.

> **She feedes mine eare with tunes of rare delight,**
> **Mine eye with louing lookes, my heart with ioy,**   (16.7–8)

> **And since her song hath fild mine eares with ioye,**
> **Hir vertues pleas'd my minde, hir face mine eye,**   (17.7–8)

The meaning of the *double thrall* in Sonnet 82 (*H'is double thrall that liv's
as Loue thinks best*) now becomes clear. This characterization of love's
power as being "double" appears in at least 6 other lines of the *Hekatompathia*.[52] In the *Dialogues of Love*, Philo says that "the love of the human

soul is double, directed not only toward the beauty of the intellect, but also towards the likeness of beauty that there is in the body."[53] The division of the cosmos into two realms, a lower sensible realm and a higher intelligible realm, is a fundamental tenet in Platonist thought.[54] Love is said to be "double" not only because it has two powers, but because it spans these two realms. This division between the phenomenal and noumenal realms, and the human apprehension of these worlds through aesthesis and noesis, respectively, is found in the *Symposium* and other Platonic dialogues, as discussed in Chapter 14. *Ex visione* love acts in the phenomenal realm, in which earthly beauty ensnares the lover, and *ex cogitatione* love acts in the noumenal realm, in which heavenly beauty grips the lover.

In Sonnet 17's headnote, Apollo (*Sol*) is reckoned to be the *cheife patron* of both visual beauty and the beauty of music (consistent with the god's mythical attributes). Thus two forms of art, painting and music, are associated with each of love's powers, *ex visione* and *ex cogitatione* love, respectively. This extends the figure of the sun, introduced in Sonnet 9 (*Sol*; HN), to include both of love's powers. In the final lines of the Series, the beloved is said to be favored by (or belong to) *Sol*.

> **Then yf you grudge, that she to** Sol **belonge,**
> **Marke but hir face, and heare hir skill in songe.**   (17.17–18)

The beloved is identified with the sun, as it is elsewhere in the sequence (for example, in Sonnets 44 and 45, an important sonnet pair, discussed in Chapter 9). The first two Series set the work's architectural foundation, and here in the last two lines, the beloved is presented as superior in her exercise of both of love's powers.

In summary, the first Subseries of the first Series poses questions about the nature of love—or as Andreas asked, *"Quid sit Amor?"* The second Subseries of the first Series answers this question with Andreas's *ex visione* love, in which love is engendered sensually by the sight of earthly beauty. The second Series answers the question about the nature of love with Andreas's *ex cogitatione* love, in which love enters the mind by the hearing of incorporeal music, which is associated with heavenly beauty. (This bifold model of love has a counterpart in the Christian model of sin, which is discussed in "Love's double nature: The Christian model of sin," Excursus 7.)

Love's double power and Renaissance cosmology

Love in the *Hekatompathia* brings both ecstasy and despair to the speaker, and at the same time, it is the fundamental force that governs the natural world—the center of the sequence's cosmological model. The poetic representation of the cosmos, or cosmopoesis, was common in this period and sometimes provided the model upon which a work is structured.[55] Paul Zumthor argues that in this period, "the design of literature fundamentally remains the expression of universal essences."[56] These "universal essences" include theology, science, and history, which Renaissance man organized into a single, complex, harmonious model of the universe. George Boas recognizes the danger that the modern reader may not recognize or appreciate these universal essences, which he calls "eternal standards":

> The observance of what are sometimes called "eternal standards" in art always eventuates in the fixation of types, and when the types are fixed, they become hieroglyphs. Since the Romantic movement we have become impatient with such an aesthetics; we demand greater fluidity of motif and theme. ... We cannot appreciate the sixteenth and seventeenth centuries, however, whether in painting or in literature, unless we rid ourselves of this prejudice.[57]

Murphy's description of the *Hekatompathia* as "'pure' literature—literature divorced from emotion, philosophy, and human nature"—results from a failure to comprehend these "hieroglyphs" as indicators of emotion, philosophy, or human nature.[58] As Robertson has noted, when such hieroglyphs are finally understood, "literary works which have heretofore seemed incoherent or meaningless become consistent, meaningful, and aesthetically attractive."[59] At the center of what Boas calls "eternal standards" is cosmology: Heninger believes that the "act of creation served as the model for all creative acts, including the composition of poetry."[60] "Art should embody the sempiternal beauty of the divine pattern. ... This tradition can be traced back through the Florentine Renaissance to St. Augustine and eventually to the Pythagorean doctrine recorded in Plato's *Timaeus* (47A–D)."[61]

From the outset, a work's genre may be associated with a certain class of cosmological system, and this may dictate a specific semiotic system. Michael Riffaterre argues for the close connection between genre and semiosis:

> Significance is regulated by reference to a literary genre's semiotic system. ... The genre sets limits to a text's potential verbal associations and allows the reader to harbor certain expectations. ... Thus it is that the genre, because it is a grammar, reorders the words and destroys or threatens their [usual] connotations in the language.[62]

Both genre and cosmology are grammars, and this is especially evident in sonnet sequences. John Porter Houston believes that one of the most important of Petrarch's innovations was his use of imagery for structural purposes. The concern for explicit structure, uncommon in classical poetry, is unmistakable in the sonnet, which is the "perfect expression of the new European regard for design in poetry."[63] Heninger sees the sonnet genre as an exemplar of this aesthetics:

> The sonnet sequence, a nonclassical genre, originated within this esthetics. Indeed, the sonnet sequence is the purest literary expression of this esthetics. The poet creates a world of passing time, a series of incidents that give the illusion of temporal dimension. There is multeity of event. But all this variety is focused on the lady, the repository of all value and therefore the unifying factor. The idea of the lady permeates and forms the sequence; she is its *ratio*, its fore-conceit, the potential that it actualizes. To use a term made current by Roman Jakobson, she is actually, not figuratively, the "dominant" of this literary system. ... We come to know the lady in all her fulness, from the mundane to the celestial, as an image of perfection, as a reflection of the divine One. In this discernment of the mistress, there is an unfolding paralleled by an infolding. By exhausting the possibilities of multeity, we paradoxically conceive unity.[64]

Our most fundamental challenge in reading the *Hekatompathia* is to perceive, as Riffaterre put it, the "presence, parallel to the text and therefore outside of it, of a preexistent model."[65]

The *Hekatompathia* seeks to understand love as a natural phenomenon, a universal, cosmological force. This treatment of love fits within a Platonic cosmological model that divided human perception into two faculties, one that assimilates sensible phenomena and the other intelligible phenomena. These faculties were considered to be distinguishable hypostases of an indivisible soul (analogous to the model of the hypostases of the trinity). Each part is associated with one of two worlds: man's sensible soul (a hypostasis) perceives objects in the material, sensible, subcelestial world; his intelligible soul (also a hypostasis) perceives entities in the nonmaterial, noetic, supercelestial world, which included thoughts, words, Platonic forms, and divinity. These two modes of passion, which correspond to Andreas's *ex visio* passion and *ex cogitatio* modes of love, are also modeled upon various medieval conceptions of mental faculties.[66]

Plato's distinction between the sensible and intelligible faculties is concomitant with his separate realms of matter and forms. The one-time-Platonist Augustine describes this duality as two eyes (or one eye with two modes of perception), with one eye perceiving the visible-corporeal world, and the other the intelligible-spiritual world. One is an "exterior" bodily eye; the other is an "interior eye" of the mind.[67] Augustine's *Vera Religione*, a lengthy letter-soliloquy, is constructed rhetorically around the division of mind and sense, light and darkness, spiritual and carnal.[68] These faculties of the mind are not wholly independent but rather work in tandem, though sometimes they seem to be in conflict with one another and at other times appear more cooperative. For example, in the twelfth century, Hugh of St. Victor, commenting on Dionysius the Areopagite, defines a "symbol" as a "coaptation of visible forms to demonstrate something invisible." "The eye of the mind" sees the physical world not directly, but through the exterior eye, and in this process the physical world is transfigured.[69] A Latin genre emerged in the Middle Ages based on this tandem processing, which features a debate between body and soul, or eye and heart, or sensuality and reason. Such debates are also found in the vernacular, for example, in Dante's *Vita Nuova* (38) and Shakespeare's *Sonnets* (24).[70]

This bifold epistemological model is consistent with certain philosophical views that were prevalent in Bacon's time. Ernst Cassirer writes of Nicholas Cusanus, an important proponent of these ideas:

> The division that separates the sensible from the intelligible, sense experience and logic from metaphysics, does not cut through the vital nerve of experience itself; indeed, precisely this division guarantees the validity of experience. ... Cusanus now works out the idea of 'participation'. Far from excluding each other, separation and participation, *chorismos* and *methexis*, can only be thought of *through* and in *relation* to each other. In the definition of empirical knowledge, both elements are necessarily posited and connected with each other. For no empirical knowledge is possible that is not related to an ideal being and to an ideal being-thus.[71]

The notion that sensible objects were divided from the Platonic forms in which they nevertheless participated (*methexis*) was prevalent in Elizabethan England. J. W. Lever argues that an "instinctive dualism" in Elizabethan England "shapes the whole character of Sidney's sequence." Also, "Spenser's poetry laid particular stress upon psychic volition and practical virtue as the integrative factors capable of reconciling nature and spirit rather than upon the transcendental powers of the soul as celebrated by Italian poets."[72] Love operates in both spheres, the visible and invisible, nature and spirit, and matter and thought, and thus can act as a bridge between these two worlds.

Another Renaissance viewpoint postulates two separate loves: an earthly, lower love and a numinous, higher love. The lower love was often considered an illness that overtakes reason, a position derived from the notion in medieval ethics that an appetitive or passionate love must be suppressed by reason. The higher love was associated with the intellect and reason, and was thought to be either a god or a demon that acts as an intermediary between heaven and earth. This belief in two opposed forms of love derives from an ancient tradition that was central to various formulations of Renaissance Platonism. Its *locus classicus* is found in Plato's *Symposium*:

> Since in fact there are two such goddesses [named Aphrodite] there must also be two kinds of Love. ... One, the elder, sprung from no mother's womb but from the heavens themselves, we will call the Uranian, the heavenly Aphrodite, while the younger, daughter of Zeus and Dione, we call Pandemus, the earthly Aphrodite. ... When the regulating principle of Love brings together those opposites of which I spoke—hot and cold, wet and dry—and compounds them in an ordered harmony, the result is health and plenty for mankind. [But] under the influence of that other Love, all is mischief and destruction.   (180d, 188ab)

The conflict between a passionate, destructive love and a divine, rational love also appears in the *Phaedrus*. Unlike medieval ethics in which passion is subordinated to reason, Socrates suggests instead that passion is superior to reason. Further, he associates passion with madness and claims that "the greatest blessings come by way of madness... that is heaven-sent" (244a). The *Hekatompathia* also treats love as a form of madness: the Puzzle Sonnet's acrostics declare that "to love is madness" (*amare est insanire*). In the context of the MLIP Subsequence, this is grounds to reject love. However, at the conclusion of the restored work, passionate, mad love is embraced. Both the *Phaedrus* and the *Hekatompathia* seek a balance between reason and mad love: in the *Phaedrus*, the charioteer must manage two horses, one prudent and the other unruly; in the *Hekatompathia*, a balance is sought between unruly love and the speaker's heart, which seeks reason and order. Eris (strife) and Eros (love), which are often indistinguishable in the *Hekatompathia*, are the foundation of the work's cosmological model.

4

The Poetics of Ruin and Restoration

In the previous chapter, we discovered that the *Hekatompathia*'s first 17 sonnets are correctly ordered and consist of two Series, one devoted to each of love's two powers. Each Series exhibits a logical progression with Sequential Ties linking one sonnet to the next. But this meticulously constructed foundation of 17 sonnets is followed by a distinct lack of order—a jumble of 83 sonnets. After visiting, as it were, the well-appointed antechambers of what we expect to be a well-constructed edifice, we instead find ourselves lost in a maze of confusion. Sonnets 18 through Sonnet 79 demonstrate almost no order, except in two instances.[1] The MLIP Subsequence that begins at Sonnet 80 also lacks order and instead presents clear anomalies.[2] A further discussion of the disorder beyond Sonnet 17 is provided in "The ruined text after Sonnet 17," Excursus 8.

The order of the sequence's remaining 83 sonnets is established by solving the Puzzle's second through fourth Stages. After restoration, the sequence exhibits a clear progression throughout, and a beginning, middle, and end can be discerned. Yet, by what authority does the puzzle-solver rewrite the text? The critic's job is to interpret texts, not rewrite them—so one would think. Unless there is evidence that other Renaissance poets intentionally disordered their texts, and that some of their contemporary readers (even if only a few) understood this literary game, then we would have to conclude that the *Hekatompathia* invents from scratch an untraditional literary mode. That would be unexpected because the *Hekatompathia* seems to be traditional: it appropriates from dozens of texts and follows the long-established poetic mode of the sonnet genre. Thus, we ought to consider prior to reordering the sequence (a difficult task that occupies the next 7 chapters) what precedents there might be for such an undertaking and what principles ought to be applied.

As discussed in the previous chapter, the concern with division, arrangement, and decorum led to the production of ordered texts, and it also led readers to order texts that exhibited disorder. In the case of Scripture, the discovery of intratextual links or concordances were used to elucidate obscure passages. In the medieval and Renaissance periods, as discussed below, certain texts include intentional disorder, incompleteness, or other formal deficiencies, and these flaws, or ruin, served as a stimulus to reader discovery. This is much like Bacon's prescription for effective pedagogy: the probative mode of insinuation supplants the direct delivery of knowledge (discussed in the first chapter).

Our discussion of the poetics of ruin begins with the sonnet genre, a natural setting for this poetics. We then turn to an example of the poetics of ruin from the twelfth century, Alan's *Anticlaudianus*, which resembles the *Hekatompathia* in that it hides its true ending in the middle of the work. Next, we consider the tradition and practices of ruin and restoration and how the *Hekatompathia* positions itself as an incomplete work. We then turn to the traditional mechanisms by which a text may guide its reader in its restoration, and the essential method that the Puzzle provides for the restoration of the *Hekatompathia*.

The tradition of the ruined text

Why would a poet deliver a ruined work to readers? The *Hekatompathia*'s ruin mirrors a world that is unstable and fragmented, a theme frequently found in mythology, and most notably, in Ovid's *Metamorphoses*.[3] According to Pierre Hadot, it reflects the Ovidian perception of the natural world as a chaotic succession of various states, always in flux rather than static.[4] Although Renaissance art is often viewed as a body of "stable, harmonious, closed artistic creations," the opposite can also be the case, according to Michel Jeanneret:

> So many great literary works of the Renaissance are presented as works-in-progress, workshops in activity. A book is published? It would seem to be finished? No, publication was just a transitory phase of a work to be corrected, supplemented, transformed. Words that seemed firmly set on the page start to move as if escaping from the realm of inert objects to return to the still flexible stage of their genesis.[5]

The "magic of the inchoate"[6] stimulates the reader's creative energies to renew or restore the text. Yet the reader is not left unconstrained in his or her attempt to interpret and restore the text: the need to resolve contradictions, to follow the author's paratextual instructions, and to maintain coherence all limit the scope of interpretation. Jeanneret believes that "the ideas and practice of transformation are constitutive of humanism" and that this "metamorphic sensibility... was widespread in the period 1480–1600."[7]

The humanists were not only concerned with the recovery and translation of ancient texts, but also with their redeployment within a new culture: *translatio imperii* (dynastic succession). (See the discussion of translation in the previous chapter.) Joachim Du Bellay, in his *Défense et illustration de la langue française*, has the new poet build upon Greek and Latin poetry, which are imagined as ruined buildings. Terence Cave writes that "the major literary works of the sixteenth century in France are all marked by an acute and persistent consciousness that they are produced in the shadow of a 'father text,' which must be in some sense destroyed if life is to continue."[8] Rebeca Helfer calls the topos of ruin "a master metaphor" of the Renaissance, arguing that its recognition is essential to the proper exegesis of many works.[9] Andrew Hui asserts that "ruin functions as a privileged cipher or master topos that marks the rupture between the world of the humanists and the world of antiquity."[10] Willy Maley, like Helfer, recognizes the topos of ruin as fundamental to Spenser's poetics, calling him a "poet of ruins."[11] Indeed, Spenser translated Du Bellay's *Antiquités de Rome* (a poem of ruins) into English and composed *The Ruines of Time*, which treats poetry as a bulwark that perseveres against the ravages of time. This concern with preservation against time is also a recurrent theme in Shakespeare's *Sonnets*. A. Kent Hieatt argues persuasively that Spenser's *Ruines of Rome: by Bellay* (his English translation) provided a model for the frequent use of images of deteriorating monuments found in the *Sonnets*.[12]

One expects a sonnet sequence to exhibit an orderly development of a theme, and to a lesser degree, a narrative. Nevertheless, disorder is also a principle of sonnet sequences, for they display a strange combination of diversity and unity: they range over a vast number of subjects, and yet virtually every sonnet points to a single entity, the beloved, an object of idolatrous worship. John Freccero argues that this deiform being appears not as a whole but as fractured and dispersed across the text:

> Her virtues and her beauties are scattered like the objects of fetish worship... Each part of her has the significance of her entire person: it remains the task of the reader to string together her gemlike qualities into an idealized unity.[13]

This scattering is an essential feature of Petrarchism; Petrarch himself referred to his poetry as *ruinae* (ruins), and the *Canzoniere* is also known as the *Rime Sparse* (scattered poetry).[14] This scattering of significance forces the reader not only to consider the meaning of individual sonnets but also to trace out ideas and images dispersed across the sequence. The reader becomes a wanderer in a labyrinth, which imitates the circumstances of the sonnet speaker's "long wandering in a blind labyrinth" (*Canzoniere* 224.1–4). The labyrinth is a symbol of disorder, and the poems of the *Canzoniere* often appear to be disordered. Thomas Greene believes the *locus classicus* of this tradition to be the *sparagmos* (dismemberment) of Osiris's body:

> How is one best to understand the creativity of fragmentation? What kind of correspondence can poetry properly aspire to? ... Osiris dismembered seems to call for an Isis impulse, working to restore the broken body piece by piece. The groping mind reforms the fragments into incipient wholes that are not contingent. The poet's mind and the reader's mind work to formulate an emergent gestalt of signs, a gestalt dependent on a new unfamiliar verbal complex which holds together and which the mind can receive in to itself.[15]

A ruined text requires an exegetical approach in which the reader discovers an internal coherence among the ideas and images scattered across the text. Exegesis of a ruined text demands a rhetorical hermeneutics, for it is by the rhetorical process of *inventio* (discovery) that the reader first becomes able to reconstruct the meaning found dispersed across the text. The ruined text necessitates that the reader, provoked by an "Isis impulse," become at once a decipherer, a restorer, and ultimately, a recipient of revelation.

Simpson's restoration of Alan's *Anticlaudianus*

In a remarkable exegesis of the *Anticlaudianus*, James Simpson finds its text to be intentionally disordered. Alan's preface suggests a deeper reading is possible, but only by the most learned of readers. Following this cue, Simpson argues that the order of the work requires a reversal: the ending books must be placed prior to the beginning books, and this rearrangement makes the work coherent.[16] (In Chapter 8, we will discover that reordering the *Hekatompathia* requires a similar reversal.) Simpson is understandably concerned about how readers may react to his study:

> An imagined reader [of Simpson's study] may be remarking how tidy my solution to the poem's difficulties is, but how preposterous (in the modern sense of the word) at the same time. Literary critics simply are not allowed to take poems apart and put them together at will.[17]

Simpson goes on to argue that his reconstruction is "entirely consistent with what Alan says about the allegory of his poem," and further, that his reading is consistent with the "cultural milieu" of Alan's time.[18] The starting point in the exegesis of these texts is the recognition that something is terribly flawed or nonsensical. Simpson explains the importance of recognizing a text's inconsistencies:

> [*Anticlaudianus* is] characterized by profound structural incoherences, which provide intriguing difficulties for a reader. In attempting to understand the sense behind these incoherences, we as readers are invited to participate in the construction of meaning, and to participate ourselves, therefore, in the processes of learning represented in the poems.[19]

Unfortunately, critics often attribute incoherences to some failure of the author rather than recognize them as signals to the reader to dig deeper. Simpson reports that critics have not been kind to the *Anticlaudianus*: C. S. Lewis describes it as "nearly worthless"; Winthrop Wetherbee argues that there is "something gratuitous and anticlimactic" about the new earthly order at its conclusion.[20] The *Anticlaudianus*, like the *Hekatompathia*, is ridiculous in its published order, which has led to these adverse critiques. Both of these ruined texts have been mistakenly subjected to literal readings; instead, they should have been read using the hermeneutic procedures subtly recommended in their prefaces. Simpson articulates the fundamental hermeneutic principle that must be applied to a corrupted text: the exegete must proceed "on the critical principle of seeking the maximum degree of formal unity in a poem only by first recognizing the maximum degree of formal disunity."[21] Simpson argues that to properly read the *Anticlaudianus*, one must carefully consider "the form of the work itself."[22] Moreover, his exegetical method closely examines the process by which the work was written:

> By understanding the way in which the poem itself is formed, we will be better placed to understand the educational 'information' it brings to its readers. Here and elsewhere in this book, I will proceed on the assumption that this formal poetic enquiry is logically prior to any investigation of the poem's philosophical or other meaning.[23]

This places the burden on the reader to give the work its formal unity. But how is the reader to discover this formal unity? Alan states in his prologue that the reader must have the courage to examine the work in the context of supercelestial forms, and he expects that only the most erudite readers will recognize the literary game that he is playing. Simpson explains Alan's game:

> In asking us to consider the 'supercelestial form' of his work, Alan is
> clearly asking us to consider his own poem as a theological artifact, and
> therefore to locate the poem's essential meaning not in the sense of
> *quem faciunt verba* (its represented action), but rather in a prior sense,
> the sense of *ex quo fiunt verba* [some sense that preceded the words].
> We are being asked in Boethius's terminology, to move from consider-
> ation of the *imago* of the poem (its outer form) to its real form, the
> informing idea behind the poem which makes sense of its outer shape.
> ... Poetic theorists contemporary with Alan [e.g., Geoffrey of Vinsauf]
> present the idea of a poetic 'archetype' which must precede the poetic
> making, as if poetic making is modelled on divine creation.[24]

The terms "poetic archetype" and "informing idea" are similar to Philip
Sidney's concept of a "fore-conceit."[25] After identifying this informing idea,
the reader must apply his or her own imagination to it, and then retrace
the path taken by the poet in creating the work. Simpson describes the
reader's re-creation of the poem:

> Alan is asking us, in the Prologue to the *Anticlaudianus*, to apply our
> intellect to the making of a poem. ... William of Conches, for example
> (again under Boethian influence) describes the role of the intellect as
> one of mentally taking apart previously joined things, or of joining
> disparate things, by virtue of its capacity to perceive the essential, in-
> tellectually separable essence of a thing. ... William [asks the reader]
> not to interpret the work according to its 'existence,' but rather accord-
> ing to our perception of its informing idea. Very crudely, it could be said
> that we are being invited to 'take the poem apart', as it were—to 'unjoin
> joined things.'[26]

Alan's informing idea is based on a well-established cosmological model,
and Simpson believes that he is "producing a Platonic poetics from within
a Boethian concept of theology."[27] Similarly, the *Hekatompathia* is based
on a Platonic poetics that articulates an established cosmological model,
though not a theological one. Its cosmology is derived from pre-Socratic
materialist philosophy and the Renaissance belief in the coincidence of
opposites. As with the *Anticlaudianus*, the *Hekatompathia*'s reader is
asked to disassemble the work ("take the poem apart") and reassemble it
in a manner consistent with a cosmological system.

Order, topical invention, and arrangement

The previous chapter considered the medieval rhetorical practices that
prescribed order; here, we consider how in the early modern period,

rhetoric advanced in its understanding of order and decorum. In the sixteenth century, Melanchthon, in his *Elementa rhetorices*, argues that readers should inquire into the argumentative purpose (*scopus*) and structural coherence (*oikonomia*) of the whole text.[28] As discussed in the prior chapter, Annabel Patterson contends that decorum may include the imitation of patterns in the natural world. Michael Hetherington argues that the *Shepheardes Calender* deserves our "attention not just for its excellence at local points but for the completeness and coherence of the whole design—Immerito's 'dewe observing of Decorum everywhere and firm knitting of sentences' mean that everything 'is well grounded, finely framed, and sternly trussed up together.'"[29] Jon Quitslund asserts that "for Spenser and other Elizabethans, poetic invention involved the arrangement of pre-existing ideas; they were not supposed to be original with the author. But the Sidneian 'right poet,' a maker whose ideas are 'eikastic' and '*architechtonike*,' had to begin with a purposeful design, establishing a foundation beneath the textual surface."[30] Yet, if decorum was mandated, then how can a ruined work be justified? Although ruined poetry appears to be indecorous, it is merely inchoate, and it contains the hints necessary for the reader to restore the work to a harmonious state. The work's decorum or structure is present but partially obscured, and it becomes the reader's responsibility to reveal the hidden part. S. K. Heninger contends that the reader must abstract "meaning by making a diagram of the relationships between its parts."[31] Moreover, he argues, a structured work begs the reader to consider authorial intention, despite its devalued status in modern critical theory.[32]

Inventio (topical invention), the starting point in rhetorical practice, is applied to *materia* (material), a word which can mean either physical matter or subject matter. One typically begins with an abundance of disorganized matter, which is often analogized as a forest: *silva* in Latin and *hyle* in Greek. Aristotle, lacking a word for "subject matter," appropriated the Greek word *hyle*, which means "wood." This metonymic use of "wood" for "subject matter" carried through to the early modern period: Ben Jonson called his commonplace book "Timber"; Bacon called his collection of miscellaneous remarks on natural history *Sylva sylvarum*, and in *Scala intellectus*, he employs the metaphor of a journey that begins in the "woods of nature."[33]

Bacon saw textual matter as analogous to physical matter and held as a fundamental principle that both are conserved. According to Gerard Passannante, Bacon "repeatedly argues for a materialist understanding of the processes of disintegration and recombination—an idea he... inherited from the Epicurean poet [Lucretius]."[34] Texts recombine material just as nature does:

> Arriving at the knowledge of subtle particles was, for Bacon, also the pleasure of knowledge reduced to its most basic possible components—the *elementa* of a language that reflected and embodied the structure of the world. This was not a vision of chaos or dissolution, but of order and calculation—a vision of reality revealed in all its clarity. ... Bacon was, in fact, operating in a long tradition of humanistic hunting and scattering that may be traced back, for example, to the compositional practices of Aulus Gellius, a second sophistic author whose notebooks became a source for the recovery of many ancient authors otherwise confined to oblivion. Through Gellius's own random quoting of "anything worth remembering... without any plan or order," the parts of previously lost texts could be put back together again, as Anthony Grafton has put it, "like the pieces of a smashed mosaic."[35]

The Puzzle's practice of recombination of text is consistent with its expression of a natural philosophy that sees the world's creation as a recombination of *elementa* (which can mean either letters or kinds of physical matter), which is derivative of the materialist natural philosophy of Epicurus and other early Greek philosophers.

Materia is subjected to *inventio*, a scientizing process that is often analogized using visual and spatial metaphors. One looks for things, or comes upon things, as the word *inventio* (*ventio*: hunt) suggests. The hunt for Pan (*venatio Panis*), discussed in the first chapter, is the scientific process by which nature was investigated. Walter Ong argues that there was an "inexorable disposition to represent thought and communication in terms of spatial models and thus to reduce mental activity to local motion."[36] *Inventio* was thought of as the discovery of places within an abundant wood or forest. Thomas Wilson, in his *The Rule of Reason* (1551) imagines *inventio* or discovery as a hunt in the woods:

> A place is, the restyng corner of argumente... Those that bee good harefinders will soone finde the hare by her fourme. ... Likewise the Huntesman in huntyng the foxe, wil soone espie when he seeth a hole, whether it be a foxe borough, or not. ... Therefore if any one will dooe good in this kinde, he must goe from place to place and by searchyng every borough he shal have his purpose undoubtedly in moste part of them, if not in al.[37]

Ong explains that this "hunt" or "logic of places" has "as their direct or indirect inspiration the *Dialectical Invention* of [Rodolphus] Agricola." His place-logic was adopted and promoted by various humanists, including Erasmus and Ramus, and made its way to England where it had a significant influence as a "practical pedagogy."[38] Because sonnet sequences consist of equal-sized poems—effectively, standard building blocks—they provide the perfect venue for the practice of place-logic. The *Hekatompathia* consists of 83 locations and 83 misplaced sonnets, and it is the puzzle-solver's job to hunt for the proper poem to fill each of its 83 locations. Bacon, in the *Advancement*, advocates a methodical distribution of knowledge—"the seats and places of learning," which he likens to the protected stations beekeepers maintain for their bee hives.[39] This image dates from antiquity, appearing in Virgil's *Georgics* (4) and Seneca's *Epistles* (84). In the *Novum Organum*, bees are again used metaphorically to describe the management of knowledge: "The bee gathers its material from the flowers of the garden and of the field, but transforms and digests it by a power of its own."[40] Knowledge is gathered, stored in compartments, and then processed.

The *Hekatompathia* is a storehouse of knowledge, gathered by the poet from his intertextual sources. This abundance of *materia* (i.e., sonnets) is available to the puzzle-solver, who must gather up this nectar and process it to produce a new sonnet sequence. The puzzle-solver's production begins with topical invention: the sequence's principal topics must be discovered among the sonnets. Each Lioness Sonnet, after the sequence is reordered, introduces a Series' theme or topic. Subsequent to the discovery of these topics, the puzzle-solver engages in the process of arrangement, restoring the order of the sonnets within each Series. These two processes, invention and arrangement, are the two principal methods required to reorder the sequence. They are essentially the same two processes described in the previous chapter as division and *ordinatio.*

Topical invention or *venatio Panis* is the counterpart to chaos or dispersal: the ruination of a text is the *pars destruens* (destructive part); topical invention and arrangement are the *pars construens* (constructive part). In the *Hekatompathia*, Bacon adhered to his pedagogical method of insinuating knowledge "in the same method wherein it was originally invented." He destroyed sonnet order (*pars destruens*) to force the reader to reinvent his sequence using the Puzzle, that is, by applying "the same method wherein" he originally composed it (*pars construens*).[41] The *Hekatompathia's materia,* its appropriated Petrarchan poetry, is transformed into a new, organic, counter-Petrarchan sequence. Bacon explains his method using an analogy in which the mind is compared with wax tablets: "On waxen tablets you cannot write anything new until you rub out the old. With the mind it is not so; there you cannot rub out the old till you have written in the new."[42] The student arrives for instruction not with a blank mind, but one filled with various beliefs: "idols" or deeply ingrained beliefs. Bacon's pedagogical trick is to initially avoid countering these beliefs and instead use them as a foundation on which to build new ideas.

In this process, the foundation may be augmented with ideas that partially conflict with it, and eventually, as this process continues, fully conflict with it. Once the new ideas are fully in place, then and only then can the old ideas be discarded—erased from the student's mind.[43] The *Hekatompathia* is an unthreatening, conventional sequence, but solving the Puzzle erases that sequence and a heterodox, if not blasphemous, counter-Petrarchan sequence emerges.

The surviving incomplete manuscript of the *Hekatompathia*, titled "A Looking glasse for Loovers," suggests that the work be read as a mirror (*speculum*) of the natural world. As a mirror or *speculum*, the *Hekatompathia* reflects the nature of love and, consistent with the didactic nature of mirrors, delivers an ethic of love. The architecture of a literary mirror or *speculum* guides interpretation: its divisions establish the framework in which the work's subject matter is interpreted. For example, Vincent of Beauvais's *Speculum naturale* is a compilation of *auctoritates* that follows the chronological order of the six days of creation. M. B. Parkes argues that by placing his diverse intertextual material into discrete chapters, which follow the *ordinatio* of creation, Vincent subordinates his intertextual borrowings to his work's structure, and they must be read in this new context.[44] Another work based on the six days of creation is Du Bartas's *La Semaine ou creation du Monde* (1578), a hexameral poem that was available in many editions and languages, including partial translations by James VI and Philip Sidney.[45] The *Shepheardes Calender* is yet another example of a work whose structural divisions are hermeneutically significant. So, too, for Spenser's *Faerie Queene*: Andrew King argues that it is divided according to a scheme of virtues, "a profoundly medieval conception of structure."[46] Division, a prolific feature of medieval works, clearly remained popular in the early modern period.

Rita Copeland refers to these divisions as "abstract 'regions' of argument, 'places' that exist in precedent, in subject, and in method." The topics of hexameral literature are the six days of creation; the topics of the *Shepheardes Calender* are the 12 months of the year, corresponding to the 12 signs of the zodiac. The topics of a sonnet sequence are not obvious—so how are we to discover them? Rhetorical invention is concerned with "a logical and discursive coherence configured in spatial terms (the notion of place or seat of argument). The forms and materials of invention are essentially logical constructs."[47] Citing the *Prologue* to *Chaucer's Legend of Good Women*, Copeland argues that the discovery of topics (*modus inveniendi*) is dependent upon the interpretation (*modus interpretandi*) of earlier texts—"the wisdom and lore preserved in old books." The *Prologue* explores "the problem of historical difference and the hermeneutics of recovery." Recovery is dependent not only upon the old books themselves, but upon a "tradition of exegetical reception," as practiced in the medieval *accessus ad auctores*.[48]

The topics that structure the *Hekatompathia* were obtained from various key texts and commentaries on those texts. The importance of Andreas's *De Amore* and Ebreo's *Dialogues of Love* was demonstrated in the previous chapter: love's double nature structures the first two Series. We will discover that the double nature of love is a key structuring mechanism employed throughout the sequence. Another structuring method is derived from the *Symposium*, which plays a pivotal role in ordering the sonnets within a Series (see Chapter 9). Another important structural model is derived from the *Phaedrus*: its pattern of three speeches is reflected in the restored work's three Subsequences. Although the *Hekatompathia* derives its structure from ideas found in intertexts, it adapts those ideas for its own purposes, and its structure is uniquely its own. Following a tradition that is derived from Proclus and other early Platonists, it is a microcosm, a small world that has its own internal logic and order. This conception of a literary microcosm can be found in Sidney's "golden world" and Philippist oratory (referring to Philip Melanchthon).[49] James Coulter refers to this as "literary organicism, i.e.[,] the belief that a work of literature is an organic microcosm created by an intelligent artisan in the light of some preexisting aim or intention."[50] This microcosm may have cosmological or philosophical underpinnings, and the reader, as part of *inventio*, may need to determine *cui parti philosphiae supponitur* (to which part of philosophy does it belong).[51] For example, the *accessus* to the *Aeneid* attributed to Bernardus Silvestris treats Virgil as both a poet and philosopher. Copeland describes Bernardus's viewpoint in this *accessus*:

> As philosopher [Virgil] writes *sub integumento*, and it is the task of the exegete to draw away the veil of fiction and expose the philosophical "plot" of the *Aeneid* as Virgil "intended" it to be read. The exegete, according to "Bernardus," thus carries out Virgil's own directives, reading according to a posited *intentio auctoris*.[52]

The restoration of the *Hekatompathia* follows a similar process: the work's philosophical plot must be discovered (*inventio*) and the work restored in accordance with the poet's intentions, as revealed by the Puzzle.

The hermeneutics of restoration

In solving the Puzzle, we practice invention as a hermeneutic procedure, yet do so under the author's guidance. Copeland identifies Matthew of Vendôme and Geoffrey of Vinsauf as early practitioners of employing invention as a hermeneutic procedure:

> [They] so prize *materia exsecuta* [the material produced] above all else
> for the difficulty that they attribute to it; in transforming invention into
> a hermeneutical procedure they prize the ingenuity of the exegetical
> performance that can disguise its own moves through a consummate
> act of textual appropriation. ... The medieval *artes poetriae* represents
> one instance of this empowered and broadened hermeneutical action.
> They constitute a crossover of grammar and rhetoric: they are products
> of the grammatical tradition of *enarratio poetarum*, but they also
> transmit ancient rhetorical precepts for composition. *They use the
> grammarian's methods of textual analysis, but they direct these meth-
> ods towards discursive production.* Their dominant discourse is that
> of hermeneutics: they lay out a system of interpretive control over text-
> ual authority, and they apply that control to contesting and appropriat-
> ing textual traditions.[53] [my italics]

Combining the traditions of grammar and rhetoric, interpretation becomes
a performative act prized for its difficulty, which imposes a system of
interpretive control that appropriates the original text. The *Hekatompathia*'s recombinative poetics requires that we apply a grammarian's
methods to interpret the text's words and images, and then apply rhetorical procedures to reorder the sequence—a "discursive production." After
reordering, a new sequence is produced (the *materia exsecuta*), an
organic, counter-Petrarchan sequence.

Ramus played an important role in disseminating this concept of
recombination, which was fundamental to his method. He adopted Agricola's division of dialectic into two parts: invention (*pars inveniendi*) and
judgment (*pars indicandi*)—judgment refers to the similarity of two terms,
i.e., similitudes.[54] Michel Foucault argues that similitude or resemblance
is fundamental to early modern discourse: "The sixteenth century superimposed hermeneutics and semiology in the form of similitude." Indeed,
Don Quixote's "whole journey is a quest for similitudes." Foucault argues
that Bacon critiques similitudes and "shows them, shimmering before our
eyes, vanishing as one draws near, then re-forming again a moment later,
a little further off. They are *idols*."[55] According to Ong, "invention and
judgment are protean in their applicability to intellectual and linguistic
activity." In the case of reading allegorical works, "a man finds something
(invention) and pronounces as a judge upon it by comparing it with something else (judgment)."[56] Ramus defines judgment as "the collocating (or
assembling) what invention has found, and of judging by this collocation
concerning the matter under consideration." Later, he will substitute "the
term disposition or arrangement for that of judgment."[57] This process of
arrangement of many and various arguments, "cohering to one another
and linked as by an unbroken chain," leads "one to a determined end."[58]

For Ramus, all linguistic activity is "a process of taking apart unit pieces by analysis and putting them back together again by genesis or synthesis"—in other words, everything revolves around arrangement.[59]

This hermeneutics of invention and judgment are the principal activities required to solve the *Hekatompathia*'s Puzzle. The puzzle-solver discovers arguments, makes judgments about the links between arguments, and then rearranges the text to progress toward a "determined end." As described later in this chapter, the work is a tissue of intratextual links that the puzzle-solver must identify (a matter of judgment). These intratextual links are between the phrase-lists that appear in certain sonnets and critical lines that appear in other sonnets. These direct the reordering of the sequence, which results in a radically different "determined end."

Although Bacon's hermeneutics is based on discovery and judgment, he was not a Ramist, and even once derided Ramus as "that hide-out of ignorance, that pestilent book-worm."[60] Clearly Bacon's experimental method and his probative rhetoric, which unite rather than divide dialectic and persuasion, were incompatible with Ramism. Marc Cogan argues that "the entire field of logic as Bacon conceived it is in fact heavily rhetorical." In contrast, Ramus separated rhetoric (persuasion) from logic. Further, Cogan asserts that "Bacon describes rhetoric in terms of its relation to, and effect on, a given set of human faculties [and by] reorienting the discussion of rhetoric to the faculties, he makes a striking innovation in rhetorical theory."[61] However, Bacon's "definition and distinction between 'invention' and 'judgment'" was, in fact, close to that of Ramus.[62]

Why is literary reception such an active and difficult process in both medieval commentaries and the *Hekatompathia*? The goal of rhetoric is persuasion: Quintilian asserts that "the art of rhetoric is realized in action."[63] A more active process of interpretation creates in the interpreter a more powerful persuasion to action. This is a fundamental argument of Sidney's *Defence*, as Robert Stillman explains:

Readers are advised imaginatively to invent (literally, to reinvent) the making of the poem, to reconstruct the conceptual design of its fictional landscape in order to profit in the very act of so doing, from its teaching. Accommodation, in the first instance, sounds mainly like the conceptual activity of adapting the text to the reader's own needs. But accommodation to the poetic text also requires simultaneously something else of equal importance. To make oneself fully at home in the poetic text, to accommodate oneself to the poet's invention requires too an affective identification—the wish to become an Aeneas in his pious rescue of Anchises or a Turnus in his courageous stand for honor. The distinctive power of the Sidneian golden world is its power to make acts of identification possible. For the world of the poetic text is golden not because it represents an "earth more lovely," nor even that it counterfeits more "excellent" kinds of heroes—heroes like Xenophon's Cyrus—but rather the "golden" eloquence of the fiction is signaled by its power to bestow "a Cyrus upon the world to make many Cyruses."[64]

The first sentence in the above quotation reminds us of Bacon's pedagogical approach: knowledge ought to "be insinuated (if it were possible) in the same method wherein it was originally invented."[65] The reader, by reinventing the making of the poem, understands it more fully and experiences it more affectively, and thus is ultimately trained not to be a "Cyrus" (a prototypical hero) but a poet, or maker of "Cyruses." Poetry becomes a metamorphic experience for the reader, having what Sidney calls "strange effects."[66] Melanchthon asserts that the power of creation, the reflection in man of the God's creative power, is the source of all arts: *Et fontes omnium artium sunt in hac potential* (And the fountain of all the arts is in this power [of making]).[67] To solve the *Hekatompathia*'s Puzzle, the reader must reinvent the work, becoming a quasi-poet, and by this powerful experience, the text is inculcated in the reader, giving it a new life that extends beyond the life of the original poet.

Lilliat's augmentation and assembly of the *Hekatompathia*

Early modern readers often modified a text by adding their own ideas: they affixed marginal notes and even reassembled a book's pages into a new order, or added new pages with material of their own creation. Elizabethan musician and poet John Lilliat created a personal compilation of the *Hekatompathia*: he removed the binding from his copy and inserted additional pages to create a new work, which has been at the Bodleian Library since the early eighteenth century. The new pages and the margins of the original pages include 163 entries, mostly verse, in his distinctive hand. When I first examined Lilliat's *Hekatompathia* at the Bodleian in 2011, I took his alterations to be an unusual practice. However, a few years later, Jeffrey Todd Knight published his *Bound to Read*, which discusses the Lilliat copy at length and finds the practice of creating such personal compilations to be common in the period.[68] This practice of compiling is derivative of the habit of keeping commonplace books, which "constituted the primary intellectual tool for organizing knowledge and thought among the intelligentsia."[69] Knight writes:

> [Mary Thomas] Crane and others have shown that the commonplace book was not simply a technology for memorizing and organizing

> aphorisms or other useful information; it was institutionalized in Ren-
> aissance schools as a model for producing texts, in particular the
> humanist-inflected verse miscellanies that had become so popular and
> influential by mid-century. This institutionalization of rhetorical
> method made commonplacing a ready model for authorial self-fash-
> ioning among Renaissance poets and playwrights, who were educated
> according to humanist precepts. ... Students were encouraged to view
> all literature as a system of interchangeable fragments, and to view the
> process of composition as centered on intertextuality rather than imi-
> tation in the usual sense.[70]

The *Hekatompathia*'s sonnets are intertextual fragments, repurposed by
Bacon to create (in its original, scrambled order) a miscellany, or what
Knight calls an "open-source composition."[71] Knight recognizes that the
Hekatompathia practices readaption and compilation throughout the work:

> Augmentation and assembly in this sense are the master tropes of the
> *Hekatompathia*. The language of compiling can be found in almost
> every poem in the sequence. [Examples are given.] The work's head-
> notes, as documents of a process of reading as writing, project over all
> such language an image of the text itself as an artifact ever subject to
> rearrangement and recontextualization. Here the complete, bound
> book is not the assumed *telos*, and in fact Watson casts the contingency
> and incompleteness of texts, especially his own, as an incitement to
> create new text.[72]

Knight, without knowledge of the work's Puzzle, finds that the *Hekatompathia* projects itself as an "artifact ever subject to rearrangement," and
that its incompleteness is an "incitement to create new text." He then considers Sonnet 1, which claims that the sequence will ultimately adhere to
the nature & true qualitie of a love passion and alludes to the poet's (supposed) unpublished *De Remedio Amoris* (HN). Knight believes that this
opening sonnet "grounds the *Hekatompathia* in the author's failure to
'perfect' an earlier text—a *Remedio* that would have precluded the need
for this anguished sequence of love poems." However, the opposite is the
case: a not-yet-complete *Remedio* hints that a sequel to the *Hekatompathia* will appear, just as Ovid's *Remedio* followed his *Amatoria*. As discussed in Chapter 8, this headnote hints at a successor text, and that by
some means, the reader must correct the published text, producing a
Remedio—a new work. Knight recognizes that this first sonnet projects
"the desire to transform, which becomes the primary structuring principle
of Watson's text."[73] Further, he reads Sonnet 67's headnote, in which the
poet claims to have added a sonnet at the last minute (*purposely compiled
at the presse*), as an indication that the *Hekatompathia*'s creation is part

of an ongoing process. Knight concludes that "the *Hekatompathia* narrates, in large and small details, the process of its own becoming."[74] This process of becoming does not end at its publication, but must be continued by the reader, as orchestrated by the Puzzle.

Paratexts and artifices inform the reader's re-creation

The *Hekatompathia* narrates "the process of its own becoming" in two ways: through such familiar methods as paratextual directives and rhetorical devices, and by a unique indexing scheme that will shortly be detailed. Poets provide paratextual and in-text hints to guide readers because they know that their words will undergo change over time and wish to nevertheless exercise some control over how they are to be read. In the *Phaedrus*, Socrates concludes that words should employ the art of dialectic such that, "instead of remaining barren [they] contain a seed whence new words grow up in new characters, whereby the seed is vouchsafed immortality, and its possessor the fullest measure of blessedness that man can attain unto" (277A). This conception of regenerative words or discourse applies to rhetoric as well as dialectic. (Boethius, a pivotal influence in the rhetorical tradition, subordinates rhetoric to dialectic, unlike Aristotle.[75]) Although rhetoric, the art of persuasion, may be used to indoctrinate fixed ideas, it is far more effective if it instead plants a seed in the reader, which is then cultivated by the reader's active participation, and ultimately results in that seed being "vouchsafed immortality."

This conception of reading as writing is integral to rhetorical theory and practice. Foremost among these practices was the accommodation of poetic interpretation to ethics. Kathy Eden sees Plutarch as an early advocate of this theory of poetic interpretation:

> [Plutarch] understands the literary interpretive process itself as *accommodation* in the radical sense of the term: as a coming to feel at home with the literary text, a process of making it familiar. ... Boldly subordinating formal to ethical concerns, Plutarch places correction of texts [Quintilian's second of four activities of *enarratio poetarum*] in the service of the correction of young moral characters.[76]

Reading, then, requires that a text be made familiar by assimilating its meaning to the reader's ethical beliefs, as, for example, *Ovide moralisé* accommodates Ovid's epic to Christian ethics. Indeed, near the end of *Ovide moralisé*, the poem warns that reading Ovid's text literally "would be of little profit and great obscurity" and that "another sense, another meaning" must be sought.[77] Likewise, the reader of the *Hekatompathia* must seek another meaning because the sequence in its published order ends bizarrely, with Cupid's repudiation and death, a blasphemy according to Sonnet 18. However, unlike *Ovide moralisé*, the *Hekatompathia* is not intended to be assimilated to the reader's preexisting beliefs, but to the concealed beliefs of the poet. To accomplish this, the reader must apply rhetorical reading practices to discover the author's intended ethos, presumably one appropriate for love poetry. Indeed, Sonnet 1's headnote suggests that although his work describes love as the product of *miserable accidentes* and the cause of *despaire*, another contrary meaning must be sought: *the contrarietie ought not to offend* the reader, *if the nature & true qualitie of a love passion bee well considered* (1.HN).

The *Hekatompathia* is stuffed with artifices: its headnotes, sidenotes, prefaces, bibliographic features, and glaring anomalies. With respect to anomalies, as discussed in the previous chapter, Michael Riffaterre recognizes their importance: any breach in decorum, error, rule-breaking, or "ungrammaticality" demands the reader's attention. Recognizing and interpreting these breaches is indispensable to our exegesis of the *Hekatompathia*. Readers often mistakenly dismiss ungrammatical texts as a lapse in the poet's workmanship. Bacon warns his reader against this in the *To the frendly Reader* preface, explaining to his readers that a poet may choose to *falter in his Poeme, when his matter requireth it*.

An ungrammatical text, though initially indeterminate, is brought to significance by the reader: "The system of inescapable ungrammaticalities makes *reading a restrictive process*," according to Riffaterre, and until the ungrammaticalities are removed, the reader's task is unfinished.[78] Ungrammatical text—for example, seemingly irrelevant digressions— occur often in the *Hekatompathia*. These are not lapses but alarm bells intended to grab the reader's attention and encourage an exegetical effort. John of Garland identifies six such "vices" to avoid in a poem:[79]

1. Incongruous arrangement of parts
2. Incongruous digression from the subject
3. Obscure brevity
4. Incongruous variation of styles
5. Incongruous variation of subject matter
6. An awkward ending

John offers the above list as faults to avoid, but we can treat it as a list of intentional breaches of decorum that may be used to provoke a reader's exegetical interest. Bacon employs each of John's listed faults at least once: the first, by scrambling 83 sonnets; the second in a longwinded story about Hebe (92); the third in a metrically truncated line (56); the fourth

in the strange alternations in meter of a Neo-Latin poem (45); the fifth in
a long discussion of labyrinths that is largely irrelevant to the sonnet's true
concern (95); the sixth in the burial of Cupid that ends the sequence (100).

That anomalies in written works require interpretation was understood by Cicero, who identifies discrepancies between a writer's words and
intentions, ambiguities, and contradictions as three hermeneutically significant anomalies.[80] Socrates, in the *Protagoras*, interprets an ode of
Simonides, and upon detecting contradiction, compares the effect of it to
getting hit by a good boxer—"things went dark and I felt giddy" (339E). A
long discussion of the meaning of various words follows, and ultimately,
it is concluded that the understanding of these words must be consistent
with "the general character and intention" of the poem, which "is indeed
an elegant and well-thought-out production" (344C). The intended meaning of Simonides's poem—the difficulty of practicing virtue—is clear
enough, and the reader must construe the meaning of various polyvalent
words to reflect the poem's intended meaning. The grammar of the whole
takes precedence over the grammar of the parts—a precept frequently
enunciated.[81] This is the most important requirement of decorum. (Puttenham claims to have written a whole book on the subject of decorum.[82])
Sometimes it seems that the *Hekatompathia*'s poet honors decorum more
"in the breach than the observance." When Bacon indulges in obfuscation,
digression, imprecise language, irrelevant glosses, and contradiction, then
beware, for he is subtly providing information that is necessary to properly
read the poem or solve the Puzzle.

The concordantial text

The Puzzle includes an indexing system that consists of hundreds of
intratextual links, which is part of both the Heuristic and Precision Systems, as described in the introductory chapter. Although the *Hekatompathia*'s application of intratextual links is unique, it is based on certain
longstanding practices that authors used in creating, and readers in interpreting, texts. Carol Kaske invented the term "concordantial reading" to
describe the practice of finding intratextual linkages: repetitions of images,
words, cadences, ideas, or anything of significance within a text. She calls
this "motif hunting" a "fruitful critical method" and applies it to the exegesis of Spenser's poetry. She identifies other critics who have applied this
method, including Northrop Frye and A. C. Hamilton, "who established
that repeated images constitute one important structure in the *Faerie
Queene*," and later, "James Nohrnberg and Stephen Barney also emphasized repeated images." She argues that this discovery of intratextual relations ought to be conducted prior to considering allegoresis or tracing

allusions.[83] The *Hekatompathia* is a tissue of such concordantial linkages created by repetition. In the previous chapter, we observed that the Sequential Ties work through the repetition of words or images. Such intratextual links are essential to reading the work: key themes such as love's double nature, the uniqueness of the speaker's love, and the paradoxical coincidence of opposites serve to "truss up" the work into an organic whole.[84]

Kaske maintains that concordantial composition and reading practices long predate Spenser. For example, Jean Leclercq postulates that monks read Scripture by the discovery of hook-words: "each word is like a hook, so to speak; it catches hold of one or several others which become linked together and make up the fabric."[85] Kaske points to the printed concordances widely available in Spenser's time and believes that they were not merely a convenience, but "constituted a statement about the common threads with which God had stitched his book together and about the proper way to read it."[86] Luther advocated that Scripture be "interpreted by a comparison of passages from everywhere." Therefore, "Renaissance exegetes urged readers to follow up internal cross-references."[87] Kaske argues that a consequence of this practice of Scriptural "image-hopping" provided the secular "poet with a divinely sanctioned model for his global structures."[88] She refers to collected concordances as "distinctions" or "*distinctiones*." (Rita Copeland refers to similar devices as *ordinatio*, as discussed in Chapter 3.) Kaske writes:

> In the Middle Ages and the Renaissance, these distinctions were sometimes culled and collected in their own freestanding book, properly called a *distinctiones*... an alphabetical dictionary of symbols, a selective concordance with quoted content and comments. Spenser composed concordantially, by which I mean that he imitated the Bible as portrayed by the *distinctiones*, in that he wrote with a concordance of his own poem in mind and expected readers to compile one too.[89]

Kaske created an index of some of the *Faerie Queene*'s repeated images, which accomplishes for it what "a *distinctiones* does for the Bible."[90] She cites Langland and Dante as predecessors in this practice of organized, repeated images.[91] The importance of repeated images extends far beyond symbol definition or other grammatical use: they often define a work's structure. Douglas Bush refers to these "sonorous and repeated key-words" as "welding rivets."[92] They may reveal the schemata that structures the work, or the poem's fore-conceit or *architektonike*.[93] In summary, cataloging a work's images, words, and themes, as Kaske did for certain images in the *Faerie Queene*, can prove valuable in the exegesis of a text.

The *Hekatompathia* is a treasury of intratextual and intertextual references, not only to the other poems explicitly cited in its headnotes but also to Renaissance systems of thought and a broad literary canon that spans from antiquity through the Renaissance. The Puzzle makes extensive use of concordantial links to reveal the true order of the sequence's sonnets (Sequential Ties and, as described below, Index Ties). The reader must engage in a close scrutiny of the text's concordantial links as they are one of the Puzzle's fundamental mechanisms. Although the meanings of the words or images in concordantial links may at times be unclear or lost due to the passage of time, the Puzzle's use of overlapping links and other redundant mechanisms creates robustness.

The significance of the images that underlie concordantial links may be either unique to a given text or based on conventional symbolic imagery. In the latter case, the puzzle-solver's effort to discern concordantial links requires that he or she make judgments about the literary or cultural context of words, images, or tropes. Often these are hallowed symbols that the reader is expected to recognize. Rosemond Tuve detects an "Elizabethan demand for a unified and coherent meaning" and, further, that these images or symbols express "a coherent meaning rationally imposed by the author and rationally apprehensible by the reader."[94] Kenneth Borris sees in this period a "distinctive new vogue for hieroglyphic signification" and "new interest in imagistic representation."[95] According to Northrop Frye, the reader must be versed in the "language of symbolism":

> One of the functions of the literary critic is to be a grammarian of imagery, interpreting the symbolic systems of religion and philosophy in terms of poetic language... In Elizabethan criticism, for instance, the importance attached to symbolic grammar comes out in the mythological hand-books, the elaborate allegorical commentaries on Virgil and Ovid, and the textbooks of rhetoric, in which every conceivable mode of utterance is studied and classified with what seems to us now the mere exuberance of pedantry.[96]

Myths, images, and archetypes were hieroglyphs whose values were known to learned Elizabethans, and the meanings of these images or symbols will prove indispensable to our reading of the *Hekatompathia*. Tuve insists that imagery must not be thought of as ornamental but as functional. Although images did play a role in producing an emotive response, their function as signs must not be overlooked. According to Borris, in this period, images are reflections of a perfect and unchanging higher reality, and this correspondence between an image and its universal meaning is defined by various venerable sources.[97] These include revered poems, prose works such as those of Ebreo and Castiglione, emblem books, iconographic handbooks, and encyclopedic compilations such as Boccaccio's *Genealogia deorum gentilium* and Natale Conti's *Mythologiae*. Bacon employed both of these compilations in his analyses of myth in *The Wisdom of the Ancients*.[98] S. K. Heninger tells us that a poet of this time has no need to "fabricate metaphors, they lie everywhere ready to his pen."[99]

The recognition of these culturally substantive images must sometimes be our starting point in interpretation. This is the case with the *Faerie Queene*, according to Frye: "To demonstrate a unity in *The Faerie Queene*, we have to examine the imagery of the poem rather than its allegory. It is Spenser's habitual technique, developing as it did out of the emblematic visions he wrote in his nonage, to start with the image, not the allegorical translation of it."[100] An earlier generation of critics (e.g., Frye, Tuve, and Edgar Wind) recognized that signifiers must often be read metonymically (that is, as culturally substantive allegoresis); in contrast, competing literary theories, including New Criticism and Leavisism, would often undervalue historical context in reading a text. Many of the *Hekatompathia*'s images are only meaningful in the context of the period's literary culture, which was indebted to the Florentine Platonism of the prior century. Tuve suggests, "The real reasons for the character of their images lie not in Renaissance poetic but in Renaissance philosophy."[101] C. S. Lewis speaks of a "philosophical iconography" appearing both in painting and literature, and documented in various sixteenth-century handbooks.[102] This principle also applies to other works of the medieval and early modern periods: for example, the images of the *Commedia* must be read within the context of its philosophical/theological system. James Simpson berates the view of Benedetto Croce, which he characterizes as follows: "What is significant about the philosophical content of Dante's *Commedia* is not what Dante learns, but what the experience of learning feels like." Simpson believes that instead, such texts should be read as the philosophical arguments that they were intended to be. Further, he complains that "Croce's hostility toward 'scientific' poetry is shared by many influential schools of twentieth-century Anglo-American criticism as well (Leavisism and the New Criticism, for example)."[103] Although New Criticism and Leavisism have long since passed their zenith, our understanding of the complex intellectual systems of this period is still incomplete, and thus we may lack the necessary historical context to comprehend some aspects of a text. An important consequence of solving the Puzzle is that it reveals the philosophical system upon which the sequence is built—no small prize for the puzzle-solver's efforts.

The *Hekatompathia*'s system of intratextual links

The *Hekatompathia* includes among its sonnets approximately a dozen that consist mostly of a list of phrases. These phrase-list sonnets are indices that aid the puzzle-solver in restoring the sequence to its proper order. According to M. B. Parkes, beginning in the mid-twelfth century, a new concern with order drove the development of new organizational techniques:

> [There was] a drive to reorganize inherited material in a new, systematic way, to make *auctoritates* not only accessible but accessible in terms of new ways of thinking. ... The application of scholastic method demanded closer scrutiny of the arguments, and the reorganization of the material according to topics produced the need for more ostensible guides to the new organization to facilitate reference. ... The notion of *compilatio* not only gave rise to a sophisticated literary form but also promoted the development of a new kind of apparatus for use alongside existing texts: the *tabula* or alphabetical index. By employing a new *ordinatio* the *tabula* provided a means of access to subordinate topics within the existing *ordinatio* of a work.[104]

The most obvious mechanism that might be used to specify the true *ordinatio* of the *Hekatompathia*'s scrambled sonnets is a *tabula* or index. The work's phrase-list sonnets, uncommon and somewhat alien to the sonnet form, are an obvious place to look for some reordering directive from the poet. Indeed, an early modern reader would likely recognize these phrase-list sonnets as ordering devices because mnemonic devices in this period, such as the *Ars Memoriae*, rely upon ordered images.[105] In the practice of the *Ars Memoriae*, images of the things to be remembered are assigned to an imagined physical place. The practitioner might visualize a building with many different rooms, and then assign a particular image or set of words to each room of the building. The practitioner then visits the rooms in a specific order, which not only reinforces memory by the use of images but also allows the recall of a collection of items in a prescribed order. The *Ars Memoriae* is fundamentally an association of images (*imagines*) and places (*loci*): place-logic is used as a recall mechanism.[106] Places act as a receptacle or treasure chest in which memories are stored. Bacon had a special interest in mnemonic mechanisms, including the *Ars Memoriae*, and the ways in which information may be organized.[107]

Sonnet sequences have a modular structure: each sonnet is a standard, independent unit within a collection of sonnets. The *Ars Memoriae* is naturally applicable to a sonnet sequence because, just as a building is divided into subunits of rooms, a sonnet sequence is divided into subunits of sonnets, and like rooms, each sonnet has a physical location in the sequence. Donne recognized an analogy between sonnets and rooms, writing, "We'll build in sonnets pretty rooms."[108] A sonnet is a *topos* in both senses of the word (place, topic): a sonnet, as is the case with any short poem, must be concerned with a single argument or topic, and it resides at a particular location within the poetic collection. The position of a sonnet within a sequence is often critical because the context of adjacent or nearby sonnets can impact our interpretation of it.

Lists and tables, employed throughout the Middle Ages, became even more popular in the early modern period, in part through the influence of Ramist rhetorical theory (although, as discussed above, Bacon was no fan of Ramus). The commonplace notebooks that were popular in this period often utilized an index to reference subject matter. The ongoing importance of these practices can be seen when, decades later, Bacon applied the *Ars Memoriae* to his program for the reform of natural philosophy. Rhodri Lewis reveals the ambitious goals toward which these practices were aimed:

> The *ars memoriae* could only realize its full potential as a means of organizing, arranging and juxtaposing natural historical data, itself a crucial stage preparatory to his new inductive methodology; Bacon labelled this phase of enquiry *experientia literata* ('literate experience'), and characterized it as a 'kind of sagacity.' ... Bacon leaves us in no doubt that he viewed the *ars memoriae* as a rationally constructed intellectual tool that provided a 'prenotion' of where one could search for a particular datum or set of data. ... Accordingly, [quoting Bacon] 'we must fashion *Tables*, and *Structured Sets of Instances* [*Coordinationes Instantiarum*], marshalled in such a way that the intellect can get to work on them.'[109]

The *Hekatompathia*'s phrase-list sonnets are called "Catalog Sonnets" throughout this study. These tables or indices are essential components of both the Puzzle's Heuristic and Precision Systems. A Catalog Sonnet is a list of intratextual links or concordances: its phrases or lines are cross-references to like images or ideas in other sonnets. One Catalog Sonnet, Sonnet 89, consists of 12 sententiae, each occupying a full line; in contrast, Sonnet 98 consists of mostly half-line phrases. Sonnet 89 is marked as a list of like items by its use of anaphora: each of its 12 sententiae begins with "Love," and each presents an image of love. Sonnet 77 makes a similar use of anaphora: it has 14 lines that begin with "Time," each describing one of time's miserable effects. Sonnet 92 lists 12 gods and their mythical attributes; Sonnet 54 enumerates the facial features of the beloved. These sonnets follow a practice similar to that found in the *Ars Memoriae*, acting as memoranda. A Catalog Sonnet provides this function for the other sonnets of the Series in which it falls, and sometimes for an adjacent Series as well. The Catalog Sonnets, which contain hundreds of intratextual links, are a critical component of the Precision System. The number and complexity of the *Hekatompathia*'s intratextual links might surprise us, but complex systems were common in the sixteenth century. In Juan de Celaya's "The Geometry of the Mind" (Fig. 4.1), for example, many topics are interlinked in a complex network, an example of an incredibly elaborate place-logic.[110]

Fig. 4.1 **The geometry of the mind (1525): place-logic with a network of link**
By permission, Bibliothèque nationale de France

In a subset of Catalog Sonnets that I call "Index Sonnets," the order of phrases is significant (in other Catalog Sonnets, it is not). Index Sonnets are ordered pointers to the sonnets in a Series that specify the order of those sonnets, as shown schematically in Fig. 4.2. The figure assumes the consecutive assignment of the numbers 1, 2, 3, and 4 to the sonnets in their original order. The Index Sonnet's phrases (depicted as arbitrary single words for convenience), like the hints in a crossword puzzle, link to sonnet lines (again, depicted as arbitrary single words). The order of the Index Sonnet's phrases, in concert with these linkages, defines a new order for the sonnets: 3, 2, 4, 1.

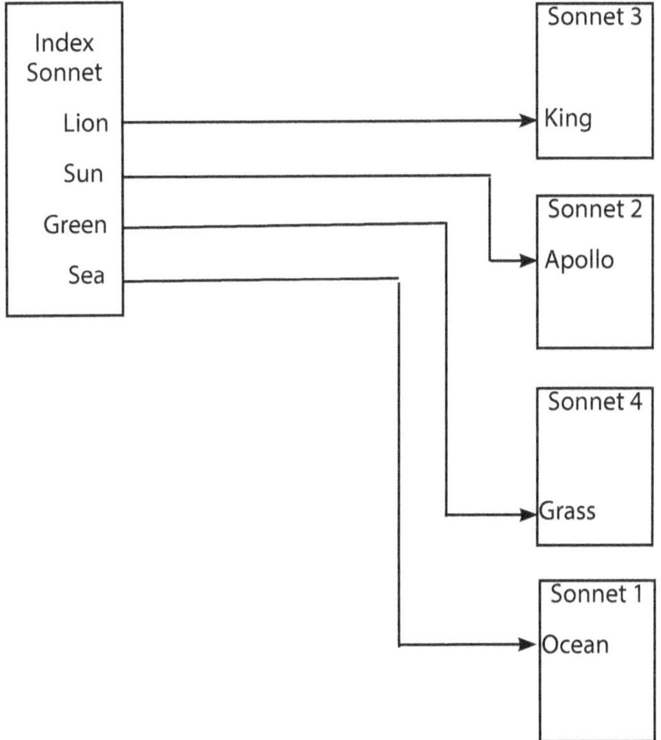

Fig. 4.2 How the Index Sonnet specifies sonnet order

Index Sonnet pointers are called "Index Ties" throughout this study. In the more general case of the Catalog Sonnet (which does not disclose order), Catalog Sonnet pointers are called "Catalog Ties," and the targeted sonnet lines to which they point are called "CipherLines." CipherLines are an essential component of the cryptographic or Precision System, which will be discussed in Chapter 6. The links between Catalog Ties and CipherLines may be obvious, such as when a common word or image is shared, or more subtly, as when a poetic conceit must be interpreted. Fig. 4.3 shows how one Catalog Tie in Catalog Sonnet 89 points to the CipherLine of Sonnet 86. The Catalog Tie, *Love is a wanton Childe and loves to brall* (89.11), shown in bold, links to the CipherLine, *And cumber heedelesse heartes with fierce assault* (86.10), also shown in bold. The subject of both lines is Cupid, and both characterize him as aggressive: *wanton* and *loves to brall* in the Catalog Sonnet and as perpetrating a *fierce assault* in the target sonnet.

The process of finding the links between Catalog Ties and their targeted CipherLines is often straightforward but sometimes subtle. The puzzle-solver must examine each of a Catalog Sonnet's pointers and find a similar image or thought among nearby sonnets, either in the same Series or an adjacent Series.

A Catalog Sonnet's determination of CipherLines is augmented by other catalogs or lists. In the Puzzle's second Stage, the Index Sonnet acts in concert with a Catalog Sonnet in selecting the CipherLine. Fig. 4.3 shows three pointers to Sonnet 86's CipherLine, one from Catalog Sonnet 89, another from Index Sonnet 98, and a third from the *Quid Amor* poem (described below), all acting in concert to identify the CipherLine. The operation of these three pointers in parallel provides overdetermination in the selection of the CipherLine. The links between these pointers and the CipherLine are strong. Both Index Sonnet 98's pointer and Sonnet 86's CipherLine use the same word, *fierce*, to describe the manner in which Cupid wields his power. Index Sonnet 98's pointer is very similar to Catalog Sonnet 89's pointer: Index Sonnet 98's first half line, *Love is a Brain-sicke Boy* (98.3), has nearly the same meaning as the Catalog Sonnet 89's *Love is a wanton Childe* (89.11). Also, *fierce by kinde* (98.3) is close in meaning to *loves to brall* (89.11).

Quid Amor is an unnumbered Neo-Latin poem of 39 hexameters that appears between Sonnets 98 and 99. It contains, by my count, 89 descriptions of love, most of which are two or three words long. This odd poem is monotonous, and few would think it has any aesthetic value. The poem's phrases often repeat phrases or images found in other sonnets, and thus it is a clear candidate for playing a role in CipherLine selection. Indeed, the *Quid Amor* poem is a special instance of a Catalog Sonnet: it serves as a master Catalog Sonnet, pointing to all CipherLines in the sequence. It will be referred to as the "*Quid Amor* Catalog" or "QA Catalog" throughout this study. The QA Catalog is reproduced in Appendix B, Fig. B.6: its 89 phrases have been assigned identifiers, starting with QA1 and ending with QA89.

For the Puzzle's second Stage, the use of the three independent pointers, as shown in Fig. 4.3, greatly improves the puzzle-solver's ability to

Catalog Sonnet (89.7-12)

Loue doth much harme through Iealosies assault; (7) ,,
Loue once embrast will hardly part againe; (8) ,,
Loue thinks in breach of faith there is no fault; (9) ,,
Loue makes a sporte of others deadly paine; (10) ,,
Loue is a wanton Childe and loves to brall. (11) ,,
Loue with his warre brings many soules to thrall. (12) ,,

Quid Amor Catalog (QA.1-8)

Quid sit amor, qualisque, cupis me scire magistro?
Est Veneris proles: coelo metuendus, et Orco;
Et levior ventis; et fulminis ocyor alis;
Pervigil excubitor; fallax comes; invidus hospes;
Armatus puer; insanus iuuenis; novitatis
Questor, belli fautor; virtuti inimicus;
Splendidus ore, nocens promisso; lege tyrannus;
Dux caecus; gurges viciorum; noctis alumnus;

Index Sonnet (98.1-6)

Harke wanton youthes, whom Beawtie maketh blinde,
And learn of mee what kind a thing is Loue;
Loue is a Brainsicke Boy, and fierce by kinde;
A Willfull Thought, which Reason can not moue;
A Flattring Sycophant; a Murd'ring Thiefe;
A Poysned choaking Bayte; a Tysing Griefe;

Target Sonnet (86.7-12): CipherLine = 10

They paint him blinde in that he cannot spy
What diffrence is twixt vertue and default.
With Boe in hand, as one that doth defie,
And cumber heedelesse heartes with fierce assault: 10
His other hand doth hold a brand of fire,
In signe of heate he makes through hot desire.

(Only a portion of each poem is reproduced.)

Fig. 4.3 CipherLine selection using Catalog, Index, and QA Ties

correctly determine the CipherLine. Although the link between any one of
the three pointers and the CipherLine may be less than certain, taken
together, the CipherLine selection is clear. In the case of the QA Catalog,
because it contains so many phrases and covers the entire work rather
than just one or two Series, its phrases will likely point to multiple lines

across the work, making it less useful in the earlier Stages of the Puzzle. However, in the later Stages of the Puzzle, after many QA Catalog pointers have been assigned, and with fewer sonnets left in the sequence to consider, its pointers to CipherLines become more useful.

The links between Catalog Ties and CipherLines may be expressed as a two-column table with the Catalog Tie phrases in the left column and the targeted CipherLines in the right column. (To a software engineer, this looks like an index in a relational database system.) These tables are essential to restoring the *Hekatompathia*. The essential act in the exegesis of this work, then, is to fill in the entries in various tables. This table-filling is fundamental to Bacon's process of scientific discovery, as discussed in the first chapter.

Surely, this process is foreign to our usual sense of what constitutes literary interpretation. Yet, that may be due to the prejudices of our own times. Jacques Derrida, with a reference to Bacon's "table of the sciences," writes, "Indexes are *specialized* dictionaries and encyclopedias [and] any possible *literary*, artistic, and *world* history must be capable of being expressed in a series of tables."[111] E. H. Gombrich, in discussing likeness in representation, argues:

> The correct portrait[,] like the useful map, is an end product on a long road through schema and correction. It is not a faithful record of a visual experience but the faithful construction of a relational model. ... I believe what we call the Renaissance artists' preoccupation with structure has a very practical basis in their needs to know the schema of things. For in a way our very concept of "structure," the idea of some basic scaffolding or armature that determines the "essence" of things, reflects our need for a schema with which to grasp the infinite variety of this world of change.[112]

Elaborate scaffolds and schemas were surely a habit of Renaissance artists, and above all for Bacon, for whom it was fundamental to his enterprise of establishing a new logic (organon) and experimental method. Throughout, the Puzzle challenges the puzzle-solver to discover the *Hekatompathia*'s schema; once discovered, the Precision System effectively confirms it.

Overdetermination, as illustrated in Fig. 4.3, provides the puzzle-solver with strong evidence for the restoration of the sonnet order; stronger evidence still is provided by the Precision System's cryptography. This overdeterminism is meant to overcome a fundamental limit in literary interpretation. According to Julianne Werlin:

> Writers mistrusted the aptitude and intentions of readers: as the period's clerics constantly warned, "private interpretation" could go

drastically awry through ignorance, willfulness, or simple error. In this respect Bacon, who felt he had "just cause to doubt" that his own work "flies too high over men[']s heads" shared his contemporaries' concerns. Bacon's philosophy is designed to give little scope to individual interpretation: only his much-touted method—rule-bound, constrained, and essentially collaborative—can transform the hermeneutic circle into a hermeneutic spiral.[113]

The links between Catalog Ties and CipherLines are effectively Baconian "tables of discovery." The reader becomes the maker (as in Sidney's *Defence*) but under the strict guidance of the poet. As in Bacon's experimental method, solving the *Hekatompathia*'s Puzzle is, by and large, the discovery of table entries.

Recognizing the Puzzle's intratextual links

The recognition of the Puzzle's intratextual links is an essential task that must be performed to solve it. For example, the discovery of a link between a Catalog Tie and a CipherLine is needed to decipher each character in the Puzzle's messages—a total of 135 links.[114] The Catalog Ties, Index Ties, Sequential Ties, and QA Ties contain, in aggregate, nearly 400 links, and account for the bulk of the work in solving the Puzzle.

Most often, recognizing a link comes down to finding a common word or image that appears in both the pointer (e.g., a Catalog Tie) and the target (e.g., the CipherLine). In the case where the target is a CipherLine, it may have special significance: it may encapsulate a sonnet's overall theme or represent a turning point in the sonnet's argument. Thus, an interpretive reading of a poem may aid in our recognition of its CipherLine. Recognition of a poem's critical lines or key conceits requires close reading. In assaying a poem, W. H. Auden asks, "Here is a verbal contraption. How does it work?"[115] Taking this contraption apart, piece by piece, and trying to understand how one part plays with another can be of great value. One approach to a formal process of evaluation is suggested by the work of Michael Riffaterre. In elaborating a poem, Riffaterre requires the recognition of a latent "hypogram," a key word or phrase that underlies a "complex network of relations" within a text. Recognizing the hypogram is an essential step in a decoding procedure that discovers significance through "restoration to a new order." The task of the reader is to recognize the "forms and hallowed symbols through a scrambled transmission." The writer has intentionally set a problem for the reader—a kind of puzzle. "Without questioning the intentional fallacy," Riffaterre writes, "the scrambled text is an icon of intention."[116] This applies to both the reading of individual poems and the architecture of the overall work.

Riffaterre's dictum of recognizing a poem's hypogram is particularly effective when reading short poems such as sonnets. In the *Hekatompathia*, repeated words or tropes often serve as a hypogram. Most sonnets are tightly composed around a single idea, with all of its elements strongly attached to that idea—even if the sonnet appears at first to be a "scrambled transmission." The hypograms of the *Hekatompathia* are usually not the arbitrary metaphors of the poet; rather, they are conventional symbols or images (see above discussion in "The concordantial text" section). Often the most essential technique in reading an individual sonnet is to identify an image or symbol that serves as the poem's hypogram, and then to recognize its conventional meaning within the appropriate Renaissance system of thought. Often a sonnet's headnote provides guidance in identifying the central image, theme, or hypogram.

Sometimes the CipherLine contains a poem's hypogram, leading to its identification. This superimposition of the Puzzle upon the work's symbols enforces their interpretation and thus indirectly provides an authorial gloss. The entanglement of the Puzzle with the recognition of symbols and images works in both directions: interpretation aids in the solution to the Puzzle, and the Puzzle adds to our literary understanding of the poem. Yes, this does present a sort of hermeneutic circle, but one in which one half, the Puzzle, is an over-constrained, quasi-mathematical system. As a result, reading is "a restrictive process," in much the same way that cryptanalysis, the unauthorized deciphering of cryptograms, is a restrictive process.[117] In cryptanalysis, the decipherer often cracks the key by recognizing the constraints upon that key. Our interpretation of a text is also subject to constraints, and only when exegesis allows the satisfaction of all constraints is the job of the reader finished.

The concept of a hypogram can also be applied at a higher level, across multiple sonnets. For example, we will find that in one Subseries, the words "fond love," or a nearly identical expression, appear in each of the sonnets of that Subseries. Upon restoration, the *Hekatompathia* is a highly structured work that is governed by a comprehensive framework built upon well-defined images and symbols. Every Series of sonnets—indeed, every individual sonnet—has its proper place and function within the highly structured framework of this elaborate and organic work.

5

Stage 2: Reason Prevails

The Puzzle's first Stage (solved in Chapter 2) defines the Puzzle's crypto-graphic system (polyalphabetic and polyphonic), specifies two types of cryptographic tables (Recta and Aversa), and allows the puzzle-solver to decipher a short message. The deciphered message reveals that the Lioness Design is an icon of love and a rubric that marks the beginning of a Series. Yet many questions remain unanswered. A third type of cryptographic table, Orchema, whose importance is emphasized in the Puzzle's instruc-tions, remains undefined. The function of the Lioness Design was revealed, but whatever function the other Designs may serve is yet unknown. Indeed, the time and difficulty spent in solving the Puzzle's first Stage seems incommensurate with the modest revelation concerning the Lioness Design's role as a rubric, and this suggests that there is more to discover. Another motivation for further investigation is the assortment of literary problems previously discussed, including the work's first head-note, strange ending, structural flaws, self-contradictions, and eccentric glosses. Clearly much work remains, both cryptographic and literary, and this pushes us to look for the Puzzle's next Stage.

The message deciphered in the Puzzle's first Stage revealed that the Lioness Design marks the lead sonnet of each Series. In Chapter 3, we found that the *Hekatompathia*'s first two Series (Sonnets 2–10; Sonnets 11–17), each headed by a Lioness Sonnet, are a carefully organized dis-course that introduces the work's fundamental model for understanding love—its twofold nature and twin powers. The logical development of the sequence's first 17 sonnets, along with the Sequential Ties that link one sonnet to the next, confirm that these sonnets are correctly ordered as published. However, the remainder of the work's sonnets exhibit disorder and we may wonder whether the *Hekatompathia* follows the practice of ruin discussed in the previous chapter. Is the poet's intentional ruin of his work on this scale possible?

The MLIP Subsequence, which the poet describes as his *long farewell to Love and all his tyrannie* (title page), is clearly demarcated by its running title, *My Love is Past*, blazoned above each of the Subsequence's 23 poems. On examination, there is considerable evidence that the presented order of these poems is wrong. The most striking example is Sonnet 90, in which the speaker recants and returns submissively to the god Love, the very god that imprisons him (10, 14–15). With its pietistic tone and expression of repentance, Sonnet 90 is directly opposed to every other poem in the MLIP Subsequence, excluding the Epilogue. It is absurdly positioned at the Subsequence's midpoint, but it should instead fall at the end, or just beyond the end, of the Subsequence.

The Epilogue also has a pietistic tone, and its headnote characterizes it differently from the other 100 poems of the sequence: *more like a praier than a Passion*. Both Sonnet 90 and the Epilogue are Neo-Latin translations of Petrarch's poems: Sonnet 90, a *paraphrastic* (HN) translation, is based on *Canzoniere* 364; the Epilogue, which is *faithfully translated* (HN), is based on *Canzoniere* 365. (There are 366 poems in the *Canzoniere*.) The adjacency of these poems in the *Canzoniere* might suggest that these two poems should be adjacent to one another in the reordered *Hekatompathia*. Indeed, as revealed below, after reordering the Subsequence using the Index Sonnet and other mechanisms, these poems end up next to each other, just as they are in the *Canzoniere*.[1]

Another striking example of disorder in the MLIP Subsequence is found in Sonnet 100, which completely contradicts the next and final poem, the Epilogue, and the apothegm immediately below it. In Sonnet 100, Cupid is killed off, and a bitter epitaph is inscribed on his grave. In contrast, in the closing apothegm, Love's *labour* is said to be *light*. How can the speaker "stomp on Love's grave" in the sequence's penultimate poem and then characterize love as *light* in the apothegm below the sequence's final poem? Although we are naturally hesitant to reorder a sonnet sequence because it would seem to usurp the poet's authority, the sequence's deep flaws require that we do so. The need to reorder the poetic text began in the first Stage, which required that we reorder the individual lines of the Puzzle Sonnet. This Stage extends that notion of reordering the poetic text to the sonnets themselves.

Reordering the sonnets of the MLIP Subsequence

Where does the second Stage of the Puzzle begin? The first Stage, which is built around the Puzzle Sonnet, appears in the first three pages of the MLIP Subsequence, making it the natural place to look for the Puzzle's next Stage. Also, the MLIP Subsequence, conspicuously demarcated by the blazoning of its running title, is an unusual feature that attracts our attention.[2] The alternative region to consider, the 62 scrambled sonnets subsequent to the first two Series and prior to the MLIP Subsequence (Sonnets 18 through 79), surely represents a more formidable task that is best deferred.

The poet provides us with three different methods by which the MLIP sonnets may be reordered, which overdetermines the new sonnet order. The most valuable of these three methods is Sonnet 98, an Index Sonnet (described in the previous chapter). A second mechanism is the MLIP Subsequence's division into three Subseries (if a group of elements can first be sorted into subgroups, the sorting process is made far easier). The MLIP Subsequence may be reordered by first sorting each sonnet into one of the three Subseries and then rearranging the sonnets within each Subseries based on the plot-like development that occurs within each Subseries. Finally, Sequential Ties, as discussed in Chapter 3, are links between adjacent sonnets that tie the end of one sonnet to the beginning of the next.

In practice, the process I used to restore the sonnets to their proper order began by printing each of the MLIP sonnets on a separate piece of paper. I then sorted these pages based on the three methods described above. I first performed a rough sort based on the three Subseries (described below). The Index Sonnet was then used to sort the sonnets at a finer level. The logical progression within each Subseries also proved valuable in this fine-level sort. Obviously, the process of shuffling pages cannot be reproduced here, nor is it necessary to do so. Instead, the sonnets are reprinted in their restored order, along with commentaries that provide evidence for their position in the restored order. The sonnets are printed on lefthand (verso) pages and the commentaries on righthand (recto) pages. This chapter includes only the texts and commentaries of the first Subseries, for the purpose of demonstrating the reordering process; Addendum 1 ("L82 Series: Reason Prevails") in the second volume includes all texts and commentaries of the MLIP Subsequence.

The MLIP Subsequence consists of 23 sonnets: Sonnet 80 (the Puzzle Sonnet instructions), Sonnets 81 and 82 (the Puzzle Sonnet in two different forms), 18 numbered poems (Sonnets 83–100), the unnumbered Neo-Latin poem titled *Quid Amor* (which follows Sonnet 98), and the Epilogue. The position and order of the first three sonnets, Sonnets 80–82, are correctly ordered, as described in the commentary pages in Addendum 1. The position of the *Quid Amor* poem is fixed as immediately following Sonnet 98 by that sonnet's headnote. The Epilogue is naturally the last poem. This leaves us with 18 scrambled sonnets, Sonnets 83–100, that must be restored to their proper order. Curiously, this challenge is comparable to the one presented in the first Stage, in which the puzzle-solver must reorder the 18 lines of a sonnet. Of course, the number 18 is significant in the *Hekatompathia*: it is the number of lines in each sonnet.

Sonnet 98, reproduced below, is an Index Sonnet, a list of phrases or Index Ties that point sequentially to the Subsequence's sonnets, specifying a new order, as described in the previous chapter (see Fig. 4.2). It consists of two introductory lines followed by 28 phrases: 24 of these phrases occupy a half line (semicolons mark the division); 4 phrases occupy a full line (3, 4, 9, 18). Of these 28 phrases, 21 point to one of 20 MLIP sonnets (two phrases point to the same sonnet) and 7 are unused. The 20 MLIP sonnets to which a phrase points are the Subsequence's 18 scrambled sonnets (83–100), *Quid Amor*, and the Epilogue. Only the correctly ordered first three sonnets, which contain the Puzzle's first Stage (instructions, Pillar Sonnet, and Puzzle Sonnet), lack Index Ties.

> **Harke wanton youthes, whome** Beawtie **maketh blinde,**
> **And learne of me, what kinde a thing is** Loue;
> Loue **is a** Brainesicke Boy, **and fierce by kinde;**
> A Willfull Thought, **which Reason can not moue;**
>   **A** Flattring Sycophant; **a** Murd'ring Thiefe;   5
>   **A** Poysned choaking Bayte; **a** Tysing Griefe;
> A Tyrant **in his Lawes; in speach vntrue;**
> A Blindfold Guide; **a** Feather **in the winde;**
> **A right** * Chameleon **for change of hewe;**
> A Lamelimme Lust; **a** Tempest **of the minde;**   10
>   **A** Breach of Chastitie; **all vertues** Foe;
>   **A** Priuate warre; **a** Toilsome webbe **of woe;**
> A Fearefull Iealosie; **a** Vaine Desire;
> A Labyrinth; **a** Pleasing Miserie;
> A Shipwracke **of mans life; a** Smoaklesse fire;   15
> A Sea **of teares; a** lasting Lunacie;
>   **A** Heauie seruitude; **a** Dropsie Thurst;
>   **A** Hellish Gaile, **whose captiues are accurst.**   (98.1–18)

Fig. 5.1 lists Sonnet 98's Index Ties and the CipherLines to which they point. To allow for easy reference, I have assigned an identification number, from 1 to 28, to each Index Tie, which appears in the first column. The Index Tie appears in the second column. The third column provides the sonnet number and line number of the CipherLine to which each Index Tie points. The fourth column contains the CipherLine text. Because the Index Ties point sequentially to the sonnets in their restored order, the restored order of the 20 sonnets can be obtained by reading down the third column: 86, 93, 88, 99, etc.

ID	Index Tie	CL	CipherLine text
1	Loue is a Brainesicke Boy, and fierce by kinde	86.10	And cumber heedelesse heartes with fierce assault
2	A Willfull Thought, which Reason can not moue	93.6	For ill once past, which cannot turn againe.
3	A Flattring Sycophant	88.18	Can drawe my witts to woes at vnawares
4	a Murd'ring Thiefe		
5	A Poysned choaking Bayte	99.9	Of her my Sonne, whose beames had made me blinde
6	a Tysing Griefe;	87.17	And since Love was cause I trode a wry
7	A Tyrant in his Lawes		
8	in speach vntrue;	95.9	False Theseus like, my credite shall I craze
9	A Blindfold Guide	97.7	Phineus I am, that so tormented was;
10	a Feather in the winde		
11	A right * Chameleon for change of hewe	96.2	In funeral attire, her woonted hew
12	A Lamelimme Lust	83.2	In chaines of roses linked all araye,
13	a Tempest of the minde	98.18	A Hellish Gaile, whose captiues are accurst
14	A Breach of Chastitie	QA.26	Virgineae zonae ruptura; dolosa voluptas;
15	all vertues Foe	94.14	By seruing such an one as reackes no right:
16	A Priuate warre		
17	a Toilsome webbe of woe		
18	A Fearfull iealosie		
19	a Vaine Desire	84.17	For if they stay, he will obtaine at last,
20	A Labyrinth		
21	a Pleasing Miserie	92.13	But what is love's delight? To hurt each where
22	A Shipwracke of mans life	91.1	Ye captiue soules of blindefold Cyprians boate
23	a Smoaklesse fire	100.5	His brand had lost his force he gan to trye
24	A Sea of teares	85.10	How error was main saile; each wave a teare
25	a lasting Lunacie	89.4	Love is distraught of wit and hath no end
26	A Heauie seruitude	90.1	Me sibi ter binos annos unumque subegit
27	a Dropsie Thurst	90.2	Divus Amor, laetusque fui, licet ignibus arsi
28	A Hellish Gaile, whose captiues are accurst	Epi.9/7	durasque procellas (9); Collapsae animae (7)

Fig. 5.1 Index Sonnet 98: Index Ties and their targets

Sometimes an Index Tie exactly replicates a phrase or easily identified idea in the sonnet line to which it points (the CipherLine). In other cases, the Index Tie offers a hint or clue that requires some deduction or inference. Index Tie 8 provides an example:

Index Tie
In speech untrue (8)

CipherLine
False Theseus **like, my credite shall I craze** (95.9)

The target sonnet's headnote (95.HN) draws special attention to the myth of Theseus, and more specifically, the breach of faith he commits against Ariadne in lying to her. In the sonnet text (95.9–10), the speaker likens himself to Theseus in his untrustworthiness (*credite* means "trustworthiness;" *craze* means "to break"). Sometimes the discovery of a link requires knowledge of an underlying myth:

Index Tie	**CipherLine**
A Blindfold Guide (9)	Phineus **I am, that so tormented was** (97.7)

The sonnet does not tell us that Phineus was a blinded king of Thrace ("guide" can mean "leader;" OED 3a). Identification of this link requires that the puzzle-solver have knowledge external to the text: the mythical story of Phineus and the Harpies. Although *A Blindfold Guide* refers to Cupid and not Phineus, and *blindfold* does not mean a blind person, a reasonably specific (though inexact) hint is provided—like a modern cross-word puzzle's hints. While most links between Index Ties and CipherLines are reasonably straightforward, others require an understanding of the sonnet's source material, or the poetic tradition from which it arose. Sometimes, the sonnet's headnote supplies an important clue.

CipherLine Selection in the MLIP Subsequence

As discussed in the previous chapter and depicted in Fig. 4.3, the selection of CipherLines is overdetermined by the Index Ties, Catalog Ties, and *Quid Amor* Ties. Although only the Index Ties specify sonnet order, the Catalog Ties indirectly aid in reordering sonnets: the Catalog Ties point to the CipherLines of each sonnet, which reinforces the links between the Index Ties and those same CipherLines. Sequential Ties and the progressive plots of each Subseries further add to our confidence in our restoration of sonnet order.

The MLIP Subsequence contains two Catalog Sonnets, Sonnets 89 and 92. Catalog Sonnet 89 specifies the CipherLines of Sonnets 80–82 and the 7 sonnets of the first of three Subseries. Catalog Sonnet 92 specifies the CipherLines of the remaining sonnets of the MLIP Subsequence. Fig. 5.2 lists each of the Catalog Ties of Catalog Sonnet 89 and the CipherLines to which they point. The first and second columns show the line number and text of each Catalog Tie. (Only the first 12 lines of the Catalog Sonnet begin with "Love," which marks them as Catalog Ties.) The third column provides the sonnet and line numbers of the linked CipherLine, and the fourth column the text of that CipherLine. Not all lines of the Catalog Sonnet act as Catalog Ties and therefore some rows have blank entries.

Line	Catalog Tie	CL	CipherLine text
1	Loue hath delight in sweete delicious fare;	87.17	And since that Loue was cause I trode a wry
2	Loue neuer takes good Counsell for his frende;	88.18	Can drawe my witts to woes at vnawares
3	Loue author is, and cause of ydle care;	80.8	such idle leasure... the Authour had, when he framed
4	Loue is distraught of witte, and hath no end;		
5	Loue shoteth shaftes of burning hote desire;	99.9	Of her my Sonne, whose beames had made me blinde
6	Loue burneth more than eyther flame or fire;		
7	Loue doth much harme through Iealosies assault;		
8	Loue once embrast will hardly part againe;	93.6	For ill once past, which cannot turn againe.
9	Loue thinks in breach of faith there is no fault;	95.9	False Theseus like, my credite shall I craze
10	Loue makes a sporte of others deadly paine;	97.7	Phineus I am, that so tormented was
11	Loue is a wanton Childe and loves to brall.	86.10	And cumber heedelesse heartes with fierce assault
12	Loue with his warre brings many soules to thrall.	81.28	[whose] hande still Tyrant like to hurte is preste.
12	Loue with his warre brings many soules to thrall.	82.18	Whose hande still Tyrant like to hurt is prest.
(Line 12 points to both forms of the Puzzle Sonnet [81 and 82])			

Fig. 5.2 Catalog Sonnet 89: Catalog Ties and targeted CipherLines

The Structure of the MLIP Subsequence

A critical step in sorting the Puzzle Sonnet's 18 lines was to recognize its bipartite structure; similarly, the solution to the second Stage is facilitated by recognizing that the MLIP Subsequence is divided into three Subseries, subsequent to the initial three pages devoted to the Puzzle's first Stage. The first Subseries, which includes 7 sonnets scattered among Sonnets 83–100, I have called the "Fond Love Subseries," based on the poet's repeated use of "fond." In this Subseries, the speaker describes his painful experiences in love and attributes them to folly, which, he asserts, comes from a failure to honor reason. "Fond," which means infatuated, foolish, or silly (OED N2, 2), appears in 5 of the 7 sonnets (or their headnotes). In the remaining 2 sonnets, the appearance of "folly" and "reason" mark the sonnet as also belonging to this Subseries. In the beginning sonnets of this Subseries, the speaker bemoans the pain caused by his decision to abandon reason in favor of following his passion; in contrast, in the latter part of this Subseries, he appears to be more joyful and further removed in time from love's tyranny. The second Subseries also consists of 7 sonnets and is referred to as the "Scoff Subseries:" in these, the speaker angrily vituperates against love. The third Subseries, the "Love Discharged Subseries," consists of 4 sonnets: the speaker bids adieu to love.

After reordering the sonnets of the MLIP Subsequence, their sonnet numbers are (obviously) no longer sequential, and it is more convenient to reference them using a new numbering system that takes into account the structure of the reordered sonnets. This new set of identifiers is based upon the Series in which a sonnet falls in the new order. The MLIP Subsequence begins with the Puzzle Sonnet (in its two forms, Sonnets 81 and 82), and in our new identification system, "L82" is the prefix that prepends the sonnet identifier for the MLIP Subsequence. "L" indicates Lioness Sonnet, and Sonnet 82 is the first sonnet of the MLIP Subsequence that appears in normal form (Sonnet 81 appears as a pillar). The second term in this new identification system designates the Subseries that the sonnet falls under, and the third term gives the sonnet's position within the Subseries. Fig. 5.3 lists each Subseries in the first column, the range of the new identifiers in the second column, and the overall position of each Subseries in the reordered MLIP Subsequence in the third column.

Subseries	New Sonnet identifer	Position in Subsequence
Puzzle Sonnet	L82.PS.1–3	1–3
Fond Love	L82.FL.1–7	4–10
Scoff	L82.Scoff.1–7	11–17
Love Discharged	L82.LD.1–4	18–21
Lioness Sonnet 90	L90.H	22
Epilogue	Epilogue	23

Fig. 5.3 Sonnet identifiers for the restored order

"Sonnet Number Converters" allow for quick translation from one numbering system to the other (located at the end of this volume and in Appendix A of Vol. II).

Sonnets and commentaries appear on facing pages

The pages that follow reproduce each sonnet of the Fond Love Subseries, along with a facing commentary page, in a fashion similar to a facing translation. This allows the poetic text to be in view at the same time that the commentary is read. Above each sonnet are two numbers: the new sonnet number, in the form presented in Fig. 5.3, and the original sonnet number as it appears in the *Hekatompathia* (however, in Arabic rather than Roman numerals). In the reproduction of each sonnet, the CipherLine is marked with the letters "CL" to the right of the line to allow for quick identification. Each commentary page is divided into six standardized paragraphs that provide evidence concerning the restoration of sonnet order and the selection of CipherLines:

Subseries: Justification for placement in the specified Subseries.

Index Tie: Identifies the link between Index Tie and CipherLine.

QA Tie: Identifies the link between the QA Tie and the CipherLine.

Catalog Tie: Identifies the link between the Catalog Tie and CipherLine.

CipherLine: Commentary on the selected CipherLine.

Sequential Tie: Identifies the link to the next sonnet.

The text and commentaries for the 7 Fond Love Subseries sonnets appear on the following 14 pages. The text and commentaries for all L82 Subseries appear in Addendum 1.

L82.FL.1　　　　　86

MY LOVE IS PAST.

The sense of this Sonnet is for the most part taken out of a letter which
Aeneas Syluius wrote vnto his friend, to persuade him that albeit he
lately had published the wanton loue of *Lucretia* and *Euryalus*, yet hee
liked nothing lesse then such *fond Loue;* and that he nowe repented
him of his owne labour ouer idlely bestowed in describing the same.

S Weete liberty **restores my woonted ioy,**
　And bids me tell, how painters set to viewe
The forme of Loue **They painte him but a** Boy,
As working most in mindes of youthfull crewe:
　　They set him naked **all, as wanting shame**　　　　5
　　To keepe his secret partes or t' hide the same.
They paint him blinde in that he cannot spy
What diffrence is twixt vertue and default
With Boe in hand, **as one that doth defie,**
And cumber heedelesse heartes with fierce assault:　　CL
　　His other hand doth hold a brand of fire,
　　In signe of heate he makes through hot desire.
They giue him winges **to flie from place to place,**
To note that all are wau'ring like the winde,
Whose liberty fond Loue **doth once deface.**　　　　15
This forme to Loue **old paynters haue assignd:**
　　Whose fond effects if any list to proue,
　　Where I make end, let them begin to Loue.

The first of the 7 Fond Love Subseries sonnets, this poem enumerates Cupid's various powers and faults. This enumeration of negative qualities of the Subseries' subject, personified Love, makes for an appropriate introduction to the Subseries.

Fond Love Subseries: "Fond" appears three times, twice in the phrase *fond love* (HN, 15) and once in the phrase *fond effects* (17). This repetition is perhaps an indication that this sonnet serves as an introduction—the first sonnet of the Fond Love Subseries.

Index Tie: *Loue is a Brainesicke Boy, and fierce by kinde* (Index 1). *Brainesicke* (OED 1: mad, foolish, frantic) points to this sonnet's description of Cupid as *wanton* (HN), *wanting shame* (5), and not knowing the difference between *vertue and default* (8). Another link between the Index Tie and this sonnet is found in the description of Cupid as a warrior (9–10)—a warrior would be *fierce by kinde* (meaning "type"). Also, there is a link through the use of the same word *fierce* in both the Index Tie and the CipherLine (10).

QA Tie: *Armatus puer* (armed boy or boy roused to war; QA8). This is close to the Index Tie's *fierce by kinde*, the Catalog Tie's *loves to brall*, and the CipherLine's *fierce assault*.

Catalog Tie: *Love is a wanton Childe and loves to brall* (89.11). This strongly resembles the Index Tie: *brainesicke* and *wanton* both imply a corrupt mind, and *fierce* aligns with *loves to brall*. *Wanton*, which can mean lascivious (OED 2), points to *cumber heedless hearts* (his wanton behavior) in the CipherLine.

CipherLine: *And cumber heedelesse heartes with fierce assault (10).* This ties to *Fierce* (Index Tie), *armatus puer* (QA8), and *wanton/brall* (Catalog Tie). This sonnet characterizes Cupid as both powerful and a promoter of lasciviousness. Only this CipherLine characterizes Cupid in both ways, strongly linking it to both the Index Tie and the Catalog Tie. As discussed in Chapter 4, the speaker's heedlessness, his acquiescence to love, is the hidden conceit of this sonnet.

Sequential Tie: The sonnet ends with the speaker's assertion that for him, love has ended (*Where I make end*; 18), even if for others love is just beginning (*let them begin to Loue*; 18). (At the end of the Subsequence, the speaker will instead call for others to end their love, as he did, which frames the Subsequence.) The next sonnet recurrently asserts that the speaker's love has ended: *My Love is Past* (1, 7, 13).

L82.FL.2   93

MY LOVE IS PAST.

In the first and sixt line of this Passion the Authour alludeth to two sen-
tencious verses in *Sophocles*; whereof the first is,

> ὦ μῶρε, θυμὸς δ' ἐν κακοῖς οὐ ξύμφορον,
> *O foole, in euills fretting nought auailes.*   In Oedipo Colonaeo.

The second,

> τὸ γὰρ   In Trachniis.
> φανθὲν τίς ἂν δύναιτ' ἀγένητον ποιεῖν;
> *For who can make vndon what once is done?*

In the other two staffes following, the Authour pursueth on his matter, beginning and ending euery line with the selfe same sillable he vsed in the
first: wherein hee imitateth some Italian Poets, who more to trie their
witts, then for any other conceite, haue written after the like manner.

MY loue is past, woe woorth the day and how'r
When **to such folly first I did** encline,
Whereof **the very thought is bitter** sow'r,
And **still would hurte, were not my soule** diuine,
  Or did not *Reason* **teach, that care is vaine**   5
  For **ill once past, which cannot turne againe.**   CL
My *Loue* is past, blessed the day and how'r.
When **from so fond estate I did** decline,
Wherein **was little sweet with mickle** sow'r.
And **losse of minde, whose substance is** diuine,   10
  Or at the lest, expence of time in vaine,
  For which expence no *Loue* **returneth gaine.**
My *Loue* is past, wherein was no good how'r:
When **others ioy'd, to cares I did** encline,
Whereon **I fedde, although the taste were** sow'r,   15
And **still beleu'd** *Loue* **was some pow'r** diuine,
  Or some instinct, which could not worke in vaine,
  Forgetting, *Time well spent was double* **gaine.**

The two sententiae in the headnote assert that ruing the past is pointless because the past is irreversible, a theme taken up in the sonnet.[3] Curiously, the sonnet contends that the mind's *substance* (or soul) *is divine* (10), but that love is not *divine* (16).[4]

Fond Love Subseries: "Fond" appears in *fond estate* (8). The sonnet's concern throughout is the *woe* that love engenders; it is described as *bitter* (3), causing *hurte* (4), an *ill* (6), *losse of minde* (10), *expence of time* (11), *sow'r* (9, 15)—all consistent with other descriptions of love in this Subseries.

Index Tie: *A willfull thought which reason cannot move* (Index 2). This sonnet's concern and that of the two sententiae is with irreversibility or immovability (*cannot move*), which may be taken as the sonnet's hypogram. This sonnet presents reason and love as opposing forces with the hope that reason will prevail. This is evident in this Index Tie, line 5, in which there is an appeal to *Reason*, and in line 14, in which the speaker says that he had been irrationally inclined to *cares* (grief; OED 1).

QA Tie: *Irrationalis motus* (irrational emotion; QA39). This aligns with the Index Tie in which reason is powerless against love's usurpation of the speaker's will. This QA Tie encapsulates the sonnet's assertion that the emotions engendered by love and reason are opposed.

Catalog Tie: *Loue once embrast will hardly part againe* (89.8). This echoes the immovability of love found in the Index Tie and the second sententia. Love makes the lover immune to reason.

CipherLine: *For ill once past, which cannot turne againe* (6). In both the Catalog Tie and Index Tie, love once embraced is irreversible; the CipherLine, equated with the second sententia in the headnote, is also a statement of irreversibility. The Index Tie's *cannot move* and the Catalog Tie's *will hardly part againe* are equivalent to the CipherLine's *cannot turne*. This CipherLine combines the *evills* of the first sententia (in *ill*) with the inability to undo the past of the second sententia. Thus both sententiae suggest that this line is the CipherLine. The hypogram of this sonnet, irreversibility, also appears in the declaration *My Love is past*, which appears three times (1, 7, 13).

Sequential Tie: The failure of those in love to live by reason (5, Index Tie, QA Tie) is taken up in the next sonnet, *I long maintayned warre gainst Reasons rule* (1). *Vaine*, which appears here 3 times (5, 11, 17), appears twice in the next sonnet's headnote: *made after the selfe same vaine* (meaning "vein"); *his late vaine* [vain] *estate and follies*. Like this sonnet, the next recalls a foolish past in the first stanza. The first two stanzas of the next sonnet show a progression from foolishness to reason and wisdom: *Discretion graunts* (10); *guile is fettred fast and wisedome rules* (11); *heau'ns have better lot assign'd* (13); *witt and will to Reason doe retyre* (16).

L82.FL.3   **88**

MY LOVE IS PAST.

This whole Sonnet is nothing els but a briefe and pithy morall, and made
after the selfe same vaine with that, which is last before it. The two
first staffes, (excepting onely the two first verses of all) expresse the
Authours alteration of minde & life, and his change from his late vaine
estate and follies in loue, by a metaphore of the shipman, which by
shipwrakes chaunce is happely restoared on a sodeine vnto that land,
which he a long time had most wished for.

I Long maintayned warre gainst Reasons rule,
  I wandred pilgrime like in Errors maze,
I sat in Follies ship, and playde the foole,
Till on Repentance rocke hir sides did craze:
       Herewith I learne by hurtes alreadie past,   5
,,   That each extreme will change it selfe at last.
This shipwrackes chance hath set me on a shelfe,
Where neither Loue can hurte me any more,
Nor Fortunes hand, though she enforce her selfe;
Discretion graunts to set me safe on shoare,   10
       Where guile is fettred fast and wisedome rules,
       To punish heedeles hearts and wilfull fooles.
And since the heau'ns haue better lot assign'd,
I feare to burne, as hauing felte the fire;
And proofe of harmes so changed hath my minde,   15
That witt and will to Reason doe retyre:
       Not Venus nowe, nor Loue with all his snares
       Can drawe my witts to woes at vnawares.   CL

The first stanza looks back to the past; then, line 7 introduces the conceit of the "lucky shipwreck." Fortune has turned, and the speaker declares that love can no longer hurt him. The reason given for his newfound immunity to love's dangers is his resistance to guile (11) and heedfulness of dangers (12). The final couplet again insists that these potential dangers—*Love with all his snares*—will not prevail against his wits.

Fond Love Subseries: Although "fond" does not appear, *Follies* (3) and *foole* (3) tie this to the prior sonnet and the theme of Fond Love. *Reason* (1, 16) and *wisedome* (11), the opposite of foolishness, also place this sonnet in the Fond Love Subseries.

Index Tie: *flattring sycophant* (Index 3). The last two stanzas declare that from now on the speaker will be wary and not be fooled by love's *guile* (11), nor entrapped by love's *snares* (17). Love's *guile* and *snares* connect to the Index Tie because *sycophant* means an imposter or deceiver (OED 4).

QA Tie: *sycophanta bilinguis* (deceitful trickster; QA40). *Sycophanta* is a trickster (LS 1); *bilinguis* (literally "two-tongued") means deceitful or treacherous (LS II). The QA Tie and Index Tie share the English-Latin cognate *sycophant*.

Catalog Tie: *Loue neuer takes good Counsell for his frende* (89.2), implying that those in love heed bad advice. A sycophant tells deceptive tales, a form of bad counsel.

CipherLine: *Can drawe my witts to woes at vnawares* (18). When love draws *wits to woes at unawares,* it is being devious and misleading. The link to the QA Tie is clear, although another possibility for the CipherLine is *Loue with all his snares* (17). However, line 18 is a closer fit with the Index Tie, QA Tie, and Catalog Tie, all of which specifically refer to a clever trickster who threatens to outwit the speaker.

Sequential Tie: The theme of this sonnet, being guiled by love, continues in the next sonnet, where the speaker remembers how he was fooled: *Loue possest my mind* (7); *could not bide* (8); *made me blinde* (9). This entrapment is attributed to a failure of will in this sonnet (*willful fooles*, 12) as well as the next sonnet, where *Will* appears in line 10. In this sonnet, the speaker pledges never to be beguiled again; in the next, he promises to *practise now the... contrary* (14), and to immediately cutoff (*choake them streight*; 16) any foolish thoughts.

L82.FL.4   99

MY LOVE IS PAST.

This passion is an imitation of the first Sonnet in *Seraphine*, & grownded vpon that which *Aristotle* writeth * of the *Aegle*, for the proofe she maketh of her birdes, by setting them to behold the Sonne. After whom *Pliny* hath written, as foloweth:

       * Lib. 9. Hist. animal.

Aquila implumes etiamnum pullos suos percutiens, Subinde cogit aduersos intueri Solis radios: et si conniuentem humectantemque animaduertit, praecipitat e nido, velut adulterinum atque degenerem: illum, cuius acies firma contra steterit, educat.

       Nat. Hist. lib. 10. Cap. 1.

THe haughtie Aegle Birde, **of Birdes the best,**
   Before the feathers, of her younglinges growe,
She liftes them one by one from out theire nest,
To vewe the Sunne, **thereby her owne to knowe;**
   Those that behold it not with open eye,   5
   She lettes them fall, not able yet to flye.
Such was my case, when Loue **possest my mind;**
Each thought of mine, which could not bide the light
Of her my Sunne, **whose beames had made me blinde,**   CL
I made my Will **suppresse it with** Despight: 10
   But such a thought, as could abide her best,
   I harbred still within my carefull brest.
But those fond dayes are past, and halfe forgotte;
I practise now the quite cleane contrary:
What thoughtes can like of her, I like them not,   15
But choake them streight, for feare of ieopardy;
   For though that Loue **to some do seeme a** Toy,
   I knowe by proofe, that Loue is long annoy.

The theme that one must be wary of love continues here with an analogy to an eagle that trains its young to be wary of the dangerous sun. The sun, of course, is metaphorically the beloved. Chapter 9 discusses this metaphor in the commentaries on Sonnets 44 and 45.

Fond Love Subseries: Once again, love is characterized as a great danger that blinds the speaker (9). *But those fond dayes are past, and halfe forgot* (13) places the time of the speaker's love further in the past. It becomes clear that there is a progression of time over the course of this Subseries.

Index Tie: *A Poysned choaking Bayte* (Index 5). The speaker, once blinded by love, describes how he now carefully avoids slipping back into love's subjugation. The speaker imagines a defense by which if one is wary of love's return, it is possible to thwart it by quickly dismissing any thought of love (15–16). Thoughts are the bait that allowed love to possess his mind (7–8). Thus, love is *A Poysned choaking Bayte.*

QA Tie: *laethale venenum* (a lethal potion/seduction; QA51). "Seduction" is a figurative meaning of *venenum*, (LS II.A.2.b)—it literally means "potion." This aligns with the Index Tie because "seduction" can mean being tricked into accepting bait (OED 4: "an allurement")—love's potion.

Catalog Tie: *Loue shoteth shaftes of burning hote desire* (89.5). Throughout the *Hekatompathia*, beams of light that originate in the beauty of the beloved instill desire, the bait by which a lover is first entrapped. In this Catalog Tie, Cupid shoots dangerous arrows, and this points to the CipherLine, in which the beloved, figured as the sun, shoots dangerous beams that entrap the speaker. This link is strengthened by the use of *shaftes*, which can mean a "beam of light" (OED 2.g), pointing to the CipherLine's *beames.*

CipherLine: *Of her my Sunne, whose beames had made me blinde* (9). The sonnet's hypogram is love's (or the beloved's) beam or shaft of light, which is the *Bayte* (Index Tie) or *venenum* (QA Tie) that entraps the lover.

Sequential Tie: The conceit that love is an insidious bait continues in the next sonnet's headnote: *Love first went beyond him, by persuading him that all was golde.* The idea that love is dangerous, even if it seems a harmless *Toy* (17) is reflected in the next sonnet's opening line: *Youth made a fault through lightnes of Beleefe.*

L82.FL.5   87

MY LOVE IS PAST.

The Authour in the firste staffe of this Sonnet, expresseth how Loue first went beyond him, by persuading him that all was golde which glistered. In the second, hee telleth, how time broughte him to trueth, and Trueth to Reason: by whose good counsell he found the way from worse to better, & did ouergoe the malice of blinde Fortune. In the third staffe, he craueth pardon at euery man for the offences of his youth; and to Loue, the onely cause of his long errour, hee geueth his *vltimum vale*.

Youth made a fault through lightnes of Beleefe,
Which fond Beleefe *Loue* placed in my brest:
But now I finde, that Reason giues reliefe;   ”
And time shewes Trueth, and Wit, thats bought, it best;   ”
   Muse not therefore although I chaunge my vaine,   5
   He runnes too farre which neuer turnes againe.
Henceforth my mind shall haue a watchfull eye,   ”
Ile scorne *Fond Loue*, and practise of the same:
The wisedome of my hart shall soone descrie
Each thing thats good, from what deserueth blame: 10
   My song shalbe; *Fortune* hath spitte her spight,
   And *Loue* can hurt no more withall his might.
Therefore all you, to whome my course is knowne,
Thinke better comes, and pardon what is past:
I find that all my wildest Oates are sowne,   15
And Ioy to see, what now I see at last;
   And since that *Loue* was cause I trode a wry,   CL
   I heere take off his Bels, and let him flie.

The headnote summarizes a three-stage progression that occurs over the course of the Fond Love Subseries: each stage is associated with one of the sonnet's three stanzas. The first stanza describes how foolish youth is entrapped by love, but then reason brings relief. The second stanza describes the need to remain *watchfull* (7) and discriminating (10) lest love once again overtake the speaker. These two stanzas point back to themes of the first 4 sonnets of this Subseries. This is yet another mechanism by which the poet aids the puzzle-solver in restoring his sonnets to their proper order. (It is similar to the sidenote mechanism used in Sonnet 7, as discussed in Excursus 6.) The third stanza introduces a new topic, which points forward to the remaining sonnets of this Subseries. The headnote describes this stanza thus: *he craueth pardon at every man for the offences of his youth; and to Loue, the onely cause of his long errour, he geveth his ultimum vale.* Here, the speaker repents and dismisses love, and this willful act is expressed in the sonnet's final line in which he takes off love's bells. "Bell" means "prize" (OED III.7a), presumably a reference to the approbation that the speaker had previously awarded to love.

Fond Love Subseries: *Fond* appears in lines 2 and 8.

Index Tie: *A Tysing Griefe* (Index 6). The headnote's recapitulation begins with love's enticement: *persuading him that all was golde which glistered.* Enticement is also evident in lines 1–2, where love places *Beleefe* in the speaker's *brest,* and in the final couplet's *Loue was cause I trode a wry.* Enticement is said to result in fortune's *malice* (HN) and fortune having *spitte her spight* (11). Thus, the theme of love's enticement and its negative consequences is concisely expressed by the Index Tie.

QA Tie: *nocens promisso* ([love] harms by means of its promise or offer; QA14). *Promissum* literally means something put forward. This is close to the Index Tie's *Tysing* (enticing) *Griefe.*

Catalog Tie: *Loue hath delight in sweete delicious fare* (89.1). Here *fare* is a bait, or in other words, something *Tysing* (Index Tie), or *promisso* (QA Tie). This points to the CipherLine's *cause,* identified here as *sweete delicious* bait.

CipherLine: *And since that Loue was cause I trode a wry* (17). The Catalog Tie's *sweete delicious fare* is bait or enticement, which is the *cause* of the speaker going down a bad path (*I trode a wry* [*trode* is the past tense of "tread"]) This also links to the Index Tie, where love is *A Tysing Griefe,* and the QA Tie, where love entices by means of a promise. The central concern of this sonnet is how the speaker was led astray.

Sequential Tie: *I trode a wry* (17) ties to the next sonnet's *at last I found the way / To leaue the doubtfull Labyrinth of Loue* (1–2). One strays, or goes awry, in a labyrinth. Thus the Sequential Tie is a link between the speaker's memory of his having gone awry, as in a labyrinth, and his having *found the way / To leaue the doubtfull Labyrinth* (next sonnet, 1–2).

L82.FL.6   **95**

MY LOVE IS PAST.

A *Labyrinth* is a place made full of turnings & creekes, wherehence, he that is once gotten in, can hardly get out againe. Of this sorte * Pliny mentioneth foure in the world, which were most noble. One in *Crete* made by *Daedalus*, at the commaundement of king *Minos*, to shut vp the *Minotaure* in: to which monster the *Atheniens* by league were bound, euery yeere to send seuen of their children, to bee deuoured; which was perfourmed, till at the last, by the helpe of *Ariadne*, *Theseus* slewe the monster. An other he mentioneth to haue beene in *Aegipt*, which also *Pomponius Mela* describeth in his first booke. The third in *Lemnos*, wherein were erected a hundreth & fifty pillers of singuler workmanship. The fourth in *Italy*, builded by *Porsenna* king of *Hetru-ria*, to serue for his sepulchre. But in this Passion the Authour alludeth vnto that of *Crete* only.   *Lib. 36. ca 13.

T Hough somewhat late, at last I found the way
  To leaue the doubtfull Labyrinth of Loue,
Wherein (alas) each minute seemd a day:
Him selfe was Minotaure; whose force to proue
    I was enforst, till Reason taught my mind   5
    To slay the beast, and leaue him there behind.
But being scaped thus from out his maze,
And past the dang'rous Denne so full of doubt,
False Theseus like, my credite shall I craze,   CL
Forsaking her, whose hand did helpe me out?   10
    With Ariadne Reason shall not say,
    I sau'd his life, and yet he runnes away.
No, no, before I leaue the golden rule,
Or lawes of her, that stoode so much my friend,
Or once againe will play the louing foole,   15
The sky shall fall, and all shall haue an end:
    I wish as much to you that louers be,
    Whose paines will passe, if you beware by me.

The headnote discusses labyrinths at length, and the sonnet's first two stanzas are concerned with the Cretan labyrinth. At first it seems that this sonnet ought to link to Index 20, *A Labyrinth*; however, this Index Tie is too far forward, well outside the range of the Fond Love Subseries. The headnote's long pedantic digression about various labyrinths should make us suspect that the poet is toying with us. Is this sonnet really about labyrinths? Even a cursory reading finds that the story of Theseus is told not to remind us of his escape from the labyrinth, but of his betrayal of Ariadne. Starting with line 9, the sonnet's concern is the maintenance of faith, the speaker asking himself rhetorically whether he will be *false* like *Theseus* (9). He answers "no" in line 13. Curiously, the headnote's tedious discussion of labyrinths ends in the statement that *the Authour alludeth unto that of Crete only.* Taken at face value, this statement is so obvious as to be unnecessary. Indeed, its true import is that the stories of the other labyrinths are irrelevant because only the story of the Cretan labyrinth includes the true subject of this sonnet, an admonition about the breaching of faith. In reading the *Hekatompathia,* we must carefully consider anomalies in the text such as spurious digressions, because they often reveal poetic significance. At the same time, we must be wary of the poet's sand traps, such as Index 20 (*A Labyrinth*). That Index Tie is ultimately unused; its only purpose may be as a trap for the unwary puzzle-solver.

Fond Love Subseries: Although "fond" does not appear, "fool" and "reason," associated with Fond Love in prior sonnets, appear in *louing foole* (15), *Reason taught my mind* (5), and *With Ariadne Reason shall not say* (11).

Index Tie: *in speach untrue* (Index 8). The sonnet's focus is the speaker's promise not to be duped again by love, as Ariadne was once duped by the *False Theseus* (9).

QA Tie: *fallax comes* (deceitful companion; QA6). This accurately describes Theseus's betrayal of Ariadne. *Fallax* exactly matches the Cipher-Line's *false.*

Catalog Tie: *Loue thinkes in breach of faith there is no fault* (89.9). Again, a breach of faith, clearly points to the CipherLine.

CipherLine: *False Theseus like, my credite shall I craze* (9) is strongly linked to the Index Tie, QA Tie, and Catalog Tie. (*My credite* means trustworthiness [OED 2]; *craze* means to break, as in a breach of faith.) The central concern of this sonnet is breach of faith.

Sequential Tie: In the third stanza, the speaker pledges to never again succumb to love. This pledge is repeated in the next sonnet's headnote, where he is *to professe vnfainedlie, that his Loue is past.* Although such declarations are common in this Subseries, this and the next sonnet make their declarations with greater certitude—not unless the *sky shall fall* (16) and *unfainedlie* (HN). This greater resolution indicates that we are reaching the end of the Fond Love Subseries.

MY LOVE IS PAST.

The Authour in this passion alludeth to the fable of *Phineus*, which is sette downe at large in the *Argonauticks* of *Apollonius*, and *Valerius Flaccus*. He compareth him selfe vnto *Phineus*; his Mistres vnto the *Harpyes*; and his thoughtes vnto *Zethes*, and his desires vnto *Calais*, the two twinnes of *Boreas*; and the voyce of *Ne plus vltra* spoaken from Heauen to *Calais* and *Zethes*, vnto the *Diuine grace*, which willed him to follow no further the miseries of a Louers estate, but to professe vnfainedlie, that his Loue is past. And, last of all, the Author concludeth against the sower sawce of *Loue* with the French prouerbe: *Pour vn plaisir mille douleurs.*

THe Harpye **birdes, that did in such despight**
　Greiue and annoy old Phinëus **so sore,**
Were chas'd away by Calais **in flight**
And by his brother Zeth **for euermore;**
　　Who follow'd them, vntill they hard on hye　　　　5
　　A voyce, that said, Ye Twinnes No **further** fly.
Phineus **I am, that so tormented was;**　　　　CL
My Laura **here I may an** Harpye **name;**
My thoughtes and lustes bee Sonnes to Borëas,
Which neuer cea'st in following my Dame,　　　　10
　　Till heau'nly Grace **said vnto me at last,**
　　Leaue fond Delightes, **and say thy loue is past.**
My loue is past I say, and sing full glad;
My time, alas, mispent in Loue I rewe,
Wherein few ioyes, or none at all I had,　　　　15
But stoare of woes: I found the prouerbe true,
　　For eu'ry pleasure that in Loue **is found,**
　　A thousand woes and more therein abound.

In the fable of Phineus, described in the headnote and first two stanzas, the harpies torment the blind Phineus until he receives relief from the sons of Boreas, Calaïs, and Zetes (brothers-in-law of Phineus). The harpies are made analogous to the speaker's mistress (HN, 8). The speaker's thoughts do not, at first, offer any aid—they follow the mistress (9–10)—until heavenly grace comes to the rescue (11–12). The headnote also mentions grace: *Diuine grace* has *willed him to follow no further the miseries of a Louers estate.* This is an indication that we have come to the end of the Subseries because grace confers a sense of finality: one does not expect to undo or retreat from grace.

Fond Love Subseries: *Fond* appears in line 12, and the themes of this Subseries appear numerous times, including the ruing of time *mispent in Loue* (14). This final sonnet of the Fond Love Subseries has the marks of an ending. The headnote uses *concludeth* and the speaker vows *unfainedlie, that his Love is past.* As discussed above in the FL.5 commentary, this Subseries has three stages; the final stage is the speaker's *ultimum vale* (FL.5.HN) to love, and this sonnet clearly belongs in that stage. This progression aids reordering, and in conjunction with the Index Sonnet and Sequential Ties, provides confidence that we have correctly reordered this Subseries.

Index Tie: *A Blindfold Guide* (Index 9). In the headnote, the *Authour... compareth him selfe unto Phineus* (see Chapter 12). Phineus was both blind and a guide or leader (OED 3a) as king of Thrace.

QA Tie: *Dux caecus* (blind guide; QA16). This is almost identical to the Index Tie, *A Blindfold Guide.* A blindfolded Cupid is effectively blind.

Catalog Tie: *Loue makes a sporte of others deadly paine* (89.10). Throughout the sonnet, love is characterized as a torment: *miseries of a Louers estate* (HN); *mille douleurs* (HN); *greiue and annoy* (2); *tormented* (7); *stoare of woes* (16); *A thousand woes and more* (18). The mistress is likened to a harpy (HN, 8), and the speaker identifies himself as Phineus, a sufferer of these woes (7). In the myth, the harpies cruelly torment blind Phineus in a manner that could be characterized as "sportive" (*sporte* in this Catalog Tie): they steal his food and drive him to the corners of the world.

CipherLine: *Phineus I am, that so tormented was* (7). The story of *Phineus* and the suffering he endured aligns with the Index Tie, QA Tie, and Catalog Tie. This line sets the analogy between the speaker's suffering and that of Phineus.

Sequential Tie: This sonnet, in its many complaints about love (see Catalog Tie section), turns toward the scoffing, which characterizes the next Subseries. In the last stanza, *sing full glad* (13) of the time *misspent in Love* (14) essentially describes the *vituperatio* of the upcoming Scoff Subseries, and thus introduces it.

Summary of Fond Love Subseries

The Fond Love Subseries, in its restored order, depicts the speaker's progressive departure from love. The Subseries' first sonnet is marked as an introduction by its triple repetition of "fond" and its description of Cupid's attributes, which defines, at the outset, the Subseries' subject matter. The second sonnet looks back to the time of love as a violation of reason, and further, recognizes that the past cannot be changed. In the third and fourth sonnets, the focus shifts from the past to the present. The speaker asserts that love cannot trick him and that he must maintain his watchfulness. The fifth sonnet describes the structure of the Subseries with each of its three stanzas pointing to the beginning, middle, or end of this Subseries. In a nod to the prior two sonnets, it vows watchfulness, and then, glancing forward, it declares a final farewell to love. The sixth sonnet proclaims that love is false, which is the speaker's final conclusion about love in this Subseries. The seventh sonnet mentions divine grace, a sign that his "conversion," that is, his departure from love, is complete; the sonnet then concludes with vows. This thematic progression from sonnet to sonnet confirms that our reordering of these scrambled sonnets was done correctly.

In summary, the order of this Subseries is overdetermined by these mechanisms: the Index Ties, which point successively to the CipherLines of each sonnet; the Catalog Ties, which reinforce the selection of those CipherLines; the Sequential Ties; and the three-stage thematic progression described in Sonnet L82.FL.5. Although there may be ambiguities or uncertainties concerning a few of the identified links, in total these intra-textual links form an adamantine fabric of interconnections that assures us that we have correctly reordered the Subseries. The *Shepheardes Calender*'s E. K. would describe the restored Fond Love Subseries as "well grounded, finely framed, and strongly trussed up together."

The Scoff Subseries

The second Subseries, the "Scoff Subseries," also consists of 7 sonnets. Here, Venus and Cupid are openly mocked, either by name-calling or the telling of derogatory stories. These sonnets are identifiable by their prolonged invective against love, following the tradition of *vituperatio* (blame), a counterpart to epideictic poetry (the poetry of praise). It is true that in the Fond Love Subseries, the speaker also engages in vituperation against love; however, in that Subseries, he also plots various strategies to resist love. In contrast, in the Scoff Subseries, such strategies are no longer discussed because he is now *secure... fully resolved* (Scoff.1.15–16) in his departure from love. "Scoff" or an equivalent phrase appears in several headnotes: *scoffing* (96), *rayling out right* (98), and *expresseth his malice* (84). The Scoff Subseries includes Index Sonnet 98, which has 28 phrases that deprecate love, and *Quid Amor,* which has 89 (mostly) deprecating phrases.

The Scoff Subseries, like the Fond Love Subseries, exhibits structure: a tripartite division. The first two sonnets imagine Cupid's loss of power: his weapons destroyed, his death, exile, and imprisonment. The next three sonnets (Scoff.3 [the Index Sonnet], Scoff.4 [*Quid Amor*], and Scoff.5) are all lists of insults or curses against Cupid. In the final two sonnets of the Subseries, the speaker recognizes that Cupid is still a threat: in Scoff.6, he imagines a defensive war against him; in Scoff.7, Cupid's powers are recalled as having been *great and forcible* (HN). Thus, the sonnet begins by imagining Cupid's loss of power, shifts to vituperation, and then ends with new concerns about the god's harmful powers.

Sonnet 92 is the Catalog Sonnet for the remainder of the MLIP Subsequence, including the Scoff Subseries, the Love Discharged Subseries, Sonnet 90, and the Epilogue. Fig. 5.4 lists the links between the Catalog Sonnet 92's Catalog Ties and the CipherLines of the targeted sonnets. Unlike Catalog Sonnet 89, Sonnet 92's Catalog Ties point to their opposite qualities in the targeted CipherLines. This inversion is implied by the sonnet's headnote, which explains that *the tyrannous delightes and deedes of blinde Cupid* are compared *with the honest delightes and deedes of other his fellow Goddesses and Gods.* Thus, each of the Catalog Sonnet's lines expresses a positive quality about a god that is intended to link to its opposite and negative quality in Cupid. The sonnets and commentary pages for the Scoff Subseries appear in Addendum 1.

The Love Discharged Subseries

The third Subseries, the "Love Discharged" Subseries, consists of four sonnets that celebrate with song the speaker's escape from love. I selected the name of this Subseries from the third sonnet: *And I reioyce, from Loue discharg'd at last* (L82.LD.3.4). *Discharged* has a double meaning: love being sent away, and love's firebrand losing its heat, or charge. This is the storyline of Sonnet 100, the second sonnet of the Subseries, in which Cupid's death is imagined and a biting epitaph is conferred. Having bemoaned his time spent in *fond love* in the first Subseries, and scoffed at love in the second, in this third Subseries the speaker's concern shifts to a call to others to dismiss love from their lives. The Subseries is characterized by both this call to others and songs of joy that love is now past. The sonnet and commentary pages for this Subseries appear in Addendum 1.

Line	Catalog Tie	CL	CipherLine text
1	Phebus delightes to view his Lawrel Tree;	94.14	By seruing such an one as reackes no right
2	The Poplar pleaseth Hercules alone;	85.10	How Error was maine saile, each waue a Teare
3	Melissa mother is, and fautrix to the Bee,	92.13	But what is Loues delight? To hurt each where
4	Pallas will weare the Oliue braunche or none;	90.13	Litis in arcendae studiis, et pace colenda
5	Of shepheardes and their flocke Pales is Queen;		
6	And Ceres rypes the corne, was lately greene;	96.2	In funerall attyre, her woonted hew/Quite chang'd
7	To Chloris eu'ry flower belonges of right;	83.2	In chaines of roses linked all araye,
8	The Dryade Nimphs of woodes make chiefe accoumpt;	84.17	For if they stay, he will obtaine at last
9	Oreades in hills haue theire delight;		
10	Diana doth protect each bubblinge Fount;	QA.26	Virgineae zonae ruptura; dolosa voluptas
11	To Hebe louely kissing is assign'd;	EPI.11	Si mea vita fuit, tamen ut claudatur honeste
12	To Zephir ee'ry gentle breathing winde.	98.18	A Hellish Gaile, whose captiues are accurst
13	But what is Loues delight? To hurt each where;		
14	"He cares not whome, with dartes of deepe desire,		
15	"With watchfull iealosie, with hope, with feare,		
16	"With nipping cold, and secrete flames of fire.	100.5	His brand had lost his force, he gan to trye
17	O happie howre wherein I did foregoe		
18	This little God, so greate a cause of woe.		

Fig. 5.4 Catalog Sonnet 92: Catalog Ties and targeted CipherLines

The final two poems of the MLIP Subsequence

Two poems appear subsequent to the Love Discharged Subseries: Sonnet 90 and the Epilogue. The sonnets and commentary pages for these two poems appear in Addendum 1. Even though these poems are clearly unrelated thematically to the rest of the MLIP Subsequence, they are nonetheless blazoned with the running title, *My Love is Past*. The reason for the inclusion of these sonnets in the MLIP Subsequence is cryptographic, as revealed in the next two chapters, in which we will complete the solution of the Puzzle's second Stage.

The accuracy of our rearrangement of the Subsequence

Is the restoration of the MLIP Subsequence in Addendum 1 correct? At this point we have no cryptographic check, as we did in the first Stage, to guarantee the accuracy of our rearrangement. However, the Heuristic System, which includes the Index Sonnet, Catalog Sonnets, and Sequential Ties—overdetermines the position of the sonnets. Further confirmation is gained from the division into three Subseries: each Subseries exhibits a further withdrawal from the life led under love. Also, within each Subseries, the speaker progressively distances himself from love.

In the first Stage, we rearranged 18 poetic lines; in this Stage, we rearranged 18 sonnets. Although there are 23 poems in the MLIP Subsequence, the first three (PS.1, PS.2, and PS.3) are fixed in their position by their headnotes (see Addendum 1), the *Quid Amor* poem is fixed by Sonnet 98's headnote, and the Epilogue clearly belongs at the end, which leaves 18 poems to be reordered. The number 18 recurs frequently in the Puzzle. Although we cannot be absolutely certain about the new sonnet order, the need to reorder these sonnets is clear, and thus we should expect that the Puzzle's creator has given us enough information to accomplish this task accurately. In Chapter 7, we will find that this new order exhibits another form of coherence, which provides further corroboration that we have correctly reordered the Series.

6

The Precision System

The first step in the solution to the Puzzle's second Stage is to reorder the MLIP Subsequence sonnets, which we performed in the previous chapter. In this chapter, we will discover the cryptographic system employed in the second and subsequent Stages. In the next chapter, we will decipher a message that is embedded in the MLIP Subsequence, completing the solution to the Puzzle's second Stage. The Puzzle's cryptographic system, the Precision System described in the first chapter, is built upon the *Hekatompathia*'s Designs. There are 97 instances of these Designs: they appear below most sonnets and in some of the work's prefatory material. There are 18 different types of Designs, some of which appear a dozen times, and others only once.

The Puzzle's first Stage provided instructions (Sonnet 80), but no instructions are available for the second Stage. A natural place to seek further guidance, however, would be the work's authorial prefaces. The importance of prefaces to the exegesis of a work cannot be overestimated because they often establish the framework in which the author intends the work to be read.[1] The *Hekatompathia*'s prefatory material includes four items penned by the author: *The Epistle Dedicatorie to de Vere, To the frendly Reader* (a preface), *the Protrepticon* (a 46-line Neo-Latin poem), and *A Quatorzain of the Authour* (a 14-line English poem).

The four authorial prefaces

The dedication to de Vere draws a parallel between Alexander the Great's high opinion of the paintings of Apelles and de Vere's favorable assessment of the *Hekatompathia*'s poems, which, it is said, he read in manuscript form. The author speaks of Apelles's *cunning hand* and *curious pensill* and then says that he would not *conferre my Poemes with Apelles Portraites for worthinesse*. Given Apelles's singular reputation, though, this comparison is a modestly presented boast. Bacon is laying claim to the importance and seriousness of his literary enterprise, which stands in contrast to the work's exterior ("Silenic") appearance as a loose collection of poems.

The *To the frendly Reader* preface is also concerned with the reception of the work and references three harsh literary critics of antiquity: Aristarchus, Momus, and Zoilus. The first was an Alexandrian grammarian who redacted from Homer what he deemed to be spurious lines; the second was a mythical figure whose name means "blame;" the third was a severe critic of Homer. The author asks the reader to *rebuke* such critics on his *behalf, saying to* Aristarchus *that my birdes are al of mine own hatching.* This claim of originality in the face of his unbroken practice of translation or *imitatio* is curious and seems intended to alert the reader that the poet's sources are merely the starting point of his poetic method. It is also a defensive move, anticipating the complaint against the *Hekatompathia* that it is merely a collection of the imitations of others' poems, a criticism that Murphy has made.[2]

In his prefatory poem, *Quatorzain*, the poet addresses the personified *Hekatompathia*, saying that if the book is disliked, it may respond in one of two ways. Either it should defend its good deeds and blame those who are critical, or *els confesse, a toye to be thy name* (11–14). This passage is similar to the one in the *To the frendly Reader* preface, in which he says that the reader may either excuse the poems as *idle toyes proceedinge from a youngling frenzie*, or instead, *defend* the poems' supposed faults, which may be purposive and required by his poetic method. Both prefaces use *toy* to describe one possible judgment of the work. In fact, superficially, the *Hekatompathia* presents itself as a *toy*: it "Englishes" the poetry of various continental poets. When the work is called "nothing but a mosaic of Petrarchan conventions" by Murphy and "a scrapbook of experiments" by Heninger, they are essentially calling the work a *toy*, exactly the response the prefaces suggest might occur.[3] Yet the author tells us that an alternative reading is available, a suggestion made by both the *Quatorzain* and *To the frendly Reader* prefaces.

While many Elizabethan poetry books contain a preface by the poet and multiple prefaces penned by friends of the poet, the appearance of four authorial prefaces is unusual, if not unprecedented. All four prefaces are focused on the critical reception of the work, often expressing anxiety, and asserting that there is more than one way for the work to be read. These prefaces, as well as the *Hekatompathia*'s intentional omissions and contradictions, challenge the reader to interpret the work in some way that elevates it beyond the level of a *toy*. Indeed, the poet has gone to great lengths in these prefaces to declare the seriousness of his artistic ambitions and the existence of an alternative mode of reading that belies his work's toy-like appearance.

The most important preface is the Neo-Latin poem, *Authoris ad Libellum suum Protrepticon* (The Author's Exhortation to his Little

Book), and like the other prefaces, it is concerned with the *Hekatom-pathia's* reception (see Vol. II, 403–404, for the complete text):

> Si quis Aristarchus mordaci laeserit ore,
>   Culparum causas ingeniosus habe   (3–4)

> (If some Aristarchus harms you with his biting mouth,
>   you must be clever in finding excuses for your faults.)[4]

The author goes on to heap praises upon his very learned sovereign (13) and obsequiously hopes that she might look at his work (17). He then speculates that his book might be read by poets Philip Sidney and Edward Dyer (23). He mentions that Edward de Vere has already seen the work (27) and hopes that he will pass it on to others of his literary circle. With the muses in mind, he refers to de Vere's literati as pious nymphs:

> Tum fortasse piis nymphis dabit ille legendum,
>   Cum de Cyprigeno verba iocosa serent.   (33–34)

> (Then, perhaps, he will give you to the pious nymphs for the reading,
>   when they bandy playful words about Cupid, that Venus-born boy.)[5]

The poet's concern with his book's reception continues, and he goes on to instruct his book on how to respond to potential criticism:

> Tetrica si qua tamen blandos damnaverit ignes,
>   Dic tu, mentito me tepuisse foco;   (37–38)

> (But if any [nymph] is hard-hearted and condemns my sweet fires,
>   Tell her that I warmed myself at a fictitious hearth;)[6]

The feminine pronoun *qua* must refer to a reader, that is, any one of the so-called "nymphs" in de Vere's literary circle. Curiously, the poet tells his book that the poet's "sweet fires" (presumably the heat of passion) come from "a fictitious hearth." This may reiterate the claim made in the *To the frendly Reader* preface that the poet's *paines in suffering* love are *but supposed.* In the next two lines, he provides the only direct reference to the *Hekatompathia's* unusual woodcut Designs, and therefore, we will consider this passage carefully.

> Tumque refer talos, et fixum calce sigillum,
>   Qua Venerem temnis, filiolumque suum   (39–40)

(Moreover, answer back your ankles and affixed woodcut from the heel,
from which place you scorn Venus and her little son.)

The figurative language of these lines presents translators with a difficult
problem (for a more detailed discussion, see "The *Protrepticon* preface,
lines 39–40," Excursus 9). The *libellum* (i.e., the *Hekatompathia*), personified throughout the *Authoris ad Libellum suum Protrepticon*, is here
being instructed in how to respond to potential criticism. We must now
consider the figurative language: what are a book's "ankles?" *Talus* (ankle)
is a metonym for foundation—that upon which something stands: *Cadat
an recto stet fabula talo* (whether the play stands on upright ankle or falls;
Horace's *Epistles*, 2.1.176). By "answer back your ankles" (*refer talos*; 39),
the poet seems to be referring to the book's foundation, either some lower
part of the book, or perhaps, metonymically, the principle or foundation
upon which it is built. The verb *refer* is also applied to *fixum calce sigillum*
(39). *Sigillum* (a stamped figure) must mean the work's woodcut Designs.
The adjective *fixum* (fixed, constant, or established) might here mean
affixed, and thus *fixum sigillum* might be translated as "affixed woodcut
stamp." *Calce*, literally a heel, can mean the lower limit of anything (LS
Calx1, II), as we use the word "foot" in English. More specifically, it can
mean the end or conclusion of a page or book.[7] The author is calling upon
his book to defend itself by the use of a Design, which is situated at the
book's lower limit of its pages (*calce*; heel). In the next line (40), we are told
that by what comes from the heel, "you [the book] scorn Venus and her
little son" (*Venerem temnis, filiolumque suum*; 40). The ferocious-looking
Lioness Design, at the "heel" of many pages, scorns personified love—
Venus and Cupid. Two other pictorial Designs also appear to scorn love, as
will be discussed shortly. The poet tells his book to defend itself by reply-
ing with its "lower parts" (ankles, heel), the place where its love-scorning
Designs are located. The next two lines describe the happy consequence
of the book thus defending itself:

> Taliter efficies, ut amet te candida turba,
>   Forsitan et autoris palma futura tui.　　　　　(41–42)

> (By this means you will induce the brilliant audience to love you,
>   and perhaps a first prize will be presented to your author.)

The *Protrepticon* may be summarized as follows. The *Hekatompathia* is
about to be released throughout the nation, and the author is concerned
about the work's reception. He mentions particular people (Queen Elizabeth, Dyer, Sidney, de Vere, and de Vere's literary circle) that he expects

might read the book. He worries that the book might be condemned, and if so, he says that it should defend itself by means of its "lower parts" (heel, ankles), the location of the Designs (*sigillum*), which scorn (*temnis*) Venus and Cupid. Only then will the "brilliant audience" (41) love the *Hekatompathia*, and the poet be given a "first prize" (42) for his work. In solving the Puzzle's first Stage, we discovered that the Lioness Design signals the start of a Series; here, we are told that a Design (or possibly Designs) that scorns love will win favor for this book. We have surely been alerted to the importance of the *Hekatompathia*'s Designs.

The Designs

The *Hekatompathia* contains 18 different woodcut Designs that appear a total of 97 times.[8] Four of the Designs are elaborate pictorials (Fig. 6.1a–d), and these appear more frequently than any of the other Designs—a total of 44 of the 97 appearances. Of the other 14 Designs, several appear to be images of flowers (Fig. 6.1e), with counts of 4, 5, 6, or 8 flowers. Two other Designs appear to me to be images of flower bulbs, with counts of 10 or 12 bulbs (Fig. 6.1f). Not all Design types are shown in Fig. 6.1.

We will now examine the 4 pictorial Designs, beginning with Fig. 6.1a, a Design filled with Daedalian imagery. I take the two feathered creatures with bird legs to be Daedalus and Icarus. Of course, Daedalus fashioned wings to escape with his son Icarus from Crete. The roundish structure at the center of the Design appears to be the open jaw of the Minotaur. The jaw's seven pairs of opposing teeth and the encircled skull likely represent the seven Athenians sacrificed to the Minotaur annually. Curiously, the torsos of the man-birds appear to be snail shells. Perhaps this is a reference to King Cocalus's request that Daedalus, while in exile, thread a string through a snail shell, a feat he accomplishes by tying a string to an ant. Daedalus, the Minotaur, the Cretan labyrinth, and the annual loss of seven Athenian children are all cited in Sonnet 95's headnote.

This "Daedalus Design" appears more frequently than any other and closes the work. Daedalus is the master of hiding things: he hides Pasiphae in the wooden cow, encloses the Minotaur in a labyrinth, and hides himself in exile to avoid the wrath of Minos. At the same time, Daedalus is the master of revelation. As the inventor of the statue, he makes the invisible gods visible. His statues take on real life, threatening to run away (Plato, *Meno*, 97d). Daedalus, as the greatest artist and craftsman, and as someone who both hides and reveals, is the perfect emblem for the *Hekatompathia*'s enterprise of hiding its true meaning by means of its labyrinthine Puzzle.[9]

Fig. 6.1b, the "Lioness Design," which the Puzzle Sonnet associates with tyrannical love, was previously discussed. Fig. 6.1c appears to show

(a) Dedalus Design

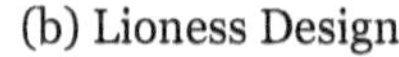

(b) Lioness Design

(c) Heart Jail Design

(d) DoubleA Design

(e) Flower Design Family

(f) Bulb Design Family

Fig. 6.1 Design types

a man's head locked into a heart-shaped structure. In the *Hekatompathia*, love is frequently depicted as a prison, and this "Heart Jail Design" seems to depict a man enclosed within a heart-shaped structure. The "DoubleA Design" (Fig. 6.1d), which has two mirrored A's, appears in other texts published both before and after the *Hekatompathia*; however, there is no consensus as to its meaning.[10] Significantly, three of these four pictorial Designs are concerned with love's capacity for terror: the Daedalus Design, which has at its center the deadly jaws of the Minotaur, suggests Pasiphae's aberrant sexuality; the Lioness Design is an icon of love's tyranny; the Heart Jail Design represents love's power to incarcerate.

The cryptographic use of designs in de Collange's *Polygraphie*

Flower designs, such as those depicted in Figures 6.1e, are common in Elizabethan books. Their purpose is often simply ornamental, but sometimes they are used to set off a section of text. In most cases, it is not known whether a design is the arbitrary choice of the printer or the careful selection of the author. With this uncertainty, most critics do not treat designs as either significant or authorial, but some dissent. Juliet Fleming believes that flower designs may sometimes be used to mark a particular genre, or the work of a particular author or coterie.[11] Kenneth Borris argues persuasively that Spenser must have had a hand in the illustration that prefaces the *Maye* eclogue in the *Shepheardes Calender*; he also cites other instances of Elizabethan writers selecting or designing the illustrations used in their texts.[12]

With respect to the *Hekatompathia*, there are several indications that the Designs are semiotic. As just noted, three of the work's pictorial Designs emblemize tyrannical love, a central theme of the *Hekatompathia*. The DoubleA Design (Fig. 6.1d) is mysteriously printed upside-down on some pages: this appears to be intentional because it occurs in two locations. Moreover, it would otherwise be an obvious error in a carefully prepared book.[13] The diversity of flower patterns, which include designs with either 4, 5, 6, or 8 flowers, appears to be another intentional signal. The Puzzle Sonnet's deciphered message suggests that the Lioness Design is a signal. Finally, the *Protrepticon* asserts that the Designs (or at least one of them) are essential to a true appreciation of the *Hekatompathia*.

In fact, the Designs are used to encipher cryptographic messages using an established cryptographic technique. Given the Puzzle Sonnet's reference to Trithemius's *Polygraphia* and the time he spent in France, Bacon may have been familiar with a French translation and augmentation of Trithemius's *Polygraphia* by Gabriel de Collange, published in 1561 and 1571. Appended to de Collange's translation is an addendum called "Tables et Figures Planispheriques," which contains dozens of cipher wheels called *volvelles* that are used to encipher and decipher messages. The *volvelles* have a rotating arm that is fastened to the center of the page by a rivet (Fig. 6.2). This arm is turned in order to select a particular Alphabet, or what we call a Transform. The *volvelles* associate each of de Collange's designs with a Recta, Aversa, or Orchema Transform. Thus, he uses designs as a signaling device: they select a cryptographic table that is then applied to a ciphertext proximate to the design.

EN la ſecóde figure planiſpherique & róde, ex-
tenſiue & dilatatiue de la recte table de tranſ-
poſition.

Fig. 6.2 A volvelle from Gabriel de Collange's *Polygraphie*[14]
Courtesy of HathiTrust

The Puzzle's cryptography in Stages 2–6

As earlier discussed, the Puzzle is similar to a multi-level, computer-based adventure game in that the earlier levels teach skills that are required in later levels. The cryptography of the Puzzle's second and subsequent Stages is built upon the cryptography of the first Stage. In the first Stage, we discovered 18 pairs of Transforms, which were specified by the Pillar Sonnet (see Figs. 2.16, 2.17, and 2.18). After restoring the lines of the Puzzle Sonnet to their proper order, we then applied these pairs of Transforms to the first and last letters of each line of the Puzzle Sonnet (Fig. 2.19). The first Transform of a pair was applied to the first letter of a sonnet line; the second Transform was applied to the last letter of the sonnet line. Applying these pairs of Transforms to the first and last letters of each line produced pairs of unresolved polyphonic plaintext letters, which we resolved to: VOCES ME. NUO LEA PESUS. In summary:

1. There are 18 pairs of Transforms derived from the Pillar Sonnet in the first Stage.

2. These pairs of Transforms are applied to the first and last letters of a sonnet line.

3. A polyphonic cipher is employed in which a choice must be made between two deciphered plaintext letters in order to produce a coherent message.

These pairs of Transforms, going forward, will be referred to as "Transform Pairs." Each of these 18 Transform Pairs consists of two Transform values from either the Recta, Aversa, or Orchema tables specified by the Pillar Sonnet. Each of the 18 Transform Pairs will be designated by the letters "TP," followed by the sonnet line to which it is applied, a number from 1 to 18. For example, referring to Fig. 2.18, for line 6 of the Puzzle Sonnet, the R10 table (i.e., the tenth Recta table) is applied to the left acrostic, and the R11 table to the right acrostic. Thus, the value of the Transform Pair TP6 is (R10, R11). The value of each of the 18 Transform Pairs is shown in Fig. 6.3; these values are identical to those in Fig. 2.18. The Transform Pair values in Fig. 6.3 are used frequently in this study and are part of a more extensive table that may be found in Fig. B.5 (Appendix B).

Because there are no explicit instructions for the second Stage, as there were for the first, we must adopt an inductive process, building upon what we already know from the first Stage. Cryptanalysis most often proceeds inductively because the cryptographic system employed by one's adversary is not usually known. We can make inferences based on the

Puzzle's first Stage, the number of Design types (18), de Collange's cryptographic use of designs, and our understanding of what constitutes a probable cryptographic system. With respect to this last point, a complex or arbitrary cryptographic system would be impossible to solve, and therefore we must assume that the cryptographic system is reasonably straightforward. Such assumptions about simplicity and solvability are required in the solution of most puzzles.

Transform Pair	First Value	Last Value
TP1	R1	R4
TP2	R5	R6
TP3	R6	R8
TP4	R8	R9
TP5	R9	R10
TP6	R10	R11
TP7	R11	R12
TP8	R12	A12
TP9	A12	A12
TP10	A11	A11
TP11	A11	A10
TP12	A10	A9
TP13	A8	A7
TP14	A7	A6
TP15	A6	A4
TP16	A3	O5
TP17	O5	O7
TP18	O7	O9

Fig. 6.3 Transform Pair values

We begin with the natural hypothesis that the cryptographic system of the second Stage builds upon that of the First Stage: that it is a polyalphabetic, polyphonic system and uses the same Transform Pairs discovered in the Puzzle's first Stage. A second hypothesis is that the Designs are a fundamental component of the cryptographic system, which is suggested by the *Protrepticon* preface, de Collange's *volvelles*, our knowledge that one of the Designs (the Lioness Design) has a semiotic purpose, and the numeric variations in the Flower Designs (4, 5, 6, and 8 flowers). We might infer that each of the 18 Design types specifies one of the 18 Transform Pairs, a mapping of one set of 18 elements to another set of 18 elements. Curiously, the reordering of the Puzzle Sonnet's 18 lines in the first Stage also required an 18-to-18 mapping (18 sonnet lines to 18 positions).

A third hypothesis is that each of the 97 Designs and their associated sonnets generates a single deciphered letter. Although the Puzzle Sonnet enciphers 18 letters, this is an unusual feat that, according to the Puzzle instructions, required *much art & study* (80.4–5). But enciphering multiple letters per Design/sonnet would hamper the poet's ability to compose freely, resulting in awkward poems skewed to serve cryptographic requirements. Our hypothesis that each of 97 Designs enciphers a single letter allows for the delivery of a 97-letter text, sufficiently long to deliver a significant message.

A fourth hypothesis is that there must be a single sonnet line, one of 18 lines, that provides the ciphertext. In the first Stage, every line of the Puzzle Sonnet provides ciphertext in its first and last letters. Consistent with our hypothesis that one letter is enciphered by each Design/sonnet, only one pair of ciphertext letters is required. This line was identified as the CipherLine in Chapter 4.

Fig. 6.4 shows how the first Stage's cryptographic system is extended in subsequent Stages. The lefthand side of Fig. 6.4 depicts the Puzzle Sonnet, in which Transform Pairs TP1 through TP18 are applied to the first and last letters of sonnet lines 1 through 18, respectively. This generates a polyphonic cipher of 18 letters that appears in parentheses to the right of the Puzzle Sonnet (only 5 of the 18 letters are shown: VOCES, which

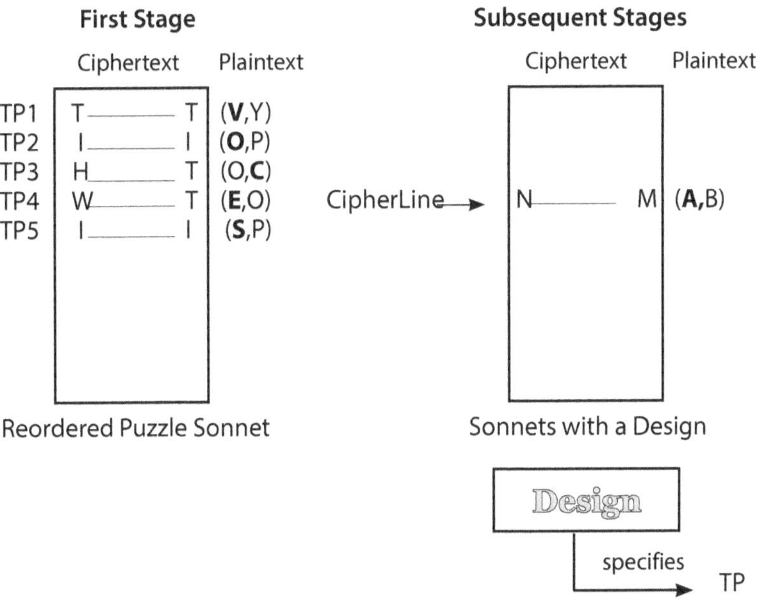

Fig. 6.4 Cryptographic model: First vs. subsequent Stages

appears in bolded letters, is the deciphered message's first word). The righthand side of Fig. 6.4 shows the cryptography of subsequent Stages: the CipherLine provides the ciphertext (the depicted letters, N and M, are arbitrary), and the Design below the sonnet specifies the Transform Pair to be used in decryption (labeled "TP"). The pair of unresolved plaintext letters is arbitrarily depicted as (A, B).

Both systems use the beginning and ending letters of poetic lines (acrostics in the first Stage) for the ciphertext; both use the same Transform Pairs that point to the cryptographic tables (Recta, Aversa, and Orchema); both are polyphonic ciphers. The righthand side of Fig. 6.4 is meant to illustrate how the first Stage's cryptographic system is extended: the Designs select the Transform Pair to be used in deciphering (second hypothesis); only one letter is produced per sonnet (third hypothesis); and a particular designated line, the CipherLine, is the site of the ciphertext (fourth hypothesis). The mechanism by which the CipherLine is determined was explained in Chapter 4.

Fig. 6.5 shows how the cryptographic system depicted in the righthand side of Fig. 6.4 is applied in each of 4 sonnets to produce a 4-letter message. The location of the CipherLine in each sonnet, marked at the left of each line with "CL," varies from one sonnet to the next (the locations of the CipherLines depicted are arbitrary). The first and last characters of each CipherLine form the ciphertext (schematically, only 4 sonnet lines are shown; the letters depicted are arbitrary). The Design below each sonnet (Flowers-6, Flowers-8, etc.) specifies the Transform Pair to be applied to the CipherLine's first and last letters. The values shown (TP6, TP7, etc.) will be discovered in the next chapter. The pair of letters shown below each sonnet is the polyphonic pair of deciphered letters. One letter of each of these polyphonic pairs must be selected based on the coherence of the message (the bolded letters), while the other is ignored. Together the 4 sonnets sequentially produce the 4-letter message POEM (an arbitrary word).

One might ask whether there are other hypothetical models for extending the cryptography of the first Stage. Upon reflection, there are very few potential models that merit consideration. The primary assumption behind our hypothesis is that it builds upon the cryptography of the first Stage, for without this assumption, the process of defining a cryptographic system would be hopelessly unconstrainted. An important characteristic of this extended cryptographic system is its flexibility (mentioned above in the third hypothesis). The sonnet form is restrictive enough without the poet being further encumbered by having to use a certain first or last letter in a line to generate a cryptographic message. Rather, the ideal cryptographic system would allow the poet to freely compose his poems and only later add cryptographic indicators someplace

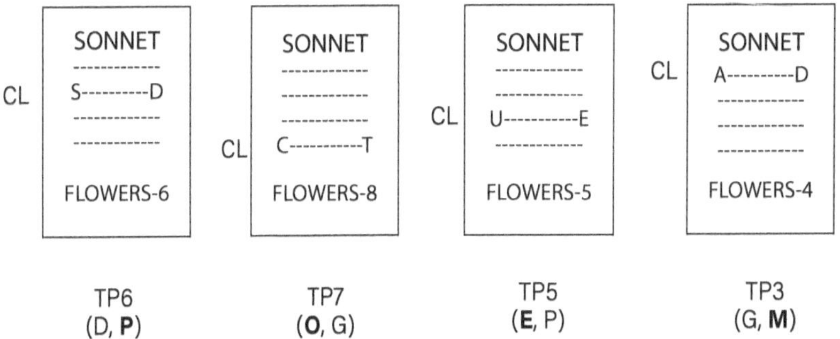

Fig. 6.5 Cryptographic model Stages 2–6

outside of the poem itself. The cryptographic system depicted in Fig. 6.5 allows precisely this: the poet may specify any Transform Pair by choosing one of the 18 Designs and placing it beneath the sonnet, and may specify the CipherLine using an external memorandum, a Catalog Sonnet. With 18 possible Designs (specifying Transform Pairs) and 18 possible CipherLines, the poet has 324 opportunities (18 x 18) to generate the letter he desires. Applying this method across multiple sonnets, the poet can generate any message he chooses.

The flexibility of Bacon's cryptographic system—more specifically, his practice of steganography—allows him to hide any message in any preexisting poem by simply adding an appropriate Design and Catalog Sonnet–based Catalog Tie. Bacon is practicing steganography with a method that he later described as *"scribendi omnia per omnia,"* which refers to the ability to hide any message (or all messages) within any ordinary text (or all texts). Bacon used these words to describe his biliteral cipher (discussed in Chapter 1), and although he wrote these words long after the *Hekatompathia*'s publication, he says that he used his biliteral cipher when in France in the late 1570s.[15]

What makes this cryptographic system (the Precision System) remarkably elegant is that it performs two functions: it delivers a cryptographic message and provides a precise check on the puzzle-solver's reordering of the sonnets. (See the introductory chapter, Fig. 1.4.) The reordering of the sonnets, performed in the previous chapter, is a heuristic process, as opposed to a precise one. Although this heuristic process is overdetermined by several methods, the methods used to reorder sonnets are based on words and are therefore imprecise. (They require either the discovery of the links between one set of words and another, i.e., Index Sonnet links and Sequential Ties, or the recognition of a plot-like progression.) But the Puzzle's cryptography overlays a precision method on top of these heuristic methods of reordering sonnets, providing not only another layer of overdetermination, but a precise one. If the puzzle-solver incorrectly reorders sonnets, the Precision System's deciphered message will be incoherent. Referring to Fig. 6.5, if the order of the 4 sonnets is incorrect, the deciphered message will not be POEM, but a spurious sequence of letters. Thus, the Precision System verifies the reordering process performed by the Heuristic System, ensuring the accuracy of our restoration.

7

Decoding the Designs

We will now apply the cryptographic model laid out in the previous chapter to the MLIP Subsequence. In that model, presented in Fig. 6.5, each Design/sonnet produces a single letter of the concealed message. Deciphering requires two pieces of information: the location of the CipherLine and the Transform Pair value specified by the Design. Having identified the CipherLines for each MLIP sonnet in Chapter 5, the remaining task is to determine the Transform Pair values specified by each of the Designs.

Mapping Designs to Transform Pairs

The Transform Pair table values were initially discovered in Chapter 2 and were entered into the table that appears in Fig. 2.18. The Transform Pair values are also shown in Fig. 6.3 and Fig. B.5. The Transform Pairs TP1 through TP15 specify either Recta or Aversa tables; TP16 through TP18 specify Orchema tables, whose values are not yet known. The reader may verify the deciphering operations presented in this chapter by consulting the Transform Pair values table (Fig. 2.18, Fig. 6.3 or Fig. B.5) and the Recta and Aversa tables (Figs 2.13 and 2.14, or Figs. B.1 and B.2, respectively).

As discussed in the previous chapter, the *Hekatompathia* contains 18 different Designs, and there are 18 different Transform Pairs. We might conjecture that this parity between the number of Designs and the number of Transform Pairs is not coincidental and that each of the 18 Designs specifies one of the 18 Transform Pairs. If true, this would be the third time that the Puzzle has required 18 items to be reordered or mapped: we previously reordered the 18 Puzzle Sonnet lines and 18 sonnets within the MLIP Subsequence. In each of these instances there were 18 factorial possible permutations, an enormous number of possibilities, which presented a considerable challenge.

Although discovering an unknown mapping of 18 items to another 18 items is not an everyday task, the mapping of one set of symbols or letters to another set is precisely the task that cryptanalysts encounter when they attempt to crack an unknown cipher. Cryptographic tables are essentially a map between one set of characters in the ciphertext and another set in the plaintext. Let us consider the practice of cryptanalysis in Bacon's time—that is, how espionage agents deciphered the cryptograms of their adversaries without access to the cipher key. Ciphers are susceptible to being cracked because language has certain patterns that repeat, allowing the cryptanalyst to guess at the plaintext. This applies at the level of individual letters (E is more common than Z), bigrams (TH is common while BZ is rare), and words (THE is extremely common, accounting for about one out of every 15 words in English). One very common cryptanalytic technique is to guess at whole phrases. In the religious wars of the sixteenth century, the Protestants became masters of these techniques. One of history's great cryptanalysts, François Viète (1540–1603)—better known for his contributions to the field of algebra—served as a privy counselor to both Henry III and Henry of Navarre. Viète noticed that the Spanish dispatches often contained guessable phrases. For example, lists of numbered articles were headed with "*memorial y instruction.*"[1] Of course, if an addressee of an enciphered letter were known and if his name could be located at the beginning of the ciphertext, this would also be of great assistance to the cryptanalyst. Such a plaintext guess is called a "crib."

This cryptanalytic technique survived long past the sixteenth century. For example, during the Second World War, the German army radioed weather reports at the same time each morning. These messages almost always began with the same exact words, announcing that a weather report was about to be sent. This was of great assistance to the British team at Bletchley Park that was responsible for deciphering messages. Having some knowledge of the contents of the plaintext is one of the most powerful tools at the cryptanalyst's disposal.

Two things made it seem obvious to me that Bacon's Puzzle must employ a crib. First, there are too many possible mappings of Designs to Transform Pairs for the problem to be solved in any other way. The pairs of letters generated (the inherent binary indeterminacy of the polyphonic cipher) and the unknown value of the Orchema Transform only added to the difficulty. Second, the blazoning of "My Love is Past" in large, bold capital letters across every page from Sonnet 80 through the Epilogue implies that these sonnets were bound together to serve some special function. The inclusion of the Epilogue among these blazoned sonnets was suspicious because it does not adhere to the "My Love is Past" theme. This unusual blazoning suggested to me that the Subsequence's 21 sonnets with Designs might encipher some phrase roughly equivalent to "My Love is Past." I assumed the phrase would be in Latin because the discovered plaintext message of the Puzzle Sonnet is in Latin. My first thought was that there was some well-known Latin *sententia*, or line from a well-known Latin work, that would quickly come to mind for an educated reader of the time. I looked for a *sententia* that included *amor* and some Latin equivalent of "past" that was 21 characters long. However, I found none. Frustrated, I began to look within the *Hekatompathia* itself for a 21-letter Latin phrase. My attention was drawn to Sonnet 98's headnote:

> The Author in this passion, telling what *Loue* is, easeth his heart, as it were, by rayling out right, where he can worke no other manner of revenge. The inuention hereof, for the most part of the particulars conteyned, is taken out of certeine Latine verses which this Author composed vpon *Quid Amor.* Which because they may well importe a passion of the writer, and aptly befitte the present title of his ouerpassed *Loue*, he setteth them downe in this next page following, but not as accomptable for one of the undredth passions of this booke.

Sonnet 98, the Index Sonnet, used to order the MLIP Subsequence in Chapter 5, contains 28 phrases that describe love in deprecating terms. The headnote tells us that many of these phrases are *taken out of certaeine Latine verses* found in *Quid Amor*, the Neo-Latin poem that appears on the page immediately following Sonnet 98. These English phrases translate some of the Latin phrases in *Quid Amor*. The headnote's phrase *the present title of his ouerpassed Loue* obviously refers to *My Love is Past*, which is blazoned across the top of the page. The use of "*ouerpassed*" here is curious: it has the effect of glossing *past* as *overpassed*. Although *overpassed* could simply indicate that the speaker's love has come to an end, that would be identical in meaning to *My Love is Past*. The poet appears to have created a new word: the OED lists this instance as the first occurrence of "overpassed." Thus, one might reasonably suspect that this new word was invented for a particular purpose. Perhaps the poet wished to recast the title as "My Love is Overpassed," with "overpassed Love" meaning an excessive love. This would be consistent with the Subsequence's central theme: the speaker's passionate love had overpassed reason. Also, the headnote's *may well importe a passion of the writer* further hints at this definition of "overpassed." Thus, an alternative reading of the Subsequence's running title is "My Love is overpassed or excessive."

Sonnet 98's headnote suggests a further place to look: *The inuention hereof… is taken out of certeine Latine verses which this Author composed vpon Quid Amor.* Perhaps one of the 89 phrases in *Quid Amor* expresses the idea that "my love is overpassed or excessive." There are 21 sonnets with Designs in the MLIP Subsequence, and according to our model

(Fig. 6.5), each enciphers a single letter. I therefore surveyed the length of each of the 89 phrases in *Quid Amor*, searching for a phrase with 21 letters. I found that only two of the phrases were 21 letters long and was excited when one of those two phrases turned out to be a very good match for *overpassed Love* (98.HN): *prodiga libertas animae.* The adjective *prodigus* means lavish or overabundant. The noun *libertas* means freedom or liberty, and here may mean "spirit of liberty" (LS IIC). In this context, I would translate *animae* as "of the mind." Thus, one might translate *prodiga libertas animae* as "an overly free state of mind," a very good description of the speaker's *overpassed Love* (98.HN). Yet another reason to select this phrase is that it is the QA Tie that points to the CipherLine of Sonnet 80, which is the Puzzle's instructions and the lead sonnet of the MLIP Subsequence (see Addendum 1, first commentary). Thus we have a pointer to this phrase at the exact location where its encryption starts, at the beginning of the MLIP Subsequence. That is, the start of the crib is "riveted" to the sonnet that enciphers its first letter (see Fig. 7.1, lower illustration). In summary, several factors suggest that this phrase deserves our attention: Sonnet 80's QA Tie, Sonnet 98's headnote, its 21-character length, and its similarity in meaning to "My love is overpassed/past." One might argue about the meaning or intent of the poet's words that I have read as pointing to *prodiga libertas animae*; however, if we are to have any chance at all to decipher a message, the crib must be included somewhere in the text. Indeed, there are few (perhaps only two) 21-character Latin phrases in the *Hekatompathia* from which to choose, and thus our cryptanalysis is not dependent upon the reading of the poet's subtle hints.

Applying the crib

The use of a crib, arguably the most common of cryptanalytic techniques, is the natural way in which to attack the Puzzle's second Stage. We will use this crib in the same way that Viète and other French Protestants used cribs, such as *memorial y instruction*, to decipher Spanish messages. They would line up the letters *MEMORIAL Y INSTRUCTION* over the ciphertext characters that headed a list of numbered articles. This superimposition of the plaintext (*MEMORIAL Y INSTRUCTION*) onto the ciphertext reveals a portion of the cryptographic key used in enciphering the message. After revealing a portion of the key, the remainder of it is often identified with relative ease.

Let us then apply Viète's cryptanalytic technique to the MLIP Subsequence. In Fig. 7.1, each sonnet of the MLIP Subsequence generates a plaintext letter, as shown in the illustration. The table in Fig. 7.1 lists each

ID	Sonnet	Design	TP Value	CL	CL First	CL Last	Crib	Possible Transforms
1	PS.1	Flowers-6	TP ?	80.8	S	D	P	S→P or D→P
2	PS.2	Flowers-5	TP ?	81.28	H	E	R	H→R or E→R
3	PS.3	Lioness	TP ?	82.18	W	T	O	W→O or T→O
4	FL.1	Heart Jail	TP ?	86.10	A	T	D	A→D or T→D
5	FL.2	Bulbs-12	TP ?	93.6	F	E	I	F→I or E→I
6	FL.3	Daedalus	TP ?	88.18	C	S	G	C→G or S→G
7	FL.4	Flowers-8	TP ?	99.9	O	E	A	O→A or E→A
8	FL.5	Flowers-6	TP ?	87.17	A	Y	L	A→L or Y→L
9	FL.6	Roots-5	TP ?	95.9	F	E	I	F→I or E→I
10	FL.7	Flowers-4	TP ?	97.7	P	S	B	P→B or S→B
11	Scoff.1	Bulbs-10	TP ?	96.2	I	W	E	I→E or W→E
12	Scoff.2	Flowers-8	TP ?	83.2	I	E	R	I→R or E→R
13	Scoff.3	Bulbs-12	TP ?	98.18	A	T	T	A→T or T→T
14	Scoff.4	Flowers-I	TP ?	QA.26	U	S	A	U→A or S→A
15	Scoff.5	Heart Jail	TP ?	94.14	B	T	S	B→S or T→S
16	Scoff.6	Flowers-I	TP ?	84.17	F	T	A	F→A or T→A
17	Scoff.7	Roots-5	TP ?	92.13	B	E	N	B→N or E→N
	LD.1	NONE						
18	LD.2	DoubleA	TP ?	100.5	H	E	I	H→I or E→I
19	LD.3	DoubleA-inv	TP ?	85.10	H	E	M	H→M or E→M
	LD.4	NONE						
20	90	Lioness	TP ?	90.13	L	A	A	L→A or A→A
21	Epilog	Daedalus	TP ?	EPI.11	S	E	E	S→E or E→E

Crib: PRODIGA LIBERTAS ANIMAE

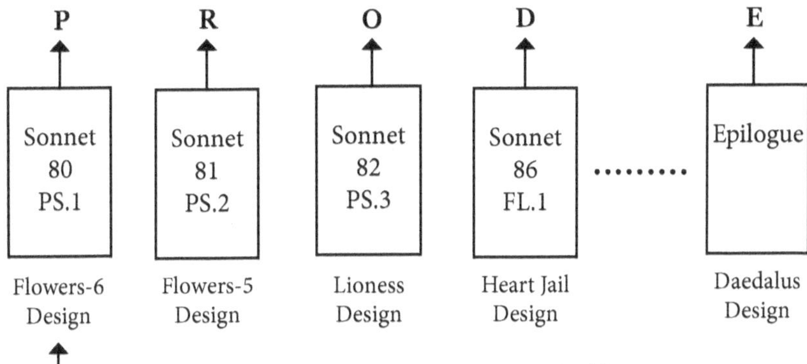

Each sonnet generates one letter based on the Design and CipherLine

Fig. 7.1 The crib allows discovery of the cryptographic process

sonnet in the restored order, beginning with the instructions to the Puzzle Sonnet (PS.1/80) and ending with the Epilogue. There are 23 sonnets in all, including two that lack a Design, which leaves 21 sonnets, and this exactly fits our 21-letter crib, PRODIGA LIBERTAS ANIMAE. The columns of Fig. 7.1 are described below:

ID	Position of letter in crib
Sonnet	Sonnet identifier
Design	Design type below each sonnet
TP value	Transform Pair value specified by Design (none yet known)
CL	CipherLine's sonnet and line number
CL First	First letter of the sonnet's CipherLine
CL Last	Last letter of the sonnet's CipherLine
Crib	Crib letter at each position (PRODIGA LIBERTAS ANIMAE)
Transforms	The two (polyphonic) Transforms that could decipher to the crib

The fourth column, "Design Type," holds the name that I have assigned to each of the work's Designs (these name assignments shall be discussed shortly). The fifth column is a placeholder for the Transform Pair associated with each Design: discovering the mapping of Designs to Transform Pairs is the primary objective of this chapter. The seventh and eighth columns contain the two ciphertext letters, that is, the first and last letters of the CipherLine (which were discovered in Chapter 5 and Addendum 1). Just as in the first Stage, this Stage employs a polyphonic cipher: one plaintext letter is deciphered from the first letter of the CipherLine, and a second plaintext letter from the last letter of the CipherLine. Our expectation is that one of the plaintext letters will match the crib letter in the last column—the practice that Viète applied in cracking Spanish ciphers. Thus, either one of the two Transform (i.e., deciphering) operations may generate the required crib letter: these two possible Transforms are listed in the ninth column.

Discovering a Design's Transform Pair value

Our task now is to determine which Transform Pair is specified by each Design. Cribs allow the cryptanalyst to work backward, using the plaintext to determine the cipher table that was used to encipher a ciphertext. In the case of the Puzzle's second Stage, knowing both the ciphertext (the Cipher-Line's first and last letters) and the plaintext (crib), and knowing the Transform Pair values, we can figure out which Design specifies which

Transform Pair. We begin by examining the first entry in Fig. 7.1, Sonnet PS.1/80—the Puzzle Sonnet instructions. This sonnet, with its Design, must decipher to the first letter of the crib, the "P" in PRODIGA LIBERTAS ANIMAE. Fig. 7.1, ID 1 (first row), columns 6 and 7, indicate that Sonnet PS.1's CipherLine begins with the letter "S" and ends with "D." The selection of the CipherLine is explained in the commentary page for Sonnet PS.1 (Addendum 1, first commentary page). From the first row, last column of Fig. 7.1, either "S" or "D" must decipher to the letter "P." These two deciphering possibilities, S→P and D→P, might occur using either the Recta or Aversa tables. Examining the Transform tables in Appendix B, Figs. B.1 and B.2, one finds that none of the Recta tables, nor any of the Aversa tables, allow the deciphering S→P. This may be easily verified by examining the "S" row of both the Recta and Aversa tables: the letter "P" never appears. This stems from a fundamental restriction in the enciphering/deciphering method: because the offset ranges only from 1 to 12, rather than 1 to 24, only half of the 24-letter alphabet may be enciphered/deciphered using a single row of either the Recta or Aversa tables.

The S→P deciphering possibility has been eliminated, and so now we turn to the other possible deciphering, D→P. We examine the "D" row of both the Recta and Aversa tables and find two possibilities for generating a "P": column 11 of the Recta table and column 7 of the Aversa table. These are the Transforms that have been designated as R11 (Recta) and A7 (Aversa), respectively. We must now consider which Transform Pairs specify these two tables. We are only concerned with the second value of the Transform Pair, the table applied to the CipherLine's last letter ("D" is the ending letter of the CipherLine). Examining Fig. 6.3 (or Fig. B.5), we find that the second value of the Transform Pair TP6 (applicable to the last letter of the CipherLine) deciphers using the R11 table. We next consider the Aversa table and find that Transform Pair TP13 deciphers the last letter of a CipherLine using the A7 table (which deciphers D→P). These findings are summarized below:

S→P   No Recta or Aversa   Transform Pair: none
D→P   R11 or A7   Transform Pairs: TP6 or TP13

The first line above specifies that a S→P Transform does not appear in either the Recta or Aversa tables. The second line specifies that the D→P Transform occurs using either the R11 or A7 Transforms, and further, that those Transforms are applicable to the last CipherLine letter in Transform Pairs TP6 and TP13, respectively.

We have now *almost* determined the Transform Pair number specified by the Flowers-6 Design, which appears below Sonnet PS.1: either TP6 or

TP13. Fortunately, we can distinguish between these two possibilities because the Flowers-6 Design also appears under Sonnet FL.5 (Sonnet 87). We repeat the same procedure just performed on PS.1 (Sonnet 80). Fig. 7.1, ID 8, indicates that the CipherLine of FL.5 begins with the letter "A" and ends with "Y." One of these two ciphertext characters must decipher to the letter "L" of the crib. We next examine the Recta and Aversa tables (Figs. B.1 and B.2), which show that R10 deciphers A→L and R12 deciphers Y→L. Examining the Aversa table, no row can decipher either A→L or Y→L. Turning to Fig. 6.3 (or Fig. B.5), we find that Transform Pair TP6 deciphers the first letter of a CipherLine with R10, and TP7 deciphers the last letter of a CipherLine with R12. Our findings for FL.5 are summarized below:

A→L	R10; no Aversa	TP6; none
Y→L	R12; no Aversa	TP7; none

Either TP6 or TP7 could produce the required crib letter "L". In our previous examination of the Subsequence's first sonnet, PS.1, either TP6 or TP13 could produce the required crib letter. Since both crib letters must be produced, and the Flowers-6 Design, which appears below both sonnets, must specify a single Transform Pair, the value specified by the Flowers-6 Design must be the intersection of the two result sets, {TP6, TP13} and {TP6, TP7}, which is TP6. Only the Transform Pair TP6 can produce the required crib letters for both PS.1 and FL.5, and thus the Flowers-6 Design specifies TP6.

The Transform Values of the Flower Designs

Of the *Hekatompathia*'s 18 Designs, 6 appear to contain flowers. These are reproduced in Fig. 7.2, along with the names that I have assigned to them. Four of the Designs in Fig. 7.2 are straightforwardly named: they consist of 4, 5, 6, and 8 flowers. The number of flowers in the Design marked Flowers-I is more difficult to determine, and consequently I used the letter "I" for "indeterminate." The final Design, Flowers-2x3 appears only once, under Sonnet 16, and in only 2 of the 10 extant copies that I have examined. The other 8 copies have a Design that I would describe as a triangular wreath under Sonnet 16.

Using the same procedure that was used to determine the Transform Pair specified by the Flowers-6 Design, we will determine the Transform Pair values specified by the other 4 Flower Designs that appear in the MLIP Subsequence. We start with the Flowers-8 Design, which appears twice, in Sonnets FL.4 and Scoff.2 (ID numbers 7 and 12, in Fig. 7.1). Using the information presented in Fig. 7.1, the Recta and Aversa tables

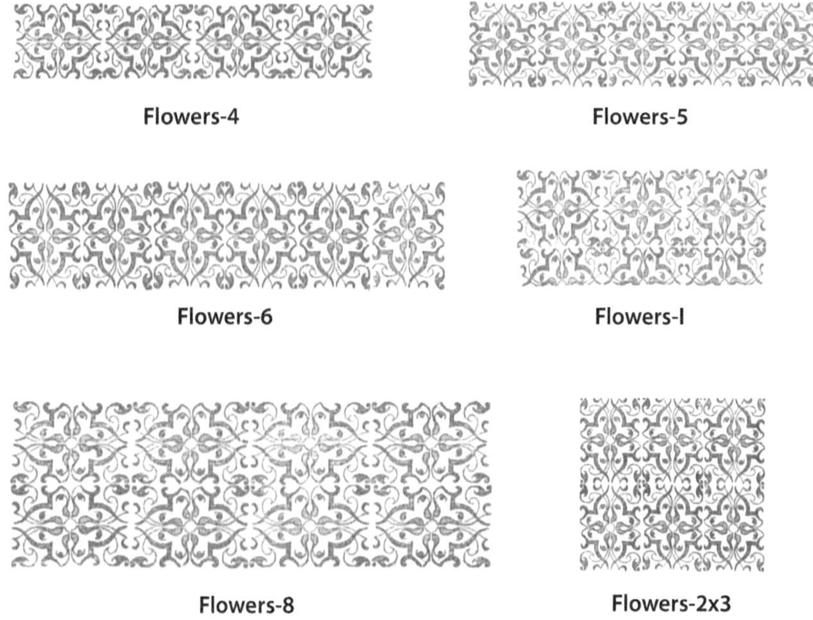

Flowers-4   Flowers-5

Flowers-6   Flowers-I

Flowers-8   Flowers-2x3

Fig. 7.2 Flower Designs

(Figs. B.1 and B.2), and the Transform Pair values table (Fig. B.5), FL.4's Flowers-8 Design may specify any of the 3 Transform Pairs listed below:

O→A	R11; A11	TP7; TP10 or TP11
E→A	No Recta; no Aversa	None; none

The reason the first line above includes both TP10 and TP11 is that both Transform Pairs have the same value for a CipherLine's first letter, Transform A11 (see Fig. B.5). We now consider the second appearance of the Flowers-8 Design, in Scoff.2:

I→R	R8; no Aversa	TP4; none
E→R	R12; A4	TP7; TP15

The Transform Pair specified by Flowers-8 is the intersection of the two sets of Transform Pair possibilities: {TP7, TP10, TP11} for FL.4 and {TP4, TP7, TP15} for Scoff.2. The only Transform Pair that appears in both sets is TP7, and thus the Flowers-8 Design must specify TP7. In our prior analysis, we determined that the Flowers-6 Design specifies TP6, which falls just before TP7. Similarly, Flowers-6 and Flowers-8 are adjacent in the numerical order of Flower Designs (there is no Flowers-7 Design). This adjacency of the Flowers-6 and Flowers-8 Designs and their Transform Pair assignments is curious, and as discussed below, a pattern begins to emerge.

The Flowers-I Design also appears twice in the MLIP Subsequence: Scoff.4 (*Quid Amor*) and Scoff.6, ID numbers 14 and 16 in Fig. 7.1, respectively. For Scoff.4:

U→A	R5; none	TP2; none
S→A	R7; A7	TP3; TP13

For Scoff.6:

F→A	None; none	None; none
T→A	R6; A6	TP2; TP14

The Transform Pair specified by Flowers-I is the intersection of the two sets of Transform Pair possibilities: {TP2, TP3, TP13} and {TP2, TP14}. The only Transform Pair that appears in both sets is TP2, and thus the Flowers-I Design must specify TP2. Curiously, the three Flower Designs examined so far, TP2, TP6, and TP7, all fall in the upper part of the Pillar Sonnet where the Recta tables reside. Next, we examine the Flowers-5 Design that appears once, in PS.2, ID number 2 in Fig. 7.1:

H→R	R9; A1	TP5; none
E→R	R12; A4	TP7; TP15

A1 does not appear in any Transform Pair and is therefore eliminated from consideration. TP7 is also eliminated from consideration because it is already assigned to the Flowers-8 Design. This leaves TP5 and TP15. Given that TP5 is adjacent to two other Flower Design values that we obtained, TP6 and TP7, TP5 seems to be a more likely possibility than TP15.

We next examine the Flowers-4 Design that appears once in FL.7, ID number 10 in Fig. 7.1:

P→B	R11; A9	TP7; none
S→B	R8; A6	TP3; TP14

A9 does not appear in any Transform Pair for the first letter and is therefore eliminated from consideration. TP7 is also eliminated from consideration because it is already assigned to the Flowers-8 Design. This leaves TP3 and TP14. Given that TP3 is adjacent to TP2 (specified by the Flowers-I Design), it appears to be the more likely possibility than TP14.

We have now found that the 5 Flower Designs that appear in the MLIP Subsequence all specify nearly contiguous Transform Pair values: TP2,

TP3, TP5, TP6, and TP7 (although TP3 and TP5 each had an alternate value). We might guess that the one Flower Design whose value remains unknown, Flowers-2x3, occupies the single missing value in the above Transform Pair values: TP4.

In Chapter 2 we found that the Puzzle Sonnet in its pillar form (Sonnet 81) has three regions: the top half of the pillar consists of Recta Transforms; the bottom half consists of Aversa Transforms; the base consists of Orchema Transforms. It appears that all 5 of the values obtained for Flower Designs fall in the first half of the Transform Pairs, which specify Recta Transforms. One might guess that flowers, which grow in an upward direction, properly belong in the Recta half of the Transform Pairs (the Recta numbers of the Pillar Sonnet increase from 1 to 12). Most other Designs, as demonstrated below, fall in the Aversa section of the Pillar Sonnet, where the numbers are decreasing—a downward direction and the direction in which roots grow. A visual pattern in the order of the Designs is beginning to emerge, which I call the "Plant Model."

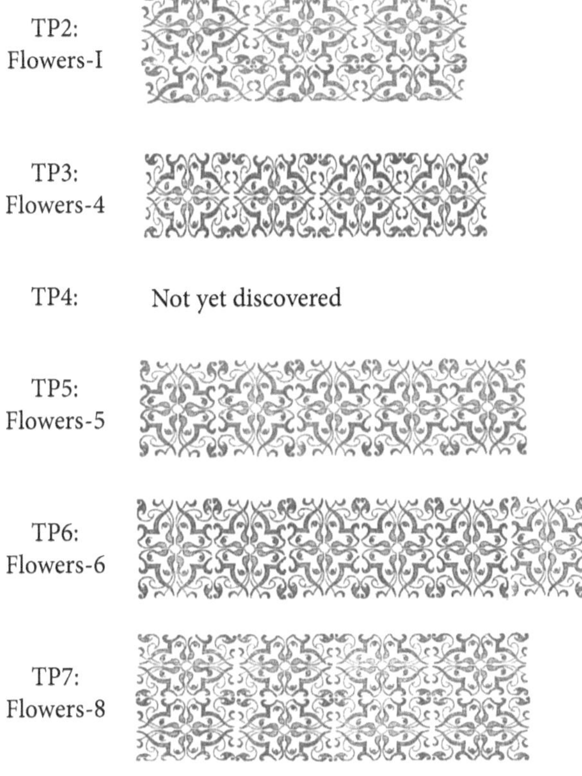

Fig. 7.3 The flower section of the "Plant Model"

Fig. 7.3 shows the mapping of Flower Designs to Transform Pairs that we have so far discovered. The number of flowers in the Designs appears to increase as the Transform Pair numbers increase. Starting at the top, the Flowers-I Design specifies TP2—here the flower count is indeterminate. Yet, the next 4 Flower Designs increase sequentially: the Designs have 4, 5, 6, and 8 flowers, which specify TP3, TP5, TP6, and TP7, respectively. There is a gap at TP4 that we might speculate is the place where the Flowers-2x3 Design belongs (the only Flower Design that does not appear in the MLIP Subsequence). The sequential order of the Flowers-4, Flowers-5, Flowers-6, and Flowers-8 Designs is not likely to be coincidental. Also, if the number of flowers is taken as a measure of width, the order of Designs follows the pattern of the top half of the Pillar Sonnet: narrow at the top and wide at the pillar's midsection.

Whether or not these Designs actually represent flowers, and whether their placement in the top half of the Pillar Sonnet is related to "*recta*" (proper, straight), implying an upward direction, is not essential to this process of deciphering. However, the clustering of the Flower Designs in a relatively narrow range, from TP2 to TP7, as opposed to scattered across the 15 Transform Pairs that are associated with Recta and Aversa tables is significant. The regularity of this pattern provides some corroborative evidence that our Design to Transform Pair assignments are correct.

The Transform Pair values of the Bulb Designs

There are two Designs that appear to me to be flower bulbs. These "Bulb Designs" are reproduced in Fig. 7.4.

Bulbs-10   Bulbs-12

Fig. 7.4 Bulb Design family

The Bulbs-10 Design occurs once in the MLIP Subsequence, in Scoff.1, ID number 11 in Fig. 7.1. The possible Transform Pairs are:

I→E	None; A12	None; TP9
W→E	R8; none	TP3; none

TP3 is already assigned, leaving TP9 as the only alternative.

The Bulbs-12 Design occurs twice in the MLIP Subsequence, in FL.2 and Scoff.3, ID numbers 5 and 13 in Fig. 7.1, respectively. The possible Transform Pairs for FL.2 are:

F→I	R3; A11	None; TP10/11
E→I	R4; A12	TP1; TP8/9

The possible Transform Pairs for Scoff.3 are:

A→T	None; A6	None; TP14
T→T	None; A12	None; TP8/9

The intersection of the two sets of possible Transform Pairs, {TP10/11, TP1, TP8/9} and {TP14, TP8/9}, is TP8/9. We are unable to distinguish between TP8 and TP9 because both Transform Pairs specify A12 for the last letter (see Fig. B.5). However, TP9 has already been assigned to Bulbs-10, and therefore Bulbs-12 must specify TP8.

The two Bulb Designs fit the proposed Plant Model. Bulbs-12, which specifies the Transform Pair TP8, falls adjacent to the last of the Flower Designs, Flowers-8, which falls at TP7. TP8 lies at the boundary between the Recta and Aversa halves of the Pillar Sonnet. This is consistent with our Plant Model: one would expect to find plant bulbs at the earth's ground level, with flowers above and roots below, as will be discussed in the next section. Immediately after Bulbs-12, which lies at TP8, we find Bulbs-10 at TP9. This looks correct in that the smaller Bulb Design, Bulbs-10, follows a decreasing pattern consistent with the tapering of the lower half of the Pillar Sonnet (excluding its base).

The Transform Pair value of the Roots-5 Design

The MLIP Subsequence has two instances of the Roots-5 Design (Fig. 7.5), which occur in FL.6 and Scoff.7, ID numbers 9 and 17 in Fig. 7.1, respectively.

Fig. 7.5 Roots-5 Design

The possible Transform Pairs for FL.6 are:

F→I	R3; A11	None; TP10/11
E→I	R4; A12	TP1; TP8/9

The possible Transform Pairs for Scoff.7 are:

B→N	R11; A11	TP7; TP10/11
E→N	R8; A8	TP3; none

The intersection of the two sets, {TP10/11, TP1, TP8/9} and {TP7, TP10/11, TP3}, is TP10/11. It is impossible to distinguish between TP10 and TP11 because both decipher the first letter using Transform A11 (see Fig. B.5). Only at a later point in the Puzzle will it be possible to choose between these two alternatives. In any case, the Roots-5 Design is located well into the Aversa half of the pillar, which fits the downward growing roots of our Plant Model.

The Transform Values of the DoubleA Designs

The two DoubleA Designs, which appear in Fig. 7.6, are identical except that one is printed upside down. In the *Hekatompathia,* there are 7 instances of the Design in which it appears upright in all copies (Sonnets 7, 14, 19, 27, 60, 72, and 100), 2 instances in which it appears upside down in all copies (under the preface by G. Peele and Sonnet 85), and 2 instances where there are press variants in which its orientation varies (Sonnets 41 and 47).[2]

DoubleA   DoubleA-inv

Fig. 7.6 DoubleA Design family

The DoubleA Design appears once in the MLIP Subsequence, in LD.2, ID 18 in Fig. 7.1. The possible Transform Pairs are:

H→I	R1; A9	TP1; none
E→I	R4; A12	TP1; TP8/9

Both TP8 and TP9 are already assigned to the Bulbs-10 and Bulbs-12 Designs, and therefore the DoubleA Design must specify TP1. This location makes it appear that the Pillar Sonnet is displaying an insignia at the very top of the pillar. Perhaps this is related to the use of a Design with two A's, similar to the DoubleA Design, that appears at the top of the title page (which is reproduced in Fig 14.1).

The DoubleA-inv Design appears once in the MLIP Subsequence, in LD.3, ID 19 in Fig. 7.1. The possible Transform Pairs are:

H→M	R4; A6	None; TP15
E→M	R7; A9	None; TP12

Both TP12 and TP15 are valid possibilities. The TP15 alternative seems most likely because there is a symmetry with respect to the position of the DoubleA Design. The TP15 location lies at the lowest point of the pillar, excluding its base, thus mirroring the position of the correctly oriented DoubleA Design, which sits at the top of the pillar. This assumption will be confirmed in the Puzzle's third Stage.

The pictorial Designs

As discussed in Chapter 4, three pictorial Designs appear to show love's capacity for terror: the Daedalus, Heart Jail, and Lioness Designs. These three Designs appear far more frequently than other Designs, accounting for 33 of the 97 Designs. We might guess that these pictorial Designs point to the Orchema ("skipping") tables: these tables are more complex than the sequentially ordered Recta and Aversa tables and therefore require more instances to discover their values. The 33 instances of these pictorial Designs would presumably provide enough information to define the Orchema tables. Put another way, if these Designs instead appeared infrequently, the values of the Orchema tables would be under-constrained and therefore indeterminate. Thus, we hypothesize that each of the three pictorial Designs specifies an Orchema table. These Orchema tables appear in the base region of the Pillar Sonnet: the Puzzle Sonnet Instructions (PS.1, Point 4) state that the Pillar Sonnet's base is orchematicall.

The Design to Transform Pair map

We have now, on a preliminary basis, identified the Transform Pair values for 9 of the 18 Designs, as shown in Fig. 7.7. Although incomplete, these results demonstrate significant coherence in the contiguous and ordered arrangements of the Flower Designs and the overall layout of the Flowers, Bulbs, and Roots Designs, in accordance with our Plant Model.

Transform Pair	Design	Uncertain
TP1	DoubleA	
TP2	Flowers-1	
TP3	Flowers-4	
TP4		
TP5	Flowers-5	
TP6	Flowers-6	
TP7	Flowers-8	
TP8	Bulbs-12	
TP9	Bulbs-10	
TP10	Roots-5?	x
TP11	Roots-5?	x
TP12		
TP13		
TP14		
TP15	DoubleA-inv	
TP16	pictorial	x
TP17	pictorial	x
TP18	pictorial	x

Fig. 7.7 Design to Transform Pair map (incomplete)

Now that we have determined the Transform Pairs specified by many of the Designs, we can update the table in Fig. 7.1, as shown in Fig. 7.8 (in a modified format). For each deciphered sonnet in the MLIP Subsequence, the updated table, column 5, shows the Transform Pair number specified by the sonnet's Design (from Fig. 7.7). Columns 6 and 7 list the two cryptographic tables specified by the Transform Pair (from Fig. B.5). Columns 8 and 9 list the CipherLine's first and last letters, and columns 10 and 11 the corresponding plaintext letters. The last column lists the deciphered letter—the crib letter. Based on which of the two possible Transforms produces the plaintext crib letter, I have bolded the cryptographic table (either column 6 or 7), the corresponding first or last ciphertext letter (either column 8 or 9), and the deciphered plaintext letter (either column 10 or 11). This bolded plaintext letter (column 10 or 11) matches the bolded crib letter in the last column. Of the 21 letters in the crib, 15 have been deciphered (shown in bold), and the remaining 6 have not because the Orchema table values are unknown. (A version of Fig. 7.8 with all entries completed appears in Appendix C, Fig. C.2.)

ID	Sonnet #		Design Type	TP value	First table	Last table	CipherLine		Plaintext		Crib
	New	Old					first	last	first	last	
1	PS.1	80	Flowers-6	TP6	R10	**R11**	S	**D**	D	**P**	**P**
2	PS.2	81	Flowers-5	TP5	**R9**	R10	**H**	E	**R**	P	**R**
3	PS.3	82	Lioness				W	T			O
4	FL.1	86	Heart Jail				A	T			D
5	FL.2	93	Bulbs-12	TP8	R12	**A12**	F	**E**	S	I	I
6	FL.3	88	Daedalus				C	S			G
7	FL.4	99	Flowers-8	TP7	**R11**	R12	**O**	E	**A**	R	**A**
8	FL.5	87	Flowers-6	TP6	**R10**	R11	**A**	Y	**L**	K	**L**
9	FL.6	95	Roots-5	TP10/11	**A11**	A11/10	**F**	E	**I**	L	**I**
10	FL.7	97	Flowers-4	TP3	R6	**R8**	P	**S**	W	**B**	**B**
11	Scoff.1	96	Bulbs-10	TP9	**A12**	A12	**I**	W	**E**	R	**E**
12	Scoff.2	83	Flowers-8	TP7	R11	**R12**	I	**E**	U	**R**	**R**
13	Scoff.3	98	Bulbs-12	TP8	R12	**A12**	A	**T**	N	**T**	**T**
14	Scoff.4	QA	Flowers-I	TP2	**R5**	R6	**U**	S	**A**	Z	**A**
15	Scoff.5	94	Heart Jail				B	T			S
16	Scoff.6	84	Flowers-I	TP2	R5	**R6**	F	**T**	L	**A**	**A**
17	Scoff.7	92	Roots-5	TP10/11	**A11**	A11/10	**B**	E	**N**	L	**N**
	LD.1	91	NONE								
18	LD.2	100	DoubleA	TP1	**R1**	**R4**	H	E	I	I	I
19	LD.3	85	DoubleA-inv	TP15	**A6**	A4	H	E	**M**	R	**M**
	LD.4	89	NONE								
20	90	90	Lioness				L	A			A
21	Epilogue	EPI	Daedalus				S	E			E

Fig. 7.8 The Stage 2 deciphering process

As discussed in the first chapter, Bacon believed that experimental science should be constructed around tables of discovery that are filled in as new experimental data becomes available. A significant part of the process of solving the Puzzle is filling in tables: the Transform Pair value table, the crib deciphering tables, and tables of Catalog Ties and the CipherLines to which they point.

Validating our Designs to Transform Pair map

How confident should we be that our Designs to Transform Pair map is correct? Let us review the assumptions that were made in the process of discovering this map. First, it was assumed that the reordering of the MLIP sonnets, determined in Chapter 5 and Addendum 1, is correct. This reordering was overdetermined by multiple mechanisms: the ordering by the Index Sonnet 98, the Sequential Ties between adjacent sonnets, the division into Subseries, and the overall logic and progression of the reordered Subsequence. A second assumption was that the CipherLine selections for each of the 15 deciphered sonnets are correct. The Cipher-Line selections are also overdetermined, based on the Index Sonnet Ties, Catalog Sonnet Ties, and *Quid Amor* Ties. A third assumption was that our crib, PRODIGA LIBERTAS ANIMAE, is the true plaintext. This assumption lacks reasonable alternatives. There are a very limited number of 21-letter Latin phrases to choose from in this primarily English work: I found only two such phrases, and Sonnet 98's headnote strongly hints that *prodiga libertas animae* is the crib. A significant restriction on this phrase is that it must be thematically close to "My Love is Past," which is blazoned above the MLIP sonnets. Finally, the crib, *prodiga libertas ani-mae*, is the QA Tie for Sonnet 80, the first sonnet of the MLIP Subsequence, which affixes the crib to its cryptographic starting point at the Subsequence's first sonnet (see the lower part of Fig. 7.1).

These assumptions produced an extraordinarily ordered result in the Design to Transform Pair map (see Figs. 7.3 and 7.7). As discussed in the first chapter, deciphered texts are validated if order emerges from the deciphering process (subject to certain conditions). The 5 ascertained Flower Design Transform Pair values all fall within a range of 6 Transform Pairs, from TP2 to TP7. If this were the result of a random process, the Flower Design values would be scattered across 15 Recta and Aversa Transform Pairs (TP1 to TP15). Moreover, these 5 Flower Designs fall sequentially in the map, as discussed above. The two Bulb Designs also fall sequentially. The DoubleA Design and its inversion appear to be positioned at antipodes, that is, the extremes of the Recta and Aversa halves of the Pillar sonnet.

Another indication of order is that the use of the crib allows us to learn the Transform Pair values of each of the 10 non-pictorial Design types that appear in the MLIP Subsequence. If the order had been random, it is likely that some Design types would lack definition or that one or more of the Design values would be superimposed on each other. Although in the course of ascertaining these values, it was sometimes necessary to assign a Design to one of two alternate values, in most instances, the assignment was uniquely determined. In summary, the foregoing indications of order are very unlikely to have arisen by chance.

Moving forward to the next Stage

Unresolved problems remain after completing the second Stage of the Puzzle, including the incomplete Designs to Transform Pairs map, the undefined Orchema tables, and, of course, we have only deciphered the 15 letters based on 15 Designs in the MLIP Subsequence (presumably, the *Hekatompathia*'s 97 Designs produce as many letters). These incomplete tasks push us to the next Stage of this complex Puzzle.

Northrop Frye identifies the "quest-myth" as "the central myth of literature, in its narrative aspect."[3] Quests are an inductive process: conjectures must be entertained, without knowing whether they are true, and sometimes they turn out to be false only after a long process of investigation. This study does not document the many false conjectures I made in the course of solving the Puzzle. These false paths, these wrong turns in the labyrinth, would always ultimately lead to a contradiction. The genius of the Puzzle's design is its system of restrictive constraints: false paths ultimately lead to dead ends. Although the inductive process is an arduous one, it is often the only path available to acquire knowledge in complex matters. Whether it be the natural world that science interrogates or the fictive world that critics investigate, inductive reasoning is usually the primary means of attaining knowledge.

The Puzzle is astonishingly complex, and the difficulties faced in solving it often seem daunting. The first Stage requires the reader to perform three manageable tasks: reordering of the scrambled sonnet, recognizing that the Pillar Sonnet is a map of Transform assignments, and inferring that the cryptogram must be polyphonic. But the bar was raised in the second Stage: the puzzle-solver must undertake the more complex task of reordering the scrambled MLIP sonnets, identifying their CipherLines, and determining the Transform Pair values of the Designs. The Puzzle's complexity increases yet again in the third Stage where an even greater number of sonnets must be reordered, and this time without the assistance of an Index Sonnet. Perhaps the ingenuity of the *Hekatompathia* is meant to impress and surprise us, which it surely does, and this is intended to inspire us to our own creative acts.

8

Stage 3:

The Restoration of the Third Subsequence

We now embark upon the Puzzle's third Stage in our quest to reorder the *Hekatompathia*'s sonnets and decipher its encrypted messages. In this Stage, the work's hidden third Subsequence is discovered. Yet how can the work contain a third Subsequence when its title page explicitly declares that it is comprised of two Subsequences? Indeed, the placement of this declaration on the title page is a clear indication of its importance:

> Divided into two parts: whereof, the first expresseth the author's sufferance in Loue: the latter, his long farewell to Loue and all his tyrannie.[1]

The first of the *two parts*, the first 79 poems, describes the speaker's misery under love's tyranny; the second *part*—what I call the MLIP Subsequence—describes his escape from love's oppression. On reaching the final poem of the first Subsequence, Sonnet 79, its headnote prepares us for the sharp break between the first and second parts:

> The Authour prepareth him selfe to fall from Loue and all his lawes as will well appeare by the sequel of his other Passions that followe, which are all made vpon this Posie, *My Loue is past.*

The second part or MLIP Subsequence (the subject of Chapter 5) is clearly delineated: every page is blazoned at the top with this *Posie* in large uppercase letters: "MY LOVE IS PAST." In the last sonnet, Cupid accidentally kills himself, after which the speaker angrily casts his ashes to the winds (Sonnet 100). Does the *Hekatompathia* really end in this way?

An absurd conclusion: the death of love

Surely this is an unusual ending for a collection of love poems. Even the unhappy lovers in Ausonius's *Cupido Cruciatus*, though they place Cupid upon a cross, release him in the end, recognizing that love is indispensable to human life. Sutton recognizes that the *Hekatompathia*'s conclusion breaks sharply with the sonnet tradition:

> Hence, although The Author employs standard Petrarchan rhetoric and imagery, the Ἑκατομπαθία leads to an unanticipated and highly untraditional conclusion: love is definitively rejected by an act of the will far more decisive than a mere momentary aberration, and the lover escapes his predicament. Reason triumphs.[2]

In the MLIP Subsequence, the speaker claims adherence to reason, but in fact does little other than express his anger. If he were sincere about abandoning love and adhering to reason, it would be incumbent upon him to provide at least a glimpse of what such a life might look like. How would the procreation of the human life continue without some sort of love? What activity would the speaker pursue instead of love? In the early modern period, was there any philosophical or theological system of thought that embraced reason alone?[3] The *Hekatompathia*, with its Greek name (Ἑκατομπαθία) on its title page, and heavily influenced by Plato (see Chapter 14), nevertheless reaches a very un-Platonic conclusion. The *Philebus* (21de) offers this view of the life of reason:

> **Protarchus:** What is the 'life of reason'?
>
> **Socrates:** Imagine one of us choosing to live in the possession of intelligence, thought, knowledge, and a complete memory of everything, but without an atom of pleasure or indeed of pain, in a condition of utter insensibility to such things.
>
> **Protarchus:** Neither of these lives seems desirable to me, Socrates, and unless I'm very much mistaken, nobody else will think them so either.

Throughout Plato's canon there is a tension between the desire to bring reason and order to human affairs, and the recognition that man is an emotional being, unable to live by reason alone.[4] The *Hekatompathia*'s ending imagines that man can live by reason alone: as if the charioteer in Plato's *Phaedrus* could stabilize his chariot by simply removing the unruly steed. Another example of the impossibility of the life of pure reason is found at the beginning of the *Republic*. Sophocles, then at a very advanced age, is asked whether the "natural force of Venus" still rages unabated within him. "No," he answers, it is "as if I had run away from a raging and savage beast of a master" (329c). Sophocles's statement implies that other than a handful of octogenarians, all citizens of a *polis* live under the rule of a raging master. This surely suggests that the difficulties of governance are formidable. At the end of the *Republic*'s Book 9, the contemplated ideal republic, a product of the many reasoned arguments in the dialogue, is judged unlikely to ever come into existence. Reason does not subsume passion in Plato's dialogues, and we should be wary of any claim that it ever does.

Another indication that the work's ending is suspect may be found in the work's closing apothegm. This apothegm appears under its last poem, called an *Epilogue* in its headnote:

The Labour is light, where Love is the Paimistres.

In the work's last 20 sonnets, love is abandoned and scorned; in Sonnet 100, which in the published order falls immediately prior to the *Epilogue*, a bitter epitaph is inscribed on love's tomb. This closing apothegm, which inexplicably declares that Love's *Labour is light*, directly contradicts the MLIP Subsequence, and it also contradicts the first Subsequence, which *expresseth the Authors sufference in Love* (title page). Throughout the work, love is characterized as a heavy burden, and there appears to be no warrant for this apothegm anywhere in the text. This arresting and unresolvable contradiction, articulated in the work's final printed words, is yet another indication that something is terribly askew.

Turning from the work's final words to its first (subsequent to the prefatory material), we find that its first headnote, which appears above Sonnet 1, provides further contradiction:

> The Author in this Passion taketh but occasion to open his estate in loue; the miserable accidentes whereof are sufficiently described hereafter in the copious varietie of his deuises: & whereas in this Sonnet he seemeth one while to despaire, and yet by & by after to haue some hope of good successe, the contrarietie ought not to offend, if the nature & true qualitie of a loue passion bee well considered.

The headnote's portrayal of the first Subsequence as the narration of *miserable accidentes*, whereof are sufficiently *described hereafter in the copious varietie of his deuises*, is accurate (*devises* refers to sonnets, which are largely variations on, or amplifications of, love's miseries). The headnote then asserts that although the first sonnet depicts *despaire*, subsequently there may be *some hope of good successe*. Four different words or phrases denote some progression or future change: *by & by*, (OED 1: "one after another in order"); *after*; *hope* (which necessarily refers to the future); *successe* (which here means "that which happens in the sequel;" OED 1a). Thus it is being heavily emphasized that a transition in the speaker's mood will occur, at some subsequent point in the sequence, from that of *despaire* to a *good* state of mind. This new state of mind (*the contrarietie*) *ought not to offend*, we are told, *if the nature & true qualitie of a love passion bee well considered*. This pushes us to ask where are these subsequent sonnets that show the speaker lifted from *despaire*? Does this transition occur somewhere within the first Subsequence, or is this a reference to the transition between the first and second Subsequence?

The sonnets of the first Subsequence consistently depict the speaker as suffering under love, in keeping with the title page's description of the first Subsequence. Although there are fleeting moments of happiness within these sonnets, virtually every sonnet portrays suffering. In any case, no thematic transition is evident, and indeed, such a transition would make no sense. If his happiness were increasing over the course of the first Subsequence, he would not then, in the last sonnet of the Subsequence, *prepareth him selfe to fall from Love* (79.HN), which he in fact does in the second Subsequence. The second alternative is that the transition referred to in the first sonnet's headnote is the transition between the first and second Subsequence. However, the sonnets of the second Subsequence express anger and vituperate against love, and more intensely than elsewhere in the sequence. This is surely not a *good* (1.HN) state of mind. Another difficulty is that the first sonnet's headnote implies that this transition will be to a mode that is consistent with *the nature & true qualitie of a loue passion*, if such a mode *bee well considered*. This suggests that love poetry follows certain conventions. But how could the second Subsequence's complete rejection of love be consistent with the conventions of love poetry? What reader would believe that Cupid's death is a conventional ending for a sequence of love poems? The promised thematic transition claimed in the first sonnet's headnote is nowhere to be found. We have reached a rather disconcerting aporia.

At the very beginning of the work, in the gloss that precedes the first poem, one would expect the poet to offer some helpful guidance to the reader, but instead, he buries us in contradiction. The second and final sentence of the first sonnet's headnote only adds to our confusion:

> And where he mentioneth that once hee scorned loue, hee alludeth to a peece of worke, whiche he wrote long since, *De Remedio Amoris*, whiche he hath lately perfected, to the good likinge of many that haue seene and perused it, though not fully to his owne fancy, which causeth him as yet to kepe it backe from the printe.

The opening sentences of a work are where one might expect to find, in keeping with rhetorical practices, an exordium that introduces the work.

Instead, we encounter a statement about another work, *De Remedio Amoris*, which he has not yet published. This is a most indecorous digression: here at the outset, the poet is telling us about a text that we cannot read, rather than the text that we are reading. Rhetoric was a fundamental discipline, drilled into the students of the day. If we take these first words of the work to be an introduction or exordium, then it ought to establish a framework for understanding the work as a whole. The poet appears to be playing a literary game in his reference to a work that does not actually exist—a game such as that played by the *Shepheardes Calender*'s E. K. and by Gabriel Harvey when he addresses Spenser in *Three Proper, and Wittie, Familiar Letters* (1580), referring to Spenser's "*Nine Comoedies,*" among other lost works.[5] Cicero distinguishes between two species of *exordia*, the direct introduction (*principium*) and the subtle insinuation (*insinuatio*).[6] What might the poet be insinuating by playing this absent-text game?

The reader is probably expected to recognize that these rhetorical insinuations in the headnote hint that the *Hekatompathia* ought to include a "cure for love" (*De Remedio Amoris*). Is this cure the second Subsequence, in which love is vanquished by reason, or something missing or hidden? Ovid's *Remedio Amoris* is a sequel to his *Ars Amatoria*, in which Ovid presents himself as a "professor of love" (freely translating *praeceptor*; I.17), and claims that through his great skill, like an adept chariot driver, he can control love (I.7-8; *arte regendus amor*, I.4). In the *De Remedio Amoris* (55–64), he claims that his sage advice, if previously available, would have saved the lives of unfortunate lovers such as Phyllis and Dido and prevented the crimes of passion of Pasiphae and Medea.[7] Ovid's reader will likely take his bald, hyperbolic claim as facetious, perhaps concluding that, in truth, there is no cure for love. Similarly, in the MLIP Subsequence, the speaker claims that by reason and watchfulness, love's troubles can be avoided, not only with respect to himself, but by those willing to listen to him. The poet is insinuating that like Ovid's *Remedio*, the cure or *remedio* found in the MLIP Subsequence ought to be understood as a *faux* cure. Curiously, he also insinuates that the true cure for love will be presented in some future publication, and indeed, the cure for love has been carefully hidden within the sequence, to be brought to light, or "published" by the puzzle-solver.

The *Hekatompathia*'s untraditional conclusion, its abandonment of love, is suspect due to the intractable contradictions found in the first sonnet's headnote and the unexplainable closing apothegm, which conflicts with the title page's description of the work. When a reader is confronted by contradictory or confusing statements in a text, it is essential to read the text in accordance with the rhetorical practices of its time. C. S. Lewis explains the importance of rhetoric to the reading of early modern poetry:

> Rhetoric is the greatest barrier between us and our [early modern]
> ancestors. ... Nearly all our older poetry was written and read by men
> to whom the distinction between poetry and rhetoric, in its modern
> form, would have been meaningless. ... This change in taste makes for
> an invisible wall between us and them.[8]

The abandonment of love in the MLIP Subsequence is not the work's true conclusion; after restoration, the work concludes in a manner that is neither eccentric nor inconsistent with *the nature & true qualitie of a love passion*. The published ending, Cupid's death and disgrace, lies not at the work's true end, but at a midpoint in the sequence. Thus, a literal reading of the *Hekatompathia* yields one meaning, but a properly practiced rhetorical reading alerts the reader to the existence of the Puzzle, which reorders the text, which then yields a very different meaning.

The third Stage: the problem of the missing sonnets

In the Puzzle's second Stage, we recognized and corrected a corruption in the sonnet order of one Subsequence, which consists of a single Series. Now, however, we will confront corruption on a far broader scale. The natural place to look for the beginning of the Puzzle's next Stage is where the previous Stage left off: at the end of the MLIP Subsequence. The last poem of the MLIP Subsequence, excluding the Epilogue, is Sonnet 90, a Neo-Latin poem. Although Sonnet 90 is part of the MLIP Subsequence cryptographically, it clearly departs from the Subsequence's theme, the rejection of love. Its tone is religious, expressing regret, self-blame, shame, and repentance, before ultimately ending in prayer. This recantation reverses the speaker's abandonment of love in the MLIP Subsequence, and one would expect that this sonnet would be followed by others that explain the speaker's change of heart. Instead, the sequence ends abruptly in this very different key.

Sonnet 90 marks a conversion in the speaker's state of mind, a significant plot point in the sequence's development, and something more than the Epilogue must follow it. Also disconcerting, the closing apothegm, in which love is characterized as a *light labor*, contradicts all that comes before it: the sequence continuously depicts love as "heavy"—a tyrannical lion whose weight presses upon the speaker (the Puzzle Sonnet). To account for the transition from the MLIP Subsequence's rejection of love to the Epilogue's apothegm, there must be a significant number of sonnets in between. The only solution to this problem is to transpose forward a significant number of sonnets from earlier in the sequence to a position subsequent to Sonnet 90, thus creating a third Subsequence.

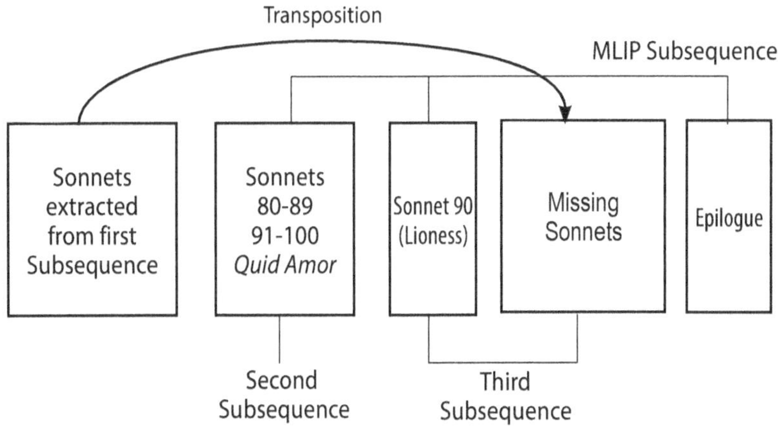

Fig. 8.1 Transposition of the missing sonnets

Fig. 8.1 depicts a hypothetical group of "Missing Sonnets" that falls between Sonnet 90 and the Epilogue. In this hypothesis, the *Hekatom-pathia* consists of three Subsequences rather than two, as claimed in its title page. This hypothetical "Third Subsequence," depicted in Fig. 8.1, would consist of sonnets taken from the first Subsequence. This hidden "remedy for love" ought to begin with Sonnet 90, a recantation, and end just prior to the Epilogue. Sonnet 90 is a translation of *Canzoniere* 364 (its antepenultimate poem); the Epilogue is a translation of *Canzoniere* 365 (its penultimate poem). Thus the missing sonnets are being inserted between the poet's translation of two sequential, closing poems of the *Canzoniere*, making it appear as if the poet is appending the *Canzoniere*.

We should now recall the poet's extravagantly highlighted couplet in Sonnet 5 (11–12), discussed at length in Chapter 3. This couplet, which violently contradicts the tenor of the rest of Sonnet 5 (a translation of *Canzoniere* 132), includes the proverb, *Selfe doe, selfe haue*. To the right is a bracket and a sidenote that reads: *Adduntur Tuscano hii duo versus* (these two verses are added to those of the Tuscan). Sonnet 5 is no ordinary sonnet: it declares the work's *circumstantiae*, and indeed Lilliat's contemporary marginalia confirm this.[9] Sonnet 5 is the sequence's rhetorical foundation, and to be certain the importance of this sonnet does not escape the reader's attention, the poet produces a second translation of *Canzoniere* 132 in Sonnet 6, this time into Latin. Sonnet sequences do not repeat whole sonnets—so why does this sonnet appear twice (albeit in two languages)? This repetition not only asserts the sonnet's importance but emphasizes the difference between the two poems, which is principally the abundantly highlighted couplet that appears in Sonnet 5, but not in

Sonnet 6 (or *Canzoniere* 132). The purpose of this heavy use of rhetorical signaling is to inform the reader that the *Hekatompathia* extends its primary intertext, the *Canzoniere*, and in this extension reverses its conclusion from the *Canzoniere*'s ending in humble supplication to some other ending that is consistent with Sonnet 5's exhortation to willfulness: *Selfe doe, selfe haue* (12).

The poet extends the *Canzoniere* by having the speaker recant at the point at which the *Canzoniere* ends (Sonnet 90/*Canzoniere* 364). The missing sonnets in Fig. 8.1 are his "addition to the Tuscan," a poetic text that presumably advocates willfulness: *Selfe doe, selfe haue*. The *Canzoniere* does not offer a cure for the lover other than perhaps the final turn to God. Thus, the *Hekatompathia* rhetorically signals that a significant piece of its text is missing. I call this missing text the third Subsequence: it is the poet's addition to, or revision of, Petrarch's treatment of love. He hides his "addition" to the *Canzoniere* within his sequence, and it is the reader's responsibility to expose this third Subsequence, this hidden *De Remedio Amoris* (hinted at in Sonnet 1's headnote). Sonnet 5's proverb suggests that this *De Remedio Amoris* is to be found in a willfulness that acts as a counterforce to love's powerful forces. Indeed, Ovid's *Remedio Amoris*, something of a self-help manual for the befuddled lover, also calls for willfulness.

Sonnet 90's missing line

The hypothesized third Subsequence begins with Sonnet 90, a translation into Latin of *Canzoniere* 364 (see Fig. 8.1). When Sonnet 90 is compared with Petrarch's sonnet, we find that it is inexplicably missing its final line. Reproduced below are the final stanza of Petrarch's sonnet, Bacon's translation of Petrarch's sonnet into Latin, and my translation of Bacon's lines into English.

> Signor che 'n questo carcer m'ài rinchiuso;
> tràmene, salvo da li eterni danni,
> ch'i' conosco 'l mio fallo, et non lo scuso.   (364.12–14)

> Ergo, summe Deus, per quem sum clausus in isto
> Carcere, ab aeterno salvum fac esse periclo.   (90.14–15)
> [   ]

> Therefore, great God, by whose power I am locked in this
> Jail, keep me safe from never ending danger.   (Tr. 90.14–15)
> [   ]

We see that Bacon has failed to translate Petrarch's final line, *ch'i' conosco 'l mio fallo, et non lo scuso* (for I recognize my fault and I do not excuse it).[10] This line is absolutely indispensable to the poem, and as we will discover, this omission was not a printer's oversight. Indeed, Bacon did translate this line in the sequence's earlier version, the manuscript titled "A Looking glasse for Loovers." In the manuscript's final page, three crossed out lines appear above the Epilogue, as shown in Fig. 8.2.[11] The first two lines, still clearly legible, are identical to 90.14–15 (shown above). The third line is clearly the missing (final) line of Sonnet 90. Although its first two words are mostly obscured, the letters that are visible, along with the last four words and knowledge of the Italian source, indicates that it surely begins with *Quam vanus*, as both Phillips and Sutton report.[12] Thus, the missing 16th line is:

Quam vanus fuerim fateor, veniamque requiro.
(I confess how false/vain I was, and I beg pardon.)

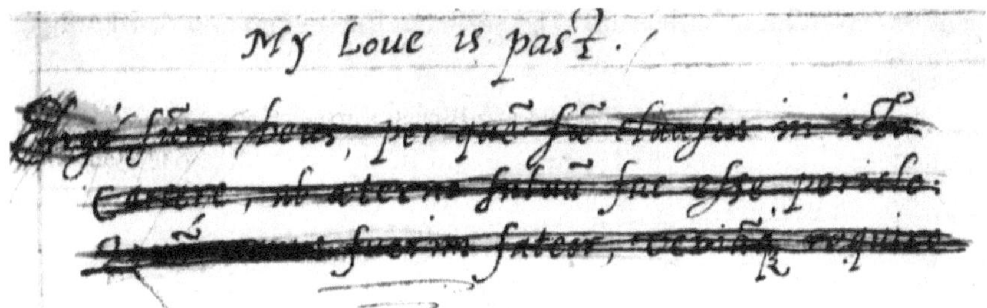

Fig. 8.2 Detail from the final page of "A Looking glasse for Loovers"
(Harley MS 3277) By permission: © The British Library Board

Just as the Puzzle's second Stage incorporates certain methods of the first Stage (e.g., the cryptographic tables), we might expect the Puzzle's third Stage to build upon the methods of the second Stage. The Precision System of the Puzzle's second Stage uses a cryptographic crib: each MLIP sonnet cryptographically generates one letter of the crib, PRODIGA LIBERTAS ANIMAE (as discussed in the previous chapter). If the third Stage builds upon the second, it, too, likely uses the Precision System and a cryptographic crib to ensure the correct reordering of sonnets. If so, then where might we find its crib? Naturally, we ought to consider the location at which we discovered the second Stage's crib, PRODIGA LIBERTAS ANIMAE. That crib was the QA Tie for the Subsequence's first sonnet, Sonnet 80 (as discussed in the previous chapter), and thus the natural place to seek the next Subsequence's crib is the first sonnet of that Subsequence, Sonnet 90.

Moreover, Sonnet 90 has a significant anomaly, as just discussed: its final line is omitted. Fig 8.3 schematically shows the presumed common architecture of the Puzzle's second and third Stages, and it depicts our hunch that the third Stage's crib may be discovered at the same relative location as the second Stage's crib, the lead sonnet of the Subsequence.

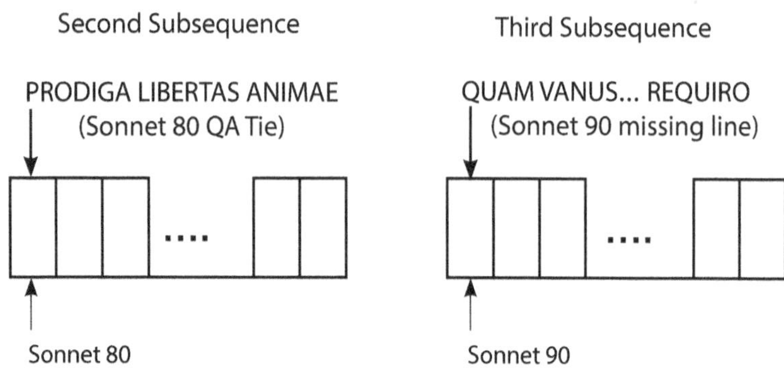

Fig. 8.3 Similar specification of the cribs in the second and third Stages

Significantly, both cribs shown in Fig. 8.3 are descriptive of the Subsequences that they regulate. Recall that in the second or MLIP Subsequence, "My Love is Past" is blazoned above each sonnet. The crib that we discovered, PRODIGA LIBERTAS ANIMAE, is descriptive of the speaker's state of mind in the second Subsequence: the speaker claims to have freed himself from love and enjoys an "overly free state of mind." *Prodiga libertas animae* was the QA Tie that pointed to the lead sonnet's CipherLine (80.8; *idle leasure*). In the third Subsequence, upon examining the lead sonnet, Sonnet 90, we ponder the omission of its final line. The carefully printed *Hekatompathia* contains few errors, and therefore this omission is unlikely to be a printer's oversight. Rather, it is an intentional breach of decorum that should be considered closely. Remembering Riffaterre's dictum that violations in grammar or decorum point to where things are hidden, we might well hypothesize that the crib is this missing line: *Quam vanus fuerim fateor, veniamque requiro*. Moreover, in this line the speaker makes an emphatic declaration, repenting for his past vanity. This repudiation of his earlier rejection of love (in the second Subsequence) summarizes the overall significance of the third Subsequence, much as *prodiga libertas animae* summarizes the speaker's state of mind in the second Subsequence.

Sonnet 90's missing line is far more likely than any other line to be the third Stage's crib. The crib or enciphered message, following the pattern of the first two Stages, is almost certainly in Latin. It could, in theory, come from any one of the work's six Neo-Latin poems, but the Neo-Latin Sonnet that heads the third Subsequence is surely the most straightforward hiding place for such a line. Moreover, as discussed above, this would follow the example of the second Subsequence in which the QA Tie to the lead Sonnet's CipherLine proved to be the crib. Should we consider any of Sonnet 90's other 15 lines? Only one of those lines could serve as a blazon for the Subsequence, that is, a description of its overall significance: *Supplice mente tibi tandem, Deus alte, repono* (10). Still, the odd omission of the final line makes it the far more likely prospect.

Assumptions must be made in the solving of any puzzle. At this point in our navigation of the labyrinth, we encounter one clearly marked path (Sonnet 90's omitted final line), a less likely path (Sonnet 90, line 10), and some unlikely paths (the lines of the other Neo-Latin poems). Fortuitously, the text of the omitted line is available from the manuscript (Fig. 8.2). Yet, even without the manuscript, we would have had a good idea of the line's content because it must translate the final line of the source poem (*Canzoniere* 364). As is the case with any inductive process, the proof only comes after the hypothesis is fully tested. In the next chapter, we will discover that the sonnets of the third Subsequence do indeed encipher the crib, QUAM VANUS... REQUIRO.

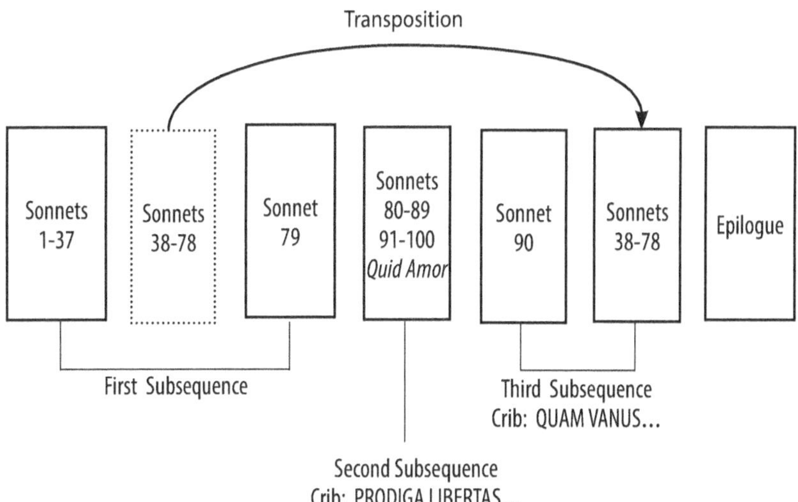

Fig. 8.4 The transposition of sonnets to form the third Subsequence

Fig. 8.4 shows where the Missing Sonnets are found. The crib, QUAM VANUS... REQUIRO, has 37 letters. If Sonnet 90 enciphers the first letter, Q, then the 36 remaining letters require 36 sonnets with Designs to encipher them. From where exactly do we transpose these 36 sonnets? Sonnet 79 lacks a design, and its headnote clearly indicates that it directly precedes Sonnet 80. However, prior to Sonnet 79, the range from Sonnet 39 through Sonnet 78, includes among them 36 sonnets with Designs (and 4 sonnets that lack Designs). Thus, this range provides exactly the 36 sonnets with Designs needed to complete the crib. Furthermore, this range begins with a Lioness Sonnet, Sonnet 39, a likely boundary point for the start of the transposition. Later in the process of solving this Stage, it became apparent that Sonnet 38, which lacks a Design, is also part of the third Subsequence. Thus, the 41 sonnets, from Sonnet 38 to Sonnet 78, must be transposed to a position subsequent to Sonnet 90, as shown in Fig. 8.4.

In our new model, the *Hekatompathia* has three Subsequences. The first Subsequence consists of the sequence's initial 37 sonnets, plus Sonnet 79. The second Subsequence, which we have so far treated as identical to the MLIP Subsequence, is slightly redefined such that it now excludes Sonnet 90 and the Epilogue. The third Subsequence includes Sonnet 90 and the 41 transposed sonnets. The Epilogue remains at its appropriate position as the last poem of the sequence. The crib, the missing final line of Sonnet 90, is enciphered starting at Sonnet 90: the first letter, "Q," of QUAM VANUS... REQUIRO is enciphered by Sonnet 90, and the last letter, "O," is enciphered by the sonnet immediately prior to the Epilogue.

What authorizes a reader to grab a large section of text from the middle of a work and append it to the end, radically altering the work's ending? As discussed in Chapter 4, a precedent for such a sweeping reordering is found in Alan of Lille's *Anticlaudianus*. This work, popular even four centuries later in Elizabethan England, expected that its most erudite readers would recognize that several of the work's books must be moved from the beginning to the end of the text, as James Simpson argues persuasively.[13] In some respects, Simpson's reversal of the order of the *Anticlaudianus*'s Books is analogous to the moving of the *Hekatompathia*'s Sonnets 38–78 from the middle to the end of the sequence. Simpson calls Books 1–6 a "Neo-Platonic theology" and Books 7–9 a "Stoic derived ethics and politics."[14] The second Subsequence, which appears last in the unrestored order, like the last three Books of the *Anticlaudianus*, expresses a quasi-stoicism in which the speaker resists love, a force of nature. He swears a resistance to love and encourages others to join him—a stoic ethics of sorts. In contrast, Sonnets 38–78, like the *Anticlaudianus*'s Books 1–6, develop a Platonist cosmology (see Chapter 14). Thus, in both works, an ending section whose concern is a stoic, or stoic-like, ethics is swapped with an earlier section that develops a Platonist cosmology.

The third Subsequence includes 5 Lioness Sonnets: 39, 50, 64, 73, and 90, each of which heads a Series. The numbering system introduced in

Chapter 5 will be used to specify the sonnets of this Subsequence in their new order. The prefix "L" is used to designate a Series name, followed by the number of the Lioness Sonnet that heads the Series. For example, the Series beginning with Sonnet 90 is designated as "L90." The first sonnet of that Series, the head Lioness Sonnet, is designated as "L90.H." Subsequent sonnets in the Series are designated L90.1, L90.2, etc.

As in the Puzzle's second Stage, the order of sonnets in the third Subsequence is scrambled. In the second Stage, the reordering process began with a sorting into three Subseries of sonnets (Fond Love, Scoff, Love Discharged); in this Stage, the first task is to sort the Subsequence's 42 sonnets into its 5 Lioness Series. I performed this task using the same method I used in the second Stage: I printed each of the 42 sonnets on a separate piece of paper and sorted them into 5 thematic piles based on the themes presented in each of the 5 Lioness Sonnets. Of course, that process cannot be captured in writing, and instead commentary pages are used to justify my sorting decisions (Addenda 2–6). The resulting third Subsequence consists of 5 Lioness Series, L90, L39, L64, L50, and L73. In performing this sort, I found that 8 sonnets belonged to the L90 Series, 13 to the L39 Series, and each of the other 3 Series contained 7 sonnets each, as shown in Fig. 8.5. I discovered the order of these Series from the overall progression of the Subsequence toward its conclusion, and from the Sequential Ties that bind the last sonnet of one Series to the beginning sonnet of the next, and a sonnet ring within each Series, as described below.

Series L90	Series L39	Series L64	Series L50	Series L73
8 sonnets	13 sonnets	7 sonnets	7 sonnets	7 sonnets
QUAM VAN	US FUERIM FAT	EOR VEN	IAMQUE	REQUIRO

Fig. 8.5 Series of the third Subsequence

Fig. 8.5 shows the letters enciphered by each Series. For example, the L90 Series enciphers the first 7 letters of the crib, QUAM VAN[US]—the final two letters of VANUS are enciphered by the next Series. The number of crib letters does not exactly match the number of sonnets in each Series because 5 of the sonnets lack Designs and therefore do not encipher letters. The 3 Series that contain 7 sonnets each (L64, L50, and L73) consist of the lead Lioness Sonnet followed by a 6-sonnet ring; the L39 Series has 13 sonnets and consists of a lead Lioness Sonnet followed by two 6-sonnet rings.

The 6-sonnet rings

The ordering of poems within a collection may be based upon either thematic or metrical considerations, practices found in both Renaissance and ancient collections of poems.[15] Some collections are organized symmetrically around a center; other collections demonstrate linear progress from the first to last poem.[16] A poem structured around a center is described as a "ring composition." A variation on ring composition, known as "interlocking ring composition," repeats a sequential pattern. Doranne Fenoaltea uses schematic diagrams to depict these two types of rings, and Fig. 8.6 was adapted from her diagrams.[17]

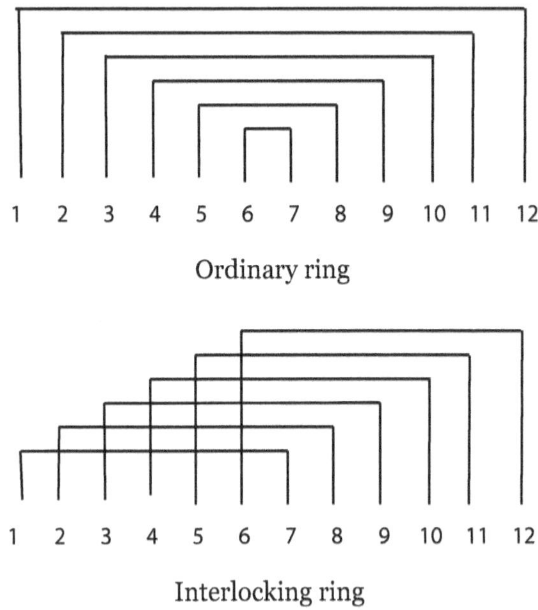

Fig. 8.6 Ring composition

The *Hekatomapthia* employs an interlocking ring structure based on a repeating pattern of 6 themes. The poet may have recognized such structures in Ronsard's 1550 *Odes* (the source for his Sonnet 83). In the three 7-sonnet Series of the third Subsequence (L64, L50, and L73), a Lioness sonnet introduces the Series, followed by 6 sonnets that cycle through 6 themes. This provides a well-defined structure for each of these Series. These rings "interlock" or repeat their pattern across multiple Series. The *Hekatompathia* defines these 6-sonnet thematic progressions in

Sonnet 47. Its headnote alerts the reader to the importance of this sonnet and suggests that it be studied carefully:

> This Passion conteineth a relation through out from line to line; as, from euery line of the first staffe as it standeth in order, vnto euery line of the second staffe: and from the second staffe unto the third. The oftener it is read of him that is no great clarke, the more pleasure he shall haue in it. And this poesie a scholler set down ouer this Sonnet, when he had well considered of it: *Tam casu, quam arte et industria.*

The cross-stanza relationship defined in the headnote distinguishes 6 groups of 3 sonnet lines each. The headnote asserts that there is a relationship among the first lines of each of the 3 stanzas, the second lines of each of the 3 stanzas, and so on through the sixth lines of each of the 3 stanzas. This makes for 6 groups that define 6 repeating themes of the ring.

The headnote's rhetorical language signals the importance of this sonnet by stating that anyone who is not a *great clarke* should read this sonnet often. The headnote further alerts us to the sonnet's significance by claiming that a scholar, upon close consideration of this sonnet, gave it this annotation: *Tam casu, quam arte et industria* (how much falls out [of this], how much art and purposefulness). *Casu* (fall out of) implies that there are significant consequences to this artful (*arte*) and purposeful (*industria*) sonnet.

Fig. 8.7 includes the text of Sonnet 47 and then sorts its lines in the manner suggested by the headnote. The first line of each stanza is grouped together (lines 1, 7, and 13), the second line of each stanza is grouped together (lines 2, 8, and 14), and so on—consistent with the poet's instructions. Each of the 6 groups presents an image or theme. We will refer to each of these 6-sonnet thematic arrangements as a "Hexameral ring" or "Hexameral."[18] Each of the Hexameral's 6 themes is denoted by the terms Hex1 through Hex6.

We will now characterize each of the Hexameral themes, as defined by the 3-line groups presented in Fig. 8.7. Examining the first group, Hex1, *yoake* appears twice along with *might* and *force*. A frequent theme in the *Hekatompathia* is love's ability to confine and exert overwhelming force. In the first of the 3 lines, a bull, a strong animal, is nevertheless confined; in the second, the might of the beloved is too great to be confined; in the third, the speaker hopes that love will overpower the beloved and bring her to recognize his suit. The image presented in all 3 lines is that of love as a great power that can control or confine the lover.

The second group, Hex2, depicts the lover as being enticed by some form of bait. In the first line, all hawks, even if untamed (*haggred*), will

In time the Bull is brought to weare the yoake;
In time all haggred Haukes will stoope the Lures;
In time small wedge will cleaue the sturdiest Oake;
In time the Marble weares with weakest shewres:
    More fierce is my sweete loue, more hard withall,   5
    Then Beast, or Birde, then Tree, or Stony wall.
No yoake preuailes, shee will not yeeld to might;
No Lure will cause her stoope, she beares full gorge;
No wedge of woes make printe, she reakes no right;
No shewre of teares can moue, she thinkes I forge: 10
    Helpe therefore *Heau'nly Boy*, come perce her brest
    With that same shaft, which robbes me of my rest.
So let her feele thy force, that she relent;
So keepe her lowe, that she vouchsafe a pray;
So frame her will to right, that pride be spent;   15
So forge, that I may speede without delay;
    Which if thou do, I'le sweare, and singe with ioy,
    That Loue no longer is a blinded Boy.

1	In time the Bull is brought to weare the yoake;	
7	No yoake preuailes, shee will not yeeld to might;	Hex1
13	So let her feele thy force, that she relent;	
2	In time all haggred Haukes will stoope the Lures;	
8	No Lure will cause her stoope, she beares full gorge;	Hex2
14	So keepe her lowe, that she vouchsafe a pray;	
3	In time small wedge will cleaue the sturdiest Oake;	
9	No wedge of woes make printe, she reakes no right;	Hex3
15	So frame her will to right, that pride be spent;	
4	In time the Marble weares with weakest shewres:	
10	No shewre of teares can moue, she thinkes I forge:	Hex4
16	So forge, that I may speede without delay;	
5	More fierce is my sweete loue, more hard withall,	
11	Helpe therefore *Heau'nly Boy*, come perce her brest	Hex5
17	Which if thou do, I'le sweare, and singe with ioy,	
6	Then Beast, or Birde, then Tree, or Stony wall.	
12	With that same shaft, which robbes me of my rest.	Hex6
18	That Loue no longer is a blinded Boy.	

Fig. 8.7 Sonnet 47 sorted into its Hexameral themes

stoope (descend) to the lure. A lure is a device used by falconers to recall their hawks and, it is claimed, all hawks will eventually succumb to the attraction of this bait. However, in the second line, the beloved is so fully fed (*beares full gorge*, another falconry term) that she does not take love's bait. In the third line, the speaker hopes that in the future she will grant (*vouchsafe*) the speaker's prayer (*pray*), or reading *pray* as "prey," that the beloved will be lured by love. The image of prey lured by the sight of bait figures the speaker's enticement by the sight of the beloved, which in the *Hekatompathia*'s twofold model of love, is *ex visione* love.

In the third group, Hex3, the wedge cleaving the oak is similar to the image of Cupid's dart piercing the lover's heart. Cupid's dart may represent either of love's two powers, as Sonnet 63 demonstrates:

> **Loue hath two shaftes, the one of beaten gold,**
> **By stroake wherof a sweete effect is wrought:**
> **The other is of lumpishe leaden mould,**
> **And worketh none effect, but what is nought;**
>> **Within my brest the latter of the twaine**
>> **Breades feare, feare thought, and thought a lasting paine.** (63.1–6)

The *sweete effect* (2) is sensory; *the other* [effect]... *worketh none effect, but what is nought* (3–4), a contradiction, except if we understand "effect" to mean material change. The import of this line must be that an immaterial change has been *wrought*. Line 6, in which *thought* appears twice, clearly depicts this change as mental rather than physical. In Hex3, the *wedge* (like a shaft) that cleaves *the sturdiest Oake* (47.3) may ultimately *frame her will* (47.15), and this signifies nonphysical *ex cogitatione* love.[19]

A shift now takes place between Hex3 and Hex4: the first 3 Hexamerals are descriptive of love's power; the next 3 Hexamerals are centered upon various means or strategies by which love's power may be either countered or co-opted for the speaker's benefit. This shift can be seen in the summary of the Hexamerals in Fig. 8.8. The fourth group, Hex4, is concerned with time: the idea that even *marble weares* over time expresses the hope that even the beloved's intransigence will subside over time, such that at some point in the future she will accept the speaker's suit. *Forge* is used in two different senses: in the first occurrence (10), it means "deceit;" in the second (16), it means to fashion or change the beloved's mind. Hex4 expresses the hope that the overwhelming and constrictive force of Hex1 will either abate with time, or that love will refashion (*forge*) the beloved's mind.

In the fifth group, Hex5, the speaker hopes that the *fierce* power of his own *sweete love* (5) will move the beloved. *Sweete* seems to signify transmission through the senses, as does Cupid's *gold* shaft (63.1). However, reading through to 47.12, the *lumpishe leaden* (63.3) shaft that causes mental anxiety (restlessness) is also indicated. In Hex5, the speaker hopes that either arrow, the sensual power of love or love's cognitive influence, will move the beloved to accept the speaker's suit.

In the first line of the sixth group, Hex6, there is a reprise of the first 4 Hexamerals. In line 12, *that same shaft which robbes me of my rest* refers to Cupid's *lumpish leaden* shaft (63.3), by which he affects the lover's mind. (*Robbes me of my rest* refers to the restlessness that comes from a lover's mental anxiety, a trope found throughout the *Hekatompathia* and the *Canzoniere*.) In Hex6, the speaker hopes that the mental effect of this *leaden* arrow, the *small wedge* that cleaves *the sturdiest Oake* in Hex3, will be turned to his advantage, piercing the beloved's *brest* and, as a result, moving her to accept his suit. When the speaker declares (conditionally based on line 17) *that Loue no longer is a blinded Boy* (18), he is expressing the hope that Cupid, rather than shooting blindly, will direct his arrow purposefully toward the beloved and that this might bring her to return his love.

The six Hexameral themes specified in Fig. 8.7 adhere to a pattern similar to that found in the six speeches of Plato's *Symposium*, as described in Excursus 10. Fig. 8.8 summarizes the 6 Hexameral themes: Hex1 through Hex3 describe how love's awesome power may subjugate the speaker; Hex4 through Hex6 describe methods by which love's powers may instead work in the speaker's favor, moving the beloved to accept his suit.

Hex1: Love's overwhelming and confining force.
Hex2: Love's sensual subjugation (*ex visione*); love initiated by visual bait.
Hex3: Love's mental subjugation (*ex cogitatione*); love acts by mental imprint.
Hex4: Changes over time; pleas to change the beloved's mind; forging.
Hex5: Hopes that love's powers will overcome beloved's intransigence.
Hex6: Hopes that love's *ex cogitatione* power will turn the beloved; a summary.

Fig. 8.8 Hexameral theme summary

The Hexameral rings significantly aid in the restoration of sonnet order within a Series. A Series of 7 sonnets consists of a Lioness Sonnet followed by 6 sonnets that form a Hexameral ring, as shown in Fig. 8.9. Subsequent to the lead Lioness Sonnet, each sonnet adheres to one of the 6 Hexameral themes in order, from Hex1 through Hex6. The 13-sonnet L39 Series consists of a lead sonnet and two Hexameral rings (see Addendum 3).

The Hexameral ring is perhaps the most effective means at the puzzle-solver's disposal to reorder the sonnets of the third Subsequence. In all,

Lioness Sonnet	Hex1 Sonnet	Hex2 Sonnet	Hex3 Sonnet	Hex4 Sonnet	Hex5 Sonnet	Hex6 Sonnet

Fig. 8.9 Hexameral ring (Series L64, L50, L73)

the puzzle-solver has three independent means to determine the restored sonnet order within each Series: the order specified by the Hexameral themes; the Sequential Ties linking one sonnet to the next; and the plot-like progression over the course of a Series. A fourth determinate of order—which functions as a check on the first three—is the crib enciphered by the Designs (the Precision System). Acting in concert, these four determinates of order provide more than enough overdetermination to ensure that the reordering is as intended by the poet.

The 5 Series of the third Subsequence encipher the crib QUAM VANUS FUERIM FATEOR VENIAMQUE REQUIRO, as shown in Fig. 8.5. Details for each of the 5 Series, L90, L39, L64, L50, and L73, appear in Addenda 2–6, respectively. The commentary pages of these addenda provide a rationale for why each sonnet was sorted into the specified Series, and for the order of sonnets within each Series. These pages also identify the Catalog Tie and CipherLine for each sonnet. The deciphering details for the sonnets of each Series appear at the end of the addendum for that Series (Figs. A2.3, A3.5, A4.2, A5.3, and A6.3, in Addenda 2–6, respectively). A summary of the deciphering details for all 5 Series appears in Appendix C, Figs. C.3a and C.3b. This summary includes the deciphering of the Lioness, Daedalus, and Heart Jail Designs, which is only possible at a later point in the Puzzle's solution.

Validating the cryptography of the Puzzle's third Stage

We may now evaluate the cryptographic results for the third Stage that appear in Addenda 2–6. If we assume that the third Subsequence has been reordered correctly, and that the CipherLine of each sonnet has been correctly identified, we may then calculate the probability that the crib was generated serendipitously, rather than intentionally enciphered by the poet. Of the 37 sonnets with Designs, 24 have Designs for which the Transform Pair values have been identified. The remaining 13 sonnets have

Designs for which the values are unknown (the Lioness, Daedalus, and Heart Jail Designs) and therefore cannot be considered. The probability that one of two polyphonic letters serendipitously generated the appropriate crib letter is approximately 1 out of 12, and the probability of such an event occurring 24 times is $(1/12)^{24}$, which is equal to approximately 1 out of 8×10^{25}, an absurdly remote event.

Yet the above calculation is based on two significant assumptions: the correctness of the sonnet reordering process and the CipherLine identification process. We may now consider a complete relaxation of the second of these assumptions, allowing the CipherLine to be any of 18 sonnet lines for each sonnet and handpicked to produce the required crib letter. Although it might seem that this would allow any plaintext letter to be produced to match the crib, in practice the restricted range of letters found at the beginning and end of sonnet lines is a limiting factor. Under this condition of the complete relaxation of CipherLine selection, the probability of a serendipitous generation of the crib would be approximately 1 out of 16 million.[20] Thus, with this loosest possible restriction on the Cipher-Line, it would be very improbable that any given reordering of the sonnets—say, one chosen at random—would produce the crib. This means that any faithful attempt to reorder the sonnets would not generate the crib unless it was the poet's intention to reorder them as such.

The only way to generate the crib without correctly reordering the sonnets would be to deliberately choose the sonnet order such that it generates the crib—essentially working backward. Further, one would need to force the selection of CipherLines such that they generated the crib. However, it would be impossible to justify any such backward-driven sonnet order because the Puzzle sets too many constraints: Sequential Ties, the Hexameral ring order, logical progression within a Series, and Cipher-Line selections.

The foregoing further confirms that the Transform Pair values discovered in the previous (second) Stage are correct. An unqualified validation, that is, one independent of the correct reordering of sonnets, is available only in subsequent Stages of the Puzzle.

9

The Third Subsequence:
A Palinode and an Epiphany

The three-Subsequence architecture of the *Hekatompathia* has some remarkable similarities to the tripartite structure of Plato's *Phaedrus*, which includes three speeches on love. The first speech is Phaedrus's recital of an oration by Lysias, which argues that a young man should surrender himself, not to a lover, but to a nonlover. The second speech, delivered by Socrates, contradicts the position of Lysias and asserts that love is a dangerous influence that can overwhelm reason. However, after finishing his speech, Socrates repudiates it and begs the gods' forgiveness for having blasphemed love. He then delivers a second speech (the work's third oration), in which he contradicts his prior speech and argues instead that love is divine and can lift man's soul. Curiously, the *Phaedrus*'s second and third orations (Socrates's two speeches) have themes similar to the *Hekatompathia*'s second and third Subsequences, respectively: Socrates's first speech, like the second Subsequence, rejects love in favor of reason; both Socrates's second speech and the *Hekatompathia*'s third Subsequence treat love as divine and beyond the realm of reason. Although the *Hekatompathia*'s vision of divine love is not the same as that presented in the *Phaedrus*, both visions associate love with the contradiction of reason, and even with madness. In both works, love's contravention of reason is initially seen as a cause to reject love, but ultimately, this irrationality is deemed to be a divine gift.

The *Hekatompathia*'s debt to the *Phaedrus* for its rhetorical structure is most evident in the abrupt turn from the rejection of love to its acceptance as divine, which is found in both works. Indeed, at the critical moment, both Socrates and the *Hekatompathia*'s speaker use equivalent words: "I acknowledge my sin" (*Phaedrus*, 242d; *Hekatompathia*, *Quam vanus fuerim fateor*—the crib and missing translation of Petrarch's line, at 90.16). Moreover, both speakers engage in prayer and ask forgiveness. After admitting he "was foolish and somewhat blasphemous," (242d),

Socrates undertakes "an ancient mode of purification" (243a)—a palinode (243b); similarly, the *Hekatompathia*'s speaker engages in ritualistic prayer in his palinode in Sonnet 90.

Following Socrates's admission of sin, he begins his second speech on love, in which a charioteer fights to control two unmatched horses—an allegorical representation of a tripartite model of the mind or soul. Prior to beginning his second speech, Socrates twice uses the word παλινῳδία (palinode; 243b), and he again uses it at the speech's conclusion (257a), which marks his extraordinary second speech on love as a palinode—a repudiation of his first speech. This implies that such wisdom about love is only gained apophatically, that is, by first ascertaining what love is not. Mistaken notions about the nature of love are found in the speech by Lysias and in Socrates's first speech. Although love is the subject of the *Phaedrus*'s discourses, the dialogue is also, at a fundamental level, concerned with rhetoric, writing, and philosophical inquiry, as is the *Hekatompathia*.

Bacon's use of the *Phaedrus* as a model may have been inspired by Spenser's eclogue, *Maye*, in the *Shepheardes Calender*. Kenneth Borris, in his analysis of the emblem that heads the *Maye* eclogue, argues convincingly that it depicts a Phaedran chariot.[1] However, this emblem depicts a chariot that is grounded on the earth, the opposite of the chariot in the *Phaedrus*, which is imagined as ascending in the sky. This ascension is an exalted vision of "the ordered rule of the philosophical life... blessed with happiness and concord" (256ab). The *Maye* eclogue features a debate between Piers and Palinode about the merits of a Christian versus a libertine life. Although the *Maye* eclogue and third Subsequence are difficult to compare directly, both are concerned with the conflict between two forms of love and between an earthly life and heavenly ideals.

Another indication that the third Subsequence transitions to a treatment of love as divine is found in the last two Subseries of the second Subsequence: Cupid is disarmed (L82.Scoff.1), imprisoned (L82.Scoff.2), and killed off by his own brand (L82.LD.2). Borris writes that the disarming of Cupid, according to "well-known literary, iconographical, and hermeneutic precedents," signifies "the ascendancy of heavenly love."[2] The second Subsequence, read in the context of the original sonnet order, is killing off both forms of love, earthly and heavenly. Yet, in the context of the restored order, only earthly love is being killed off in the second Subsequence, and in the third Subsequence, a vision of numinous love prevails.

The third Subsequence's shift to a numinous view of love is accompanied by a change in poetic style and iconic content. A Neo-Latin poem, Sonnet 45 (L90.2) has an unusual meter that oscillates between hexameters, the meter of epic, and glyconics, which is associated with lyric. Many of the L90 Series sonnets are concerned with the actions of the pagan gods as they affect human life, also a characteristic of epic. Moreover, Sonnet 72 (90.5) describes a royal wedding and pageant that inaugurates a new dynasty, which is a conventional topic in epic. Elizabethan poetry often mixes together the features of different genres, and such shifts have significant exegetical implications. Here, the shift to an epic voice is indicative of the seriousness and scope of the *Hekatompathia*'s third and final Subsequence.

The L90 Series: Two Suns (Addendum 2)

The first three poems of the L90 Series introduce the third Subsequence. The Lioness Sonnet 90 is followed by a pair of poems, Sonnets 44 and 45, that present the beloved as a second sun. These three pivotal poems appear on the next three pages, one poem per page, followed by translations of the two Neo-Latin poems (90, 45). These three poems also appear in Addendum 2, along with facing commentary pages.

In Sonnet 90, the speaker, having been subjugated to *Diuus Amor* (Divine Love; 2) for seven years, calls upon what appears to be the Christian God, *Deus alte* (high God; 10), using pietistic words that demonstrate his faith in God (10). *Diuus* and *Deus* are orthographically and etymologically close, the effect of which is to conflate the Neoplatonic love god (*Amor*) and the Christian God. In the closing lines, the speaker addresses *summe Deus* (highest God; 14), declaring that this god is holding the speaker in "this jail" (*isto carcere*; 14–15), making it appear that the pagan love god is being addressed (love is characterized as a jailer throughout the *Hekatompathia*). However, in these final lines, the speaker also begs protection using words appropriate to prayer to the Christian God. This conflation of the Christian God with a pagan god appears to be blasphemous.

Sonnet 44 introduces the conceit that the speaker's beloved is *a Second Sunne* (HN), which also appears in Sonnet 45 and elsewhere in the third Subsequence.[3] This second sun is imagined to have two powers with opposite effects, melting and stiffening, both harming the speaker. He describes his suffering, unable to live either with love (*meltinge away*; HN) or without it (*growing stiffe*; HN). In contrast to the second Subsequence, in which he claimed to have happily removed himself from love, he is once again bound to it. The third stanza introduces the speaker's hope that somehow (*perchaunce*) the beloved's power will restore his heart, which he analogizes to the rebirth of the phoenix. This hope of a rebirth, of restoration to a happy life, is found throughout the third Subsequence. The death and revival described in the final line foreshadows the climax of the Subsequence.

L90.H   90

MY LOVE IS PAST.

In this Latine passion, the Authour translateth, as it were, paraphrasti-
cally the Sonnet of *Petrarch*, which beginneth thus.

> *Tennemi Amor anni vent' vno ardendo,*   Sonnet. 313.
> *Lieto nel foco, e nel duol pien di speme. &c.*

But to make it serue his owne turne, he varieth from *Petrarches* wordes,
where he declareth, howe manie yeares he liued in loue, as well before,
as since the death of his beloued *Lawra*. Vnder which name also the
Authour, in this Sonnet, specifieth her, whom he lately loued.

ME *sibi ter binos annos vnumque subegit*
 Diuus Amor; laetusque fui, licet ignibus arsi;
 Spemque habui certam, curis licèt ictus acerbis.
Iamque duos alios exutus amore perêgi,
 Ac si sydereos mea Laura volârit in orbes,   5
 Duxerit et secum veteris penetralia cordis.
Pertaesum tandem vitae me paenitet actae,
 Et pudet erroris penè absumpsisse sub vmbra
 Semina virtutum. Sed quae pars vltima restat,
 Supplice mente tibi tandem, Deus alte, repono,   10
 Et malè transactae deploro tempora vitae,
 Cuius agendus erat meliori tramite cursus,
 Litis in arcendae studiis, et pace colenda.
Ergò summe Deus, per quem sum clausus in isto
Carcere, ab aeterno saluum fac esse periclo.   15
[Quam vanus fuerim fateor, veniamque requiro.]   Missing line

L90.1   **44**

In this Passion the Authour misliketh one while his estate, & by and by after liketh of the same againe, vppon hoape and likelyhoode of amend-
ment, & throughout the whole Sonnet hee fayneth his Mistres to bee
a *Second Sunne*: and by expressinge his priuate infelicitie, in either
alwayes meltinge away with *Loue*, or growinge stiffe throughe Death
approachinge neere him by reason of dayly cares, hee maketh allusion
vnto the diuerse effectes of the Sunne, whiche maketh the clay much
harder, and the wax softer, then it was before.

T Hat Second Sunne, whose beames haue dimd my sight,
  So scorched hath my hart and senses all,
That cloggd with cares, and voide of all delight,
I onely seeke, and sue to be her thrall;
    Yet soe this heate increaseth day by day,   5
    That more and more it hast'neth my decay.
Sometimes I melt, as if my limmes were wex,
Sometimes grow stiffe, as if they were of clay;
Thrise happy he whome Loue doth neuer vexe,
Nor any Second Sunne doth mealt away: 10
    Nay cursed I blaspheme the fayrest Light
    That euer yet was seene by day or night.
Perchaunce her parching heates will once repaire
My hart againe, and make me all anew:
The Phenix so reuiues amids the ayre   15
By vertue of that Sunne which all men view:
    The vertue of my Sunne exceedes the skye,
    By her I shall reuiue, though first I die.

L90.2   **45**

The Authour vseth in this Passion the like sense to that which he had
in the last before it, calling his Mistres a *Second Sunne* vpon earth,
wherewith Heauen it selfe is become in *Loue*: But when he compiled
this Sonnet, he thought not to haue placed it amongst these his English
toyes.

F Oelices alii iuuenes, quos blandula Cypris
  Aptos fecit amoribus,
Exoptare solent tenebrosa crepuscula noctis,
  Aurorae maledicere:
At multo est mihi chara magis pulcherrima coniux 5
  Tythoni gelidi senis,
Dum venit in prima surgentis parte diei,
  Et Soles geminos mihi
Apperit, & maesto foelices reddit ocellos,
  Quod Soles videam duos, 10
Qui simili forma, simili sic luce coruscant,
  Et mittunt radios pares,
Vt Polus ipse nouo Terrae laqueatus amore
  Flammis inuideat meis,
Solis & ignoto se torreat igne secundi, 15
  Oblitus decoris sui,
Haud secus atque olim, Cum veris prima venustas
  Multo flore superbiit,
Et nitidos primùm strophiis ornâre capillos
  Pulchri Naïadum chori. 20

Translation of Sonnet L90.H (90)

He subjugated me for thrice two plus one years,
    Divine Love himself, and I was happy though burning with fire
    And I held certain hope, even though stricken with bitter woes.
Even now, deprived of love, I have lost two more years,
    And if my Laura were to fly up to the heavenly spheres,   5
    She would bring the innermost parts of an old heart with her.
Having wearied, finally, I regret the life that I have lived,
    And I am ashamed to have nearly consumed, in the darkness of error,
    the seeds of virtue. Yet what last part of my life remains,
    Finally, high God, I give back submissively to you;   10
    and I deplore my life of poorly spent time,
    whose course should have taken a better path,
    in the pursuit of avoiding strife and in cultivating peace.
     [alternatively, "in studying the prevention of lawsuits..."]
Therefore, great God, by whose power I am locked in this
    Jail, keep me safe from never ending danger.   15
    [I confess how false/vain I was, and I beg pardon.]   Missing line

Translation of Sonnet L90.2 (45)

Other fortunate young men, whom alluring Venus
    has made suitable for love,
are wont to crave the dusky dark of night
    and curse the dawn.
far dearer to me is the fair consort   5
    of chilly old man Tithon
when she comes at the start of the rising day,
    bringing for me two suns,
gladdening this gloomy fellow's eyes,
    since I see two suns   10
with similar form [or beauty] and thus similarly glittering with light
    and dispersing equal rays
such that the Pole itself, ensnared by new love for the earth
    envies my flames,
scorching itself with strange light of a second sun   15
    forgetful of its own beauty
not otherwise than the time when springtime's delight first waxed
    wanton with many a flower
and garlands first decorated the shining hair
    of the fair choruses of the Naiads.   20

In Sonnet 45, the beloved's brilliance and beauty is said to rival that of the heavenly sun (10–11). This conceit is also found in Spenser's *Shepheardes Calender*, published three years earlier, in which Elisa's "angelick face" (April.64) inspires these words of Hobbinol:

> I sawe *Phoebus* thrust out his golden hedde,
> vpon her to gaze:
> But when he sawe, how broade her beames did spredde,
> it did him amaze.
> He blusht to see another Sunne belowe,
> Ne durst againe his fyrye face out showe:
> Let him, if he dare,
> His brightnesse compare
> With hers, to haue the ouerthrowe.   (April.73–81)

In both Hobbinol's speech and in the sonnet pair (44, 45), a second sun is portrayed as a rival to the heavenly sun, one that may even surpass it. This elevation of the beloved is significant when considered in the context of the prolific and extensive sun symbolism found in both Christian and Platonist writings. The sun was considered the source of life and was used metaphorically to represent God, knowledge, and goodness. Ficino, in *Sopra lo Amore* (the Tuscan version of *de Amore*), writes:

> And not without good reason does Dionysius liken God to the Sun; for just as the Sun illumines and warms our bodies, so does God bestow the light of Truth and the fire of Love upon our souls. This comparison, as you will hear, is undoubtedly drawn from Book 6 of Plato's Republic.[4]

In a similar vein, Ebreo calls the sun "the simulacrum and corporeal image of the incorporeal Godhead."[5] Commenting upon Plato's solar symbolism and its Renaissance influence, Borris writes:

> Ficino's adaptations of Plato's solar epistemological analogy combine it with biblical comparisons of God to the sun and light, as well as with comparable statements from earlier Christian Platonists such as "Dionysius" and Nicholas of Cusa, so that this celestial luminary anagogically correlates with God, Truth, Goodness, and the brilliance of the divine Ideas.[6]

Making the beloved a god—if not *the* god—is the audacious conceit that animates the sonnet genre. In many sequences, the sonnet beloved is held as preeminently beautiful and virtuous in comparison to any example from the past or anyone that may come in the future. The beloved, like the Incarnation, is a unique historical event, one without precedent, and never to recur. Although the beloved is clearly not God, as she is mortal and part of the created world, she rivals the noumenal world, and this rivalry can be found throughout the L90 Series. The beloved so draws the attention of the sonneteer that it seems that the Christian God is entirely absent.

The L90 Series compares and conflates the beloved with the celestial and divine sun; it also conflates the Neoplatonic love god (*Diuus Amor*; 90.2) and the Christian God (*Deus alte*; 90.10), addressing them as if they were one and the same. At one moment the speaker addresses this god/God with pietistic language; at another he sees him as his jailor (90.14–15). This apparent blasphemy continues with the *Second Sunne* conceit in the pair of sonnets (44, 45) that follows. In the first of the pair, after making an accusation against love and the beloved, the speaker says, *Nay cursed I blaspheme the fayrest Light / That euer yet was seene by day or night* (44.11–12). In the second of the pair, the equivalence between the earthly and celestial suns is emphasized: "with similar form/beauty, and thus similarly glittering with light and dispersing equal rays" (translation of 45.11–12). Further evidence of such blasphemy is found in the concluding couplet of the first of the pair:

> **The vertue of my** Sunne **exceedes the skye,**
> **By her I shall reuiue, though first I die.**　　　　　　(44.17–18)

Here, not only is the *Second Sunne* ranked above the heavens, but it acts as the redeemer or savior of the speaker. This revival from death adumbrates a conversion that takes place near the close of the third Subsequence, in the L50 Series. This heretical view, an overturning of the medieval cosmological model in which the numinous world stands above the material, sublunar world, presents a problem for the reader that must be solved in the course of the third Subsequence. In medieval and Renaissance cosmological models, there is a natural hierarchy that extends from God above, down through the spheres of heaven, and then further down into the sublunar, changeable world of mortal beings. This "golden chain" orders the world, extending downward from the goodness and purity of the heavens and ending in the privation of the sublunar sphere.[7] The beloved violates this order by rivaling the noumenal world. This essential feature of most sonnet sequences, although blasphemous, enables the poet to make the divine visible. Just as Renaissance man believed that the reflection of the divine could be seen in nature and man, the sonneteer, in his creation of the beloved, presents a reflection of the divine to his reader.

Sonnet L90.2 (45) is a revealing and unusual Neo-Latin poem. According to its headnote, when the poet first wrote this poem, he *thought not to haue placed it amongst these his English toyes*. This may be the poet's modestly made claim for the poem's artistic merit or significance to the sequence, accomplished by depreciating the rest of the poetic collection (*toyes*). Its unusual meter alternates between hexameters and glyconics, which would be striking in any poetry collection; in the context of the constrictive form of the sonnet genre, it is a glaring anomaly that pushes the reader to ask why this weird meter was employed. Another reason to consider this poem carefully is that it is written in Latin: Bacon appears to turn to Latin for important poems such as Sonnet 6 (paired with Sonnet 5), Sonnet 90, and the Epilogue. Moreover, devoting a pair of poems (44, 45) to the conceit that his beloved is a *second sunne*, critically positioned at the beginning of the third Subsequence, is surely an indication of this pair's importance.

As discussed above, Socrates delivers two speeches in the *Phaedrus*, the second of which contradicts the first. After Socrates breaks off from his first speech, he says, "My dear good man, haven't you noticed that I've got beyond dithyramb, and am breaking out into epic verse, despite my faultfinding?" (241e). Dithyrambs are associated with Dionysian lawlessness, and poetic inspiration: more or less the opposite of the grandeur and virtue of epic verse. Socrates's change to epic meter is a change in diction that prefigures the reversal from his first (false) speech to his second speech, which begins with a palinode. Sonnet 45's sporadic use of glyconics comes shortly after the palinode, Sonnet 90, which introduces the sequence's "third act" (third Subsequence). Similarly, Socrates's dithyrambs occur at the beginning of the *Phaedrus*'s third act (the first act is Lysias's speech delivered by Phaedrus; the second and third acts are Socrates's two speeches). In both works, this momentary metrical shift is an indication of a critical turning point, an embarkation on the third leg of the journey (or plot), that leads to the work's conclusion.

In the *Hekatompathia*, the mixing of epic's hexameters with glyconics (a meter associated with lyric) may suggest that this third Subsequence is concerned with the topics common to epic—worldly rather than personal matters—even if subsequently the meter returns to a lyrical mode, the norm for sonnet sequences. It seems that Bacon, by the sudden inclusion of hexameter meter, heralds the third Subsequence's new focus: its attempt to understand love as a cosmic force. The sonnet genre's tendency to conflate lyric and epic modes is taken up in the final chapter. Another possible explanation for this extreme alternation in meter is that it reflects a discord arising from the juxtaposition of two opposed cosmic worlds: the earthbound sun of the beloved and the celestial sun—although these suns glitter with equal brightness, they belong to disparate spheres.

At the poem's outset, the speaker distinguishes his love from that of other men: he loves the day at sunrise while others crave the dark of night. The uniqueness of the speaker's love—a theme found throughout the work—appears to be linked here to the light of the sun and not to dark night. This provides us with insight into the distinguishing characteristic of the speaker's love, which the poet here links to the heavenly beauty of the sun/beloved. In Platonist philosophy, copies, which reside in the world of matter, are inferior to the immaterial Platonic forms. Yet, here the speaker insists on an equality between these two worlds, claiming that the two suns are equal: *simili* (similar) appears twice in line 11 and *pares* (equal) in the next line. Indeed, the second sun is so powerful that it even scorches (*torreat*; 15) the Pole itself—the second sun, the beloved, operates on a celestial scale, exceeding the natural laws of the sublunar world. Other men are concerned with earthly love, the speaker with heavenly love.

The final four lines hark back to a golden age, or the beginning of creation, when flowers first bloomed and pretty goddesses wore shining flowers in their hair—a point in time when numinous beauty and earthly beauty existed side by side and were perhaps indistinguishable. The speaker finds this golden age comparable to his present time due to the pristine, cosmic beauty of his human beloved. This imagined equality between earthly and heavenly beauty—an impossibility in most Platonist cosmologies—serves as an introduction to the concerns of the third Subsequence. The speaker is grappling with the strange nature of love, which is at once terrestrial and numinous, immanent and transcendent—an unfathomable contradiction. This *coincidentia oppositorum* lies at the heart of much Renaissance Platonism. However, as discussed below (the L73 section of this chapter and Chapter 14), the *Hekatompathia* goes a step further, ultimately collapsing the distinction between the terrestrial and the numinous.

The L39 Series: Link of the Universe (Addendum 3)

Throughout the L39 Series, love is characterized as a conjoining of opposites: heat and cold, hope and fear, joy and sorrow, life and death. In the Series' lead sonnet, the speaker asks: *What man doth live in more extreemes than these* (39.17). This conjoining of extremes has its roots in the *Symposium*, medieval philosophy and theology, and ancient mysticism, as discussed in Chapter 14. The speaker explores the nature of love and finds it to be a fundamental cosmic force that mysteriously binds opposites together. Love is both a reckless god that causes pain and a positive force that delivers pleasure. The *Hekatompathia*'s many paired opposites, including peace/war, joy/sorrow, bitter/sweet, and hope/fear, all evoke this

Platonist conception, and the ultimate point of resolution for these contrarieties is the Plotinian godhead: "contradictions coincide in the nature of the One." Ficino called love "the perpetual knot and link of the universe" (*amor nodus perpetuus, et copula mundi*).[8] The sonnet immediately preceding this Series, the last of the L90 Series, contains an encomium to the features of the beloved, which includes the peace/war opposition:

> **Her Eyes, one making Peace, the other Warres;**
> **By** Venus **one, the other rul'd by** Mars;   (L90.7.11–12)

Pico, citing Plutarch, says that "Harmony was born from the union of Venus and Mars," two gods that were often perceived as opposites. Indeed, Venus and Mars appear on opposite sides of the *Hekatompathia*'s title page (Fig. 14.1). Pico finds support among various other authorities including Heraclitus, Empedocles, the Pythagoreans, and Plato.[9] In the above lines, the beloved embodies that union of opposites and demonstrates that Bacon's deeper concern is with the principle by which unity is found in multeity. Although the *Hekatompathia*'s beloved is the human object of the speaker's love, she is also a cosmological construct, a unity that emerges from the strife of opposites. The *Canzoniere* describes Laura as a coincidence of opposites, a fountain from which both the bitter and the sweet flow.[10] Ebreo, in his *Dialogues of Love*, practices this Petrarchan trope: the beloved, Sophia, is portrayed as a coincidence of bitter and sweet:

> **Sophia:**   I cannot agree with your statements, Philo. At one time you make me divine and greatly desired by you, and at another you find me poisonous.
>
> **Philo:**   Both statements are true and compatible: for your poison is caused by your divinity.[11]

This extraordinary characterization of divinity as poisonous seems to run against the Augustinian belief that evil is not an entity, but an absence or rejection of goodness. In the *Hekatompathia*, a love that conjoins good and evil is the divinity that rules the speaker's life. The most significant conjoining of opposites in the *Hekatompathia* is the pairing of life and death. The speaker frequently describes himself as partaking of both at the same time—a living death or a dying life—or being at the boundary between the two, as when he is at the bank of the river Styx (L64.2). This state is perhaps reminiscent of Dante in the *Inferno*, who says, "I did not die and was still not living" (34.25). This half-alive state is where the speaker resides until the end of the penultimate Series, L50, in which he confronts a personification of death in the sequence's climax.

Bacon's fondness for *coincidentia oppositorum* is not unique among Elizabethan poets. As discussed in Chapter 2, in Spenser's *Faerie Queene*, Venus is described as hermaphroditic:

> But for, they say, she hath both kinds in one,   (IV.x.41)
> Both male and female, both under one name:
> She syre and mother is her selfe alone,
> Begets and eke conceives, ne needeth other none.

Alastair Fowler, quoting this passage, writes:

> Spenser's most obvious expression of his philosophical vision takes the form of representing aspects of the divine image by sexually coupled contraries. He repeatedly imagines the divine as a union combining opposites in love—a thought in the same tradition with Dionysius's use of the word *henosis* both for divine unity and for sexual intercourse.[12]

Edgar Wind finds *coincidentia oppositorum* in the works of Ben Jonson and describes how knowledge of Cusanus was spread in England by the visit of Giordano Bruno. He notes that the correspondence between Harvey and Spenser (1579–80) shows that they were studying the works of Pico, who often quotes Cusanus. Wind writes that "Bruno's *Eroici furori* (1585), with its dedication to Sidney, played a crucial role in 'naturalizing' the coincidence of opposites among Elizabethan writers."[13]

The L64 Series: *Canso* (Addendum 4)

The theme of the L64 Series is the speaker's effort to persuade the beloved to accept his suit: unbreakable causal chains bind the speaker to the beloved, and his only hope of escaping his torment is if the beloved reciprocates his love. As the Series progresses, the speaker increasingly recognizes the inescapability of his bondage. The intensity of the speaker's pleas also increases: he tearfully implores the beloved, worships her, makes prayers to heaven, and finally, begs heaven for her life. In the final sonnet, the speaker recognizes that his confinement is inescapable and so concludes with his vow of unwavering devotion.

Some of this Series' sonnets follow the tripartite rhetorical structure of a *canso*, an epistolary song to the beloved: *captatio benevolentiae* (seeking goodwill), which consists of praise of the beloved; a *narratio,* which relates the lover's suffering; and finally a *petitio*, a plea for mercy.[14] The speaker seeks reciprocation—that is, he seeks to convince the beloved to accept his suit.

The L50 Series: Epiphany (Addendum 5)

Having failed in his suit to the beloved in the prior Series (L64), the speaker now calls upon personified Love to aid him directly in his attempt to win the beloved's favor. When this plan fails, the speaker becomes increasingly desperate, his tone more dramatic and personal. As this last hope of gaining the beloved's favor is dashed, he comes to believe that death is the only means to gain relief. In the penultimate sonnet of the Series, L50.5, he enters into a dialog with Love and Death, which leads to an epiphany, and ultimately, conversion.

The *locus classicus* of conversion stories, Augustine's *Confessions*, is an important intertext for Petrarch, who imitates Augustine's conversion in his ascent of Mont Ventoux. John Freccero believes that Augustine, the master of "literary self-creation," is "the founder of the [sonnet] genre," which he calls "a narrative of conversion." As he further explains, "In the text of *Confessions*, conversion is always a literary event, a gloss on an anterior text."[15] The epiphany that occurs in Sonnet L50.5 leads to a resolution of the fundamental conflict set at the sequence's outset, the separation of the speaker's heart *from his owne body, and remoued into a darksome and solitarie wildernes of woes* (2.HN). In the final L73 Series, the speaker's heart or soul reaches a compromise with the tyrannical "lioness"—love.

In the headnote of the L50 Series' first sonnet, the speaker asserts that his love is unique:

> In this Passion is effectually set downe, in how straunge a case he liveth that is in loue, and in how contrary an estate to all other men, which are at defiaunce with the like follye. And this the Authour expresseth here in his owne person: therewithall calling upon *Loue*, to stand his frend; or if he faile, vpon death to cut off his wearysome life.

Remarkably, the *Authour* expresses himself *in his owne person*. This headnote, as most of the *Hekatompathia*'s headnotes, is written in the third person, which creates a small, if unconvincing, distance between the poet and the glosser. In contrast, this sonnet's headnote instructs us to treat the speaker as if he and the poet (*Authour*) are one; this baldly declared breach of the separation between speaker and poet must be considered significant. The headnote explains that in the sonnet, the speaker—the poet himself—calls upon Death to end his *wearysome life* (HN) should his suit fail, a dramatic and personal statement. In the final line, he addresses the beloved directly, and seemingly emphatically, using italics and parentheses: (*Deere Dame*).[16] This is difficult to square with the poet's statement that his *paines in suffering* [*these louepassions*] is *but supposed* (*To the frendly Reader* preface). There is no apparent means to resolve this contradiction, and to be sure, such tensions between the poet and speaker are often found in sonnet sequences. Significantly, the sequence includes one other clear exception to this separation between speaker and poet, which occurs in Sonnet 3:

> This passion is all framed in manner of a dialogue, wherein the Author talketh with his owne heart, beeing nowe through the commandement and force of loue separated from his bodie miraculouslie, and against nature, to follow his mistres, in hope, by long attendance vpon her, to purchase in the end her loue and fauour, and by that meanes to make him selfe all one with her owne hearte. (3.HN)

Sonnet 3, in conjunction with Sonnet 2, initiates the sequence's primary conceit, the separation of the speaker from his heart. In both the introduction of this conceit at the work's beginning, and its resolution in this and the final Series, the speaker adopts a personal voice. The climactic moment of resolution occurs in Sonnet L50.5, which like Sonnet 3, *is all framed in* [the] *manner of a dialogue* (3.HN). Thus the sequence's primary conceit begins and ends in the poet's personal voice presented in dialogue form.

Sonnet L50.5 is a dialog with three participants: the speaker, Death, and Love. Here, the speaker undergoes an epiphany that is signaled by a breach in decorum, a violation of metric grammar that alerts the reader that exegesis is required.[17] The breaking of metrical rules, which Annabel Patterson calls "metrical disturbances," is an indication of unruly or disruptive emotions. She cites a stanza from *Willobie his Avisa* (1594) that has two extrametrical lines and, in the margin, this explanation: "These verses exceed measure, to show that his affections keepe no compasse, and his exceeding love."[18] Patterson describes "the extent to which decorum of style branches out into the finest details of diction, meter, and rhythm." She then quotes the *Hekatompathia*'s *To the frendly Reader* preface at length because of its comments about the relationship between emotional and metrical disruption:

> I hope thou wilt in respect of my trauaile in penning these louepassions, or for pitie of my paines in suffering them (although but supposed) so suruey the faultes herein escaped, as eyther to winke at them, as ouersightes of a blinde Louer; or to excuse them, as idle toyes proceedinge from a youngling frenzie; or lastlie, to defend them, by saying, it is nothing *Praeter decorum* for a maiemed man to halt in his pase, where his wound enforceth him, or for a Poete to falter in his Poeme, when his matter requireth it. Homer in mentioning the swiftnes of the

> winde, maketh his verse to runne in posthaste all vpon *Dactilus*: and
> Virgill in expressing the striking downe of an oxe, letteth the end of his
> hexameter fall withall, *Procumbit humi bos.* Therefore if I roughhewed
> my verse, where my sense was vnsetled, whether through the nature of
> the passion, which I felt, or by rule of art, which I had learned, it may
> seeme a happie fault; or if it were so framed by counsell, thou mayest
> thinke it well donne; if by chaunce, happelie.[19]

Patterson sees this as an "important passage," evidence that decorum of
style in late sixteenth-century poetry, and breaches thereof, require
"detailed study."[20] In the above passage, Bacon claims that *it is nothing
Praeter decorum* (contrary to decorum) for a *Poete to falter in his Poeme.*
Thus, a breach in decorum of style, a "fault" (*falter*), does not truly breach
decorum because such intentional breaches are a poetic device meant to
signal the reader. If we read carefully, we will notice that Bacon is cunningly breaching decorum in his discussion of breaching decorum (similarly, Puttenham breaches decorum while discussing decorum).[21] In the
above-quoted preface, Bacon provides two examples of how a poet may
falter ("stumble," OED 1), the first in the *Iliad* and the second in the *Aeneid.*
The first is a canard. There is no fault or breach in form when a Homeric
verse (*Iliad* 9.4) is composed purely of six dactyls: it is a normal or "legal"
variant in epic meter. One translator of Homer, Oliver Crane, writes:

> Virgil rarely admits a pure dactylic line... while Homer, particularly in
> the Iliad, gives freer rein to his choice; and both—when sprightliness
> and spirited action invite it, as in the rush of thought in stirring descrip-
> tions—avail themselves of the dactylic movement as an element of life.[22]

A poet's choice of different proportions of dactyls and spondees in a line
of dactylic hexameter is an example of how metrical variation is meant to
induce an emotional response in the reader, but it is *not* an example of a
poet *falter*-ing or breaching decorum; rather, such metric variation is a
normal and fundamental property of epic meter. Bacon intentionally fal-
ters by spuriously implying that Homer's dactylic line is a fault, and the
effect of this is to highlight his second example, the *Aeneid*'s metric fault.
Even so, just in case the reader misses his intentional flaw, he highlights
it in another way. In the above quotation from the *To the frendly Reader*
preface, Bacon uses the phrase "*a maiemed man to halt in his pase*" and
the word "*falter*" (stumble—implying a slow pace) to characterize Homer's
portrayal of swift-paced winds. This seeming contradiction, even if super-
ficial, should further alert an attentive reader.

Why does the preface quoted above point to Virgil's breach of decorum in the *Aeneid*? Virgil's *procumbit humi bos,* which is metrically short, is a well-known example of metrical breach. Even poor Latin students (such as I) remember reading this line. In a class where students take turns reading lines, I read this line and paused, thinking that I had mis-scanned it:

sternitur exanimisque tremens procumbit humi bos.   (*Aeneid* 5.481)

(and flung down, the trembling ox fell forward to the ground, lifeless.)

But my instructor corrected me and explained that this line is not one of the *Aeneid*'s unfinished lines; rather, it is intentionally truncated. As the bull keels over, its life cut short, so too does the poetic line fall short—metrically. Bacon has carefully drawn our attention to Virgil's intentional breach of metric decorum, by which he enhances his portrayal of death's suddenness and finality. Turning to his own poetry, Bacon curiously states: *Therefore if I roughhewed my verse, where my sense was vnsetled... it may seeme a happie fault.* Yet, Bacon rarely *roughhew*[s] ("give crude form to") his verses in the *Hekatompathia*, rather, his metrical practice "is notable for the unwavering regularity of its meter."[23] He then hints at his purpose: *if it were so framed by counsell, thou mayest thinke it well donne.* Here we are informed that the line was intentionally corrupted (*framed by counsel*) alerting us to watch out for any wavering in his almost constantly unwavering meter. Furthermore, by his choice of Virgil's metrically short line as an example, he has specified the fault for which we must be on the lookout.

In the headnote of Sonnet L50.5 (56), the poet states that in the third stanza, he entreats *Death a new, to ende his dayes.* Line 14 of this sonnet is a tetrameter, one of only four unmetrical lines in the work.[24] The speaker, after requesting that Death *dispatch* him, enacts his own death by metric fault:

And thou, O Death, when I possesse my Hart,
Dispatch me then at once: Why so?   (L50.5.13–14)

Like Virgil's metrically short line, this one evokes death. The reader has been forewarned in the *To the frendly Reader* preface that a metrically short line may be an intentional fault that emphasizes death's suddenness and finality. Bacon thus draws our attention to the sequence's most critical plot point, the moment of epiphany that leads to the speaker's conversion.

Speakers in sonnet sequences are often characterized as pilgrims, and in mythopoetic terms, the speaker, by enacting his own death, makes a journey to the underworld (*descensus ad infernos*). The literary precedents for such a downward journey include Orpheus's descent to Hades, Odysseus's visit to the underworld in the *Odyssey*, and Aeneas's descent in search of his father in *Aeneid* 6. According to medieval commentaries, Aeneas's descent depicts a virtuous man transcending life's *temporalia* and attaining philosophical wisdom.[25] In the next and final Series, the speaker attains such wisdom.

In the medieval period, the *descensus ad infernos* is theological rather than philosophical. A Christian *descensus* is a descent into humility, the first stage of a pilgrimage guided by grace.[26] There is a death of the former self—one must die in order to be reborn. In *Confessions*, the moment of death and rebirth takes place near a fig tree. Freccero characterizes it this way:

> In effect, the Augustinian solution of the epistemological problem of confession was identical with the Pauline solution of the moral problem facing all Christians. All confession, literary or sacramental, is either a lie or the record of a conversion, a descent into Hell, while self-expression in its profoundest sense is necessarily re-birth.[27]

Dante's sonnet sequence is the story of a conversion to a new life, as its title, *Vita Nuova*, indicates. In the *Hekatompathia*, the speaker's moment under the Augustinian fig tree, that point of discontinuity in time when a new life begins, occurs in this sonnet (L50.5). The Series is defined by the speaker's petition to Love to aid him in his pursuit of the beloved's favor. He calls upon Love to *stand my friend*, an expression that appears several times in the Series. He asks that if he is unsuccessful in his suit, Death make a speedy end to his life. In many of the earlier sonnets of this Subsequence, the speaker stands at the threshold between life and death, and in this Series, the choice between life and death comes to a head.

This sonnet consists of three dialogs: between Death and the speaker in the first stanza, between Love and the speaker in the second, and then once again, between Death and the speaker in the third. The dialogic breaks between interlocuters often occur mid-line; such enjambment is also found in Sonnet 25's quasi-dialog between the Author and Echo. Sonnet 25 is printed with names of the interlocuters inserted into the middle of the poetic lines—an unusual practice. Perhaps the reader is expected to recall this practice in Sonnet 25 and recognize the need to read this sonnet as if the interlocuters names were inserted here as well. In Fig. 9.1, for the sake of convenience, I have reformatted this sonnet into its dialogical form, which is printed below the sonnet in its normal form.

Come gentle Death; who cals? one thats opprest:
What is thy will? that thou abridge my woe,
By cutting of my life; cease thy request,
I cannot kill thee yet: alas, why soe?
    Thou want'st thy Hart. Who stoale the same away?   5
   Loue, whom thou seru'st, intreat him if thou may.
Come, come, come *Loue*: who calleth me so oft?
Thy Uassall true, whome thou should'st know by right.
What makes thy cry so faint? my voyce is softe,
And almost spent by wayling day and night.   10
    Why then, whats thy request? that thou restore
    To me my Hart, and steale the same no more.
And thou, O Death, when I possesse my Hart,
Dispatch me then at once: why so?
By promise thou art bound to end my smart.   15
Why, if thy Hart returne, then whats thy woe?
    That brought from colde, It neuer will desire
    To rest with me, which am more hote then fire.

Speaker:	Come gentle Death.	(Stanza 1)
Death:	Who cals?	
Speaker:	One thats opprest.	
Death:	What is thy will?	
Speaker:	That thou abridge my woe, by cutting of my life.	
Death:	Cease thy request, I cannot kill thee yet.	
Speaker:	Alas, why soe?	
Death:	Thou want'st thy Hart.	
Speaker:	Who stoale the same away?	
Death:	*Loue*, whom thou seru'st, intreat him if thou may.	

Speaker:	Come, come, come *Loue*.	(Stanza 2)
Love:	Who calleth me so oft?	
Speaker:	Thy Vassall true, whome thou should'st know by right.	
Love:	What makes thy cry so faint?	
Speaker:	My voyce is softe, and almost spent by wayling day and night.	
Love:	Why then, whats thy request?	
Speaker:	That thou restore to me my Hart, and steale the same no more.	

Speaker:	And thou, O Death, when I possesse my Hart, dispatch me then at once.	(Stanza 3)
Death:	Why so? [end of tetrameter line]	
Speaker:	By promise thou art bound to end my smart.	
Death:	Why, if thy Hart returne, then whats thy woe?	
Speaker:	That brought from colde, it neuer will desire to rest with me, which am more hote then fire.	

Fig. 9.1 Sonnet 56 (L50.5) as published, and reformatted as a dialog

In the first stanza, the speaker calls upon Death to end his life; how-ever, Death refuses to kill him because he lacks his heart, which resides with the beloved. In the second stanza, the speaker entreats Love for the return of his heart, in order that Death might then kill him. In the third stanza, the speaker again calls for Death to take his life when his heart is returned: *when I possesse my Hart / Dispatch me then at once* (13–14). The separation of the speaker from his heart begins in Sonnet 2 and we have now reached the sequence's climactic moment: the return of the speaker's heart is contemplated and perhaps even imminent. In the tetrameter line (14), he asks Death to *dispatch* him, and then within the same line, Death asks, *Why so?* The speaker nevertheless insists that Death is bound to keep his promise and end his life (15). Death persists in his questioning: *Why, if thy Hart returne, then whats thy woe?* (16). The return of his heart is the relief that the speaker has sought throughout the sequence, beginning with the opening sonnets, and yet, apparently this will not cure him. The difficulty, we are told, is that the return of the speaker's heart would in no way lessen his heart's desire. At this moment, the speaker recognizes the true nature and place of that desire, when he declares: *That brought from colde, it neuer will desire / To rest with me, which am more hote then fire* (17–18). It seems that somehow the heart is not actually the true seat of desire.

On first consideration, the speaker's assertion that he is *more hote then fire* is just another instance of the prolific trope equating desire and fire. Yet, with the contemplated return of the speaker's heart, the whole cause of the speaker's woe, so frequently rehearsed, has suddenly evapo-rated. The third Subsequence began with several sonnets in which the beloved is characterized as a source of overwhelming heat, a second sun, and the speaker's heart lies with that second sun. Now, he finally realizes that this fire is not external to himself: it truly lies within himself and not in his beloved. This is the point of discontinuity between the speaker's past and future self—that Augustinian moment under the fig tree.

How are we to understand the beloved? Significantly, she has no spe-cific physical characteristics or mental temperament, nor does she partici-pate in any action other than her general intransigence. Indeed, the beloved is far removed from any historical human being that the poet may have loved; rather, she is the poet's construct (the headnote of Sonnet 50 col-lapses the distinction between historical and poetical, but that lies outside the poetic text itself). Freccero asserts that in the sonnet genre, the subject matter is its own act: the poet makes the beloved and the beloved makes the poet.[28] The speaker's boundless desire is reflected in the object of his own creation, a literary device that provides the poet a means of self-expression that is extraordinarily powerful. This reflexive poetics is a new means by which an interior self may be represented. The beloved is ultimately a poetic construct that allows the poet to better describe the love that resides within himself, whether it be his love for another, his love of God, or the love of poetic creation. The heat within the speaker, although it may be triggered by beauty's bait, not only resides within himself, but is native to himself, and the nativity of this desire is found in the work's denouement, the final Series of the sequence.

The L73 Series: Love's Double Destiny (Addendum 6)

In this final Series, the speaker discovers that love resides not only in nature but also within himself. The lead sonnet's headnote explains that the *Author* is *faining a quarrel betwixt Loue and his Heart* and declares that fault lies on both sides: although love maliciously enslaves its victims, the speaker's heart enables his own *imprisonment,* a *heedlesse follie.* In the first Subsequence, the speaker lives under love's tyranny, and in the second Subsequence, he escapes it, choosing instead to live according to reason. Neither of these approaches work, and in the third Subsequence, the speaker pursues various strategies aimed at understanding love or winning the beloved's favor. These strategies also fail, and ultimately, the speaker learns to accept that love and his heart must live in conflict. In this Series, which ends the third Subsequence and the sequence, the speaker finds a middle ground between the extremes of the first and second Subsequences: neither the helpless suffering experienced in the first Subsequence nor willpower's victory over love in the second Subsequence provide sensible models for leading one's life. Thus, as the lead sonnet's headnote makes clear, a compromise must be struck between love's *wilfull malice* and the heart's *heedlesse follie.* In this Series, the speaker, now wiser, recognizes that living in love, with all of the good and bad that it brings, is mankind's natural and unalienable state.

The lead sonnet provides some clues as to how the speaker came to his newfound acceptance of love. It rehearses (yet again) the trope of imprisonment—love locks up the speaker's heart in the beloved's breast. Yet, in contrast to most earlier treatments of this trope, the speaker lays the blame squarely on himself, a *bird, that willingly choaseth a golden cage for liberty* (17–18). The speaker's responsibility for his own life, and his own ability to effect change, is suggested at the beginning of the sequence in Sonnet 5's proverb, *Selfe doe; selfe haue* (see Chapter 3). The speaker attributes his newfound wisdom to *experience* (15): *Beawties bates can make the simple wise* (16). Throughout the sequence, the speaker exhibits a commanding intellect that ranges over vast spaces of literary precursors and intellectual history: he is anything but simple. In

Matthew 11:25, Jesus says, "I thank thee, O Father... because thou hast hid these things from the wise and prudent, and hast revealed them unto babes." In this last Series, there is a recognition that love cannot be intellectually dissected, but only accepted as the world's predominant natural force. A few verses later, the Matthew chapter concludes: "For my yoke is easy, and my burden is light" (11:30). The *Hekatompathia* ends with a similar sentiment in its closing apothegm: *The Labour is light, where Loue is the Paimistres.* The speaker is yoked to Love, his pay-mistress, throughout the sequence, and the labor is heavy, but at the end, with newfound wisdom, love's burden is now light.

Love's Labour's Lost, written only a decade after the *Hekatompathia*, begins with sonnet-writing young men in a Neoplatonic academy, committed to three years of isolated study. Yet, love quickly intrudes, vows of isolation fail, and odd strategies are followed in the pursuit of ladies (the men are disguised as Russians). By the end of the play, this over-thinking has led the young men nowhere. Ironically, the ladies, more "simple" than the men by measure of their education, prove themselves to be the wiser. As the play ends, they advocate simple Christian charity, and the young men agree to begin a year of penance. As in the *Hekatompathia*, the extensive intellectualizing, the complex strategies for gaining happiness in love, and the desire to fit love into some rational scheme, are not successful. In the *Hekatompathia*'s Epilogue, *more like a praier than a Passion* (HN), there is penance for past errors. Perhaps these unproductive paths were necessary to finally arrive at the simple truth. One might see a parallel in Augustine's journey down what he later concluded to be false paths, Manicheism and Platonism, but which in retrospect were nonetheless necessary detours in the process of his true conversion to a Christian life.

In this Series' second sonnet (L73.1), the speaker recognizes love as an overwhelming force that rules the natural world and human life as well. Love is called a *Consuetudo* (HN) or *Second Nature* (17), and it is compared to a region's climate:

The man that dwelles farre North, hath seldome harme
With blast of winters wind or nipping frost:
The Negro **seldome feeles himselfe too warme**
***If he abide within his native coast;**   (L73.1.13–16)

> *for both experience teacheth & Philosophical reason approoveth, that an Ethyopian may easily in Spaine be smothered with the heat of the countrey though Spaine be more temperate than Ethiopia is.

Just as Northerners are adapted to the cold, and those in equatorial climes to the heat, so too must mankind accept love as the habitat into which he or she is born—as immutable as the laws of nature. In the work's longest sidenote, reproduced above, an *Ethyopian*, accustomed to heat, would be smothered in temperate *Spaine* (i.e., by the lack of adequate heat). This strikingly recants all prior Series' characterization of love as an oppressive weight—for example, in the Puzzle Sonnet's final couplet; instead, an insufficiency of love smothers. For without love, *life would soone decay* (L73.1.5). The war waged against love in so many of this work's sonnets, here, gives way to surrender. This sidenote succinctly expresses the sequence's final verdict about love, the results obtained from its two methods of argumentation: *Philosophical reason* (e.g., process physics) and *experience* (affective rhetorical arguments). In this sidenote, the *Hekatompathia* follows its usual practice of hiding critical statements in what appears to be an inconsequential or digressive piece of text.

The Series' third sonnet (L73.2) declares that love resides within the speaker himself. Although love is a great force in the natural world, its force within himself is even greater. In the climactic, metrically deficient sonnet of the prior L50 Series, the speaker reveals the great heat within himself:

> **That brought from colde, it neuer will desire**
> **To rest with me, which am more hote then fire.**   (L50.5.17–18)

The heat that was once ascribed to the beloved—as when she was likened to a second sun—is now, instead, found within the speaker. In this sonnet (L73.2), the speaker declares that the strength of love within himself is comparable to that found within the gods themselves:

> **If** Neptunes **waues were all dride vp and gone,**
> **My weeping eyes so many teares distill,**
> **That greater Seas might grow by them alone;**
> **Or if no flame were yet remayning still**
> > **In** Vulcans **forge, he might from out my brest**
> > **Make choise of such as should befit him best.**
> **If** Aeole **were depriu'd of all his charge,**
> **Yet soone could I restore his windes againe,**   (L73.2.7–14)

Sonnet speakers typically experience love (or God) through the mediatrix-beloved, but here the source of love is not an entity external to the speaker, but rather an internal reservoir of great energy. The speaker's energy rivals that of the gods: he imagines that he could himself replenish the power of any god that lost his potency. This reverses the Christian and Platonist concept of God or a demiurge creating, or dispersing into, the natural world; instead, the speaker imagines himself a god, dispersing love's great power into the natural world.

The Series' penultimate sonnet (L73.5) makes another extraordinary claim about the speaker's love: it arises not, as before, with the sight of beauty, but from Cupid himself. In this sonnet's *jeu d'esprit*, the physician Aesculapius treats Cupid's bee sting with herbs, which after being tinged with Cupid's blood, are thrown aside, landing upon the speaker's heart (or the decayed heart's place). The speaker is then cured by this infusion of Cupid's blood:

> **By haplesse hap did breed my hartes decay:**
> **For there they fell, where long my hart had li'ne**
> **To waite for *Loue*, and what he should assigne.**   (L73.5.16–18)

The cure for love's losses is love itself. This image of the speaker being infused with Cupid's blood reinforces the idea that love is resident within the speaker himself. The sonnet's final line surprises us: the speaker is now available for whatever love may *assigne* (18). Does this mean that a new beloved may be assigned? If this is the intent, it would be a spectacularly anomalous ending for a sonnet sequence. The reader cannot help but notice that the beloved has virtually disappeared in this final Series: she is mentioned in passing on only three occasions.[29] The speaker's heart undergoes *decay* (16), and not from suffering, as is common in the sequence, but from the blood-tinged herbs that cure him. His heart no longer lies *where long* [it] *had li'ne* (17), that is, where it has been continuously since the sequence's second sonnet. The speaker's heart must now wait for a new assignment from love—whatever love *should assigne* (18). Thus, the beloved is discharged in the sequence's penultimate sonnet. Although cured by love, he is still subject to its power, the subject of the next and final sonnet.

In Sonnet L73.6, the speaker now sees love as a deliverer of destiny—both good and evil—that cannot be escaped. This double destiny is most evident in the enumeration of contrarieties with which the Series closes: *my sighes, my songes; my feare, my hoping minde* (L73.6.16). Remarkably, in this final Series, the beloved evaporates: the poet closes shop, and the beloved, his stage prop and the very foundation of the sequence, is packed away. In the final sonnet's last stanza, only her eyes remain:

> **From out my** Mistres **eyes, two lightsome starres,**
> **He destinates estate of double kinde,**   ["He" refers to love]
> **My teares, my smyling cheere, my peace, my warres;**
> **My sighes, my songes; my feare, my hoping minde;**
> **My fire, my frost; my ioy, my sorrowes gall;**
> **My curse, my prayse; my death, but life with all.**   (L73.6.13–18)

Why has the beloved disappeared? S. K. Heninger, in his comparison of the *Canzoniere* with Dante's *Vita Nuova*, argues that Petrarch subtly shifts the focus or "dominant" of the sonnet sequence from "the ethereal essence of the lady herself [to] the response of the lover to her."[30] The *Hekatompathia* moves even further in this direction, for throughout the sequence, the beloved is far less visible than the *Canzoniere*'s Laura. In this final Series, the poet acknowledges that the beloved is a conventional construct, and unlike most fictional characters, she is characterless—a device that allows the speaker to present his arguments.

Why are her eyes described as *lightsome starres* (13)? Elsewhere in the sequence, the beloved's eyes represent paired opposites, favorable and unfavorable consequences, and eight such pairs are presented in this sonnet's final four lines. *Lightsome* (13) may mean either "radiant with light" (OED a2.1) or "light-hearted" (OED a1.2). The latter definition aligns with the work's closing apothegm, in which love is characterized as a light labor (below the *Epilogue*). The subject of this final stanza is destiny: love *destinates* (14); *starres* (13) is a metonym for destiny. *He* (14) who controls destiny (or fate or providence) is at the apex of divinity; here, the speaker accepts love as the highest god (*summe Deus*; 90.15). Unlike Petrarch's wandering speaker, this speaker exits the labyrinth.

The speaker's exit from the labyrinth becomes visible only after the puzzle-solver navigates the Puzzle's labyrinth, restoring the sonnets to their proper order. Thus reader and puzzle-solver are both cast as wanderers who seek the end of their respective journeys. They both must navigate a narrow path, avoiding any wrong turns, or otherwise be condemned to endless wandering.

The journey's end

Unlike the *Canzoniere*, the *Hekatompathia* has a clear resolution: the lover-pilgrim accepts that love governs both the physical world and, to a great extent, the speaker's life. In contrast, the pilgrimage of Petrarch's speaker is set forth in *Canzoniere* 16, which contrasts the speaker's search for the longed-for true form of Laura with the journey of an elderly pilgrim making his way to Rome to gaze upon the Veil of Veronica, a celebrated relic. Thomas Greene takes this sonnet as a point of departure to contrast the speaker's journey with that of the elderly pilgrim:

> [*Canzoniere* 16] places more stress on the *dissimilarities* that separate the two protagonists. One difference is temporal. The old man has made a single pilgrimage, distinct in time, to a specific destination, a pilgrimage narrated in the historical present, whereas the speaker's

pursuit... is repetitive, temporally indefinite, lacking closure, narrated not in the historical but iterative present tense, the basic verb tense of the entire *Canzoniere*. Thus the pilgrim's quest has an ending, but the lover's has none, and will not have even at the close of the volume. That is one reason why Petrarch is ultimately so wearying to read: there is never any resolution, and this failure to resolve anything is acted out in the iterative present tense: "I burn, I freeze, I suffer, I yearn." The speaker's experience is repetitive and endless. The old pilgrim has a goal and reaches it; he is not trapped in the lover's deadly circularity.[31]

The *Hekatompathia's* speaker, like the elderly pilgrim, reaches an end, and remarkably, peregrination leads to conversion. The sequence frequently alludes to conversion by its pairing of life and death, and by its use of the phoenix, a symbol of conversion. The *Hekatompathia* contains three conversions: in the first conversion at the start of the MLIP Subsequence, love is abandoned; in the second at the start of the third Subsequence, that abandonment is reversed and love is recognized as a great power—metonymically, a sun; the third and final conversion occurs in the final Series of the third Subsequence, in which love's power is recognized as the supreme force that not only pervades the cosmos but also lies within the speaker as well.

The third Subsequence lays the groundwork for the speaker's conversion in the final Series. After the descent to earth in the Subsequence's first Series (L90), the next Series begins with the speaker blaming his predicament on his *heedlesse hart* (L39.A1.1) and misplaced *wilfulness* (L39.A2.HN). The speaker's movement toward taking responsibility for his own life marks this Subsequence as different from Petrarchan discourse; the speaker's call for self-reliance is what the poet "adds to the Tuscan" (Sonnet 5, sidenote). The speaker directs his energies toward winning the beloved's heart, but without success. The moment of epiphany, which occurs in his dialogue with Love and Death in the sonnet with the tetrameter line (L50.5), is a prelude to conversion but not the conversion itself, for the speaker is still resigned to death at the end of the L50 Series. Then, surprisingly, at the start of the final Series, we find that the speaker has reached a verdict concerning the *quarrell betwixt Love and his Heart* (L73.H.HN), the conceit that began the sequence with the speaker's separation from his heart (Sonnets 2 and 3). In the final Series' second sonnet, he appears cheerful, thinking his *Woes are Blisse* (L73.1.18).

The moment of conversion occurs outside of the text, in the "gutter" or gap between the final sonnet of the penultimate Series and the first sonnet of the final Series. Comic strip writers are advised "not to write the gutter" (the gap between images) because leaving a gap engages the reader, forcing him or her to imagine what takes place between images. In the gap between the penultimate and final Series, the *Hekatompathia*'s reader is pushed to imagine that which is not presented, and indeed, cannot be presented. The moment at which faith, a prerequisite of conversion, is acquired is a point of discontinuity in the life of the convert. Faith does not derive from reason, but from grace: the old soul dies and a new one is reborn. This point in time can only be represented as a gap in the text, or a discontinuous or mysterious moment in the narrative.

Conversion, the most essential of religious acts, is a move from an externally focused perspective to an internally focused one. Augustine turns inward, finds the divine within himself, and then comes to rest in God. The *Hekatompathia*'s speaker turns inward to find his god, love, within himself. Previously, in the second Subsequence, the speaker abandoned love, embraced reason, and contended that love's power is not *divine* (93.16). However, in the first sonnet of the third Subsequence, the pivotal Sonnet 90, he recants and returns to his god, *Divus Amor* (90.2). Consistent with this, he acknowledges that love is indeed a divine power in the final Series. Further, he comes to rest in nature, love's cosmic order:

> **A ling'ring vse of *Loue* hath taught my brest**
> **To harbor strife, and yet to liue in rest.**   (L73.1.11–12)

Patrick Cheney argues that "Petrarch awakens to the mega-paradox at the heart of his sequence; it is unrequited love for Laura that is salvific. 'I see it was for the best that she resisted my desire' (289.5–6). For Petrarch, in other words, unrequitedness is itself providential." Cheney then compares this to a very different sort of Petrarchism in Spenser's *Amoretti*: "The master-stroke of Spenser's counter-Petrarchism is to make requitedness at once providential and salvific."[32] Bacon's counter-Petrarchism is like Spenser's: salvation comes from his making peace with the world—by accepting the inevitability of strife and uncertainty.

10

The Precision System's Orchema Tables

Solving the first three Stages revealed most of the details of the Precision (or cryptographic) System. Stage 1's discoveries include the Transform Pair mechanism and the values of the Recta and Aversa tables (though not the Orchema tables). In Stages 2 and 3, we discovered that the MLIP Subsequence enciphers the crib PRODIGA LIBERTAS ANIMAE and the third Subsequence enciphers the crib QUAM VANUS... REQUIRO. Knowing that each sonnet with a Design generates a particular letter in the Subsequence's crib allowed us to determine the Transform Pair values of many of the Designs. These Transform Pair values were presented in Fig. 7.7, which has been updated in Fig. 10.1. Two entries have been added: the TP values for the Diamond and Diamond-B Designs, discovered using the third Stage's crib (in Addendum 2 and Addendum 3, respectively).

We now know the value of 12 of the 18 Design types (excepting the small uncertainty with respect to the value of Roots-5). Of the 6 Designs whose values remain to be discovered, 3 appear infrequently and only in the fourth and fifth Stages; their values will be determined in the next chapter. The other 3 Designs with unknown values are the frequently appearing pictorial Designs: the Lioness, Heart Jail, and Daedalus Designs. We now have enough information to discover the Transform Pair values of these Designs and the value of the Orchema tables to which they point.

The Design to Transform Pair map (Fig. 10.1) is a fundamental building block of the Puzzle, and our job is to fill in the remaining open entries of this table. As mentioned in Chapter 7, and first discussed in Chapter 4, Bacon believed that experimental science was practiced, in part, by filling in tables of discovery. The Design to Transform Pair map and Orchema deciphering tables are two such tables that must be filled in to solve the Puzzle—a task brought near to completion in this chapter.

In the second and third Stages, 57 Designs, in conjunction with CipherLines, generated two cribs.[1] Of these, 40 Designs generated crib letters using Recta or Aversa tables; the remaining 17 Designs were one of the three pictorial Designs that specify Orchema tables (see the last three rows of Fig. 10.1). One of these 17 Designs, Sonnet 90's Lioness Design, produced two crib letters. As a result, 18 rather than 17 crib letters are produced. Figure 10.2 lists these 18 instances in which plaintext letters are produced from either a Lioness, Heart Jail, or Daedalus Design. The values in each row of Fig. 10.2 were taken from Chapter 7 and Addenda 1–6. The specific table (Fig. 7.8, A2.3, etc.) is specified in the second column of Fig. 10.2.

Transform Pair	Table First Letter	Table Last Letter	Design	Where Discovered
TP1	R1	R4	DoubleA	Ch. 7
TP2	R5	R6	Flowers-1	Ch. 7
TP3	R6	R8	Flowers-4	Ch. 7
TP4	R8	R9		
TP5	R9	R10	Flowers-5	Ch. 7
TP6	R10	R11	Flowers-6	Ch. 7
TP7	R11	R12	Flowers-8	Ch. 7
TP8	R12	A12	Bulbs-12	Ch. 7
TP9	A12	A12	Bulbs-10	Ch. 7
TP10	A11	A11	Roots-5?	Ch. 7
TP11	A11	A10	Roots-5?	Ch. 7
TP12	A10	A9	Diamond-B	Add. 3
TP13	A8	A7		
TP14	A7	A6	Diamond	Add. 2
TP15	A6	A4	DoubleA-inv	Ch. 7
TP16	A3	O5	pictorial	
TP17	O5	O7	pictorial	
TP18	O7	O9	pictorial	

Fig. 10.1 Design to Transform Pair map (updated)

Mapping the pictorial Designs to Transform Pairs

The information in Fig. 10.2 can now be used to determine the Transform Pair values of the three pictorial Designs and the values of the underlying Orchema tables. The Puzzle employs the pictorial Designs in a calculated manner: the 18 instances in Fig. 10.2 provide the puzzle-solver enough information to discover the Orchema table values. Said another way, the 36 possible Transforms listed in the last column can be reduced logically to the Orchema table values. For instance, "T" appears 13 times among the 36 entries in the "CL first" and "CL last" columns, which has the effect of eliminating several possible Transforms and validating others.

Row ID	Ref. Fig.	Ref. Row	Sonnet	Design	CL First	CL Last	Crib	Possible Transforms
1	7.8	3	PS.3	Lioness	W	T	O	W→O or T→O
2	7.8	4	FL.1	Heart Jail	A	T	D	A→D or T→D
3	7.8	6	FL.3	Daedalus	C	S	G	C→G or S→G
4	7.8	15	Scoff.5	Heart Jail	B	T	S	B→S or T→S
5	7.8	20	L90.H	Lioness	L	A	A	L→A or A→A
6	7.8	21	EPI	Daedalus	S	E	E	S→E or E→E
7	A2.3	1	L90.H	Lioness	L	A	Q	L→Q or A→Q
8	A2.3	2	L90.1	Daedalus	S	L	U	S→U or L→U
9	A2.3	3	L90.2	Heart Jail	Q	T	A	Q→A or T→A
10	A3.5	1	L39.H	Lioness	S	S	U	S→U or S→U
11	A3.5	9	L39.B2	Daedalus	T	E	M	T→M or E→M
12	A4.2	1	L64.H	Lioness	L	E	E	L→E or E→E
13	A5.3	1	L50.H	Lioness	T	T	I	T→I or T→I
14	A5.3	5	L50.4	Daedalus	I	D	Q	I→Q or D→Q
15	A5.3	7	L50.6	Daedalus	O	T	E	O→E or T→E
16	A6.2	1	L73.H	Lioness	T	T	R	T→R or T→R
17	A6.2	2	L73.1	Heart Jail	T	T	E	T→E or T→E
18	A6.2	5	L73.4	Heart Jail	T	D	I	T→I or D→I

Column Descriptions

Row ID	Used to reference a row in this table
Ref. Fig.	Figure in Chapter 7 or Addenda 2–6 that provides row's data
Ref. Row	Row ID of the above referenced Figure
Sonnet	Sonnet number (restored order numbering system)
Design	Sonnet's Design type
CL First	First letter of CipherLine
CL Last	Last letter of CipherLine
Crib	Crib letter (plaintext)
Pos. Transforms	The two possible Transforms that would produce the crib letter

Fig. 10.2 Pictorial Design Transforms list (Stages 2 and 3)

Our first task is to map each of the three unassigned pictorial Designs to one of the three open Transform Pair positions in the last three rows of Fig. 10.1.[2] The Puzzle instructions (Sonnet 80) declare that the base of the Pillar Sonnet is *orchematicall*, and these three pictorial Designs, which are most likely adjacent to one another, are probably located in the base of the Pillar Sonnet, which corresponds to positions TP16, TP17, and TP18 (see Chapter 7, "The pictorial Designs" section). There are only 6 (3 factorial) possible mappings of the three Designs to the three Transform Pair values. Often in cryptanalysis, one breaks a cipher by eliminating possibilities, and this applies here as well. The most promising place to start is with TP16 because we already know one of its values: the first Transform of this Transform Pair is A3 (see Fig. 10.1). We begin by arbitrarily assuming that the Lioness Design specifies TP16. We then examine two Lioness Design instances, Row ID 13 and 16 of Fig. 10.2, and find that the following two statements must then be true.

A3(T) = I [false]	or	O5(T) = I	Row ID 13
A3(T) = R [false]	or	O5(T) = R	Row ID 16

We know that A3(T) = D (Aversa table, Fig. B.2), and therefore, we can mark the left-hand side of both above statements as false. If the left-hand sides of both above statements are false, then the right-hand sides of both above statements must be true. Yet, this leads to a contradiction: O5 (T) cannot be equal to both I and R. Therefore, our original hypothesis that the Lioness Design specifies TP16 must be false. Let us now hypothesize that the Heart Jail Design specifies TP16 and apply the same process to the Heart Jail Designs in Row IDs 2 and 4 of Fig. 10.2:

A3(A) = D [false]	or	O5(T) = D	Row ID 2
A3(B) = S [false]	or	O5(T) = S	Row ID 4

Once again, the left-hand sides of both statements fail: the A3 table specifies different values (Fig. B.2). Therefore, the right-hand sides of the statements must be true. But O5(T) cannot be equal to both D and S, a contradiction, and therefore the Heart Jail Design cannot specify TP16. The only remaining possibility is that the Daedalus Design specifies TP16. Let us now apply TP16 to all 6 instances of the Daedalus Design in Fig. 10.2:

A3(C) = G [false]	or	**O5(S) = G**	Row ID 3
A3(S) = E [true]	or	O5(E) = E	Row ID 6
A3(S) = U [false]	or	**O5(L) = U**	Row ID 8
A3(T) = M [false]	or	**O5(E) = M**	Row ID 11
A3(I) = Q [false]	or	**O5(D) = Q**	Row ID 14
A3(O) = E [false]	or	**O5(T) = E**	Row ID 15

In 5 of the 6 above instances, the left-hand sides of the statements are false, and this necessitates that the right-hand sides of the statements are true, which is indicated by the bolded font. We have obtained 5 values of the O5 table. (The one instance above in which the left-hand side is true provides no information about the Orchema tables.)

We return to the problem of assigning pictorial Designs to Transform Pair positions. With TP16 assigned to the Daedalus Design, then the Lioness Design must be either TP17 or TP18. Let us assume it is TP17. Then:

O5(L) = A [false]	or	O7(A) = A	Row ID 5
O5(L) = Q [false]	or	O7(A) = Q	Row ID 7

Once again, the left-hand sides of both statements are false because in the earlier examination of the Daedalus Design, we determined that O5(L) = U (Row ID 8). Therefore, the right-hand sides of the above statements must be true. However, this results in a contradiction because O7(A) cannot equal both A and Q. By this process of elimination, we now know that the Lioness Design specifies TP18. The one remaining open slot, TP17, must then be specified by the Heart Jail Design. Fig. 10.3 updates the last three rows of Fig. 10.1.

The ordering of these three pictorial Designs makes sense aesthetically. The Lioness Design, the icon of love and the most fundamental force in the cosmos, surely belongs at the lowest level of the base. Although the position of the Lioness Design is firmly established by the above cryptographic deductions, its aesthetically pleasing position provides a small but welcome measure of confirmation for the puzzle-solver.

Perhaps it also makes aesthetic sense that the Heart Jail, which represents the speaker's imprisonment by tyrannical love, lies adjacent to the Lioness Design. One might further speculate that the Daedalus Design, which lies at the boundary or gateway between the Aversa section and Orchema section (subterranean, in our plant model) mimics Daedalus's station at the gates of Hades in *Aeneid* 6. However, it is the cryptographic deductions that establish the position of these Designs.

Transform Pair	Table First Letter	Table Last Letter	Design	Where Discovered
TP1	R1	R4	DoubleA	Ch. 7
TP2	R5	R6	Flowers-l	Ch. 7
TP3	R6	R8	Flowers-4	Ch. 7
TP4	R8	R9		
TP5	R9	R10	Flowers-5	Ch. 7
TP6	R10	R11	Flowers-6	Ch. 7
TP7	R11	R12	Flowers-8	Ch. 7
TP8	R12	A12	Bulbs-12	Ch. 7
TP9	A12	A12	Bulbs-10	Ch. 7
TP10	A11	A11	Roots-5?	Ch. 7
TP11	A11	A10	Roots-5?	Ch. 7
TP12	A10	A9	Diamond-B	Add. 3
TP13	A8	A7		
TP14	A7	A6	Diamond	Add. 2
TP15	A6	A4	DoubleA-inv	Ch. 7
TP16	A3	O5	Daedalus	Ch. 10
TP17	O5	O7	Heart Jail	Ch. 10
TP18	O7	O9	Lioness	Ch. 10

Fig. 10.3 Design to Transform Pair map (updated)

Discovering the remaining entries in the Orchema tables

We discovered 5 values for the O5 table in our work above, and now that we know the Transform Pair values of the three pictorials, we can discover certain values of the O7 and O9 tables. We begin with one instance of the Heart Hail Design:

O5(T) = I   [false]   or   **O7(D) = I**   Row ID 18

We already determined that O5(T) = E, and thus O5(T) ≠ I. Therefore O7(D) = I, which is shown in bold to indicate that it is true. Next, we examine two instances of the Lioness Design, in which both the beginning and ending letters are "T:"

O7(T) = I   [false]   or   **O9(T) = I**   Row ID 13
O7(T) = R   or   O9(T) = R [false]   Row ID 16

Because O7(D) = I, and we would not expect two different ciphertext letters to map to the same plaintext letter, then O7(T) ≠ I and is marked above as false. Consequently, O9(T) = I (bolded as true). A consequence of O9(T) = I, is that O9(T) ≠ R, and therefore O7(T) = R (bolded). Next, we examine 3 instances of the Heart Jail Design in which the last ciphertext letter is "T:"

O5(A) = D   or   O7(T) = D   [false]   Row ID 2
O5(B) = S   or   O7(T) = S   [false]   Row ID 4
O5(Q) = A   or   O7(T) = A   [false]   Row ID 9

Because O7(T) = R, all three right-hand sides of the above statements are false, and all three left-hand sides of the statements are true. We have now discovered all 8 values for the O5 table. We now turn to the two Lioness instances listed below:

O7(L) = A   or   O9(A) = A   Row ID 5
O7(L) = Q   or   O9(A) = Q   Row ID 7

At this point, we cannot distinguish between these alternatives; however, the above statements necessitate that the two statements below are true. This ambiguity will be resolved in a later Stage.

O7(L) = A or Q
O9(A) = A or Q

We next consider the two Lioness instances below. We previously determined O7(L) = A or Q and that O9(T) = I. This provides two new values:

O7(W) = O   or   O9(T) = O [false]   Row ID 1
O7(L) = E   [false]   or   **O9(E) = E**   Row ID 12

We next return to the Puzzle's first Stage in which the final two letters of the Puzzle Sonnet's plaintext message, VOCES ME NUO LEA PESUS, were assumed without proof. The letters "US" were a guess (see Chapter 2, "The final letters of the deciphered message" section). If we examine the last two rows of Fig. 2.19, knowing that the last two letters are "US," we find that:

O5(N) = U [false]   or   **O7(N) = U**   Fig. 2.19, line 17
O7(N) = S [false]   or   **O9(N) = S**   Fig. 2.19, line 18

In the first statement above, O5(N) ≠ U because we already determined that O5(L) = U. As a result, O7(N) = U, which makes the left-hand side of the second statement, O7(N) = S, false. Therefore, O9(N) = S. Finally, we examine the remaining Lioness instance in Row ID 10:

O7(S) = U [false]   or   **O9(S) =U**   Row ID 10

Because O7(N) = U, O7(S) is not also equal to U, and so the right-hand side of the statement is true.

We have now exhausted all but one row (17) of the 18 rows in Fig. 10.2 (Row 17 confirms that O5(T) = E). All Orchema table values discovered in the foregoing work and shown in bold have been entered into the appropriate Orchema table column (O5, O7, or O9) in Fig. 10.4. For convenience, it also appears in Appendix B, Fig. B.3 (with the A/Q ambiguity resolved).

Observations about the Orchema tables

The process that we used to discover the Orchema tables is a deductive process. This contrasts with most processes used in solving the Puzzle, which are inductive. The deductions that produced the Orchema table entries are based on simple syllogisms—well understood in the early modern era, especially by cryptanalysts for whom they were an essential tool. To discover the tables by which a message was enciphered, one typically eliminates various alternatives, finding the truth by a process of elimination. Indeed, Bacon recognized the value of elimination in the hunt for the truth. Although I may have used modern notation or terms in describing this process, nothing presented would surprise an experienced sixteenth-century cryptanalyst. Bacon almost certainly knew that the use of exclusions and negatives is extremely valuable in cryptanalysis. Indeed, Bacon uses Cupid as an example of an entity only detectable by negative inference: "For all the knowledge of him which is to be had proceeds by exclusions and negatives" (*Works*, 5.463). This *via negativa* means to knowledge has ancient roots in pre-Socratic philosophy and apophatic theology. In navigating Bacon's labyrinthine Puzzle, negative instances often exclude fruitless pathways, and by this process of elimination, the correct path through the Puzzle can be found.

The Puzzle's design is extraordinarily clever: the set of information presented in Fig. 10.2, those 18 instances of pictorial Designs, reduce perfectly to the set of Orchema table entries presented in Fig. 10.4. This considerable coherence in the information in Fig. 10.2 cannot be accidental and provides yet further validation of our puzzle-solving efforts. To summarize, sufficient information is available for us to assign the three pictorial Designs to Transform Pairs, and further, 18 specific Orchema table entries were discovered. Only one minor unresolved value was

Ciphertext	O5 table plaintext	O7 table plaintext	O9 table plaintext
A	D		A or Q
B	S		
C			
D	Q	I	
E	M		E
F			
G			
H			
I			
K			
L	U	A or Q	
M			
N		U	S
O			
P			
Q	A		
R			
S	G		U
T	E	R	I
U			
W		O	
X			
Y			
Z			

Fig. 10.4 The Orchema tables

encountered, the "A or Q" table entries (Fig. 10.4). If the information that we began with in Fig. 10.2 had been random or included serious errors, we would have almost certainly encountered unresolvable contradictions or indeterminacies, and most likely both. The Puzzle communicates exactly the information needed to progress toward its solution. This is yet another example of the work's organicism, and once again, we are reminded of E. K.'s remark in the *Shepheardes Calender*: everything is "Well Grounded, Finely Framed, and Strongly Trussed up Together."

The Orchema tables provide another example of the *Hekatompathia's* recurrent use of the number 18: there are exactly 18 Orchema Transforms (see Fig. 10.4). The Orchema table was constructed using the 18 instances of pictorial Design decryptions available from the second and third Stages (see Fig. 10.2). If we examine the Design to Transform Pair map (Fig.10.3), we find that exactly 18 of the 24 potential Recta and Aversa Transforms are used (R2, R3, R7, A1, A2, and A5 do not appear). We rearranged 18 Puzzle Sonnet lines in the first Stage and 18 sonnets in the second Stage.

The Orchema tables presented in Fig. 10.4, unlike the Recta and Aversa tables, lack entries in many locations. This is disconcerting at first, as one might expect them to resemble the Recta and Aversa tables. My assumption upon beginning the process of their discovery was that the Orchema tables would follow some pattern that would allow the remaining open entries to be filled in by inference. Trithemius presents a few examples of Orchema tables in his *Polygraphia*, and each follows a different pattern. In contrast, the *Hekatompathia's* Orchema tables exhibit no repeated pattern, which is obvious from even a casual glance at Fig. 10.4. However, even though Trithemius's Orchema tables exhibit a pattern, he points out that the possible arrangements of these tables is virtually limitless.[3] Indeed, arbitrariness in cryptographic tables is a virtue, not a vice: it makes it harder for a cryptanalyst to break the cipher. Indeed, the lack of any repeating pattern is the norm in cipher keys.

The reason that the *Hekatompathia's* Orchema tables exhibit no pattern emerges on further consideration. The pictorial Designs that specify Orchema Transforms appear more frequently than other Designs, which likely necessitates that they require a greater flexibility in pairing cipher-text and plaintext letters than the simple shifts of the Recta and Aversa tables allow. The ending letters of sonnet lines are particularly unvaried: "E" and "T" are very common. These common ending letters must map to high frequency letters in Latin (such as vowels, which are extremely common in Latin) to allow plaintext messages to be enciphered. Examining the O7 and O9 columns in Fig. 10.4, 7 of the 10 entries are vowels. One also observes that the ciphertext letters (first column) for which there are entries include letters that commonly end a word. If the Orchema tables are to be frequently employed, then common letters must map to common letters. But the common letters of the alphabet (vowels, "T," "N," and "S") do not appear at set intervals. Thus, it would have been difficult to implement repeating patterns in the Orchema tables and also use those tables more frequently than Recta and Aversa tables. There are only 3 Orchema tables (O5, O7, and O9) but 18 Recta and Aversa tables.[4] Although the Orchema tables represent 14% of the tables (3/21), they are employed more frequently—approximately 30% of the time. As a result, the limited number of Orchema table entries (Fig. 10.4) must specify Transforms for relatively common letters.

There was another benefit of implementing the Orchema tables in this manner. An important design goal in the Puzzle's construction is the locking between Stages (i.e., the prevention of skipping past any Stage). The Puzzle restricts the puzzle-solver to a well-defined path, and if he or she strays, then no progress is made. This follows the model of a labyrinth: if you take a wrong turn, you will never exit the labyrinth. The path through the Puzzle is narrow: one wrong turn in the labyrinth, and one cannot exit.

The Puzzle locks its Stages in various ways, and here, at the beginning of Stage 4, it does so by means of the Orchema tables. The fourth Stage produces a new message, not a crib, and that message cannot be deciphered without knowledge of the Orchema tables (the incidence of Orchema table use is high in the fourth and fifth Stages). Unless the puzzle-solver has completed the second and third Stages, and correctly compiled the information listed in Fig. 10.2, he or she cannot advance through the next Stage of the Puzzle. Indeed, critical parts of the plaintext messages in the Puzzle's later Stages are enciphered using the Orchema tables in order to positively enforce this restriction.

With the discovery and completion of the Orchema table values (Fig. 10.4), with the exception of one minor unresolved value, we have a nearly complete picture of the Puzzle's cryptographic system, and the Design-to-Transform Pair map (Fig. 10.3) is complete, with the exception of a few entries. It is now possible to compile complete deciphering tables for the second and third Stages. These appear in Appendix C, Figs. C.2 and C.3 (a,b), respectively. With the Puzzle's cryptographic system almost entirely revealed, we are in a position to tackle the Puzzle's fourth Stage.

Accuracy in CipherLine selection

Our discovery of Orchema values in this chapter was dependent upon the correct identification of CipherLines in the second and third Stages. The 18 entries in Fig. 10.2 relied solely on the Heuristic System because without knowing the Orchema table values, the Precision System could not function as it had for the Recta and Aversa Transforms, which were matched to the crib. In the second Stage, the Index Ties provided some overdetermination, but in the third Stage, CipherLine selection was based only on Catalog Ties. When I suspended my puzzle-solving at the end of the third Stage and published the first edition of *Labyrinth of Ruins*, my CipherLine selections for those 17 sonnets in Fig. 10.2 were based only on the Heuristic System, as I then had no knowledge of the Orchema table values. This effectively provides a test of how accurate I was in selecting CipherLines using the

Heuristic System alone. Of the 17 CipherLine selections (Sonnet 90 is used twice, thus accounting for all 18 rows of Fig. 10.2), I got 15 correct. Both errors were off by just a single line—a line adjacent to the true CipherLine. For Row ID 15, I erroneously selected line 14 as the CipherLine, rather than 13: indeed, the meanings of the two adjacent lines are nearly identical, although line 13 proved to be the superior choice.[5] For Row ID 12, I selected line 7 as the CipherLine, rather than 8: I missed a subtle distinction between these two lines.[6] My "test score," 15 of 17 correct, should provide some confidence in the process of identifying CipherLines.

My two erroneous selections and their correction demonstrate the interplay between the Heuristic and Precision Systems, the process at the heart of the Puzzle's design. In the case of my erroneous CipherLine selection in Row ID 15, it led to a contradiction when I began my work on the Orchema tables. This is an example of how the Precision System can inform the puzzle-solver of incorrect choices. This interplay between the Heuristic and Precision Systems also occurs when reordering sonnets: reordering errors fail to generate the crib (the Precision System), and then one must reevaluate the sonnet order. This mimics Bacon's model for experimental science: one collects experimental data, from which one derives axioms, but then new experiments may require the correction of those axioms. This shuttling back and forth between experimental data and axioms is prolific in the sciences and occurs in virtually any inductive process. This is not circular reasoning but the process of discovery. Discoveries are then validated by measuring the coherence of the solution, and in cryptography, this is defined by a formal (mathematical) process.

11

Stages 4 and 5:
The Poet's New Instructions

The *Hekatompathia* contains 97 Designs, which generate 98 letters, of which 58 were deciphered in the second and third Stages.[1] The location of the remaining 40 undeciphered Designs is shown in Fig. 11.1. Three consecutive Design-less sonnets, Sonnets 8–10, make for a conspicuous gap, as there are no other instances of even two consecutive sonnets lacking Designs. This gap appears to be a signal that there are two separate enciphered messages, and I have therefore treated these messages as belonging to two independent Stages, as shown in Fig. 11.1. As discussed in Chapter 3, the first 17 sonnets are correctly ordered, but the subsequent sonnets are not. Seeking to embark on the Puzzle's fourth Stage, it seemed to me that the next logical step was to finish the reordering of the remaining scrambled sonnets (18–37). I therefore designated those sonnets following the gap, Sonnets 11–37 and the Design-less Sonnet 79, as the next or fourth Stage of the Puzzle (Sonnet 79's headnote marks it as the last sonnet of the first Subsequence). Stage 5 consists of those Designs prior to the gap: there are 13 Designs spread across the prefaces and first 7 sonnets.

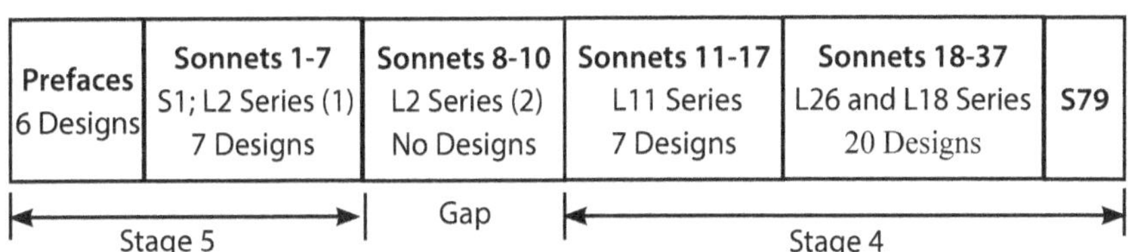

Fig. 11.1 Stages 4 and 5: the prefaces and first Subsequence

The fourth Stage (Addenda 7–9)

The 27 Sonnets of Stage 4 consist of 3 Series: L11 (Addendum 7), L26 (Addendum 8), and L18 (Addendum 9). The subject of the correctly ordered L11 Series (Sonnets 11–17) is music, as discussed in Chapter 3. Sonnets 18–37, all of which are scrambled, divide into two Series, the L18 and L26 Series. I began the reordering process by recognizing the themes of each of these two Series. From the Sequential Ties, it was apparent that the L26 Series preceded the L18 Series. The L26 Series sonnets (Addendum 8) are encomia to the beloved. However, this praise of the beloved is accompanied by the speaker's *distressed heauines* (L26.H.HN), due to the beloved's failure to accept his suit. In the lead Lioness Sonnet 26, the speaker compares himself to the nightingale, which sings beautiful songs of sorrow at night. The order of the next 6 sonnets is based on the Hexameral ring thematic structure and the Sequential Ties between adjacent sonnets.

The L18 Series (Addendum 9), which follows the L26 Series, consists of the lead Lioness Sonnet 18 and a double Hexameral ring, a structure also found in the third Stage's L39 Series (see Fig. A3.1). Sonnet 79, which introduces the MLIP Subsequence, is the last sonnet of the L18 Series. Lioness Sonnet 18 has a two-part structure, which reveals the organization of the pair of Hexameral rings that follow. Sonnet 18's first two stanzas blame love in 25 deprecating phrases. The third stanza begins with a recantation: *Yet mightie Loue regard not what I saye* (13). In this stanza, blame is instead directed at the beloved, and love is held blameless. The two-part structure of Sonnet 18 reveals the structure of the Series: the first Hexameral ring ("A" Subseries) blames love, and the second Hexameral ring ("B" Subseries) blames the beloved.

The reordering of Sonnet 18 through 37 is determined by its Hexameral rings, Sequential Ties, and for the L18 Series, an Index Sonnet. In the second Stage, Index Sonnet 98 aided in our reordering of the MLIP Subsequence (Chapter 5). The third Stage lacks any Index Sonnet. In this fourth Stage, the last sonnet, Sonnet 79, is an Index Sonnet that specifies the order of the L18 Series (see Fig. A9.1). Sonnet 79's 18 enumerated themes, one per sonnet line, provide 18 potential Index ties. They also act as a second set of Catalog Ties, overdetermining the selection of CipherLines.

In this fourth Stage, we decipher an entirely new text for the first time since Stage 1—the poet's concealed message rather than a crib. The cribs in the second and third Stages allowed us to determine the cryptographic values of most Designs and the values of the Orchema tables. But with those tasks now complete, the poet is free to encipher whatever message he chooses.

Adden-dum	Sonnet #		Design Type	TP val-ue	First table	Last table	CipherLine		Plaintext	
	New	Old					first	last	first	last
7	L11.H	11	Lioness	TP18	O7	O9	B	E	*	E
7	L11.1	12	Diamond-B	TP12	A10	A9	M	T	D	X
7	L11.2	13	Heart Jail	TP17	O5	O7	A	D	D	I
7	L11.3	14	DoubleA	TP1	R1	R4	T	L	U	P
7	L11.4	15	Daedalus	TP16	A3	O5	O	E	I	M
7	L11.5	16	Flowers-2x3	TP4	R8	R9	I	D	R	N
7	L11.6	17	Bulbs-10	TP9	A12	A12	T	E	T	I
8	L26.H	26	Lioness	TP18	O7	O9	T	Y	R	*
8	L26.1	37	Diamond	TP14	A7	A6	O	L	E	I
8	L26.2	21	Heart Jail	TP17	O5	O7	B	E	S	*
8	L26.3	20	Flowers-5	TP5	R9	R10	W	D	F	O
8	L26.4	33	Roots-5	TP11	A11	A10	B	D	N	M
8	L26.5	29	Flowers-4	TP3	R6	R8	T	E	A	N
8	L26.6	34	Heart Jail	TP17	O5	O7	S	T	G	R
9	L18.H	18	Lioness	TP18	O7	O9	W	T	O	I
9	L18.A1	32	Daedalus	TP16	A3	O5	F	E	R	M
9	L18.A2	24	Flowers-5	TP5	R9	R10	B	T	L	E
9	L18.A3	23	Flowers-I	TP2	R5	R6	A	T	F	A
9	L18.A4	22	Daedalus	TP16	A3	O5	T	D	D	Q
9	L18.A5	19	DoubleA	TP1	R1	R4	I	E	K	I
9	L18.A6	28	Bulbs-10	TP9	A12	A12	S	Y	U	P
9	L18.B1	27	DoubleA	TP1	R1	R4	S	E	T	I
9	L18.B2	35	Flowers-8	TP7	R11	R12	O	E	A	R
9	L18.B3	25	Flowers-6	TP6	R10	R11	N	T	Y	F
9	L18.B4	31	Flowers-4	TP3	R6	R8	T	E	A	N
9	L18.B5	36	Daedalus	TP16	A3	O5	T	E	D	M
9	L18.B6	30	Flowers-4	TP3	R6	R8	T	E	A	N

Fig. 11.2 Stage 4: deciphering process
(derived from Figs. A7.2, A8.1, and A9.2)

One Catalog Sonnet, Sonnet 18, provides Catalog Ties for all 27 sonnnets in Stage 4 (see Addendum 7 and Fig. A7.1). Sonnet 18 includes 25 phrases in its first two stanzas and 6 lines in its third Stanza that serve as Catalog Ties. In all, 31 Catalog Ties are provided that point to the Cipher-Lines of 27 sonnets, leaving 4 Catalog Ties unused. Texts and commentaries for each of the fourth Stage's 28 sonnets may be found in Addenda 7–9.

After identifying the order of the sonnets of the fourth Stage and the CipherLine in each sonnet, we are able to decipher its message. The sonnets of the fourth Stage are listed in their restored order in Fig. 11.2. Each row includes the addendum number in which the sonnet appears, the sonnet number (new and old), Design type, Transform Pair value, corresponding tables, the first and last letter of the CipherLine, and the two deciphered (polyphonic) plaintext letters. An asterisk indicates that the Orchema table is empty (indeterminate) for that value, in which case, the alternate polyphonic value must provide the deciphered letter.

One new Design appears in this Stage, the Flowers 2x3 Design, which appears only once in the sequence, under Sonnet 16. We previously suspected that its value was TP4, which would place it among the other Flower

Transform Pair	Table First Letter	Table Last Letter	Design	Where Discovered
TP1	R1	R4	DoubleA	Ch. 7
TP2	R5	R6	Flowers-1	Ch. 7
TP3	R6	R8	Flowers-4	Ch. 7
TP4	R8	R9	Flowers-2x3	Ch. 11
TP5	R9	R10	Flowers-5	Ch. 7
TP6	R10	R11	Flowers-6	Ch. 7
TP7	R11	R12	Flowers-8	Ch. 7
TP8	R12	A12	Bulbs-12	Ch. 7
TP9	A12	A12	Bulbs-10	Ch. 7
TP10	A11	A11		
TP11	A11	A10	Roots-5	Ch. 7/11
TP12	A10	A9	Diamond-B	Add. 3
TP13	A8	A7		
TP14	A7	A6	Diamond	Add. 2
TP15	A6	A4	DoubleA-inv	Ch. 7
TP16	A3	O5	Daedalus	Ch. 10
TP17	O5	O7	Heart Jail	Ch. 10
TP18	O7	O9	Lioness	Ch. 10

Fig. 11.3 Design to Transform Pair map (updated)

Designs, and we now enter it into the updated Design to Transform Pair map in Fig. 11.3 (confirmed below by the correct plaintext letter that it generates). One other new entry has been made in the Design to Transform Pair map: the value of the Roots-5 Design. That Design was known to be either TP10 or TP11 (Chapter 7), and we now know from its use in Sonnet L26.4 that its value is TP11 (only then does it generate the correct plaintext letter). The updated Design to Transform Pair map appears in Fig. 11.3.

Fig. 11.4 reproduces the final two columns of Fig. 11.2 horizontally, for convenience. The puzzle-solver must now select the correct letter from each of the two polyphonic alternatives. Fig. 11.4 shows the letters that I selected in bold (as does Fig. C.4, which duplicates the content of Fig. 11.2).

*	**D**	D	**U**	I	**R**	T	**R**	E	S	F	N	**A**	G	**O**	R	L	F	**D**	K	U	T	**A**	Y	**A**	D	**A**
E	**X**	I	P	M	N	I	*	I	*	**O**	M	N	**R**	I	**M**	E	**A**	Q	I	**P**	I	R	**F**	N	**M**	N

Fig. 11.4 Stage 4 deciphered message

The message then reads:

EXI [or EDI] VIRI RES. O MARO. ME ADI PIA FAMA.

We defer translation for the moment to first consider the context in which this and other enciphered messages are delivered: who is speaking and for what purpose? All four authorial prefaces, two in verse and two in prose, are focused on the work's reception. The two verse prefaces, the *Protrepticon* and *Quatorzain*, personify the *Hekatompathia* as a speaking book: the poet dispatches his book into the world and instructs it on how to defend itself against criticism. The published book is thus not presented as a static text, but as engaged in a conversation with the reader or puzzle-solver. This may remind us of the humanist practice of deep engagement with antiquity's texts, which often led to a new understanding of the text. The concept of a dynamic text is also found in Plato's *Phaedrus*: "The dialectician... sows his words founded on knowledge, words which can defend both themselves and him who planted them, words which instead of remaining barren contain a seed whence new words grow up in new characters" (277a).

When the personified *Hekatompathia* speaks to us via its encrypted messages, it either refers to itself (i.e., the book or Puzzle) in the first-person singular, or it addresses the puzzle-solver in the second-person singular. Its first words, VOCES ME (deciphered in the Puzzle's first Stage), do both: it requests that the puzzle-solver call (VOCES; second-person singular, subjunctive mood) upon the book (ME; first-person singular pronoun). NUO LEA PESUS informs us that it also communicates by gestures (NUO; first-person singular indicative verb) using its Lioness Designs (LEA). In the *Protrepticon*, the poet instructs his little book (*libellus*) to defend itself: *Tumque refer talos, et fixum calce sigillum* (Moreover, answer back your ankles and affixed woodcut from the heel). The translation of this line confounded two of the work's editors: in fact, its enigmatic and figurative language is incomprehensible without context (see Chapter 6 and Excursus 9). This line can only be understood as an aid to the solution of the Puzzle, alerting us to the significance of the Designs. The deciphered words of this speaking book must be read within the unusual context of the work's Puzzle.

In the above-deciphered message, the second letter may be either of the two polyphonic alternatives, D or X, as both will produce a valid text. Examining the message's first sentence, we consider first the "D" alternative:

EDI VIRI RES   (I consumed things of poison)

RES (things) can only refer to the book's sonnets. They are poisonous—figuratively evil—because they deprecate love. Cupid's darts and the beloved's sun-like rays are characterized as poisonous throughout the sequence (e.g., love is characterized as a *laethale venenum* [QA51]). The poet consumed these sonnets—these intertextual borrowings—that deprecate love, but provides instructions for their reuse in a new (reordered) sonnet sequence. We now consider the "X" alternative:

EXI VIRI RES   (Bring forth [imperative] things of nobility/goodness)

The imperative verb EXI (second-person singular) addresses the puzzle-solver. VIRI is the genitive form of both *virus* (poison) and *vir* (man/nobility): I read VIRI as *virus* in EDI VIRI RES but as *vir* in EXI VIRI RES. Using this overlap of lexical forms in VIRI, in conjunction with the polyphonic ambiguity of EDI and EXI, the poet has cleverly delivered two sentences in the space of one. These paired sentences eloquently describe the process by which the book is reborn: the seemingly ignoble (*virus*) sonnets (RES) are consumed and transformed into noble (*vir*) sonnets through the reordering performed by the puzzle-solver. Thus, the joint mission of the puzzle-solver and the speaking book is to consume the bad and deliver the good.

This reading is consistent with the *Quatorzain* preface, in which the book is told that if it is disliked, it should *Say thou, that deedes well donne to evill wrest* (12). The puzzle-solver's work, if *well donne*, will *wrest* the book from its poisonous (*virus*) or *evill* state and bring it to a noble (*vir*) state—from disparaging love to praising it.

In a sense, the published state of the *Hekatompathia* resembles the disorder found in the natural world. The puzzle-solver is engaged in a process of discovery analogous to the investigation of nature (*venatio Panis*; see Chapter 4). The puzzle-solver, under the guidance of the speaking book, is a demiurge or craftsman who "brings forth" (EXI) by consuming (EDI) the material of the ruined sequence. The message continues:

O MARO   (O! Maro)

The exclamation "O" serves to create separation from the previous words, as punctuation cannot be enciphered. It also suggests that the next word, MARO, be read in the vocative case.[2] MARO, a reference to Virgil (Vergilius Maro), was used to praise someone as a fine poet. The literati associated with de Vere were likely themselves poets, and by extension, MARO may refer to the puzzle-solver—a person who has a significant understanding of poetry. Thus, as I read it, the message calls out to the puzzle-solver, praising him or her as a poet (of sorts). The next four words also address the puzzle-solver:

ME ADI PIA FAMA   (Approach/assist me with a pious reputation)[3]

By "approach me" (ADI; second-person singular, imperative), the personified book refers to the reader's approach in interpretive reading, and obviously not the book's physical proximity. If we read PIA FAMA as an ablative of manner, then "pious reputation" is adverbial: the puzzle-solver is to read in a manner consistent with good (PIA) character (FAMA; LS II).[4] Indeed, to have arrived at this point, the puzzle-solver must have reordered the work so that it ends on a good note (Sonnet 65's allegiance to Cupid, instead of Sonnet 100's extermination of Cupid). Reading in a pious (PIA) manner echoes the initial part of this Stage's message, EXI/ EDI VIRI RES, that tasks the puzzle-solver with bringing the text from a poisonous to a noble state. It also echoes the *Quatorzain* preface's instruction: *Say thou, that deedes well donne to evill wrest* (discussed above).

The fifth Stage (Addendum 10)

Only 13 of the *Hekatompathia*'s Designs remain to be deciphered in this, the Puzzle's fifth Stage. The work's prefaces contain 6 Designs, and the first 7 Sonnets each contain one Design. Two Designs appear under the *Quatorzain* preface, the only instance in which two Designs appear on the same page. A single CipherLine is applied to both Designs. The prefaces and sonnets in this Stage were not scrambled by the poet (see Chapter 3).

Sonnet 7, an encomium to Venus that lists her attributes, serves as the Catalog Sonnet for this Stage, identifying the CipherLines of both the prefaces and sonnets. As in earlier Stages, the *Quid Amor* Ties aid in Cipher-Line selection. At this late point in the Puzzle, there are a limited pool of QA Ties left available, and this makes the QA Ties more valuable in identifying CipherLines. With 77 of the original 89 QA Ties having been used in the prior Stages, only 12 QA Ties remain unassigned, exactly matching the number of CipherLines that must be identified.[5] The Catalog and QA Ties, in concert, overdetermine the selection of CipherLines, which adds to our confidence in deciphering this Stage's message.

This Stage, unlike earlier ones, contains prefaces, which obviously have a different format than the 18-line sonnets. Nevertheless, the same cryptographic principle applies: the first and last letters of the CipherLine provide the ciphertext. I use the identifiers P1 through P5 to identify the 5 prefaces with Designs; the identifiers P5a and P5b are used to distinguish between P5's two Designs.

This Stage contains two Designs that appear only once in the work: the Roots-4 Design and the "Humus" Design (see Fig. 11.5). The Roots-4 Design, a variant on the Roots-5 Design, appears under Sonnet 4; the Humus Design appears under Sonnet 5. I chose the name "Humus" because the Design appears to me to combine bulbs and leaves, which in the context of the "plant model" (Chapter 7), seemed to me to be soil—decayed organic material.

Roots-4 Design (Sonnet 4)   Humus Design (Sonnet 5)

Fig. 11.5 Roots-4 and Humus Designs

If we examine the Design-to-Transform Pair map in Fig. 11.3, we find that there are two unassigned slots. The Roots-4 Design surely belongs next to Roots-5, and thus we assign it to TP10. However, we might have thought that the order of Roots-5 and Roots-4 in the table would be reversed, decrementing downward in the bottom half of the table, just as Bulbs-12 decrements to Bulbs-10. The reason for this curious anomaly will be apparent in the seventh Stage (see Excursus 11). The final remaining Design, the Humus Design, may now be assigned to the only remaining open slot—TP13. Fig. 11.6 updates the previous Design to Transform Pair map (Fig. 11.3) with these two new entries.

Transform Pair	Table First Letter	Table Last Letter	Design	Where Discovered
TP1	R1	R4	DoubleA	Ch. 7
TP2	R5	R6	Flowers-1	Ch. 7
TP3	R6	R8	Flowers-4	Ch. 7
TP4	R8	R9	Flowers-2x3	Ch. 11
TP5	R9	R10	Flowers-5	Ch. 7
TP6	R10	R11	Flowers-6	Ch. 7
TP7	R11	R12	Flowers-8	Ch. 7
TP8	R12	A12	Bulbs-12	Ch. 7
TP9	A12	A12	Bulbs-10	Ch. 7
TP10	A11	A11	Roots-4	Ch. 11
TP11	A11	A10	Roots-5	Ch. 7/11
TP12	A10	A9	Diamond-B	Add. 3
TP13	A8	A7	Humus	Ch. 11
TP14	A7	A6	Diamond	Add. 2
TP15	A6	A4	DoubleA-inv	Ch. 7
TP16	A3	O5	Daedalus	Ch. 10
TP17	O5	O7	Heart Jail	Ch. 10
TP18	O7	O9	Lioness	Ch. 10

Fig. 11.6 Design to Transform Pair map (final)

Does the assignment of the Humus Design to TP13 make sense in the context of the plant model? If one counts downward from TP9 (Bulbs-10 Design), decrementing by one bulb per table row, one arrives at TP13 (Humus Design) at the count of 6. Examining the Humus Design in Fig. 11.5, there appear to be 6 bulbs. If one takes the downward Bulb count further, to the table's last row, TP18, one ends with a count of "Bulbs-1." This equates a single bulb with the Lioness Design (whose value is TP18). A bulb is the place where plant generation starts, and in the *Hekatom-pathia*, love, emblemized as the Lioness, is the source from which everything in the natural world flows. True, this plant model is not perfectly consistent: the Bulbs-12 entry at TP8 is an increment of two, not one, above the Bulbs-10 entry at TP9. However, this likely results from the need for symmetry between the two horizontal rows of bulbs. In any case, the number of bulbs in these three Designs shows a decreasing trend, which is consistent with the decreasing Aversa half of the Pillar Sonnet. Similarly, the Flower Designs show an increasing trend, which is consistent with the increasing Recta half of the Pillar Sonnet. Whether the foregoing rationales were intended or not, the mapping of Designs to Transform

Pairs is complete, with each of the 18 Designs specifying one of the 18 Transform Pairs.

Curiously, the two unique Designs, Roots-4 and Humus, fall next to each other (Sonnets 4 and 5) at the tail end of Stage 5's message, and as we will shortly discover, it is here that a critical secret is revealed. This positioning of the two unique Designs enforces the locking of Stages, as their values are unknown prior to completing most of the entries in the Design to Transform Pair map. This imposes a single progressive path through the Puzzle's Stages, preventing the puzzle-solver from skipping ahead to this Stage before completing the earlier Stages.

There is one anomalous feature in Stage 5 that deserves our scrutiny: unlike any other Design in the *Hekatompathia,* Sonnet 1's Design is positioned above the headnote, rather than below the sonnet. This positioning of the Flowers-4 Design above the work's very first sonnet breaches decorum. In the next chapter, we will discover that this is an important signal that directs the puzzle-solver to the next (sixth) Stage. The question we might now ask ourselves is whether the position of Sonnet 1's Design has any implication for its Transform Pair value. The poet may have intended that we imagine the page as inverted, that is, rotated 180°, bringing the Design to the bottom of the page. The effect of this inversion makes the sonnet's last line its first and makes all lines read backward, from right to left. A consequence of the latter is that the position of the first and last letters of the CipherLines would be reversed. In this treatment, we would need to apply the first table value of the Flowers-4 Transform Pair to the last letter of the CipherLine (instead of the first), and the second table value of the Transform Pair to the first letter of the CipherLine (instead of the last). The effect of this is to change the value of the Flowers-4 Transform Pair, TP3, from (R6, R8) to (R8, R6). As this is only a hypothesis, both alternatives for Sonnet 1 should be considered. This results in four alternative plaintext letters, rather than the usual two, as shown in the seventh row of Fig. 11.7.

Figure 11.7 presents the 13 Designs in the fifth Stage, the Cipher-Line letters for each of the pages with Designs, and the deciphered plaintext letters. The information presented here is extracted from Addendum 10, which details the CipherLine selection for each of the 12 prefaces and sonnets.

We can now resolve the "A or Q" ambiguity for O7(L) and O9(A) in the Orchema tables (see Fig. 10.4). From the second row of Fig. 11.7, we know that O9(A)≠Q (the alternative is undefined) because the next letter (third row) cannot be a U, and thus O9(A)=A and O7(L)=Q. The fully resolved Orchema table is presented in Fig. B.3.

Fig. 11.8 presents Fig. 11.7's last two columns horizontally, and we must now select one letter from each pair of polyphonic plaintext letters to

Adden-dum	Sonnet #	Design Type	TP value	First table	Last table	CipherLine		Plaintext	
						first	last	first	last
10	P1	Diamond	TP14	A7	A6	Y	R	U	C
10	P2	Lioness	TP18	O7	O9	U	A	*	A
10	P3	Daedalus	TP16	A3	O5	P	S	H	G
10	P4	DoubleA-I	TP15	A6	A4	F	E	O	R
10	P5a	Flowers-5	TP5	R9	R10	T	T	D	E
10	P5b	Heart Jail	TP17	O5	O7	T	T	E	R
10	1	Flowers-4-i	TP4	R6/8	R8/6	W	E	C, E	N, L
10	2	Lioness	TP18	O7	O9	W	E	O	E
10	3	Daedalus	TP16	A3	O5	A	T	X	E
10	4	Roots-4	TP10	A11	A11	A	S	O	W
10	5	Humus	TP13	A8	A7	A	E	R	O
10	6	Heart Jail	TP17	O5	O7	Q	T	A	R
10	7	DoubleA	TP1	R1	R4	E	S	F	X

Fig. 11.7 Stage 5: deciphering process
(derived from Fig. A10.3)

U	*	H	O	D	E	C, E	O	X	O	R	A	F
C	A	G	R	E	R	N, L	E	E	W	O	R	X

Fig. 11.8 Stage 5 deciphered message

obtain a coherent message. The selected letters are shown in bold (as they are in Fig. C.5, which includes content from both Figs. 11.7 and 11.8). The seventh letter selected, "E," was produced by the (R8, R6) alternative for Flowers-4, the result of inverting Sonnet 1.[6] The message reads:

VAH. RERE. EX ORA X.   (Wow! Think! Ten from the coast/edge.)

I take the message's first word, VAH (wow), to be an expression of approbation to the puzzle-solver for having reached this point in the Puzzle. The next word, RERE, is the verb "think" (second-person singular, either indicative or imperative mood). I saw this as an alert to the puzzle-solver that some considerable intellectual challenge lies ahead. Finally, EX ORA X (Ten from the coast/edge), appears to be an instruction concerning the Puzzle's next Stage. Of course, acrostics—first and last letters—are central to the Puzzle. ORA, then, must refer to the text's edge, which provides the ciphertext (a sonnet's first and last letters are its edge). Bacon seems to be indicating that something is hidden 10 letters in from one sonnet edge or the other, or more likely, a polyphonic choice between the two. But to what sonnets or other text should this be applied? Are these letters deciphered by a Design? These questions are taken up in the next chapter.

Before deciphering this message, I believed that the fifth Stage would be the last, because with the supply of Designs exhausted, there seemed to be nothing left to decipher. I expected to decipher an impressive final message and was sorely disappointed when I instead obtained this cryptic message—clearly the Puzzle had not reached its conclusion. Worse yet, the meaning of the message was hard to comprehend and the path forward from this point was not at all evident. I had reached an aporia and was overtaken by the fear that having come so far, and expending years of effort in doing so, I would be unable to discover the device or trick that allows one to advance. I would be left standing at this threshold, with the prize of completing this amazing journey just beyond my reach. I took the imperative RERE to be a provocative challenge from the preternaturally talented poet who created the Puzzle, and it unnerved me. Until, that is, I found the blemish, that signpost, that breach of decorum, that allowed me to pass on to the next Stage.

Validation of the messages of Stages 4 and 5

The Stage 4 and Stage 5 messages may now be validated. After completing the third Stage and determining the Orchema table values (Chapter 10), our knowledge of the Puzzle's cryptographic system was nearly complete: the Design to Transform Pair map had only a few open entries that required completion. We are now positioned to authenticate the completed cryptographic system and the new messages it delivered in the fourth and fifth Stages.

In the fourth and fifth Stages, only half of the deciphered text is produced by reordered Designs: the 20 Designs in the prefaces and Sonnets 1–17 are not scrambled; the other 20 sonnets (18–37) were reordered. The order of the 20 reordered sonnets is robustly defined: the 7 sonnets of the L26 Series are overdetermined by two methods, the Sequential Ties and the Hexameral themes; the 13 sonnets of the L18 Series are overdetermined by three methods, the Sequential Ties, the Hexameral themes, and

Index Sonnet 79. The order of the 40 sonnets in these two Stages is thus almost certainly correct: 20 are in the original order, 7 are twice overdetermined, and 13 are thrice overdetermined.

We must also consider the specification of the CipherLines. Approximately half of the CipherLines (13/27) are overdetermined by Index Sonnet 79, which points to the CipherLines in concert with the Catalog Ties. Overdetermination is also provided by the *Quid Amor* (QA) Ties, which become more reliable in the Puzzle's later Stages, as one begins to exhaust the 89 QA Ties available at the beginning of the Puzzle.

We will now perform a mathematical validation of the fourth and fifth Stage's deciphered messages. The standard method of validating cryptograms, described in Chapter 2 and Excursus 3, must account for three factors: the absolute rate of language (the full range of the ciphertext), the number of potentially valid messages, and the range of the key (known as key equivocation). To validate our 40 letters worth of plaintext messages, we first calculate the probability that a coherent and relevant plaintext message is produced by a randomly generated 40-letter text. Using a Shannon information value of 25% pure information and 75% redundancy, the number of potentially valid texts is equal to $24^{(25\% \text{ of } 40)} = 24^{10}$ = approximately 6.3×10^{13}. We now divide the number of valid texts by the absolute rate of language, which for our 40-letter ciphertext is 24^{40}, or approximately 1.6×10^{55}:

$$\text{Ratio of valid texts to all possible texts} = 6.3 \times 10^{13} / 1.6 \times 10^{55} = 4 \times 10^{-42}$$

We now must account for the indeterminacy in polyphonic ciphers, which requires a choice between one of two plaintext letters. For 40 letters, that is 2^{40} or approximately 10^{12}. This increases the ratio calculated above to 4×10^{-30} or 1 in 2.5×10^{29}. This is the probability of serendipitously producing a valid and relevant text by a random process, which is roughly equivalent to winning a one-in-a-trillion lottery every second since the universe began.

The above calculation is dependent upon two conditions: (1) that the scrambled sonnets in the fourth Stage have been correctly reordered, and (2) that the CipherLine selections are correct. With respect to the order of the 39 sonnets and prefaces, only 20 have been reordered and the order of 13 of these is triply redundant (by a double Hexameral ring, Sequential Ties, and an Index Sonnet). With respect to CipherLine selection, there is also overdetermination: Catalog Ties, QA Ties, and, for 13 of the sonnets, Index Ties. These work in concert to increase the reliability of CipherLine selection. Furthermore, the practice of CipherLine selection was firmly established in Stage 2, in which Catalog and Index Ties pointed to CipherLines for all sonnets except the first three. Stage 3 further increased our confidence in the process of CipherLine selection. Also, as discussed in the previous chapter, my selections of 17 CipherLines (those associated with pictorial Designs) in the second and third Stages, were later subject to verification in the derivation of the Orchema table. I found that I made the correct selection for 15 of 17 CipherLines, and the two errors were subtle ones in which the selection was made to an adjacent line.

Nevertheless, we might wish to make a more conservative calculation with respect to CipherLine selection. We assume that for each of the 40 deciphered letters, two different CipherLine selections might have been made, even though I think this greatly overstates the ambiguity in Cipher-Line selection. Assuming all 40 CipherLine selections could be any 2 of the 18 sonnet lines, the previously calculated probability of 1 in 2.5×10^{29} must be increased by a factor of 2^{40}, or about 10^{12}, which results in a probability of 1 in 2.5×10^{17}. This is still an absurdly remote event, roughly equivalent to flipping a fair coin and getting heads each time, once per second, since the universe began. At this probability, our cryptographic validation of the fourth and fifth Stages is incontrovertible.

An interesting comparison may be made to the pseudo-cryptography discussed in the first chapter. The pseudo-decipherer works backward, beginning with a preconceived message (usually the name of a person of interest), and then construes methods or keys to produce that preconceived message. With the Puzzle's multistage architecture, that is not possible because each Stage produces a message and/or new table entries that are then used in the next Stage to advance. This highly structured architecture cannot be operated in reverse. The Puzzle's coherence is the result of its careful construction by the poet, the work's master architect, who had the necessary control over the poetic text, the placement of Designs, the content of Catalog Sonnets, and the content of headnotes and sidenotes that frequently provide essential hints on how to proceed.

Another important difference between the cryptography presented here and the many pseudo-cryptographic claims that have been made is the length of the messages presented. At this point in the Puzzle, we have deciphered 98 characters. The inherent order displayed by the deciphered messages, all generated by the same basic cryptographic system, is over-whelming. In contrast, pseudo-cryptographic results are usually very short, often a dozen characters or less. The effect of this difference between a dozen and nearly one hundred characters is not linear but expo-nential (see Excursus 3).

Although mathematical methods are best suited to validate crypto-grams, a qualitative evaluation of the deciphered messages may better resonate with some readers of this study. One's sense from reading the messages of these Stages is that they are directly responsive to our obvious questions about the purpose of the Puzzle. The clever overlay of EDI VIRI RES and EXI VIRI RES (I consumed things of poison; bring forth things of nobility) perfectly describes, in an extraordinarily concise sentence of only 10 letters, the poet's ruin of his sequence and the puzzle-solver's restoration of it. The first 7 of these 10 letters were deciphered from Sonnets 11–17, which did not require any reordering, and are thus free of any possible reordering error. Indeed, the devising of this eloquent Latin trick is far beyond my skill and could only be the brainchild of the poet.

The remainder of the fourth Stage's message is again contextually relevant: the puzzle-solver is praised, and the next words fit the context established by the *Protrepticon* preface. The fifth Stage's message again compliments the puzzle-solver (VAH; "wow") and demands that further mental effort (RERE; "think") be applied to a mysterious instruction (EX ORA X; "10 from the edge"). These last words reveal an essential secret that is revealed in the next chapter.

The Puzzle is without precedent, astonishingly extensive and complex, and uniquely melds the disparate disciplines of poetry and cryptography. It sets its own rules; it creates its own "golden world." Our reflexive reaction to claims of singular events or ideas is often rejection because our expectations are geared toward the norm: unicorns are summarily dismissed—an unfortunate error. Here, we must recognize that the cryptographic evidence trumps any reflexive judgments. Thus, we now possess a previously unknown sixteenth-century sonnet sequence, and its authenticity is mathematically corroborated.

The *Restored Hekatompathia*

The *Hekatompathia*, like a jigsaw puzzle, has two states: scattered pieces and a restored, properly ordered whole. The last of the scrambled sonnets were reordered in the solution to the fourth Stage, which completes the restoration of the sequence. The poet wrote exactly those sonnets needed to form a structured, coherent sequence and then intentionally ruined his sequence with the expectation that it would later be restored (EDI VIRI RES; EXI VIRI RES). The poet disrupts the sequence at a critical point: he bizarrely assigns a sonnet number (80) to an itemized list of instructions and challenges the reader to decipher a message (see Chapter 2). The Pillar Sonnet definitively specifies a set of cryptographic tables. Further instructions for restoration appear in headnotes, sidenotes, Index Sonnets, Catalog Sonnets, and various rhetorical devices. The puzzle solver's role is to follow those instructions to the conclusion they impose. Now, centuries after the first appearance of the sonnets in their corrupted order, the poet's authentic sonnet sequence is revealed. The second volume of this study includes the *Restored Hekatompathia*, uninterrupted by commentary pages.

The *Hekatompathia*'s astonishing feat of self-transformation into an organic work is an aesthetic wonder. The restored sequence's Series, marked by the Lioness Sonnets, exhibit an ordered development in the speaker's exploration of the nature of love. Each sonnet dovetails to the next, linked by Sequential Ties. Two double and four single Hexameral rings are another architectural mechanism that imposes order. The restored work is perfectly framed: it begins with a series of questions about the nature of love; it ends with the L73 Series, in which the speaker recognizes love as all-powerful, disbursed across the cosmos, and essential to the speaker's own being. In traversing the Puzzle, table entries in the Design-to-TP mapping table, the Orchema tables, and the QA Tie list are progressively filled in, and at this point in the Puzzle, each of these tables stand complete. This process of progressively adding table entries coincides with Bacon's vision of the new experimental science, in which scientists begin with incomplete tables of collected data and then successively add new table entries or revise previous ones. In the *Hekatompathia*, the completion of all table entries might be expected to signal the end of our journey, except for the strange message deciphered in the fifth Stage, which pushes us to look further.

12

Stage 6:

The Hidden Labyrinth

Having deciphered all 97 of the *Hekatompathia*'s Designs, it seems that we have reached an aporia. Yet, Stage 5's deciphered message directs us to "think" (RERE), which seems to indicate that something must follow, but is otherwise uninstructive. The next words, EX ORA X ("10 from the edge"), presumably reveal how we are to proceed. The first and last letters of a CipherLine, which form the edges or acrostics of a sonnet, might be thought of as "one from the edge." My first thought was to apply the Designs to the known CipherLines of each sonnet using new ciphertext letters located 10 letters in from the beginning and end of each CipherLine. However, this produced gibberish. On reflection, I realized that reuse of CipherLines in this way would severely constrain the poet's choice of words, making it an unattractive method to encipher another message. It seemed that the Designs would in some way be reused, but it was unclear how this was to be done.

Not knowing how to proceed, I wondered if the fifth Stage might provide a second clue (besides EX ORA X) that allows the puzzle-solver to advance. I thought back to the aporia I faced at the end of the second Stage: from the end of the MLIP Subsequence there is no apparent path forward. But the Subsequence's final sonnet, Lioness Sonnet 90, is a signpost that marks the beginning of the third Subsequence and the third Stage. As a Lioness Sonnet, Sonnet 90 must start a new Series, and therefore the only solution is to transpose sonnets forward (Chapter 8). Sonnet 90 is an anomaly, a Neo-Latin poem with a uniquely religious tone that is missing its final line. The Puzzle often presents an anomaly or contradiction that provides a hint as to how the puzzle-solver is to advance. The challenge is to detect that breach of decorum—what Riffaterre called an "ungrammaticality"—that serves as "the index to the solution."[1]

The fifth Stage contains an obvious breach of decorum: Sonnet 1's Flowers-4 Design appears above, not below, the sonnet, the only one of the 97 Designs so positioned. This cannot be a capricious decision or the choice of the printer because this positioning inverted the value of the

Transform Pair TP3 in this instance, from (R6, R8) to (R8, R6), as discussed in the previous chapter. Only with this inversion was Stage 5's deciphered message coherent. Why this unique and elaborate difference in the positioning of Sonnet 1's Design? Why not simply choose a different Design, positioned normally, that produces the required plaintext letter?

My first thought was to try inverting other sonnets and see if reversing the two tables specified by the Transform Pairs produced a coherent message somewhere. It did not. Finally, I realized that the anomalously placed Flowers-4 Design performs a second function in addition to its cryptographic one, just as the Lioness Design performs a second function in signaling the beginning of a Series. The Flowers-4 Design appears 5 times in the sequence, above Sonnet 1 and under Sonnets 29, 30, 31, and 97. The consecutive appearance of three Flowers-4 Designs (29, 30, and 31) is an anomaly: nowhere else in the sequence is any Design repeated even once. This reminds us of the anomalous absence of Designs in Sonnets 8–10, which signals the division between the fourth and fifth Stages, as discussed in the previous chapter. I thought that perhaps Sonnet 1's Flowers-4 Design might be a signpost meant to direct the puzzle-solver to Sonnet 29, the first of the three adjacent Flowers-4 sonnets. I decided to examine the letters that are "10 from each edge" of Sonnet 29. I did this for all the sonnet's lines, not just its CipherLine: I extracted the 10th letter from the beginning of each line and the 10th from the end of each line. These 18 pairs of letters will be referred to as "In-10 Acrostics." Sonnet 29's In-10 Acrostics are rendered below in a horizontal format, beginning with the pair of letters from the sonnet's first line (S, E) and ending with the pair of letters from the sonnet's last line (L, E):

S	**E**	**T**	H	**U**	X	S	O	S	L	**U**	**I**	**E**	E	O	O	I	L
E	T	E	**S**	C	**E**	**A**	**R**	T	**E**	E	S	N	A	K	O	A	E

The In-10 Acrostics must be subjected to a polyphonic selection process, choosing one letter from each pair of letters to form a coherent message. This is the same polyphonic selection process applied to the first and last letters of CipherLines in all prior Stages of the Puzzle. In the above horizontal display of Sonnet 29's In-10 Acrostics, the letters I selected are shown in bold. The resulting message is:

ET SUE ARTE; VIE (And sew with skill; weave)

This 12-letter message begins with the second letter of the In-10 Acrostics and leaves the last 5 letters unused. This message and others we will discover consist of a contiguous subset of the available letters, typically beginning after the sonnet's first line and ending before its last. These messages appear in each of the 39 sonnets and prefaces of Stages 4 and 5.

The hiding of a secret text within an open (clearly readable) text is an example of steganography (see Chapter 1 and Excursus 2). In previous Stages of the Puzzle, the first and last letters were stripped from the Cipher-Lines to form a ciphertext—a steganographic process. However, these letters were subsequently deciphered using tables. In contrast, in this process, the In-10 Acrostics are in plaintext, and no deciphering is required. The hiding of plaintext at various predetermined locations within an open text was commonly practiced in the sixteenth century. A device called a Cardan grille—a grid or piece of paper with cutouts—specified the position of the secret text on a page.[2] A sonnet's fixed structure makes it a natural vehicle for this form of steganography. The Puzzle's sixth Stage can be thought of as a simple implementation of the Cardan Grille method: the extraction of the 10th letter from the beginning and end of each line.

These steganographic messages were likely embedded in a previously composed sonnet on an opportunistic basis. The poet would find a promising place in his sonnet to embed his message and then modify spelling and sometimes make minor adjustments to the text to produce the desired In-10 Acrostics. The flexibility in Elizabethan-era spelling provided many opportunities to modify the sonnet text such that the desired letters of the hidden text would fall at either the front end or back end of the In-10 Acrostics.

Resolving these In-10 Acrostics to a Latin word or phrase is more difficult than the resolution of the polyphonic messages of deciphered letters practiced in prior Stages. One difference is that the starting and ending points of the In-10 Acrostics message are unmarked: the message can fall on any contiguous sequence of letters within the In-10 Acrostics. Another difference is that the resolution of the polyphony is more difficult because the two letters one chooses between are not arithmetically generated. In cryptographic polyphony, the choice is between two arithmetically generated (effectively random) letters, which would sometimes include an easily excluded letter such as "Z." In contrast, In-10 Acrostics consist entirely of letters that appear in the text, and therefore the excluded letter is unlikely to be an easily excluded letter such as "Z." It must be acknowledged that the foregoing makes our confidence in the resolved message less certain. However, the message is only used as a pointer to another sonnet, as discussed below, and as will become apparent, this places significant constraints on the range of the message. In fact, we will find that the messages embedded in the In-10 Acrostics are mostly unambiguous. This may be tested by examining the In-10 Acrostics of sonnets that fall outside the range of the Stage 6 sonnets (which have no embedded messages), or by examining acrostics at a distance of other than 10 letters, as discussed in the last section of this chapter. In such examinations, few Latin words appear by chance, and in the rare cases that they do, they are unlikely to be meaningful, as explained below.

A 40–room labyrinth

Sonnet 29's In-10 Acrostics message begins with ET (and), which suggests a continuation of Stage 4's message, EX ORA X (ten from the edge). Thus the puzzle-solver is instructed to extract the In-10 Acrostics and then sew something together skillfully (SUE ARTE). The importance of SUE (sew) is emphasized by the further command to weave (VIE). SUE and VIE, both second-person singular imperative verbs, instruct the puzzle-solver to create a new text. The idea that a text is woven is etymologically grounded: "text" was thought to be derived from *textus* (a woven fabric).[3] The verb *vieo, viere* (VIE) was also associated with the production of a text, according to Varro's fanciful etymology: "antiquos poetas vates appellabant a versibus viendis" (they used to call the ancient poets "vates" because of the weaving [*viendis*] of verses).[4] Moreover, in some notable instances of ekphrasis, a woven fabric recounts a portion of the poetic story in which it appears: Arachne's weaving in *Metamorphoses* 6, Helen's in *Iliad* 3, and the purple coverlet on the marriage bed of Peleus and Thetis in Catullus 64.

In the previous Stages, solving the Puzzle required the reordering of sonnets. Naturally, having exhausted the supply of sonnets, one would think that there was no further reason to reorder sonnets. After all, having already brought the sequence to its proper literary order, what further purpose could be served by "sewing" together sonnets to produce yet another order? However, in order to encipher yet another message, it is necessary to reuse sonnets that already produced messages in earlier Stages. This new reordering of sonnets is not for any literary purpose, but to provide new ground for enciphering another message.

In Stage 6, the In-10 Acrostics direct us from one sonnet to the next, establishing a new ground upon which a message may be enciphered. Each one of Stage 6's sonnets or prefaces has a message embedded in its In-10 Acrostics, which I call the "In-10 Sequential Tie." An In-10 Sequential Tie is a contiguous message extracted from the polyphonic In-10 Acrostics. The In-10 Sequential Ties direct the puzzle-solver to the next sequential sonnet in a new order. The puzzle-solver's task is to determine the new order of these sewn-together sonnets and use them to decipher a new message. Stage 6 reuses the 27 sonnets of Stage 4 and the 12 sonnets or prefaces of Stage 5. In all, 39 sonnets or prefaces, containing 40 Designs (preface P5 has two Designs), encipher a new 40-letter message.

The number 40 has numerological significance: Moses spent 40 days on Mount Sinai receiving God's law; the Israelites spent 40 years wandering in the Sinai; Christ was led by the Spirit for 40 days in the wilderness where he was tested; Lent lasts 40 days. The number 40 symbolizes a period of wandering and testing. The sixth Stage, one of the Puzzle's more difficult Stages, is a 40-room or 40-turn labyrinth that must be first navigated and then deciphered. Successful transversal of this Stage reveals the instructions for the seventh and final Stage. Only then can the *Hekatompathia*'s "seventh seal" be broken and the work's final words uncovered. In making the sixth Stage so difficult, one might speculate that Bacon was following the pattern found in the breaking of the sixth seal in *Revelation*, which is complex and detailed (*Revelation* 6:12–17; 7:1–17).

Our first task is to determine the new order of these 40 sonnets/prefaces (counting the preface P5, with its two Designs, twice). Fig. 12.1 depicts schematically the first four sonnets and the final two sonnets of this new order, connected by arrows. In the upper left-hand corner, Sonnet 1, with its Flowers-4 Design at the top, is the signpost that sends us to the first sonnet of the sixth Stage, Sonnet 29, as earlier discussed. From Sonnet 29, we advance to the next sequential sonnet, Sonnet 30, the second in this new order. We are then directed on a labyrinthine path by the In-10 Sequential Ties, each of which points to the next sonnet in order. Sonnet 30's In-10 Sequential Tie directs us to sonnet 32, and that sonnet's In-10

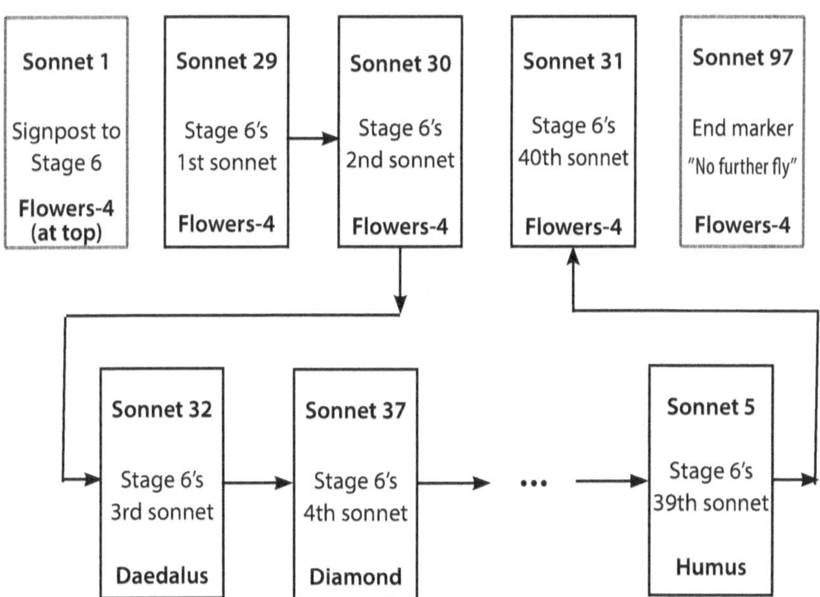

Fig. 12.1 Schematic drawing of the Stage 6 sonnet labyrinth

Sequential Tie directs us to Sonnet 37, and so on, as shown. The Stage ends at Sonnet 31, the last of the three contiguous Flowers-4 sonnets. Sonnet 31's In-10 Acrostics informs us that it is the last sonnet, as discussed below. Sonnet 97, the fifth and last Flowers-4 Sonnet, indicates that one has overgone the limit of Stage 6, as later discussed.

This 40-room labyrinth is presented in the second volume, Addendum 11. There, each sonnet and preface of Stage 6 is reproduced along with a resolution of its In-10 Sequential Ties from its In-10 Acrostics. To give a sense of how these In-10 Sequential Ties work, several examples are provided below, beginning with Sonnet 30:

H	O	S	M	O	R	O	S	I	A	**A**	**O**	A	I	**S**	U	**N**	**A**
K	H	E	O	G	T	T	**H**	**O**	**R**	D	H	**R**	O	A	**E**	O	I

In-10 Sequential Tie: HORA, ORIS ENA. (At this time, swim out from the shores). Rather than continue linearly to Sonnet 31, the puzzle-solver is told to swim away from the "shores," which are presumably Sonnets 30 and 31, as shown in Fig. 12.1. Sonnet 30 begins the labyrinthine journey, and Sonnet 31 ends it. The puzzle-solver is told to swim out (ENA), but to where? The obvious target is the nautical adventure of Strozza's poem, "Somnium," found in Sonnet 32 (HN). Also, Thetis, a water god, appears in Sonnet 32's first line. There is another link that connects these two sonnets: the poet's name, Strozza, appears in Sonnet 30's headnote as well as in Sonnet 32's headnote. We now examine Sonnet 32's In-10 Sequential Tie:

A	G	E	G	H	A	**A**	**U**	E	**T**	N	N	**A**	D	N	E	W	A
O	L	D	I	T	S	F	O	D	B	**O**	**U**	T	O	**A**	U	H	T

In-10 Sequential Tie: AVETO VADA. (All desire the fords/crossings). VADA is a place through which one can cross: shallow water or shoals. This points to Sonnet 37, in which various gods, overcome by desire for mortals, all leave their natural homes (heaven, hell, etc.) to visit mortal women on Earth. For example, Neptune removes himself from the seas and seeks the sands (37.3–4).

The navigation of this sonnet-labyrinth is detailed in Addendum 11, and we now skip to the penultimate sonnet of the labyrinth, Sonnet 5 (see Fig. 12.1):

L	E	C	H	L	Y	D	M	C	**T**	**N**	B	G	**U**	**R**	**E**	U	R
A	H	S	E	A	W	L	H	**A**	E	M	**E**	**U**	L	D	I	A	N

In-10 Sequential Tie: AT NEU URE (and burn or not). This points to Sonnet 31, whose last line is *Whilst I both frie and freeze twixt flame and frost.*

We have now reached the final sonnet of Stage 6, Sonnet 31 (see Fig. 12.1). Its In-10 Acrostics do not point to another sonnet but instead acknowledge that the end has been reached:

O	A	T	E	L	A	U	L	I	T	L	**A**	E	N	U	E	**E**	**T**
S	A	R	L	H	O	T	B	E	**E**	D	E	**M**	E	T	**R**	R	M

In-10 Sequential Tie: EDA ME. URET. (Disclose me [imperative]. It will vex.)[5] EDA ME refers to the seventh and final Stage, in which the poet's identity is revealed. Finally, URET (it will vex) foretells that the seventh Stage will be difficult.

How do we know that we have reached the end of the sixth Stage? We have traversed 40 sonnet/Designs, and this likely signals the end of wandering, the metonymic value of the number 40. Moreover, Sonnet 31's In-10 Sequential Tie seems to refer to the next Stage. Perhaps most significant of all, we have now looped back to where we began: the last of the three consecutive sonnets with Flowers-4 Designs (29, 30, and 31), and this signals the completion of our journey.

Nevertheless, we may be tempted to visit the last of the five Flowers-4 Designs, Sonnet 97 (see Fig. 12.1). The sonnet's headnote explains that *this passion alludeth to the fable of Phineus* (HN) in which Calais and Zethes, *the two twinnes of Boreas* (HN), are told by *the voyce, Ne plus ultra* (nothing further beyond), *spoaken from Heaven* (HN) that they should *No further fly* (6). The motto *plus ultra* was used by Charles V and appears in Claude Paradin's *Devises heroïques* (Lyons, 1557; 29), along with an illustration of the twin pillars of Hercules. In myth, these twin pillars marked the western extreme of the Roman world at the strait of Gibraltar: *Ne plus ultra* meant that there was "nothing further beyond." Leaving out the "Ne" in Paradin's device implies that the new empire of Charles V exceeds the limits of antiquity. In Sonnet 97, *Ne plus ultra* is applied to the eastern (rather than western) extreme of the Roman empire, which was Thrace. In the Phineus myth, which is recounted in the sonnet's first stanza, Calais and Zethes chase away the Harpies that have been torturing Phineus, driving these vengeful creatures to and past the eastern limit of Thrace. Beyond that border lies only the north wind, Boreas. Thus, Calais and Zethes are told by heaven to *No further fly* (6). The implication for the puzzle-solver is that the limit of Stage 6 has been reached—there is nothing further. Bacon famously used the image of the twin pillars of Hercules and a boat sailing past them in the frontispiece of his *Instauratio magna*

(1620). He adopted the motto *plus ultra*, which served as an image of his desire to go "further beyond" the limits of current knowledge by means of his inductive scientific method.[6]

The setting of Sonnet 97 in Thrace creates an interesting echo of the *Authoris ad libellum suum Protrepticon* preface. The *Protrepticon's* image of the poet speaking to his "little book" (*ad libellum*), the *Hekatompathia*, which is being sent off on a journey, is clearly based on Ovid's *Tristia* 1.1. The "little book" theme is also found in another authorial preface of the *Hekatompathia*, the *Quatorzain*. Both the *Protrepticon* and *Tristia* 1.1 use the same word *libellus* (little book), have the book speak as if it were a person, and declare that the poet is suffering hard times. Bacon was suffering due to the recent death of his father (1579) and a dispute with his older half-brothers over his father's estate, which left him financially vulnerable. Ovid's *Tristia* recounts Ovid's overwhelming sorrow over his exile to Thrace. (Ovid's exile is mentioned in Sonnet 8's headnote.) Thus, Thrace provides a link between the *Protrepticon* and Sonnet 97. Ovid hoped that his letters or work might earn him Augustus's sympathy, and that the exile order would be rescinded. Essentially, Sonnet 97 is a boundary, marking a hard stop after Stage 6's last sonnet: Thrace, whether in Sonnet 97 or *Tristia* 1.1., is metonymically a limit or end. We have reached the end of the sixth Stage.

The sixth Stage's cryptic message

This Stage's 40-letter encrypted message is enciphered using the same method as that used in earlier Stages. However, a new CipherLine must be identified for each of the 39 sonnets/prefaces (counting preface P5 once). Reuse of the previously identified CipherLines would have made for a difficult, if not impossible, constraint in producing a new message. Thus, a new set of CipherLines is specified by using Catalog Sonnets or equivalent devices. As in previous Stages, the first and last letters of a CipherLine contain a ciphertext that can then be deciphered using the Transform Pair value specified by the Design below the sonnet.

The sixth Stage is divided into 4 "Sections" of sonnets/prefaces, which I have designated as Sections A through D. Each Section has a Catalog Sonnet, or equivalent device, that provides a list of Catalog Ties. Addendum 11 devotes a single page to each of the Stage's 39 sonnets/prefaces. Each page identifies the Catalog Tie and CipherLine for that sonnet, and the In-10 Sequential Tie that links it to the next sonnet. The Stage's 40 Designs generate a 40-letter message (each of preface P5's two Designs produces a letter).

In Section A, a Catalog Tie list appears in the headnote of one of the Section's sonnets. The headnote of Sonnet 30 (the second sonnet of Section A) is reproduced below:

In the first part of this Passion the Author prooueth, that hee abideth more vnrest and hurt for his beloued, then euer did *Laeander* for his *Hero*: of which two paramours the mutuall feruency in Loue is most excellently set foorth by *Musaeus* the Greeke Poet. In the second part he compareth himselfe with *Pyramus*, and *Haemon* king *Creons* Sonne of *Thebes*, which were both so true hearted louers, that through Loue they suffered vntimely death, as *Ouid metam. lib.* 4. writeth at large of the one, And the Greeke Tragedian *Sophocles in Antig.* of the other. In the last, in making comparison of his paynes in Loue to the paines of *Orpheus* descendinge to hell for his *Eurydice*, he alludeth to those two verses in *Strozza*,

> Tartara, Cymba, Charon, Pluto, rota, Cerberus, angues,
> Cocytes, Phlegeton, Stix, lapis, vrna, sitis.

In the sonnet's text, the speaker complains that the pain that he suffers in love surpasses that of the lovers in various classical stories, recounted by the poets Musaeus (sixth century), Ovid, and Sophocles. Curiously, the headnote describes the last stanza, which cites the story of Orpheus and

ID #	Old Sonnet #	Design Type	TP value	First table	Last table	CipherLine		Plaintext		Plaintext Select
						first	last	first	last	
1	29	Flowers-4	TP3	R6	**R8**	I	**E**	P	**N**	**N**
2	30	Flowers-4	TP3	**R6**	R8	**T**	E	**A**	N	**A**
3	32	Daedalus	TP16	A3	**O5**	I	**E**	O	**M**	**M**
4	37	Diamond	TP14	A7	**A6**	I	**L**	K	**I**	**I**
5	28	Bulbs-10	TP9	A12	**A12**	O	**E**	Z	**I**	**I**
6	12	Diamond-B	TP12	**A10**	A9	**E**	S	**L**	Y	**L**
7	11	Lioness	TP18	O7	**O9**	M	**E**	*	**E**	**E**
8	P2	Lioness	TP18	O7	**O9**	U	**A**	*	**A**	**A**
9	23	Flowers-I	TP2	**R5**	R6	**H**	T	**N**	A	**N**
10	27	DoubleA	TP1	R1	**R4**	O	**E**	P	**I**	**I**
11	34	Heart Jail	TP17	**O5**	O7	**S**	E	**G**	*	**G**
12	24	Flowers-5	TP5	**R9**	R10	**H**	S	**R**	D	**R**
13	6	Heart Jail	TP17	**O5**	O7	**Q**	T	**A**	R	**A**

Fig. 12.2 Section A deciphered message
(appears as Fig. A11.2 in Addendum 11)

Euridice, as an allusion to two verses from Strozza, which he quotes. Yet, if one consults these two verses in Strozza's text, as William Murphy did, their connection to Orpheus and this sonnet is not clear. Murphy argues that this shows "the apparent irrelevance of some of Watson's sources."[7] However, this spurious reference to Strozza's poem (which is not even about Orpheus) is another one of the poet's decorum-breaking signposts: it draws our attention to the quotation of these two verses. Indeed, their purpose is entirely cryptographic: each word in these two verses is a Catalog Tie, one for each of the 13 sonnets in Section A. In concert with the Designs, these produce Section A's enciphered message. The deciphering of this message is shown in Fig. 12.2. This polyphonic cipher is resolved as follows:

> NAM II LEA NIGRA
> (For I proceeded by means of the doleful lioness.)

NAM is a conjunction that introduces an explanation—a word one might expect as a bridge between the prior Stage and this one. On examining Fig. 12.2, rows 4–8, one notices that the next two words (II LEA), the most critical part of the message, are easily distinguished: the polyphonic alternative letters are either rare in Latin (Y and Z), not Latin at all (K), or indeterminate (*). We deciphered LEA (lioness in the ablative case) previously, in the Puzzle's first Stage, which alerted us to the special function of the Lioness Design. Remarkably, the poet has perfectly framed his Puzzle: near its end, he returns to the Lioness Design that played such an important role in the Puzzle's first Stage. The deciphered message describes the Puzzle's journey: the poet proceeded (II) in his Puzzle by means of the Lioness-demarcated Series. The speaker suffered under love and hence the lioness is called "doleful" (NIGRA).

After Section A's use of a specialized list in Sonnet 30's headnote, Section B returns to the use of a normal Catalog Sonnet. It reuses Catalog Sonnet 7, which served as the Catalog Sonnet in Stage 5. This Section contains 12 sonnets, which appear with commentaries in Addendum 11. Three of these sonnets (1, 2, and 7) appeared in Stage 5, in which Sonnet 7 specified their Catalog Ties. As might be expected, the CipherLines for these three sonnets in Stage 6 are identical to the CipherLines previously identified in Stage 5. The deciphering of Section B's enciphered message is shown in Fig. 12.3. This polyphonic cipher is resolved as follows:

> IRE FORE XI EMI   (Proceed by gateway, 11 are procured.)[8]

The first sentence of Stage 6's deciphered message (see Section A above) informs us that the poet "proceeded" (II) by means of the "doleful lioness"

ID #	Old Sonnet #	Design Type	TP value	First table	Last table	CipherLine		Plaintext		Plaintext Select
						first	last	first	last	
14	14	DoubleA	TP1	R1	**R4**	T	**E**	U	**I**	**I**
15	35	Flowers-8	TP7	R11	**R12**	T	**E**	F	**R**	**R**
16	25	Flowers-6	TP6	R10	**R11**	D	**S**	O	**E**	**E**
17	7	DoubleA	TP1	**R1**	R4	**E**	S	**F**	X	**F**
18	16	Flowers-2x3	TP4	R8	**R9**	H	**E**	Q	**O**	**O**
19	26	Lioness	TP18	**O7**	O9	**T**	Y	**R**	*	**R**
20	2	Lioness	TP18	O7	**O9**	W	**E**	O	**E**	**E**
21	36	Daedalus	TP16	**A3**	O5	**A**	E	**X**	M	**X**
22	17	Bulbs-10	TP9	A12	**A12**	M	**E**	B	**I**	**I**
23	1	Flowers-4-i	TP3-i	**R8**	R6	**W**	E	**E**	L	**E**
24	15	Daedalus	TP16	A3	**O5**	S	**E**	E	**M**	**M**
25	19	DoubleA	TP1	R1	**R4**	T	**E**	U	**I**	**I**

Fig. 12.3 Section B deciphered message
(appears as Fig. A11.4 in Addendum 11)

(LEA NIGRA), a clear reference to the Lioness Sonnets. This second sentence uses the same verb ("proceed") in its infinitive form (IRE) and again asserts that the Lioness Sonnets provide the means of progression: FORE ("gateway") refers to the Lioness Sonnets, which are the gateways that mark the start of each Series. This sentence also specifies 11 (XI), which is the number of Lioness Designs that appear in the *Hekatompathia*. These references to the Lioness Sonnets surely indicate that these sonnets play an essential role in the Puzzle's next and final Stage. Indeed, in the next chapter, we will discover that one letter is deciphered from each of the sequence's 10 Lioness Sonnets and one Lioness preface.

This second sentence employs the historical infinitive mode twice (IRE and EMI). In this mode, past events are presented in a vivid and immediate manner—a dramatic reenactment of the past. Stage 6 comes near the end of the long process of solving the Puzzle: a climactic moment for which this emotive mode of expression is appropriate. Furthermore, this mode is well-suited for describing the shared mission of poet and puzzle-solver. In the first Stage, VOCES ME suggests that the poet and puzzle-solver are engaged in a joint mission: the poet discloses the method by which he enciphered the message, and this allows the puzzle-solver to decipher the encrypted message. In the fourth Stage, the EDI/EXI overlap has the poet destroying (EDI) in the perfect tense and the puzzle-solver bringing forth (EXI) in the present tense. The poet constructed the Puzzle in the past; the puzzle-solver solves the Puzzle in the present. The historical infinitive mode is conveniently unspecific: infinitive verbs are not conjugated to either the "I" of the poet or the "you" of the puzzle-solver, and in a sense, the historical infinitive melds the past and present tenses. Thus IRE and EMI may be applied to both the poet and puzzle-solver: both must "proceed" (IRE) through the Lioness Sonnets and "collect up" (EMI) 11 in all. The historical infinitive tense allows this message to be applied to either the poet or the puzzle-solver.

Sections C and D combine to produce one message. Section C consists of 6 sonnets and 3 prefaces, and these contain 10 Designs (preface P5 has two Designs). Like Section A, Section C uses an enumerated list rather than a Catalog Sonnet to specify Catalog Ties. This list appears in the headnote of the Section's first sonnet, Sonnet 4, whose headnote reads:

> The Authour sometime wrote these three Latine verses.
>
> *Mons Erycinus, Acidalius fons, alba columba,*
> *Hesperus, ora Pathos, Rosa, Myrtus, & insula Cyprus,*
> *Idaliumque nemus; Veneri haec sunt omnia sacra.*   (4.HN)

The 9 items ("all sacred to Venus") enumerated in these verses are the Catalog Ties that specify the Section's CipherLines.

Section D contains only 5 texts: one preface (P1) and 4 sonnets (5, 18, 31, and 33). Sonnet 18, which served as a Catalog Sonnet in Stage 4, also serves as a Catalog Sonnet for this Section. Three of Section D's 5 CipherLines were previously specified by Sonnet 18's Catalog Ties in Stage 4: Sonnets 18, 31, and 35. These three Catalog Ties apply in this Stage as well. The CipherLines of the remaining two sonnets/prefaces, P1 and Sonnet 5, are specified by two of Sonnet 18's Catalog Ties that were not used in Stage 4. The message in Sections C and D is deciphered in Fig. 12.4 (see Addendum 11 for further details). This polyphonic cipher is resolved as follows:

BEO ESU VERA IN DIA

(I bless divine truths by consuming in the true goddess.)[9]

In the fourth Stage's message, VIRI performed a double duty, meaning *virus* (poison) in one extracted sentence and *vir* (nobility) in the other. Here, a similar trick is employed to achieve extraordinary concision: VERA... DIA can mean either "divine truths" or "true goddess." ESU is an

ID #	Sec	Old Sonnet #	Design Type	TP value	First table	Last table	CipherLine first	CipherLine last	Plaintext first	Plaintext last	Plain-text Select
26	C	4	Roots-4	TP10	**A11**	A11	**N**	E	**B**	K	**B**
27	C	20	Flowers-5	TP5	R9	**R10**	W	**T**	F	**E**	**E**
28	C	3	Daedalus	TP16	**A3**	O5	**I**	E	**O**	M	**O**
29	C	P5a	Flowers-5	TP5	R9	**R10**	B	**T**	L	**E**	**E**
30	C	P5b	Heart Jail	TP17	**O5**	O7	**B**	T	**S**	R	**S**
31	C	P3	Daedalus	TP16	**A3**	O5	**C**	U	**U**	*	**U**
32	C	13	Heart Jail	TP17	**O5**	O7	**L**	E	**U**	*	**V**
33	C	21	Heart Jail	TP17	**O5**	O7	**T**	E	**E**	*	**E**
34	C	22	Daedalus	TP16	**A3**	O5	**F**	E	**R**	M	**R**
35	C	P4	DoubleA-I	TP15	**A6**	A4	**T**	E	**A**	R	**A**
36	D	18	Lioness	TP18	O7	**O9**	W	**T**	O	I	**I**
37	D	33	Roots-5	TP11	**A11**	A10	**B**	D	**N**	M	**N**
38	D	P1	Diamond	TP14	**A7**	A6	**P**	E	**D**	P	**D**
39	D	5	Humus	TP13	**A8**	A7	**I**	E	**I**	O	**I**
40	D	31	Flowers-4	TP3	**R6**	R8	**T**	E	**A**	N	**A**

**Fig. 12.4 Sections C and D deciphered message
(appears as Fig. A11.7 in Addendum 11)**

ablative derivative of the Latin verb meaning to "consume" (*edo, edere, edi, esus*). This verb was employed in the fourth Stage in its first-person perfect form: EDI VIRI RES (I consumed things of poison). In this message, the poet says that he blesses divine truths (BEO... VERA... DIA) by consuming in the true goddess (...ESU VERA IN DIA). In my translation, I read VERA... DIA twice, and in two different senses. The poet, limited to a short message, uses words twice to obtain remarkable concision. Similarly, in Stage 4's deciphered message (EDI/EXI VIRI RES), VIRI RES was read twice, in two different senses, to produce two sentences.

The true goddess (VERA... DIA) is, of course, love, which suggests its emblem, the Lioness Design. Both of this Stage's two prior messages also refer to the Lioness Sonnets (LEA NIGRA in the first; FORE in the second). This strange message provides a critical hint to the solution of the Puzzle's seventh and final Stage, as discussed in the next chapter.

Sixteenth–century information technology

One must admire Bacon's virtuosic performance in creating this complex Stage. He found the means to overlay a new 40-letter message on the same ground that he used in the fourth and fifth Stages. He accomplished this by specifying a new sonnet order using the In-10 Sequential Ties, and by designating new CipherLines for many sonnets, by either reusing the prior Stage's Catalog Sonnets or using the embedded lists that appear in two headnotes. The reuse of the 40 Designs reminded me of software subroutines, which are run multiple times with different arguments. Bacon seems to have understood certain principles of information technology long before the information age began. As discussed in the first chapter, the Puzzle's mechanisms, though constructed upon various medieval textual practices (e.g., indices), resemble features found in present-day computer software: a network of interdependent tables, redundant indices, linked lists, inheritance, and recursion. Its complex system of links (e.g., its Catalog Ties) and the arithmetic and tabular processing of both numbers and symbols almost constitute a software program. While the Puzzle's basic mechanisms are all well-known early modern devices, what is unprecedented is their integration into a complex information-based system that can only be processed in a series of progressive steps.

Independent validation of the authenticity of the Puzzle

This Stage's In-10 Sequential Ties validate the discovery of the Puzzle in a way that is completely independent of the cryptographic methods used in earlier Stages. We have directly extracted plaintext messages from the In-10 Acrostics without recourse to any Designs, Transform Pairs, CipherLines, or cryptographic tables. Thus, this new evidence is independent of the mathematical techniques and underlying assumptions used in the validations provided earlier in this study. The validity of the In-10 Sequential Ties may be tested by attempting to extract messages at different distances from the edges of Stage 6's sonnets—say, 5, 6, 7, 8, 9, 11, or 12 letters off from each edge. Although scattered Latin words may appear, longer texts such as those that appear in some sonnets will not. Moreover, any serendipitously produced Latin words will not be meaningful in the context of the Puzzle, and they will prove useless in any attempt to reorder the Stage's 40 sonnets.

13

Stage 7:

The Seventh Seal

The sixth Stage yielded three messages that—as we might expect—contain clues to help us solve the Puzzle's seventh and final Stage. The first hurdle we confront is to determine the location of the next Stage. We faced a similar difficulty after the fifth Stage: we had already deciphered a single letter from each sonnet with a Design, and it was unclear where to turn next. We overcame that obstacle when we discovered the sixth Stage's mechanism of reusing sonnets to produce another letter. The seventh Stage similarly reuses sonnets to produce additional letters.

We begin our search for the final Stage's location by considering the three messages we deciphered in the sixth Stage:

NAM II LEA NIGRA   (For I proceeded by means of the doleful lioness)

IRE FORE XI EMI   (Proceed by gateway, 11 are procured)

BEO ESU VERA IN DIA (I bless divine truths by consuming in the true goddess.)

Significantly, all three messages refer to the Lioness Designs. The first message includes LEA (lioness), which also appeared in the first Stage's message (NUO LEA PESUS). The second message refers to a gateway (FORE), which accurately describes the Lioness Sonnets that begin each Series. This reference to the Lioness Sonnets is confirmed by the mention of the number 11 (XI), an exact count of the *Hekatompathia*'s Lioness Designs (found in 10 Lioness Sonnets and one preface). It also alerts us to the fact that preface P2 is included in this Stage's cryptography. The third message, which provides the most important clue, refers to "the true goddess," which in the context of the *Hekatompathia* can only be personified Love, represented by the Lioness Design, the emblem of love.

Given this repeated emphasis on the Lioness Sonnets, it seems likely that the 10 Lioness Sonnets and one Lioness preface hold an 11-letter enciphered message. This answers the question of which sonnets contain the seventh Stage's message, but it leaves three essential questions unanswered. First, in what order are we supposed to read the Lioness Designs: in their published order, in the restored order, or in some other order? The second question concerns the method of encryption: does it follow the pattern of earlier Stages? Third, how are the CipherLines distinguished? Is there a Catalog Sonnet as in prior Stages, or is some other method employed? We now address these three questions.

In what order are we to read the Lioness Sonnets? The original and restored orders provide no flexibility in enciphering the message. We know from the sixth Stage that some flexibility is required because sonnets are restricted in the plaintext letters that they can produce. We should recall that the Puzzle frequently builds upon the knowledge gained in earlier Stages. The Puzzle's sixth Stage provided complete flexibility in ordering sonnets through the use of embedded directives: the In-10 Sequential Ties. An examination of the In-10 Acrostics of those Lioness Sonnets that fall outside of Stage 6 reveals that they too contain In-10 Sequential Ties. Thus we can conclude that the sonnet order in the seventh Stage is specified by In-10 Sequential Ties, the same method that was used in the sixth Stage.

The second question concerns the method by which the message is encrypted. We might initially presume that the seventh Stage follows the practice of Stages 2–6, in which the first and last characters of the Cipher-Line were deciphered using a Transform Pair specified by each sonnet's Design. However, all Designs in this Stage are Lioness Designs, which specify TP18 (O7, O9). These two Orchema tables, O7 and O9, have a very limited range: they can only produce the plaintext letters A, E, I, O, Q, R, S, and U. This would place a severe limit on the enciphered message, with only 8 letters of the alphabet available. Thus, the encryption method used in Stages 2–6 is unlikely to be the one employed.

Unfortunately, the three messages we deciphered in the sixth Stage do not offer any clues about the encryption method. However, we should again recall that the Puzzle frequently builds upon the knowledge gained in earlier Stages. If the deciphering method used in Stages 2–6 is inapplicable to Stage 7, then the only alternative prior method that we might call upon is the first Stage's method. Indeed, it would make aesthetic sense for Stages 1 and 7 to share a common deciphering method, as it follows the artistic practice of framing. This hypothesis is reinforced by the special significance of the Lioness Design in both Stages 1 and 7, and the appearance of LEA in both Stage 1's deciphered message and the instructions for Stage 7 (delivered in Stage 6). As described below, the Transform Pairs are applied sequentially to Lioness Sonnets; they were also applied sequentially in the first Stage, but to each line of the Puzzle Sonnet.

The third question concerns the identification of CipherLines. If, as in earlier Stages, a Catalog Sonnet identifies CipherLines, that sonnet could only be Sonnet 18, the only Lioness Sonnet that contains a list of phrases. However, a search for links between Sonnet 18 and the other Lioness Sonnets fails in most cases. Instead, we should look closely at Stage 6's deciphered messages for clues as to how we might identify CipherLines.

The third message, BEO ESU VERA IN DIA, declares that "by consuming" (ESU) "in the true goddess" (VERA IN DIA), the poet "blesses" (BEO) "divine truths" (VERA... DIA).[1] The "true goddess" must refer to the Lioness Sonnets (as in the first two messages). But what is to be consumed? Recall that the Puzzle's third Stage begins with Sonnet 90, a recantation that parallels Socrates's recantation in the *Phaedrus* (see Chapter 8), and whether in the *Hekatompathia* or the *Phaedrus*, it is essential to recant, indeed erase, false speech. As discussed in the first chapter, Bacon believed that one must give false arguments to initially gain the reader's or listener's attention, playing upon their existing beliefs and prejudices. Then, having gained a beachhead, it will hopefully be possible, over time, to erase those prejudices and ultimately replace them with truths. The idea that knowledge is gained through negative instances is a principle found in Bacon's work, ancient Greek philosophy, and cryptanalysis.

Thus, if "divine truths" are to be blessed and something is to be consumed, that something must be falsehoods. Most sonnet lines depict the speaker suffering under love's power, and if this constitutes a false appraisal of love, then these lines must be erased or "consumed." The remaining line or lines then present a true representation of love. Therefore, the puzzle-solver's task must be to recognize an exception within each Lioness Sonnet—a counterpoint to the other lines, most of which complain about love. This counterpoint is a reversal, a mini-palinode, hidden within each Lioness Sonnet. The Lioness Sonnets follow the Silenic literary model described in the first chapter, in which the ugly outside of a statue hides the beautiful and divine truth within. The puzzle-solver must again modify the poetic text, not by reordering, but by erasing lines that defame love, so that only the "blessed" truth remains.

The process of deciphering the final message

I began by following the poet's instruction: I "consumed" or erased those lines that depicted the speaker as suffering under love or that otherwise deprecated love. I examined each Lioness Sonnet and found that, like most other sonnets in the *Hekatompathia*, the majority of lines describe the speaker's *sufferance in Love* (title page). On average, 15 of the 18 lines in each Lioness Sonnet could be eliminated as CipherLine candidates on this basis.[2] In the section below that includes the Lioness Sonnet texts and commentaries, I specify the lines that I eliminated under the paragraphs titled "Eliminations." Of course, I had hoped that this criterion would eliminate 17 of the 18 lines in each sonnet; instead, some lines were neutral and sometimes a positive viewpoint was split between two lines. In those cases, I selected the line that seemed to me to express the most positive regard for love. In my first attempt to distinguish CipherLines, I got about half the lines right. Although the first step, the elimination process, was accurate, my ability to distinguish among the remaining lines, three on average, was not always reliable.

Nevertheless, I then began a cryptanalytic attack with only about half the CipherLines correctly identified. Despite this degree of uncertainty, the restrictions on CipherLine selection were sufficient to allow me to decipher the message using the usual bag of codebreakers' tricks. Certain infrequent letters and unlikely bigrams could be thrown out (see Fig. E3.3, the second and third levels of the trapezoid above the base). As in almost all codebreaking, I looked for likely words. For example, Sonnet 2 has only one candidate line and was thus a good place to start. Immediately prior to that, Sonnet 26, has 4 candidates; however, I suspected that line 4 (*And lovely Nature smiles...*) was the CipherLine. It associates "love" (reading *lovely* as a portmanteau of "love") with *Nature* and a positive disposition (*smiles*). With these two CipherLine selections, Sonnet 26 deciphers to N or U and Sonnet 2 deciphers to M or U (see details below). This allows for 4 possible bigrams: NM, NU, UM, and UU. All are possible in Latin, but UM is a particularly common word ending. Indeed, it turned out to be the ending of ERUM in the deciphered message. Following the usual codebreaking practices, I alternately guessed at the most likely CipherLine among the candidates, examined the resulting decryptions, and guessed at likely words. By this process, I was able to decipher Stage 7's message. Although this process allowed me to decrypt the message, surely the poet intended that the puzzle-solver would engage in a more precise process, one that would point to a unique CipherLine in each sonnet—as was the case in previous Stages of the Puzzle. Heuristic analysis of the text and cryptography were entangled in the first 6 Stages, and therefore we should not be surprised to find them again entangled here. Indeed, I was able to discern a better process for CipherLine selection, which is presented in the section immediately below.

The process of working back and forth between guessing keys and plaintext is the fully justified standard practice of codebreakers. Indeed, Bacon describes this process of shuttling between hypotheses and trials (or experiments), and we have frequently found it necessary to adopt this process to solve the Puzzle (see Excursus 12). I have recounted my deciphering process here to allow the reader of this study to see how I arrived at my revised arguments for CipherLine selection. Although they occurred ex post facto with respect to deciphering the message and thus could reasonably be suspect as nothing more than rationalizations for choices I already made, the coherence of the results, which can be measured using Shannon information, will justify my process.

Refinement of the CipherLine selection process

Throughout the *Hekatompathia*, we are alerted to critical information by the appearance of an exception to the norm. We perceive signals from counterpoint—a reversal in direction or some anomaly—which may take the form of "blemishes" in otherwise decorous material. In this Stage, we discover singular truths amongst the false matter that defames love. After my identification of the CipherLines, I found that each of the Lioness Sonnets contained some reversal. This is not surprising as sonnets are a dialogic form, but what I noticed was that the CipherLines usually appear at the point of reversal. In my examination of these sonnets, I found that they either (1) start with an appreciation of love and then descend into suffering or vituperation, or (2) begin by disparaging love but then end on a hopeful or happy note. In 5 of the Lioness Sonnets, the CipherLine comes near the beginning (lines 1, 2, 2, 3, and 4); in the other 5 sonnets, the CipherLine comes either in the concluding couplet (4 cases) or, in one case, in line 16. Lines 5–15 have no incidences of CipherLines. After deciphering the message and knowing which lines were CipherLines (with some ambiguity where lines end or begin with the same letter), I defined a set of criteria for distinguishing CipherLines subsequent to the initial process that eliminates those lines that deprecate love.

Throughout the sequence, until the final L73 Series, the speaker wanders in a labyrinth of pain, seeking relief. Each Series is a progressive step in the speaker's quest to understand love, but each Series prior to the final one ends in failure. Yet, each Lioness Sonnet, the gateways to these Series, provides a glimpse of the conception of love reached at the sequence's end. These glimpses run contrary to the Lioness Sonnet's basic argument: they are palinode-like reversals that foreshadow the sequence's final L73 Series. Indeed, the final Series is itself a palinode: it runs counter to the work's other Series. It finds that love is, after all, a source of pleasure and the natural condition of human existence. In the second sonnet of the final Series: *the Authour... rebuketh all... others whatsoever* that *pitie his estate in Love* (L73.1.HN). Although the poet rebukes *others*, he is effectively rebuking himself and his former attitude toward love.

Recantation, or a palinode, occurs three times in the sequence: between the first and second Subsequences (Sonnet 79), in the first sonnet of the third Subsequence (Sonnet 90), and in the concluding Series (see Chapters 9 and 11). At a lower architectural level—within each Lioness Sonnet—we also find reversals, or mini-palinodes. An organic entity that repeats the same pattern at different architectural levels might be called "self-similar," a term I borrow from mathematics. Fractals are an example of self-similarity and are generally considered to be aesthetically pleasing. Reversal or recantation may be practiced within any sonnet (not just Lioness Sonnets). Indeed, the sonnet form is dialogical, and the fundamental structure of the *Hekatompathia*'s three-stanza sonnets, Shakespearean sonnets, and Petrarchan sonnets are all designed as a platform for competing discourse.

The complete process by which CipherLines are identified can now be set forth. The first Stage 6 message, NAM II LEA NIGRA, refers to the Lioness as "wicked" or "doleful" (NIGRA). Indeed, all 10 Lioness Sonnets depict the speaker as suffering under love. Even the last Lioness Sonnet, L73.H, which heads a Series in which the speaker appears happy, is principally devoted to remembering a painful past. The first step in identifying CipherLines is described above as the "Eliminations" process, in which false representations of love are erased. This eliminates, on average, all but 3 lines.

In the second step, we must recognize the one true or "blessed" line (BEO) among the remaining (non-erased) lines in each sonnet. These are what the deciphered message calls "divine truths" (VERA... DIA). Our poet blessed these lines as the work's final representation of the nature of love. This end-state knowledge of love is the wisdom expressed by the speaker in the L73 Series. What most distinguishes these final Series truths is the speaker's "cheerful" state and his recognition that love, like the climate, is an ineradicable condition of human existence (L73.1.HN, 13–18). In this second step, we must distinguish the one line that presents the true nature of love as revealed in the final Series. That Series recognizes that love is a source of joy and that it resides within the speaker himself—a condition native to himself (L73.1.17). Moreover, the strength of that resident love is comparable to the strength of love found in the gods themselves (L73.2).

Another fundamental truth asserted in the final Series concerns the necessity of exercising one's own willpower. This is adumbrated at the sequence's outset by the elaborately highlighted proverb *Selfe doe; selfe have* (5.11–12). In the lead sonnet, the speaker acknowledges his failure to assert his will: *he not excuseth his Heart, for desiring a faire imprisonment, when he needed not* (L73.H.HN). He claims that now he freely exercises his will and chooses to lead his life in love (L73.2.17–18).

The final Series insists that love's force reigns supreme in the cosmos: Love hath no leaden heeles (L73.3.HN, 18); love prevails over time (L73.4); the only cure for love is love (L73.5); the greatest pagan gods must obey love (L73.6.1–6). In the sequence's concluding sonnet, the speaker recognizes that love is the dispenser of destiny (L73.6.14) and that he must submit to its influence (*a maiori ad minus*; HN). Every Stage 7 CipherLine expresses one of the foregoing truths—that is, each CipherLine has its warrant in the final Series. For convenience in identifying CipherLines, the above "final Series truths" are listed below:

1. Life under love's reign is happy or sweet.
2. The great force of love, a raging fire, resides within the speaker himself.
3. One must choose to exercise one's willpower.
4. Love is the supreme cosmic force, a raging unquenchable fire.
5. One must submit to love's greater power (*a maiori ad minus*).

Examination of the Lioness Sonnets

With which sonnet should we start? At this point, our decision is completely arbitrary because we have no indication of a starting point among the 10 Lioness sonnets and one preface. I chose to start with Sonnet 26, a reasonably clear example of the CipherLine selection process, but could have started with any Lioness Sonnet.

L26.H   **26**

Here the Author as a man ouertaken with some deepe melancholie, compareth him selfe vnto the *Nightingale*, and conferreth his vnhappie estate (for that by no meanes his *Mistresse* will pitie him) with her nightly complaints: to whose harmonie all those that giue attentive eare, they conceiue more delight in the musicall varietie of her noates, then they take iust compassion vpon her distressed heauines.

W Hen Maye is in his prime, and youthfull spring
   Doth cloath the tree with leaues, and ground with flowres,
And time of yere reuiueth eu'ry thing;
And louely Nature smiles, and nothing lowres: CL7
   Then Philomela most doth straine her brest   5
   With night-complaints, and sits in litle rest.
This Birds estate I may compare with mine,
To whom fond loue doth worke such wrongs by day,   CL
That in the night my heart must needes repine,
And storme with sighes to ease me as I may;   10
   Whil'st others are becalm'd, or lye them still,
   Or sayle secure with tide and winde at will.
And as all those, which heare this Bird complaine,
Conceiue in all her tunes a sweete delight,
Without remorse, or pitying her payne: 15
So she, for whom I wayle both day and night,
   Doth sport her selfe in hearing my complaint;
   A iust reward for seruing such a Saint.

Eliminations: The first 4 lines are neutral or positive, and are therefore "retained." Lines 5–6 are eliminated because they introduce Philomela, whose songs complain about love. All lines in the second stanza, which compares the speaker's unhappy state to that of Philomela (also unhappy), are eliminated. In the third stanza, Philomela's complaint (13) is conceived as sweet (14–15) but this turns out to be false (it only appears to be sweet) and thus these lines are eliminated. Lines 16 and 17 are eliminated because the speaker is wailing and complaining. In line 18, the beloved listens to the speaker speaker's complaint, and though this is said to be a deserved *reward*, the speaker is nevertheless still complaining. Thus, only lines 1–4 are retained.

CipherLine: *And louely Nature smiles, and nothing lowres* (4). The first three lines present a pretty picture of spring, but are not about love and assert no final Series truths. Love is subtly introduced in line 4: lovely Nature smiles. This reminds us of Sonnet L73.1, in which love is called an *altera natura* (HN) or *Second Nature* (17). Love (visible in lovely) is portrayed as happy (*smiles*). Nothing lowres runs against Philomela's distressed heauines (HN): it suggests the opposite of the heavy, burdensome love found throughout the sequence (e.g., the Lioness's hand, pressed to hurt in the Puzzle Sonnet). This lightness may be tied to the sequence's closing apothegm, in which love's *Labour is light*. Philomela's song may be doleful, but it does not eclipse Nature's beauty or love's power (found in music). Within this doleful sonnet, line 4 presents the happiness and lightness of love.

In-10 Acrostics:

S	H	Y	N	M	**C**	**E**	**D**	N	W	H	C	H	N	M	H	H	R
F	I	H	H	N	N	R	R	**E**	**S**	**E**	**I**	**D**	E	N	A	Y	S

In-10 Sequential Tie: CEDE SE ID (withdraw/concede it from oneself). Here, our work is already done for us: in Stage 6, Sonnet 26's In-10 Acrostics (CEDE SE ID) pointed to Sonnet 2, a Lioness Sonnet. This link between two Lioness Sonnets in Stage 6 must, for reasons of consistency, apply in Stage 7 as well. The argument in Stage 6, set forth in the commentary page for Sonnet 26, was that "withdraw it from oneself" refers to the sequence's fundamental conceit, set forth in Sonnet 2, that the speaker's heart no longer rests with himself and instead resides with the beloved (see Addendum 11).

L2.H   **2**

In this passion the Author describeth in how pitious a case the hart of a
louer is, being (as he fayneth heere) seperated from his owne body, &
remoued into a darksome and solitarie wildernes of woes. The conuey-
ance of his inuention is plaine & pleasant enough of it selfe, and therefore needeth the lesse annotation before it.

MY harte is sett him downe twixt hope & feares
    Upon the stonie banke of high desire,
      To view his own made flud of blubbering teares
      Whose waues are bitter salt, and hote as fire:
    There blowes no blast of wind but ghostly grones   5
    Nor waues make other noyse then pitious moanes
As life were spent he waiteth Charons boate,
And thinkes he dwells on side of Stigian lake:
But blacke despaire some times with open throate,
Or spightfull Ielousie doth cause him quake,   10
    With howlinge shrikes on him they call and crie   CL
    That he as yet shall nether liue nor die:
Thus voyde of helpe he sittes in heauie case,
And wanteth voyce to make his iust complaint.
No flowr but Hiacynth in all the place,   15
No sunne comes there, nor any heau'nly sainte,
    But onely shee, which in him selfe remaines,   CL7
    And ioyes her ease though he abound in paines.

Eliminations: The description of a lover's suffering is clearly present in every line of the first two stanzas and the first two lines of the third stanza. Line 15 is a reference to the myth of Hyacinthus, in which Apollo's lover is murdered and turned into a flower (hyacinth). Lines 15–16 express the speaker's dreary condition, and in line 18, the speaker *abounds in pain.* Thus only line 17 is retained.

CipherLine: *But onely shee, which in him selfe remains* (17). This dreary sonnet recounts the moment when the speaker's heart is first separated from his body, removed into a *solitarie wildernes of woes* (HN). Line 17 sets a problem for the reader: who is *shee?* (The problem of determining a pronoun's antecedent occurs frequently in Shakespeare's *Sonnets*.)[3] The previous line informs us that *no sunne* or *heav'nly sainte* is present. *Sunne* is often used as a metonym for the beloved; *saint* is used on 10 occasions to refer to the beloved.[4] This seems to be contradicted by the next line: who is the *shee, which in him selfe remaines*? Could it be an image or memory of the beloved? No, a difficulty is encountered with *joyes her ease* (18), which an image cannot do. The only candidate for *shee* is a feminine, personified love. This should not surprise us, knowing the sequence's end: love resides within the speaker himself (the second of the final Series truths). It also reminds us of the moment of epiphany in Sonnet L50.5, in which the speaker recognizes that love's fire resides within himself, even in the absence of his heart. As in other Lioness Sonnets, the CipherLine contains some joy (reading on to the next line), a counterpoint to the suffering that dominates the poem.

In-10 Acrostics:

S	**O**	O	**S**	**E**	A	E	S	D	U	N	E	O	H	T	M	H	E
O	H	**R**	H	S	**I**	A	T	P	S	A	L	H	T	L	U	F	N

In-10 Sequential Tie: SORS, EI (Fate, alas). In Stage 6, this In-10 Sequential Tie points to Sonnet 36, whose headnote blames fate for the *ouerhardnes* of the beloved's heart, attributing it to the *froward constellation of his owne natiuitie* (the sign under which the speaker was born). In the seventh Stage, Sonnet 2 cannot point to Sonnet 36 because it is not a Lioness Sonnet. Instead, it points to Sonnet 50, in which the speaker's fate (*Fortune*; 4) hangs in the balance. The speaker notes his unusual fate: *in how straunge a case he liueth that is in loue, and in how contrary an estate to all other men* (L50.H.HN). Throughout the L50 Series, the speaker's fate teeters between life and death.

L50.H   50

In this Passion is effectually set downe, in how straunge a case he liueth
that is in loue, and in how contrary an estate to all other men, which
are at defiaunce with the like follye. And this the Authour expresseth
here in his owne person: therewithall calling vpon *Loue*, to stand his
frend; or, if he faile, vpon death, to cut of his wearysome life.

W Hile others feede, my fancy makes me fast;
   While others liue secure, I feare mischaunce;
I dread no force, where other stand agast;   CL7
I follow sute where Fortune leades the Daunce,
   Who like a mumming mate so throwes the Dice,   5
   That Reason leesing all, Loue winnes the price;
Which Loue by force so worketh in my brest,
That needes perforce I must encline my will
To die in dreames, whiles others liue in rest,   CL
And liue in woes while others feele none ill.   10
   O gentle Death let heere my dayes haue ende,
   Or mightie Loue, so vse me as thy frend.
Mine eyes are worne with teares, my wittes with woe,
My coulour dride with cares, my hart with paines,
My will bewitcht, my limmes consumed soe,   15
That scarsely bloud, or vitall breath remaynes:
   While others ioy, or sleepe, I wayle and wake:
   All this (*Deere Dame,*) I suffer for thy sake.

Eliminations: Skipping ahead to the second stanza, love applies force to bend the speaker's will, which causes him to live in *woes*, thus eliminating lines 7–10. In line 11 the speaker calls upon *Death* to end his days—surely not the CipherLine. In line 12, he calls upon love's aid in his pursuit of the beloved (which plays out unsuccessfully over the course of the Series). The third stanza describes suffering in every line, eliminating all. We return to the first stanza, observing that in the headnote the speaker claims that he lives in a state contrary to that of all other men. In the first two lines, that state is inferior to that of others (*fast* vs. *feed*; *feare* vs. *secure*). These lines may be eliminated, but then there is a curious reversal in the third line: the speaker's state is superior to that of other men: he is fearless (*dread no force*) while others fear (*stand agast*). The fourth line expands upon this fearlessness: he is willing to follow his fortune, even to the point that he goes beyond any reason, willing to bet everything: love wins over reason. Only lines 3–6 are retained.

CipherLine: *I dread no force, where other stand agast* (3). In line 3 we find the reversal we seek: in the two prior lines, the speaker's circumstances are inferior to other men; in this line, his circumstances are superior to others. This line is consistent with the final Series, in which the speaker no longer fears love (*force* is unlikely to refer to anything other than love). In the end, the speaker accommodates to love and accepts its greater power (L73.6). What of lines 4–6, which were also not eliminated? Although the speaker appears fearless in these lines, he bets all on *Fortune*, which indicates that he is foolish. The image of mummers (performers) playing dice suggests recklessness. Worse yet, the speaker gives up on *Reason* altogether (6). True, the sequence portrays the limits of reason: it fails in the second Subsequence, and its strategies geared to win the beloved are unsuccessful in the third Subsequence. However, in the sequence's final sonnet, when the speaker yields *him selfe to the imperie of Love*, he does so based on reason: proven *examples, ... by manner of argument*, and *with good reason* (L73.6.HN). The turn toward blind fortune and against reason in lines 4–6 is inconsistent with the sequence's end, and thus they do not contain the CipherLine.

In-10 Acrostics:

R	R	O	T	U	N	B	S	E	W	**A**	L	**R**	D	I	E	**R**	E
A	M	S	S	W	E	H	L	**L**	E	E	**A**	T	W	O	T	Y	F

In-10 Sequential Tie: LEA ARDI. ERE. (Those parched/made poor by the Lioness. Master [vocative]).[5] This points to Sonnet 18, whose first two stanzas list 25 ways in which the lover is oppressed. Sonnet 18's third stanza then turns to a recantation: *Yet mightie Love* (13), which effectively calls out to personified Love as a master, just as this Sequential Tie does: ERE.

L18.H   **18**

This sonnet is perfectly patheticall, and consisteth in two principall
points: wherof the first conteyneth an accusation of Loue for his hurt-
full effects and vsuall tyrannie; the second part is a sudden recantation
or excuse of the Authors euill words, by castinge the same vpon the
necke of his beloued, as being the onely cause of his late frenzy and
blaspheamous rage so lauishly powred forth in fowle speaches.

L Oue is a sowr delight; a sugred greefe;
A liuinge death; an euerdying life;
A breache of Reasons lawe; a secret theefe;
A sea of teares; an euerlasting strife;
   A bayte for fooles; a scourge of noble witts;   5
   A Deadly wound; a shotte which euer hitts.
Loue is a blinded God; an angry boye;
A Labyrinth of dowbts; an ydle lust;
A slaue to Beawties will; a witles toy;
A rauening bird; a tyraunt most vniust;   10
   A burning heate; A cold; a flattringe foe;
   A priuate hell; a very world of woe.
Yet mightie Loue regard not what I saye,
Which lye in traunce bereft of all my witts,
But blame the light that leades me thus astraye,   15
And makes my tongue blaspheme by frantike fitts.
   Yet hurt her not, lest I susteyne the smart,
   which am content to lodge her in my heart.   CL/CL7

Eliminations: All lines in the first two stanzas dispraise love and are therefore eliminated. The headnote calls the turn at line 13 *a sudden recantation.* But the speaker's mindset does not shift from angry *accusation* (HN) against love to its accommodation; rather, the object of his *evill words* shifts to the *beloved* (HN). Thus the speaker remains in a distressed state, and in lines 14–16, he is frantic. Thus, lines 13–16 are eliminated. In lines 17 and 18, we find a second recantation, introduced by the same word, *yet,* as the first recantation (13). This second recantation (actually, more of a qualification) reverses *But blame the light* [the beloved] *that leades me thus astraye* (15), requesting that Love not *hurt* the beloved (17). Only lines 17 and 18 are retained.

CipherLine: *which am content to lodge her in my heart* (18). Line 17 has no warrant in the final Series, as the beloved is almost entirely absent. *Content* (18) is consistent with the speaker's happy accommodation to love in the final Series—the restful state depicted in L73.1.12. But does the speaker *lodge* the beloved *in* his *heart* (18) in the final Series? *A ling'ring use of Love hath taught my brest / To harbor strife, and yet to live in rest* (L73.1.11–12) suggests that the beloved is not entirely gone—that some memory of her remains in his heart.

In-10 Acrostics:

W	E	F	R	F	**U**	**I**	H	**E**	B	**E**	E	E	N	H	Y	R	N
G	R	C	T	N	H	N	**A**	**A**	**M**	T	W	T	A	H	N	N	R

In-10 Sequential Tie: VIA EME (Gain by the journey). This points to Sonnet 33 in the sixth Stage, and there I resolved the polyphonic In-10 Acrostics to UNA EME. Here, however, I have resolved them to VIA EME (only the second letter is changed). This points to Sonnet 73, in which the speaker recounts his sorry experience in love and then says that he has learned his lesson: *Where now (alas) Experience doth tell* (15). The sequence is an odyssey that ends in the L73 Series, and there the speaker finally reaps the benefits of his labyrinthine voyage, learning to live happily only at the end of a long journey.

L73.H   73

Here the Author, by faining a quarrell betwixt *Loue* and his *Heart*, vnder a
   shadow expresseth the tyrannie of the one, & the miserie of the other:
   to sturre vp a just hatred of the ones iniustice, and cause due compassion of the others vnhappines. But as he accuseth *Loue* for his readines
   to hurt, where he may; so he not excuseth his *Heart*, for desiring a faire
   imprisonment, when he neded not: thereby specifying in *Loue* a wilfull
   malice, in his *Heart* a heedlesse follie.

I Rue to thinke vpon the dismall day
  When Cupid first proclamed open warre
Against my Hearte; which fledde without delay,
But when he thought from Loue to be most farre,
    The winged boy preuented him by flight,   5
    And led him captiuelyke from all delight.
The time of triumph being ouerpast,   CL
He scarcely knewe where to bestowe the spoile,
Till through my heedlesse Heartes desire, at last,
He lockt him vp in Tower of endlesse toyle,   10
    Within her brest, whose hardned wil doth vexe
    Her silly ghest softer then liquid wex.
This prison at the first did please him well,
And seem'd to be some earthly Paradise,
Where now (alas) Experience doth tell,   15
That Beawties bates can make the simple wise,
    And biddes him blame the bird, that willingly   CL7
    Choaseth a golden cage for liberty.

Eliminations: This introduction to the final Series mostly laments the past instead of setting forth the speaker's newfound wisdom. This failure to properly summarize the Series' subject matter is only understandable in the context of the seventh Stage's CipherLine selection process. If this sonnet had been devoted to expressing the speaker's resolved mental state and newfound knowledge of love, then few lines would be eliminated and no unique CipherLine indicated. This is why the first two stanzas and the first two lines of the third stanza recount the speaker's past foolishness. Although lines 13 and 14 depict the speaker as happy, he is imprisoned, and thus love is still, regrettably, his jailor. Then in line 15, the speaker admits that his past life was lived in error; however, *alas* indicates he is still complaining. In the last three lines, the speaker tells us what he has learned, so only lines 16–18 are retained.

CipherLine: *And biddes him blame the bird, that willingly* (17). Line 16, though true, mostly reflects upon the past. The final couplet expresses one of the final Series truths, the need to exercise one's will. The speaker *blames the bird*—himself—for *willingly* making a poor choice (17). Sonnet 16 presents an image of the speaker's entrapment that is similar to the one presented in line 18 of this sonnet: *And wheras som do keepe their birds in cage / My bird* [the beloved] *keeps me, and rules me as hir page* (16.5–6). (In this sonnet, *bird* refers to the speaker; in Sonnet 16 it refers to the beloved.) Line 18 points to past failure. But line 17 expresses the sequence's primary lesson about love, foregrounded in the proverb at 5.11–12: the speaker now accepts *blame* for his past failure to exercise his will.

In-10 Acrostics:

N	F	H	T	B	C	T	Y	G	M	B	H	**N**	**O**	**L**	**I**	H	G
D	D	T	E	I	A	**N**	**E**	**S**	**L**	**I**	**N**	**A**	L	C	S	**T**	F

In-10 Sequential Tie: NOLIT (He may be unwilling). The other bolded letters, the overlapped NES LINA, will be discussed later (in the section titled "Deciphering the seventh Stage's message"). NOLIT points to Sonnet 39, whose headnote draws attention to the sonnet's second stanza by quoting its source in the *Canzoniere*. This is known as the inexpressibility *topos*: the writer is either unable or unwilling to write. In the L39 Series, the speaker vacillates between hope and fear, unable to move forward. The speaker's inability to exercise his will is particularly apparent in Sonnet 39's third stanza, in which the speaker is jostled between *extreemes* (17). The issue of the speaker's will, first signaled in Sonnet 5, is resolved in the third Subsequence. Of the 5 Lioness Sonnets in that Subsequence, only Sonnet 39 can be the target of NOLIT. The other 4 Lioness Sonnets attempt progress: Sonnet 90 through recantation, Sonnet 64 by appealing to the beloved, Sonnet 50 by appealing to love itself, and Sonnet 73 by embracing love. Series 39 depicts love as process physics, pairs of opposite forces, that control the speaker because he does not exercise his will ("unwilling").

L39.H   39

The second part of this Passion is borrowed from out the fifte Sonnet in
Petrarch part. I. whose wordes are these,

Piu volte gia per dir le labbra apersi:
  Poi rimase la voce in mezz'l petto:
  Ma qual suon poria mai salir tant' alto?
Piu volte incominciai di scriuer versi,
  Ma la penna, e la mano, e lo'ntelletto
Rimaser vinto nel primier assalto.

When first these eyes beheld with great delight   CL7
The Phoenix of this world, or second Sunne,
Her beames or plumes bewitched all my sight,
And loue encreast the hurte that was begunne:
    Since when my griefe is grow'ne so much the more,
    Because I finde no way to cure the soare.
I haue attempted oft to make complainte,
And with some dolefull wordes to tell my griefe,
But through my fearefull heart my voyce doth fainte,
And makes me mute where I shoulde craue releife: 10
    An other while I thinke to write my paine,
    But streight my hand laies downe the pen againe.
Sometimes my mind with heapes of doubtefull cares   CL
Conioyn'd with fawning hoapes is sore opprest,
And sometime suddeine ioy at vnawares   15
Doth moue to much, and so doth hurte my brest;
    What man doth liue in more extreemes then these,
    Where death doth seeme a life, and paines doe please?

Eliminations: Subsequent to the first two lines, the first stanza recounts the speaker's capture by love. In the second stanza, the speaker tells of his pain and his attempts to express it. The third stanza recalls suffering: *heapes of doubtefull cares* (13); *hoapes opprest* (14); *hurte my brest* (16); *life in extreemes* (17); *paines* (18). Only lines 1, 2, and 15 are retained.

CipherLine: *When first these eyes beheld with great delight* (1). Line 15 recalls *joy*, but line 16 explains that the over-intensity of this joy results in pain, eliminating it from consideration. Line 2 contains only a subject, the beloved or *second Sunne*, but the predicate, which falls on the next line, refers to the speaker's capture by love. Line 1 expresses only the *great delight* of beholding the beloved. Of course, the experience of love is a delight in the final Series—even turning the speakers *Woes* into *Blisse* (L73.1.18).

In-10 Acrostics:

T	X	O	C	M	I	M	M	H	**E**	**I**	H	**M**	**I**	M	O	T	H
E	E	A	W	U	R	C	L	**D**	A	**I**	**E**	E	O	**A**	**R**	**S**	S

In-10 Sequential Tie: DEI EMI ARS (the art of the divine is to be acquired). This points to Sonnet 11 and the L11 Series more generally. In Sonnet 11, music is treated as a gift derived from heaven, bestowed upon various mortals, including the beloved.

L11.H   11

In this sonnet is couertly set forth, how pleasaunt a passion the Author one day enioyed, when by chance he ouerharde his mistris, whilst she was singinge priuately by her selfe: And sone after into howe sorrowfull a dumpe, or sounden extasie he fell, when vpon the first sight of him she abruptlie finished her song and melodie.

O Goulden bird and Phenix of our age,
  whose sweete records and more then earthly voice   CL7
    By wondrous force did then my griefe asswage   CL
    When nothing els could make my heart reioyce,
    Thy teunes (no doubt) had made a later end,   5
  If thou hadst knowen how much they stood my frend.
When silence dround the latter warbling noate,
A sudden greife eclypst my former ioye,
My life it selfe in calling Carons boate
Did sigh, and say, that pleasure brought anoy;   10
    And blam'd mine eare for listning to the sound
    Of such a songe, as had increast my wound.
My heauie heart remembring what was past
Did sorrowe more then any tounge can tell;
As did the damned soules that stoode agast,   15
when Orpheus with his wife return'd from hell:
    Yet who would think, that Musike which is swete,
    In curing paines could cause delites to fleete?

Eliminations: The first stanza describes the wonder of the beloved's song, but the final two lines of the stanza express regret that the song ended prematurely. So, the first 4 lines are retained, but the last two are eliminated. The second stanza describes the pain that results from the song's premature end and are thus eliminated. The third stanza finds the speaker with *heavie heart* (13) thinking of Orpheus's sad tale. The only line that should not obviously be eliminated is line 17. But calling music *swete* is not the same as calling love sweet, and in any case, is merely an afterthought to the loss of *delites* in the next line. Only lines 1–4 are retained.

CipherLine: *whose sweete records and more then earthly voice* (2). The first 4 lines depict the wonder and relief offered by music. Of course, the concern of the final Series is love and not music, but lines 2–3 attribute to music an unearthly and *wondrous force*, which can only be love. We must now distinguish between these two lines. Line 2 contains *sweete*, an attribute applied to love, and *more then earthly voice* connotes divinity, another attribute of love in the final Series. Although *wondrous force* (3) is also a characteristic of love, it is not necessarily a positive. Also, to *my griefe asswage* (3) indicates unhappiness, even if it is being ameliorated. So we eliminate line 3. In line 4, the force behind the music makes the speaker's *heart rejoyce*. This is consistent with the portrayal of love in the final Series. We are now left with two qualifying lines: 2 and 4. This would be a problem except that both lines begin with a "W" and end with an "E." Thus since there is no cryptographic distinction between them, I have arbitrarily listed line 2 as the CipherLine.

In-10 Acrostics:

I	T	S	N	N	S	C	E	E	D	**I**	N	**E**	E	**A**	U	L	**A**
I	R	E	A	E	O	B	**F**	**A**	**R**	T	**A**	H	**N**	T	N	**I**	E

In-10 Sequential Tie: FARI AENA VIA. (Speaking in a strong manner.) This links to Preface P2, a link that was established in the sixth Stage. Preface P2 is concerned with poetic representation: the poet, full of passion, paints things better than they actually are (men are *of greater affection then iudgement* [11–12]).

P2   **P2**

constant in their passions: Loue would either shortly be worne 31
out of vse, or men out of loue, or women out of lightnes. I cā cō-
demne none but by cōiecture, nor commend any but by lying,
yet suspicion is as free as thought, and as farre as I see as neces-
sary, as credulitie. 35

    Touching your Mistres I must needes thinke well, seeing
you haue written so well, but as false glasses shewe the fairest
faces, so fine gloses amēd the baddest fancies. Apelles painted
the Phenix by hearesay not by sight, and Lysippus engraued
Vulcan with a streight legge, whome nature framed with a CL
poult foote, which proueth men to be of greater affection then
iudgement. But in that so aptly you haue varied vppon wo-
men, I will not vary from you, for confesse I must, and if I
should not, yet mought I be compelled, that to Loue were the CL7
sweetest thing in the earth: If women were the faithfullest, & 45
that women would be more constant if men were more wise.
And seeing you haue vsed mee so friendly, as to make me ac-
quainted with your passions, I will shortly make you pryuie to
mine, which I woulde be loth the printer shoulde see, for that
my fancies being neuer so crooked he would put thē in straight 50
lines, vnfit for my humor, necessarie for his art, who setteth
downe, blinde, in as many letters as seeing.

Farewell.

Eliminations: This preface by Lyly expresses misgivings about love and the genuineness of lovers, asserting that he can only *commend any* [lovers] *but by lying* (3). He then suggests that the *Hekatompathia*'s poet has painted an overly fine picture of love and gives the examples of Apelles and Lysippus, who create images that do not accurately portray reality. Curiously, Lyly seems to have read the *Hekatompathia* as glorifying love, which is completely at odds with the published version, but consistent with the restored work. In any event, Lyly's disapproval of love runs through to line 43, but then he launches into a short palinode, introduced as follows: *for confesse I must, and if I should not, yet mought I be compelled* (43–44). Then, varying from his earlier criticism of love, he declares that it is *the sweetest thing in the earth* (44–45). *Sweetest thing* is the hidden nugget—the first of the final Series truths identified above. These two lines stand out for their praise of love. Then Lyly returns to his dispraise of love: the failures of men and women (46) and the publishing of Lyly's passions (47–52), which he characterizes as *crooked* (50). All lines except 44 and 45 are eliminated.

CipherLine: *should not, yet mought I be compelled, that to Loue were the* [*sweetest thing*] (44). Of the two remaining lines, line 44 contains subject and verb but the predicate runs onto the next line. However, that line (45) also begins a new line of questioning about the genuineness of lovers: *if women were the faithfullest*. Thus line 44 is the better choice. As it happens, it is unnecessary to distinguish between these two lines as they are cryptographically identical: they both begin with the letter "S," and the last letter of line 45 is an ampersand, cryptographically undefined, and thus may be ignored.

In-10 Acrostics:

N	R	B	I	D	O	**I**	**N**	B	H	**E**	B	O	Y	H	W	Y	I	I	B	T	D
T	H	B	E	C	W	T	L	**U**	**R**	**E**	E	M	O	I	R	O	O	S	I	W	R

In-10 Sequential Tie: INURE. (Scorch [imperative].) In Stage 6, this Sequential Tie pointed to Sonnet 23 (scorched by the beloved's reflection in a mirror), but Sonnet 23 is not a Lioness Sonnet and therefore cannot be our target sonnet this time. Also, we would not expect it to point to any of the Lioness Sonnets present in Stage 6, because then its use in Stage 6 would be ambiguous. That leaves us to choose from among 6 Lioness Sonnets: 39, 50, 64, 73, 82, and 90. INURE points to Sonnet 90: *laetusque fui, licet ignibus arsi* (and I was happy though burning with fire; 2). (In the third Stage, Sonnet 90 leads into the critical sonnet pair of Sonnets, 44 and 45, which are concerned with the sun's overwhelming power to burn or scorch.)

L90.H　　　　　90

MY LOVE IS PAST.

In this Latine passion, the Authour translateth, as it were, paraphrasti-
cally the Sonnet of *Petrarch*, which beginneth thus.

> *Tennemi Amor anni vent' vno ardendo,*　Sonnet. 313.
> *Lieto nel foco, e nel duol pien di speme. &c.*

But to make it serue his owne turne, he varieth from *Petrarches* wordes,
where he declareth, howe manie yeares he liued in loue, as well before,
as since the death of his beloued *Lawra*. Vnder which name also the
Authour, in this Sonnet, specifieth her, whom he lately loued.

ME *sibi ter binos annos vnumque subegit*
　　　Diuus Amor; laetusque fui, licet ignibus arsi;　　　CL7
　　　Spemque habui certam, curis licèt ictus acerbis.
Iamque duos alios exutus amore perêgi,
　　　Ac si sydereos mea Laura volârit in orbes,　　　5
　　　Duxerit et secum veteris penetralia cordis.
Pertaesum tandem vitae me paenitet actae,
　　　Et pudet erroris penè absumpsisse sub vmbra
　　　Semina virtutum. Sed quae pars vltima restat,
　　　Supplice mente tibi tandem, Deus alte, repono,　　　10
　　　Et malè transactae deploro tempora vitae,
　　　Cuius agendus erat meliori tramite cursus,
　　　Litis in arcendae studiis, et pace colenda.　　　CL
Ergò summe Deus, per quem sum clausus in isto
Carcere, ab aeterno saluum fac esse periclo.　　　15
[Quam vanus fuerim fateor, veniamque requiro.]

Eliminations: In the first line, the speaker is subjugated (*subegit*); in the third line, he is stricken (*ictus*). The second stanza includes the loss of two more years (4) and the beloved's flight to the heavens, which means her death and separation from the speaker (5–6). In these lines, love is clearly a hardship, and this continues in the third stanza, which includes "having wearied" (*pertaesum*; 7), "darkness of error" (*erroris ...sub umbra*; 8), "what last part of my life remains" (9), and "I deplore my life" (11). In the final two printed lines, the speaker is still locked in a jail (14–15). All lines except 2, 10, 12, 13, and the missing line (16) are eliminated.

CipherLine: *Diuus Amor; laetusque fui, licet ignibus arsi* (Divine Love himself, and I was happy though burning with fire; 2). This line is consistent with both the first and second of the final Series truths: happiness (*laetus*) and the fire burning within (*ignibus arsi*). There are four other lines that were not eliminated: "I give back submissively to you" (10); "[I] should have taken a better path (12); the speaker's regret at not avoiding strife (13); and if we are to count it, the missing 16th line that admits fault. All four lines express regret; however, regret is not expressed in the final Series: the closest the speaker comes to that sentiment is to say that he does not excuse his heart's past faults (73.H.HN). Furthermore, regret is an unhappy state.

In-10 Acrostics:

B	L	B	S	**E**	S	**T**	R	T	E	N	D	C	D	A	F
Q	G	T	**M**	R	**A**	N	**S**	**T**	**A**	M	M	A	U	S	Q

In-10 Sequential Tie: MEAT. STA. (It moves along. Stand still [imperative].) First, we consider MEAT, which points to Sonnet 64, one of two sonnets that practice *reduplicatio*: the end of one line is repeated at the beginning of the next to create a sense of continuous motion. Sonnet 64's headnote explicitly references Sonnet 41, which also practices *reduplicatio* (41.HN). These two sonnets demonstrate poetic flow from line to line and, as earlier discussed (Chapter 3), suggest the Sequential Tie mechanism used throughout the *Hekatompathia*.

Although we began our examination of the Lioness Sonnets at an arbitrary point, not knowing where the message started or ended, the second word, STA (stand still), indicates completion, the end of the message. Thus, we can project that STA marks the endpoint of the seventh Stage's circular message. As described below, this sonnet enciphers the 11th and final letter of the message. Thus, the next sonnet, Sonnet 64, enciphers the first.

L64.H   **64**

This Passion is of like frame and fashion with that, which was before vnder the number of XLI. whetherto I referre the Reader. But touching the sense or substance of this Passion, it is euident, that herein the Authour, by layinge open the long continued grieuesomnes of his misery in *Loue*, seeketh to moue his Mistres to some compassion.

MY humble sute hath set thy minde on pride,
Which pride is cause thou hast me in disdaine,
By which disdaine my woundes are made so wide,
That widenesse of my woundes augmentes my paine,
    Which Paine is cause, by force of secreate iarres,   5
    That I sustaine a brunt of priuate Warres.
But cease deere Dame to kindle further strife,
Let Strifes haue ende, and Peace enioy their place;   CL
If Peace take place, Pitie may saue my life,
For Pitie should be show'ne to such as trace   10
    Most daung'rous wayes, and tread their stepp's awry,
    Or liue in woes: and such a one am I.
Therefore My Deere Delight regard my *Loue*,
Whome *Loue* doth force to follow Fond Desire,
Which Fond Desire no counsell can remoue;   15
For what can counsell doe, to quench the fire
    That fires my hart through fancies wanton will?   CL7
„   Fancie by kind with Reason striueth still.

Eliminations: The first stanza recounts suffering or the beloved's intransigence: *pride, disdaine, wounds, paine, iarres, warres.* In the second stanza, lines 7, 8, 11, and 12 clearly express hardship: *strife, daung'rous ways, woes.* In lines 9 and 10, the speaker is begging the beloved to take pity upon him, indicative of his unhappy, unrequited love. In the third stanza, line 13, the speaker again calls on the beloved to accept his suit (*regard my Love*), and thus the speaker still suffers from the singular cause of his pain. Lines 14 and 15 are concerned with foolish choices (Fond Desire) and are therefore eliminated. Only the final three lines (16–18) remain candidates.

CipherLine: *That fires my hart through fancies wanton will?* (17). Lines 16–17 pose a rhetorical question, to which the answer is "nothing." This reflects our second final Series truth, that the desire within the speaker is an overwhelming force, beyond his control. In Sonnet L73.2, the speaker's desire is so great *that from out* his Hart *croswounded with desire* (4), he could replenish the energy of Jove's spent thunderbolts (1–3). This sonnet's last line has *Reason* still in a battle with *Fancie* (desire). Reason warred with desire in the MLIP Subsequence and lost; in this L64 Series, the speaker is still pursuing a strategy in which he argues reason to the beloved. While the last line is appropriate to this Series, it has no warrant in the sequence's final Series—reason fails in its battle with love. Line 17 expresses the speaker's key discovery that love lies within his own heart. Buried within this sonnet, whose concern is winning the beloved's favor, is the essence of the sequence's ending: nothing can quench love's fire— the fourth of the final Series truths.

In-10 Acrostics:

U	**E**	**S**	E	E	A	E	S	K	H	R	O	M	D	D	N	M	I
N	I	M	T	E	U	T	T	S	U	T	U	G	F	L	N	W	I

In-10 Sequential Tie: NES (You weave.) As discussed in the previous commentary page, STA marks the previous sonnet (90) as the endpoint of Stage 7's message. If the 11 Lioness Sonnets in Stage 7 form a loop, then the loop's last sonnet should point to its first sonnet. Is there any indication to confirm that this sonnet is the first in the loop? Its In-10 Sequential Tie suggests that we should weave (NES), which mimics the first sonnet of Stage 6, Sonnet 29: its In-10 Sequential Tie also instructs us to sew and weave (SUE ARTE VIE), as described in the previous chapter. As SUE ARTE VIE marks the sonnet that contains the first letter of Stage 6's encrypted message, we have good reason to suspect that NES marks the sonnet that contains the first letter of Stage 7's encrypted message.

Yet, NES is an In-10 Sequential Tie and therefore must also point forward to the next sonnet. In which of the Lioness Sonnets did we have to weave together a new text? The solution to the Puzzle Sonnet (82) required that we reorder (or "weave") its 18 lines to produce a new poem.

L82.PS3   82

MY LOVE IS PAST.

Expansio Columnae praecedentis.

t   The life I ledde in Loue deuoyd of rest
I   It was a Hell, where none felt more than I,
"   *His double thrall that liu's as Loue thinks best
"   Whose hand still Tyrant like to hurt is prest.   CL
i   I'le choose a path that shall not leade awri.   5
a   And Reason bids me leaue olde wellada,
s   Since therefore now my woes are wexed less,
a   And Ciprya la nemica mia
s   So frames it with me now, that I confess
A   At last, though late, farewell olde wellada;   10
e   Els must thou proue how Reason can by charme
m   Mirth for mischaunce strike vp a newe alarm;
r   Retyre to Cyprus Ile and cease thy warr,
E   Enforce to flight thy blyndfold bratte and thee.
r   Rest then with me from your blinde Cupids carr   15
e   Each one of you that serue and would be free.   CL7
n   No longer shall the world laugh me to scorn:
n   Nor any with like miseries forlorn.

* τόν τόι τύραvον
εὐσεβεῖν οὐ
ῥᾴδιον. Sophoc. in
Aia. flagell.

Eliminations: The sonnet that appears on the opposite page is the reordered version of the Puzzle Sonnet (the line order has no cryptographic effect). The poem has a two-part structure, as discussed in Chapter 2. The first 8 lines describe the speaker's bitter experience in love, and clearly disparage it: *devoyd of rest* (1); *it was a Hell* (2); *double thrall* (3); *Tyrant* (4); *leade awri* (5); *wellada* (a lamentation; 6); *woes* (even if now less intense; 7); *la nemica mia* (8). The first half clearly shows the speaker in conflict with love. Line 9 introduces the speaker's farewell to love in line 10, which again calls love *wellada*. In the poem's second half, the speaker declares himself free from of love, which also conflicts with the sequence's end. Lines 12–15 include words that disparage love: *newe alarm* (12); *warr* (13); *blyndfold bratte* (14); *blinde Cupids* (15). Lines 17–18 declare his independence from love (to avoid the pain it causes). Lines 11 and 16 are the only lines retained.

CipherLine: *Each one of you, that serue and would be free* (16). Here, the speaker calls out to those who still live under love; the poem otherwise concerns the speaker's departure from love. In the context of the speaker's delivery of this line, he invites others to leave love, for then they *would be free*. But if we consider the context of the final Series, serving love is not bad, but good (fifth of the final Series truths). Also, if we read *would* as introducing a coinciding condition, the line suggests that one can both freely exercise one's will and serve love. This foreshadows the sequence's final sonnet, in which the *Author* says *that he may with good reason yeeld him selfe to the imperie of Love* (HN). In the final Series, the speaker's will and his submission to love do not conflict. Line 16, in the context of the MLIP Subsequence suggests to others that they be free from love, but read outside of that context, it fits perfectly with the sequence's end. The only other retained line (11) hypothesizes about a return to an unhappy struggle with love (*strike up newe alarm*; 12), which has no warrant in the L73 Series.

In-10 Acrostics:

U	I	L	Y	O	F	T	E	L	H	E	B	H	A	I	Y	T	S
L	A	A	A	A	T	**A**	**U**	**T**	**I**	E	L	H	T	C	O	T	U

In-10 Sequential Tie: AUTI (Increases). This points to the first stanza of Sonnet 26, in which Spring causes *leaves* and *flowres* (2) to grow, *reuiueth eu'ry thing* (3), and *nothing lowres* (4), but rather, increases. Spring is a time of increase. We have now returned to Sonnet 26, the starting point in our study of this group of 10 Lioness Sonnets and one Lioness preface. Thus, the 11 Lioness Sonnets of this Stage form a circular group, a loop, as discussed both above (Sonnet 64 commentary) and below.

Deciphering the seventh Stage's message

Having ordered the Lioness Sonnets and identified their CipherLines, we may now decipher the seventh Stage's message. As discussed above, the cryptography of the seventh Stage returns to the relatively simple cryptographic model used in the first Stage. In that Stage, the Transform Pairs, TP1 through TP18, were applied in numerical order to each of the 18 lines of the Puzzle Sonnet. This produced the message: VOCES ME NUO LEA PESUS. We now adopt a similar approach for this Stage: the Transform Pairs TP1 through TP11 are applied to the CipherLines of each of this Stage's 11 texts (10 sonnets and one preface) in the order determined by the In-10 Sequential Ties. Those Sequential Ties produce a loop of 11 sonnets. We arbitrarily started that loop at Lioness Sonnet 26:

$$\rightarrow S26 \rightarrow S2 \rightarrow S50 \rightarrow S18 \rightarrow S73 \rightarrow S39 \rightarrow S11 \rightarrow P2 \rightarrow S90 \rightarrow S64 \rightarrow S82 \rightarrow$$

As described in this chapter's commentary pages, we found that the In-10 Sequential Ties specified a starting point and an ending point for the loop. The starting point was Sonnet 64: its In-10 Sequential Tie, NES, instructs the puzzle-solver to "weave," as did the In-10 Sequential Tie of the first sonnet of the sixth Stage (Sonnet 29). The ending point appears to be specified by STA (stand still) in Sonnet 90's In-10 Sequential Tie, marking it as the final sonnet. Therefore, we postulate that the order of the above sonnet loop should be shifted right by two places:

$$S64 \rightarrow S82 \rightarrow S26 \rightarrow S2 \rightarrow S50 \rightarrow S18 \rightarrow S73 \rightarrow S39 \rightarrow S11 \rightarrow P2 \rightarrow S90$$

NES   STA

Having determined the starting and ending points of the sonnets loop, we can now associate each of the Lioness Sonnet CipherLines with a Transform Pair, TP1 through TP11, as shown in Fig. 13.1.

S64	S82	S26	S2	S50	S18	S73	S39	S11	P2	S90
TP1	TP2	TP3	TP4	TP5	TP6	TP7	TP8	TP9	TP10	TP11

Fig. 13.1 Assignment of Transform Pairs to Lioness Sonnets (preliminary)

Using the assignment in Fig.13.1, I deciphered the Lioness Sonnet CipherLines, hopeful that this reasonable plan would succeed. However, it produced only gibberish. What now? Just as the sequence of sonnets is viewed as a loop, the Transform Pairs, TP1 through TP11, may also be viewed as a loop. Although I had correctly identified the starting place of the message (the sonnet loop), this does not coincide with starting point of the Transform Pair loop. Instead, the Transform Pair loop begins at an offset to the sonnet loop's starting point: the relation between the sonnet loop and Transform Pair loop depicted in Fig. 13.1 must be modified. This is not surprising because occasionally difficult restrictions are placed on the CipherLine's first and last letters for certain offsets.[6] I determined the offset—the start of the Transform Pair loop—by simply trying all 10 possible offsets. In cryptanalysis, when confronted with only 10 possibilities, it is often expeditious to just try each possibility, hoping that one produces a coherent message.

Even though I found the Transform Pair loop's starting point by trial and error, the Puzzle does provide a pointer to its location. Sonnet 73's In-10 Sequential Tie includes an extra set of words, NES LINA (You weave the linens; see Sonnet 73's commentary page). NES (you weave) also appears in Sonnet 64's In-10 Sequential Tie (NES), which marks the sonnet loop's starting point. As such, this second appearance of NES in Sonnet 73's In-10 Sequential Tie is a hint that the Transform Pair loop starts at Sonnet 73 (see Fig. 13.2). Additionally, *linum* (LINA is the plural) was used by Romans to refer to "the thread with which letters were bound and legal instruments sealed" (LS IIA). Typically, a few words were written on these threads or linens, perhaps the author's name, so that the document could be identified without breaking its seal, again suggesting that NES LINA marks the starting point of the Transform Pair loop. Fig. 13.2 shows the starting points of both the sonnet loop and Transform Pair loop.

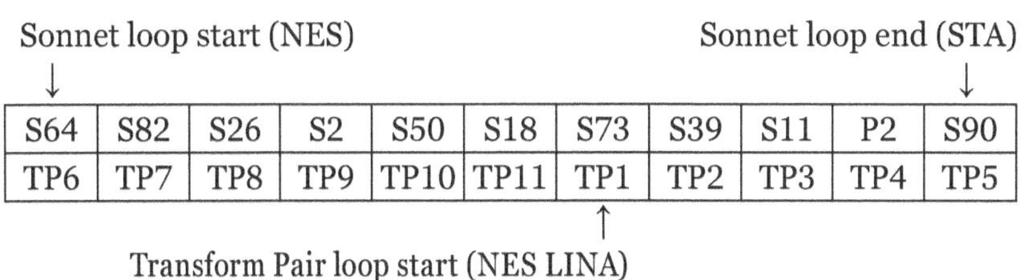

S64	S82	S26	S2	S50	S18	S73	S39	S11	P2	S90
TP6	TP7	TP8	TP9	TP10	TP11	TP1	TP2	TP3	TP4	TP5

Fig. 13.2 Assignment of Transform Pairs to Lioness Sonnets (final)

We now have done everything necessary to decipher Stage 7's message, as shown in Fig. 13.3.

ID #	Lioness Sonnet #	TP value	First table	Last table	CipherLine		Plaintext		Plaintext
					first	last	first	last	
1	64	TP6	**R10**	R11	**T**	E	**E**	Q	**E**
2	82	TP7	R11	**R12**	E	**E**	Q	**R**	**R**
3	26	TP8	R12	**A12**	A	**S**	N	**U**	**U**
4	2	TP9	**A12**	A12	**B**	S	**M**	U	**M**
5	50	TP10	**A11**	A11	**I**	T	**F**	U	**F**
6	18	TP11	**A11**	A10	**W**	T	**S**	W	**S**
7	73	TP1	**R1**	R4	**A**	E	**B**	I	**B**
8	39	TP2	R5	**R6**	W	**T**	B	**A**	**A**
9	11	TP3	**R6**	R8	**W**	E	**C**	N	**C**
10	P2	TP4	R8	**R9**	S	E	B	**O**	**O**
11	90	TP5	**R9**	R10	**D**	I	**N**	T	**N**

Fig. 13.3 Stage 7 deciphered message

The final column of Fig. 13.3 resolves the polyphonic cipher to:

ERUM FS BACON   (the master, Fs. Bacon)

ERUM is the accusative case of *erus, eri*, which may be translated as "master of a house, or family, lord, owner, or proprietor" (LS I, II). I read this as an accusative of place (or goal).[7] Thus, ERUM answers the question: to where have we come, now that we have reached the end of the Puzzle? We have come to the house of the master who wrote the book, FS BACON. Having journeyed through 7 Stages of this extraordinary labyrinth, we have finally reached its endpoint: the poet's home.

An alternative reading of ERUM is to treat it as an accusative of exclamation (master!). *Erus* is foregrounded by its use (in different forms) in two previous In-10 Sequential Ties: (1) AI ERI (speak of the master) in Stage 6, Sonnet 19, a reference to personified love (see Addendum 11), and (2) LEA ARDI ERE (those parched or made poor by the Lioness. O Master) in Stage 7, Sonnet 50, again a reference to personified Love (see above).

If this reading was intended, it provides a fitting image for the Puzzle's conclusion as it aligns with the sequence's final sonnet (L73.6), in which the poet accepts Love as his master.

I believe that Bacon meant ERUM in both ways, yet another display of his ability to compress multiple meanings into one or two words. He had only 4 letters with which to work after expending 7 of the 11 available letters on his name. We might consider what alternatives Bacon had for the remaining four letters. The word SUM (I am) would fit (using FRA to abbreviate Francis, making a total of 11 letters) but would hardly be elegant. There is not enough space for either POETA or AUCTOR. Bacon's use of the word ERUM allowed him to pull off yet one last clever trick: a cryptographic symbol on the work's title page implies that Bacon's name should be placed there, as described in Excursus 11.

Francis was commonly abbreviated as Fr., Fs., and Fra., and Bacon's letters show his use of both Fr. and Fs. as a signature. Sometimes (to my eye) he wrote the second letter of the abbreviation to be indistinguishable, either "r" and "s." I have examined only a few facsimiles of his signature, so I do not know which abbreviation was more common. Consulting a standard edition of his works and letters may not be definitive on this point: the transcriber of his signature would not likely spend much effort to distinguish between "r" and "s," as the difference would not matter. In any case, using the first and last letters of a first name as an abbreviation was very common: Wm. for William, Hy. for Henry, and so forth.

With ERUM FS BACON, we have reached the end of Bacon's extraordinary Puzzle. The revelation of Bacon's name is accomplished with great elegance, blazoning his name on the cornerstones of the sequence: the sonnets with Lioness Designs—the emblem of love. Yet, what is most extraordinary is the ingenious method that he adopted to select the CipherLines that encipher the seventh Stage's message: the erasure of 17 lines in each sonnet that misrepresent (or fail to acknowledge) the nature of love, leaving only a single line that reflects the true nature of love as expressed at the sequence's end. This is yet another variation on the work's central rhetorical practice: to first blame love, then recant and erase the previous blame, and end with praise for love and acceptance of its primacy. This mimics the rhetorical technique of the *Phaedrus*, in which Socrates recants—effectively erasing—his first speech against love (see Chapter 9). It is also consistent with the primary purpose of the Puzzle, which is to convert the *Hekatompathia* from a diatribe against love (its published form) to a sequence that praises love (its restored form). This pattern of a false statement, which is then erased, followed by the truth is central to Bacon's rhetorical method (see Chapter 4). He conceived of poetry as a didactic art that ought to fully engage the reader in the poet's thought processes.

The *Hekatompathia*: a pseudepigraphic work

The practice of hiding the authorship of a work under a false name—pseud-epigrapha—was widely practiced in the early modern period. Elizabethan authors had many reasons for writing pseudonymously or anonymously—in fact, a culture of literary anonymity prevailed during the Elizabethan era (see Chapter 1). However, the extent of this practice has neither been adequately recognized nor studied, according to Martin Mulsow.[8] In the seventeenth century, the desire to reveal the true authors of inflammatory or heterodox books led to the publication of dictionaries that unmasked the authors of anonymous and pseudonymous works. Vincentius Placcius's monumental *Theatrum anonymorum et pseudonymorum*, published in 1708, nine years after his death, unmasks 2,777 anonymous works and 2,930 pseudonymous works. It resulted from a collaborative effort of at least 40 contributors, some prominent—Leibniz is among them.[9] The unmasking of pseudonymous authors was also undertaken in the prior century by Joseph Scaliger and Isaac Casaubon—Huguenots with strong connections to English protestants. They wished to expose for theological reasons works attributed to figures such as Hermes Trismegistus as for-geries.[10] Political danger also prompted pseudonymous publication. When Henry III learned of Stephanus Junius Brutus's *Vindiciae contra tyrannos* (1579), which questioned a king's authority, he engaged an envoy to dis-cover the author's true identity. The author of this pseudepigraphic publi-cation remains an open question; one of two prominent candidates is Hubert Languet, a mentor and close friend of Philip Sidney.[11]

Scholars have never seriously considered whether the *Hekatompathia* might be pseudepigraphic. Perhaps the prefaces that congratulate Watson and the commentaries that mention him mitigate against this. However, the writers of those prefaces and commentaries may have assumed Wat-son's authorship based on the title page, or might have been participants in a literary game. Prefaces frequently appropriate names as a matter of editorial convenience. For example, scholars usually attribute the dedica-tion signed by actors Hemings and Condell in Shakespeare's *First Folio* to Ben Jonson (who contributed other prefaces).[12] Names may easily be appropriated with or without consent. For example, a dedicatory poem in Henry Peacham's *Minerva Britanna*, undersigned "E. S.," appears by its style to be written by Edmund Spenser. An Elizabethan reader would quickly attribute the poem to Spenser except for one serious difficulty: the poem references Queen Elizabeth's death (she died several years after Spenser). Someone "borrowed" Spenser's initials and style, and this obvi-ous impersonation suggests that the signatures under prefatory material should not necessarily be taken at face value.[13]

The culture of literary anonymity was prevalent due partly to aristocratic custom, but also due to the inherent dangers in expressing unorthodox religious or political views. Bacon might well have decided not to risk publishing the *Hekatompathia* under his own name for this reason. Even in its unrestored order, it is blasphemous: it fails to acknowledge the Christian God, instead pledges fealty to Venus and Cupid, and treats a human beloved as a divinity. The work's obvious engagement with materialist philosophy and pagan ideas would have made all but the most reckless of authors choose to publish it anonymously or pseudonymously. Indeed, over the next century, works that advocated radical philosophical ideas such as pantheism were seen as "pagan traps" that threatened the theologically critical separation between the Creator and His creations. The efforts to unmask the true author of these works were intended to discredit or suppress their further publication.[14] For Bacon, given his position and aspirations, pseudonymity would have been a natural choice.

Another indication that the *Hekatompathia* is pseudonymous is Watson's record of criminal behavior. How likely is it that such a man is also an erudite poet—an "apostle of Continental culture"?[15] Further, the de Vere dedication suggests a relatively familiar relationship, which Watson would be less likely to have than Bacon, due to class differences (Bacon and de Vere had strong family ties). It is also worth noting that both Bacon and Watson, under the aegis of England's spymaster, Francis Walsingham, operated in France during a time of intense religious conflict and were therefore likely skilled in deception and the maintenance of secrecy.

The *Hekatompathia*'s hiding of its author's name is consistent with the work's suppression of its own true text. The Puzzle, a labyrinth, is a veiling device, and the puzzle-solver must lift veil after veil to reveal the truth. This follows the Silenic literary model, in which a work's exterior presents a false appearance that obscures the truth that lies hidden within (see the section titled "Erasmus's Silenic literary model" in the first chapter). The *Hekatompathia*'s title page declares that the work is *divided into two parts* and ends with *a long farewell to Love and all his tyrannie.* However, we now know that the work contains three, not two parts or Subsequences, and that it ends with the speaker's acceptance, rather than rejection, of love. Immediately following this false statement, we find: *Composed by Thomas Watson Gentleman.* Why accept this statement of authorship if the immediately prior statement has been demonstrated to be false? Paratextual material—prefaces and sometimes the title page—can be part of a text's fiction. We must recognize such false exteriors as "Silenic": Erasmus's *Praise of Folly,* despite its title, does not really praise folly; Montaigne's *In Defense of Raymond Sebond* is not truly a defense of

Raymond Sebond; and *Pantagruel* was not written by Alcofribas Nasier (the name on its cover, an anagram of François Rabelais).[16] *Caveat lector.*

In the case of the *Hekatompathia*, the revelation of the author's name at the completion of the Puzzle is foregrounded in the preface that immediately precedes the first sonnet:

> **In all thou mai'st tender thy father's fame,**
> „   Bad is the Bird, that fileth his own nest.
> **If thou be much mislik't, They are to blame,**
> **Say thou, that deedes well donne to euill wrest:**
>   **Or els confesse,** A Toye **to be thy name;**
> „   **This trifling world** A Toye **beseemeth best.**
>
> *(Quatorzain,* 9–14)

In all may refer to the endpoint of the Puzzle; *thou* refers to the personified book; *father* denotes the author. *Mai'st tender* expresses the hope that at some endpoint (*In all*), the book will deliver *fame* to the author. As Watson's name appears on the title page, nothing needs to be completed to *tender* his *fame*. Further, we are provided a reason for the poet's suppression of his name in line 10. The importance of this line is emphasized by its being set in a standard serif font rather than the Old English font used in the poem's other lines (see Appendix D). The alternative to the tendering of thy *father's fame* (9) is for the book to admit it is a *Toye* (13)—the unrestored text that ludicrously ends with the death of Cupid. With the restoration of the sequence, the work is no longer a *Toye*; with the deciphering of Bacon's name in the seventh Stage, the poet's *fame* is realized.

The authenticity of the Puzzle and restored text

As I desire that the restored sequence be accepted as the *Hekatompathia's* true text, I summarize here the evidence for the Puzzle and the restored sequence that it has produced. Although the Puzzle is utterly unique and therefore seemingly improbable, the evidence for it and the restored sequence are incontrovertible. The Puzzle forthrightly presents itself in Sonnets 80–82, promising that something may be deciphered. Messages can indeed be deciphered and validated from the cryptographic tables that the text specifies (see Chapter 2). We validated the deciphered messages of the fourth and fifth Stages using a standard and well-established test (see Chapter 11). The combined length of 40 letters from these two Stages produced a definitive result: the odds against a serendipitous or false deciphering are 1 in 2.5×10^{17}, an absurdly remote event. This alone guarantees that the Puzzle is not a mirage and that it allows us to reorder the sequence.

In addition to cryptographic validation of the fourth and fifth Stages, the validity of the Puzzle and the restored sequence is supported by the numerous steps taken in solving the Puzzle that produced coherent results. In Chapter 5, we found that multiple methods specified a new sonnet order for the MLIP (second) Subsequence, and this new order was both overdetermined and showed consistent plot development. In Chapter 7, we found that our analysis produced a consistent mapping of Designs to Transform Pairs for 10 of the Designs. In Chapter 10, we discovered that the sonnets with pictorial Designs produced a set of Boolean equations that precisely specified the Orchema tables.

In Chapter 12, we discovered the unencrypted In-10 Sequential Ties, which are independent of all cryptographic mechanisms—the hidden text is obtained by a simple polyphonic selection between two unenciphered letters. This mechanism has no heuristic components (such as Cipher-Lines) and uses no cryptographic tables. Any doubter can test the validity of the In-10 Sequential Ties by exploring sonnets that fall outside the range of the sixth and seventh Stages (or by using an arbitrary offset other than 10). The In-10 Sequential Ties also reconfirm the validity of part of the Stage 5 message: EX ORA X (10 from the edge).

There are other pieces of independent evidence. For example, the link between the Puzzle's fifth and sixth Stages: Sonnet 1's oddly placed Flowers-4 Design points to the anomalous sequence of three Flowers-4 Designs (Sonnets 29–31), which form the beginning and endpoints of the sixth Stage. Throughout our traversal of the Puzzle, we found internal consistencies among the headnotes, sonnets, prefaces, and sidenotes that propelled us to new discoveries of the Puzzle's mechanisms.

The seventh Stage provides yet another independent confirmation of the Puzzle's validity. Most of the cryptographic mechanisms employed in the earlier Stages, including Catalog Ties, the Design-to-Transform Pair map, and the Orchema tables, are absent. This Stage depends only upon the tables associated with TP1–TP11 (established by the Pillar Sonnet), the In-10 Sequential Ties, and the singular CipherLines that praise love. Through the 7 Stages of the Puzzle, we deciphered 167 characters (see Appendix C). The Puzzle's Stages are deeply interconnected by their common methods and enciphered messages, and this cohesion across Stages adds further to our confidence that the individual validations performed for various Stages are correct.

We now know with certainty that the *Hekatompathia* is a unique text that guides its reader in an extensive and minutely detailed reconstruction of itself. The work is truly a marvel of technical wizardry, a complex information system well ahead of its time (see Chapter 12). It is a work of grand ambition that builds upon and integrates various poetic and philosophical traditions of the preceding two millennia. Further, this discovery is of great consequence because it provides an inside view of how a poet constructs a poetic collection, employs intertextual material, and communicates through a rhetorical system.

Unmasking the poet

Even prior to deciphering the seventh Stage, we might easily suspect that *Hekatompathia*'s authorship is uncertain due to the prevalence of pseudepigrapha, Watson's criminal behavior, and the Puzzle itself, which abounds in false semblances that the reader must resolve. But if not Watson, then who wrote it? Bacon is an obvious candidate: what we know (or think we know) about Watson's life coincides with established facts of Bacon's life. Given these parallels, the choice of "Thomas Watson" as a pseudonym might have subtly signaled the possibility of Bacon's authorship to his contemporaries. Both men spent time in France in the late 1570s, shared a strong connection to Francis Walsingham, possessed legal training, participated in the Sidney-Leicester literary circle, and (purportedly) authored plays or masques. Another reason to suspect that Bacon is the true author of the *Hekatompathia* is the *Protrepticon* preface's obvious echoes of *Tristia* 1.1, in which Ovid is devastated by his exile. This aligns with the hardship that Bacon experienced in the years during which the *Hekatompathia* was written (see the discussion of Sonnet 97's connection to Thrace in the previous chapter).[17] Indeed, Sonnet 97 includes Bacon's motto, *Ne plus ultra* (97.HN). Nor is it particularly surprising that Bacon wrote poetry: he wrote a letter in which he refers to himself as a "concealed poet" (see Chapter 1).

Among the strongest reasons for suspecting Bacon's authorship is the intellectual gifts on display in both the *Hekatompathia*'s text and the Puzzle. The Puzzle employs Bacon's rhetorical methods, which often rely on exceptions to uncover the truth. Even prior to restoration, the *Hekatompathia* is clearly the work of a very gifted polymath and polyglot; with the Puzzle and restored sequence in hand, the author's gifts seem preternatural. Bacon's genius is most evident in the Puzzle, a complex information-based system that employs mechanisms that foreshadow present-day technology (see the "Sixteenth-century information technology" section in the previous chapter). The Puzzle's architecture—its Heuristic and Precision Systems—functions much like Bacon's experimental method: the puzzle-solver must formulate hypotheses and then test them using the Precision System (see Chapter 1). Are we to believe that Watson was also such a visionary and harbinger of the future? If one attributes the work to Watson, then we have the unlikely coincidence that two men, Watson and

Bacon, possessed rare intellectual gifts, were visionaries and harbingers of the future, and also shared the common life histories discussed above.

Validation of the seventh Stage's deciphered message

The validation of our deciphered message will consist of a preliminary validation followed by further steps that refine the validation. This arises from certain challenges encountered in any mathematical validation of a short (11-letter) message, as later discussed. We begin by listing the initial assumptions made in our validation.

The first assumption to consider is whether the order in which we have deciphered the Lioness Sonnets (determined by the In-10 Sequential Ties) is correct. Might a different extraction or interpretation of the Sequential Ties have led to a different ordering of the Lioness Sonnets? The In-10 Sequential Ties in this Stage can point to only one of 10 other Lioness Sonnets, which is far more restrictive than Stage 6's range of 39 sonnets/prefaces. While it could be argued that, in a few instances, an In-10 Sequential Tie points to another sonnet, this would rarely produce a sequential loop of 11 Lioness Sonnets. Instead, the loop would likely be broken because, as one incrementally assigns Lioness Sonnets, the decreasing pool of unassigned sonnets limits the discovery of new linkages. Said another way, the requirement that each sonnet link point forward in a chain (i.e., never back to any previously linked sonnet) is extremely restrictive and therefore provides a sufficient check on our interpretation of the In-10 Sequential Ties.

A second assumption is the use of the Transform Pair values discovered in the first Stage. These values were directly taken from the mapping that the Pillar Sonnet specifies (see Chapter 2). These values were then used to produce Stage 1's message, and subsequently, in Stages 2–6, they also produced coherent messages. Thus, we can be sure of their validity.

Finally, the accuracy of our identification of the CipherLines in the Lioness Sonnets is the most critical issue in validating the deciphered message. Our first step in their identification was to eliminate those lines that depict the speaker suffering at the hands of love or disparaging love, which the poet suggests by his instruction to "consume" (ESU) lines. This first step eliminated all but three lines on average. This elimination is a straightforward process that is consistent with the practice of recantation we find at other critical moments in the sequence. In the second step of the identification process, some interpretation was required to select a unique CipherLine: we recognized the palinode-like reversals that run counter to a sonnet's overall thrust. The unique lines that we selected characterize love as it is presented in the sequence's final L73 Series. In our preliminary validation, we will assume the CipherLine selections are correct; later, we will allow for some ambiguity in the selection process.

Using the validation procedure practiced in earlier Stages, we first calculate the absolute rate of language for the 11 letters in our message, which is 24^{11}, or approximately 1.52×10^{15}. We must divide this by 2^{11} (2,048), the arbitrary choice between the two polyphonic alternatives. Finally, we must consider the range of possible messages, which is calculated using Shannon Information Theory: we assume 25% pure information and 75% redundancy. For a 24-letter alphabet, the absolute rate is $\log_2 24 \approx 4.6$. Then, 25% of 4.6 = 1.15, and from this, the Shannon information per character is $2^{1.15} \approx 2.22$. This must be raised to the 11th power, as the message is 11 characters: $(2.22)^{11} \approx 6,500$. Thus, we estimate that there are 6,500 valid and contextually relevant 11-letter messages.[18] Using these results, there is a probability of approximately 1 in 114 million that our deciphering was serendipitous:

$$1.52 \times 10^{15} / (2048)\,(6500) \approx 114,000,000$$

Of course, this probability represents a very remote event. We will now take further steps to refine this validation, beginning with our initial assumption that there was no ambiguity in the CipherLine selection process. My refinement of the CipherLine selection process occurred subsequent to my deciphering the message, and therefore, working backward, I knew the true CipherLines (except in a few instances where lines begin or end with the same letter). This helped me to formulate a better selection process. My working backward is merely a variation on the usual cryptanalytic process of shuttling back and forth between keys and plaintext (as discussed above and in Excursus 12). Although some heuristic judgment is required in the selection of this Stage's CipherLines, this was also the case in prior Stages. Indeed, the architecture of the Puzzle, with its Heuristic and Precision Systems, was designed to push the puzzle-solver to make heuristic judgments for pedagogical purposes and then allow him or her to test those judgments with the Precision System (see Chapter 1).

In our preliminary validation of the deciphered message, I assumed that it was possible to correctly identify all 11 CipherLines, which does not account for any key equivocation (i.e., incorrect selections of CipherLines). Using my initial (and inferior) CipherLine selection process, I got 5 of 11 CipherLines wrong. Using this as a benchmark, we might assess key equivocation to be the uncertainty between one of two lines for 5 of the 11 sonnets. This would imply a key equivocation of 2^5 (32) and changes the previously calculated probability of serendipitous deciphering from 1 in 114 million to approximately 1 in 3.5 million. My more refined CipherLine selection process, if I had thought of it prior to first deciphering the message, may have scored better. Yet, for the purposes of validation, we should push in the opposite direction, toward a more conservative assessment of key equivocation. If we assume a one-of-two-line ambiguity for all 11 sonnets, then the chance of a serendipitous deciphering increases by a factor of 2,048 (2^{11}), to 1 in 55,000.

We now turn to the number of potential messages, or more accurately, "the probabilities of the various possible messages," which was 6,500 in our prior calculation.[19] This number was based on a 25% to 75% ratio of information to redundancy, a standard which is more appropriately applied to messages that have several words, including a subject and predicate. Therefore, we must tailor our calculation to the special circumstances of this Stage's short 11-letter message. We begin by considering the context and the likelihood of various messages that might reasonably appear, that is, the relevance or probability of these messages. I provide an example of this in Excursus 3: if one intercepts an enemy's military communications, one expects that the subject matter is more likely to be about troop movements than, say, the Homeric epics.

The seventh Stage's message may only be deciphered after we complete our rite of passage: traversing the 40-turn labyrinth of the sixth Stage. After completing this arduous journey, we fully expect that something significant, if not spectacular, will be revealed. The Puzzle is a step-by-step revelation of secrets, and it can hardly end on any other note. What might we expect in the short space of 11 letters? I can think of only three categories of messages: the name of the true author, the name of the beloved, or a statement about love. Beginning with the last, it is hard to imagine that anything limited to 11 letters would impress us. If we were to decipher a message such as DEUS EST AMOR (God is love) or OPTIMUS AMOR (most noble love), it would surely be anticlimactic as well as an aesthetic disappointment. Revealing the name of the beloved would disclose a secret, but throughout the sequence the beloved has no discernable characteristics that are not wholly conventional. If a lover were to be revealed, we would expect this to be foregrounded somewhere in the text, but it is not.[20] On the other hand, the revelation of the author's name is foregrounded in the *Quatorzain* preface, as discussed above.

We must now estimate the number of messages that would disclose the work's true author. We assume that we need a short word such as ERUM or SUM that indicates authorship, followed or preceded by an abbreviated first name and a last name. If we take the broadest possible view—that anyone then living in England could have written the *Hekatompathia*—then the number of possible messages is very large. We might guess that there are 5,000 possible last names and 200 possible first names—one million possible names in all, and perhaps 20 possible ways of abbreviating first names and adding a word such as ERUM or SUM that indicates authorship. The result is 20 million possible messages, far more than the 6,500 possible messages used in the above calculation. This increases the chances of a false deciphering from 1 in 55,000 to about 1 in 18. This probability of a serendipitous result is unacceptably high, and thus validation fails.

If the Puzzle's creator had expected us to consider one million possible authors, he would have designed the Puzzle to allow for a longer and more descriptive final message. Indeed, the *Hekatompathia*'s prefaces suggest that the poet was a member of the Sidney-Leicester literary circle, and thus we might reasonably limit ourselves to a few dozen candidate poets. Or looked at another way, the author was a poet, polyglot, polymath, and expert cryptographer—a very rare individual. We will conservatively round up our estimate of a few dozen candidates to 100. Next, we might guess that there are 4 words other than ERUM that would suggest the named person wrote the *Hekatompathia*—5 possible words in total. That word could either precede or follow the name—two possibilities. There might be two possible abbreviations for the first name. Thus with 100 candidates and 20 other permutations (ERUM or alternative [5]; first name abbreviation [2]; precede/follow [2]), there are 2,000 possible messages.[21] This is less than the 6,500 messages assumed earlier and yields a probability of approximately 1 in 180,000 of a false deciphering.[22] Under these assumptions, we have validated the seventh Stage's deciphered message: Bacon is our poet.

This validation may be further refined by considering what Shannon calls the "probabilities of the various possible messages" in which Bacon's name appears, which is a subset of all possible messages.[23] What probability should we assign to this subset (i.e., this branch in a probability tree)? Bacon is a far more probable candidate than any of the other 99 candidates in our estimate of 100 possible authors. The reasons for over-weighting of Bacon's candidacy includes the biographical coincidences between Watson's purported life and Bacon's (see Chapter 1), the appearance of Bacon's motto in Sonnet 97, the echoes of Ovid's *Tristia*, Bacon's close relationship with Walsingham and key members of the Leicester circle, the Puzzle's practice of Bacon's experimental method (the Heuristic and Precision Systems), and the *Hekatompathia*'s practice of Bacon's rhetorical and pedagogical methods. Most strikingly, the astonishingly complex mechanics of the Puzzle—so far ahead of its time—argue that a preternatural genius created it. Bacon's contributions span diverse fields: he made pivotal contributions to philosophy and law; he envisioned the modern university devoted to research; his experimental method is at the center of the scientific revolution; and his literary achievements include his *Essays* and his shrewd reading of myth in the *Wisdom of the Ancients*. With these inimitable talents, this uniquely talented polymath is by far the most likely candidate for the creator of the *Hekatompathia*'s extraordinary Puzzle.

We might now revise our previous calculation, which used 100 equiprobable potential authors and 20 "other permutations." The estimate of 20 permutations is reasonable and will be retained. However, for the reasons given in the previous paragraph, we will estimate that the probability that Bacon is the poet is 10 times higher than the average probability of the other 99 candidates. This is equivalent to estimating that there are 10 equiprobable candidates. This reduces the previously calculated probability of an erroneous deciphering from 1 in 180,000 to 1 in 1.8 million. This is equivalent to saying that we are 99.9999% certain that the deciphering is correct. If we had instead assumed that Bacon was one of a thousand equiprobable candidates, we would still be 99.99% certain that our deciphering is valid.

Libellus returns home to its "father"

The *Protrepticon* and *Quatorzain* prefaces personify the *Hekatompathia* as *libellus* and *my little booke*, respectively. The author sends his book out to the world (*goe hye thee hence away*), hoping that it will be well received and, at some later point, *tender* its *father's fame* (*Quatorzain* 1, 9). With the disclosure of the work's true "father" in the seventh Stage, the book has fulfilled its ultimate mission of revealing the author's name.

Bacon has engraved his name into those lines that praise love in the sequence's cornerstones, the Lioness Sonnets—the emblems of love that are the very foundation of his poetic enterprise. Thus, the message bearing his name is deeply interwoven into the poetic text. His signature is the mathematical product of those poetic lines and the cryptographic system defined in the first Stage, and thus could only have been created by the poet himself. Like the interwoven security threads and watermarks in modern documents, this signature cannot be forged. Thus, in this, the Puzzle's grand finale, the poet, with extraordinary flair and imagination, has indelibly signed his work.

The *little booke* has returned home in another sense: the restoration of the work from a ruined pile of sonnets is now complete. We have exited the labyrinth! We may look back and admire the beauty of its architecture. The Puzzle is perfectly framed: the first Stage discloses that the Lioness Sonnets are the sequence's cornerstones, which mark the start of each Series; the last Stage uses the Lioness Sonnets to reveal the poet's hidden identity. The work's conflicted self-representation as both a "toy" that dismisses love and a serious work that embraces love is now resolved. Lyly's preface, which reads the work as praising love, may now be appreciated. The poet's promise of his everlasting allegiance to love in the fourth sonnet (praising Venus) and the Epilogue have now been honored.

14

The Ontology of Love

Throughout the sequence, the speaker seeks an answer to the question posed at its beginning: *what kind of thing is love?* (5.2). This same question initiates the discussion in Plato's *Symposium*, and both works seek answers through dialectical argument: in the *Hekatompathia*, the speaker debates with himself; in the *Symposium*, competing speeches are delivered. But what is this investigation of the nature of love truly about? Neither work's concern is with the commonplace issues that arise between lovers; rather, they both pose an ontological question about love, and thus, their wide-ranging discussions include topics such as cosmology, human desire, beauty, immortality, and what constitutes a happy life. Are these then philosophical works? Certainly, yes, even though their arguments often turn to myth rather than the logical discourse that predominates in modern philosophy.

This ontological question about love's nature is concomitant with questions about how we come to know things. Love appears to be an animating or enabling force in inquiry itself. Stanley Rosen offers this overview of the *Symposium*:

> There is a connection between Eros and what we now call "epistemology" and "ontology." The connection becomes explicit in Diotima's instruction, but it is present throughout the *Symposium* in the dramatic exhibition of the psyche's daimonic nature. For example, the speakers at the banquet are themselves emblems of the daimonic, intermediaries to the gods. ... Phaedrus, "the father of logos" [177d5] is turned toward the past in his emphasis on the antiquity of Eros. ... Agathon [is] the advocate of youth and innovation. ... In general, then, the *Symposium* is an evocation of the past, not in a historical but in a mythical sense. As is explicitly stated by Aristophanes, the erotic desire for wholeness is a longing for our "original nature."[1]

Both the *Hekatompathia* and the *Symposium* ask whether love is an "old god," that is, an eternal cosmological principle, or an unpredictable young god (as Cupid is so often depicted) associated with the changeable material world, or some demonic intermediary between the divine and the material realms. Phaedrus, the first of the *Symposium*'s speakers, calls love the greatest of the gods and further claims that "Love is unbegotten, nor is there mention of his parentage to be found" (178b). Thus, love, eternal and old, is like physical matter, which was considered eternal by Greek atomist philosophers such as Democritus. Later, Agathon (in the fifth speech) disagrees with Phaedrus's claim that Love is "older than even Cronus" and instead asserts that "Love in his imperishable youth, is, I repeat, the youngest of them all" (195c). In Socrates's speech, in which he recalls what he learned about love from Diotima, he asserts that love is "halfway between mortal and immortal... a very powerful spirit (*daimon*)":

> [These spirits] are the envoys and interpreters that ply between heaven and earth, flying upward with our worship and our prayers, and descending with the heavenly answers and commandments, and since they are between the two estates they weld both sides together and merge them into the one great whole. They form the medium of the prophetic arts, of the priestly rites of sacrifice, initiation, and incantation. (202de)

Here love is described as a messenger or angel that mediates between heaven and earth. Renaissance Platonism often identified cosmic love with the world soul or the Holy Spirit. Yet Ficino, whose readings of the *Symposium* and *Phaedrus* had a decisive impact on the treatment of love in the Renaissance, concluded otherwise, according to Michael J. B. Allen. Love is neither a Platonic form nor a participant in a form, and therefore, "it cannot be adequately defined as either god-like or demonic, being logically and ontologically prior to the possibility of that distinction." Love is a mystery, and Ficino believed that both the *Phaedrus* and the *Symposium* were derivative of Orphic mysteries and Pythagorean cosmogony.[2]

Does the *Hekatompathia* ultimately conclude that love is a daemon, an old god, or a young god? An "old god," figurative language for the "eternal," is associated with the philosophical notion of being; "young god," a poetic description of ever-changing flux, is associated with the notion of becoming. The sequence iterates through these opposing formulations and finally settles in a place that breaks with medieval traditions. The *Hekatompathia*'s ontology of love, essentially a representation of the human condition, is surprisingly modern and fundamentally materialist. Having restored the sequence, we can now traverse it in its proper order, reading the philosophical story that it tells.

The master trope of the absconded heart (Sonnets 1–3)

The sequence begins with love's capture of the speaker (Sonnet 1) and the separation of the speaker's heart from his body (Sonnets 2 and 3). Love mysteriously oppresses the speaker's will and leaves him in a melancholic state. The speaker experiences *amathia*, a "dis-knowledge" of the self, for the speaker does not know the location of his own heart (*where is thy dwelling place?* [3.1]). The sequence is the story of the speaker's three attempts to cure himself by acquiring self-knowledge. In the first Subsequence, he seeks a cure by exploring the pathos within himself; in the second, he rejects pathos and turns to logos; in the third, he recognizes himself as an inherently composite creature, an amalgam of pathos and logos. In the work's final sonnet, the speaker concludes that his destiny is an *estate of double kinde* (L73.6.14), which makes for a conflicted life, but one that may, nevertheless, be happy.

The sequence in its restored order is perfectly framed: it begins with the separation of the body and heart and ends with a reconciliation or compromise *betwixt Love and his Heart* (L73.H.HN). In the final Lioness Sonnet (73), the word *Love* correlates with the speaker's body, for love is often portrayed as a powerful physical or cosmological force—a constituent part of all matter. This materialist view defines love as what might be called "process physics."[3] Various materialist conceptions of love are found in the first three speeches in the *Symposium*, and the third speech by the physician Eryximachus is especially close to the *Hekatompathia*'s portrayal of love as a coincidence of opposites in the L39 Series. The framing of the sequence by the division of the speaker's self at the outset, and the reconciliation of the divided parts at the sequence's conclusion in the L73 Series, makes for an organic work.

The sequence ends with the speaker in a healthy state, in which the parts of the self are in balance. This ideal is found in the *Republic*, which describes a man bound "together and made of himself a unity, one man instead of many, self-controlled and in unison" (443e). Referring to this passage, Gadamer argues that this "internally well-ordered soul is the true measure of Dasein's self-understanding, i.e., of *sophia*. Conversely, the destruction of the soul is *amathia* (444a), the diminution and darkening of this inner capacity to govern oneself."[4] Prior to the final Series, the speaker lives in a state of *amathia*: "a person turned away from himself in curiosity."[5] The *Hekatompathia* progresses from disease to cure, a journey whose destination is knowledge of the human condition—a fulfillment of the Oracle's imperative to "know thyself."

The cause of the self's disunity is represented mythically by the figure of Cupid: *An other now is mistris of my minde / Cupid hath clapt a yoake upon my necke* (1.8–9). Cupid is a personification of the transience and conflict found in nature, depicted in the L39 Series as a coincidence of opposites. As mankind is constructed from matter, and matter is transient, conflict is an irradicable feature of postlapsarian human existence.[6] The separation of the speaker's heart and body is a poetic representation of the mind-body dualism that holds a central place in the Western philosophical tradition. Rosen offers this generalization: "In essence, the dualism implicit in the beginnings of modern philosophy is a secularized version of the Judeo-Christian teaching of the separateness of body and soul."[7] The *Hekatompathia* establishes this philosophical dualism at its outset, first, in the trope of the absconded heart and, then in the first two Series, by presenting two epistemic modes, aesthesis and noesis.

Aesthesis and noesis (Subsequence 1, Series L2 and L11)

The first two Series, the sequence's foundation, depict love as having two powers, or two epistemic modes, *ex visione* love and *ex cogitatione* love, as discussed in Chapter 3. The L2 Series (especially the second part) describes the speaker's captivation through the visual perception of the beloved (*ex visione* love); the L11 Series (Sonnets 11–17) describes the beloved's singing as an otherworldly force (*ex cogitatione* love) that binds the speaker to her. Thus the sequence's central dilemma is the disjunction between one mode of human cognition associated with sense, matter, appearance, ephemerality, and selfish interest, and a second mode associated with reason, mind, substance, the eternal, and virtue.

The division between things sensed (*ex visione*) and things "*nous*-ed" (*ex cogitatione*), aesthesis and noesis, is fundamental to both the *Hekatompathia*'s cosmology and the structuring of its poetic journey. The sequence's structure is determined by this epistemic division at both a lower architectural level within a Series and the higher level of the Subsequences. Within the hexameral-based Series, Hex2 sonnets are concerned with aesthesis, while Hex3 sonnets treat noesis (see Chapter 9). At the higher architectural level, although both epistemic modes are evident in all three Subsequences, each has a different focus. The first Subsequence (subsequent to the first two Series) is primarily concerned with aesthesis or the speaker's emotive response: the speaker vacillates between hope and fear as his perceptions (aesthesis) dictate his emotional state. In the second or MLIP Subsequence, sense and emotion are made subservient to the mind's logic and reason (noesis). In the third Subsequence, the speaker recognizes that neither epistemic mode can rule the other and a compromise must be reached.

The division between aesthesis (visual) and noesis (intelligible) is found in Plato's *Republic* (VI:509d) and is central to his philosophy. According to Gadamer, the Pythagoreans failed to distinguish between aesthesis and noesis, and a decisive turn in Plato's thought occurs when he defines the relationship between appearance and idea as participation, or *methexis*.[8] This *methexis* is a "mixing" of the aesthetic and noetic realms, and this mixing or compromise between sense and reason allows for the cure at the *Hekatompathia*'s end—the cure rhetorically promised in the first sonnet's headnote (the poet's claim of having written an unpublished *De Remedio Amoris*). The speaker's will, which emerges in the final Subsequence, effects a compromise between sense and reason, much like Plato's image in the *Phaedrus* of the charioteer with his two steeds, one reasonable and the other unruly, that pull in different directions. The charioteer's challenge is to manage the two steeds as best he can.

The encomium to love (Subsequence 1, Series L26)

Having established the work's ontological foundation in the first two Series, the speaker embarks upon his philosophical journey in the third. Each sonnet of this Series is an encomium to the beloved—a common practice in the sonnet genre. At first this seems to conflict with the overall theme of the rest of the first Subsequence, which recounts the speaker's *sufferance in Loue* (title page), but the poet avoids contradiction by cleverly contextualizing his encomium in the Series' first sonnet: *the poet compareth him selfe vnto the Nightingale* (26.H.HN). In myth, Philomela, a rape victim, is turned into a nightingale who sings beautiful songs of grief. Although those that *heare this Bird complaine, conceiue in all her tunes a sweete delight* (26.H.13–14), in truth the speaker is grief-stricken for his beloved (*for whom I wayle both day and night*; 16). Thus, the encomium is delivered in the context of the speaker/nightingale's despair.

In the Series' second sonnet, the three Olympian gods that rule over heaven, the seas, and the underworld are subordinated to mortals:

> IF Ioue **himselfe be subiect vnto** Loue
> **And range the woodes to finde a mortall praie:**
> If Neptune **from the seas himselfe remoue,**
> **And seeke on sandes with earthly wightes to plaie:**
> **Then may I loue my peerelesse choise by right,**
> **Who farre excels each other mortall wight.**
> If Pluto **could by loue be drawne from hell,**
> **To yeeld him selfe a silly** Virgins **thrall:**   (L26.1.1–8)

This restages the Titanomachia (the war between the Titans and Olympians), in which three Olympic gods, Jupiter, Neptune, and Pluto, each ascend to be the ruler of a world. However, in the *Hekatompathia*'s reenactment, the Olympians lose rather than win, and in Sonnet L26.1, they are depicted as subordinate to mortals. The *Symposium* also restages the

Titanomachia, and as in the *Hekatompathia*, the Olympians lose.[9] But why restage the Titanomachia in either work? Plato's goal was to replace piety to the pagan gods with reverence for "the Good" (a Platonic form). The *Hekatompathia*'s *Epilogue* rejects "empty ephemeral things" (*mortalia vana*; 2) and offers a prayer to God or a divine love. The ever-rapacious Olympic gods here represent the ephemeral or process physics. Both Plato and Bacon seek to replace them with a new order.

Sonnet L26.1 in conjunction with the sequence's final sonnet, L73.6, form a frame: in both sonnets, Jupiter, Neptune, and Pluto are toppled from their rule and made subordinate to another power. In L26.1's opening frame, these gods are rendered powerless by their pursuit of mortal beloveds, for if the higher honors the lower, the lower becomes the higher, and by this, humankind ascends above the gods. Throughout the L26 Series, pagan divinities are portrayed as inferior to the beloved in an encomiastic mode known as *synkrisis*—praise by comparison. The beloved is described as combining the gifts of Juno, Athena, and Venus (L26.2.1–9), and furthermore, it is claimed that had she been alive at the time of the judgment of Paris, she would have won that contest (L26.4.1–6). This exalted praise continues with Sonnet L26.5, in which the great artists of antiquity are left dumfounded by the beloved and so daunted that they are unable to represent her (L26.5). In the ending frame, the sequence's final sonnet (L73.6), the three Olympian gods are also subordinated:

> **Who knoweth not, how often** Venus **sonne**
> **Hath forced** Iuppiter **to leaue his seate?**
> **Or els, how often** Neptune **he hath wunne**
> **From seaes to sandes, to play some wanton feate?**
> **Or, howe he hath constraind the Lord of** Stix
> **To come on earth, to practise louing trickes?**
> **If heau'n, if seaes, if hell must needes obay,**
> **And all therein be subiect vnto** Loue;   (L73.6.1–8)

The three Olympic gods, Jupiter, Neptune, and Pluto, each ruler of one of the three spheres in ancient cosmology, are again snared by mortal beloveds, as in the opening frame. But here, in the sequence's final sonnet, *Love* is crowned as the new ruler of all three spheres (8). In Bacon's *On Principles and Origins according to the Fables of Cupid and Coelum*, he similarly makes Cupid the ruler of three (nearly the same) spheres: "The keys of ether, land and sea" were "entrusted to him."[10] Love's victory is complete.

The encomiastic sonnets of Series L26 share a similar perspective with the encomium delivered by Phaedrus in the *Symposium* (the first speech). Phaedrus, like the *Hekatompathia*'s speaker, praises the beloved rather than the lover. (Phaedrus adopts a similar position in Plato's *Phaedrus*, in which he reads a speech by Lysias that praises the nonlover rather than the lover.) Phaedrus, quoting Hesiod and Parmenides, defines love as unbegotten (without parents), the oldest of the gods, and as having arisen from primordial "Chaos" (178b). Similarly, Series L26 describes the beloved as a product of *Natures cunning skil* (L26.2.1). Although the beloved is obviously not unbegotten, several of the encomia are set in antiquity, which establishes that her qualities, if not her person, reign supreme across time. The first three speakers in the *Symposium* (Phaedrus, Pausanias, and Eryximachus) and three of the *Hekatompathia's* Series (L26, L18, and L39) treat love as a natural phenomenon or process physics—flux, chaos, or the coincidence of opposites.[11] However, this relegation of love to a physical phenomenon empties it of the higher qualities that we associate with love such as its association with virtue. The materialism or technicism of the *Symposium's* first three speakers is repudiated by the fourth through sixth speeches (by Aristophanes, Agathon, and Socrates), which present a more human-centric view of love.

Love vs. the beloved (Subsequence 1, Series L18)

Love's realm is not peaceful: the speaker's emotions alternate between fear and hope. The lead sonnet's first two stanzas castigate love; the third stanza recants and instead blames the beloved. This sets the structure of the double Hexameral ring that follows: love is blamed in the first Subseries, the beloved in the second. The next sonnet (L18.A1), based on Tito Strozzi's "Somnium," juxtaposes two dreams, which offer two alternative visions of love. The headnote strongly suggests that the reader *peruse* Strozzi's poem *with due attention* (see the extended commentary in Addendum 9). In this sonnet's first dream, *false darkned clouds* foretell a *dolefull doome* (L18.A1.12–14); in the second, an angelic woman, personified *Hope*, presents a vision of rescue (15–18). Dreams, commonly seen as indicators of destiny, may serve as a literary foreshadowing device. For example, in *Odyssey* 19, Penelope presents her dream to the disguised Odysseus, which foretells the battle against the suitors and Odysseus's victory. Here, this pair of dreams adumbrates the speaker's alternation between fear and doubt (*Quid dubitas? Quid nunc vult timor iste tibi?*; "Somnium", 88) on the one hand, and hope and faith on the other.

This conflict between hope and fear is central to the sequence, appearing repeatedly from this point forward through to the sequence's last sonnet. It is also apparent in the difference between the endings of the published and restored versions of the sequence. The former ends in the MLIP Subsequence, in which the speaker, fearing love, uses reason as a bulwark against any possible return of love. His fear is so great that in the concluding sonnet (100) he imagines Cupid's death, scattering his ashes to the wind. In the restored sequence's ending, hope prevails over fear: *If Loue were past, my life would soone decay / Loue bids me hoape, and hoape is all my stay* (L73.1.5–6). The express words, *If Loue were past*, repudiate *My Love is Past*, the blazon at the top of every MLIP Subsequence sonnet. Nevertheless, in the final sonnet (L73.6), the speaker realistically acknowledges that his double destiny includes both *my feare* and *my hoping minde* (16). In the restored version, the framing of the conflict between hope and fear begins with L18.A1 and ends with the last sonnet, L73.6, a span of approximately 75 sonnets, the final three-quarters of the sequence.

Although hope triumphs at the sequence's end, fear wins battles along the way. As the L18 Series concludes, the speaker rues that his destiny (*the froward constellation of his owne natiuitie*; L18.B5.HN) is *a webbe of endlesse strife* (18). In the final two sonnets of the Series, the speaker rues that *hope* is *blowne out with feare* (L18.B6.6) and *inconstant hope is often drown'd in feares* (L18.C1.14). He has reached an aporia and *requests an untimely death* (L18.B5.HN). This is the first of three aporias (one appears in each of the three Subsequences); the second occurs at the end of the second Subsequence; the third occurs in the penultimate L50 Series, when the speaker also calls for an early death. In these aporias, the speaker undergoes what is effectively a *katabasis*—a visitation to the underworld such as that undertaken by Odysseus and Aeneas. A *katabasis* is a confrontation with death—an essential moment in the protagonist's progress in his journey.

In the Series' final sonnet (L18.C1), the speaker *prepareth him selfe to fall from Love* (HN). This sonnet serves as a bridge to the second (or MLIP) Subsequence, as its headnote indicates. It lists 18 *particular miseries which befall him that loueth* (HN), one per sonnet line. The headnote explains that these *miseries* are taken from *a Theame diducted out of the bowelles of Antigone in Sophocles (which he lately translated into Latine, and published in print) he writeth in very like manner as followeth*. Several Latin lines excerpted from his *Antigone* follow, which accurately reproduce the published text. This theme, extracted from the poet's Latin *Antigone*, induces the careful reader to consider its context within that work.

Antigone consists of a translation of Sophocles's text (mostly lifted from an earlier translation), followed by four pomps, a short procession of speakers, who summarize the moral lesson that should be gleaned from each of four of the play's characters: Creon, Antigone, Haemon, and Ismene.[12] Next follow four themes in verse, which offer the same moral lessons for each of the same four characters.[13] The pomps treat the four characters in the order given above, but the four themes skew that order by reversing the last two characters: Creon, Antigone, Ismene, and

Haemon. Sutton calls this an "obvious error," which it certainly is, and corrects the order in his edition.[14] The headings above the themes include the names Haemon and Ismene, leaving us to wonder how the printer could be so careless, or whether something else is afoot.

The pomps and themes devoted to Creon and Antigone assert that both were wrong: Creon is said to be guilty of blind self-love and Antigone of uncontrolled emotion and disregard for the law.[15] Haemon is condemned as an erotomaniac, and the poet's speech in the pomp devoted to him warns that it is nearly impossible to both love and be wise.[16] This theme, a condemnation of love, is excerpted in the Latin lines in Sonnet 79's headnote and in the enumerated *miseries* (HN) listed in each sonnet line. Consistent with the headnote's claim, this theme aligns perfectly with the MLIP Subsequence, as both present the same images of love's untenable *miseries*.

Having used Creon, Antigone, and Haemon as examples of what not to do, Ismene is made the work's hero. She is praised for her prudence, piety, calmness in the face of adversity, and self-restraint. Curiously, in a preface to this Latin *Antigone* addressed to the reader (*Ad Lectorem*), Philip Harrison asserts that "Watson's muse made Ismene speak with a Latin tongue."[17] This oddly singles out Ismene, rather than Antigone, and seems to treat her as the principal character. This preface's highlighting of Ismene contrasts with the two other prefaces that have similar expressions: "For he taught Sophocles' Antigone to speak in our tongue" (John Cooke preface), and "I taught Antigone how to speak Latin" (Thomas Watson's preface in honor of Philip Howard).[18] The Harrison preface's direct address of the reader (*Ad Lectorem*) surprises us: it seems odd that a contributed preface is addressed to the reader rather than performing its usual function, which is to address and congratulate the author. This suggests that we should carefully consider Harrison's highlighting of Ismene.

Antigone's pomps and themes are thoroughly didactic, upholding Ismene as virtuous and the other three characters as moral failures. The lesson of Haemon's failure, presented on the text's last page, is that love itself is evil: the reader is advised to let wicked love depart (*Ergo cedat amor, si sapis, improbus*).[19] Is this really the lesson to be learned from either this Latin *Antigone* or Sophocles's *Antigone*? The pomps and themes uphold both love of family and duty to country. The fault of Creon, Antigone, and Haemon lies not with their love, but with their overzealous, extreme love. Ismene represents the course of moderation (*Seque res recte modicae coercent*) and wariness of greater powers (*Quae supra vires mala sunt, relinquas*).[20] Thus, we see that the inconsistent ordering of the pomps and themes is not a printer's error but rather a test set for the reader that asks whether the work's ultimate and essential lesson is about love's abandonment or its moderation. We must choose between the order presented in the pomps and that found in the themes. The alert reader, recognizing these signposts, will deduce that the order of the third and fourth themes must be reversed. After this correction, the work ends with its proper, authorially intended conclusion.

This stratagem of expecting the alert reader to swap poetic material to create a different ending is the same strategy practiced in the *Hekatompathia*—the Puzzle provides a new ending. As discussed above, Haemon's theme aligns perfectly with the MLIP Subsequence, the faux ending of the *Hekatompathia*. Ismene's theme aligns with the true ending of the *Hekatompathia*: coexistence with love and recognition of its greater power. *A maiori ad minus* (the lesser must submit to the greater; L73.6.HN) aligns with Ismene's deference to authority. Both works bury the end in the middle and expect the reader to restore proper order. Indeed, L18.C1 (Sonnet 79) hints at the corruption of order in *Antigone* when its headnote asserts that the theme of love's miseries was *diducted out of the bowelles of Antigone*. This statement is false, for in the published order, this excerpted theme appears not in its *bowelles*, but on the work's last page. Instead, it should appear earlier (i.e., in the *bowelles*) where it belongs. Thus L18.C1's headnote alerts the reader to *Antigone*'s corrupted order. Indeed, both *Antigone* and the *Hekatompathia* are similarly corrupted: love is castigated at the end of the published order, but in the restored order, love triumphs. Bacon, who I presume to be the author of this *Antigone*, gave Sophocles's *Antigone* a Petrarchan makeover: its lack of faith to the original is abundantly clear.[21] The influence of Petrarchism in this period is considerable.[22]

In the *Hekatompathia*'s conclusion and in the corrected conclusion of the Latin *Antigone*, love is triumphant and the speaker practices moderation (sophrosyne). But at this point in the speaker's journey (the end of the first Subsequence), he reaches the first of three aporias. Not yet ready to compromise with love, he turns not to moderation but to extremity.

My Love is Past (Subsequence 2, Series L82)

In this Subsequence, the speaker rejects love entirely. It consists of a single Series that is divided into three Subseries: Fond Love, Scoff, and Love Discharged (see Chapter 5). The Fond Love Subseries provides analyses that critique love as foolish; the Scoff Subseries turns to invective and mockery; the last Subseries imagines Cupid's death and then attempts to prove Cupid's guilt through a recitation of authorities. The Series ends ludicrously with L82.LD.4, which includes 12 sententiae, each from a different authority, meant to prove love's guilt. This final sonnet is a good example of Bacon's practice of intentionally misquoting his sources, which the reader is expected to recognize and interpret. The first authority, Saint Jerome, is hilariously misquoted: *In deliciis difficile est seruare castitatem* (Amongst pleasures/darlings, it is difficult to serve chastity; L82. LD.4.HN). The poet loosely translates this as *Love hath delight in sweete delicious fare* (1). Saint Jerome obviously said no such thing.[23] This is a corruption of *Difficile est, inquit, Haereticum reperire qui diligat castitatem* (It is said that it is difficult to find a heretic who chooses chastity).[24] The second authority quoted is Ausonius, from his *Cupido Cruciatus* (46). The meaning of this sententia is misconstrued: in Ausonius's text, *inconsultus amor* (HN) refers to Cupid's ill-advised appearance, which leads to his capture; in contrast, the sonnet's sententia (*Loue neuer takes good Counsell for his frende*; 2) suggests that those in love never accept good advice.[25] The third authority, Seneca, is another spurious quotation.[26] Of the remaining 9 sententiae, some are accurate while others are not.

What is the purpose of these misquoted sententiae? One possibility is that because they are part of a Catalog Sonnet (L82.LD.4) and point to Catalog Ties, modifications could have been made to accomplish that function. However, this did not require the reversal of meanings, and instead we should consider what poetic purpose is being served. These corrupt quotations reflect the speaker's state of mind, a desperation that peaks in this final sonnet of the Love Discharged Subseries. The speaker imagines Cupid's death in L82.LD.2, then engages in a deranged appeal to various authorities in L82.LD.4. He rejects desire and human carnality in favor of pure logic—a psychologically dubious proposition. The speaker's obviously delirious mental state signals that this rejection of love is absurd, and that we have arrived again at an aporia (the sequence's second). In the next Subsequence, the speaker returns to his god, Love.

The return of love (Subsequence 3, Series L90)

In the first Subsequence, the speaker says that he has *proueth by probabilities that he* [Cupid] *neither is a childe (as they say) nor blinde... nor (to conclude) anie God at all* (L18.A5.HN). In the second Subsequence, Cupid is scourged and then imagined dead. Now suddenly, in the first sonnet of the third Subsequence (L90.H), the speaker submissively returns to his god (10). How did this come about? The second Subsequence ends in a frenzy: the speaker grasps at straws and misquotes or misinterprets various authorities to justify his rejection of love (L82.LD.4). In this aporic state, he reconsiders his time spent in love: though "subjugated" (*subegit*; L90.H.1), "I was happy" (*laetusque fui*; 2) and "I held certain hope" (*spemque habui certam*; 3). Thus, hope returns, the speaker recognizes his "error" (8), and "deplores" his "life of poorly spent time" (11).

Following Sonnet 90, a pair of sonnets (L90.1–2) present two suns (see Chapter 9). Remarkably, there appear not one god but two: an incorporeal god and its equal, the earthbound beloved. This repudiates the second Subsequence's dismissal of love and reassesses the argument made by the speaker in the first Subsequence that love is not divine and is opaque. (For example: *And yet when he hath said al he can to this end, he cryeth out vpon the secret nature and qualitie of Loue, as being that, whereunto he can by no meanes attaine, although he haue spent a long & tedious course of time in his seruice* [L18.A5.HN]). In the L90 Series, the poet vests the earthbound beloved with divine powers, and this, it is hoped, will provide a path by which he may acquire knowledge of love. This deification of the beloved is the essential conceit or construct that empowers a Petrarchan sonnet sequence.

The sun is the most important image that Plato employs: it is a symbol of the good, which "is indeed the cause of all things[,] of all that is right and beautiful, giving birth in the visible world to light, and the author of light and itself in the intelligible world being the authentic source of truth and reason" (*Republic* 517c).[27] By declaring the beloved a sun, the speaker makes the sensible world the equivalent of the intelligible world. This violates a fundamental tenet of Platonist philosophy: the division and hierarchy of the intelligible and sensible worlds. In the *Hekatompathia*'s formulation, the intelligible world of being and the sensible world of becoming are still differentiated, but they are, surprisingly, declared equivalent. Renaissance Platonist thought often sought a bridge between these two worlds that could be attained through a mystical ascent of a *scala amoris*. The *Hekatompathia* goes beyond Renaissance Platonism when it collapses the ontological distinction between these two worlds. The poet appears to have adopted a monist materialist philosophy; however, a psychological and epistemological distinction remains.

In the course of the L90 Series, there is a descent from the heavenly vision of two suns to a feigned wedding in which the gods descend to the *faire Citty of London* (L90.5.HN). (See the discussion in Addendum 2.) The Series ends with a return to traditional encomiastic sonnets that praise the beloved by comparison (L90.6–7). The final sonnet emphasizes the sensual pleasure of the beloved: *the Authour boasteth, howe sound a pleasure he lately enioyed in the companie of his Beloued, by pleasing effectually all his fiue senses exterior* (L90.7.HN). Thus, the L90 Series begins with a recantation (L90.H), moves to the intelligible world in which the speaker gazes upon two suns (L90.1–2), and then descends back to the sensible world (L90.3–7). The beginning of the L90 Series is equivalent to that point in the *Republic* (book 7) in which the prisoners in the cave burst their chains and look directly at the sun. However, those who view the sun directly are nevertheless expected to return to the cave and its shadows. Similarly, in this Series, the speaker, after gazing upon not one but two suns, then returns to the sensible world. Why is there a descent back to the sensible world in both the *Hekatompathia* and the *Republic*?

Socrates says that when those who have turned to the sun and "reached the heights and taken an adequate view," they should not be permitted to "linger there [nor] refuse to go down again among the bondsmen and share their labors and honors" (519d). Those who have ascended should return to bind together the commonwealth and serve as "king bees and leaders in the hive" (520ab). In this view, life is not meant to be lived in the heavens; instead, knowledge gained from the direct observation of the intelligible world should be applied to the practical matters of life on earth.

The "two suns" sonnet pair (L90.1–2) establishes an equal relationship between the sensible and intelligible worlds, which did not exist prior to this point in the sequence. In the first Subsequence, the sensible world dominates: throughout, the speaker is sensually battered. Although the intelligible world is discussed, it is presented as a complete enigma: music is characterized as mysterious in the L11 Series; Cupid is impossible to fathom in the L18 Series. In the second Subsequence, the speaker banishes love and shifts to an embrace of pure reason. Although his raging against love is passionate, he believes that he is being entirely rational, embracing the pure logos of the intelligible world. In the third Subsequence, these two worlds are placed on an equal footing for the first time. Love itself represents the intelligible world, and the beloved represents the sensible world, and both are characterized as a sun. Throughout this Subsequence, the focus alternates between the intelligible and sensible worlds. Plato likens this shifting from one world to another to a theatrical device, a "scene-shifting periactus" (*Republic* 518c). Insight is gained by shifting between the sensible and intelligible worlds, which are represented by the beloved and love itself, respectively. The third Subsequence builds an epistemological model that encompasses both worlds.

At the end of the *Republic*, it is judged that the Kallipolis, the ideal city, will never come to existence as it is too near the gods.[28] Thus, mankind's home lies not with the gods, and yet, man cannot live without the divine. The notion of the heroic and noble depend upon something external to the world of becoming, and this is essential to human life. In the penultimate sonnet of the first Subsequence (L18.B6), the speaker compares himself to those lovers that have died for their beloveds (Pyramus for Thisbe; Haemon for Antigone). Nothing in the first Subsequence provides grounds for this altruism or nobility, which is one reason why the first Subsequence ends in aporia. Nor are there any grounds offered in the second Subsequence, for love has been altogether abandoned. But the "two suns" sonnet pair that launches the third Subsequence is an *anabasis*, a visit to the divine, for that is the only place upon which the grounds for nobility may be found.

For Socrates, philosophy and the Good begin in wonder when men turn their eyes upward toward the stars in an almost erotic desire for knowledge. In contrast, Aristophanes is concerned with the erotics of men looking downward at themselves.[29] This unresolvable dualism is at the core of Petrarchan sonnet sequences. In the third Subsequence, it is as if a periactus turns the reader back and forth between heavenly and earthly perspectives, as represented by love and the beloved. This occurs within each Hexameral Series: Hex1–3 treat love itself, and then in Hex4–6, the speaker attempts to gain the beloved's acceptance. The L90 Series begins with the celestial divine and then makes a downward progression to the earthly and material (see Addendum 2). The next Series presents a materialist process physics.

Love as process physics (Subsequence 3, Series L39)

The L39 Series presents a cosmology in which love is a primordial force that acts to conjoin extremes: heat and cold, hope and fear, joy and sorrow, life and death. An image of this cosmological model appears on the *Hekatompathia*'s title page: Venus and Mars are situated opposite each other in the left and right panels (Fig. 14.1). According to Gordon Teskey, the adultery of Mars and Venus (*Odyssey* 8.267) was read allegorically in the Renaissance: the adulterers were "exposed when they were caught in the net of Hephaestus, and this was interpreted as an allegory of the divine creator binding the forces of opposition and concord in the net of the logos."[30] This view of love is what Ficino called "the perpetual knot and link of the universe," and was derived, in part, from Cusanus but also from the physics of antiquity, including Heraclitean flux and pre-Socratic atomism (see Chapter 9). This point of view had a considerable influence on Renaissance thinking.[31] The *Symposium*'s third speaker, the physician Eryximachus, presents love as based on this process physics: health is a matter of achieving a balance between opposing forces. The ascent toward the comprehension of love is not through myth, poetry, or mysticism, as presented by subsequent speakers, but by the habits of a healthy life and the munificence of a healthy cosmos that maintains an equilibrium (*isonomia*) between love's conflicting forces.[32] Love is at the center of Eryximachus's cosmological model, and Bacon adopted a similar model. Sophie Weeks describes Bacon's cosmological model as "creation *ex chao*":

> Cupid is, Bacon says, "coeval" with chaos. In other words, in the beginning there is *materia prima* and its appetitive power (both signified

by Cupid). The chaos refers to matter's lack of form *in toto*: as a whole, chaos is dark, mysterious and incomprehensible. ... During this phase, matter's productive power is unrestrained and nothing lasts; things are generated and immediately devoured. ... However, there comes a point at which concord becomes "powerful and predominant." Cupid's "principal and peculiar power is effective in uniting bodies; and the keys of ether, land and sea were also entrusted to him."[33]

Bacon calls this great cohering power "the great schematism," and, according to Weeks, "the presence of chaos or system is determined by the balance of *discordia* and *concordia*."[34] For both Bacon and Eryximachus, concord emerges through the notion of harmony: Eryximachus replaces the two Eroses of Pausanias with a double Eros in which opposites may be harmonized.[35] Eros for him is a means of effecting a sympathy between things in conflict (187a–c). Music is similarly characterized as a mysterious instrument of harmonization in the L11 Series. Eryximachus, according to Rosen, "goes beyond Heraclitus and Empedocles in suggesting that man is able to reduce strife to harmony."[36] Bacon was likewise optimistic in his belief that the forces of nature could be brought under control for the benefit of mankind.

While the conflict between opposites appears in most of the L39 Series' 13 sonnets and is the dominant theme in 6 of them, the remaining 7 sonnets present images of perpetual motion, another feature of this process physics.[37] Endless motion is an essential construct in Petrarchan sonnet sequences, and this endlessness is often figured as an inescapable labyrinth. Sonnets in which this theme appears include L39.A4, which provides an example of *reduplicatio* (HN): the ending of one sonnet line links to the beginning of the next. Another such sonnet, L39.A6, defines the circular Hexameral themes. Sonnet L39.B1 features the repetitive and endless tortures of Tantalus, Ixion, and Sisyphus. Sonnet L39.B4 is a Latin translation of a key Petrarch sonnet that recounts endless suffering: "I suffer one thousand deaths, and after each, I resume life that day" (13). Three other sonnets are constructed around the theme of endlessness.[38] Socrates presents perpetual motion in the *Theaetetus*:

All the things we are pleased to say 'are,' really are in a process of becoming, as a result of movement and change and of blending one with another. We are wrong to speak of them as 'being,' for none of them ever is; they are always becoming. In this matter let us take it that, with the exception of Parmenides, the whole series of philosophers agree—Protagoras, Heraclitus, Empedocles—and among the poets... Homer. (152de)

Laurence Lampert asserts that, according to Socrates's interpretation, Homer presents a process physics—"a totality of becoming, while veiling it in a poetic theology of ostensibly immortal beings." Further, Socrates claims that the secret of these wise men is that they practiced esotericism: "They never said what they meant."[39] In the *Symposium*, becoming is presented as Eros by Diotima: he is homeless and "neither mortal nor immortal... alive and blooming, and now dying, to be born again. [He stands] midway between ignorance and wisdom" (203de). Eros, both in the *Symposium* and the *Hekatompathia*, is presented as process physics in a materialist cosmology.

The two-millennia history of this process physics (or becoming) is surveyed in Michel Jeanneret's remarkable *Perpetual Motion*. One important example Jeanneret explores is Ovid's *Metamorphoses*, which "conveys manifestations of a world delivered up to flux, continuous creation" and "presents primitive matter as a knot of discordant forces, doomed to disorder and war."[40] Of course, this pagan cosmogony conflicts with the Christian worldview, and yet some found a path to coexistence. For example, Maurice Scève writes: "His great Chaos unfolded in light visible / To show what was his primal power."[41] Yet, too much candor risked getting oneself burned at the stake.[42]

The L39 Series' concern with the process physics of perpetual motion and the conflict of opposites may be contrasted with the thematic content of the sequence's other double Hexameral ring, the L18 Series (first Subsequence). In both Series, hope is present only in the "A" ring, with fear and gloom predominating in the "B" ring. Otherwise, the differences between the two Series are stark: the L18 Series is not marked by either the conflict of opposites or perpetual motion, except in two sonnets that occur late in the Series (L18.B4 and L18.B5).[43] Although these two sonnets appear to adumbrate the process physics of the later L39 Series, in the L18 Series, the speaker primarily attempts to understand the nature of love by citing classical myths rather than turning to process physics. These two alternative approaches, one based on myth and the other on a logos of process physics, are also found in the *Symposium*: in the first three speeches, logos predominates, and in the last three, mythos does (discussed below).

Process physics was known in Elizabethan England from the atomist doctrines of Epicurus, who lived a century after Democritus. Sonnet L18.B4 appears to signal Bacon's interest in atomism: it describes the Milky Way as the product of many stars and the sun's light as a stream of particles (*moates*; 5).[44] The influence of Epicurus's materialist philosophy was expanded in the first century BCE by Lucretius's hexameter poem, *De rerum natura*. The poem was rediscovered in the fifteenth century and studied by Ficino, although he later burned his essays on it. In the next century, Erasmus wrote a dialogue, the *Epicure*, which introduced Epicureanism to a larger audience.[45] The dialog at first appears to be an attack on Epicureanism, but according to Adam Rzepka, a close reading reveals it "to be a defense of Epicureanism and not simply a screed against it." It employs a "crafted stratagem that uses the apparent subsumption of Epicureanism in Christianity to open the door to a philosophy that the period rarely hesitated to condemn as 'atheism.'" *Epicure* was translated and printed in English in 1545; however, its complex rhetorical strategy—its "double or triple layers of discursive camouflage"—has meant that the introduction of Epicureanism to England has not received sufficient attention, even though its influence was considerable.[46] For example, the first 23 lines of *De rerum natura*, its invocation to Venus, appears in translation in book 4 of the *Faerie Queene*; Spenser seems to stay true to the original's ideas, if not its actual language.[47] Epicureanism was also central to Harriot's work in optics, and it appears to be an important influence in Shakespeare's *King Lear*.[48]

The Epicurean and Christian worldviews cannot be realistically reconciled, which makes "discursive camouflage" necessary. The process physics in the L39 Series is evident in the restored sequence, but in the published sequence, the Series' 13 sonnets are scattered over a range of 40 sonnets, from Sonnet 39 to Sonnet 78. Thus disbursed, the references to endlessness and the conflict of opposites may be taken as figurative or emotive language rather than cosmological constructs. But in the restored sequence, the L39 Series adheres to the rigid structure of the double Hexameral ring, and every sonnet depicts some feature of process physics. The *Hekatompathia*'s practice of ruin and restoration thus camouflages its heretical cosmology.

In this Series' final sonnet, the speaker is completely at the mercy of love's power: *For Love Dame Natures foe, without remorse / Thus coopleth contraries in me by force.* (L39.B6.17–18). Love's process physics lacks nobility and compassion but is unavoidable because it forcibly resides within the speaker (*in me*). The speaker's exploration of process physics concludes here, and in the next Series he will turn to the beloved, hoping to find either compassion or some form of love besides process physics.

The return of mythos (Subsequence 3, Series L64)

The *Hekatompathia* depicts love from two perspectives, and each perspective might be called a "theater": the theater of the love, that is, love as Cupid—a cosmic force; and the theater of the beloved—a deiform entity. The speaker attempts to understand the nature of love either as a cosmic force or as a human desire, as when he attempts to gain the beloved's favor. The first two introductory Series contain both theaters, but in most subsequent Series, one theater or the other is predominant. The third Series, L26, is an encomium to the beloved; the next Series, L18, is concerned with love as a natural force. The L82 (MLIP) Series that follows also treats love as a natural force, a danger that the speaker must guard against. The L90 Series begins with love and ends with the beloved: a recantation and prayer are made to love (L90.H); love and the beloved are then equated in the paired "two suns" sonnets (L90.1–2); the last sonnet (L90.7) is a traditional encomium to the beloved. The L39 Series switches back to the investigation of love as a natural force. Then the L64 Series returns to the theater of the beloved, as the speaker attempts to win her favor. This series closely adheres to an important tradition in sonnet sequences, the *canso*, which is an epistolary song to the beloved (see Chapter 9). The L50 Series combines love and the beloved in a love triangle (after Cupid is struck by his own arrow), and in the final L73 Series, the beloved fades and the sequence reaches its conclusion about love itself.

Though the speaker fails to win over the beloved in the L64 Series, in its final sonnet, he reaches two conclusions: as to the nature of love, he can only answer *nought* (L64.6.5); as to the beloved, hope remains, and he pledges endless love should she *salve* his *wound* (L64.6.15–16). The attempt to develop a comprehensive ontology (or logos) of love fails because process physics cannot elucidate the higher form of love. Whatever it is that drives lovers to die for their beloveds requires a vision of the Good that process physics cannot deliver. The search for a logos of love is unsuccessful, and the quest to gain the beloved's favor has nearly reached an aporia.

An alliance with love (Subsequence 3, Series L50)

The sequence reaches its climax in this Series when the speaker fails in his final attempt to win over the beloved. In the Series' lead sonnet, the speaker attempts to gain the beloved's favor with the help of personified Love (HN). Love, so often depicted as an adversary in the sequence, is here seen as a possible ally, shooting a golden arrow at the beloved on the speaker's behalf. However, Cupid's arrow ricochets off the beloved's *hard brest* and instead lodges in Cupid himself (L50.2.11–12). The theaters of love and the beloved converge here. The speaker then seeks a speedy death in a dialogue with personified Death and Love (L50.5), as discussed in Chapter 9.

The power of the human will becomes evident in this Series as the speaker plots *with* Cupid in his pursuit of the beloved. He is conscious of his willfulness: *That needes perforce I must encline my will* (L50.H.8); *I will enforce my selfe to liue content* (L50.4.8). A similar turn toward self-empowerment occurs at the beginning of the *Symposium*'s fifth speech, delivered by the tragedian Agathon.[49] For him, love is a poet or maker, and human love is a creative or poetic act. Agathon is a proto-Sidneian in his exalted view of poetry's power and importance. This Series begins with an arresting declaration of self-expression: *the Authour expresseth here in his owne person* (L50.H.HN). The speaker characterizes his love as *straunge*, and a *contrary* state to that of *all other men* (L50.H.HN). The speaker, a poet, is unlike others: he *dies in dreames, whiles others liue in rest* (L50.H.8–9), and it is this assertion of will that allows the sequence to reach its conclusion. Strikingly, for the first time in this Subsequence, Cupid is depicted as having diminished powers: *Cupid, where is thy golden quiver nowe? / Where is thy sturdy Bowe? and where the fire*[?] (L50.3.1–2). Although Cupid was also portrayed as having lost his power at the end of the second Subsequence, that occurred in the context of the speaker's complete rejection of love. In this Series, the power of love and that of the speaker exist side by side, which foreshadows the sequence's end in the next and final Series.

The beloved appears to take precedence over the love-god as the speaker pledges his everlasting allegiance to her (L50.4.13–16). Love is not presented here as process physics but as a mystery described through poetry and myth: it is a priceless nectar that flows from a magical spring in Boeotia, *the well of the Muses* (L50.1.HN, 13–16). This reminds us of Agathon's contention that Love is a poet rather than a physician, and contra Phaedrus, he asserts that Love is the youngest of the gods, a store of "imperishable youth" (195ab). Unlike any previous speaker, Agathon subordinates the body to the psyche's poetic fire. Rosen asserts that words, cosmology, and process physics are concerned with necessity, while "poetry is the genuinely erotic activity of freedom."[50] As in Plato's *Phaedo*, the soul is separated from the body and "freed from its shackles" (67cd). Love is the force behind the Augustinian model of Christian conversion: the soul's weight is measured in love (*pondus meum amor meus*).

The discussion of this Series in Chapter 9 emphasized its *katabasis*, the confrontation with personified Death that takes place in L50.5. But an *anabasis* develops in parallel, an interior journey that discovers man's power of creation. The link between this *katabasis* and *anabasis* is found in the final lines of L50.5, when Death asks the speaker why the return of his heart (the sequence's master trope) will not end his *woe*. The speaker answers: *That brought from colde, It neuer will desire / To rest with me, which am more hote then fire* (17–18). The heat (metaphorically, the speaker's heart) never really resided in the beloved; rather, her beauty activated what was always native to the speaker. Just as Augustine discovers at the moment of conversion that God lies within himself, the speaker likewise discovers that Eros, the heat of desire, lies within himself.

The ontological collapse (Subsequence 3, Series L73)

Throughout the sequence, the *Hekatompathia* presents symmetrical pairs of Manichean cosmic images—what Carol Kaske calls images *in bono et in malo*.[51] This new philosophy appears to be a kind of pantheism: everything is in flux, and generation rests not with a god in heaven but in a divinity that is everywhere dispersed. Giordano Bruno believed that there is but one divinity whether it is called love, Venus, *anima mundi*, or Nature:

> You see then that there is one simple Divinity found in all things, one fecund Nature, preserving mother of the universe insofar as she diversely communicates herself, casts her light into diverse subjects, and assumes various names.[52]

This philosophy is a seemingly odd combination of an idealist philosophy, Platonism, and a materialist philosophy, such as that found in Democritus or Lucretius.[53] Jon Quitslund sums up Bruno's philosophy as follows:

> Bruno's cosmos may be de-centered and de-mythologized, but it is not normless. The place of the Christian God is taken by Fate, enigmatic but rational; the ways of Fate and Fortune, together with the old pantheon, are subject to interpretation by Sophia [an interlocuter in *Expulsion*] in the name of ideal truth and virtue. Nature is an intrinsic norm unifying all existing phenomena.[54]

This is similar to the position taken in this final Series, in which the speaker's god, higher love, is *a Second Nature* (L73.1.17) that resides within himself. The placement of divine love within the material existence of the speaker essentially collapses the distinction between the sublunar and supralunar worlds. This contradicts Plato's cosmology in which eternal, unchangeable, divine forms reside in one cosmic sphere, while material, mutable instantiations of those forms reside in another. Nor is this compatible with Aristotelianism or Scholastic philosophy, which likewise maintain separate spheres. Instead, contrarieties are dispersed across the cosmos, as in the cosmology of Bruno, in which "the conventional distinction between a mutable sublunary world and an immutable supralunary one, an article of faith elaborately supported by the Aristotelean tradition of philosophy, is utterly disregarded."[55] Love, or process physics, is dispersed throughout the material world, which includes the speaker himself. Yet, he is more than process physics, for as we learned in the L50 Series, willpower and limitless desire also reside within the speaker, who is *more hote then fire* (L50.5.18). Two loves, immanent process physics and transcendent desire, coexist within the speaker. These two loves are referred to as *Love* and *Heart* in the headnote of the lead sonnet of the L73 Series: *Love* is the wanton tyrant of process physics; the *Heart* is the speaker's will, which in earlier Series pursued the beloved—*a heedlesse follie* (HN). In this head-note, the poet defines his sequence as the *faining* of *a quarrell betwixt Love and his Heart*, and now at the sequence's conclusion, he effects a compromise between these two forces, immanent and transcendent love.

This conception is different from the Renaissance Platonism in which one climbs a *scala amoris* through transcendent realities, ending in the Plotinian One. In the *Hekatompathia*'s cosmology, the hierarchy between the sublunar material world and the supralunary divine world is collapsed: the physical world and the intelligible world of the human mind are not separate spheres. In Sonnet L73.2, the passion within the speaker is depicted as capable of replacing the powers of the Olympic gods. This collapse is foreshadowed in the prior Series when Cupid's arrow boomerangs and penetrates himself rather than the intended target, the beloved (L50.2). As a result, Cupid himself comes under the power of the beloved, and the speaker's longstanding double hurt becomes a *triple hurt* (16). Love itself is subordinated to the immanent beloved, which adds to the speaker's pain. However, an equitable balance is achieved in the final Series: process physics love is no longer a god, but instead likened to a habitat, or climate, that is, the natural environment in which one lives (L73.1). In the sequence's final stanza, love, a *coincidentia oppositorum*, is imagined as radiating from the beloved's eyes:

> **From out my** Mistres **eyes, two lightsome starres,**
> **He destinates estate of double kinde,**
> **My teares, my smyling cheere, my peace, my warres;**
> **My sighes, my songes; my feare, my hoping minde;**
> > **My fire, my frost; my ioy, my sorrowes gall;**
> > **My curse, my prayse; my death, but life with all.** (L73.6.13–18)

Love (*He*; 14) determines destiny, through the dialectical pairs that emanate from the beloved's eyes. This breaks with the Christian tradition, in which destiny is ordained by God. The oneness and simplicity (a theological term) of the Christian God is replaced by a scattered divinity dispersed across the natural world. Sonnet L73.6, the last of the sequence, answers the question posed at the work's beginning: "What is the nature of love?" (Sonnet 5). Love is not Nature, but a *Second Nature* (L73.1.17), a condition of existence that is likened to the climate (*consuetudo*; L73.1.HN).

In the *Symposium*, Socrates claims that love is not a thing in and of itself, but a relation between things: "Love is always the love of something" (200e). Diotima sees an errant tendency "to give the name of Love to what is only one single aspect of it" (205b). Socrates's definition of love is broad, encompassing some of the conceptions of love presented by the earlier speakers. It includes both the beauty of the beloved and the goodness of a lover who sacrifices his life for a beloved. Seth Benardete argues, "This twofold immanence of Eros [beauty, goodness] is so complete that the god disappears into his human counterparts [lover and beloved]. Eros, which begins as subject, ends up as predicate."[56] In the *Hekatompathia*, love is also a predicate rather than a subject, an ever-present natural force, an interaction between things, that resides both within the natural world and the speaker himself: *If Aeole were depriu'd of all his charge / Yet soone could I restore his windes againe* (L73.2.13–14).

This ever-present natural force is neither psyche nor body, but a striving for wholeness—the fulfillment of desire. Nature, in this view, "includes both body and mind as the central and irreducible dualism of human existence."[57] In Hex1–3 and the *Symposium*'s first three speeches, love is a tyrannical process physics; in Hex4–6 and the *Symposium*'s last three speeches, love may act as a friend, and in this conjunction with human agency, may allow for a happy life.[58] Agathon, the fifth speaker, eschews process physics and embraces complete poetic freedom: the old gods, who confer Necessity, are eclipsed by the young god, Love, a poet and the author of virtue (197bc). He asserts that divinity, without process physics or Necessity, has descended into man. But for Socrates, this goes too far, because man cannot shed his corporeality. Although he may ascend to the gods as he does in Diotima's *scala amoris*, his true nature includes both his corporeality and psyche.

The *Hekatompathia* presents a double Eros in its first two Series (*ex visione*; *ex cogitatione*) but ends with man as double—a material body and a material psyche. Although the psyche is an epiphenomenon of the body in this final Series, it is also the seat of the will. Like the *Symposium*, the *Hekatompathia* begins and ends with corporeal Eros, but at the same time, the speaker exercises his will, despite the strength of corporeal Eros.[59] Indeed, the exercise of will is the cure for love. In the sequence's first headnote, the poet claims to have written an unpublished *De Remedio Amoris* (1.HN), which presumably would furnish a cure for love. As the sequence begins, love wounds the speaker by stealing his heart; at the sequence's end, this very wound (*selfe same ground*) is the site at which Aesculapius's *Herbes*, tinged with Cupid's *force*, release the speaker from his imprisonment (L73.5). Paradoxically, love both causes the wound and effects the cure. This paradox is resolved by recognizing love as double:

process physics love causes the wound, but higher love, associated with the psyche and human will, allows for a cure. As discussed in Chapter 3, Sonnet 5 establishes the sequence's purpose, its inquiry into the nature of love. Its headnote declares that *(two verses only excepted)*, it is *wholly translated out of Petrarch*. These two verses contain the proverb, *Selfe doe, selfe have* (12); they are heavily highlighted, and a sidenote next to them reads: *Adduntur Tuscano hii duo versus* ("two verses added to those of the Tuscan"). Sonnet 6, a Neo-Latin translation of the same Petrarch sonnet, is also a faithful translation, but it lacks these two added verses, which are not only absent in Petrarch's sonnet, but a sentiment foreign in nature to the *Canzoniere.* By translating Petrarch's sonnet twice and highlighting the two added verses that only appear in Sonnet 5, Bacon defines the difference between his sequence and Petrarch's as the exercise of human will.

Sonnet 5's highlighted proverb suggests that the assertion of human will is the mainspring behind higher love. A fundamental difference between the *Canzoniere* and the *Hekatompathia* is that in the former, the speaker does not escape his labyrinth, but in the latter he does. In a letter to Henry Saville (n.d., circa 1596–1604), Bacon reveals his view of the will. He begins by denying that men, by their will, can make their own fortunes ("Faber quisque suae fortunae") because life's accidents are beyond our control. However, he suggests that this sententia may profitably be turned to "Faber quisque ingenii sui" (Maker of his own intellect), for then...

> It would teach men to bend themselves to reform those imperfections in themselves, which now they seek but to cover. ... But certain it is, whether it be believed or no, that as the most excellent of metals, gold, is of all other the most pliant and most enduring to be wrought; so of all living and breathing substance, the perfectest (Man) is the most susceptible of help, improvement, impression, and alteration. ... And as to the will of man, it is that which is most [manageable] and obedient; as that which admitteth most medicines to cure and alter it. The most sovereign is Religion, which is able to change and transform it in the deepest and most inward inclinations and motions.[60]

Bacon optimistically insists that man is malleable, and that his will may be managed in a way that allows for cure and transformation of his inclinations. He believed that although the will inclines toward desire or "appetite," it is open to other remedies:

> Therefore it is no marvel though this faculty of the mind of will and election, which inclineth affection and appetite, being but the

inceptions and rudiments of will, may be so well governed and managed, because it admitteth access to so divers remedies to be applied
to it and to work upon it.[61]

The *Hekatompathia* offers a secular cure (rather than the above "most
sovereign [cure of] Religion") for the primitive inclination of the will,
which is overly tilted toward the satisfaction of base desire. Bacon's hope
is that man may be a second creator, the "maker of his own intellect." The
Hekatompathia's noetic journey defines a path by which man, through the
exercise of his will, may be brought to a happier state. Although man cannot counter the world's constant change and instability—he cannot be the
maker of his own fortune (*suae fortunae*)—he can learn to be happy under
this condition by recognizing within himself the sovereignty of his own
intellect (*ingenii sui*). That self-sovereignty, which includes both sophrosyne (self-moderation) and the speaker's recognition of the great power of
love within himself, is attained in the last Series:

> If Aeole **were depriu'd of all his charge,**
> **Yet soone could I restore his windes againe,**
> **By sobbing sighes, which forth I blow at large,**
> **To moue her mind that pleasures in my paine;**
> > **What man, but I, could thus encline his will**
> > **To liue in** *Loue*, **which hath no end of ill?**   (L73.2.13–18)

The speaker claims god-like powers, which ensue, ironically enough, from
the very source of his pain, the beloved's unmoving *mind* (16). He leverages this pain, through the exercise of *his will* (17), to escape the torment
of the world of becoming. He believes that this willfulness makes him
unique: *what man, but I* (17). Speakers in sonnet sequences often lay
claim to the uniqueness of their love.[62] In the Platonic dialogues, Socrates
claims that he has a unique knowledge of love, or at least that it is the one
thing that he understands.[63] Poets and philosophers are exceptional in that
they create (*poiesis*), which is not only a willful act, but in the context of a
love poet telling his story, an act of self-creation. The exercise of will is
most evident in the *Symposium*'s ending: Socrates refuses Alcibiades's
advances, outlasts his interlocutors who succumb to the soporific effects
of the wine, and sets off for the baths at the Lyceum, a purification ritual.
The *Symposium* ends with the renewal of the self (223d). In Diotima's
speech, men renew themselves by "every day... becoming a new man," and
she also claims that the cosmos maintains itself through a process of perpetual renewal.[64] In the *Hekatompathia*, the speaker reaches the brink of
death in the L50 Series but renews himself in the L73 Series. The cure for

the world of becoming, like the Nietzschean concept of eternal return, lies in self-renewal.

Agathon declares that "Love is himself so divine a poet that he can kindle in the souls of others the poetic fire, for no matter what dull clay we seemed to be before, we are every one of us a poet when we are in love" (196e). *Poiesis*, making or creating, is a willful act. Love, then, is the cure for love: it is a *pharmakon* (potion) that can either poison or cure (see L39.A3). Agathon goes on to elaborate how Apollo is the god of both medicine and the arts, and a "scholar in the school of Love" (197a). Rosen argues that "Apollo represents the harmony between the disharmony of body and psyche."[65]

In the *Hekatompathia*'s final sonnet, the speaker crowns love as ruler of an *empire* that subsumes *Juppiter in heaven, Neptune in the seas, and Pluto in hell* (L73.6.HN). As in the *Symposium*, the Olympic gods, who ascended in the Titanomachy, are now themselves overthrown, and Love becomes the archon. In the sonnet's final stanza (quoted above), the dialectical pairs of process physics rule, but the *double hurt* (10) experienced throughout the sequence is now recognized as the coupling of *sweet* and the *sow'r* (12). The soul cannot break free of process physics, but can assert its own volition. Love, as the *Hekatompathia* finally defines it, is divine and encompasses both the process physics of nature and human agency. The Neo-Latin *Epilogue* that concludes the work—more of *a praier then a Passion* according to its headnote—places all hope in divine Love (*in te quam spes mea tota reposta est*; 14). The ontological and epistemic division into two worlds that began with the speaker's body-soul disunity at the sequence's beginning, concludes in a new order of Love.

The new ontology

The *Hekatompathia* ignores the Christian deity and crowns an all-pervading love-physics as the new god. Destiny flows from the flux emanating from the beloved's eyes, dialectical pairs *in bono et in malo*. We may wonder whether the *Hekatompathia*'s new cosmology is consistent with Bacon's later philosophical works. Were such heterodox views more prevalent in Elizabethan England than is generally assumed? If God is process physics, then what is the source of nobility and virtue? Of course, this study can no more than glance at these difficult questions. Yet, having spent much effort in traversing this most deliberately calculated sonnet sequence, its philosophical ideas deserve our attention, for it offers an unusual window into the intellectual history of its time.

The *Hekatompathia*'s cosmology is pantheistic: the love-god is distributed everywhere in nature. A decade earlier, we can find such pantheism in Ronsard's "Le chat": *Dieu est par tout, par tout se mesle Dieu* (God is everywhere, everywhere God mixes in).[66] Pantheism's origins lie in antiquity: Plato's *Phaedrus* identifies the "self-mover" as the first principle of motion and asserts that "this is the essence and definition of soul, to wit, self-motion" (245de). The creator "put intelligence in soul, and soul in body" and thus "the world came into being—a living creature truly endowed with soul and intelligence by the providence of God" (*Timaeus* 30b). This disbursal of intelligence into the material world conflicts with our usual understanding of Platonism as an idealist philosophy in which eternal and unchanging forms are instantiated in the material world—a tension in Plato's thought. The tension between idealist and materialist formulations in Plato's thought has led to deep rifts among Plato scholars: the majority accept Plato as a Platonist (idealist), but a minority believe that his eternal and unchanging forms are intended as noble lies.[67] Disbursed intelligence is also found in Aristotelian philosophy, in which forms are a potential in matter.

What precedents exist for the *Hekatompathia*'s pantheistic philosophy? Although Nature was not a prominent goddess in antiquity, she emerges in the medieval period as a significant figure, particularly in Chartrian Platonism. In the sixteenth century, according to Quitslund, "*natura* is distinguished from *materia* and refers to the formative vivifying and regenerative principles in physical phenomena," and this is consistent with its characterization as a *daimon*.[68] Unlike poets who usually veil divine mysteries, Levinus Lemnius, a physician, openly characterizes nature in his 1559 treatise on nature's secrets. For him, nature is (i) a quality infused in things from their beginning and birth, (ii) the temperature and mixing of the four elements, (iii) the virtue and efficient cause and preserver of all things, and (iv) the order and continuation of the divine works, which obeys God's power and his word and commandments.[69] The *Hekatompathia* follows the first of these three points. This conception of nature appears to have been an important influence on other Elizabethan poets.[70]

Is this natural philosophy heretical in its claim that God's power lies within nature rather than with Him alone? In the case of Bruno, who wrote that *natura est deus in rebus* (nature is the god in things), a verdict was rendered by his contemporaries.[71] At one time or another he was in trouble with the Calvinists, Lutherans, and the Catholic Church—a heretical hat-trick that eventually cost him his life. Yet, rather than see God in nature, an alternative was to see nature as an order prescribed by God. Then the critical question becomes how the operations of nature are related to God's *ex nihilo* creation of the world. The Chartrian Platonists regarded nature as a handmaiden of God, a force that acts upon created things but does not itself create.[72] Another explanation found in medieval thought identifies nature's forces with God's love, a vestige of creation that permeates God's creatures—*vestigium divinae caritatis*.[73] This formulation of love and nature as expositions or images of God may, for some, reconcile Platonist conceptions of nature with Christian beliefs in God's omnipotence.[74] For Calvinists, however, these beliefs were no better than gnostic heresies. In their view it was essential to maintain the distinction between God and his works, which the natural philosophies of Aristotle, Plato, and the Stoics all failed to do.[75]

The *Hekatompathia*'s title page (Fig. 14.1) reprises its cosmology and answers a question raised early in the sequence: whether love is an "old god," that is, an eternal cosmological principle, or an unpredictable young god associated with the changeable material world.[76] The left panel depicts two love gods: an infantile Cupid stands at the feet of Venus, barely reaching her knee. The bottom panel shows a mature Cupid, sitting on a throne and wearing a crown. Archers at the left and right extremes arise from plants, showing that love's powers, wielded though its arrows, are a part of the natural world. Two peacocks (long-tailed birds perched on the hands of Cupid) represent beauty, the mysterious source of love's power. Two wild boars (or possibly some other long-horned animal) that appear in the far bottom corners of the panel represent erotic desire. In the sonnet that defines the Hexameral rings, the speaker expresses the hope *That Love no longer is a blinded Boy* (L39.A6.18). Cupid is not blindfolded in either his depiction as an infant in the left panel, or as a mature god in the bottom panel. Both the *Symposium* and the *Hekatompathia* see the question of whether love is a young god or old god as pivotal. The bottom panel depicts him as a mature king, as genesis—the primal origin of life. Yet, it also depicts him as the generator of new life: the archers, vines, and flowers represent generation—the continuous production of new life. This panel indicates that love is both young—that is, a continuous process of new creation and destruction—and old, a primordial force in the natural world.

The *Hekatompathia*'s materialist portrayal of love or Cupid as the root of all causation, both material and mental, is laid out in the sequence's first two Series and the L39 Series. As discussed above, Lucretius and Epicurus, both of whom were rediscovered in the late Renaissance, had a significant influence on early modern thought. In Lucretius, we see an infinity of atoms forming complex structures in a process of creation and destruction. Similarly, in *Wisdom of the Ancients*, Bacon identifies Cupid as "the original and unique force that constitutes and fashions all things out of matter."[77] The atom, equivalent to Cupid, is the "cause of causes—itself without cause."[78] Baconian matter is also appetitive or procreative, and "by repetition and multiplication produces all the variety of nature."[79] Weeks characterizes Bacon's views as "an extreme form of materialism."[80]

Fig. 14.1 The *Hekatompathia*'s title page

For Bacon, there is not one love but two: the parent-less Love, which arose from "Chaos," that "begot all things, the gods included," and a second "Love, the youngest of the gods, son of Venus, to whom the attributes of the elder are transferred."[81] He describes the younger love god as forever an infant, blind and naked, and an archer, and the elder love god as the "cause of causes," an "appetite or instinct of primal matter; or to speak more plainly, *the natural motion of the atom*."[82] Bacon goes on to describe Democritus's view of the atom, which he characterizes as "narrow." In contrast, Bacon believes that atoms are responsible for all motion, though they act blindly, that is, without purpose, and they are "peculiarly empty and destitute of providence."[83] Nevertheless, he argues that they produce all "order and beauty of the universe," in accordance with divine Providence. Bacon then describes the younger Cupid:

> In the description of him, the allegory changes its aim and passes to morals. And yet, there remains a certain conformity between him and the elder Cupid. For Venus excites the general appetite of conjunction and procreation; Cupid, her son, applies the appetite to an individual object. From Venus therefore comes the general disposition, from Cupid the more exact sympathy. Now the general disposition depends upon causes near at hand, the particular sympathy upon principles more deep and fatal, and as if derived from that ancient Cupid, who is the source of all sought-after [*exquisita*] sympathy.[84]

In Bacon's materialist cosmology, human potential is high because "the body of man is of all existing things both the most mixed and the most organic... and this is indeed the reason [why man] is capable of such wonderful powers and faculties." Man's broken nature is "counteracted by mixture," and the result is "abundance and excellence of power."[85] At the base of Bacon's cosmology is plenipotentiary matter that may be mixed to produce new forms of matter, and as man is "the most mixed," he has the power of a second creator.[86]

Bacon is using myth (and perhaps sophistry) to present a scientific cosmology that nevertheless accounts for human creativity and nobility. His cosmology rests upon an amoral process physics, and he never resorts to the dualism of materialist and idealist spheres. Bacon's division between the noumenal and phenomenal is not ontological but psychological and epistemological. His bifurcation of Venus is necessary because "morals" cannot be derived from physics, nor mind from matter. The elder Venus is associated with genesis and the younger with generation.[87] Primal matter is productive by an attraction or sympathy among atoms, and that "general disposition" remains an operative force in the more "exact" or "particular sympathy" found in human love and generation. This strategy of delineating two different loves originates in the *Symposium*. It first appears when Pausanias corrects Phaedrus's error of conflating love-physics with the love of the altruistic lover who dies for his beloved.[88] Recognizing the gap between Phaedrus's two descriptions of love, Pausanias declares that there are two Aphrodites: an older heavenly Aphrodite who is unbegotten (parent-less) and arises from the sea, and a younger, earthly Aphrodite, who is the daughter of Zeus (180de). In both Pausanias's and Bacon's scheme, both love gods exhibit a form of "sympathy" (*sympathia*; literally, a feeling or passion in common).

Although the first three speakers in the *Symposium* may call love a god, in fact, they deny love's divinity by depicting it as process physics. Plato likely assumed that his readers would recognize Phaedrus and Eryximachus as impious figures, for both were implicated in the desecration of the Hermae and the profanation of the Eleusinian mysteries, which occurred around the time that the *Symposium* is set, in approximately 416 BCE.[89] There is a close connection between the "atheistic" process physics of the atomist cosmologists and the Sophists who were Plato's chief philosophical opponents.[90] What unites the *Symposium* speakers is their overthrow of the Olympic gods—the cosmology presented in the Homeric epics—but they differ in what they believe ought to replace those gods. The first three speakers replace the Homeric gods with a technicism based on process physics; the latter three speakers, two playwrights and Socrates, replace the Olympic gods with something more human-centric. Bacon's thought embraces both the materialist and the human-centric views in both the *Hekatompathia* and his later writings. The speaker cannot free himself of his composite and conflicted nature (as in his unsuccessful attempt to escape from love in the second Subsequence). However, Bacon is optimistic about the potential of human willpower—man's ability to become a second creator. Unlike the inherent disorder and unpredictability found in Lucretian atomism, the human will can impose order.[91]

In the sequence's final stanza (quoted above), the beloved vanishes except for her eyes—*starres* that disburse the dialectical pairs that comprise cosmic love. This departs radically from the Petrarchan model in which the beloved is the terminal point of all references, the epitome of beauty and goodness that the speaker idolatrously worships.[92] The Petrarchan beloved may be seen as an "ontological mezzanine" between heaven and earth, or what Spenser calls "the image of the heavens in shape humane."[93] But at the *Hekatompathia*'s conclusion, the beloved is no longer a mirror of heaven's perfection, but eyes that transmit the flux of process physics. Cosmic power is not directed from heaven, but resides in nature, including within the speaker himself. This conflicts with ancient and medieval cosmological models, which were bifold: they were divided between heaven and earth, sublunar and supralunar, or forms and their instantiations (Platonism). Instead, in *Hekatompathia* we find a monist primal flux everywhere present: the antique model of two distinct ontological spheres has collapsed into a single natural world that includes the human psyche. The discarding of the hierarchy of heaven and earth is most evident in Sonnet L90.2 (the Neo-Latin poem near the beginning of the third Subsequence), in which the beloved and the sun are judged equal. The beloved, no longer a mediatrix or an incarnate deity, is equivalent to the divine. The divine and human merge, and the speaker, the beloved, and the natural world are all reservoirs of love's cosmic energy (L73.2).

This collapsed ontology has been detected in other Elizabethan poets. In Shakespeare's *Sonnets*, the beloved (the speaker's male friend) is characterized as a triune deiform entity, the archetype of beauty, goodness, and truth. Sonnet 105 explicitly presents the friend as this triad of Platonic forms, using overtly Christian language. And yet this directly contradicts both Christian theology and Platonist philosophy. Long ago, J. B. Leishman detected an "inverted Platonism" throughout much of the *Sonnets* and was surprised to find that the transcendental had descended into the immanent. In the friend, says Leishman, "the distinction between human and divine, terrestrial and celestial, nowhere appears"—an ontological collapse.[94] Leishman contrasts Shakespeare's treatment of the friend with other literature, both ancient and Renaissance, and finds little precedence for this inverted Platonism.[95]

In the *Sonnets*, the friend is prefigured by ancient models of beauty, and after his death, true beauty will disappear. This casts the friend as the Incarnation, a singular point in time in which the transcendent and immanent meet. This represents a single point of ontological collapse, as opposed to the complete collapse of ontological spheres found in pantheism and the ending of the *Hekatompathia*. At times, Petrarch's Laura seems to represent a single point at which the divine and material intersect. A single point of ontological collapse is apparent in Spenser's *Amoretti*:

> That is true beautie: that doth argue you
> > to be divine, and borne of heavenly seed:
> > deriv'd from that fayre Spirit, from whom al true
> > and perfect beauty did at first proceed.   (79.9–12)

Patrick Cheney, quoting the above passage, explains that "Spenser sees the bosom of his fiancée, Elizabeth Boyle, as more than the site of physical and moral beauty: her breast is also the 'sacred harbor' of the holy Ghost." Indeed, "Elizabeth's body incarnates the deity." Further, he asserts that in this "stunning epiphany," Spenser runs counter to both Petrarchism and "Augustine's stern authority."[96] This conflation of the immanent and the transcendent, the earthly and the heavenly, incarnates the beloved, which is surely blasphemous. Cheney believes that "every book of Spenser's national epic dilates on Petrarchism, with Book III a virtual index of Spenser's counter-Petrarchism."[97] An image of surpassing Petrarch is found in Sir Walter Ralegh's Commendatory Verse to the 1590 *Faerie Queene*:

> All suddenly I saw the Faery Queene
> At whose approch the soule of *Petrarke* wept
> And from thenceforth those graces were not seene.
> For they this Queene attended, in whose steed
> Oblivion laid him downe on *Lauras* herse: (6–10)

Cheney argues that "without Petrarch, there could be no Spenser," and obviously, the same applies to Bacon and his *Hekatompathia*. He further asserts that Spenser's Petrarchism and counter-Petrarchism have been significantly undervalued by critics.[98]

Although the complete ontological collapse that occurs in the *Hekatompathia* is not found in Petrarch's sequence, Laura often appears to be a singular point of collapse between two ontological spheres—an incarnation. Petrarch spurned the old hierarchical cosmology by prioritizing the physical over the spiritual.[99] In Petrarch's dialogue, the *Secretum*, Franciscus (essentially Petrarch himself) is accused of idolatry for allowing the love of one of God's creatures, Laura, to distract him from the love of God. Although Franciscus claims that he has not "loved her body more than her soul," Augustinus (patterned after Augustine) wins the debate when he asserts that Franciscus would not have loved her soul so much if she had been ugly.[100] Citing these lines, Richard Strier argues that in the *Canzoniere*,

> There is a sustained insistence on the importance and value of the bodily and the mortal. ... Petrarch's task as a poet is to celebrate, even after her death, Laura's earthly existence... Petrarch sees his (unachievable) poetic goal as quite literally incarnational—"Nor with my style her beautiful face can I incarnate" [308.8]. [In the *Canzoniere*'s final poem, a prayer to the Virgin,] he offers as his most promising feature his ability "to love with such a marvelous faith a bit of frail mortal earth."[101]

Petrarch's poetics, grounded to earthly beauty rather than heavenly beauty, is incompatible with his Platonist cosmology, according to Strier:

Petrarch resists the ethical implications of the Platonism—or the Platonized Christianity—to which he is, metaphorically and religiously, committed. He accepts the soul-body dualism of Platonism, but he refuses to give the soul an absolute priority and to dismiss and devalue the body. He refuses, in other words, to adopt a transcendental perspective.[102]

The *Hekatompathia* completes the ontological shift that Petrarch began by rejecting the dualism of Platonism and replacing it with the habitat of process physics (*consuetudo*; L73.1.HN). The *Hekatompathia* is not a mirror of universal essences, as might be found, for example, in the works of the Chartrian Platonists. As suggested by its manuscript title, "A Looking glasse for Loovers," it is a mirror of the consciousness of a lover. The beloved points not to the noumena of heaven but to human consciousness with its willpower—the only potentially noumenal entity in the *Hekatompathia*'s materialist cosmology. This radically departs from Christianity's and Platonism's ontological model of separate transcendent and immanent realms that rarely intersect—the Christian exceptions are the Incarnation and the sacrament of the Eucharist. The *Hekatompathia*'s poetics is not that of a *vates* (prophet/poet), but a humanist poet. "The subject of the *vates* is god; the subject of [Sidney's] right poet is man," asserts Stillman.[103] Rather than practicing a "Protestant poetics" (a loose term that implies the influence of Reformed theology), the *Hekatompathia* practices a Sidneian humanist poetics. This poetics, according to Stillman, is primarily Philippist—the humanist tradition that Melanchthon initiated.[104]

Love: logos and mythos

The ontological collapse into process physics leaves us without any understanding of higher love. Why are lovers, such as Pyramus and Leander, willing to die for their beloveds (Sonnet 30)? Upon what ground can Phaedrus claim that love "is the ancient source of all of our highest good" and that it is the beacon that "a man must steer by when he sets out to live the better life" (178c)? The *Symposium*'s speakers struggle to bridge the vast chasm between lower and higher love, and a coherent explanation remains elusive.[105] Nor can Bacon, in his later writing, provide an adequate explanation of higher love, except through myth (see prior section).

In Petrarchan sequences, the mysterious and perfect beloved is an embodiment of this higher love—a theophany that is visible through the senses but cannot be grasped through noesis. In the L26 Series, the speaker is unable to directly behold the divine (sun-like) beloved:

> ***But sobbes, and sighes, and saith I am vndonne;**
> **No bird but** Ioues **can looke against the sunne.**   (L26.2.17–18)

This gulf between the lover and the beloved—the *amathia* of Sonnets 2 and 3, in which the speaker is separated from his heart—and the division of love into two forms (*ex visione* and *ex cogitatione*) in the first two Series, present a philosophical or theological problem. The speaker's unrequited love for the beloved—a poetic correlative of the impossibility of direct access to the divine—is the fundamental motif upon which Petrarchan sequences rest. An ontology that accounted for higher love would have to be based on a logos of permanence, unlike process physics, which is transient, and the existence of such a logos is doubtful.[106] Sonnet L26.2 (whose final couplet is quoted above) is an explicit statement of the beloved's ineffable nature, her incomprehensibility. Likewise, in the *Phaedo*, Socrates compares the limits of human comprehension to gazing directly at the sun during an eclipse, the effect of which would be to blind him, and metaphorically, to blind his soul. He says that instead, one must look at the sun indirectly, observing its reflection (or image) in water or some other medium (99d). This might serve as a statement of the core strategy of the sonnet genre, for the Petrarchan beloved is a mirror of ineffable, higher love.

With the adoption of process physics and pantheism—the dispersal of God throughout the natural world—how does one account for nobility, virtue, or the nomos of the ideal city? Having replaced a sovereign deity with the philosophy of Lucretius and Epicurus, we are left without a teleological account of the world. Stephen Greenblatt describes Lucretius's worldview:

> There is no master plan, no divine architect, no intelligent design. ... There is no reason to think that the earth or its inhabitants occupy a central place, no reason to set humans apart from all other animals, no hope of bribing or appeasing the gods, no place for religious fanaticism, no call for ascetic self-denial, no possibility of triumphing over nature, no escape from constant making and unmaking and remaking of forms. ... What humans can and should do is to conquer their fears, accept the fact they themselves and all the things they encounter are transitory, and embrace the beauty and the pleasure of the world.[107]

Lucretian materialism—the world of becoming—presents a hard epistemological barrier to knowledge of any possible world of being (or denial of its existence). The *Hekatompathia* hits this same barrier when it attempts to comprehend love through a logical dissection of its attributes (which begins in Sonnet 5). The *Symposium* also confronts this barrier, and both works ultimately turn away from the praxis of logos, which cannot account for higher love, to a human-centered investigation that employs poetic sensibility and mythos.

The *Symposium* is instructive in this interplay between logos and mythos. As discussed above, the first speaker, Phaedrus, defines love as process physics and later as something entirely different, the "source of all of our highest good" (178c), but fails to connect these two different conceptions of love. Pausanias recognizes the incoherence in Phaedrus's definition of love and resolves it by dividing love in two: lower and higher love. Next, Eryximachus, presents his logos of love, a technicism. Logos is central to the arguments of these first three speakers, but the next two speeches, by playwrights Aristophanes and Agathon, turn to mythos. Aristophanes offers his cosmogonic myth of the double humans; while Agathon contends that love is a poet (196e).[108] The final speaker, Socrates, presents both logos, in his own words, and mythos via Diotima's speech-within-a-speech. This combining of logos and mythos also occurs in the *Hekatompathia*: Hex1–3 present a logos of natural forces; Hex4–6 are human-centric and utilize myth or poetry in the pursuit of the beloved, an image of higher love.

This interplay between logos and mythos, a two-pronged approach aimed at arriving at the truth, is practiced throughout the Platonic dialogues. For example, the divide between logos and mythos gives rise to different theoretical cities in the *Republic*, and the famous "quarrel between philosophy and poetry" (607b). For Plato, neither mythos nor logos alone can give an adequate account of the whole, and he uses love as an epistemic device that can encompass both of them, pulling them together. E. R. Dodds explains:

> Eros has a special importance in Plato's thought as being the one mode of experience which brings together the two natures of man, the divine self and the tethered beast. For Eros is frankly rooted in what man shares with the animals, the physiological impulse of sex. ... Yet Eros also supplies the dynamic impulse which drives the soul forward in its quest of a satisfaction transcending earthly experience. It thus spans the whole compass of human personality, and makes the one empirical bridge between man as he is and man as he might be.[109]

The sonnet genre is built upon a similar opposition: the beloved is an image of a divine self that transcends earthly experience, and the speaker is a figure of unfulfilled desire, a tethered beast—mankind as it is. The great danger is that with the gods having drifted into irrelevance (as happens in both the *Hekatompathia* and the *Symposium*), mankind is left with nothing more than a radically temporal life. Human life is reduced to unbounded desires (pleonexia) and the basis for piety is left in doubt (Plato's *Euthyphro* presents an unsuccessful inquiry into the nature of piety).[110]

The *Symposium* answers this vexing problem first with a faux solution, followed by an implied solution. Diotima describes an ascent to beauty itself (211e–212a), however, the principles by which one ascends this *scala amoris* to the transcendent realm of the beautiful and the good are not disclosed. A beautiful speech, indeed, but is it true? One might wonder whether Diotima's speech is akin to the noble lie in the *Republic*, a myth that must be prescribed for a world that lacks teleological guidance.[111] Socrates harbors some doubt about Diotima's arguments at one point (208b) but, in the end, says that he has been persuaded and will promote this vision of love (212b). Yet did he truly believe her, or did he claim to be persuaded to promote a noble lie? Just prior to his persuasion, Diotima speaks of the true contemplation of beauty itself and virtue itself, which elevates one to the status of a "friend of god" and holds out the possibility of immortality (212a). This contradicts Socrates's contention in the *Phaedo* (99d, discussed above) that one is blinded by the sight of beauty itself. Diotima's speech, especially the grandeur of its epistemological vision, ought to leave us skeptical. Indeed, prior to this ascension to the divine, she first descends to the level of corporeality of man and beasts— why was this necessary?[112] Perhaps Diotima's *scala amoris* is a faux conclusion and the *Symposium*'s teaching about love is actually incomplete.[113] We have further reason to doubt Diotima's tale of epistemic ecstasy as its end is harshly punctuated by the noisy entrance of an impious man of extraordinary excess. Alcibiades arrives drunk, staggering, shouting, wearing a wreath of ivy, and to the sound of flutes (212d). The Dionysiac figure of Alcibiades is perfectly antithetical to Diotima's Apollonian vision of the beautiful and the good.[114]

Socrates is notoriously ugly, poor, sober (no matter how much he drinks), and an unerotic figure; Alcibiades is notoriously handsome, rich, passionate, and an erotomaniac.[115] According to Diotima, Eros is the offspring of Poverty and Plenitude (203c), but no love arises between Socrates, a figure of poverty, and Alcibiades, a figure of plenitude. (Alcibiades's describes his unsuccessful attempt to seduce Socrates.) In the *Symposium*, Eros is presented as the "desire for completeness, and the adjunct of synoptic vision," and therefore, it "must encompass the ugly as well as the beautiful, or somehow make peace between them."[116] The *Symposium*'s teaching about love is incomplete, for Socrates's love of the divine and eternal is not reconciled with Alcibiades's love of the earthly and temporal. Although higher and lower love remain divided, the potential for their reconciliation is implied by Socrates's final argument in the *Symposium*, that "the same man might be capable of writing both comedy and tragedy" (223d). Mythical vision, whether Diotima's *scala amoris* or the myth of Er that concludes the *Republic*, is comic in the sense of a happy ending—the arrival at an eschaton. Process physics and pleonexia (as represented by Alcibiades's degenerate life) are tragic. A complete understanding of love must by synoptic, integrating the tragic with the comic. Alcibiades recounts Socrates's effort to educate him, that is, to reform his soul, but he instead returns to his base pursuits (216ab). If Socrates's attempt at education had been successful, the mixture of the poverty of Socrates and the plenitude of Alcibiades might have produced a complete man—an Alcibiades that understood love.

Both the *Symposium* and the *Hekatompathia* conclude with a synoptic vision of love: logos and mythos must be mixed to achieve a complete understanding. Mankind is divided by nature, part process physics and part poet or mythographer of a higher love. The speaker's moment of anagnorisis comes when he recognizes this divided nature, what he calls his *consuetudo* or *Second Nature* (L73.1.HN,17). When the Oracle advises: *gnōthi seauton* (know thyself), it is not prescribing knowledge of something, but the recognition of the epistemological limit that prevents access to the world of being.[117] Socrates explicitly claims to lack wisdom (*Apology* 21a–24a), a position he takes in opposition to the Sophists; his only claim to knowledge is with respect to love (*Symposium* 177d, 198d), which is actually a recognition of the limits of human knowledge, as a metaphysical description of higher love is not available.[118] The *Hekatompathia* reaches a similar conclusion: in its last sonnet, the gods of the heavens, earth, and seas are all made *subject unto Love* (L73.6.1–8). The speaker claims that he has *proveth by examples, or rather by manner of argument, A maiori ad minus* (HN): everything, including the speaker himself, falls within love's realm. The ontology of the *Hekatompathia* is grounded in a Socratic knowledge of the limits of human knowledge.[119]

The *Hekatompathia* is structured by, and progresses in according with, its central epistemic argument that man is divided in his acquisition of knowledge. The headnote of the final Series' lead sonnet summarizes the work's central conflict:

Here the Author, by faining a quarrell betwixt Loue and his Heart, under a shadow expresseth the tyrannie of the one, & the miserie of the other: to sturre up a just hatred of the ones injustice, and cause due compassion of the others unhappines. (L73.H.HN)

Love refers to lower love—transient and tyrannical process physics; the *Heart* is a metonym for the psyche or soul, which seeks permanence and fulfillment. The sequence investigates transient process physics through logos or logical discourse, especially in the L39 Series (the coincidence of opposites). But in the L64 and L50 Series, attempts to find a logos of higher love fail: the beloved, a poetic correlative of the world of being, remains beyond reach. The work then turns to myth, the *descensus ad infernos* in the L50 Series. Poetry or myth is the only epistemic mode by which higher love can be effectively treated. In the final L73 Series, logos and poetry are combined to achieve a compromise between *Love* and the *Heart*. In the final sonnet (L73.6), the dialectical pairs of process physics still rule (last stanza), but through the myth of the restaged Titanomachia (first two stanzas), the rule of *Love*, though sometimes *sow'r*, is also *sweet* (12). Mankind must live with this disorder, and the sequence culminates in a poetic celebration of love's mixed blessings.[120]

Like the *Symposium* and the *Republic*, the *Hekatompathia* is a contest between poetry and philosophy that ends in a draw or compromise.[121] Philosophy's logos cannot supply the telos or purposefulness that humans desire; only poetry can provide that.[122] But poetry alone is dangerous because it releases unbridled passions. In the *Republic*, "elaborate precautions... are required to preserve the best city from destruction, in particular from the passions, [and] the *thumos* of the guardians. ... *Thumos* must be regulated by the *dianoia* [discursive or logical thought]."[123] According to Rosen, the Platonic dialogues "suggest that this quarrel is not, and cannot be, resolved. Instead, to employ a Hegelian term, it is sublated into a demiurgic discourse that is neither poetry nor philosophy but philosophical poetry."[124] The *Hekatompathia* is such a demiurgic discourse.

The reader as demiurge

In the fourth Stage's deciphered message, the poet explains that he "Consumed things of poison" (EDI VIRI RES) in order that the reader might "Bring forth things of nobility/goodness" (EXI VIRI RES). Bacon drew from a diverse collection of Petrarchan and other poetic material to create a precisely structured organic work, which he then destroyed in order that the reader might repeat his process of creation. Writing poetry, then, is a process that begins with disorder—heterogenous intertextual material— and ends in order. Similarly, the reader who solves the Puzzle turns disordered material—the scrambled sonnets—into an ordered and organic work.

The original disorder resembles process physics love; the final ordered work resembles the desire for wholeness that is associated with higher love. The restoration of sonnet order follows a Lucretian strategy: the recombination of elements. Lucretius frequently makes an analogy between atoms forming material entities and letters forming words.[125] In the *Birth of Physics*, Michel Serres writes "that for linguistic atoms, as well as for the letters of matter, a given element placed here or located in such and such a vicinity is not the same as the same element elsewhere and in a different context or structure."[126] In the case of the *Hekatompathia*, the recombination of its elements—its sonnets—produces a structured, carefully staged philosophical argument. According to Robert Schuler, "Bacon habitually found his atomic physics in the scientific poem of Lucretius," and he adopted "striking Lucretian metaphors with which to conclude the first major division" of both the *Advancement* and the *Novum Organum*.[127] In Lucretius, creation arises from a combination of elements, which provides a model for both literary creation and the natural processes of the physical world. The *Hekatompathia* thrusts the reader into the role of creator: it provides the textual *materia* from which the reader, by means of recombination, restores the scrambled text to a coherent poetic collection.

As discussed in the above section on Series L73, love is a striving for wholeness, which reminds us of Aristophanes's myth in which divided lovers seek reunification. Writing poetry drawn from intertextual sources and reading a ruined text to discover its hidden order are both erotic endeavors—willful acts aimed at achieving completeness. No literary work was more willfully conceived than the *Hekatompathia*: its elaborate structure and complex network of intratextual links are a wonder to behold. It is the brainchild of an Apollonian poet (Sonnet L90.2 suggests this; see the discussion in the next chapter). Agathon describes the central role of love in Apollonian art:

> And who will deny that the creative power by which all living things are begotten and brought forth is the very genius of Love? Do we not, moreover, recognize that in every art and craft the artist and the craftsman who work under the direction of this same god achieve the brightest fame, while those that lack his influence grow old in the shadow of oblivion? It was longing and desire that led Apollo to found the arts of archery, healing, and divination—so he, too, was a scholar in the school of Love. (*Symposium*, 197a)

In this model of art, higher love drives inquiry or discourse toward a harmonious solution to the problem or conflict defined at the work's outset. In the *Hekatompathia*, the separation of heart and body that begins the sequence ultimately resolves in a compromise in the final Series. Its inquiry includes both Apollonian and Dionysian art—logos and mythos, respectively. Although the Apollonian viewpoint does not triumph over the Dionysian, the sequence when viewed as a whole presents itself as carefully crafted and organic—the characteristics of Apollonian art. The purpose of the Puzzle is to train the reader in the "school of love," to force him or her into the role of a demiurge, for only then will the work's esoteric teachings be truly understood and appreciated.

15
Conclusions

The *Hekatompathia*'s elaborate practice of concealment is stunning in its scope and complexity. Although unique in this and other respects, its poetics are derivative of continental humanist poetics, medieval exegetical methods, and long-standing rhetoric practices.[1] Its strict construction upon a cosmological foundation, sophisticated use of rhetoric, elaborate structures, and extensive use of metonyms and similitudes, can shed light on the poetic practices of other early modern works. The poet's purpose and application of these methods is more visible than in other works because the *Hekatompathia* adheres to a precisely defined structure that is fully revealed by solving its Puzzle. The *Restored Hekatompathia* presents scholars with an extraordinary opportunity to extend our knowledge of early modern poetry.

Hermeneutics: concealment and semiosis

The *Hekatompathia* continuously warns its readers that interpretation is required through its paratexts, structural incoherences, and rhetorical devices. The challenge faced by the reader is to select the proper hermeneutic procedure and apply it carefully to these authorial signals. But how can we know that a literary interpretation is consistent with these subtle signals and not the product of the interpreter's imagination? How do we practice exegesis and avoid eisegesis? In his preface to *Wisdom of the Ancients* (discussed in the first chapter), Bacon acknowledges that readers often place meanings upon a work that "it was never meant to bear." Yet, he often finds "a conformity and connexion with the thing signified, so close and so evident, that one cannot help believing such a signification to have been designed and meditated from the first, and purposely shadowed out."[2] Bacon explains the reason for this shadowing or concealment:

> Parables have been used in two ways, and (which is strange) for contrary purposes. For they serve to disguise and veil the meaning, and they serve also to clear and throw light upon it. ... I mean the employment of

parables as a method of teaching. ... If anyone wish to let new light on any subject into men's minds, and that without offence or harshness, he must still go the same way and call in the aid of similitudes.[3]

Bacon's teaching method seeks to avoid contradicting a student's preexisting, deeply ingrained beliefs (discussed in Chapter 4, "Order, topical invention, and arrangement" section). The introduction of new ideas, especially if radical, requires concealment: only over time will students allow new principles to replace preexisting beliefs. Concealment also has the advantage that if a significant effort has been expended to unveil the new ideas, they will be prized all the more.

The unfolding of concealed significance requires the recognition of what Bacon calls "similitudes." The *Hekatompathia*'s use of similitudes could not be more extensive: the links that bind Catalog, Index, and QA Ties to CipherLines; the Sequential Ties between sonnets; the In-10 Sequential Ties in Stage 6; the Hexameral themes that point to the location of sonnets within a Series; myths and pagan gods that figure a state of mind or a natural force; headnotes and sidenotes that explicitly point to external texts; the dual epistemic modes that bear significance throughout the work; and the process physics behind dozens of paired opposites. The identification of similitudes is the matching of signifiers to significands. Michel Foucault argues that for sixteenth-century literature, hermeneutics is a matter of reading signs:

> Let us call the totality of the learning and skills that enable one to make the signs speak and to discover their meaning, hermeneutics; let us call the totality of the learning and skills that enable one to distinguish the location of the signs, to define what constitutes them as signs, and to know how and by what laws they are linked, semiology: the sixteenth century superimposed hermeneutics and semiology in the form of similitude. To search for meaning is to bring to light a resemblance. To search the law governing signs is to discover the things that are alike. The grammar of beings is an exegesis of these things. ... 'Nature' is trapped in the thin layer that holds semiology and hermeneutics one above the other; it is neither mysterious nor veiled, it offers itself to our cognition, which it sometimes leads astray, only in so far as this superimposition necessarily includes a slight degree of non-coincidence between the resemblances.[4]

The hermeneutics of early modern poetics, then, is the practice of semiosis. Foucault cites Bacon in his critique of similitudes: "He shows them, shimmering before our eyes, vanishing as one draws near, then re-forming again a moment later, a little further off. They are *idols*."[5] Yet, interpretation is not simply a matter of deciphering of individual signs but also the discovery of an underlying "grammar," a "network of signs" that connects the poet's imagined world to the natural world. A cosmological model provides cohesion, for it is the glue that holds together this network of signs. Thus, the deciphering of signs is constrained by both the resemblance between signifier and significand, and its place within a work's grammar, which, in certain poetry, is a model of the natural world. Once that model is identified, it sharply constrains the range of possible meanings for a text's signs, which increases our confidence that we have read the signs correctly.

The *Hekatompathia*'s cosmology is established upfront, in the first two Series, which provides the reader with critical guidance for reading the rest of the text, a practice essential to solving the Puzzle (see Chapter 3). In this poetics, the identification of a work's cosmology or natural philosophy is the first and most essential step in the hermeneutic process, and any misidentification of this foundational grammar will result in an inaccurate reading. For example, if we assume a cosmology consistent with Reformed theology, but the work's foundation is instead an Epicurean materialism, we will likely misread its signs. For scientific poetry (discussed below), one begins by identifying the work's underlying cosmology or natural philosophy. In Chapter 3, our analysis of the first 17 (unscrambled) sonnets revealed two types of love and the two epistemic modes (without solving the Puzzle). Also, the coincidence of opposites is apparent in the sequence even prior to restoration. However, the work's strong embrace of Epicurean materialism is not apparent prior to solving the Puzzle.

The identification of a work's underlying cosmology may be difficult to make if that cosmology is heterodox, as it will likely be hidden to avoid conflict with prevailing Christian beliefs. Bacon warns of the danger of speaking openly in the first fable of *Wisdom of the Ancients*, in which he claims that Cassandra unintentionally harmed her people by divulging too much (see Chapter 1). The practice of esotericism frequently goes unrecognized, according to Stanley Rosen. "The skepticism of many contemporary scholars toward the practice of esotericism in previous epochs is not supported by an accurate knowledge of the history of Western thought prior to the Enlightenment."[6]

For Bacon, rhetoric, that is, the delivery of arguments, is inseparable from logical argument (contra Ramus) because it has such a powerful effect on human faculties.[7] The reader must be sensitive to the subtle, and not so subtle, signals that rhetoric provides. In *Wisdom of the Ancients*, Bacon argues that one such stimulus to interpretation, a "sign, and one of no small value," is that "these fables contain a hidden and involved meaning; which is, that some of them are so absurd and stupid upon the face of the narrative taken by itself, that they may be said to give notice from afar and cry out that there is a parable below."[8] Of course, the *Hekatompathia*'s faux ending, in which Cupid is killed off, is "absurd and stupid." Bacon's use of concealment and rhetorical signals owes much to Plato, who, according to Montaigne, wrote in a veiled mode, a deception that often goes unrecognized by critics.[9] The reader's task then is to uncover what is hidden by recognizing the authorial signals that rhetorical and other devices (e.g., paratextual material) may provide. An analysis of the work's structure is perhaps the most powerful tool available to the critic because form follows function: the poet designed the structure to serve the work's argument. In our examination of the *Hekatompathia*'s structure, an analysis of the first 17 sonnets proved decisive. A work's beginning and end points are particularly valuable to understanding its path and aims.

In the Bacon quotation that began this section, parables are said to be employed for the purpose of teaching. The identification of a work's signs and the uncovering of its concealed knowledge are cognitive challenges meant to ensnare the reader's mind. This study began with Nietzsche's dictum: "everything deep loves the mask." What we ourselves uncover is more deeply valued, and the process of digging out the truth, one shovelful at a time, makes it all the more memorable. The *Hekatompathia* is an extreme case, but this poetics—really an educational rhetoric—runs deep in the Elizabethan era.

Sidney's *Defence* begins with an anecdote about his instructor in horsemanship, John Pietro Pugliano. He extolls, with the "fertileness of the Italian wit," the virtues of his faculty, praising horsemanship as mankind's noblest profession. He then proceeds to praise the horses themselves in the most laudatory terms. Sidney says that if he had not been grounded in reason, "I think he would have persuaded me to have wished myself a horse." The skilled horseman respects the horse and gently guides it. In the *Defence*, rider and horse are being implicitly compared to poet and reader: the rider guides his horse in a manner that allows the horse to feel that it still exercises control. The poet must similarly guide the reader in a manner that sustains his belief that he is in control and avoids infringing on his ego. Sidney concludes "that self-love is better than any gilding to make that seem gorgeous wherein ourselves are parties."[10] R. W. Maslen argues that everyone in the *Defence* is "equally addicted to self-love—the text is populated with Puglianos."[11] Bacon's educational method also leverages self-love: each step in solving the Puzzle provides the puzzle-solver with a moment of gratification. Bacon's educational model is derived from Plato's educational model. Socrates acts as a "midwife" and not a dispenser of doctrine because this allows the disciple to enjoy for himself the pleasurable act of discovery and creation. The creative function, at least in part, has been transferred from author to reader. Sidney's strategy is not to make a Cyrus (a prototypical hero), but to make a maker of Cyruses.[12] Poetry, then, is a form of husbandry: the breeding of a poet, philosopher, or other thinker.

Another tenet of Plato's educational method that the *Hekatompathia* practices is the requirement that philosophy be veiled. As Laurence Lampert explains, "The mix of high pleasure and vast ambition definitive of the philosopher is bound to appear as vice if paraded in public."[13] And just as essential, veiling engages the reader in the process of unveiling. In the *Hekatompathia*, the puzzle-solver must fully embrace Bacon's marvelous, complex system to solve it. For then, as Socrates informs us in the *Phaedrus*, a discourse's knowledge will be "written in the soul of the learner" (276A). Similarly, Sidney argues that poetry has "strange effects," meaning that it has a metamorphic effect upon the reader. The object of the Puzzle, then, is to harness the metamorphic powers of poetry to forcefully engrave the poet's message in the reader's "soul." The Puzzle is an intensification, taken to extraordinary lengths, of what poetry has always done.

Scientific poetry and the literary microcosm

Bacon and his contemporaries considered scientific poems such as Lucretius's *De rerum natura* and Virgil's *Georgics* to be a didactic form of poetry. Written in epic meter, these poems were valued just as highly as epic.[14] According to Andrew Wallace, Bacon's *The Advancement of Learning* shows evidence of "a protracted engagement with Vergil's [*Georgics*]."[15] In *Advancement*, Bacon quotes the *Georgics* (3.289–90) and compares its purpose to that of the *Aeneid*:

> To instruct and suborne Action and active life, these Georgickes of the mind concerning the husbandry & tillage therof, are no lesse worthy then the heroical descriptions of vertue, duty, & felicity wherefore the maine & primitive division of Morall knowledge seemeth to be into the EXEMPLAR or PLATFORME of GOOD, and the REGIMENT or CULTURE OF THE MIND; The one describing the nature of Good the other prescribing rules how to subdue, apply and accomodate the will of man thereunto.[16]

Though read as an agricultural manual, Bacon rates the *Georgics* as worthy as the *Aeneid*, for it raises the minds of men, not through an example of goodness such as Aeneas, but as a practical guide that develops or cultivates the mind.[17] The *Hekatompathia* is a "Georgickes of the mind": its purpose is to teach the reader to accept and acclimate to the harsh world of becoming—love's oppressive process physics—and to utilize his or her willpower to rise to action. The mode of representation in the *Georgics* and the *Hekatompathia* is unlike traditional allegory (even in its use of myth). The *Hekatompathia* practices a more direct poetics in which philosophy and poetry are not easily distinguishable. Montaigne believed that "Philosophy is nothing else but a sophisticated poesie."[18] Sidney sees Plato as the source of this tradition: he argues that Plato recognized poetry's great power and "therefore made mistress Philosophy very often borrow the masking raiment of Poesy."[19]

In scientific poetry (works built upon a cosmological model), all meaning derives from a preexisting, unified model, as James Coulter describes it:

> Knowledge, that is philosophical knowledge, and apparently of both substantive points *and* method—*must* precede any art. [The artist is] a creator of organisms which parallel the Great Living Thing, the Cosmos, which had been fashioned by the divine Demiurge. This model of artistic creation, with its strong emphasis on the conscious intellect of the creator, when added to the general tendency of a Platonic literary aesthetic to emphasize intention, made a conception of unity rooted in the artist's directing consciousness even more prevalent.[20]

The poet is an architect who deliberately constructs a literary microcosm or paracosm, an image of the world, based on a preexisting cosmological model. Robert Stillman argues that this paracosm is not an allegory, but a fictive world or "epistemic construct" built in accordance with the poet's cosmological model.[21] Sidney's concept of a paracosm, a "golden world," assumes that the cosmos adheres to a plan or order (such as the coincidence of opposites) and that this order is transparent to investigation.[22] However, the Sidneian poet is not strictly bound to nature, rather "he goeth hand in hand with Nature, not enclosed within the narrow warrant of her gifts, but freely ranging only within the zodiac of his own wit."[23] With this new role assigned to the imagination, Stillman claims that "the *Defence* advances arguments on behalf of the preeminence of poetry that are unprecedented in the history of European poetics."[24] The *Hekatompathia* follows the basic principles that Sidney outlined in his *Defence* and provides an extraordinary example of his poetics: the sequence's cosmological model of love as the coincidence of opposites, operating through two powers, dictates sonnet order, the progress of the speaker's quest, and the deciphering of cryptographic messages.

Stillman asserts that Sidney is committed to "a universalizing epistemology: the poet's 'golden world' achieves its legitimacy and power only because the Ideas to which it lends rhetorical substance have the status of natural law."[25] S. K. Heninger makes a similar argument in his study of the poetics of Sidney and Spenser: the poet is a "maker" who constructs a fictive world in imitation of the natural world.[26] This poetics is radically different from Aristotle's theory of tragedy, which rests upon the playwright's intuitive "ability to organize plots" that follow a reasonable or necessary path.[27] It is also distinct from traditional allegory, which is not grounded in natural law.[28] Of course, this poetics is foreign to present-day poetic sensibilities as modern poetry is rarely founded upon a cosmological model.

One consequence of understanding a poem as a paracosm is that it must form an organic, unified whole, like the natural world that it reflects. The belief that a literary composition must be constructed as an organic entity is found in Plato, who believed that a properly written work is constructed in a manner such that its parts bear an appropriate and necessary relationship to each other.[29] The *Hekatompathia*, with its clearly defined Series, Hexameral rings, cryptographic backbone, and multiple indexing devices, is surely organic. Plato's advocacy of structure influenced Basil, whose *Hexameron* is patterned on the six days of creation, a literary tradition that persisted through to Bacon's time (e.g., Du Bartas's *La Semaine ou creation du Monde*). Organic works must be interpreted using a hermeneutics in which the exegete discovers the *status* or *causa* of a work—its central argument (see Chapter 3). According to Stillman, the exegete must be committed "to reading whole books to recover complete arguments."[30] Solving the Puzzle enforces a nearly exhaustive close reading of the *Hekatompathia*'s text.

The poet's paracosm is not identical to the natural world but an imitation of it, governed by laws internal to its own organization. The poet was thought to engage in a process analogous to that of the Creator, producing a microcosm shaped rationally by number and measure. The blend of scientific and literary modes of inquiry is foreign to our Romantic and post-Romantic aesthetic sympathies; however, to an early modern reader, nature, art, and mathematics were all components of a universal system of knowledge (quadrivium and trivium). In organic works, the poet is a maker, an artisan, who consciously and deliberately creates his work with a purpose in mind. Stillman argues that the microcosm is "a world in which the maker's intentions, at once clear and demonstrably coherent, both can and must be recovered by the best hermeneutic means available—by means, that is, of dialectic and rhetoric." A universal truth "stands at the center of the narrative [which] is simultaneously associated, like Melanchthon's *loci*, with the author's intention (*voluptas*), chief cause (*summam causam*) or main argument (*status dicendi*)."[31] Sidney calls this the work's "fore-conceit," which Stillman describes:

> Sidney conceives of the Idea [i.e., fore-conceit] as innate to that same erected wit as an impression remaining from his Maker inscribed within (hence, innate to) what the *Defence* calls (in good Philippist [i.e., Philip Melanchthon] fashion) the mind's own divine essence. ... When Sidney writes about "notions" of virtue and vice, he treats them as *notitiae* (innate ideas), which poetic images are best able to bring to consciousness. Meaning is not something separable from the poem—lodged in some transcendental order of Ideas veiled by textual symbols that required allegorical decoding. Meaning happens in the verbal dynamic of the poem itself, as sparks of truth are fanned into flames of knowledge, as speaking pictures give substance to Ideas innately unknowable apart from their exemplification. ... Such "notions," in turn, are authoritative because they are inscribed by the divine hand, they are powerful because they recall us to our nature (our Nature as the Maker first made it), and they are necessary, because they enable what Sidney calls *architectonike*, "the knowledge of a man's self."[32]

The essential goal of this poetics is to uncover "the mind's own divine essence," which follows not from transcendental entities such as Platonic forms, but from our innate human nature. Sidney's "right poet," according to Stillman, "has a purpose inextricably connected to God—since self-knowledge entails in Sidney's distinctively Christian anthropology, an enjoyment of what is divine in one's own nature."[33] In the *Hekatompathia*, this anthropology, rather than Christian, is a reflection of the natural world's process physics—what Sonnet L73.1 calls our *Second Nature* (17) or *consuetudo* (HN). In this new poetics, poetry is reconceptualized as an "autonomous form of knowledge"; it "transcends the categories of the sacred and the secular since its scope is awareness of one's own divine essence, an 'architectonic' species of knowledge."[34] Tasso, in his *Discourses on the Heroic Poem*, suggests that the encoding of *discordia concors* into a literary work (which the *Hekatompathia* does) elevates the work's "status [to that] of a creative demigod."[35]

The *Hekatompathia* presents two domains: the macrocosm, which is dominated by process physics, and the microcosm, the world of the speaker's mind. The sequence's tension arises from the speaker's thwarted desire for fulfillment in the macrocosm. In the final Series, he recognizes that the microcosm (himself) consists of the same primordial "flux"—love-physics—as the macrocosm. Although the macrocosm is overpowering, the microcosm includes the speaker's willpower, which he compares to the macrocosm's natural forces (L73.2). The final Series defines the relationship between the macrocosm and microcosm, a departure from traditional medieval philosophy in favor of a new Renaissance worldview. Harry Berger Jr. describes this new worldview:

Man is in two worlds, but they are no longer the medieval worlds of flesh and spirit, or nature and grace, which, even when antithetical, were hierarchically ordered in a single universe: now there is a world around man hemming him in and a world within pressing out from the center of self, and these two worlds are discontinuous, for the first is actual, and the second is imaginary or hypothetical. What is important here is the awareness that the first world must be articulated, the limit asserted, to make the second world significant.[36]

The speaker recognizes his own limit, that is, his inferiority to the powers of the macrocosm in the sequence's final sonnet: *a majori ad minus* (L73.6.HN). This is what Berger calls the "Axiom of Self-Limitation," the necessity of recognizing the outside force as the greater. In Berger's view, this makes the "golden world," and more generally, the Renaissance imagination, possible.[37] By asserting this limitation, the speaker has carved out a space for himself, in which he may exercise his willpower. This fulfills the promise of going beyond Petrarch's worldview; he sets forth his worldview in the counter-Petrarchan proverb, *selfe doe, selfe have* (5.12).

A revised Petrarchism

Patrick Cheney claims that "three grids [were] central to [Spenser's] literary career: a generic grid linking epic and lyric; a gender grid linking the beloved and God; and a theological grid linking fame and glory."[38] This provides a useful framework for our analysis because the *Hekatompathia* employs all three grids. The *Canzoniere* also employs these grids, though with significant differences. These three grids will now be taken up in order.

The sonnet genre mixes the worldly topics of epic with the more personal concerns of lyric poetry—what Thomas Greene calls the "lyricization of epic materials."[39] Sonnet sequences are a form of lyric poetry in which the speaker, in his pursuit of the beloved, undertakes an *itinerarium mentis* or soteriological journey. Although a personal journey, its topics are those found in epic: fundamental questions about the nature of the world, man, virtue, and love. Augustine's *Confessions* is the *sui generis* of this fusing of a personal narrative with cosmic concerns. It is not an autobiography in the modern sense (despite its biographical content) but the recounting of a spiritual journey that completes long before the work's end—the remainder of the work is devoted to theological and philosophical issues.[40] By turning inward, Augustine discovers God; in the *Hekatompathia*, an inward turn reveals the cosmic love and willpower that lie within the speaker himself. A sonnet sequence may include discursive argument or mimetic representation, but it is primarily an affective rhetoric: its "epic materials" are viewed through the affective lens of the speaker's experience. The *Hekatompathia* is relentlessly reductive: in its process physics, love dominates both the macrocosm and microcosm (the speaker's mind), and this singular physical principle makes the work organic, concise, and encyclopedic. The sonnet genre is indebted to Alexandrian epyllion, a form promoted by Callimachus, who argued that epic was overlarge: "big book, big evil" (*mega biblion, mega kakon*). The compactness of lyric is applied to the expansive range of epic, which is made possible by a universalizing love.

Representation occurs not through mimesis but arises from structure, and by means of amplification through repetition—variation on a well-defined theme or themes. The *Hekatompathia* employs amplification prodigiously, for example, in its Hexameral rings and assertion of love's two powers. The widespread use of repetition and variation is stylistically mannerist (if mannerism is narrowly defined as "a combinatory order of recurrent schemes").[41] Jon Quitslund believes that although Spenser, unlike mannerists, subordinated art to nature, he nonetheless was "clearly mannerist in his representation of nature."[42] Tasso describes the relationship between a theme and its variants in his *Discourses on the Heroic Poem*:

> Yet the poem that contains so great a variety of matters none the less should be one, one in form and soul; and all these things should be so combined that each concerns the other, corresponds to the other, and so depends on the other necessarily or verisimilarly that removing any one part or changing its place would destroy the whole. And if that is true, the art of composing a poem resembles the plan [*ragione*] of the universe, which is composed of contraries, as that of music is. For if it were not multiple it would not be a whole or a plan, as Plotinus says.[43]

The *Hekatompathia* precisely adheres to a "plan"—the structure of the restored sequence, as revealed by the Puzzle. Like epic, it is both expansive ("a variety of matters") and reductive to "one in form and soul" (organic). This epic-lyric form is not unique to the *Hekatompathia* but a characteristic of Petrarchan sonnet sequences. As discussed in the previous chapter, Patrick Cheney argues that Petrarch exerted a profound influence on Spenser and that every book of the *Faerie Queene* "dilates on Petrarchism, with Book III a virtual index of Spenser's counter-Petrarchism."[44]

The *Hekatompathia* mixes not only epic and lyric, but tragedy and comedy. In the *Symposium*, the first three speeches present a tragic vision in which love is process physics; the next three speeches present a comic vision in which love is a potential cure. It ends with Socrates's argument that "the same man might be capable of writing both comedy and tragedy—that the tragic poet might be a comedian as well" (223d). Socrates has concisely encapsulated the underlying theme of the *Symposium*: the division between tragedy and comedy is concomitant with the division between mankind's rational self (noesis) and sensual self (aesthesis).[45] Poetry must engage in both the rational logos of philosophy and the intoxication of Eros (desire), and then harmonize these two epistemic modes. Yes, intoxication is an epistemic mode—a Dionysian one—and integral to this poetics. Whether the drunkenness in the *Symposium* or the frenzied desire for the beloved in sonnet sequences, the merger of tragic and comic modes requires intemperance. In the *Hekatompathia*, the merger begins in the penultimate Series (L50) and is complete before the start of the final Series. The work's tragic component is the inescapable process physics; the comic component is the speaker's discovery of his willpower and the cosmic energy that resides within himself.

Bacon's dismemberment of his sonnet sequence presents the reader with a tragedy: it ends with the speaker in a frantic mental state, having just scattered Cupid's ashes to the winds. This leaves the reader or puzzle-solver in the role of Isis, who collects up Osiris's scattered members. The *Restored Hekatompathia* exhibits a comedic form, moving from disorder to an ending in which the speaker happily accepts the human condition (*consuetudo*; L73.1).[46] The puzzle-solver's job, then, was to make a tragic work into a comic one. Petrarchan sonnet sequences, the *Hekatompathia* included, are necessarily a tragic-comic form, proving Socrates's observation, quoted above, that "the tragic poet might be a comedian as well" (223d).

What makes the *Hekatompathia* counter-Petrarchan is its equitable balance between the inner and outer worlds, which is expressly set forth in the two-sun Neo-Latin poem (L90.2/45) and in the final Series. This builds upon the *Canzoniere*, which takes the revolutionary step of demarcating the inner world, the microcosm, and through Petrarch's rich imagination, making it the center point of the work's poetics.[47] Petrarch accepts the macrocosm/microcosm dualism of Platonism, but Laura's earthly existence remains separated from his conscious experience of her, a division that is never resolved. Despite his acceptance of dualism, Petrarch "refuses to give the soul an absolute priority" over the material world.[48] In contrast, the *Hekatompathia* makes the inner world the ontological equal of the outer world; further, it is given a measure of independence through the human faculty of the will.

Examining the difference between Laura and the *Hekatompathia*'s beloved is instructive. Laura lives in the world of becoming: her hair is a "thousand sweet knots" (90.2); she ages and dies; she is alleged to be a historical person that Petrarch saw on a particular day.[49] In contrast, the *Hekatompathia*'s beloved is transcendent: she has no name; her physical characteristics are depicted only in a wholly conventional manner; she neither ages nor dies; we are told she is "but supposed" in a preface. This beloved is a mirror of the poet's consciousness and has no discernable existence that is independent of the poet. In the final Series, only her eyes remain as a ghostly dispenser of fate (L73.6). The speaker is cured not by any change in his relationship to the beloved but by the elevation of the ontological status of his own consciousness to a level commensurate with the overwhelming power of love (or flux) in the physical world. In contrast, in the *Canzoniere*, the earthly Laura and the speaker's divine image of her remain divided and unresolved. The speaker's inner self does not undergo any change in its ontological status. Cheney's second grid, the link between the beloved and God (or, more generally, the transcendent), diverges sharply in these two works. The *Hekatompathia* ends with the poet's transformed consciousness: the speaker's mind accommodates itself to the outer world. In contrast, the *Canzoniere* ends with the poet weeping over the time spent loving a mortal thing (365.1–2). Petrarch's beloved, an earthbound image of the divine, does not ultimately amend his consciousness; a peace between the inner and outer worlds is never achieved, and the only hope that remains is with God (365.14).

Cheney's third grid, the "theological grid linking fame and glory," refers to the poet's desire for personal fame, which, in the *Canzoniere*, conflicts with the humble reverence that he owes to God (the central topic in the *Secretum*). Of course, poets often lay claim to the immortality of their verse: as discussed in Chapter 3's section on translation, E. K., the glosser of the *Shepheardes Calender*, asserts that "monuments of Poetry abide for ever." He then quotes celebrated lines of Ovid and Horace.[50] In contrast, Bacon, in his *Protrepticon*, expresses the hope that the queen will take notice of his work, but then pulls back, warning his book not to hope "for so great future developments: the Attic ear does not approve of vain roaring" (21–22).[51] By his reference to a purported Athenian dislike of poetic self-aggrandizement, he appears to be rejecting that habit of vanity found in other poets. However, though he makes no high claim for his sequence, he surely must have had high hopes for its reception given the work's scope, evidence of learning, and, of course, the unprecedented Puzzle.

Yet perhaps he has engaged covertly in poetic self-aggrandizement. The two prefaces written by "C. Downhalus" (see Chapter 3) claim the *Hekatompathia* as the worthy descendent of antiquity's great poetry, and further, that its poet, "excellent in both talent and art, taught the Muses to speak British words," implying that other English poets, up to that point, had failed to do so.[52] Scholars have assumed "Downhalus" to be a Latinization of Downhall and found one candidate with that last name but whose first name does not begin with "C." None of the other prefaces are undersigned with a Latinized name. Further, "Downhallus" would be a more appropriate Latinization. Oddly, Downhalus's first preface conforms to the *Hekatompathia*'s unique 18-line sonnet structure (including ababcc rhymes). As such, his style may coyly suggest that this preface's author is actually the *Hekatompathia*'s poet and that Downhalus is a pseudonym. "Down" can mean hill or an elevated pastureland; "halus" is a Middle English spelling of "hallowed." Downhalus's first poem, addressing the muses, suggests a transfer of artistic talent from Mount Helicon to an English hill:

> Is Helicon **your onely paradise?**
> Hath Britan **soyle no hill, no heath, no well,**
> **No wood, no wit, wherein you list to dwell?**   (4–6)

The muses reside on a hallowed hill. The subject of both Downhalus prefaces is the *Hekatompathia*'s foundation in the hallowed poetry of antiquity, making "Downhalus" a particularly appropriate name for the author of these two prefaces. Curiously, a preface by "Downhalus" also appears in the poet's Latin *Antigone*, and it too praises the poet. Hallowed ground—the burial mound that Antigone desires for her brother—is, of course, central to the play. Is "Downhalus," then, a pseudonym? Paratextual material such as prefaces do not guarantee historical fact, and as often as not, slyly carry the fiction of the poetical text into the external world. "Downhalus," if a paratextual fiction, cleverly allows the poet to openly declare his grand ambition for his work without engaging in the "vain roaring" that the ancient Athenians disliked. In contrast, Ovid and Horace openly and loudly declare their ambitions.[53] Petrarch is open about his poetic ambitions, but also uneasy about them—an important topic in his *Secretum*.

An Apollonian poetics

The *Hekatompathia*'s speaker often declares that his love is different from that of others, an assertion also found in the *Canzoniere*. The speaker's most revealing declaration of uniqueness is found in the "two suns" Neo-Latin poem:

> Other fortunate young men, whom alluring Venus
>   has made suitable for love
> are wont to crave the dusky dark of night
>   and curse the dawn.
> far dearer to me is the fair consort
>   of chilly old man Tithon
> when she comes at the start of the rising day,
>   bringing for me two suns.   (Tr. of L90.2.1–8)

Nighttime is when one practices Bacchic rites; daytime is the hour when one drinks from Helicon's learned well. In Bacchus-inspired poetry, the prophetic poet leads the reader to epiphany; Apollonian poetry, in contrast, is ordered and normally obedient to rules and form.[54] The sonnet genre, with its strict obedience to a preset form, is Apollonian in character. The *Restored Hekatompathia* is highly ordered, and when rules are broken, it is done with a specific intent and within the context of its overall plan. A comparison is made between these two poetic modes in Sonnet 15, in which the rude songs of satyrs are compared with the beloved's voice. The beloved's singing is ranked as a *science* (4), and it is imagined that if Apollo were to judge her in a music contest, she would win against any contestant:

> **For though rude** Satyres **like** Marsias **songs,**
> **And** Choridon **esteem his oaten quill:**
> **Compare them with hir voice, and both are ill.**   (15.10–12)

The beloved's refined music is superior to the Bacchanal song of a satyr and the rustic sound of a shepherd's pipe (*oaten quill*). The reference to *Marsias* alludes to the well-known myth in which Apollo and the satyr Marsyas engage in a music contest: Apollo wins the contest and is crowned with laurel; Marsyas is flayed. Edgar Wind offers an insightful interpretation of this myth (as portrayed in Raphael's fresco in the Stanza della Segnatura):

> In the drunken speech of Alcibiades [*Symposium*, 215ab], Socrates himself was called a Marsyas, and that this dubious appellation followed immediately after his description as a 'Silenus figure', in which he was compared to a deceptive contraption in statuary shops which shows outwardly the face of an ugly man, but, when opened, proves to be full of gods. Like Silenus, Marsyas was a follower of Bacchus, and his flute was the Bacchic instrument of arousing the dark and uncontrollable passions which conflict with the purity of Apollo's lyre. The musical contest between Apollo and Marsyas was therefore concerned with the relative powers of Dionysian darkness and Apollonian clarity; and if the contest ended with the flaying of Marsyas, it was because flaying was itself a Dionysian rite, a tragic ordeal of purification by which the ugliness of the outward man was thrown off and the beauty of his inward self revealed. That Socrates, who was a disciple of Apollo and had adopted from an inscription on Apollo's temple at Delphi his own maxim, 'Know thyself', should be figuratively described as a Silenus and a Marsyas, meant that his ruthless pursuit of bewildering questions was but the disguise of an inward clarity—a disguise which was indispensable because it reckoned with the twofold nature of man.[55]

Bacon, like Socrates, is a "disciple of Apollo," practicing a poetics that seeks clarity and whose aim is to understand the true nature of the self. The beloved is a thoroughly Apollonian figure: she is equated to the sun in the "two suns" Neo-Latin poem (quoted above). At the same time, may we not say that the speaker is "flayed," that is, suffers, throughout most of the sequence? His suffering under love is a "tragic ordeal of purification," for without some ordeal, it seems unlikely that he would ever recognize the strength and willpower that resides within himself.[56] To "know one-self," one must endure a painful peregrination—the traversal of an oppressive labyrinth. Pico, according to Wind, believes that Apollonian inspiration "requires in us the dismemberment of Osiris, whom he identified with Bacchus."[57] Michael J. B. Allen, citing Rabelais's *Quart Livre*, Plato's *Laws*, and Ficino's letters, finds that "it is this Bacchic wine that paradoxically gives us the sobriety of soul to interpret Apollonian mysteries, the nine hypotheses of the *Parmenides*."[58]

The *Hekatompathia* does not lack Dionysian art: the speaker is "flayed" in the second sonnet when his heart is separated from his body; in the second Subsequence, the frenzied speaker dismisses love and calls for others to revel with him; throughout, affective language is used to persuade. Yet, the work's precise and logical structure, carefully crafted arguments, and clearly articulated conclusion demonstrate the practice of Apollonian poetics. The *Hekatompathia* is structured like the deceptive Silenus statues discussed in the first chapter, which outwardly display the ugly wine-god, the satyr Silenus, but contain a hidden beauty on the inside. The reader must solve the Puzzle to discover the sequence's true Apollonian nature.

Hermeneutics, old and new

The *Hekatompathia*'s poetics did not arise *ex nihilo*—it is deeply rooted in the poetic practices of antiquity and the medieval period. James Simpson, in his study of Alan's *Anticlaudianus* and Gower's *Confessio Amantis*, describes their poetics, which might also serve as a description of the *Hekatompathia*'s essential poetic practices.

> Both poems... are characterized by profound structural incoherences, which provide intriguing difficulties for a reader. In attempting to understand the sense behind these incoherences, we as readers are invited to participate in the construction of meaning, and to participate ourselves, therefore, in the processes of learning represented in the poems. The ultimate aim of both Alan and Gower is not so much to represent the formation of the soul, but to enact that formation in the

reader. The meaning of both works is to be located less in their represented narratives, than in the sense of those narratives, a sense which
is understood only through the reader's act of interpretation. Their
mode of meaning is, in short, literary rather than discursive. So, although they both provide philosophic and educative 'information' in
the more neutral sense of that word, that is not their prime function;
the essential and, I think, intended effect of these literary structures
is to inform the soul of the reader—to bring the soul of the reader to its
own ideal state, or 'form.' [The] fundamental principle by which my
argument is directed is that an understanding of literary shaping is the
premise of understanding the philosophical meaning of a work.[59]

Like the *Anticlaudianus* and *Confessio Amantis*, the *Hekatompathia*
exhibits "profound structural incoherences," requires extensive interpretation on the part of the reader, has a deeply embedded philosophical
meaning, and seeks to enact the "formation of the soul" in the reader. Each
of these three pillars of the *Hekatompathia*'s poetics is considered below.

The *Hekatompathia* contains extensive and "profound structural
incoherences," including its faux ending and the scrambling of its sonnets.
The reader is explicitly "invited to participate in the construction of meaning" by the careful rearrangement of its sonnets to form a perfectly
ordered sequence.[60] Meaning cannot be separated from order, as Frank
Kermode reminds us: "I cannot make sense of a part without placing it in
relation to a whole: that is common sense, and also a basic principle of
interpretation-theory."[61] Unfortunately, commentators often try to force a
text to fit into a simple narrative model, or they attribute incoherences to
errors in transmission or lapses in the quality of writing. The attempt to
save a text from its own complexity is misguided; instead, the commentator should recognize the difference between meaning and truth—between
a literal reading and the reconstruction of the text that the poet expects
the reader to perform. The reader must recognize that any "structural
incoherence" or elaborate internal structure is a call to exegesis.[62] Kermode believes that "there must be supra-literary forces [or] cultural pressures, which tend to make us seek narrative coherence, just as we expect
a conundrum to have an answer, and a joke a point. Our whole practice of
reading is founded on such expectations."[63]

Too often critics approach works with a preexisting set of normative
expectations, based on a work's genre, or some social or cultural model.
They then assume that it follows a particular set of rules or adheres to
certain premises. Instead, each work has the power to define its own set
of rules, often varying or inverting those rules from what is commonly
practiced. Aesthetic norms "are never simply given," according to Gerald

Bruns. "They are in any case *not* presiding universals; they emerge in the hermeneutic identity of the singular, irreplaceable work itself."[64] The *Hekatompathia* defines its "presiding universals," its love-physics and epistemic model in its first seventeen sonnets. The Puzzle is a unique system designed for the special purposes of this and only this sonnet sequence. It allows for a precision exegesis and guards against eisegesis. It defines its methods explicitly in Sonnet 80's prose instructions, implicitly through its rhetorical devices, and most importantly, by means of its precisely defined structure. The poet is the architect of a "golden world," and the proper procedure to determine its rules is not by reference to an external set of standards, but by a careful analysis that uncovers its internal coherence.

Internal coherence is also the goal when reading a work's rhetorical passages. The *Hekatompathia* contains many silly digressions, intentional misquotations, odd sidenotes, and other violations of decorum. This forces the alert reader to interpret, fill in missing links, reconsider the presented argument, recognize irony, or understand the significance of a joke. The *Hekatompathia* presents the reader with a set of mental gymnastics to be performed—the hundreds of steps necessary to solve the Puzzle. This is much like the process one undertakes to solve a difficult mathematical problem or write a computer program. This model of reading runs against current trends in criticism. For example, a Derridean critic will focus on the difficulty of stabilizing meaning—the text's undecidability. This mode of interpretation is irreconcilable with Gadamer's mode, the hermeneutics in which the poet and reader seek a common understanding through a process of interpretation. The reading of early modern poetry, I believe, is best served by Gadamer's approach.

The second pillar of the *Hekatompathia*'s poetics is its philosophical substrata. Solving the Puzzle would have been impossible without ascertaining the philosophical model upon which the work is built. This structuring of a literary work upon a philosophical foundation is found in other Elizabethan works, for example, those of Spenser. Ayesha Ramachandran argues that diagnosing Spenser's "philosophic commitments is central to an understanding of his poetic project." Indeed, the *Hekatompathia*'s philosophical model has much in common with that of Spenser. Ramachandran argues that for Spenser "eros is the origin of the cosmos and erotic union is a microcosmic figure for cosmic harmony and order."[65]

Bacon's use of a literary vehicle to deliver philosophical arguments may remind us of Plato, who used dramatic dialogues to deliver his philosophical beliefs. Although Bacon is obviously not a metaphysical Platonist, he is a rhetorical Platonist, that is, a disciple of Plato's educational rhetoric. In this rhetoric, ideas must be conveyed indirectly, by similitudes, irony, or other subterfuge. Both Plato and Bacon were responding to the cultural disasters of their time. Plato, writing after the fall of Athens, invents the forms that, in effect, replace the Homeric gods: the Good is "a kind of monotheistic ruler topping a hierarchy of gods."[66] Bacon, writing in a time of religious strife and uncertainty, wishes to introduce a new atomistic science that conflicts with orthodox Christian beliefs. In the *Hekatompathia*, he places love (rather than the Good) at the apex of his cosmology. Both Plato and Bacon practiced concealment both for its value as an educational method and to avoid accusations of blasphemy. Unfortunately, concealment or esotericism is often wrongly associated with mysticism or eccentrism. Goethe wrote, "Whoever wants to understand the poet must go to the poet's land."[67] For the *Hekatompathia* and other Elizabethan works, the "poet's land" is the heterodox cosmological model that structures the work, and until that model is identified, the work is likely to be unreadable.

If, as Simpson argues, "an understanding of literary shaping is the premise of understanding the philosophical meaning of a work," then an analysis of its formal and structural design is the essential step in reading it.[68] This enforces the reader to undertake a highly proactive form of reading. In the exceptional case of the *Hekatompathia*, the Puzzle enables the reader to discover the order or *architectonike* of the paracosm, to reconstruct the text's "golden world." Stillman, as earlier quoted, describes this process of discovery as understanding the speaking pictures as exemplifications of *notitiae*, the innate ideas of the microcosm, which are derived from the macrocosm. This requires that the reader be an architect, or structural analyst, at almost every moment. In Bacon's Sidneian poetics, the reader is instructed in the design of a little world, a paracosm, the very work being read. Essentially, the reader is taught how to be a poet, a maker of Cyruses.[69]

The third pillar of the *Hekatompathia*'s poetics is its plan "to inform the soul of the reader."[70] Bacon's goal, like Alan's in the *Anticlaudianus*, is to educate the reader's soul through "the reader's act of interpretation." Both the *Hekatompathia* and the *Anticlaudianus* tell the story of a noetic journey, an *intinerarium mentis*, in which the soul perceives its own origins.[71] Self-knowledge, in both Alan's and Bacon's time, was derivative of a knowledge of the cosmos. Simpson describes this aspect of the *Anticlaudianus*:

> The poem's primary 'meaning' is to be found not so much in its represented action, but rather in the self-knowledge it provokes in its reader. ... The reader is the central focus of the text (as we would expect, after all, from the thoroughly reader-centred poetic culture of the late Middle Ages). The poem's first commentator, Ralph of Longchamps, describes the poem's 'final cause' [as gaining] an understanding of one's origin.[72]

The *Hekatompathia* is also "reader-centred," and like the *Anticlaudianus*, its purpose is to develop the reader's self-knowledge. The work ends with the speaker's recognition that the great power that he perceives in nature and the beloved, love-physics, is also present within himself. The book's manuscript title, "A Looking glasse for Loovers," suggests that the work is a mirror or a science (as the word was then understood), a form of didactic poetry like the *Georgics* or the *Anticlaudianus*.[73] These works map the self to a cosmological model, and through an anatomization of the human, the reader gains self-knowledge.

This poetics has ancient roots. In the *Republic*, Book 10, mimetic art is criticized as being "far removed from the truth" because it is "at the third remove from truth and reality."[74] Homer is then criticized for being a poor educator, as having merely stirred the passions of his audience, rather than attempting to "educate men and make them better" (600c). Plato argues for a different mode of education, a new paideia, which, according to Gadamer, shapes "an inner harmony in the soul of a person."[75] An "unbridgeable chasm" separates this new "paideia from all other existing education" in ancient Greece, and we are the "heirs of [this] Greek humanism."[76] This new education seeks the harmony of two warring halves of human beings, "the bestial and the peaceful."[77] The key to achieving this harmony is self-knowledge and sophrosyne, which preserves phronesis, a lasting governance of the self.[78] Sophrosyne or phronesis is the cure sought after throughout the *Hekatompathia*: the integration of a divided self. The work begins with a divided self and ends with the compresence of two selves, a harmony between the aesthetic and noetic selves. In the resulting balance or temperance, the speaker learns to live within the limits of the human condition.

Socrates in the *Phaedo* argues that most people gain temperance not by giving up on all self-indulgence, but by accepting another pleasure in place of the one that has been lost:

> They control themselves, in a sense, by self-indulgence. [However,] it is wisdom that makes possible courage and self-control and integrity. ... The true moral ideal, whether self-control or integrity or courage, is really a kind of purgation from all these emotions, and wisdom itself is a sort of purification. (68e–69c)

The *Hekatompathia*'s speaker attains the wisdom achieved in the final Series as the result of the ordeal he experiences throughout the sequence. He learns to accept the loss of one pleasure, the beloved, and to look forward to some other pleasures that love may yet *assigne* (L73.5.18). The speaker learns to abandon the desire for what is unattainable. What is most instrumental in the speaker's cure is his epiphany concerning his true nature and his acceptance of love's sovereignty. The *Hekatompathia* ends in a celebration of love's great power and a newfound acceptance of living in the world of becoming.[79]

The *Hekatompathia* mixes physical science and poetry: the first is characterized by necessity, the second by the free exercise of the will. In the *Symposium*, the first three speakers are weighed down by love-physics, but the subsequent speakers, two of whom are poets, give rise to a human-centric vision of the world. Agathon accepts that the physical world operates by necessity, but then quotes Homer, who says that *Ate* (mischief) is divine and dainty, and walks upon the heads of men (195cd)—the psyche is the principle of freedom.[80] Agathon then gives "pride of place to [his] own vocation: Love is himself so divine a poet that he can kindle in the souls of others the poetic fire, for no matter what dull clay we seemed to be before, we are everyone of us a poet when we are in love" (196e). Poetry, then, is an erotic activity, a freely exercised expression of ourselves; it is the antithesis of, and the antidote to, the necessity of love-physics. Poetry gives rise to the human.[81]

In both the *Symposium* and the *Hekatompathia*, poetry "is conceived as originating in the spontaneous activity of human imagination as directed by the will."[82] This follows Sidney's model in which the imagination allows the creation of a "golden world." It is also consistent with the Apollonian poetics discussed above, as well as the willful and imaginative mind that created the Puzzle. Will and imagination are also essential to solving the Puzzle: the puzzle-solver must imagine the work in its organic, coherent form, a frequent step in the process of its restoration. With the reader acting as an apprentice or midwife to the writer, exegesis and eisegesis become nearly indistinguishable: both poet and reader are together engaged in producing the text.

Socrates says that a discourse's knowledge should be "written in the soul of the learner" (*Phaedrus* 276A, as discussed above). This is equivalent to Sidney's argument that poetry has "strange effects," a metamorphic effect upon the reader. Gadamer asserts that a "work of art has its true being in the fact that it becomes an experience that changes the person who experiences it."[83] In this aesthetics, a work of art is not a museum piece to be dissected, characterized, and then classified as if it were a zoological specimen; rather, it can only come into being when the reader makes it his or her own.[84] "It is an event in which the work claims a place in the world *we* inhabit—indeed, it is right to say that the work claims a piece of us and insists on belonging to our lives."[85] Plato, Bacon, Sidney, Nietzsche, and Gadamer all share this belief in the metamorphic power of art.

The *Hekatompathia* and its Puzzle take this conception of art to its extreme limit. The Puzzle, like no other literary device, harnesses the metamorphic powers of poetry, writing the poet's text into the "reader's soul." Poetry conceived under this poetics is a robust vehicle for communicating ideas in a way that withstands the erosion of time. Rome may have been in ruins, but the Elizabethans were given a steady diet of its Latin poets from their earliest age. They thus recognized that while marble monuments are ground to dust, poetry survives. A poem survives as a parasite does, only by the nourishment provided by a living host, its reader. Until now, the *Hekatompathia* has only survived as a trifling miscellany of Petrarchan poetry—a historical curiosity. However, embedded within it is a mechanism that allows for its resurrection. The *Hekatompathia* impresses the reader into the poet's service with its captivating Puzzle, and when the text has been restored, new life nourishes old words and thus sustains the spirit of the poet.

Notes (Vol. I)

Chapter 1 » Introduction: A Systematically Concealed Text

1   "Deciphering and the Exhaustion of Recombination," in *A Material History of Medieval and Early Modern Ciphers: Cryptography and the History of Literacy*, ed. Katherine Ellison and Susan Kim (New York: Routledge, 2018), 202.

2   *The Shakespearean Ciphers Examined: An Analysis of Cryptographic Systems Used as Evidence That Some Author Other Than William Shakespeare Wrote the Plays Commonly Attributed to Him* (Cambridge: Cambridge University Press, 1958).

3   I am aware of only one systematic cryptographic claim among those claiming an alternative authorship of the works of Shakespeare. However, this system did not actually operate on a Shakespearean text but employed Bacon's biliteral cipher invention to recognize supposed differences in the fonts used in printing the First Folio. The so-called "Gallup cipher" is described and debunked in Friedman and Friedman, *Shakespearean Ciphers Examined*, 188–278.

4   Rollett presents his claim on two occasions, in "The Dedication to Shakespeare's Sonnets," *Elizabethan Review* 5.2 (1997): 93–122, and later in "Secrets of the Dedication to Shakespeare's Sonnets," *Oxfordian* 2 (1999): 60–75. In the first publication, he assessed the probability that his deciphering could arise serendipitously at 1 in 270,000, for which he does provide a calculation. In the second publication, he assessed the probability at 1 in 20,000, without providing a calculation. Apparently, he realized that he had missed some of the possible variations (they are easy to overlook). In my analysis, the additional variations I found made a serendipitous deciphering very probable, which thoroughly undermines the validation.

5   See note directly above. My calculation, with the necessary explanations, would require a dozen pages, far beyond the space available here. Suffice it to say that the degrees of freedom that I have identified (called variations in the above note) produce a high probability of a serendipitous deciphering.

6   Correctly calculated, the probability is a function of negative, not positive, instances. I have simplified the calculation, which results in an insignificant difference.

7   The 100 poem count is not exact. There are precisely 100 pages labeled with Roman numerals. However, the page marked LXXX contains the puzzle instructions, not a poem. There is also a poem labeled as the *Epilogue* that appears subsequent to the last numbered poem, and another poem, titled *Quid Amor,* consisting of 39 Latin hexameters, which is unnumbered and appears between XCVIII and XCIX. The poet refers to the poems as "passions" three-quarters of the time and as "sonnets" the remainder of the time, according to Phillips (Phillips Dissertation, 30).

8   Oddly, Bacon refers to his Neo-Latin poem 45 as a sonnet in its headnote.

9   See A. E. B. Coldiron, "Watson's *Hekatompathia* and Renaissance Lyric Translation," *Translation and Literature* 5.1 (1996): 7–8.

10   Murphy Dissertation, abstract, 5. The abstract is a separate document stored with the dissertation, available at the Harvard Archives.

11   Coldiron, "Watson's *Hekatompathia* and Renaissance Lyric Translation," 7.

12   Frank Ardolino, "Thomas Watson, Shadow Poet of Edmund Spenser," *Notes and Queries* 61.2 (2014): 225–29. Also, Phillips Dissertation, 43.

13   Heninger Edition, xvii–xviii. See also Vol. II, Appendix D, "Notes on the Text."

14   Thomas Watson, "A Looking glasse for Loovers," Manuscript: (British Library: Harleian 3277, n.d.). The British Library has available a microfilm of the manuscript from which copies may be ordered.

15   Wendy Phillips, "No More Tears: Thomas Watson Absolved," *Comitatus: A Journal of Medieval and Renaissance Studies* 20.1 (1989): 75. However, there are four lines that break metrical form: an 11-syllable line (48.9), two tetrameters (56.14; 77.1), and a hexameter (92.3). See 246–47; II 67, 109, 165, 179, 383–84.

16   Thomas Watson, *Thomas Watson Poems*, ed. Edward Arber (London: English Reprints, 1870), 3–4.

17   Murphy Dissertation, abstract, 4; xcvii. The abstract is a separate document stored with the dissertation, available at the Harvard Archives.

18   See the discussion of translation in Excursus 4.

19   "Ma il petrarchista non è un plagiario nel senso moderno della parola: è un poeta rinascimentale, e cioè un razionale imitatore di quello che egli riteneva essere il meglio delle opere che prendeva a modello." *Thomas Watson e la tradizione petrarchista*, Messina G. Principato, 1969, 266. Translation: Phillips Dissertation, 45.

20   Phillips Dissertation, 78.

21   "Watson's *Hekatompathia* and Renaissance Lyric Translation," 22, 9.

22   "Thomas Watson's *Hekatompathia* and European Petrarchism," in *Petrarch in Britain: Interpreters, Imitators, and Translators Over 700 Years*, ed. M. L McLaughlin, Letizia Panizza, and Peter Hainsworth, Proceedings of the British Academy 146 (Oxford, UK: Published for the British Academy by Oxford University Press, 2007), 223–27.

23   *Pagan Mysteries in the Renaissance* (London: Faber and Faber, 1958), 151.

24   On the influence on later sonnet sequences, see Sutton Edition, 135N3. On the influence on Shakespeare's sonnets, see. E. Pearlman, "Watson's *Hekatompathia* [1582] in the Sonnets and Romeo and Juliet," *English Studies* 74.4 (1993): 343–51.

25   Phillips Dissertation, 69–74.

26   *English Literature in the Sixteenth Century Excluding Drama: The Completion of the Clark Lectures, Trinity College, Cambridge, 1944* (Oxford: Clarendon Press, 1962), 483.

27   *The Elizabethan Sonnet Sequences: Studies in Conventional Conceits* (New York: Russell & Russell, 1966), 17.

28   Sutton Edition, vi.

29   Ibid., xiv–xv.

30   "Thomas Watson, Playwright: Origins of Modern English Drama," in *Lost Plays in Shakespeare's England*, ed. D. McInnis and M. Steggle (New York: Palgrave Macmillan, 2014), 198.

31 Ibid., 187.

32 Wendy Phillips argues that "Watson's first madrigal reads like an autobiographical account of a first meeting with Sidney, leading to a close friendship" (Phillips Dissertation, 63–66). With respect to Spenser, see Harry Morris, "Richard Barnfield, 'Amyntas,' and the Sidney Circle," *PMLA* 74.4 (1959): 318–24. Also, William Ringler, "Spenser and Thomas Watson," *Modern Language Notes* 69.7 (1954): 484–87.

33 Sutton Edition, vN2. The words "and apostle of Continental culture" appear only in the online edition.

34 Hirrel, "Thomas Watson, Playwright: Origins of Modern English Drama," 198.

35 Ibid.

36 Ibid., 199.

37 See the section titled "The Significance of Bacon's Pseudonyms" in Richard Serjeantson, "Francis Bacon's Valerius Terminus and the Voyage to the 'Great Instauration,'" *Journal of the History of Ideas* 78.3 (2017): 348–57.

38 *Works*, 10.65

39 Georg Cantor, *Resurrectio Divi Quirini, Francisci Baconi, Baronis de Verulam…* (Cura Et Impensis G.C. [Georg Cantor], 1896).

40 Opinion of James Spedding (*Works*, 8.325–26).

41 *The Anonymous Renaissance: Cultures of Discretion in Tudor-Stuart England* (University of Chicago Press, 2003), 3–4.

42 "Ignoto in the Age of Print: The Manipulation of Anonymity in Early Modern England," *Studies in Philology* 91.4 (1994): 393, 397, passim 390–416.

43 Marcy North, "Anonymity's Revelations in 'The Arte of English Poesie,'" *Studies in English Literature, 1500–1900* 39.1 (1999): 1–2.

44 Ibid., 5–7.

45 Ibid., 13–14.

46 Serjeanston, "Francis Bacon's *Valerius Terminus* and the Voyage to the 'Great Instauration,'" 348–49. Serjeanston provides this note: See Lisa Jardine and Alan Stewart, *Hostage to Fortune: The Troubled Life of Francis Bacon* (London: Gollancz, 1998), esp. 55–58.

47 *Works* 8.109.

48 *Reading Memory in Early Modern Literature* (Cambridge: Cambridge University Press, 2011), 220.

49 *Works*, 4.444-447. Bacon writes that this invention "I devised myself when I was at Paris in my early youth" (445).

50 Ibid., 445.

51 James Gleick, in *The Information: A History, a Theory, a Flood* (New York: Pantheon, 2011), identifies the first instance of Information Theory as the biliteral cipher (159–61). However, he misattributes Bacon's invention to John Wilkins, who appropriated it without attribution in 1641. Gleick writes, "The essential idea of information theory poked to the surface of human thought, saw its shadow, and disappeared again for four hundred years" (161).

52 *Works* 4.84.

53 See Benjamin Farrington, *The Philosophy of Francis Bacon: An Essay on Its Development from 1603 to 1609, with New Translation of Fundamental Texts* (Chicago: University of Chicago Press, 1966), 111.

54 *Theogony*, 27–28.

55 "Suspicion, Deception, and Concealment," *Arion: A Journal of Humanities and the Classics* 1.2 (1991): 121. Plato reference: *Republic*, III, 389b.

56 Leo Strauss, *Persecution and the Art of Writing* (Glencoe: Free Press, 1952), 57–58. I wish to thank Palle Yourgrau for suggesting this work.

57 Ibid., 61–62.

58 Ibid., 67.

59 Arthur F. Kinney, *Continental Humanist Poetics: Studies in Erasmus, Castiglione, Marguerite De Navarre, Rabelais, and Cervantes* (Amherst: University of Massachusetts Press, 1989), 46. Second quotation: Desiderius Erasmus to Justus Jonas, May 10, 1521, in *Correspondence*, 8:203.

60 See David Weil Baker, *Divulging Utopia: Radical Humanism in Sixteenth-Century England*, Massachusetts Studies in Early Modern Culture (Amherst: University of Massachusetts Press, 1999), 25–26.

61 See Martin Mulsow, *Knowledge Lost: A New View of Early Modern Intellectual History*, tr. H. C. Erik Midelfort, Bilingual edition (Princeton: Princeton University Press, 2022). Mulsow argues that historians of the early modern period have often failed to uncover the knowledge that is intentionally hidden in many texts. Indirect forms such as commentary and annotation are often used to subtly express heterodox views (14).

62 *Works*, 4.450.

63 See Rhodri Lewis, "Francis Bacon, Allegory, and the Uses of Myth," *Review of English Studies* 61.250 (2010): 367.

64 "Ethics and Politics in the *New Atlantis*," in *Francis Bacon's New Atlantis: New Interdisciplinary Essays*, ed. Bronwen Price (Manchester: Manchester University Press, 2002), 73.

65 In the *To the frendly Reader* preface, the sonnets may either be defended, or excused as *idle toyes proceedinge from a youngling frenzie* (second paragraph). In the final stanza of the *Quatorzain* preface, the personified book may either declare its worth or *confesse* that it is *a Toye*. The *Protrepticon* preface also suggests two alternative reading modes (see Chapter 6).

66 See Daniel S Russell, *The Emblem and Device in France*, French Forum monographs 59 (French Forum, 1985), 48. Russell is referring to emblems, but I believe the principle applies more generally to poetry.

67 Bartolomeo Fontius (1455–1513). Quoted from Concetta Carestia Greenfield, *Humanist and Scholastic Poetics, 1250-1500* (Lewisburg: Bucknell University Press, 1981), 288.

68 *Summa theologiae* I.Q. I, a9, r.2.

69 *On Christian Doctrine*, 2.6.8, tr. Rev. J. F. Shaw; Golding, "Too the Reader," in Ovid, *Metamorphosis*, tr. Golding (London, 1567), A2v (STC 18956).

70 His preface to Henry Savile's translation of Tacitus (1591), STC 23642.

71 *Visionary Spenser and the Poetics of Early Modern Platonism* (Oxford: Oxford University Press, 2017), 70.

72 *Boccaccio on Poetry*, tr. Charles Osgood (New York: Liberal Arts Press, 1956), 60–62.

73 *The Discarded Image: An Introduction to Medieval and Renaissance Literature* (Cambridge: Cambridge University Press, 1964), 10.

74 Erasmus's *Adages*, translated into English, appeared in 11 editions in the sixteen century. Claudia Corti argues that Erasmus was at "the very core of

the extraordinary co-textual and inter-textual experience of the English Renaissance." *Silenos: Erasmus in Elizabethan Literature*, Studi di letterature moderne e comparate 1 (Ospedaletto [Italy]: Pacini, 1998), 9–10.

75 Thomas More, *Utopia: With Erasmus's the Sileni of Alcibiades*, tr. David Wootton (Indianapolis: Hackett Publishing Company, Inc., 1999), 169.

76 Ibid., 169–70.

77 Quoted from Arthur F. Kinney, "Rhetoric as Poetic: Humanist Fiction in the Renaissance," *ELH* 43.4 (1976): 422–23. Kinney quotes the English translation of Sir Thomas Chaloner (1549): E3.

78 Ibid., 426.

79 *Utopia: With Erasmus's the Sileni of Alcibiades*, 24–25.

80 "Prologue of the Author," in *Gargantua and Pantagruel*, tr. Michael Andrew Screech (London: Penguin Books, 2006), 207.

81 Quoted from Ronald Levao, "Francis Bacon and the Mobility of Science," *Representations*, 40 (1992): 5.

82 The quotation is from Laurence Lampert, *Nietzsche and Modern Times: A Study of Bacon, Descartes, and Nietzsche* (New Haven: Yale University Press, 1993), 276. Lampert points to the first sentence of Descartes's *Discourse*, a direct quotation from Montaigne: "Good sense is most evenly distributed in the world, for each thinks himself so well endowed therewith that even those who are most difficult to please in all other things are not wont to desire more of it than they have." He argues that both Montaigne and Descartes know this declaration to be false and that to the contrary, people struggle to distinguish the true from the false. Indeed, according to Lampert, Descartes eventually tells his reader that "almost all people are deficient with respect to distinguishing the true from the false" (207). Thus, both Montaigne and Descartes brazenly state a bold lie in their rhetorical approach to argument. Bacon applies a similar rhetorical approach in both the *Hekatompathia* and his *Essays*. On his use of rhetoric in the *Essays*, see Stanley Fish, *Self-Consuming Artifacts: The Experience of Seventeenth-Century Literature* (Berkeley: University of California Press, 1972), 78–155.

83 See Stephen Clucas, "A Knowledge Broken": Francis Bacon's Aphoristic Style and the Crisis of Scholastic and Humanist Knowledge-Systems," in *English Renaissance Prose: History, Language, and Politics*, ed. Neil Rhodes (Tempe: Medieval & Renaissance Texts & Studies, 1997), 147–72. See also Lampert, *Nietzsche and Modern Times*, 19–26, for his discussion of Bacon's esoterism.

84 "Francis Bacon and the Mobility of Science," 5.

85 Ibid., on Bacon's poetics, see 5–8, passim, 1–32.

86 *Novum Organum*, civ. *Works*, 4.97.

87 "Francis Bacon and the Mobility of Science," 19.

88 The quoted words are Levao's, Ibid., 20.

89 "The Collapse of the Religious Hieroglyph: Typology and Natural Language in Herbert and Bacon," *Renaissance Quarterly*, 45.1 (1992): 112.

90 Ibid., 112.

91 "Refashioning Fable through the Baconian Essay: *De sapientia veterum* and Mythologies of the Early Modern Natural Philosopher," in *The Essay: Forms and Transformations*, ed. Dorothea Flothow et al., (Heidelberg: Universitätsverlag, Winter 2017), 25.

92 *Science and the Secrets of Nature: Books of Secrets in Medieval and Early Modern Culture* (Princeton: Princeton University Press, 1994), 288.
93 Ibid., 289–90.
94 "Francis Bacon and the Rhetorical Reordering of Reality," *Rhetor* 6 (2016), 12.
95 Quoted from *Nietzsche and Modern Times*, 277 (Daybreak, preface 5).
96 An acrostic is formed by the first letter of each chapter forming a message that includes the name Francesco Colonna; however, the identity of the author is uncertain.
97 *The Cornucopian Text: Problems of Writing in the French Renaissance* (Oxford: Oxford University Press, 1979), 181–82.
98 Ibid., 164.
99 *Works*, 4.449.
100 From "Thoughts and Conclusions," in Farrington, *The Philosophy of Francis Bacon*, 75–76.
101 David Colclough, "'Non Canimus Surdis, Respondent Omnia Sylvae': Francis Bacon and the Transmission of Knowledge," in *Textures of Renaissance Knowledge*, eds. Philippa Berry and Margaret Tudeau-Clayton (Manchester: Manchester University Press, 2003), 86.
102 *Works* 4.449.
103 "Francis Bacon, Allegory and the Uses of Myth," *Review of English Studies* 61.250 (2010): 369.
104 *Explorations in Ancient and Modern Philosophy*, Vol. 2 (Cambridge: Cambridge University Press 2012), 27.
105 See the discussion in the final chapter: Sidney's goal is not to create a Cyrus (a prototypical hero) but a maker of Cyruses.
106 "Rabelais's Realism, Again," in *François Rabelais: Critical Assessments*, ed. Jean-Claude Carron (Baltimore: Johns Hopkins University Press, 1995), 37.
107 "Francis Bacon and the Art of Misinterpretation," *PMLA* 130.2 (2015): 246, 243.
108 "Francis Bacon, Allegory and the Uses of Myth," 381.
109 "Ethics and Politics in the New Atlantis," 72.
110 "'Non Canimus Surdis, Respondent Omnia Sylvae'," 88.
111 "The Hermeneutical Anarchist: *Phronesis*, Rhetoric, and the Experience of Art," in *Gadamer's Century: Essays in Honor of Hans-Georg Gadamer*, ed. Jeff Malpas et al., (Cambridge, MA: MIT Press, 2002), 61.
112 Quoted from "The Hermeneutical Anarchist," 61 (*Truth and Method*, 116).
113 "The Hermeneutical Anarchist," 61–62.
114 Quoted from Stanley Rosen, *The Ancients and the Moderns: Rethinking Modernity* (New Haven: Yale University Press, 1989), 212.
115 See *The Ancients and the Moderns*, 213.
116 Ibid., 211.
117 Ibid., 232.
118 "Francis Bacon and the Art of Misinterpretation," 238.
119 See Pierre Hadot, *The Veil of Isis: An Essay on the History of Idea of Nature*, tr. Michael Chase (Cambridge, MA: Harvard University Press, 2006), 93, passim.
120 *Works* 6.713.

121 Sophie Weeks, "The Role of Mechanics in Francis Bacon's Great Instauration," in *Philosophies of Technology: Francis Bacon and His Contemporaries* (2 Vols.), ed. Claus Zittel et al., Vol. 1 (Koninklijke Brill NV, 2008), 140.

122 Ibid., 163–64.

123 Ibid., 180.

124 Ibid., 174, 180, 184–85.

Chapter 2 » Stage 1: The Puzzle Sonnet

1 Two poems fall outside of the *Hekatompathia*'s numbering scheme: *Quid Amor* and the Epilogue. The headnote of Sonnet 98 (which precedes *Quid Amor*) states that the poet placed *Quid Amor* on the *next page following, but not as accomptable for one of the hundreth passions of this booke*, thus excluding it from being counted. The headnote of the Epilogue also appears to exclude it from being counted as one of the 100 passions: *more like a praier than a Passion*. Thus no poem replaces Sonnet 80 in the sonnet count, and the title's promise of 100 passions falls short by one.

2 Trithemius uses "*transpositionis*" to mean the change or enciphering from a plaintext alphabet to a ciphertext alphabet ("*mutationem seu transpositionem;*" Oii). He labels both his *Recta* and *Aversa* tables (at the top of the page) as "*tabula transpositionis*" (Oii, Oiiv). In his "*Explanatio in quintum librum polygraphiae nostrae brevis*" (explanation of the fifth book; Biv), which is an appendage to the 1518 edition, he uses "*transpositionem*" a dozen times. "*Orchema*" is the title given to his irregular enciphering table (Pii, but the page number is mislabeled). "*Orchema*" appears about 10 times in his "*Explanatio in quintum librum polygraphiae nostrae brevis.*" Thus the Puzzle's instructions make the reference to *Polygraphia* 5 extremely clear.

3 The reference to "the syllabic count of each line increasing by odd instead of consecutive numbers" refers to the "orchematicall" base of the Pasquine Pillar featured in Sonnet 81. Phillips Dissertation, 424.

4 In steganography, an ordinary, readable text forms the ciphertext (ciphertexts are normally gibberish), which is deciphered to produce the (secret) plaintext. Typically, only a modest percentage of the ordinary text—say the first letter of every sentence—is used in deciphering. Here, a small percentage of the letters of the acrostic (*amare est insanire*) would amount to only one or two letters, hardly sufficient for a message. In the course of this chapter, we will discover that Bacon, through his prodigious skill (*how much art and study the Author hath bestowed*; Sonnet 80), managed to utilize 50% of each acrostic, an impressive accomplishment.

5 Post-Petrarchism Origins and Innovations of the Western Lyric Sequence (Princeton: Princeton University Press, 1991), 102–6. Roland Greene recognizes correctly that the Puzzle Sonnet marks a significant turning point in the work, and such an event could be marked by ritual. However, an acrostic sonnet is neither mystical nor a sacrament.

6 Of the 100 numbered poems, 4 are Neo-Latin poems (6, 45, 66, and 90) and 3 are devoted to the Puzzle Sonnet (the instructions and the two versions of the Puzzle Sonnet). This accounts for 94 English language sonnets, counting the two Puzzle Sonnet versions as one sonnet.

7 Phillips Dissertation, 421.

8   I calculate the average number of lines that intermediate a rhyme pair or triplet: zero is the value for adjacent lines and one for alternating rhyme lines, etc. The scheme is a b a c b d e f g h e a h g c d f f. Examining the first "a" rhyme (a triplet), its first gap (one intervening "b" line) is equal to 1; the second gap (these lines intervene: c b d e f g h e) is equal to 8. The calculated gap values are: a: 1, 8; b: 2; c: 10; d: 9; e: 3; f: 0, 8; g: 4; h: 2. The average of these 10 gaps is 4.7.

9   I calculated what the average gap value would be for a randomly ordered poem consisting of 6 rhyme pairs and 2 triplets. For rhyme pairs, the maximum gap is 16 and the average gap is (1 to 16) $\sum$ ((1 to 16)$\sum$ N) / (1 to 17) $\sum$ N = 5.33. For triplets, the maximum gap, averaged across the two gaps, is 7.5, and the average gap is .5 (1 to 15) $\sum$ ((1 to 15)$\sum$ N) / (1 to 16) $\sum$ N = 2.5. A weighted average between the 6 pair gaps and the 4 triplet gaps yields an average gap of 4.2.

10   Examples of sonnet structure include the three-quatrain-plus-couplet Shakespearean sonnet (actually Wyatt's invention), the octave-plus-sestet Petrarchan sonnet, and the *Hekatompathia*'s three-sestet sonnet.

11   *The Literary Riddle before 1600* (Westport: Greenwood Press, 1948), 3.

12   The couplet would be forced to play some role of intermediation between the two octaves, and it is too small to do so. In a Shakespearean sonnet, the third quatrain often intermediates between the first two quatrains. In a Petrarchan sonnet, no couplet follows the two sections, the octave and the sestet.

13   "For" may be a misprint: Sonnet 81 reads "or" and Sonnet 82 "for." However, the manuscript's Sonnet 81 reads "for," and thus three of four instances read "for." Here, "for" likely means "under the influence of" (OED 20a) and thus *mirth* is said to arise from *mischance*.

14   In the reordered poem's rhyme scheme, abaab cdcdc eefgfg hh, all rhyming end words either fall in adjacent lines or are separated by only one line, with the one exception of the "b" rhymes, which are separated by two lines. But abaab is a reasonable rhyme scheme for a combined triplet and pair. Rhyme schemes of abba are, of course, common. True, the rhyme scheme overlaps the bipartite structure of the sonnet. But given the pairs and triplets with which we have to work, this rhyme scheme is certainly reasonable.

15   *Polygraphia* 5, Oii.

16   The Recta tables include 25 rather than 23 tables, but this includes 2 erroneous tables that fill up what would otherwise be empty columns on the page titled "*Quinta figura expansionis tabulae rectae*." These 2 extra tables are actually Orchema tables and are clearly out of place. Most of my references to *Polygraphia* 5 are made by page title or other means because many of the work's page numbers are misprinted.

17   *Polygraphia* 5, second page: "And if, on account of a multitude of difficulties, the family of alphabets which we have noted are not sufficient, or if some of them seem too open and too obvious, we will be able to introduce various new transpositions of which the number is large, and the mode of the secrecy remains always concealed." (The original text begins with "Quod si prae multitudine" and ends with "occultus.")

18   Trithemius uses a 24-letter alphabet that includes the non-Latin letters K and W. It is identical to the 24-letter Elizabethan alphabet except that Trithemius's

alphabetic order places "W" as the last letter of the alphabet, as was the custom in the German language. The Puzzle uses the standard order of the 24-letter Elizabethan alphabet, in which W follows U/V.

19   Trithemius's master Aversa Table, titled *Tabula transpositionis aversa* appears on the fourth page of *Polygraphia* 5. This master table is rendered oddly and is inconsistent with his expansion into the 23 tables that appear on the tenth through fourteenth pages of *Polygraphia* 5. My version uses the values from the 23-table expansion. Also, my version, following the Puzzle, is modified such that "W" is the 21st letter of the alphabet.

20   A late sixteenth-century dialogue on love, *Contramours*, was published under the pseudonym Battista Fregoso. The acrostic in a fourteen-line prefatory poem spells out THOMAS SEBILLET.

21   Phillips Dissertation, 427.

22   Ibid., 427–29.

23   In this assignment of tables, only two binary assumptions have been made. The first is the assignment of the increasing numbers to the Recta tables and the decreasing numbers to the Aversa tables, as opposed to vice versa, which would be an unnatural choice. With respect to the Recta tables, one can read them either as encryption or decryption tables, also a binary choice.

24   Alberti embedded letters in the ciphertext itself that signaled which alphabet would be used.

25   If in cryptanalysis, one makes too many arbitrary and elaborate assumptions about the cryptographic system, the validity of any deciphered message may be called into question. For example, if one's conjecture about a cryptographic system arbitrarily settles on one of a million possible systems, this reduces confidence in the validity of the deciphered message. Here we have made only a handful of assumptions; if the assumptions had instead been numerous, it would be necessary to factor this into the mathematical validation at the conclusion of this chapter.

26   Credited to mathematician David Silverman, this was reportedly published in August 1970 in *Kickshaws* (no further information is available).

27   Aloys Meister, *Die Geheimschrift im Dienste der Päpstlichen Kurie von ihren Anfänge bis zum Ende des 16. Jahrhundert* (Paderborn: Schöningh, 1906), 297. The table below provides references to some sixteenth-century polyphonic ciphers documented in *Die Geheimschrift*.

Year	Correspondent	Page in *Die Geheimschrift*
1544–50	Bishop of Ajaccio	178
1579	Camillo Capozucca	296
1582	Vincenzo Vitelli	296
15??	Cardinal Sabellus	200
1583	Cardinal Sabellus	297
1585	Cardinal Sabellus	298
1585	Bishop of Amalfi	350
1586(?)	Anonymous	255

28   For each letter, the absolute rate of language is 4.6 bits ($\log_2 24$). To compare the information content of the absolute rate of language with the output of a polyphonic cipher with one bit of indeterminacy, divide the information content of each: (4.6-1) / 4.6 ≈ 78%.

29   Katherine Ellison, "Deciphering and the Exhaustion of Recombination," in *A Material History of Medieval and Early Modern Ciphers: Cryptography and the History of Literacy*, ed. Katherine Ellison and Susan Kim (New York: Routledge, 2018), 187.

30   *The Book of Memory: A Study of Memory in Medieval Culture*, 2nd ed. (Cambridge: Cambridge University Press, 2008), 230–31, 245.

31   He is depicted as either possessing powers, symbolized as arrows or a brand, or as dispossessed of these powers (Sonnets 70 and 100).

32   Sonnet 25, line 8 where the fabricated pronoun "*he" represents he or she. This is necessary in the poem to account for the change in the gender of the person referenced in the echo.

33   *Blyndfold bratte and thee* (M, F); *Blind cupids carr* (M); *Ciprya la nemica mia* (F).

34   See Clive S. Lewis and Alastair Fowler, *Spenser's Images of Life* (Cambridge: Cambridge University Press, 2013), 16.

35   Ibid., 15.

36   "Emanations of Glory: Neoplatonic Order in Spenser's *Faerie Queen*," in *A Theatre for Spenserians: Papers of the International Spenser Colloquium, Frederiction, New Brunswick, October, 1969*, ed. Judith M. Kennedy and James A. Reither (Toronto: University of Toronto Press, 1973), 54.

37   The *Polygraphia* 5's Orchema tables, printed on a single page labeled "*Orchema*," consist of 6 tables or Alphabets. The first and second tables skip 1 and 3 letters, respectively, between entries. The third and fourth tables exhibit a wholly different pattern consisting of sequential letters with periodic reversals of direction. The fifth and sixth tables are *recta* tables, an error.

38   The OED lists *pesum* (*pensum*), the neuter gender of this masculine verbal adjective, *pesus*, in its entry for "avoirdupois."

39   A hypogram is a key word or phrase that underlies a complex network of relations within a text.

40   The final word, PESUS, was only a guess because the value of the Orchema Transforms is unknown. Therefore, it is not included in our validation test.

41   It should be noted that Shannon's figure of 25% is based on experiments he conducted in which his subjects made successive guesses at each letter of a text that was 100 letters in length. On average, they had 50 letters of prior context to help them in their guessing. This is significantly longer than our 13-letter text. As evident from Fig. E3.3, meaning, grammar, and context are implicit in this 25% information rate. The reason that I believe that the 25% rate is applicable to our plaintext message, even though it is short, is that it is meaningful, grammatically correct, and fits perfectly with its larger context, the Puzzle Sonnet from which it emerged. The Puzzle Sonnet, the circumstance of the *Hekatompathia*'s poet addressing a reader, and the necessity of giving a clue to the Puzzle's next stage, all severely limit what text we might expect to find. The plaintext message is four words forming two sentences. The compactness of Latin allows for this amazingly concise message. Despite its short length, the message exhibits grammatic structure. Most importantly, its words precisely fit the context of the Puzzle Sonnet from which it emerged.

42   The probability of an event occurring at least once if repeated n times is not actually the product of n and the probability of the event, p. However, when p<<1 and n<<p, n times p is a close approximation.

43 There are 18 Puzzle Sonnet lines, which generate a 13-letter message, and thus there are 18!/5!, or approximately 5.3 x 10^{13} permutations or reorderings (without restriction). The vast majority of these will fail to maintain logical coherence, adhere to an appropriate rhyme scheme, exhibit appropriate structure, or make sense in the context of the MLIP Subsequence. I estimated the number of poetically valid reorderings by making the following judgment: for any given line in the Puzzle Sonnet, only 3 of the 17 remaining lines could appropriately follow it. This results from the need to maintain logical and grammatic flow from line to line, and the requirement that a reasonable rhyme scheme be maintained. The judgment that only 3 of 17 lines are appropriate successors is based on (1) examining each sonnet line for potential successors, and (2) knowing that the requirement for rhyme will often allow for only one possible successor line. The value of 3 possible successor lines is an average of greater and lesser values incurred during a traversal from the first sonnet line to the 13th. Of course, it is an impractical task to map out each of what are likely thousands of traversals.

   This successor line estimate may now be used to estimate the number of valid reorderings. For each successive line after the first, there is a 3 out of 17 chance that that line is valid, logically and poetically. This is true even as the supply of remaining lines decreases as one progresses toward the 13th and last line. My calculation assumes that only 6 lines are appropriate to begin the sonnet, and then each of 12 successive lines has only a 3/17 chance of being valid. The probability of a valid reordering is then (6/18) $(3/17)^{12} \approx 1$ in 3.3 x 10^{9}. Multiplying this probability by the total number of permutations (5.3 x 10^{13}), we obtain approximately 16,000 valid reorderings. This estimate does not account for all restrictions on reordering the Puzzle Sonnet, as previously discussed (e.g., the requirement that the reordered sonnet exhibit structure).

Chapter 3 » The *Hekatompathia*'s Foundation: Sonnets 1–17

1 Just prior to the 1580s, Spenser's *Shepheardes Calender* (1579) used an Old English font for the poetry and a more modern font for the commentary, the same practice adopted by the *Hekatompathia*. That choice also appears to have been made in order to cast the text in an antiquarian light.

2 An exception is Spenser's *Shepheardes Calender*—its glosses perform a function similar to those found in the *Hekatompathia*.

3 The gloss that appends the December eclogue states: "This poet in his Epilogue sayth he hath made a Calendar, that shall endure as long as time etc. following the ensample of Horace and Ovid..." (folio 52). According to Patrick Cheney, Spenser imagines a poetic career patterned after Virgil (the concept of the "Virgilian wheel" in which a poet's career progresses from eclogues, to georgics, and finally to epic). See "Spenser's Pastorals: *The Shepheardes Calender* and *Colin Clouts Come Home Againe*," in *The Cambridge Companion to Spenser*, ed. Andrew Hadfield (Cambridge: Cambridge University Press, 2001), 79–80. See further discussion in this study's final chapter.

4 Exceptions include Dante's *Vita Nuova*, which includes commentary; Scève's sequence has elaborate designs.

5 Rita Copeland, *Rhetoric, Hermeneutics and Translation in the Middle Ages* (Cambridge: Cambridge University Press, 1991), 66, 70–71.

6   Ibid., 67, 69.
7   "Continental Poetics," in *A Companion to Rhetoric and Rhetorical Criticism*, ed. Walter Jost and Wendy Olmsted (Malden: Blackwell Publishing, 2004), 81.
8   Ibid., 80. Cicero's influence on Renaissance rhetorical theory is discussed later in this study.
9   *Rhetoric, Hermeneutics and Translation in the Middle Ages*, 70.
10   Ibid., 77.
11   Ibid., 187–88, 77–78.
12   Quoted from Kathy Eden, *Hermeneutics and the Rhetorical Tradition: Chapters in the Ancient Legacy and Its Humanist Reception* (New Haven: Yale University Press, 2009), 83–84.
13   *Rhetoric, Hermeneutics and Translation in the Middle Ages*, 82.
14   Parkes, "The Influence of the Concepts of *Ordinatio* and *Compilatio* on the Development of the Book," in *Medieval Learning and Literature: Essays Presented to Richard William Hunt*, ed. J. J. G. Alexander and Margaret Gibson (Oxford: Clarendon Press, 1976), 117–19.
15   Ibid., 130–32.
16   "'Well Grounded, Finely Framed, and Strongly Trussed up Together' the 'Medieval' Structure of 'The Faerie Queene,'" *Review of English Studies* 52.105 (2001): 28, 26.
17   *Odyssey* 5.193.
18   *Hermeneutics and the Rhetorical Tradition*, 58.
19   *Hermogenes and the Renaissance: Seven Ideas of Style* (Princeton: Princeton University Press, 1970), 9–10.
20   III.23. *The Art of English Poesy: A Critical Edition*, ed. Wayne A. Rebhorn and Frank Whigham (Ithaca: Cornell University Press, 2007), 348.
21   *Hermeneutics and the Rhetorical Tradition*, 17–18.
22   7.10.16–17. Quoted from Ibid., 29–30.
23   *De inventione* 2.40.117. Quoted from Ibid., 18.
24   *Hermogenes and the Renaissance: Seven Ideas of Style*, 12–13.
25   "Epistle," 125. *The Yale Edition of the Shorter Poems of Edmund Spenser*, ed. William Oram et al. (New Haven: Yale University Press, 1989), 17.
26   In the first translation, I have associated *lea* with the participle *pesus*, and in the second, with the verb *nuo*.
27   Translating short Latin expressions, such as those that appear in emblems and impressa, is often problematic. In both translations, LEA is taken as a metonym for love (surely not an actual lioness). In the second translation, LEA is also taken to be the image of the lioness, the Lioness Design.
28   Sonnet 1's headnote provides an overall description of the work's content: *miserable accidentes... described hereafter in the copious varietie of* [the poet's] *deuises* [i. e., sonnets]. It suggests that the work progresses toward an end that is consistent with *the nature & true qualitie of a loue passion*. Yet the sequence ends (in its published order) with the death of Cupid, which seems inconsistent with *the nature & true qualitie of a* sonnet sequence. Reordering the sequence will resolve this contradiction, as discussed in Chapter 8.
29   Sonnet 1 describes the speaker's pitiful state: *despaire* (6); *yoake vpon my necke* (9); *live in servile kinde* (10); *live her thrall* (17). Sonnet 2's headnote acknowledges this state when it declares *how pitious a case the hart of a lover is*. A more specific Sequential Tie between these sonnets is found in the

link between *I now cry creake* (1.11), which can mean to "confess oneself beaten" (OED 5) or, literally, "a strident cry," and *blubbering teares* (2.3; *blubbering* means "sobbing noisily and unrestrainedly" [OED 2]).

30 *Dialogues of Love* (Toronto: University of Toronto Press, 2009), 68, 176.

31 II.8. Translation from *Commentary on Plato's Symposium on Love*, tr. Sears Reynolds Jayne (Dallas: Spring Publications, 1985), 144.

32 *Dialogues of Love*, 68.

33 *The Book of the Courtier*, ed. Virginia Cox, tr. Thomas Hoby (London: Everyman, 1994), 343.

34 See the note after the next.

35 See the sections that treat the L39 Series in Chapters 9 and 14.

36 The sidenote reads: *Materna redimitus tempora Mirto*, which may be a corrupted quotation from the *Aeneid* (*Sic fatus, velat materna tempora myrto*; 5.72), or from the *Georgics* (*cingens materna tempora myrto*; 1.28). The latter is a reference to Augustus, a supposed descendent of Aeneas and Venus.

37 Jeffrey Todd Knight, *Bound to Read: Compilations, Collections, and the Making of Renaissance Literature* (Philadelphia: University of Pennsylvania Press, 2013), 115.

38 See the discussion in Appendix D, "Notes on the Text".

39 William Murphy sees this proverb as similar to one quoted by Michael Drayton in his *Idea*: "Fortune assists the boldest" (*Idea*, 59.7) (Murphy Dissertation, 134).

40 See Kaske, *Spenser and Biblical Poetics* (Ithaca: Cornell University Press, 1999), 24.

41 *Semiotics of Poetry* (Bloomington: Indiana University Press, 1978), 161.

42 Michael Riffaterre, *Text Production* (New York: Columbia University Press, 1983), 111–12.

43 "Andreas Capellanus's Scholastic Definition of Love," *Viator* 25 (1994): 209–10. Monson provides the following note: "According to Aristotle, *De anima* 1.5 (410a25–26), thinking, like sense perception, is a kind of passion; that is, in perceiving or thinking the soul both acts and is acted upon. Cf. Aquinas, *Summa theologiae* la2ae.22.1, contra: 'sentire et intelligere est quoddam pati'" (210N53).

44 Hearing is a poetical representation of the intellectual (as opposed to sensual) acquisition of knowledge. This is the "coaptation of visible forms to demonstrate something invisible" (Dionysius the Areopagite, as discussed later in this chapter). A nonphysical, spiritual event is given a physical representation. In the Annunciation, it is a dove—symbolically the Holy Ghost—that enters through Mary's ear.

45 *Dialogues of Love*, 177–78.

46 Book 1, 1.1. Translation: *The Art of Courtly Love*, tr. John Jay Parry (New York: W.W. Norton, 1969), 28.

47 "The Subject of the 'De Amore' of Andreas Capellanus," *Modern Philology* 50.3 (1953): 152.

48 4377–84. See Charles Dahlberg, "Macrobius and the Unity of the 'Roman de la Rose,'" *Studies in Philology* 58.4 (1961): 579.

49 Douglas Kelly, "Courtly Love in Perspective: The Hierarchy of Love in Andreas Capellanus," *Traditio* 24 (1968): 147.

50 In *De Amore*, the cognitive process is what distinguishes courtly love from sensual love. Douglas Kelly writes: "For as both Paul Zumthor and Schlosser

have shown, the difference between Andreas' conception of courtly love and other forms of sensual love lies in the rational control the courtly lover exercises over his senses when directing his love to only one person" (Ibid., 131–32).

51   Sweet: 11.2; 11.17; 12.8; 13.HN; 14.10; 16.HN; 16.1. Delight: 12.14; 13.4; 14.12; 16.7; 17.12.

52   Six other instances of love's double power:

For nowe my life is double dying still,	(31.11)
But I feele paines, though blinde and double deade	(35.15)
And to my double hurt his pow'r do proue?	(65.10)
Am now twise free, and all my loue is past.	(85.18)
Though now my selfe twise free from all such care.	(89.18)
Forgetting, Time well spent was double gaine	(93.18)

53   *Dialogues of Love*, 191.

54   An interesting view on the philosophical development of these two categories, sense and intellect, and their treatment in Petrarch can be found in Edward Cranz, "A Common Pattern in Petrarch, Nicholas of Cusa, and Martin Luther," in *Humanity and Divinity in Renaissance and Reformation: Essays in honor of Charles Trinkaus*, ed. John W O'Malley et al. (Leiden: E. J. Brill, 1993), 53–70.

55   See S. K. Heninger, *Touches of Sweet Harmony: Pythagorean Cosmology and Renaissance Poetics* (San Marino: Huntington Library, 1974), 287–397. Heninger argues that in early modern poetics the poet is a "maker," analogous to the demiurge in Plato's *Timaeus*, which is the *locus classicus* of this tradition (291). He further argues that poetry may be a literary microcosm patterned after creation. In this way, the poet is not an imitator of imitation, a criticism that Plato makes in the *Republic*, but a revealer of the true nature of things (364). See also Coulter, *Literary Microcosm: Theories of Interpretation of the Later Neoplatonists* (Leiden: Brill, 1976), 32–126. For cosmopoesis in Spenser, see Kenneth Borris, *Visionary Spenser and the Poetics of Early Modern Platonism* (Oxford: Oxford University Press, 2017), 50–53, passim.

56   "From the Universal to the Particular in Medieval Poetry," *MLN* 85.6 (1970): 822.

57   Horapollo Niliacus, *The Hieroglyphics of Horapollo* (Princeton: Princeton University Press, 1993), 28. Introduction by George Boas.

58   Murphy Dissertation, xcvii.

59   *Essays in Medieval Culture* (Princeton: Princeton University Press, 1980), 19.

60   *The Subtext of Form in the English Renaissance: Proportion Poetical* (University Park: Pennsylvania State University Press, 1994), 41.

61   *Touches of Sweet Harmony*, 5–6. See also S. K. Heninger, "Sequences, Systems, Models: Sidney and the Secularization of Sonnets," in *Poems in Their Place: The Intertextuality and Order of Poetic Collections*, ed. Neil Fraistat (Chapel Hill: University of North Carolina Press, 1986), 69–71.

62   *Semiotics of Poetry*, 115, 154, 160.

63   *The Rhetoric of Poetry in the Renaissance and Seventeenth Century* (Baton Rouge: Louisiana State University Press, 1983), 8–10, 15. Houston argues that Scève, as Petrarch's heir, takes this use of images for structural purpose even further (32–33).

64   "Sequences, Systems, Models: Sidney and the Secularization of Sonnets," 71.

65 "The Mind's Eye: Memory and Textuality," in *The New Medievalism*, ed. Marina Scordilis Brownlee, Kevin Brownlee, and Stephen G. Nichols (Baltimore: Johns Hopkins University Press, 1991), 31.

66 Underlying this model is Aristotelean causality and scholastic psychology, according to Don Monson's "Andreas Capellanus's Scholastic Definition of Love," 209–11.

67 See Robert J. O'Connell, *Images of Conversion in St. Augustine's Confessions* (New York: Fordham University Press, 1996), 126–27.

68 See Brian Stock, *Augustine's Inner Dialogue: The Philosophical Soliloquy in Late Antiquity* (Cambridge: Cambridge University Press, 2010), 102.

69 See Winthrop Wetherbee, *Platonism and Poetry in the Twelfth Century: The Literary Influence of the School of Chartres* (Princeton: Princeton University Press, 1972), 59.

70 For the *Vita Nuova*, see Peter Dronke, *Dante's Second Love: The Originality and the Contexts of the Convivio* (Exeter: Society for Italian Studies, 1997), 8.

71 *The Individual and the Cosmos in Renaissance Philosophy* (Chicago: University of Chicago Press, 1963), 22.

72 *The Elizabethan Love Sonnet* (London: Methuen, 1966), 135–36.

Chapter 4 » The Poetics of Ruin and Restoration

1 Sonnets 44 and 45 are an obvious pair. Sonnet 79, which refers to the forthcoming MLIP Subsequence, is properly placed immediately prior to Sonnet 80.

2 Order is evident in two cases: Sonnets 80–82, which form the Puzzle Sonnet, are in their proper order; Sonnet 98 and the unnumbered *Quid Amor* poem are also correctly adjacent. However, elsewhere disorder is evident. As discussed in Chapter 5, at the Subsequence's midpoint, Sonnet 90 directly contradicts the theme of all other sonnets in the MLIP Subsequence. Also, the *Epilogue* and its closing apothegm controverts the sequence's last sonnet, which immediately precedes it.

3 See Michel Jeanneret, *Perpetual Motion: Transforming Shapes in the Renaissance from Da Vinci to Montaigne*, tr. Nidra Poller (Baltimore: Johns Hopkins University Press, 2001), 104–5.

4 *The Veil of Isis: An Essay on the History of Idea of Nature*, tr. Michael Chase (Cambridge, MA: Belknapp Press of Harvard University Press, 2006), 25–26. See also the extensive treatment in *Perpetual Motion*, 11–103.

5 *Perpetual Motion*, 1.

6 Ibid., 2.

7 Ibid., 6.

8 Terence Cave, *The Cornucopian Text: Problems of Writing in the French Renaissance* (Oxford: Oxford University Press, 1979), 179–180, 68–69.

9 *Spenser's Ruins and the Art of Recollection* (Toronto: University of Toronto Press, 2012), xii, *passim*.

10 *The Poetics of Ruins in Renaissance Literature* (New York: Fordham University Press, 2016), 2.

11 "Spenser's Languages: Writing in the Ruins of English," in *The Cambridge Companion to Spenser*, ed. Andrew Hadfield (Cambridge: Cambridge University Press), 175.

12 "The Genesis of Shakespeare's Sonnets: Spenser's *Ruines of Rome:by Bellay*," *PMLA* 98.5 (Oct. 1983): 800–14. See also Anne Ferry, *All in War with Time:*

Love Poetry of Shakespeare, Donne, Jonson, Marvell (Cambridge, MA: Harvard University Press, 1975).

13   "The Fig Tree and the Laurel: Petrarch's Poetics," *Diacritics* 5.1 (1975): 39, passim.

14   For *ruinae*, see Thomas M. Greene, *The Light in Troy: Imitation and Discovery in Renaissance Poetry*, Elizabethan Club series 7 (New Haven: Yale University Press, 1982), 92.

15   *Poetry, Signs, and Magic* (Newark: University of Delaware Press, 2005), 256.

16   The argument of his *Sciences and the Self in Medieval Poetry: Alan of Lille's Anticlaudianus and John Gower's Confessio Amantis*, Cambridge Studies in Medieval Literature 25 (Cambridge: Cambridge University Press, 1995).

17   Ibid., 67.

18   Ibid.

19   Ibid., 14.

20   Ibid., 25–26.

21   Ibid., 138.

22   Ibid., 29–30.

23   Ibid., 31.

24   Ibid., 69–70.

25   See the discussion of "fore-conceit" in Chapters 3 and 15.

26   Ibid., 72–74.

27   Ibid., 70. Simpson quotes Geoffrey of Vinsauf's *Poetria nova*, which describes "the initial creative act as the formation of an idea." Geoffrey writes: "The measuring line of his mind first lays out the work, and he mentally outlines the successive steps in a definite order" (70).

28   Michael Hetherington, "Renaissance Rhetorical Theory," in *Edmund Spenser in Context*, ed. Andrew Escobedo (Cambridge: Cambridge University Press, 2017), 172. See discussion in Chapter 3.

29   Ibid., 173.

30   *Spenser's Supreme Fiction: Platonic Natural History and The Faerie Queene* (Toronto: University of Toronto Press, 2001, 14.

31   *Sidney and Spenser: The Poet as Maker* (University Park: Pennsylvania State University Press, 1989), 55.

32   Heninger bemoans the legacy of New Criticism for its undervaluation of authorial intention, which he characterizes as distancing the artifact from the artificer (Ibid., 39–41).

33   See Sophie Weeks, "The Role of Mechanics in Francis Bacon's Great Instauration," in *Philosophies of Technology: Francis Bacon and His Contemporaries* (2 Vols.), ed. Claus Zittel et al., Vol. 1, (Koninklijke: Brill NV, 2008), 189–90.

34   "Homer Atomized: Francis Bacon and the Matter of Tradition," *ELH* 76.4 (2009): 1029.

35   Ibid., 1031–32.

36   *Ramus, Method, and the Decay of Dialogue: From the Art of Discourse to the Art of Reason* (Cambridge, MA: Harvard University Press, 1958), 119.

37   Ibid., 120. Quotation from 1553 edition, 37r.

38   Ibid., 124–25. Agricola argued for the orderly arrangement of *argumenta* within places or *loci* (ibid., 237).

39   *Works* 3.323. See Andrew Wallace, "Virgil and Bacon in the Schoolroom," *ELH* 73.1 (2006): 174. See also Rhodri Lewis, "Francis Bacon and Ingenuity,"

Renaissance Quarterly 67.1 (2014): 122. For the use of this metaphor by Ronsard and Erasmus, see *Perpetual Motion*, 247–48, and by Quintillian, Macrobius, Montaigne, 253–54. For use by Seneca, Lucretius, and Horace, see Greene, *Light in Troy*, 73–74.

40 *Works*, 4.93.
41 *Works*, 4.449.
42 "The Masculine Birth of Time," in *The Philosophy of Francis Bacon: An Essay on Its Development from 1603 to 1609, with New Translation of Fundamental Texts*, tr. Benjamin Farrington (Chicago: University of Chicago Press, 1966), 72.
43 See David Colclough, "Ethics and Politics in the New Atlantis," in *Francis Bacon's New Atlantis: New Interdisciplinary Essays*, ed. Bronwen Price (Manchester: Manchester University Press 2002), 68–69. Also, see his "'Non Canimus Surdis, Respondent Omnia Sylvae': Francis Bacon and the Transmission of Knowledge," in *Textures of Renaissance Knowledge*, ed. Philippa Berry and Margaret Tudeau-Clayton (Manchester: Manchester University Press, 2003), 83–88.
44 M. B. Parkes, "The Influence of the Concepts of Ordinatio and Compilatio on the Development of the Book," in *Medieval Learning and Literature: Essays Presented to Richard William Hunt*, ed. J. J. G. Alexander and Margaret Gibson (Oxford: Clarendon Press, 1976), 128–29.
45 Katherine Jackson, "Sylvester's 'Du Bartas,'" *Sewanee Review* 16.3 (1908): 317. Joshua Sylvester published a full translation in 1605.
46 "'Well Grounded, Finely Framed, and Strongly Trussed up Together' the 'Medieval' Structure of 'The Faerie Queene,'" *Review of English Studies* 52.205 (2001): 26.
47 Copeland, *Rhetoric, Hermeneutics and Translation in the Middle Ages*, 152.
48 Ibid., 190.
49 Robert Stillman, "The Scope of Sidney's *Defence of Poesy*: The New Hermeneutic and Early Modern Poetics," *English Literary Renaissance* 32.3 (2002): 372.
50 James Coulter, *The Literary Microcosm: Theories of Interpretation of the Later Neoplatonists* (Leiden: Brill, 1976), 84, passim, 95–126.
51 Copeland, *Rhetoric, Hermeneutics and Translation in the Middle Ages*, 108–9.
52 Ibid., 124.
53 Ibid., 174–75.
54 See *Ramus, Method, and the Decay of Dialogue*, 112.
55 *The Order of Things: An Archaeology of the Human Sciences* (New York: Vintage Books, 1970), 29, 32, 47, 51 (his italics).
56 *Ramus, Method, and the Decay of Dialogue*, 113.
57 Ibid., 184–85.
58 Ibid., 187.
59 Ibid., 267.
60 "The Masculine Birth of Time," in *Philosophy of Francis Bacon*, 64.
61 "Rhetoric and Action in Francis Bacon," *Philosophy & Rhetoric* 14.4 (1981): 213.
62 See Craig Walton, "Ramus and Bacon on Method," *Journal of the History of Philosophy* 9.3 (July 1, 1971): 291.
63 *Rhetoric, Hermeneutics and Translation in the Middle Ages*, 153. *Institutio oratoria* 2.17.26; 18.1–2.
64 *Philip Sidney and the Poetics of Renaissance Cosmopolitanism* (London:

Routledge, 2008), 114. The quotation from Sidney's *Defence* may be found in *An Apology for Poetry or The Defence of Poesy*, ed. Geoffrey Shepherd (London: T. Nelson and Sons, 1965), 101. For a similar view on Sidney, and also on Pontano, see Victoria Kahn, *Rhetoric, Prudence, and Skepticism in the Renaissance* (Ithaca: Cornell University Press, 1985), 41, 40.

65   *Works*, 4.449.

66   See Stillman, "Scope of Sidney's *Defence of Poesy*", 383. The quotation from the *Defence* ("strange effects") may be found in *An Apology for Poetry* (Shepherd), 114.

67   Stillman's translation of Melanchthon, *Corpus Reformatorum* XIII, 138: "Scope of Sidney's Defence of Poesy," 380N44.

68   *Bound to Read: Compilations, Collections, and the Making of Renaissance Literature* (Philadelphia: University of Pennsylvania Press, 2013), 95–96; passim, 94–116.

69   Ibid., 93; 220N30. Moreover, interleaved books were relatively common in the sixteenth century: the printer could easily add blank pages in between the pages of a book in the printing stage—be that "on demand" for a prospective customer or, which frequently occurred, for commercial reasons in religious texts that invited extensive glossing well beyond the page margins. See Petra Feuerstein-Herz: "Weiße Seiten. Durchschossene Bücher in alten Bibliotheken," in *Idee. Zeitschrift für Ideengeschichte* XI/4 (Winter 2017): 101–14. My appreciation to Gerhard F. Strasser for this insight.

70   *Bound to Read*, 93–94.

71   Ibid., 106.

72   Ibid., 111.

73   Ibid., 12.

74   Ibid., 113.

75   See Copeland, *Rhetoric, Hermeneutics and Translation in the Middle Ages*, 153.

76   *Hermeneutics and the Rhetorical Tradition: Chapters in the Ancient Legacy and Its Humanist Reception* (New Haven: Yale University Press, 2009), 31–32.

77   Copeland, *Rhetoric, Hermeneutics and Translation in the Middle Ages*, 124–25.

78   *Semiotics of Poetry*, 150 (italics in original).

79   Chapter 5, lines 4–8. Translation of Traugott Lawler, *The "Parisiana poetria" of John of Garland* (New Haven: Yale University Press, 1974), 85.

80   See Eden, *Hermeneutics and the Rhetorical Tradition*, 8.

81   Augustine insists the *res* or doctrine is set although the words or *signa* (signs) are not (Copeland, *Rhetoric, Hermeneutics and Translation in the Middle Ages*, 157–58). Eden cites the *Clavis scripturae sacrae* (1567) of Matthias Flacius, which recognizes that "a discrepancy between the writer's words and her or his intention" must be resolved. Eden concludes: "The ultimate aim of interpretation, in other words, is to establish authorial intention, the *mens authoris*: to look beyond the meaning or signification of the words to what the writer meant (*magis in mentem, quam in verba Scriptoris, respicere*) (2.31)" (*Hermeneutics and the Rhetorical Tradition*, 93–94).

82   George Puttenham, *The Art of English Poesy: A Critical Edition*, ed. Wayne A Rebhorn and Frank Whigham (Ithaca: Cornell University Press, 2007), 347N1; 360.

83   *Spenser and Biblical Poetics* (Ithaca: Cornell University Press, 1999), 18–19.

84   "Truss up" is taken from E. K.'s "well grounded, finely framed, and strongly trussed up together," discussed in the previous chapter.

85 *Spenser and Biblical Poetics*, 20. The Leclercq quotation is from *The Love of Learning and the Desire for God*, 91.

86 Ibid., 21.

87 Ibid. Luther quotation is from *World and Sacrament 3* (Vol. 37 of *Works*), 21.

88 *Spenser and Biblical Poetics*, 21.

89 Ibid., 27.

90 Ibid., 27. Kaske's index, which appears in her study in Appendix 2, covers the images that she treats in her book.

91 Ibid., 59.

92 Bush is referring to the works of Donne and Andrewes: *English Literature in the Earlier Seventeenth Century, 1600–1660* (London: Oxford University Press, 1945), 305.

93 *Spenser and Biblical Poetics*, 60.

94 *Elizabethan and Metaphysical Imagery: Renaissance Poetic and Twentieth-Century Critics* (Chicago: University of Chicago Press, 1947), 44.

95 "Allegory, Emblem, and Symbol," in *The Oxford Handbook of Edmund Spenser*, ed. Richard A McCabe (Oxford: Oxford University Press, 2010), 442.

96 "Yeats and the Language of Symbolism," *University of Toronto Quarterly* 17 (October 1947): 1.

97 See Kenneth Borris, *Visionary Spenser and the Poetics of Early Modern Platonism* (Oxford: Oxford University Press, 2017), 68–69.

98 See Charles Lemmi, *The Classic Deities in Bacon: A Study in Mythological Symbolism* (Baltimore: Johns Hopkins Press, 1933).

99 *Touches of Sweet Harmony: Pythagorean Cosmology and Renaissance Poetics* (San Marino: Huntington Library, 1974), 338.

100 *Fables of Identity: Studies in Poetic Mythology* (New York: Harcourt, Brace & World, 1963), 71.

101 *Elizabethan and Metaphysical Imagery*, 24–26.

102 *Spenser's Images of Life* (Cambridge: Cambridge University Press, 1967), 8–10.

103 *Sciences and the Self in Medieval Poetry*, 11, 11N22.

104 "The Influence of the Concepts of *Ordinatio* and *Compilatio* on the Development of the Book," 117, 131.

105 The *Ars Memoriae* is founded on the idea of an ordered, itemized list of short phrases that act as a mnemonic device. Simonides of Ceos (556–468 BCE) is credited as the founder of this art. He was said to have attended a banquet, and when called outside the building to meet others, narrowly escaped death when the building collapsed. The diners' bodies were so disfigured that they could not be identified. However, Simonides, aware of their positions at the banquet table, was able to identify the bodies by remembering where they were seated.

106 The *Ars Memoriae* was an essential tool of the rhetorician. Cicero's five parts of rhetoric include *dispositio* (arrangement) and *memoria* (memory). The *dispositio* of a work—the order in which an argument is presented—was considered critical to whether an argument would prevail. The *Ars Memoriae* can also utilize images or short phrases as an aid in the recall of texts. For example, it was used to recall Scripture: often one biblical phrase provided sufficient stimulus to allow the recall of a far longer passage. Ordered lists of phrases were also used by orators to remember the sequence in which to deliver the order of a speech's arguments or topics. The delivery of topics in their

proper or ideal order, *kairos*, was considered essential for a speech to be persuasive.

107 See Rhodri Lewis, "A Kind of Sagacity: Francis Bacon, the *Ars Memoriae* and the Pursuit of Natural Knowledge," *Intellectual History Review* 19.2 (2009):155–175. Watson wrote a treatise on the *Ars Memoriae: Compendium Memoriae Localis* in the early 1580s. See Sutton Edition, Vol. 2, 11. I have not examined the issue of whether this might instead be the work of Francis Bacon.

108 *The Canonization*, 32. In Ramism, topics or *loci* are "pictured as individual structures in real-estate developments, separated from one another according to 'Solon's Law' by a clear space of so many feet" (*Ramus, Method, and the Decay of Dialogue*, 121).

109 "A Kind of Sagacity," 156, 169, 172.

110 *Expositio magistri Joannis de Celaya, Valentini, in primum tractatum Summularum magistri Petri Hispani*, Bibliothèque nationale de France, 1525, folio M3r.

111 *Dissemination* (Chicago: University Press, 1981), 51 (his italics).

112 *Art and Illusion: A Study in the Psychology of Pictorial Representation* (New York: Pantheon Books, 1960), 90, 155.

113 "Francis Bacon and the Art of Misinterpretation," *PMLA* 130.2 (2015): 238.

114 In the Puzzle's first 6 Stages, 138 characters are encrypted using 135 CipherLines. There are 3 cases of double use of a CipherLine: Sonnet 90 and one preface with two Designs, employed twice. The seventh Stage uses a different method to specify CipherLines.

115 *The Dyer's Hand and Other Essays* (New York: Vintage Books, 1962), 50.

116 *Semiotics of Poetry* (Bloomington: Indiana University Press, 1978), 168N16, 70, 165, 150.

117 As quoted in the above section, "Paratexts and artifices inform the reader's re-creation."

Chapter 5 » Stage 2: Reason Prevails

1   However, the relative position of these two poems is later modified in a subsequent Puzzle Stage, as revealed in Chapter 8.

2   Running titles are present in Sidney's sequence and Shakespeare's, but not most others. In the case of the *Hekatompathia*, the appearance of running titles only over the second Subsequence arouses our curiosity.

3   The headnote states that the sonnet's first and sixth lines allude to the headnote's two Sophoclean *sententiae*; however, the first Sophoclean quote aligns not with the first line but the fifth line, which I presume to be an unintentional error.

4   This adumbrates the conclusion of sequence in the restored order. As discussed in Chapter 14, love is "process physics," a Heraclitan flux, which is not divine. In contrast, the speaker's mind is characterized as divine.

Chapter 6 » The Precision System

1   Two particularly useful studies that discuss prefaces are Gérard Genette, *Paratexts: Thresholds of Interpretation*, Literature, Culture, Theory 20

(Cambridge: Cambridge University Press, 1997), and Jacques Derrida, *Dissemination* (Chicago: University Press, 1981).

2   See discussion in Chapter 1.

3   See discussion in Chapter 1.

4   Sutton's translation.

5   A revision of Sutton's translation. Sutton identifies *cyprigeno* (Venus-born) as Cupid; Heninger claims it is Venus; however, *cyprigeno* means Venus-born, not Cyprus-born (Cupid was not born in Cyprus).

6   Sutton's translation; however, I have modified his translation of *qua* from "any girl" to "any Nymph." *Qua*, which appears in both lines 35 and 37, surely refers back to *piis Nymphis* (33). The whole passage is about readers in the literary circle, who are called nymphs, and therefore would use the feminine *qua*.

7   LS *calx* (2), II.B; also, Quintilian 8.5.30.

8   The 18 Designs include 4 pictorial Designs (Figs. 6.1a–6.1d), the DoubleA Design printed inverted (Fig. 7.6), 6 Flower Designs (Fig. 7.2), 2 Bulb Designs (Fig. 7.4), 2 Root Designs (Fig. 7.5; Roots-4 appears with Sonnet 4), a diamond-shaped Design (see Sonnet 42/L90.6), a diamond with a border Design (see Sonnet 52/L64.5), and a Design that appears to be a combination of bulbs and flowers that appears only once (Sonnet 5).

9   On Daedalus, see Yves Bonnefoy, *Greek and Egyptian Mythologies* (Chicago: University of Chicago Press, 1992), 88–90.

10   According to Peter Dawkins, the image of a "Double-A" first appeared in 1577 in Christopher Platin's edition of Andrea Alciato's *Emblemata* (Antwerp), Emblem XLV (*The Shakespeare Enigma* [London: Polair Publishing, 2004], 328–29).

11   "Changed Opinion as to Flowers," in *Renaissance Paratexts*, ed. Helen Smith and Louise Wilson (Cambridge: Cambridge University Press, 2011), 63.

12   *Visionary Spenser and the Poetics of Early Modern Platonism* (Oxford: Oxford University Press, 2017), 87–92, 87N16.

13   The two locations are below the prefatory poems of Royden and Peele, and below Sonnet 85. There are press variants at other locations (see Appendix D, Notes on the Text), which may be an attempt to correct the orientation to the author's specification. We will discover in the second and subsequent Stages of the Puzzle that the normal and inverted printings of this Design signal different Transform Pairs (cryptographic tables). See further discussion in Chapter 7.

14   *Polygraphie, et vniuerselle escriture cabalistique*, de M. I. Tritheme abbé ; traduicte par Gabriel de Collange, natif de Tours en Auuergne (Paris: Pour Iaques Keruer, 1561), Clavicle et interpretation, Kv.

15   See Spedding's comment in *Works*, 2.501. From *De Augmentis Scientiarum* (1623), Book VI, chapter 1.

Chapter 7 » Decoding the Designs

1   Peter Pesic, "François Viète, Father of Modern Cryptanalysis-Two New Manuscripts," *Cryptologia* 21.1 (1997): 12.

2   See discussion in Appendix D, Notes on the Text.

3   *Fables of Identity: Studies in Poetic Mythology* (New York: Harcourt Brace & World, 1963), 18.

Chapter 8 » Stage 3: The Restoration of the Third Subsequence

1   Prominently located at the center of the title page, as shown in Fig. 14.1.
2   Sutton Edition, 139.
3   The adherence strictly to reason is not a tenet of Christian, Platonist, or Aristotelean thought. Although Stoic philosophy advocates reason, the MLIP Subsequence cannot easily be cast in this light: the speaker's emotions are in high gear.
4   See E. R. Dodds, *The Greeks and the Irrational* (Berkeley: University of California Press, 1951). Chapter 7 is especially relevant: "Plato, the Irrational Soul, and the Inherited Conglomerate," 207–35.
5   Ardolino, "Thomas Watson, Shadow Poet of Edmund Spenser," *Notes and Queries* 61.2 (2014): 227.
6   Monson, *Andreas Capellanus, Scholasticism, and the Courtly Tradition* (Washington, DC: Catholic University of America Press, 2005), 56.
7   See Robert M. Durling, *The Figure of the Poet in Renaissance Epic* (Cambridge, MA: Harvard University Press, 1965), 35.
8   *English Literature in the Sixteenth Century Excluding Drama: The Completion of the Clark Lectures, Trinity College, Cambridge, 1944*, Clark lectures 1944 (Oxford: Clarendon Press, 1962), 61.
9   See the discussion in Chapter 4.
10   Durling's translation.
11   Sonnet 90 does not appear elsewhere in the manuscript. Only these three lines appear, above the Epilogue, on the manuscript's last page.
12   Phillips Dissertation, 471; Sutton Edition, 275–76.
13   As discussed in Chapter 4.
14   *Sciences and the Self in Medieval Poetry: Alan of Lille's Anticlaudianus and John Gower's Confessio Amantis*, Cambridge Studies in Medieval Literature 25 (Cambridge: Cambridge University Press, 1995), 31.
15   For antiquity, see William S. Anderson, "The Theory and Practice of Poetic Arrangement from Vergil to Ovid," in *Poems in Their Place: The Intertextuality and Order of Poetic Collections,* ed. Neil Fraistat (Chapel Hill: University of North Carolina Press, 2011). For the early modern period, see Earl Miner, "Some Issues for Study of Integrated Collections," also in *Poems in Their Place.*
16   Anderson, "Theory and Practice of Poetic Arrangement from Vergil to Ovid," 49.
17   These diagrams appear in Doranne Fenoaltea, "A Poetic Monument: Arrangement in Book 1 of Ronsard's 1550 Odes," in *The Ladder of High Designs: Structure and Interpretation of the French Lyric Sequence,* ed. Doranne Fenoaltea and David Lee Rubin (Charlottesville: University Press of Virginia, 1991), 55, *passim,* 54–72.
18   The term "Hexameral" is only meant to mean "six of something" and is not related to the hexameral literature that organizes around the six days of Creation.
19   The conceit that Cupid has two arrows, one gold and one lead, can be found in Ebreo's *Dialogues of Love*; however, his symbolism is entirely different from the symbolism in Sonnet 63. *Dialogues of Love*, tr. Rossella Pescatori and Cosmos Damian Bacich (Toronto: University of Toronto Press, 2009), 142–43, 164.

20   In this calculation, we completely relax the conditions of CipherLine selection such that any line may be handpicked to produce the appropriate crib letter. This relaxation does not permit any plaintext letter to be produced because of restrictions in the Transform tables and the restricted range of letters that are typically found at the beginning and end of sonnet lines. I examined the first and last letters of each of the 18 lines of the 24 sonnets in the Puzzle's third Stage (excluding those sonnets with Designs for which the Transform Pair value is unknown). I found that, on average, there were only about 8 different letters that were used to begin a sonnet line, and only about 4 letters that ended a sonnet line. Not surprisingly, the first letters of sonnet lines have a limited range over the 24-letter Elizabethan alphabet—certain letters such as, say, "T" are far more common than, say, "Q." There was even less variation in the ending letters of sonnet lines. In Elizabethan spelling, the letter "E" ends many words. Furthermore, given that lines end in rhymes, certain letters such as "S," "T," and "Y" are particularly common.

   The following analysis approximates the range of plaintext letters that may be generated. (A stricter analysis would utilize the actual text of the 24 sonnets to calculate the range of plaintext letters; in this analysis, I found the range to be more restricted, and thus my approximate calculation here is more conservative.) If, on average, there are 8 different first letters in a sonnet's lines and 4 different last letters, then there are 12 different ciphertext letters that can be generated (allowing the CipherLine to be any one of the 18 sonnet lines). The number of possible plaintext letters, each deciphered from a single ciphertext letter, is thus also limited to a range of 12 different letters. However, the crib has a full range of 24 possible letters for each crib letter, and thus for any given sonnet, there is only a 12 out of 24 chance, equal to a 1 out of 2 chance, that 1 of those 12 plaintext letters will match the required crib letter. The probability that this 50/50 event would occur for the 24 sonnets that generate a crib letter is equivalent to tossing a coin 24 times and getting heads each time. The probability that one would win a 50/50 bet 24 times in a row is approximately 1 out of 16 million.

Chapter 9 » The Third Subsequence: a Palinode and an Epiphany

1   *Visionary Spenser and the Poetics of Early Modern Platonism* (Oxford: Oxford University Press, 2017), 106–10, passim, 83–121.
2   "(H)eroic Disarmament: Spenser's Unarmed Cupid, Platonized Heroism, and *The Faerie Queene*'s Poetics," *Spenser Studies* 31–32 (2018): 97, 117.
3   39.2 and 78.3.
4   *On the Nature of Love: Ficino on Plato's Symposium*, tr. Arthur Farndell (London: Shepheard-Walwyn Publishers, 2016), 16 (Speech 2, chapter 2).
5   *Dialogues of Love*, tr. Rossella Pescatori and Cosmos Damian Bacich (Toronto: University of Toronto Press, 2009), 324.
6   *Visionary Spenser and the Poetics of Early Modern Platonism*, 160; passim, 127, 136, 160–65.
7   The classic study on this subject is Arthur O. Lovejoy, *The Great Chain of Being: A Study of the History of an Idea* (Cambridge, MA: Harvard University Press, 1936).

8   *De amore*, 3.3. A translation of the Tuscan version, *Sopra lo Amore*: "This is why all the parts of the cosmos—being the works of a single craftsman, parts of a single mechanism, and mutually alike in being and living—are bound together by means of a reciprocal love, in such a manner that Love may rightly be called the everlasting knot and bond of the cosmos, the unmoving support of its parts, and the firm foundation of the whole mechanism" (*On the Nature of Love*, 38 [Speech 3, chapter 3]).

9   See Edgar Wind, *Pagan Mysteries in the Renaissance* (London: Faber and Faber, 1958), 82.

10   Petrarch Sonnet 164.

11   *Dialogues of Love*, 194.

12   Alastair Fowler, "Emanations of Glory: Neoplatonic Order in Spenser's Faerie Queen," in *A Theatre for Spenserians*, ed. Judith Kennedy and James A Reither, Papers of the International Spenser Colloquium, Frederiction, New Brunswick, October, 1969 (Toronto: University of Toronto Press, 1973), 54.

13   Wind notes the interweaving of opposites in a perfect maze in Jonson's *Pleasure Reconciled to Virtue* (*Pagan Mysteries in the Renaissance*, 168) and in the riddle that the Sphinx proposes to Cupid in *Love freed from Ignorance and Folly* (180). On the spread of knowledge to England: 181–82.

14   Don A Monson, *Andreas Capellanus, Scholasticism, and the Courtly Tradition* (Washington, DC: Catholic University of America Press, 2005), 108–9.

15   "The Fig Tree and the Laurel: Petrarch's Poetics," *Diacritics* 5.1 (1975): 34, 36.

16   The use of italics in the *Hekatompathia*'s sonnets is uncommon, as discussed in Appendix D.

17   Michael Riffaterre writes, "Ungrammaticality is a sign of literariness" and a call to exegesis (*Semiotics of Poetry* [Bloomington: Indiana University Press, 1978], 139).

18   Annabel M. Patterson, *Hermogenes and the Renaissance: Seven Ideas of Style* (Princeton: Princeton University Press, 1970), 11–12.

19   Patterson's quotation from the *Hekatompathia* appears on pages 12–13 (Ibid.).

20   Ibid., 13.

21   Puttenham expresses hostility toward carnivalesque (in Bakhtin's sense of the word) poetry, at length, but then indulges in the very same in his treatise on poetry, breaking the decorum that he advocates. See Wayne A. Rebhorn, "'His Tail at Commandment': George Puttenham and the Carnivalization of Rhetoric," in *A Companion to Rhetoric and Rhetorical Criticism*, ed. Walter Jost and Wendy Olmsted (Malden: Blackwell Publishing, 2004), 96–99, passim.

22   *Virgil's Aeneid*, tr. Rev. Oliver Crane (New York: Baker & Taylor Company, 1888), x.

23   Previously quoted in Chapter 1: Wendy Phillips, "No More Tears: Thomas Watson Absolved," *Comitatus: A Journal of Medieval and Renaissance Studies* 20.1 (1989): 75.

24   The other three metrical faults are L82.Scoff.7/92.3 (hexameter) and corruptions at 48.9 and 77.1. See commentaries on these sonnets in Vol. II.

25   John Freccero, *In Dante's Wake: Reading from Medieval to Modern in the Augustinian Tradition*, ed. Melissa Swain and Danielle Callegari (New York: Fordham University Press, 2015), 60–61.

26   Ibid., 67.

27   Ibid., 207.

28 "The Fig Tree and the Laurel," 34, 37.
29 She is mentioned in a reference to the past in L73.H.11 and hypothetically in L73.2.16. Her eyes become dispersers of love's power in L73.6.13.
30 "Sequences, Systems, Models: Sidney and the Secularization of Sonnets," in *Poems in Their Place: The Intertextuality and Order of Poetic Collections*, ed. Neil Fraistat (Chapel Hill: University of North Carolina Press, 1986), 73.
31 *Poetry, Signs, and Magic* (Newark: University of Delaware Press, 2005), 247, 256. Also, the rest of this intriguing chapter titled, "Poetry and the Scattered World," 245–59. Although Greene asserts that Petrarch's speaker does not reach an end, one could argue that he does in the final three poems of the *Canzoniere*, in which he places himself in God's hands. However, Greene's claim that the *Canzoniere* never reaches a resolution seems to me to be correct because the speaker's attachment to Laura (and poetic fame, symbolized by laurel) is never truly abandoned. As in Petrarch's *Secretum*, this conflict never resolves.
32   "Petrarch," in *Edmund Spenser in Context*, ed. Andrew Escobedo (Cambridge: Cambridge University Press, 2017), 239–40.

Chapter 10 » The Precision System's Orchema Tables

1   Stage 2's 21-letter crib and Stage 3's 37-letter crib were generated from 57 sonnets/Designs (Sonnet 90 and its Lioness Design were used twice).
2   TP4 and TP13 are also unassigned. However, TP4 is among the Flower Designs and so its likely value is the Flowers-2x3 Design. TP13 is unassigned, but its value (A8, A7) is unlikely to accommodate one of the frequently appearing pictorial Designs. Also, either TP10 or TP11 is unassigned: the Roots-5 Design must be assigned to either TP10 or TP11, but we do not yet know which one (because the first Transform of both TP10 and TP11 is A11). However, we would naturally expect that the Roots-4 Design lies adjacent to the Roots-5 Design, and therefore neither TP10 nor TP11 is likely available. See also Chapter 7, "The pictorial Designs" section.
3   The *Hekatompathia*'s reference to the Orchema tables in *Polygraphia* 5 directs us to a single page (Oii, 1518 edition, but the page numbering is corrupt). This page includes 6 tables of two columns each, followed by these two sentences, translated from the Latin:
    > In these Orchema tables, a flexible alphabet [what I call a Transform] is presented through transposition and skipping, as much as by the pattern of succession as by the position of the letters. These together suffice through the example of their arrangements: their method and form resist discovery because they can be varied without limit.

    The *Polygraphia*'s back matter includes "brief explanations" of each of its books. In the section titled "EXPLANATIO IN QUINTUM LIBRUM polygraphiae nostrae brevis," the last sentence (page C, my translation) refers to the Orchema tables:
    > And it is a great secret that few will understand, to be able to find out all the senses of the transposition of letters, however they are hidden.
4   Recta: R1, R4, R5, R6, R8, and R9 through R12; Aversa: A3, A4, and A6 through A12.

5   See the first edition of this study, pages 394–95, for my erroneous selection of line 14. The correct CipherLine selection for Sonnet L50.6 is line 13. The argument for why line 13 is the correct selection may be found in Addendum 5.
6   See the first edition of this study, pages 320–21, for my erroneous selection of line 7. The argument for why line 8 is the correct CipherLine selection for Sonnet L64.H may be found in Addendum 4. As it happens, the distinction between lines 7 and 8 is inconsequential: both lines end with "E," and it is the last letter of the CipherLine that produces the required plaintext letter.

Chapter 11 » Stages 4 and 5: The Poet's New Instructions

1   Sonnet 90 is used twice, once in the MLIP Subsequence and once in the third.
2   There is another polyphonic alternative available here, for if one looks at the 12th through 15th columns of Fig. 11.4, MAGI can be formed. But as this would be read as a *plural* second-person vocative, it conflicts with the second-person *singular* imperatives of EXI and ADI, and thus I rejected it.
3   See LS I.B.1 for "approach" and "assist."
4   Another possible reading of ME ADI PIA FAMA is "Assist me with [gaining] a pious reputation."
5   See Addendum 10. There are 13 Designs, but only 12 CipherLines, because the CipherLine on the *Quatorzain* preface, which has two Designs, is used twice.
6   This inversion is discussed above. The reason for this anomaly is taken up in the next chapter.

Chapter 12 » Stage 6: The Hidden Labyrinth

1   As previously quoted in Chapter 3. Also discussed in Chapter 4.
2   A Cardan or Cardano grill is described in David Kahn, *The Codebreakers: The Story of Secret Writing* (Toronto: Macmillan, 1967), 144.
3   Servius calls the *Aeneid* a text when he refers to the "totius libri textum" of Book 7 (ad 7.601). See Shadi Bartsch, "Ars and the Man: The Politics of Art in Virgil's *Aeneid*," *Classical Philology* 93.4 (1998): 322–42.
4   Varro was frequently read by humanist scholars (*De Lingua Latina* 7.36). My thanks to Chris Cochran for this insight.
5   URET: LS II.B.1: "to vex; annoy."
6   On Bacon's use of this motto, see Richard Serjeantson, "Francis Bacon's *Valerius Terminus* and the Voyage to the 'Great Instauration,'" *Journal of the History of Ideas* 78.3 (2017): 341–368.
7   Murphy Dissertation, 185. *Strozii Poetae Pater Et Filius* [Titus Vespasianus Stroza; Hercules Stroza] (Parisiis: Ex officina Simonis Colinaei, 1530) 224b–225b.
8   I read IRE and EMI as historical infinitives. Alternatively, the message could be read with different word boundaries: I RE FORE XI EMI. In this reading, RE FORE is an ablative of attendant circumstances and might be translated: "Proceed [imperative], in the circumstance of the thing (i.e., sonnet) being a gateway. I acquired 11." However, reading IRE and EMI as historical infinitives better fits the context.

9   BEO might instead be read in the historical present tense: "I blessed." This would fit with the use of the historical infinitive mode in the prior sentence, as described above.

Chapter 13 » Stage 7: The Seventh Seal

1   The double use of VERA... DIA is explained in Chapter 12.
2   The number of lines not excluded were, beginning with Sonnet 26 and ending with Sonnet 82, as follows: 4, 1, 4, 2, 3, 3, 4, 2, 5, 3, 2. The sum of the foregoing numbers is 33, or an average of 3 lines per sonnet (33 divided by 11 sonnets).
3   For example, the value of the feminine pronouns in Sonnet 126 shift near the poem's end. See Helen Vendler, *The Art of Shakespeare's Sonnets* (Cambridge, MA: Belknap Press, 1997), 534.
4   17.1, 25.11, 26.18, 29.1, 29.14, 32.15, 52.8, 55.18, 75.11, and 76.7.
5   ARDI can refer to a meager manner of living (LS, *aridus*, IIA).
6   I performed an analysis of the ciphertext letters required to generate the actual plaintext message (ERUM FS BACON) for each possible offset. For example, in the case in which the Transform Pair loop starts at an offset of one (at the second sonnet letter), a difficulty is encountered when trying to encipher the tenth letter, which is the "O" in BACON. To generate an "O" using TP9 (A12, A12) requires that either the first or last letter of the CipherLine be "Z," a very severe restriction. About half of the possible offsets were likely unusable (1, 2, 3, 7, 8, and 10). Of the remaining ones, some would have provided the poet with greater flexibility than others in constructing appropriate CipherLines.
7   See E. C. Woodcock, *A New Latin Syntax* (Mundelein, IL: Bolchazy-Carducci Publishers, 1959), 3–4 (paragraph 5).
8   See "Practices of Unmasking: Polyhistors, Correspondence, and the Birth of Dictionaries of Pseudonymity in Seventeenth-Century Germany," *Journal of the History of Ideas* 67.2 (2006): 219–50. Mulsow argues that literary scholars have been focused on literary issues such as Foucault's "author-function" and seem to be unaware of Vincentius Placcius's monumental *Theatrum anonymorum et pseudonymorum* (220N1). See also Mulsow, *Knowledge Lost: A New View of Early Modern Intellectual History*, tr. H. C. Erik Midelfort, bilingual edition (Princeton: Princeton University Press, 2022). He argues that the obscuration of authorship was widespread during the early modern period: "Pseudonyms were used, and publishers posted false information about the printer or place of publication; titles were falsified as well" (15). I wish to thank Sarah A. Lang for recommending Mulsow's work.
9   Ibid., 231–34.
10   Ibid., 222.
11   Ibid., 219. See also Ernest Barker, "The Authorship of the *Vindiciae Contra Tyrannos*," *Cambridge Historical Journal* 3.2 (1930): 167.
12   Although commendations may be part of a literary game, they may also be written to satisfy a printer's requirements (printer refers to the publisher). See Clara Gebert, *Elizabethan Dedications and Prefaces* (New York: Russell and Russell, 1966), 23–24.
13   See Michael Bath, *Speaking Pictures: English Emblem Books and Renaissance Culture* (London: Longman Group, 1994), 110.

14 See "Practices of Unmasking," 223–24, 224N15–17.

15 Sutton's comment; see Chapter 1.

16 On *Praise of Folly*, see Chapter 1. With respect to Montaigne's work, P. J. Hendrick argues, "Sebond appears to be forgotten, and the value of his work undermined by the sustained attack of the *Apologie* on human reason in general. This apparent betrayal of Sebond... has given some credibility to those who would argue for an ironic, anti-religious design in Montaigne's *Apologie*. If he entitles an important essay 'Apologie de Raimond Sebond', and goes on to destroy the whole foundation on which Sebond's work is built, it might seem legitimate to suppose that a certain irony is intended" ("Montaigne, Lucretius and Scepticism: An Interpretation of the 'Apologie de Raimond Sebond,'" *Proceedings of the Royal Irish Academy: Archaeology, Culture, History, Literature* 79 [1979]: 143).

17 Bacon's father died in 1579, and the estate could not provide adequately for Francis, his mother, his brother Anthony, and his half-brothers.

18 Although an 11-letter sequence is short for the purposes of this calculation, the context is extraordinarily restrictive. Any message that appears after such a long journey (solving the Puzzle) would be ridiculous if it did not have great import. Surely a significant secret must be revealed.

19 Shannon speaks of "the probabilities of the various possible messages" (see Excursus 12).

20 One possible exception is the enigmatic headnote to Sonnet 74: *The Author in this passion, vpon a reason secret vnto him selfe, extolleth his Mistres vnder the name of a Spring.*

21 A more detailed explanation of the number of possible messages that would reveal Bacon's name is provided here. Bacon signed letters either Fr. Bacon or Fs. Bacon, as discussed earlier in this chapter. The remaining 4 letters may have used a word or words other than ERUM to describe Bacon's role. For example, SUM (I am) could have been used instead, though this leaves us a letter short. Yet, I cannot think of any appropriate four-letter words other than ERUM. Furthermore, ERUM is foregrounded by its earlier appearance (in other forms) among the Stage 6 Sequential Ties (AI ERI and LEA ARDI. ERE.) and is thus more probable than any other word that indicates authorship. Nevertheless, to be conservative, we imagine that there are 4 alternatives that have not come to mind and further treat them as equiprobable, for a total of 5 possibilities. Bacon's name, FS BACON, could have either preceded or succeeded the 4-letter word. In all, there are 5 possibilities for the word indicating authorship, 2 possible orders of the 4-letter word, and 2 alternative abbreviations for Bacon's first name (FS and FR). Multiplied together, this gives us 20 possibilities.

22 The earlier estimate of 1 in 55,000 multiplied by 2,000/6,500.

23 See the discussion in Excursus 12.

Chapter 14 » The Ontlogy of Love

1 *Plato's Symposium*, 2nd ed. (New Haven: Yale University Press, 1987), 2–3.

2 "Cosmogony and Love: The Role of Phaedrus in Ficino's Symposium Commentary," *Journal of Medieval and Renaissance Studies Durham, NC* 10.2 (1980): 152.

3   Rosen's term. For example, *Plato's Symposium*, 44.
4   Hans-Georg Gadamer, *Dialogue and Dialectic: Eight Hermeneutical Studies on Plato*, tr. P. Christopher Smith, (New Haven: Yale University Press, 1980), 86.
5   Ibid., 86N4 (P. Christopher Smith's description).
6   A glimpse of prelapsarian human existence is found in the first four lines of Sonnet 1 and the last four lines of the Neo-Latin poem, Sonnet 45/L90.2.
7   *The Ancients and the Moderns: Rethinking Modernity* (New Haven: Yale University Press, 1989), 22.
8   See Andrew Fuyarchuk, *Gadamer's Path to Plato: A Response to Heidegger and a Rejoinder by Stanley Rosen* (Eugene, OR: Wipf and Stock, 2010), 68–69.
9   According to Rosen, the *Symposium*'s first speaker, Phaedrus, has the Titans prevail over the Olympic gods (*Plato's Symposium*, 50). The Titans represent forces of the natural world; the Olympic gods are, as Ezra Pound characterized them, eternal states of mind manifested by poets.
10 The *Oxford Francis Bacon*. Vol. 6, *Philosophical Studies, c.1611–c.1619*, ed. Graham Rees (Oxford: Oxford University Press, 1996), 197. Rees suggest that Natalis Comes may be Bacon's source (416–17).
11 See Rosen, *Plato's Symposium*, 48–49.
12 With respect to the use of other translators' work, see note 3 in Sutton's "Introduction" to *Antigone*. Available at www.philological.bham.ac.uk/watson/antigone), or Sutton Edition (see "List of Primary Sources"), 3–15.
13 On the form of the pomps and themes, see Sutton's "Introduction" (Ibid., notes 10 and 11).
14 Ibid., note 10.
15 Ibid., notes 12–14.
16 Ibid., notes 9, 22.
17 The complete verse is "Musa Sophoclaeas Watsoni imitata Camoena Ismenidem Latio reddidit ore loqui."
18 Sutton's translations of Cooke's Greek preface and the author's Latin preface addressed to Howard, respectively. These are avaialble online or the Sutton Edition (see my note 12 above).
19 Fourth pomp, 30th line.
20 Third pomp, 30th line and 41st line, respectively.
21 Sutton, a Hellenist, at times bristles at this usurpation of Sophocles's play (which is fair enough), but he also recognizes that Elizabethans had their own agenda. See his "Introduction" to *Antigone*, notes 6–10 (op. cit., my note 12 above).
22 For example, Shakespeare, in *Troilus and Cressida*, similarly applies a thick coat of Petrarchan paint to his source material. See my discussion of Sir Walter Ralegh's *Commendatory Verse* to the 1590 *Faerie Queene* below. See also *Petrarch in Britain: Interpreters, Imitators, and Translators Over 700 Years*, ed. M. L McLaughlin, Letizia Panizza, and Peter Hainsworth, Proceedings of the British Academy 146 (Oxford, UK: Published for the British Academy by Oxford University Press, 2007), especially Stephen Clucas's "Thomas Watson's *Hekatompathia* and European Petrarchism" (217–28). Other sources include Gordon Braden, "Shakespeare's Petrarchism," in *Shakespeare's Sonnets: Critical Essays*, ed. James Schiffer (New York: Garland, 2000), 989; and Thomas Roche, *Petrarch and the English Sonnet Sequences* (New York: AMS Press, 1989).

23 See Sutton's notes on this line, 89.1 online, or print Sutton Edition, 266).
24 The quotation I cite is from a work published one year after the *Hekatom-pathia*: Petrus Canisius, *Commentariorvm De Verbi Dei Corrvptelis, Tomi duo* (Sartorius, 158), 204. It provides a corrupted quotation followed by Je-rome's "true" words: "Rursus vero Hieronymus: Difficile est, inquit, Haereti-cum reperire qui diligat castitatem." Apparently, Bacon was not the only one to corrupt this line. A substantially similar version of Jerome's words appears in Thomas Gascoigne's fifteenth-century theological dictionary, *Loci E Libro Veritatum*: "difficile enim est haereticum reperiri qui diligat castitatem."
25 *Cupido Cruciatus*: "Quas inter medias furvae caliginis umbram /dispulit inconsultus Amor stridentibus alis" (45–46).
26 Sutton reports that this is "evidently not a quote from Seneca (Senior or Ju-nior)." See his notes for 89.3 (online) or print Sutton Edition, 266.
27 On the relationship between the sun and the Good, see *Republic* 509b.
28 See Jacob Howland, *The Republic: The Odyssey of Philosophy* (Toronto: Twayne, 1993), 148.
29 Rosen, *Plato's Symposium*, 147–48.
30 *The Spenser Encyclopedia* (Abingdon: Routledge, 1996), 18.
31 Edgar Wind's summary of this cosmology is worth quoting at length:

> Among Renaissance theologians it was almost a commonplace to say that the highest mysteries transcend the understanding and must be apprehended through a state of darkness in which the distinctions of logic vanish. The 'negative theology' of Dionysius the Areopagite had developed the argument in ecstatic language; and by the dialectical skill of Nicolaus Cusanus 'the portentous power of the negative' had been refined to a 'learned ignorance.' One did not need to turn to Pico's *Conclusiones* to learn of this particular principle. Any Platonist knew it as 'the One beyond Being,' to which Plato had pointed in the *Parmenides*; any Cabbalist knew it as 'the absconded God' (*Ensoph*). And all agreed with the Areopagite that the ineffable power of the One could be described only by contradictory attributes, that is, by negating those traits which would render it finite and thereby accessible to the intellect. In another part of the *Conclusiones* Pico himself had already stated the principle in strictly philosophical terms: 'Contradictoria conincidunt in natura uniali.' [Contradictions coincide in the nature of the One.] And in this form, so closely reminiscent of the Areopagite and of Cusanus, the proposition did not yet contain any 'Orphic' secret. It was only by association with the image of Blind Love, as the power 'above the intellect', that Pico's argument acquired an unexpected 'Orphic' twist. Unexpected, because the blind Eros was known as a wanton god, a demon befuddling man's intelligence by arousing his animal appetites. The common *voluptas*, which gratified these desires, was known as blind pleasure unguided by the counsels of reason, and hence deceptive, corrupting, and short-lived. How could the god responsible for these delusions be transformed into a force superior to reason, a guide to delights that are secure? (*Pagan Mysteries in the Renaissance* [London: Faber and Faber, 1958], 57–59).

32 See Rosen, *Plato's Symposium*, 92, 95.
33 "Francis Bacon and the Art-Nature Distinction," *Ambix*, 54.2 (2007), 127–28.

34 Ibid., 128.
35 Rosen, *Plato's Symposium*, 98; *Symposium* 186ab.
36 Rosen, *Plato's Symposium*, 112.
37 The 6 sonnets in which the conflict of opposites dominates are L39.H, A3, A5, B3, B5, and B6. The conflict of opposites is subtle in L39.A3: the poisonous wound of Telephus made by Achilles is both potentially fatal and potentially a cure—analogous to love, which is both disease and cure, as discussed below.
38 The remaining three sonnets that feature endless motion are A1, A2, and B2: Sonnet A1's concern is the Cretan maze, a figure of endlessness; Sonnet A2's concern is *endlesse toyle* (16); Sonnet B2 features *a lasting warre* (16).
39 *How Socrates Became Socrates: A Study of Plato's Phaedo, Parmenides, and Symposium* (Chicago: University of Chicago Press, 2021), 179.
40 *Perpetual Motion: Transforming Shapes in the Renaissance from Da Vinci to Montaigne*, trans. Nidra Poller (Baltimore: Johns Hopkins University Press, 2001), 105, 85.
41 *Perpetual Motion*, 84 (*Microcosme*, 25–26).
42 *Perpetual Motion*, 86.
43 Sonnet L18.B4 alludes to the conflict of opposites (e.g., *flame and frost*; 18). This sonnet also depicts atomism, as discussed below. Sonnet L18.B5 may suggest perpetual motion in *endlesse strife* (18) .
44 This description of the Milky Way as consisting of many stars is surprising as it predates Galileo's 1610 telescopic observations of the Milky Way.
45 Adam Rzepka, "Discourse Ex Nihilo: Epicurus and Lucretius in Sixteenth-Century England" in *Dynamic Reading: Studies in the Reception of Epicureanism*, ed. Brooke Holmes and W. H. Shearin (Oxford: Oxford University Press), 120, 122.
46 Ibid., 123–24. See also Stephen Greenblatt, *The Swerve: How the World Became Modern* (New York: W. W. Norton & Company, 2012).
47 "Discourse Ex Nihilo," 124–29.
48 Ibid., 130–32.
49 Rosen, *Plato's Symposium*, 169.
50 Ibid., 177.
51 *Spenser and Biblical Poetics* (Ithaca: Cornell University Press, 1999), 63–64.
52 *The Expulsion of the Triumphant Beast*, ed. Arthur D. Imerti (New Brunswick, NJ: Rutgers University Press, 1964), 238.
53 Rosalie Colie asserts, "One Renaissance philosopher was able to marry the Platonic and Democritan worlds, in language at least, to achieve a fusion of Being and Becoming in which the concepts were mutually inextricable. Bruno presents the puzzling portrait of a philosopher and poet who was at once a pantheist—for which, among other things, he was terribly burned—and an atomist, a man who quite deliberately attempted the fusion of these utterly different traditions, with their utterly different concepts of the value of materiality" (*Paradoxia Epidemica the Renaissance Tradition of Paradox* [Princeton: Princeton University Press, 1966], 330).
54 *Spenser's Supreme Fiction: Platonic Natural History and The Faerie Queene* (Toronto: University of Toronto Press, 2001), 292.
55 Ibid., 291–92. Quitslund finds a similar philosophy in Spenser's *Mutabilitie Cantos* (287–92). Nor does Sidney accept the division between the sublunary

and supralunary spheres, according to Robert Stillman, who asserts that Sidney "is not readily characterized as a neoplatonist [because he] does not conceive of Ideas as deriving from or participating in some transcendent realm of meaning and value" (*Philip Sidney and the Poetics of Renaissance Cosmopolitanism* [London: Routledge, 2008], 109).

56   Benardete, *Plato's Symposium* (University of Chicago Press, 1993), 189.

57   Rosen, *Plato's Symposium*, 214–15.

58   Ibid., 136.

59   Ibid., 196.

60   *Francis Bacon*, ed. Brian Vickers (Oxford: Oxford University Press, 1996), 115, 117.

61   Ibid., 117.

62   For example, Shakespeare's Sonnet 124. The uniqueness of the beloved in the sonnet genre goes hand in hand with the speaker's singular vision of love.

63   As previously discussed, Socrates claims a lack of knowledge except with respect to love. In the *Symposium*, Alcibiades asserts that Socrates "is absolutely unique" and that his ideas are his own creation and unlike any other's (*Symposium* 221c).

64   *Symposium* (207cd). See Rosen, *Plato's Symposium*, 253.

65   Ibid., 192.

66   *Le sixiesme livre des poemes de Pierre de Ronsard* (1569), 1.

67   Montaigne believed that Plato wrote in a veiled mode, as discussed in the next chapter. See the accompanying note.

68   *Spenser's Supreme Fiction*, 104.

69   Levinus Lemnius (1505–68) was a Dutch physician. The text quoted here is Quitslund's translation (*Spenser's Supreme Fiction*, 104) of a French translation (*Des occultes merveilles et secretz de nature* [1574], 12r).

70   According to Quitslund, "Spenser goes a long way toward accepting Bruno's vision of a cosmos in flux, with everything in heaven and earth made of eternal substances, shaped from within by mutable formative principles" (*Spenser's Supreme Fiction*, 295). S. K. Heninger asserts that "by the mid-fifteenth century in Ficino's Italy there had begun to emerge an ambiguous interpretation of mimesis: while art must be truthful to the ideal order prescribed by the deity, it may shamelessly imitate the world that lies open to our senses. ... As the location of ultimate reality shifted from the Christianized version of Plato's realm of essences to the empiricist's world of observable nature, a work of art became a representation of what exists in fact, rather than a presentation of what is *supposed* to be in ideal principle. ... By the time of Sidney and Spenser, the relocation of reality was well under way; they lived, in fact, when the conflict was at crisis" (*Sidney and Spenser: The Poet as Maker* [University Park: Pennsylvania State University Press, 1989], 64). Indeed, Spenser appears to be under the influence of Cusanus. Alastair Fowler argues that "Spenser's most obvious expression of his philosophical vision takes the form of representing aspects of the divine image by sexually coupled contraries" ("Emanations of Glory: Neoplatonic Order in Spenser's Faerie Queen," in *A Theatre for Spenserians*, ed. Judith Kennedy and James A Reither, Papers of the International Spenser Colloquium, Fredericton, New Brunswick, October 1969 [Toronto: University of Toronto Press, 1973], 54).

71   *The Expulsion of the Triumphant Beast*, 235.

72 See F. J. E. Raby, "Nuda Natura and Twelfth-Century Cosmology," *Speculum* 43.1 (1968): 72–73.

73 See D. W. Robertson, "The Subject of the "De Amore" of Andreas Capellanus," *Modern Philology* (1953), 148, N21, N22. Robertson quotes Ailred of Rievaulx: *Quod in omnibus creaturis quoddam vestigium divinae charitatis appareat.* He asserts that a similar idea can also be found in Augustine's *De genesi ad litteram.*

74 C. S. Lewis argues that such an explanation may be found in Cusanus, and that others, such as Spenser, should not necessarily be viewed as blasphemous when in their works nature assumes the appearance of God (*Spenser's Images of Life* [Cambridge: Cambridge University Press, 1967], 42–43).

75 Quitslund cites the work of Genevan theologian Lambert Daneau (1530–95) as an example of Calvinist condemnation of pagan natural philosophy. His work was translated into English in 1578. Natural philosophers were said to be at fault for confining their study to the phenomenal world—that is, secondary causes—and neglecting the primary causes, which are found in the Creator (*Spenser's Supreme Fiction*, 126–27).

76 See the beginning of this chapter.

77 *Works*, 6.729 (*Wisdom of the Ancients*, "Cupid; or the Atom").

78 Ibid.

79 Ibid., 730.

80 "Francis Bacon and the Art-Nature Distinction," 122.

81 *Works*, 6.729 (*Wisdom of the Ancients*, "Cupid; or the Atom").

82 Ibid., italics in original.

83 Ibid., 6.730–31.

84 Ibid., 6.731. Spedding translates *exquisita* as "exquisite," which I have changed.

85 *Works*, 6.747.

86 See "Francis Bacon and the Art-Nature Distinction," 142.

87 Rosen, *Plato's Symposium*, 48.

88 Phaedrus's speech is incoherent in several respects. He argues that the beloved is more praiseworthy than the lover but then later contradicts himself when he praises lovers who have died for their beloveds, concluding that the lover "is always nearer than his beloved to the gods" (180b). Rosen argues that by this Phaedrus has deviated from his major premise (*Plato's Symposium*, 58).

89 Rosen, *Plato's Symposium*, 7–8.

90 Ibid., 40.

91 I wish to thank Adam Rzepka for his insights into Lucretian atomism, here and elsewhere in this chapter.

92 For Augustine, says John Freccero, "all things are signs [and] God is the terminal point in the referential chain" ("The Fig Tree and the Laurel: Petrarch's Poetics," *Diacritics* 5.1 [1975]: 38). With respect to Petrarchism, he writes: "The love must be idolatrous for its poetic expression to be autonomous; the idolatry cannot be unconflicted, any more than a sign can be completely nonreferential if it is to communicate anything at all" (Ibid., 40). Shakespeare, in his sonnet 105, raises the issue of idolatry: "Let not my love be called idolatry / Nor my beloved as an idol show."

93 The expression "ontological mezzanine" is borrowed from Kenneth Borris, *Visionary Spenser and the Poetics of Early Modern Platonism* (Oxford:

Oxford University Press, 2017), 201. For Spenser, see *Colin Clouts Come Home Againe*, line 351.

94 *Themes and Variations in Shakespeare's Sonnets* (London: Hutchinson, 1961), 151.

95 Leishman found this inverted Platonism difficult to explain and wondered whether Shakespeare had serious philosophical intent or was merely careless with his ideas. Subsequent *Sonnets* scholarship has largely ignored Leishman's concern, with the exception of Richard Strier, as discussed below.

96 "Petrarch," in *Edmund Spenser in Context*, ed. Andrew Escobedo (Cambridge: Cambridge University Press, 2017), 239.

97 Ibid., 236.

98 Ibid., 243, 242.

99 Freccero sees Laura as incarnational: "As all desire is ultimately a desire for God, so all signs point ultimately to the Word. In a world without ultimate significance, there is no escape from the infinite referentiality of signs. Signs, like desire, continually point beyond themselves. ... Short of the Word made flesh, there can be no bridge between words and things" ("The Fig Tree and the Laurel," 35). In contrast to Dante's Beatrice, who is a mediatrix to God, Petrarch makes "his 'God' the lady Laura, the object of his worship" (Ibid., 38). Laura is the endpoint of referentiality, like the Word made flesh.

100 *My Secret Book*, tr. Nicholas Mann (Cambridge, MA: Harvard University Press, 2016), 169.

101 Strier also notes that sonnet 4 contains "a direct parallel between the circumstances of Christ's birth and those of Laura's" (*The Unrepentant Renaissance: From Petrarch to Shakespeare to Milton* [Chicago: University of Chicago Press, 2012], 60, 73–74, 76).

102 Ibid., 60.

103 *Philip Sidney and the Poetics of Renaissance Cosmopolitanism*, 163.

104 Ibid., 166–68. Stillman believes that critics have misapprehended Sidney's poetics because it has been viewed in "a critical context within which Reformed theology has been mistakenly identified as dogma proceeding from the writings of a single person, John Calvin" (xi).

105 According to Rosen, "the cosmic Eros of pre-Socratic physics is difficult if not impossible to reconcile with the human Eros ostensibly being praised [by Phaedrus]" (*Plato's Symposium*, 44).

106 Rosen argues that a true logos must exhibit "the unchanging form it describes. Moving logoi are in fact mythoi. ... The Platonic dialogues give ample reason to doubt the possibility of such a logos. ... There can be no logos of Eros, which perpetually comes to be and passes away. ... The *Phaedrus*, *Phaedo*, and *Timaeus* all teach us that it is impossible to grasp the immortal and divine by means of logos. ... Eros is not merely moving but is formless; hence the extraordinary difficulty in speaking about it at all" (*Plato's Symposium*, 207–10).

107 *Swerve*, 6.

108 Regarding Aristophanes, see Rosen, *Plato's Symposium*, 131.

109 *The Greeks and the Irrational* (Berkeley: University of California Press, 1951), 218.

110 Lampert argues that Plato attempts to hide the radical temporal life because "the truth about Eros is terrifying." To speak the truth directly is profane. Lambert reminds us that "both the frame and the core of the *Symposium* is

drenched in the religious crime of profanity" (the historical event of the desecration of the Hermae). The work is ring-fenced by multiple interlocuters. The truth must be hidden (*How Socrates Became Socrates*, 153–55).

111 See Stanley Rosen, "Are We Such Stuff as Dreams Are Made On?," in Jeff Malpas, Ulrich Arnswald, and Jens Kertscher, eds., *Gadamer's Century: Essays in Honour of Hans-Georg Gadamer* (Cambridge, MA: MIT Press, 2002), 262–63.

112 Rosen, *Plato's Symposium*, 251–52.

113 According to Rosen, "The absence of the eternal is a mark of the incompleteness of the teaching of the *Symposium*" (*Plato's Symposium*, 219). "If we restrict our attention merely to the *Symposium*, the result is a distorted understanding of Plato's conception of philosophy." Indeed, Diotima "is not the final stage of Socrates' teaching as presented in the corpus of Platonic dialogues." A complete teaching on Eros "must encompass the ugly as well as the beautiful or somehow make peace between them," which does not occur in Diotima's speech (Ibid., 221). Rosen argues that "the philosopher must neither scorn the ugly nor mistake it for the beautiful" (Ibid., 223). He quotes Kierkegaard: "[Plato] starts out from the concrete and arrives at the most abstract, and there, where the investigation should now begin, he stops" (Ibid., 278). Unlike the ascensions that take place in Hegelian and Christian thought, Plato does not have Diotima explain how an ascension up the *scala amoris* might impact our life. See further discussion below.

114 According to John Lepage, Bacchus and Apollo are together instillers of good health (*Revival of Antique Philosophy in the Renaissance* [New York: Palgrave Macmillan, 2012], 37–43).

115 Eros is "harsh and arid, barefoot and homeless, sleeping on the ground... and always partaking of his mother's (Penuria) poverty" (203cd). Socrates is poor and typically shoeless—his ugliness is a form of poverty.

116 Rosen, *Plato's Symposium*, 221.

117 According to Laurence Lampert, "Parmenides turns Socrates toward an ontological psychology." This psychology limits human knowledge: "Knowledge of ignorance is knowledge of the soul in its way of 'knowing'" (*How Socrates Became Socrates*, 131–32).

118 Lampert argues that Socrates (and Nietzsche) "recognize the need to inquire first into the inquirer and his fitness to know—epistemology—and only then a properly prepared inquiry into being as far as it is knowable—ontology. ... Ultimately, knowledge of the self and the human pointed each of them [Socrates and Nietzsche] to an ontology that could never be more than inferential." Lampert argues that Eros, and its equivalent in Nietzsche's philosophy, the will to power, is "the most fundamental fact [quoting Strauss]" (*How Socrates Became Socrates*, 223).

119 Lampert makes this argument with respect to the *Symposium* and the philosophy of Nietzsche (*How Socrates Became Socrates*, 221–22).

120 Rosen offers a fascinating discussion of what he calls "the two main types of philosophical thinking... the mathematical and the poetical." He argues that "the poetic mode culminates in a celebration of transience" (*Gadamer's Century*, 259–60, *passim*, 257–77).

121 Rosen, *Plato's Symposium*, 37. The *Republic* explicitly refers to this trial as the "quarrel between philosophy and poetry" (607b). Although the poets are thrown out of the ideal city, music is not.

122 According to Rosen, "The proper ordering of Eros depends upon a vison of, or friendship for, the good. ... Eros alone is insufficient to make a man a philosopher (*Plato's Symposium*, 84). In the *Republic*, "The city cannot be founded upon, or preserved by, the unmitigated truth because the 'goodness' of the Ideas, and so too of the god of the philosophers, has nothing to do with everyday human existence" ("Suspicion, Deception, and Concealment," *Arion: A Journal of Humanities and the Classics* 1.2 [1991]: 122).

123 Ibid.

124 *Quarrel Between Philosophy and Poetry: Studies in Ancient Thought* (New York: Routledge, 1988), 26.

125 Ibid., 117. The Latin language conveys this sense: *elementum* can mean either letter or element.

126 Michel Serres, David Webb, and William Ross, *The Birth of Physics* (London: Rowman & Littlefield, 2018), 170.

127 "Francis Bacon and Scientific Poetry," *Transactions of the American Philosophical Society* 82.2 (1992): 27, 25N38. Schuler provides further evidence of the importance of Lucretius to Bacon in his discussion of *Wisdom of the Ancients* (34–35) and *Cogitationes de natura rerum* (35–36).

Chapter 15 » Conclusions

1   Chapter 4 discusses the poetics of ruin, the hermeneutics of restoration, and the importance of rhetoric.

2   *Works*, 6.695–96.

3   Ibid., 6.698.

4   *The Order of Things: An Archaeology of the Human Sciences* (New York: Pantheon Books, 1971), 29.

5   Ibid., 51, italics in original.

6   *Plato's Symposium*, 2nd ed. (New Haven: Yale University Press, 1987), liv. In contrast, Rosen adds, "Philosophers like Leibniz, Hume, Rousseau and Nietzsche were better informed" (ibid.). See also Chapter 1, sections titled "The obscured text" and "Erasmus's Silenic literary model."

7   See Marc Cogan, "Rhetoric and Action in Francis Bacon," *Philosophy & Rhetoric* 14.4 (1981): 213. "The entire field of logic as Bacon conceived it is in fact heavily rhetorical. ... Bacon describes rhetoric in terms of its relation to and effect on, a given set of human faculties. By reorienting the discussion of rhetoric to the faculties, he makes a striking innovation in rhetorical theory."

8   *Works*, 6.697.

9   Montaigne argues that philosophers "wrote for the needs of society, like their religions; and on that account it was reasonable that they did not want to bare popular opinions to the skin, so as not to breed disorder in people's obedience to the laws and customs of their country. Plato treats this mystery with his cards pretty much on the table. For where he writes on his own, he makes no certain prescriptions. When he plays the lawgiver, he borrows a domineering and assertive style, and yet mixes in boldly the most fantastic of his inventions, which are as useful for persuading the common herd as they are ridiculous for persuading himself; knowing how apt we are to accept any impressions, and most of all the wildest and most monstrous" (Michel de Montaigne,

The Complete Essays, tr. Donald Frame, II:12 [Stanford: Stanford University Press, 1958], 379). Stanley Rosen claims that "throughout the Platonic dialogues, one finds a continuous interest in falsehood, suspicion, deception, and concealment, an interest that is curiously unnoticed in the secondary literature" ("Suspicion, Deception, and Concealment," *Arion: A Journal of Humanities and the Classics* 1.2 [1991]: 121). Most Plato scholars read literally, that is, they consider Plato to be a Platonist (Lloyd P. Gerson makes this argument in *From Plato to Platonism* [Ithaca: Cornell University Press, 2013], 3–33). However, in the last century, beginning with Gadamer, a dissenting group of scholars have recognized Plato's deception and read his dialogues through a hermeneutic lens. These scholars include Leo Strauss, John Herman Randall Jr., Stanley Rosen, Seth Benardete, and Laurence Lampert.

10 *An Apology for Poetry: Or, The Defence of Poesy*, ed. Geoffrey Shepherd (London: T. Nelson and Sons, 1965), 95.

11 Philip Sidney, *An Apology for Poetry, or, The Defence of Poesy*, ed. R. W Maslen (Manchester: Manchester University Press, 2002), 39.

12 See the discussion in "The hermeneutics of restoration" section of Chapter 4.

13 *Nietzsche and Modern Times: A Study of Bacon, Descartes, and Nietzsche* (New Haven: Yale University Press, 1993), 236.

14 See Robert M. Schuler, "Francis Bacon and Scientific Poetry," *Transactions of the American Philosophical Society* 82.2 (1992): 43–46.

15 "Virgil and Bacon in the Schoolroom," *ELH* 73.1 (2006): 167.

16 *Works*, 3.419. *Georgics* 3.289–90: "Nor doubtfully know how hard it is for words to triumph here, and shed their luster on a theme so slight" (tr. Greenough).

17 Schuler writes, "Bacon shows that he—like most English readers of the period—considered the *Georgics* to be a didactic poem containing practical, technical information on agriculture" ("Francis Bacon and Scientific Poetry," 46).

18 *The Essays Translated by John Florio* (London: M. Bradwood for E. Blount & W. Barret, 1613), 301.

19 *Apology for Poetry* (Shepherd), 114.

20 *The Literary Microcosm: Theories of Interpretation of the Later Neoplatonists* (Leiden: Brill, 1976), 75, 77. Italics in original.

21 *Philip Sidney and the Poetics of Renaissance Cosmopolitanism* (London: Routledge, 2008), 110.

22 See Stillman's description of Sidney's "golden world," upon which my description is based (Ibid., 163).

23 *Apology for Poetry* (Shepherd), 100.

24 Stillman, *Philip Sidney and the Poetics of Renaissance Cosmopolitanism*, 121. See commentary page for Sonnet L50.1: the poet prefers the inspiration of his beloved to that of the muses.

25 *Philip Sidney and the Poetics of Renaissance Cosmopolitanism*, 215.

26 *Sidney and Spenser: The Poet as Maker* (University Park: Pennsylvania State University Press, 1989), 207, passim.

27 See Coulter, *Literary Microcosm*, 76.

28 Stillman argues for "the development of an early modern poetics in England that stood apart conspicuously and self-consciously from the allegorical tradition. ... Sidney clearly belongs to an alternative, non-allegorical history of hermeneutics" (*Philip Sidney and the Poetics of Renaissance Cosmopolitanism*, 72).

29 See Coulter, *Literary Microcosm*, 74. He cites *Phaedrus* 268d.

30 *Philip Sidney and the Poetics of Renaissance Cosmopolitanism*, viii.

31 Ibid., 110–11.

32 Ibid., 117, 119. Quotation from Sidney, *An Apology for Poetry* (Shepherd), 104.

33 Ibid., 164.

34 Ibid., 223, 162.

35 Kenneth Borris, *Visionary Spenser and the Poetics of Early Modern Platonism* (Oxford: Oxford University Press, 2017), 51. Borris references *Discourses on the Heroic Poem*, tr. Mariella Cavalchini and Irene Samuel (Oxford: Clarendon Press, 1973), 77–78. He also cites Coulter, *Literary Microcosm* (in its entirety), and S. K. Heninger, *Touches of Sweet Harmony: Pythagorean Cosmology and Renaissance Poetics* (San Marino: Huntington Library, 1974), 287–397.

36 *Second World and Green World: Studies in Renaissance Fiction-Making* (Berkeley: University of California Press, 1990), 49.

37 Ibid. 45, passim, 49–50.

38 "Petrarch," in *Edmund Spenser in Context*, ed. Andrew Escobedo (Cambridge: Cambridge University Press, 2017), 235.

39 *The Light in Troy: Imitation and Discovery in Renaissance Poetry*, Elizabethan Club Series 7 (New Haven: Yale University Press, 1982), 115.

40 See Marjorie O'Rourke Boyle, "A Likely Story: The Autobiographical as Epideictic," *Journal of the American Academy of Religion* 57.1 (April 1, 1989): 25–26, passim, 23–51.

41 See Jean-Pierre Maquerlot, *Shakespeare and the Mannerist Tradition: A Reading of Five Problem Plays* (Cambridge: Cambridge University Press, 1995), 19.

42 *Spenser's Supreme Fiction: Platonic Natural History and* The Faerie Queene (Toronto: University of Toronto Press, 2001), 16.

43 *Discourses on the Heroic Poem*, tr. Mariella Cavalchini and Irene Samuel (Oxford: Clarendon Press, 1973), 78.

44 "Petrarch," 235–36.

45 See Rosen, *Plato's Symposium*, 326.

46 J. V. Cunningham argues that "the direction of the action in tragedy is from order to disorder; in comedy the converse" (*Woe or Wonder: The Emotional Effect of Shakespearean Tragedy* [Denver: University of Denver Press, 1951], 38).

47 A good example is Petrarch's *Canzoniere* 164, which Bacon translates in Sonnet L39.B4 (66). The world is peaceful while the poet's mind is full of turmoil. The poet's focus on his own emotive engagement with the world, rather than producing a mimesis of the world, is a revolutionary change.

48 Richard Strier, as quoted in the previous chapter (*Unrepentant Renaissance*, 60).

49 See Teodolinda Barolini, "The Self in the Labyrinth of Time," in *Petrarch: A Critical Guide to the Complete Works*, ed. Victoria Kirkham and Armando Maggi (Chicago: University of Chicago Press, 2009), 49.

50 *Shepheardes Calender* (London: Hugh Singleton, 1579) edition, folio 52.

51 *Hic tamen, hic moneo, ne speres tanta futura: / Attica non auris murmura vana probat* (21–22).

52 *Ingenio tandem praestans Watsonus, et arte / Pieridas docuit verba Britanna loqui* (13–14). The translation is Sutton's. For other English poets' failings, see lines 15–16.

53 The *Shepheardes Calender* (folio 52) quotes Horace ("Exigi monimentum aere perennius, / Quod nec imber nec aquilo vorax &c") and Ovid ("Grande Opus exegi quae nec Iouis ira nec ignis, / Nec ferum poterit nec edax abolere vetustas &c.").

54 See Northrop Frye, *Fables of Identity: Studies in Poetic Mythology* (New York: Harcourt Brace & World, 1963), 17.

55 *Pagan Mysteries in the Renaissance* (London: Faber and Faber, 1958), 143.

56 There is an intrinsic value to suffering in the soteriological scheme presented in the New Testament. See Thomas More, *Utopia: With Erasmus's the Sileni of Alcibiades*, tr. David Wootton (Indianapolis: Hackett Publishing, 1999), 9.

57 *Pagan Mysteries in the Renaissance*, 144.

58 "De Libro Sexto Cum Commento," in *François Rabelais: Critical Assessments*, ed. Jean-Claude Carron (Baltimore: Johns Hopkins University Press, 1995), 190.

59 *Sciences and the Self in Medieval Poetry: Alan of Lille's* Anticlaudianus *and John Gower's* Confessio Amantis, Cambridge Studies in Medieval Literature 25 (Cambridge: Cambridge University Press, 1995), 14–15.

60 See the block quote immediately above.

61 Frank Kermode, *The Genesis of Secrecy: On the Interpretation of Narrative*, Charles Eliot Norton Lectures 1977–1978 (Cambridge: Harvard University Press, 1979), 5.

62 Ibid., 131, 116.

63 Ibid., 53.

64 "The Hermeneutical Anarchist: *Phronesis*, Rhetoric, and the Experience of Art," in *Gadamer's Century: Essays in Honour of Hans-Georg Gadamer*, ed. Jeff Malpas, Ulrich Arnswald, and Jens Kertscher (Cambridge: MIT Press, 2002), 64–65.

65 "Cosmology and Cosmography," in *Edmund Spenser in Context*, ed. Andrew Escobedo (Cambridge: Cambridge University Press, 2017), 328.

66 See Laurence Lampert, *How Socrates Became Socrates: A Study of Plato's Phaedo, Parmenides, and Symposium* (Chicago: University of Chicago Press, 2021), 225.

67 "Wer den Dichter will verstehen, Muss in Dichters Lande geben" (Noten auf West–östlicher Divan).

68 As quoted above, *Sciences and the Self in Medieval Poetry*, 14–15.

69 As quoted earlier in this chapter, *Apology for Poetry*, (Shepherd) 101.

70 As quoted above, *Sciences and the Self in Medieval Poetry*, 14–15.

71 On the "noetic plot" of the *Anticlaudianus*, Ibid., 31, 34, 122–27.

72 Ibid., 125.

73 Ibid., 62.

74 "At the third remove," that is, a copy of something that is itself a copy of a form (598b, 599d).

75 Hans-Georg Gadamer, *Dialogue and Dialectic: Eight Hermeneutical Studies on Plato*, tr. P. Christopher Smith (New Haven: Yale University Press, 1980), 54.

76 Ibid., 53.

77 Ibid., 54.

78 Ibid., 88–89.

79 See: *What man, but I, could thus encline his will / To live in Love, which hath no end of ill* (L73.2.17–18); *Love hath no leaden heeles* (L73.3.18); *Nor any time can make me cease to love* (L73.4.18); *A majori ad minus* (L73.6.HN).

80 See Rosen, *Plato's Symposium*, 177.

81 According to Rosen, "The poetry of Agathon is an attempt to transform traditional religion into a religion of poetry" (Ibid., 200). This view has much in common with Nietzsche's religion of art (Ibid., 132).

82 Rosen's words, in the context of Aristophanes's speech (132).

83 See Bruns, "Hermeneutical Anarchist," 65. He quotes Gadamer from *Truth and Method*, tr. Joel Weinsheimer and Donald Marshall, 2nd rev. ed. (New York: Continuum, 1989), 102.

84 Bruns writes: "In Gadamer's aesthetics, the event of the work of art is not a museum event in which we simply gape at the thing" ("Hermeneutical Anarchist," 65).

85 Ibid. Bruns references *Truth and Method*, 126–28.

List of Primary Sources

The *Hekatompathia*

The *Hekatompathia* has been republished five times since its original edition in 1582 and twice reproduced in dissertation editions. All published editions are listed in chronological order, followed by the two dissertations. I abbreviate references to these editions, as shown in bold below.

Original Edition: *The Hekatompathia or Passionate centurie of loue, diuided into two parts: whereof, the first expresseth the authors sufferance in loue: the latter, his long farewell to loue and all his tyrannie. Composed by Thomas Watson Gentleman; and published at the request of certaine gentlemen his very frendes.* London: imprinted by Iohn Wolfe for Gabriell Cawood, in Paules Churchyard at the signe of the Holy Ghost, 1582. [STC 25118a]

1869 Edition: *The Hekatompathia* [Romanized form], *or, Passionate centurie of love.* Printed for the Spenser Society, 1869.

Arber Edition: *Poems: Viz.: — The Ekatompathia [Romanized form] or passionate centurie of love 1582.* Ed. Edward Arber. London: English Reprints, 1870.

Cecioni Edition: *Hekatompathia.* Ed. Cesare Giulio Cecioni. Catania: Universitá di Catania, 1964.

Heninger Edition: *The Hekatompathia; or, Passionate centurie of love (1582).* Ed. S. K. Heninger. Delmar: Scholars' Facsimiles & Reprints, 1964.

Sutton Edition: *The Complete Works of Thomas Watson (1556–1592).* Volume 1. Ed. Dana Sutton. Lewiston: Edwin Mellen Press, 1997. An online edition is available at www.philological.bham.ac.uk/watson

Murphy Dissertation: William Michael Murphy, "Thomas Watson's Hecatompathia, or the Passionate Centurie of Loue [1582]." 1947. Dissertation, Harvard.

Phillips Dissertation: Wendy Phillips, "Thomas Watson's *Hekatompathia* or Passionate Centurie of Love, 1582: A facsimile edition with notes and commentary." 1989. Dissertation, UCLA.

Other primary sources including translations

Andreas, Capellanus. *The Art of Courtly Love.* Translated by John Jay Parry. New York: W. W. Norton, 1969.

Augustine of Hippo. *On Christian Doctrine.* Tr. Rev. J. F. Shaw. Edinburgh: T. & T. Clark, 1873.

Bacon, Francis. *The Works of Francis Bacon.* Edited by James Spedding, Robert Leslie Ellis, and Douglas Denon Heath. London: Longmans and Co., 1857.

———. "The Masculine Birth of Time." In *The Philosophy of Francis Bacon: An Essay on Its Development from 1603 to 1609, with New Translation of Fundamental Texts.* Tr. Farrington, Benjamin. Chicago: University of Chicago Press, 1966.

——. The *Oxford Francis Bacon*. Vol. 6, *Philosophical Studies, c.1611–c.1619*. Ed. Graham Rees. Oxford: Oxford University Press, 1996.

——. *Francis Bacon: the Major Works*. Ed. Brian Vickers. Oxford: Oxford University Press, 1996.

Boccaccio, Giovanni. *Boccaccio on Poetry*. Tr. Charles Osgood. New York: Liberal Arts Press, 1956.

Bruno, Giordano. *The Expulsion of the Triumphant Beast*. Tr. Arthur D. Imerti. New Brunswick: Rutgers University Press, 1964.

Castiglione, Baldassarre. *The Book of the Courtier*. Edited by Virginia Cox. Tr. Thomas Hoby. London: Everyman, 1994.

Celaya, Joannis, "de." *Expositio magistri Joannis de Celaya, Valentini, in primum tractatum Summularum magistri Petri Hispani*. Bibliothèque nationale de France, 1525.

Cooper, Thomas. *Thesaurus Linguae Romanae & Britannicae*. Ed. Thomas Cooper. London, 1565.

Dante. *Dantis Alagherii Epistolae: The Letters of Dante*. Edited by Paget Jackson Toynbee. Oxford: Clarendon Press, 1920.

Ebreo, Leone. *Dialogues of Love*. Tr. Rossella Pescatori and Cosmos Damian Bacich. Toronto: University of Toronto Press, 2009.

Ficino, Marsilio. *Commentary on Plato's Symposium on Love*. Tr. Sears Reynolds Jayne. Dallas: Spring Publications, 1985.

——. *On the Nature of Love: Ficino on Plato's Symposium*. Tr. Arthur Farndell. London: Shepheard-Walwyn Publishers, 2016.

Forcatuli, Stephani. *Epigrammata*, Ioan. Tornaesium, 1554.

Heywood, Thomas. *The Dramatic Works of Thomas Heywood: Edward IV, pt. 1–2*. London: Shakespeare Society, 1850.

Horapollo. *The Hieroglyphics of Horapollo*. Princeton: Princeton University Press, 1993. Introduction by George Boas.

John of Garland. *The "Parisiana Poetria" of John of Garland*. Tr. Traugott Lawler. New Haven: Yale University Press, 1974.

Montaigne, Michel de. *The Complete Essays*. Tr. Donald Frame. Stanford: Stanford University Press, 1958.

——. *The Essays Translated by John Florio*. London: M. Bradwood for E. Blount & W. Barret, 1613.

More, Thomas. *Utopia: With Erasmus's the Sileni of Alcibiades*. Tr. David Wootton. Indianapolis: Hackett Publishing, 1999.

Ovid. *Metamorphosis*. Tr. Arthur Golding. London, 1567. STC 18956.

Petrarch, Francesco. *My Secret Book*. Tr. Nicholas Mann. Cambridge: Harvard University Press, 2016.

——. *Petrarch's Lyric Poems: The Rime Sparse and Other Lyrics*. Tr. Robert M. Durling. Cambridge: Harvard University Press, 1976.

Plato. *The Collected Dialogues*. Eds. Edith Hamilton and Huntington Cairns. Princeton: Princeton University Press, 1961.

Plutarch. *Essays and Miscellanies: Comprising All His Works Collected Under the Title of "Morals."* Edited by William W. Goodwin. New York: Little, Brown, 1909.

Puttenham, George. *The Art of English Poesy: A Critical Edition*. Edited by Wayne A. Rebhorn and Frank Whigham. Ithaca: Cornell University Press, 2007.

Rabelais, Francois. *Gargantua and Pantagruel.* Tr. Michael Andrew Screech. London: Penguin Books, 2006.

Ronsard, Pierre "de". "Le" Sixièsme Livre Des Poèmes De Pierre De Ronsard. France: Par Iean Dallier Libraire, 1569.

Selenus, Gustavus (Duke August of Wolfenbüttel). *Cryptomenytices et Cryptographiæ libri IX.* Lunaeburgi, 1624.

Sidney, Philip. *Shepheardes Calender.* London: Hugh Singleton, 1579.

———. *An Apology for Poetry or The Defence of Poesy.* Ed. Geoffrey Shepherd. London: T. Nelson and Sons, 1965.

———. *An Apology for Poetry or The Defence of Poesy.* Ed. R. W Maslen. Manchester: Manchester University Press, 2002.

Spenser, Edmund. *The Faerie Queene.* Ed. Thomas P. Roche, Jr. New Haven: Yale University Press, 1978.

———. *The Yale Edition of the Shorter Poems of Edmund Spenser.* Ed. William Oram et al. New Haven: Yale University Press, 1989.

Stroza, Titus and Hercules. *Strozii Poetae Pater Et Filius.* Parisiis: Ex officina Simonis Colinaei, 1530.

Tasso, Torquato. *Discourses on the Heroic Poem.* Tr. Mariella Cavalchini and Irene Samuel. Oxford: Clarendon Press, 1973.

Trithemius (Johann Heidenberg, a German Benedictine abbot). *Polygraphiae libri sex Ioannis Trithemii.* Editions in 1518, 1550, 1564, and 1571.

———. *Polygraphie, et vniuerselle escriture cabalistique,* de M. I. Tritheme abbé; traduicte par Gabriel de Collange, natif de Tours en Auuergne. Paris: Pour Iaques Keruer, 1561. Clavicle et interpretation [de Collange's addition, appending the work].

Virgil. *Virgil's Aeneid.* Tr. Rev. Oliver Crane. New York: Baker & Taylor Company, 1888. (For introduction only.)

Watson, Thomas. *Compendium memoriae localis. The Complete Works of Thomas Watson (1556–1592).* Volume 2. Ed. Dana Sutton. Lewiston: Edwin Mellen Press, 1997.

———. "A Looking glasse for Loovers; wherem are contayned two sortes of amorous passions: the one expressing the trewe estate and pertubations of him that is overgon with love: the other a flatt defyance of love and all his laws." Manuscript: British Library: Harleian 3277, n.d.

List of Secondary Sources

Allen, Michael J. B. "Cosmogony and Love: The Role of Phaedrus in Ficino's Symposium Commentary." *Journal of Medieval and Renaissance Studies Durham, NC* 10.2 (1980): 131–53.

———. "De Libro Sexto Cum Commento." In *François Rabelais: Critical Assessments*. Ed. Jean-Claude Carron. Baltimore: Johns Hopkins University Press, 1995.

Anderson, William S. "The Theory and Practice of Poetic Arrangement from Vergil to Ovid." In Neil Fraistat, *Poems in Their Place: The Intertextuality and Order of Poetic Collections*, Chapel Hill: University of North Carolina Press, 2011.

Ardolino, Frank. "Thomas Watson, Shadow Poet of Edmund Spenser." *Notes and Queries* 61.2 (2014): 225–29.

Auden, W. H. *The Dyer's Hand and Other Essays*. New York: Vintage Books, 1962.

Auerbach, Erich. *Dante: Poet of the Secular World*. Tr. Ralph Manheim. NYRB Classics, 2007.

Baker, David Weil. *Divulging Utopia: Radical Humanism in Sixteenth-Century England*. Massachusetts Studies in Early Modern Culture. Amherst: University of Massachusetts Press, 1999.

Barker, Ernest. "The Authorship of the *Vindiciae Contra Tyrannos*," *Cambridge Historical Journal* 3.2 (1930): 164–181.

Barksdale-Shaw, Lisa M. "'That You Are Both Decipher'd': Revealing Espionage and Staging Written Evidence in Early Modern England." In *A Material History of Medieval and Early Modern Ciphers: Cryptography and the History of Literacy*. Ed. Katherine E Ellison and Susan Kim. New York: Routledge, 2018.

Barolini, Teodolinda. "The Self in the Labyrinth of Time." In *Petrarch: A Critical Guide to the Complete Works*. Eds. Victoria Kirkham and Armando Maggi. Chicago: University of Chicago Press, 2009.

Bartsch, Shadi. "*Ars* and the Man: The Politics of Art in Virgil's *Aeneid*," *Classical Philology* 93.4 (1998): 322–42.

Bath, Michael. *Speaking Pictures: English Emblem Books and Renaissance Culture*. London: Longman Group, 1994.

Benardete, Seth. *Plato's Symposium*. Chicago: University of Chicago Press, 1993.

Berger, Harry, Jr. *Second World and Green World: Studies in Renaissance Fiction-Making*. Berkeley: University of California Press, 1990.

Bonnefoy, Yves. *Greek and Egyptian Mythologies*. Chicago: University of Chicago Press, 1992.

Borris, Kenneth. "Allegory, Emblem, and Symbol." In *The Oxford Handbook of Edmund Spenser*. Ed. Richard A. McCabe. Oxford: Oxford University Press, 2010.

———. "(H)Eroic Disarmament: Spenser's Unarmed Cupid, Platonized Heroism, and *The Faerie Queene*'s Poetics." *Spenser Studies* 31–32 (Jan. 1, 2018): 97–135.

———. *Visionary Spenser and the Poetics of Early Modern Platonism*. Oxford: Oxford University Press, 2017.

Borris, Kenneth, Jon Quitslund, and Carol Kaske, eds. "Spenser and Platonism Issue of Spenser Studies." *Spenser Studies* 24 (2009).

Boyle, Marjorie O'Rourke. "A Likely Story: The Autobiographical as Epideictic." *Journal of the American Academy of Religion* 57.1 (1989): 23–51.

Braden, Gordon. "Shakespeare's Petrarchism." In *Shakespeare's Sonnets: Critical Essays*. Ed. James Schiffer. New York: Garland, 2000.

Briggs, John. *Francis Bacon and the Rhetoric of Nature*. Cambridge: Harvard University Press, 1989.

Bruns, Gerald. "The Hermeneutical Anarchist: *Phronesis*, Rhetoric, and the Experience of Art." In *Gadamer's Century: Essays in Honor of Hans-Georg Gadamer*. Ed. Jeff Malpas et al. Cambridge: MIT Press, 2002.

Burnyeat, M. F. *Explorations in Ancient and Modern Philosophy*, Vol. 2. Cambridge: Cambridge University Press, 2012.

Bush, Douglas. *English Literature in the Earlier Seventeenth Century, 1600-1660*. London: Oxford University Press, 1945.

Cantor, Georg. *Resurrectio Divi Quirini, Francisci Baconi, Baronis de Verulam...* Cura et Impensis G.C. (Georg Cantor), 1896.

Carruthers, Mary. *The Book of Memory: A Study of Memory in Medieval Culture*. 2nd ed. Cambridge: Cambridge University Press, 2008.

Cassirer, Ernst. *The Individual and the Cosmos in Renaissance Philosophy*. Chicago: University of Chicago Press, 1963.

Cave, Terence. *The Cornucopian Text: Problems of Writing in the French Renaissance*. Oxford: Oxford University Press, 1979.

Cecioni, Cesare Giulio. *Thomas Watson e la Tradizione Petrarchista*. Milano: Messina G. Principato, 1969.

Cheney, Patrick. "Petrarch." In *Edmund Spenser in Context*. Ed. Andrew Escobedo. Cambridge: Cambridge University Press, 2017.

———. "Spenser's Pastorals: The Shepheardes Calender and Colin Clouts Come Home Againe." In *The Cambridge Companion to Spenser*. Ed. Andrew Hadfield. Cambridge: Cambridge University Press, 2001.

Christie, E. J. "The Cryptographic Imagination: Revealing and Concealing in Anglo-Saxon Literature." In *A Material History of Medieval and Early Modern Ciphers: Cryptography and the History of Literacy*. Ed. Katherine Ellison and Susan Kim. New York: Routledge, 2018.

Cipolla, Gaetano. "Labyrinthine Imagery in Petrarch." *Italica* 54.2 (1977): 263–89.

Clody, Michael C. "Deciphering the Language of Nature: Cryptography, Secrecy, and Alterity in Francis Bacon." *Configurations* 19.1 (2011): 117–42.

———. "Limited by Their Letters: Alphabets, Codes, and Gesture in Seventeenth-Century England." In *A Material History of Medieval and Early Modern Ciphers: Cryptography and the History of Literacy*. Ed. Katherine Ellison and Susan Kim. New York: Routledge, 2018.

Clucas, Stephen. "'A Knowledge Broken': Francis Bacon's Aphoristic Style and the Crisis of Scholastic and Humanist Knowledge-Systems." In *English Renaissance Prose: History, Language, and Politics*. Ed. Neil Rhodes. Tempe: Medieval & Renaissance Texts & Studies, 1997: 147–72.

———. "Thomas Watson's *Hekatompathia* and European Petrarchism." In *Petrarch in Britain: Interpreters, Imitators, and Translators Over 700 Years*. Ed.

M. L McLaughlin, Letizia Panizza, and Peter Hainsworth, 217–28. Proceedings of the British Academy 146. Oxford: Published for the British Academy by Oxford University Press, 2007.

Cogan, Marc. "Rhetoric and Action in Francis Bacon." *Philosophy & Rhetoric* 14.4 (1981): 212–233.

Colclough, David. "Ethics and Politics in the *New Atlantis*." In *Francis Bacon's New Atlantis: New Interdisciplinary Essays*. Ed. Bronwen Price. Manchester: Manchester University Press, 2002.

———. "'Non Canimus Surdis, Respondent Omnia Sylvae': Francis Bacon and the Transmission of Knowledge." In *Textures of Renaissance Knowledge*. Eds. Philippa Berry and Margaret Tudeau-Clayton. Manchester: Manchester University Press, 2003.

Coldiron, A. E. B. "Watson's *Hekatompathia* and Renaissance Lyric Translation." *Translation and Literature* 5.1 (1996): 3–25.

Colie, Rosalie. *Paradoxia Epidemica: The Renaissance Tradition of Paradox*. Princeton: Princeton University Press, 1966.

Cooper, Andrew, M. "The Collapse of the Religious Hieroglyph: Typology and Natural Language in Herbert and Bacon." *Renaissance Quarterly* 45.1 (1992): 96–118.

Copeland, Rita. *Rhetoric, Hermeneutics and Translation in the Middle Ages*. Cambridge: Cambridge University Press, 1991.

Corti, Claudia. *Silenos: Erasmus in Elizabethan Literature*. Studi Di Letterature Moderne e Comparate 1. Ospedaletto, Italy: Pacini, 1998.

Coulter, James. *The Literary Microcosm: Theories of Interpretation of the Later Neoplatonists*. Leiden: Brill, 1976.

Cranz, Edward. "A Common Pattern in Petrarch, Nicholas of Cusa, and Martin Luther." In *Humanity and Divinity in Renaissance and Reformation: Essays in Honor of Charles Trinkaus*. Ed. John W. O'Malley, Thomas M. Izbicki, and Gerald Christianson. Leiden; New York: E. J. Brill, 1993.

Crosbie, Christopher. "Refashioning Fable through the Baconian Essay: *De sapientia veterum* and Mythologies of the Early Modern Natural Philosopher." In *The Essay: Forms and Transformations*. Ed. Dorothea Flothow et al. Heidelberg: Universitätsverlag, Winter 2017.

Cunningham, J. V. *Woe or Wonder: The Emotional Effect of Shakespearean Tragedy*. Denver: University of Denver Press, 1951.

Dahlberg, Charles. "Macrobius and the Unity of the 'Roman de La Rose.'" *Studies in Philology* 58.4 (1961): 573–82.

Dawkins, Peter. *The Shakespeare Enigma*. London: Polair Publishing, 2004.

Daybell, James. *The Material Letter in Early Modern England: Manuscript Letters and the Culture and Practices of Letter-Writing, 1512–1635*. New York: Palgrave Macmillan, 2012.

Defaux, Gérard. "Rabelais's Realism, Again." In *François Rabelais: Critical Assessments*. Ed. Jean-Claude Carron. Baltimore: Johns Hopkins University Press, 1995.

Derrida, Jacques. *Dissemination*. Chicago: University Press, 1981.

Dodds, E. R. *The Greeks and the Irrational*. Berkeley: University of California Press, 1951.

Dronke, Peter. *Dante's Second Love: The Originality and the Contexts of the Convivio*. Ed. Society for Italian Studies. Exeter: Society for Italian Studies, 1997.

Dupont, Quinn. "The Printing Press and Cryptography: Alberti and the Dawn of a Notational Epoch." In *A Material History of Medieval and Early Modern Ciphers: Cryptography and the History of Literacy*. Ed. Katherine Ellison and Susan Kim. New York: Routledge, 2018.

Durling, Robert M. *The Figure of the Poet in Renaissance Epic*. Cambridge: Harvard University Press, 1965.

Eamon William. *Science and the Secrets of Nature: Books of Secrets in Medieval and Early Modern Culture*. Princeton: Princeton University Press, 1994.

Eden, Kathy. *Hermeneutics and the Rhetorical Tradition: Chapters in the Ancient Legacy and Its Humanist Reception*. New Haven: Yale University Press, 2009.

Ellison, Katherine. "Deciphering and the Exhaustion of Recombination." In *A Material History of Medieval and Early Modern Ciphers: Cryptography and the History of Literacy*. Ed. Katherine Ellison and Susan Kim. New York: Routledge, 2018.

Farrington, Benjamin. *The Philosophy of Francis Bacon: An Essay on Its Development from 1603 to 1609, with New Translation of Fundamental Texts*. Chicago: University of Chicago Press, 1966.

Fenoaltea, Doranne. "A Poetic Monument: Arrangement in Book 1 of Ronsard's 1550 Odes." In *The Ladder of High Designs: Structure and Interpretation of the French Lyric Sequence*. Ed. Doranne Fenoaltea and David Lee Rubin. Charlottesville: University Press of Virginia, 1991.

Ferry, Anne. *All in War with Time: Love Poetry of Shakespeare, Donne, Jonson, Marvell*. Cambridge: Harvard University Press, 1975.

Fish, Stanley. *Self-Consuming Artifacts: The Experience of Seventeenth-Century Literature*. Berkeley: University of California Press, 1972.

Fleming, Juliet. "Changed Opinion as to Flowers." In *Renaissance Paratexts*. Ed. Helen Smith and Louise Wilson. Cambridge: Cambridge University Press, 2011.

Foucault, Michel. *The Order of Things: An Archaeology of the Human Sciences*. New York: Vintage Books, 1970.

Fowler, Alastair. "Emanations of Glory: Neoplatonic Order in Spenser's *Faerie Queen*." In *A Theatre for Spenserians*. Ed. Judith Kennedy and James A Reither. Papers of the International Spenser Colloquium, Fredericton, New Brunswick, October, 1969. Toronto: University of Toronto Press, 1973.

Fraistat, Neil. *Poems in Their Place: The Intertextuality and Order of Poetic Collections*. Chapel Hill: University of North Carolina Press, 2011.

Freccero, John. "The Fig Tree and the Laurel: Petrarch's Poetics." *Diacritics* 5.1 (1975): 34–40.

———. *In Dante's Wake: Reading from Medieval to Modern in the Augustinian Tradition*. Ed. Melissa Swain and Danielle Callegari. New York: Fordham University Press, 2015.

Friedman, William, and Elizebeth Friedman. *The Shakespearean Ciphers Examined: An Analysis of Cryptographic Systems Used as Evidence That Some Author Other than William Shakespeare Wrote the Plays Commonly Attributed to Him*. Cambridge: Cambridge University Press, 1958.

Frye, Northrop. *Fables of Identity: Studies in Poetic Mythology*. New York: Harcourt Brace & World, 1963.

———. "Yeats and the Language of Symbolism." *University of Toronto Quarterly* 17 (October 1947): 1–17.

Fuyarchuk, Andrew. *Gadamer's Path to Plato: A Response to Heidegger and a Rejoinder by Stanley Rosen*. Eugene, OR: Wipf and Stock, 2010.

Gadamer, Hans-Georg. *Dialogue and Dialectic: Eight Hermeneutical Studies on Plato*. Tr. P. Christopher Smith. New Haven: Yale University Press, 1980.

———. *Truth and Method*. Tr. Joel Weinsheimer and Donald Marshall. 2nd rev. ed. New York: Continuum, 1989.

Gebert, Clara. *Elizabethan Dedications and Prefaces*. New York: Russell and Russell, 1966.

Genette, Gérard. *Paratexts: Thresholds of Interpretation*. Literature, Culture, Theory 20. Cambridge: Cambridge University Press, 1997.

Gerson, Lloyd. *From Plato to Platonism*. Ithaca: Cornell University Press, 2013.

Gildenhard, Ingo and Andrew Zissos. "Ovid's Narcissus (Met. 3.339–510): Echoes of Oedipus." *American Journal of Philology* 121.1 (2000): 129–47.

Gleick, James. *The Information: A History, a Theory, a Flood*. New York: Pantheon, 2011.

Gombrich, E. H. *Art and Illusion: A Study in the Psychology of Pictorial Representation*. New York: Pantheon Books, 1960.

Greenblatt, Stephen. *The Swerve: How the World Became Modern*. New York: W. W. Norton & Company, 2012.

Greene, Roland. *Post-Petrarchism Origins and Innovations of the Western Lyric Sequence*. Princeton: Princeton University Press, 1991.

Greene, Thomas M. *The Light in Troy: Imitation and Discovery in Renaissance Poetry*. Elizabethan Club Series 7. New Haven: Yale University Press, 1982.

———. *Poetry, Signs, and Magic*. Newark: University of Delaware Press, 2005.

Greenfield, Concetta Carestia. *Humanist and Scholastic Poetics, 1250–1500*. Lewisburg: Bucknell University Press, 1981.

Hadot, Pierre. *The Veil of Isis: An Essay on the History of Idea of Nature*. Tr. Michael Chase. Cambridge: Harvard University Press, 2006.

Hamilton, Albert Charles. Ed. *The Spenser Encyclopedia*. Abingdon: Routledge, 1996.

Hankins, John. *Source and Meaning in Spenser's Allegory: A Study of The Faerie Queene*. Oxford: Clarendon Press, 1971.

Hardison, O. B. *The Enduring Monument: A Study of the Idea of Praise in Renaissance Literary Theory and Practice*. Chapel Hill: University of North Carolina Press, 1962.

Harris, Stephen J. "Anglo-Saxon Ciphers." In *A Material History of Medieval and Early Modern Ciphers: Cryptography and the History of Literacy*. Ed. Katherine Ellison and Susan Kim. New York: Routledge, 2018.

Helfer, Rebeca. *Spenser's Ruins and the Art of Recollection*. Toronto: University of Toronto Press, 2012.

Hendrick, P. J. "Montaigne, Lucretius and Scepticism: An Interpretation of the 'Apologie de Raimond Sebond.'" *Proceedings of the Royal Irish Academy: Archaeology, Culture, History, Literature* 79 (1979): 139–152.

Heninger, S. K. *The Cosmographical Glass: Renaissance Diagrams of the Universe*. San Marino: Huntington Library, 1977.

———. "Sequences, Systems, Models: Sidney and the Secularization of Sonnets." In *Poems in Their Place: The Intertextuality and Order of Poetic Collections.* Ed. Neil Fraistat. Chapel Hill: University of North Carolina Press, 1986.

———. *Sidney and Spenser: The Poet as Maker.* University Park: Pennsylvania State University Press, 1989.

———. *The Subtext of Form in the English Renaissance: Proportion Poetical.* University Park: Pennsylvania State University Press, 1994.

———. *Touches of Sweet Harmony: Pythagorean Cosmology and Renaissance Poetics.* San Marino: Huntington Library, 1974.

Hetherington, Michael. "Renaissance Rhetorical Theory." In *Edmund Spenser in Context.* Ed. Andrew Escobedo. Cambridge: Cambridge University Press, 2017.

Hieatt, A. Kent. "The Genesis of Shakespeare's Sonnets: Spenser's *Ruines of Rome: by Bellay*" *PMLA* 98.5 (Oct., 1983): 800–14.

Hirrel, Michael. "Thomas Watson, Playwright: Origins of Modern English Drama." In *Lost Plays in Shakespeare's England.* Ed. D. McInnis and M. Steggle. Palgrave Macmillan, 2014.

Hiscock, Andrew. *Reading Memory in Early Modern Literature.* Cambridge: Cambridge University Press, 2011.

Honig, Edwin. *Dark Conceit: The Making of Allegory.* London: Faber and Faber, 1959.

Houston, John Porter. *The Rhetoric of Poetry in the Renaissance and Seventeenth Century.* Baton Rouge: Louisiana State University Press, 1983.

Howland, Jacob. *The Republic: The Odyssey of Philosophy.* Toronto: Twayne, 1993.

Hui, Andrew. *The Poetics of Ruins in Renaissance Literature.* New York: Fordham University Press, 2016.

Jackson, Katherine. "Sylvester's 'Du Bartas.'" *Sewanee Review* 16.3 (July 1908): 316–26.

Jardine, Lisa, and Alan Stewart, *Hostage to Fortune: The Troubled Life of Francis Bacon.* London: Gollancz, 1998.

Jeanneret, Michel. *Perpetual Motion: Transforming Shapes in the Renaissance from Da Vinci to Montaigne.* Tr. Nidra Poller. Baltimore: Johns Hopkins University Press, 2001.

John, Lisle Cecil. *The Elizabethan Sonnet Sequences: Studies in Conventional Conceits.* New York: Russell & Russell, 1966.

Junker, William. "Plato and Platonism." In *Edmund Spenser in Context.* Ed. Andrew Escobedo. Cambridge: Cambridge University Press, 2017.

Kahn, David. *The Codebreakers: The Story of Secret Writing.* Toronto: Macmillan, 1967.

Kahn, Victoria. *Rhetoric, Prudence, and Skepticism in the Renaissance.* Ithaca: Cornell University Press, 1985.

Kaske, Carol V. *Spenser and Biblical Poetics.* Ithaca: Cornell University Press, 1999.

Kelly, Douglas. "Courtly Love in Perspective: The Hierarchy of Love in Andreas Capellanus." *Traditio* 24 (1968): 119–47.

Kennedy, Judith M., and James A. Reither. *A Theatre for Spenserians: Papers of the International Spenser Colloquium, Fredericton, New Brunswick, October, 1969.* Toronto: University of Toronto Press, 1973.

Kermode, Frank. *The Genesis of Secrecy: On the Interpretation of Narrative.* Charles Eliot Norton Lectures 1977–78. Cambridge: Harvard University Press, 1979.

Kerrigan, John. "The Editor as Reader: Constructing Renaissance Texts." In *The Practice and Representation of Reading in England.* Ed. James Raven, Helen Small, and Naomi Tadmor, 102–24. Cambridge: Cambridge University Press, 1996.

King, Andrew. "'Well Grounded, Finely Framed, and Strongly Trussed up Together': The 'Medieval' Structure of 'The Faerie Queene.'" *Review of English Studies* 52.205 (2001): 22–58.

Kinney, Arthur F. "Continental Poetics." In *A Companion to Rhetoric and Rhetorical Criticism.* Ed. Walter Jost and Wendy Olmsted. Malden: Blackwell Publishing, 2004.

——. *Continental Humanist Poetics: Studies in Erasmus, Castiglione, Marguerite De Navarre, Rabelais, and Cervantes.* Amherst: University of Massachusetts Press, 1989.

——. "Rhetoric as Poetic: Humanist Fiction in the Renaissance." *ELH* 43.4 (1976): 413–43.

Knight, Jeffrey Todd. *Bound to Read: Compilations, Collections, and the Making of Renaissance Literature.* Philadelphia: University of Pennsylvania Press, 2013.

Lampert, Laurence. *Nietzsche and Modern Times: A Study of Bacon, Descartes, and Nietzsche.* New Haven: Yale University Press, 1993.

——. *How Socrates Became Socrates: A Study of Plato's Phaedo, Parmenides, and Symposium.* Chicago: University of Chicago Press, 2021.

Leishman, J. B. *Themes and Variations in Shakespeare's Sonnets.* London: Hutchinson, 1961.

Lemmi, Charles. *The Classic Deities in Bacon: A Study in Mythological Symbolism.* Baltimore: Johns Hopkins Press, 1933.

Lepage, John. *Revival of Antique Philosophy in the Renaissance.* New York: Palgrave Macmillan, 2012.

Levao, Ronald. "Francis Bacon and the Mobility of Science," *Representations,* 40 (1992): 1–32.

Lever, J. W. *The Elizabethan Love Sonnet.* London: Methuen, 1966.

Lewis, C. S. *The Discarded Image: An Introduction to Medieval and Renaissance Literature.* Cambridge: Cambridge University Press, 1964.

——. *English Literature in the Sixteenth Century Excluding Drama: The Completion of the Clark Lectures, Trinity College, Cambridge, 1944.* Oxford: Clarendon Press, 1962.

——. *Spenser's Images of Life.* Ed. Alastair Fowler. Cambridge: Cambridge University Press, 1967.

Lewis, Rhodri. "A Kind of Sagacity: Francis Bacon, the *Ars Memoriae* and the Pursuit of Natural Knowledge." *Intellectual History Review* 19.2 (2009): 155–75.

——. "Francis Bacon, Allegory, and the Uses of Myth," *Review of English Studies* 61.250 (2010): 360–389.

——. "Francis Bacon and Ingenuity," *Renaissance Quarterly* 67.1 (2014): 113–163

Loomis, Catherine. "Bear Your Body More Seeming." In *The Emblematic Queen: Extra-Literary Representations of Early Modern Queenship.* Ed. Debra Barrett-Graves. New York: Palgrave Macmillan, 2013.

Looze, Laurence de. "Signing Off in the Middle Ages: Medieval Textuality and Strategies of Authorial Self-Naming." In *Vox Intexta: Orality and Textuality in the Middle Ages*. Ed. Alger Nicolaus Doane and Carol Braun Pasternack, 162–78. Madison: University of Wisconsin Press, 1991.

Lovejoy, Arthur O. *The Great Chain of Being: A Study of the History of an Idea*. Cambridge: Harvard University Press, 1936.

Maley, Willy. "Spenser's Languages: Writing in the Ruins of English." In *The Cambridge Companion to Spenser*. Ed. Andrew Hadfield. Cambridge: Cambridge University Press, 2001.

Maquerlot, Jean-Pierre. *Shakespeare and the Mannerist Tradition: A Reading of Five Problem Plays*. Cambridge: Cambridge University Press, 1995.

Meister, Aloys. *Die Geheimschrift im Dienste der Päpstlichen Kurie von ihren Anfänge bis zum Ende des 16. Jahrhundert*. Paderborn: Schöningh, 1906.

Miner, Earl. "Some Issues or Study of Integrated Collections." In Neil Fraistat, *Poems in Their Place: The Intertextuality and Order of Poetic Collections*. Chapel Hill: University of North Carolina Press, 2011.

Monson, Don A. *Andreas Capellanus, Scholasticism, and the Courtly Tradition*. Washington, DC: Catholic University of America Press, 2005.

———. "Andreas Capellanus's Scholastic Definition of Love." *Viator* 25 (1994): 197–214.

Morris, Harry. "Richard Barnfield, 'Amyntas,' and the Sidney Circle." *Publications of the Modern Language Association of America*, 1959, 318–24.

Mulsow, Martin. *Knowledge Lost: A New View of Early Modern Intellectual History*. Tr. H. C. Erik Midelfort. Bilingual edition. Princeton: Princeton University Press, 2022

———. "Practices of Unmasking: Polyhistors, Correspondence, and the Birth of Dictionaries of Pseudonymity in Seventeenth-Century Germany." *Journal of the History of Ideas* 67.2 (2006): 219–250.

Neely, C. T. "The Structure of English Renaissance Sonnet Sequence." *ELH* 45.3 (1978): 359–89.

Nicholl, Charles. *The Reckoning: The Murder of Christopher Marlowe*. Chicago: University of Chicago Press, 1995.

North, Marcy. *The Anonymous Renaissance: Cultures of Discretion in Tudor-Stuart England*. Chicago: University of Chicago Press, 2003.

———. "Ignoto in the Age of Print: The Manipulation of Anonymity in Early Modern England." *Studies in Philology* 91.4 (1994): 390–416.

———. "Anonymity's Revelations in 'The Arte of English Poesie.'" *Studies in English Literature, 1500–1900* 39.1 (1999): 1–18.

Ong, Walter, J. *Ramus, Method, and the Decay of Dialogue: From the Art of Discourse to the Art of Reason*. Cambridge: Harvard University Press, 1958.

O'Connell, Robert J. *Images of Conversion in St. Augustine's Confessions*. New York: Fordham University Press, 1996.

Parkes, M. B. "The Influence of the Concepts of Ordinatio and Compilatio on the Development of the Book." In *Medieval Learning and Literature: Essays Presented to Richard William Hunt*. Ed. J. J. G. Alexander and Margaret Gibson. Oxford: Clarendon Press, 1976.

Parry, David. "Francis Bacon and the Rhetorical Reordering of Reality," *Rhetor* 6 (2016): 1–17.

Passannante, Gerard. "Homer Atomized: Francis Bacon and the Matter of Tradition." *ELH* 76.4 (2009): 1015–1047

Patterson, Annabel M. *Hermogenes and the Renaissance: Seven Ideas of Style.* Princeton: Princeton University Press, 1970.

Pearlman, E. "Watson's *Hekatompathia* [1582] in the *Sonnets* and *Romeo and Juliet.*" *English Studies* 74.4 (1993): 343–51.

Pesic, Peter. "François Viète, Father of Modern Cryptanalysis-Two New Manuscripts." *Cryptologia* 21.1 (1997): 1.

Phillips, Wendy. "No More Tears: Thomas Watson Absolved." *Comitatus: A Journal of Medieval and Renaissance Studies* 20.1 (1989).

Quint, David. *Origin and Originality in Renaissance Literature.* New Haven: Yale University Press, 1983.

Quitslund, Jon A. *Spenser's Supreme Fiction: Platonic Natural History and* The Faerie Queene. Toronto: University of Toronto Press, 2001.

Raby, F. J. E. "Nuda Natura and Twelfth-Century Cosmology." *Speculum* 43.1 (1968): 72–77.

Ramachandran, Ayesha. "Cosmology and Cosmography." In *Edmund Spenser in Context.* Ed. Andrew Escobedo. Cambridge: Cambridge University Press, 2017.

Rebhorn, Wayne A. "'His Tail at Commandment': George Puttenham and the Carnivalization of Rhetoric." In *A Companion to Rhetoric and Rhetorical Criticism.* Ed. Walter Jost and Wendy Olmsted. Malden: Blackwell Publishing, 2004.

Riffaterre, Michael. "The Mind's Eye: Memory and Textuality." In *The New Medievalism.* Ed. Marina Scordilis Brownlee, Kevin Brownlee, and Stephen G Nichols. Baltimore: Johns Hopkins University Press, 1991.

———. *Semiotics of Poetry.* Bloomington: Indiana University Press, 1978.

———. *Text Production.* New York: Columbia University Press, 1983.

Ringler, William. "Spenser and Thomas Watson." *Modern Language Notes* 69.7 (1954): 484–87.

Robertson, D. W. *Essays in Medieval Culture.* Princeton,: Princeton University Press, 1980.

———. "The Subject of the 'De Amore' of Andreas Capellanus." *Modern Philology* 50.3 (1953): 145–61.

Roche, Thomas. *Petrarch and the English Sonnet Sequences.* New York: AMS Press, 1989.

Rollett, John. "The Dedication to Shakespeare's Sonnets," *Elizabethan Review* 5.2 (1997): 93–122.

———. "Secrets of the Dedication to Shakespeare's Sonnets," *Oxfordian* 2 (1999): 60–75.

Rosen, Stanley. *The Ancients and the Moderns: Rethinking Modernity.* New Haven: Yale University Press, 1989.

———. "Are We Such Stuff as Dreams Are Made On?" In *Gadamer's Century: Essays in Honour of Hans-Georg Gadamer.* Eds. Jeff Malpas, Ulrich Arnswald, and Jens Kertscher. Cambridge: MIT Press, 2002.

———. *Plato's Symposium.* 2nd ed. New Haven: Yale University Press, 1987.

———. *Quarrel Between Philosophy and Poetry: Studies in Ancient Thought.* New York: Routledge, 1988.

———. "Suspicion, Deception, and Concealment." *Arion: A Journal of Humanities and the Classics* 1.2 (1991): 112–127.

Rosenheim, Shawn. *The Cryptographic Imagination: Secret Writing from Edgar Poe to the Internet.* Baltimore: Johns Hopkins University Press, 1997.

Russell, Daniel S. *The Emblem and Device in France.* French Forum Monographs 59. Lexington: French Forum, 1985.

Rzepka, Adam. "Discourse Ex Nihilo: Epicurus and Lucretius in Sixteenth-Century England." In *Dynamic Reading: Studies in the Reception of Epicureanism.* Eds. Brooke Holmes and W. H. Shearin. Oxford: Oxford University Press, 2012.

Schuler, Robert M. "Francis Bacon and Scientific Poetry." *Transactions of the American Philosophical Society* 82. 2 (1992).

Serjeantson, Richard. "Francis Bacon's Valerius Terminus and the Voyage to the 'Great Instauration.'" *Journal of the History of Ideas* 78.3 (2017): 341-368.

Serres, Michel et. al. *The Birth of Physics.* London: Rowman & Littlefield, 2018.

Shannon, Claude. "Communication Theory of Secrecy Systems." *Bell System Technical Journal* 28.4 (1949): 656–715.

———. "A Mathematical Theory of Communication." *Bell System Technical Journal* 27 (July and October 1948): 379–423 and 623–56. Reprinted in *The Mathematical Theory of Communication*, University of Illinois Press, 1964.

———. "Prediction and Entropy of Printed English." *Bell System Technical Journal* 30.1 (1951).

Simpson, James. *Sciences and the Self in Medieval Poetry: Alan of Lille's* Anticlaudianus *and John Gower's* Confessio Amantis. Cambridge Studies in Medieval Literature 25. Cambridge: Cambridge University Press, 1995.

Stillman, Robert E. *Philip Sidney and the Poetics of Renaissance Cosmopolitanism.* London: Routledge, 2008.

———. "The Scope of Sidney's *Defence of Poesy*: The New Hermeneutic and Early Modern Poetics." *English Literary Renaissance* 32.3 (2002): 355–85.

Stock, Brian. *Augustine's Inner Dialogue: The Philosophical Soliloquy in Late Antiquity.* Cambridge: Cambridge University Press, 2010.

Strasser, Gerhard F. "Diplomatic Cryptology and Universal Languages in the Sixteenth and Seventeenth Centuries." In *Go Spy the Land.* Ed. Keith Neilson and B. J. C. McKercher, 73–97. Praeger, 1992.

———. "The Noblest Cryptologist." *Cryptologia* 7.3 (1983): 193.

———. "The Rise of Cryptology in the European Renaissance." In *The History of Information Security: A Comprehensive Handbook.* Ed. Karl de Leeuw and J. A Bergstra, 277-325. London: Elsevier, 2007.

Strauss, Leo. *Persecution and the Art of Writing.* Glencoe: Free Press, 1952

Strier, Richard. *The Unrepentant Renaissance: From Petrarch to Shakespeare to Milton.* Chicago: University of Chicago Press, 2012.

Taylor, Archer. *The Literary Riddle before 1600.* Westport: Greenwood Press, 1948.

Teskey, Gordon. "Renaissance Literary Theory." In *Edmund Spenser in Context.* Ed. Andrew Escobedo. Cambridge: Cambridge University Press, 2017.

Tuve, Rosemond. *Elizabethan and Metaphysical Imagery; Renaissance Poetic and Twentieth-Century Critics.* Chicago: University of Chicago Press, 1947.

Usher, Jonathan. "Boccaccio's Experimentation with Verbal Portraits from the 'Filocolo' to the 'Decameron.'" *Modern Language Review* 77.3 (1982): 585-596

Vendler, Helen. *The Art of Shakespeare's Sonnets*. Cambridge: Harvard University Press, 1997.

Vickers, Nancy J. "This Heraldry in Lucrece's Face." *Poetics Today* 6.1/2 (1985): 171–84.

Virgil. *Virgil's Aeneid*. Tr. Rev. Oliver Crane. New York: Baker & Taylor Company, 1888. (For introductory notes only.)

Wallace, Andrew. "Virgil and Bacon in the Schoolroom." *ELH* 73.1 (2006): 161-185.

Walton, Craig. "Ramus and Bacon on Method." *Journal of the History of Philosophy* 9.3 (July 1, 1971): 289–302.

Weeks, Sophie. "The Role of Mechanics in Francis Bacon's Great Instauration." In *Philosophies of Technology: Francis Bacon and His Contemporaries*. Two vols. Ed. Claus Zittel et al. Koninklijke Brill NV, 2008.

———. "Francis Bacon and the Art-Nature Distinction." *Ambix*, 54.2 (2007): 117–145.

Werlin, Julianne. "Francis Bacon and the Art of Misinterpretation." *PMLA* 130.2 (2015): 236–251.

Wetherbee, Winthrop. *Platonism and Poetry in the Twelfth Century: The Literary Influence of the School of Chartres*. Princeton: Princeton University Press, 1972.

Wind, Edgar. *Pagan Mysteries in the Renaissance*. London: Faber and Faber, 1958.

Winnick, R. H. "'Loe, Here in One Line Is His Name Twice Writ': Anagrams, Shakespeare's Sonnets, and the Identity of the Fair Friend." *Literary Imagination* 11.3 (2009): 254–77.

Woodcock, E. C. *A New Latin Syntax*. Mundelein, IL: Bolchazy-Carducci Publishers, 1959.

Zumthor, Paul. "From the Universal to the Particular in Medieval Poetry." *MLN* 85.6 (December 1970): 815–23.

List of Figures (Vol. I)

List of Figures (Vol. II)

Appendices

Addenda

Excursus

General Index

Volumes I and II

Sonnet Index

The location in Volume II of the pair of text and commentary pages is listed in the third column.

First Subsequence

| Sonnet Number | | Vol. II | Description | Additional References |
Restored	Orig.	page		
1	1	266	Cupid clasps a yoke on neck	133, 213, 280, 287–88, 291, 346, 418, 435, II 307, 346
L2.H	2	268	Heart is now separated	99–101, 107, 143, 245, 250, 304, 309–11, 346, 378, 418, II 355
L2.1	3	270	Speak gentle heart	101–2, 107, 245, 346, 378
L2.2	4	272	Invocation to Venus	102–3, 107, 278, 298
L2.3	5	274	What is love? ("Self do" proverb)	102, 104–7, 217–18, 251, 256, 278, 292, 298, 306, 317, 365, 367, 378, II 26
L2.4	6	276	Latin: what is love?	104, 108, 217–18, 240, 367
L2.5	7	278	Blazon of beloved	108, 167, 278, 296, II 49, 253, 298, 349–53
L2.6	8	416	Acteon sees Diana naked	107–8, II 350–53
L2.7	9	417	Marigold and the sun	107–8, II 350–53
L2.8	10	418	Tiresias and others blinded	107–8, II 350–53
L11.H	11	188	Musical phoenix of our age	109, 112, 320, II 188
L11.1	12	190	Song of the mistress	109, 112, II 26
L11.2	13	192	Miraculous effects of music	109, 112
L11.3	14	194	Love, by music, enters his will	109, 111–12
L11.4	15	196	Music contest, Apollo judges	109, 398
L11.5	16	198	My bird keeps me as her page	109, 112, 274, 317, II 28
L11.6	17	200	She, phoenix, is basis of poetry	97, 108–9, 112–13
L26.H	26	204	Nightingale song: grief and joy	272, 304, 307–9, 349
L26.1	37	206	Gods chase mortal prey	292, 349–50
L26.2	21	208	Her gifts: Juno, Pallas, Venus	378
L26.3	20	210	Breath, speech and kissing	
L26.4	33	212	She wins judgment of Paris	350
L26.5	29	214	Great artists fail to portray	350
L26.6	34	216	She is peerless among ladies	

Second Subsequence

Third Subsequence

| Sonnet Number | | Vol. II | Description | Additional References |
Restored	Orig.	page		
L64.H	64	136	My humble suit is met by disdain	99, 317, 326, II 26, 136
L64.1	60	138	I see what is better but do the worse	II 26, 135
L64.2	49	140	Heat of love dries and consumes me	242
L64.3	76	142	In frost I burn; I freeze in flame	
L64.4	59	144	Help in time before i further faint	
L64.5	52	146	Acrostic: *amor me pungit & urit*	
L64.6	38	148	Love grows madder; lives accurst	362, II 25–26, 135
L50.H	50	154	Reason loses all; love overpowers	312, 317, 362–63, II 26, 360
L50.1	74	156	Secret spring: beauty forceth love	363, 434, 443, II 360
L50.2	63	158	Love has two shafts: gold & lead	80, 227–28, 362, 428, II 360
L50.3	70	160	Cupid, where are thy weapons now?	363
L50.4	46	162	Hopes that loue will be his friend	362–63
L50.5	56	164	Dialogue with Death and Love	244–45, 247–50, 253, 256, 362–63, II 26, 151, 243, 360, 383
L50.6	69	166	He wishes to die in sight of her	II 151, 360
L73.H	73	170	Quarrel between love and his heart	251, 256, 306, 316–17, 347, 381, II 360
L73.1	57	172	So, Loue in me a Second Nature is	252–53, 256–57, 306, 315, 364–65, 381, 392, 395, II 26, 224
L73.2	61	174	His heart restores a god's lost power	253, 306, 365–66, 368, 375, 392, II 27
L73.3	67	176	Loue hath no leaden heels	307
L73.4	77	178	Time cannot make me cease to love	141, 307, II 169, 385
L73.5	53	180	Aesculapius's herbs & Cupid's blood	254, 307, 366, II 26, 80
L73.6	65	182	He destinates estate of double kind	254–55, 307, 333, 347, 350, 352, 365, 369, 381–82, 393, 396
Epilogue	Epi	78	Hopes to live more honorably	213, 222, 369

Sonnet Number Converter: restored to original

First Subsequence		
Sonnet Number		Vol. II
Restored	Orig.	page
1	1	266
L2.H	2	268
L2.1	3	270
L2.2	4	272
L2.3	5	274
L2.4	6	276
L2.5	7	278
L2.6	8	416
L2.7	9	417
L2.8	10	418
L11.H	11	188
L11.1	12	190
L11.2	13	192
L11.3	14	194
L11.4	15	196
L11.5	16	198
L11.6	17	200
L26.H	26	204
L26.1	37	206
L26.2	21	208
L26.3	20	210
L26.4	33	212
L26.5	29	214
L26.6	34	216
L18.H	18	220
L18.A1	32	226
L18.A2	24	228
L18.A3	23	230
L18.A4	22	232
L18.A5	19	234
L18.A6	28	236
L18.B1	27	238
L18.B2	35	240
L18.B3	25	242
L18.B4	31	244
L18.B5	36	246
L18.B6	30	248
L18.C1	79	250

Second Subsequence		
Sonnet Number		Vol. II
Restored	Orig.	page
L82.PS.1	80	34
L82.PS.2	81	36
L82.PS.3	82	38
L82.FL.1	86	40
L82.FL.2	93	42
L82.FL.3	88	44
L82.FL.4	99	46
L82.FL.5	87	48
L82.FL.6	95	50
L82.FL.7	97	52
L82.Scoff.1	96	54
L82.Scoff.2	83	56
L82.Scoff.3	98	58
L82.Scoff.4	QA	60
L82.Scoff.5	94	62
L82.Scoff.6	84	64
L82.Scoff.7	92	66
L82.LD.1	91	68
L82.LD.2	100	70
L82.LD.3	85	72
L82.LD.4	89	74

Third Subsequence		
Sonnet Number		Vol. II
Restored	Orig.	page
L90.H	90	84
L90.1	44	86
L90.2	45	88
L90.3	71	90
L90.4	58	92
L90.5	72	94
L90.6	42	96
L90.7	54	98
L39.H	39	104
L39.A1	55	106
L39.A2	48	108
L39.A3	68	110
L39.A4	41	112

Third (continued)		
Sonnet Number		Vol. II
Restored	Orig.	page
L39.A5	40	114
L39.A6	47	116
L39.B1	62	118
L39.B2	78	120
L39.B3	51	122
L39.B4	66	124
L39.B5	75	128
L39.B6	43	130
L64.H	64	136
L64.1	60	138
L64.2	49	140
L64.3	76	142
L64.4	59	144
L64.5	52	146
L64.6	38	148
L50.H	50	154
L50.1	74	156
L50.2	63	158
L50.3	70	160
L50.4	46	162
L50.5	56	164
L50.6	69	166
L73.H	73	170
L73.1	57	172
L73.2	61	174
L73.3	67	176
L73.4	77	178
L73.5	53	180
L73.6	65	182
Epilogue	Epi	78

Sonnet Number Converter: original to restored

Sonnet Number Orig.	Restored	Vol. II page
P1	P1	256
P2	P2	258
P3	P3	260
P4	P4	262
P5	P5	264
1	1	266
2	L2.H	268
3	L2.1	270
4	L2.2	272
5	L2.3	274
6	L2.4	276
7	L2.5	278
8	L2.6	416
9	L2.7	417
10	L2.8	418
11	L11.H	188
12	L11.1	190
13	L11.2	192
14	L11.3	194
15	L11.4	196
16	L11.5	198
17	L11.6	200
18	L18.H	220
19	L18.A5	234
20	L26.3	210
21	L26.2	208
22	L18.A4	232
23	L18.A3	230
24	L18.A2	228
25	L18.B3	242
26	L26.H	204
27	L18.B1	238
28	L18.A6	236
29	L26.5	214
30	L18.B6	248
31	L18.B4	244

Sonnet Number Orig.	Restored	Vol. II page
32	L18.A1	226
33	L26.4	212
34	L26.6	216
35	L18.B2	240
36	L18.B5	246
37	L26.1	206
38	L64.6	148
39	L39.H	104
40	L39.A5	114
41	L39.A4	112
42	L90.6	96
43	L39.B6	130
44	L90.1	86
45	L90.2	88
46	L50.4	162
47	L39.A6	116
48	L39.A2	108
49	L64.2	140
50	L50.H	154
51	L39.B3	122
52	L64.5	146
53	L73.5	180
54	L90.7	98
55	L39.A1	106
56	L50.5	164
57	L73.1	172
58	L90.4	92
59	L64.4	144
60	L64.1	138
61	L73.2	174
62	L39.B1	118
63	L50.2	158
64	L64.H	136
65	L73.6	182
66	L39.B4	124
67	L73.3	176

Sonnet Number Orig.	Restored	Vol. II page
68	L39.A3	110
69	L50.6	166
70	L50.3	160
71	L90.3	90
72	L90.5	94
73	L73.H	170
74	L50.1	156
75	L39.B5	128
76	L64.3	142
77	L73.4	178
78	L39.B2	120
79	L18.C1	250
80	L82.PS.1	34
81	L82.PS.2	36
82	L82.PS.3	38
83	L82.Scoff.2	56
84	L82.Scoff.6	64
85	L82.LD.3	72
86	L82.FL.1	40
87	L82.FL.5	48
88	L82.FL.3	44
89	L82.LD.4	74
90	L90.H	84
91	L82.LD.1	68
92	L82.Scoff.7	66
93	L82.FL.2	42
94	L82.Scoff.5	62
95	L82.FL.6	50
96	L82.Scoff.1	54
97	L82.FL.7	52
98	L82.Scoff.3	58
QA	L82.Scoff.4	60
99	L82.FL.4	46
100	L82.LD.2	70
Epi	Epilogue	78